Illinois Central College
Learning Resources Center

Index to motion pictures reviewed by VARIETY, 1907-1980

by

MAX JOSEPH ALVAREZ

THE SCARECROW PRESS, INC.
Metuchen, N.J., & London • 1982

Library of Congress Cataloging in Publication Data

Alvarez, Max Joseph, 1960-
  Index to motion pictures reviewed by Variety, 1907-
1980.

    1. Moving-pictures--Reviews--Periodicals--Indexes.
2. Variety--Indexes. I. Variety. II. Title.
PN1995.A39   011'.37   81-23236
ISBN 0-8108-1515-X   AACR2

INTRODUCTION

There just isn't another motion picture publication as reliable as Variety.

No other film magazine or newspaper has kept us in constant touch with the world film industry for as many years as Variety, and no other has reviewed as many movies.

Variety was first published on December 6, 1905, but film reviews did not appear until January 19, 1907, when editor Sime Silverman decided to include a thumbnail review of a current "moving picture" entitled The Life of a Cowboy. Thus began a feature that was to continue for the next eight decades, the goal being to inform the trade of the merits and shortcomings of new releases.

What were the films about? Were they any good? Would exhibitors profit from showing them? Since it was impossible for any one person to answer all of those questions, due to the hundreds and hundreds of pictures being released annually, Variety found it necessary to organize a small group of reviewers to keep tabs on current film product. (The critics signed their reviews by abbreviating their names, a practice that continues today.)

Although the film reviews were eventually given their own territory in August 1909, Variety did not consider them as important as the vaudeville and "legit" news. Convinced that movies were merely a passing fad, the publication discontinued the reviews in March 1911 and did not revive them until January 1913. (Frank Wiesberg's detailed account, "Why Variety Discontinued Film Reviews in 1911-12," appeared in the paper's December 24, 1915, issue on page 16.)

As the dusty California plains evolved into the legendary land of Hollywood, <u>Variety</u> gradually realized the importance of the new art form of motion pictures, and news of the film industry slowly began to dominate its pages. Reviews grew in length; credit boxes listing actors, producers, directors, and writers were introduced in April 1922, and running times in March 1923. The latter element was independently calculated by the critics themselves, not by the distributors, and these figures remain an important firsthand source for film scholars.

On January 15, 1930, Variety inserted capsule reviews for impatient readers. These capsules briefly summed up the critic's opinion of the film and initially ran alongside the complete review. Finally, in June 1951, the editors decided to position the capsules on top of the accompanying reviews, and this system is still in use.

Now, for the first time ever, <u>Variety</u>'s film reviews from 1907 to 1980 are readily available for scholarly study. These criticisms represent history in the making. <u>Variety</u> was there when an American film debuted on Broadway. It was there when a foreign film debuted in its European homeland. It was there when an experimental film process was publicly demonstrated.

Many films were reviewed more than once, either from different countries at various lengths, or during the film's re-release. This index includes every review a film received and also provides a cross-referencing guide for American films that were remade in foreign languages for overseas release during the 1930s. I have also cited all short subjects (running under thirty minutes) reviewed by <u>Variety</u> dating back to the 1920s.

It should be noted that this index would not have been possible without the assistance and encouragement of Robert R. and Lee L. Alvarez, Steven Dhuey, Professor J. Douglas Gomery, Christine Steinhage, the Milwaukee Public Library System, and Multi-Cultural Community High School. I would also like to give an additional nod to Professor Szymon St. Deptula.

Of the tens of thousands of motion picture reviews <u>Variety</u> has published over the seventy-three years covered here, some are timely and others are amusingly dated. But there isn't a dull paragraph in any of them.

HOW THE INDEX WORKS

All motion picture features and short subjects reviewed by
Variety from January 19, 1907, to December 31, 1980, are
alphabetized from A to Z on the following pages.   The title
of the film is followed by the month, day, year, and page
number in which the review appeared.   Thus,

Citizen Kane   4-16-41:16

indicates that the film "Citizen Kane" was reviewed by Variety
on April 16, 1941, page 16.   When more than one date follows a film's title, this means that Variety reviewed the film
on more than one occasion.

Short Subjects

The American Film Institute defines a short subject as any
film that runs under thirty minutes.   Since Variety did not
begin listing actual running times until March 1923, this index only differentiates between full-length features and short
subjects released after that date.   A film reviewed after
March 1923 running less than thirty minutes is followed by
the letter "s" in parentheses, designating "short."   Most of
the films reviewed between 1907 and 1911 rarely exceeded
lengths of ten minutes, but these cannot truly be considered
short subjects because their running times were standard for
their years.

Foreign Films

In some instances, Variety reviews a foreign film in the
United States under its new American title, but in most situa-
tions a film is reviewed in its European capital under its
original foreign title.   To aid readers in search of foreign

• vi

films known only by American titles, I have supplied cross-references. An example: for the French film "State of Siege," the index reads

State of Siege (See: <u>Etat de Siege</u>)

Alphabetizing foreign films has always been a problem. In English, titles that begin with "A," "An," and "The" are always alphabetized by the words that follow. The same method will be used for all foreign film titles beginning with the following words:

Das (German)	Il (Italian)
Den (Swedish)	L' (French)
Der (German)	La (Italian/French)
Des (German/French)	Las (Spanish)
Die (German)	Le (French)
Ein (German)	Les (French)
El (Spanish)	Lo (Italian)
En (Swedish)	Los (Spanish)
Ett (Swedish)	Un (French/Spanish)
Gli (Italian)	Una (Spanish)
I (Italian)	Une (French)

I should also point out that we are following <u>Variety</u>'s policy of omitting accent marks from foreign-language film titles.

Cross-Referencing

The cross-referencing in this index is limited mostly to foreign-language films, but an exception has been made with American titles that were abbreviated by the <u>Variety</u> editors when first reviewed. One such example is the 1938 film "The Adventures of Robin Hood," which was reviewed as "Robin Hood." In the index, the title reads

Adventures of Robin Hood, The (See: <u>Robin Hood</u>).

Misprints

On three rare occasions, <u>Variety</u> printed incorrect date listings on certain issues. This could lead to confusion, so the following key has been added to guide readers:

Two stars (**) following a title and date indicate that the page on which the review appears bears the incorrect date of February 27, 1935.

Three stars (***) indicate that the page of the review bears the incorrect date of June 14, 1923.

Four stars (****) indicate that the page of the review bears the incorrect date of September 20, 1923.

INDEX TO MOTION PICTURES
REVIEWED BY VARIETY,
1907-1980

● A ●

A and P Gypsies (s) 4-10-29:16
  and 6-05-29:15
ABC Del Amor 4-12-67:6
A Belles Dents 8-17-66:6
A Bor 10-03-33:15
A Bout du Souffle 1-27-60:6
A Brivele der Mamen 9-20-39:27
A Cama ao Alcance de Todos
  8-27-69:18
A Cavallo della Tigre 3-07-62:6
A Chacun Son Enfer 2-16-77:21
  and 2-16-78:24
A Ciascuno il Suo 5-03-67:6
A Coeur Joie 7-26-67:22
A Compadecida 4-09-69:8
A Confederacao--O Povo e Que
  Faz a Historia 10-10-79:24
A Culpa 10-15-80:66
A Cruz de Ferro 4-09-69:41
A Csunya Lany 9-11-35:17 and
  10-23-35:31
A Dama Do Lotacao 5-31-78:26
A Derrota 8-09-67:6
A Donto Pillanat 4-27-38:23
A Double Tour 9-09-59:6
A Falecida 9-01-65:6
A Falu Rossna 2-16-38:25
A Ferfi Mind Orult 10-27-37:19
A Flor Da Pele 9-29-76:34
A Grande Cidade 9-14-66:24
A-Haunting We Will Go 7-08-42:8
A Holgy Kisse Bogaras 11-09-38:
  19
A Hora e Vez de Augusto Matraga
  5-25-66:24
A Idade Da Terra 9-17-80:23
A. K. A. Cassius Clay 11-04-
  70:24
A Kedves Somszed 2-28-79:22
A Kiralylany Zsamolya 3-02-77:26
A Kiralyno Huszarja 1-15-36:19
A Kis Valentino 2-28-79:22
A La Guerre Comme a la Guerre
  8-09-72:20
A Lenda de Ubirojara 4-07-76:32
A Los Cuatro Vientos 8-03-55:6
A Marcia Nuziale 3-04-36:27
A Megfagyott Gyermek 10-20-37:27

A Mezzanotte Va La 3-26-74:20
A Miniszter Baratja 12-13-39:52
A Morte Da Comanda Do Cangaco
  7-12-61:7
A Mulher de Todos 4-01-70:26
A Navalha Na Carne 4-29-70:180
A Noite de Espantalho 10-02-74:22
A Noszty Fiu Este Toth Marival
  2-23-38:14
A Nous a l'Americane 1-26-32:27
A Nous Deux 6-06-79:22
A Nous Deux la France 5-27-70:22
A Nous la Liberte 1-05-32:23 and
  5-31-32:15
A Nous les Petites Anglaises 1-14-
  76:20
A-009 Missione H. K. 6-14-67:7
A L'Ouest Rien de Nouveau 12-24-
  30:29 (Also see: All Quiet
  on the Western Front)
A Paty Jezdec de Strach 7-27-66:24
A Pied, a Cheval et en Voiture 10-
  23-57:18
A Piros Bugyellaris 9-21-38:25
A Pozdravuji Vlastovsky 8-09-72:20
A Primeira Missa 5-24-61:17
A Promessa 5-23-73:18
A Queda 4-05-78:23
A Quelques Jours Pres (See: Matter
  of Days, A)
A Repulo Arany 12-27-32:54
A Sangre Fria 8-06-47:12
A Sori Sdesi Tihje 9-06-72:18
A Tizedes Meg a Tobbiek 9-14-66:26
A Toda Maquina 11-21-51:18
A Toi de Faire Mignonne 10-23-63:
  6
A Tout Casser 10-30-68:26
A Tout Coeur 10-20-31:27
A Tout Coeur a Tokyo Pour OSS
  117 11-23-66:26
A Tout Prendre 8-28-63:18
A Trombitas 2-28-79:22
A Un Dios Desconocido 9-28-77:24
A Ven Gazember 1-17-33:17
A Vereb Is Madar 6-11-69:40
A Vida Provisoria 5-14-69:32
AWOL 5-17-72:28
AABA--The Movie 12-14-77:13
Aarohi 8-04-65:28
Aaron Loves Angela 12-24-75:16
Aaron Slick from Punkin Crick
  2-20-52:6
Aaronson's Commanders (s) 12-05-
  28:12 and 12-18-29:22
Aarti 10-02-63:6
Aashirwaa 8-05-70:22
Aasman Manal 7-27-66:7

Abajo El Telon   12-28-55:6
Abandoned   10-05-49:8
Abarembo Kaido   7-31-57:6
Abbott & Costello Go to Mars
    3-25-53:6
Abbott & Costello in Hollywood
    8-22-45:20
Abbott & Costello in Society
    8-09-44:12
Abbott & Costello in the Foreign
    Legion   7-12-50:6
Abbott & Costello Meet Captain
    Kidd   11-26-52:6
Abbott & Costello Meet Franken-
    stein   6-30-48:10
Abbott & Costello Meet the Key-
    stone Cops   2-09-55:10
Abbott & Costello Meet the Invisi-
    ble Man   3-07-51:18
Abbott & Costello Meet the Killer,
    Boris Karloff   8-03-49:16
Abbott & Costello Meet the Mummy
    5-11-55:8
Abby   1-01-75:14
Abdication, The   9-18-74:19
Abductors, The   2-02-72:26
Abdul the Damned   3-19-35:27 and
    5-13-36:14
Abdulla the Great   4-04-56:16
Abe Lincoln in Illinois   1-24-40:14
Abe Lyman and Orch. (s)   6-13-
    28:12 and 9-12-28:12
Abel Twoj Brat   7-15-70:15
Abelha Na Chuva, Una   8-02-72:24
Abenteuer Des Werner Holt, Die
    3-03-65:7
Abenteuer in Wien   10-29-52:24
Abenteuerin von Tunis   11-03-31:
    27
Abenteuer in Engadine   12-23-36:
    62
Abfahrer, Die   5-23-79:26
Abicinema   8-27-75:24
Abie's Irish Rose   4-25-28:28
Abie's Irish Rose   12-26-28:27
Abie's Irish Rose   11-27-46:14
Abilene Town   1-09-46:79
Abilene Trail   3-14-51:7
Abismos de Pasion   8-14-63:6
Able Minded Lady   3-03-22:40
Abnae el Samte   8-16-75:17
Abominable Doctor Phibes, The
    5-26-71:23
Abominable Snowman   10-30-57:6
About Face   4-15-42:8
About Face   4-16-52:6
About Mrs. Leslie   5-05-54:6

Above and Beyond   11-17-52:6
Above Suspicion   4-28-43:8
Above the Clouds   1-09-34:17
Above Us the Waves   4-06-55:6
Abraham Lincoln   1-24-24:26
Abraham Lincoln   8-27-30:21
Abraham Lincoln's Clemency   11-
    12-10:16
Abroad With Two Yanks   7-26-44:10
Abschied (See: Farewell)
Abschied   10-29-69:17
Abschied von den Wolken   12-23-
    59:6
Abschied von Gestern   9-14-66:24
Absences Repetees   9-06-72:26
Absent Minded (s)   4-02-30:18
Absent Minded Professor, The   2-
    22-61:6
Absentee, The   5-14-15:19
Absolute Quiet   5-06-36:19
Absturz, Der   8-09-23:45
Abu El Banat   10-24-73:16
Abu Raihan Beruni   6-18-80:24
Abuna Messias   1-03-40:42
Abus de Confiance   12-24-38:15
Abusuan   8-29-73:14
Abwege   11-14-28:17
Abysses, Les   1-16-63:6
Abyssinia   7-22-36:34/12-16-36:15
AC/DC: Let There Be Rock   10-01-
    80:26
Acadie, L'Acadie, L'   6-09-71:17
Accattone   9-06-61:18
Accent on Youth   8-14-35:15
Accident   2-15-67:17
Accidental Honeymoon, The   5-17-
    18:44
Accidents Will Happen (s)   10-01-
    30:19
Accidents Will Happen   4-27-38:23
Accomplice   9-25-46:10
Accomplished Mrs. Thompson, The
    6-19-14:22
According to Advice   3-21-13:13
According to Hoyle   6-16-22:43
According to Law   3-17-16:32
According to Miss Hoyle   6-20-51:20
According to St. John   2-18-16:23
According to the Code   7-21-16:23
Accordion Joe (s)   6-23-31:18
Accused   8-12-36:19 and 12-30-36:
    11
Accused, The   11-17-48:13
Accused of Murder   1-30-57:6
Accusee-Levez Vous   10-01-30:34
Accusing Finger   11-18-36:13
Accusing Voice, The   5-22-14:23

Ace Eli and Rodger of the Skies
4-25-73:18
Ace High 6-28-18:28
Ace in the Hole 5-09-51:6
Ace of Aces 11-14-33:30
Ace of Cards 10-20-26:66
Ace of Hearts 10-28-21:35
Ace of Spades (s) 3-25-31:16
Aces and Eights 8-12-36:19
Aces High 10-01-69:28
Aces High 5-26-76:18
Aces Up 4-22-31:18
Aces Wild 1-27-37:24
Achalta Ota 5-28-80:14
Achilleshaelen er Mit Vaaben 3-
28-79:20
Acht Maedels Im Boot 11-15-32:23
Acht Tage Glueck 7-28-31:24
48 Stunden Bis Acapulco 2-07-68:12
Acid Mantra, or Rebirth of a
Nation 10-09-68:26
Acosada 5-13-64:6
Acquittal, The 12-20-23:22
Acquitted 1-28-16:22
Acquitted 12-11-29:39
Acrobate, L' 4-28-76:21
Across 110th Street 12-27-72:6
Across the Atlantic Via Zeppelin
(s) 2-20-29:14
Across the Badlands 9-20-50:6
Across the Border (s) 8-29-28:15
Across the Bridge 8-28-57:6
Across the Continent 4-28-22:42
Across the Deadline 1-20-22:35
Across the Deadline 4-08-25:40
Across the Divide 10-02-09:13
Across the Island of Ceylon 11-
06-09:13
Across the Isthmus 11-20-09:13
Across the Ocean on the Lusitania
11-02-07:11
Across the Pacific 11-10-26:14
Across the Pacific 8-19-42:8
Across the Plains 6-07-39:12
Across the Rio Grande 8-31-49:8
Across the River 9-09-64:24
Across the Sierras 4-16-41:18
Across the Wide Missouri 9-19-
51:6
Across the World 1-22-30:17 and
(s) 10-22-30:23/9-29-31:14
Across to Singapore 5-02-28:14
Act of Love 12-26-53:6
Act of Murder, An 8-25-48:8
Act of the Heart 9-30-70:15
Act of Vengeance 6-12-74:18
Act of Violence 12-22-48:6
Act One 12-18-63:7

Actas de Marusia 5-19-76:23
Acteon 8-04-65:32
Action 2-20-80:19
Action for Slander 8-04-37:25
Action Immediate 5-22-57:20
Action in Arabia 2-16-44:10
Action in the North Atlantic 5-19-
43:8
Action Man (See: Soleil Des Voyous,
Le)
Action of the Tiger 8-21-57:6 and
8-28-57:6
Action: The October Crisis of 1970
2-26-75:20
Actions Speak Louder Than Words
2-05-30:19
Activist, The 12-03-69:20
Acto da Primavera 8-04-65:6
Actor, The (s) 9-18-29:15
Actors and Sin 5-28-52:22
Actors' Fund Field Day 10-15-10:
12
Actorul Si Salbaticii 7-30-75:22
Actress, The 7-11-28:25
Actress, The 8-05-53:6
Ad Ogni Costo (See: Grand Slam)
Ada 7-26-61:13
Adalen '31 5-21-69:6
Adam and Eve (See: Adan y Eva)
Adam and Evelyne 6-08-49:18
Adam and Evil 8-10-27:21
Adam at 6 A.M. 9-23-70:22
Adam Becomes a Man 9-14-60:21
Adam 11 2-12-10:16
Adam Had Four Sons 2-19-41:16
Adam 2 10-22-69:32
Adamo ed Eva 1-25-50:18
Adam's Apple 9-26:28:27
Adam's Eve 2-05-30:19
Adam's Rib 3-01-23:32
Adam's Rib 11-02-49:10
Adam's Woman 4-08-70:22
Adan y Eva 11-28-56:6
Adding Machine, The 9-24-69:15
Addio, Alexandra (See: Love Me--
Love My Wife)
Addio, Fratello Crudele 2-23-72:6
Addio Mia Bella Napoli (See: Fare-
well, My Beautiful Naples)
Address Unknown 4-19-44:12
Adela Jeste Nevecreta 6-21-78:23
Adelaide 5-01-68:26
Adelantados, Los 7-17-74:16
Adele 1-31-19:52
Adele Le Marr (s) 9-05-28:14
Adele Rowland (s) 8-15-28:17
Adieu, l'Ami 8-28-68:6
Adieu Les Beaux Jours 5-01-34:15

Adieu Mascotte 9-18-29:29
Adieu Philippine 11-22-61:6
Adieu Poulet 12-24-75:14
Adios Alicia 12-28-77:22
Adios, Amigo 1-14-76:20
Adios, Ciguena, Adios 11-17-71:
22
Adios Gringo 1-31-68:23
Adios Juventud 10-11-44:12
Adios Sabata 9-01-71:26
Adjutant, Der 3-06-29:15
Admirable Crichton, The 6-19-57:
6
Admiral Nakhimov 8-13-47:22
Admiral Was a Lady, The 5-10-
50:6
Admirals All 7-03-35:15
Admission 5¢ (s) 10-17-23:19
Admission Free (s) 5-17-33:14
Adolescente, L' 1-31-79:24
Adolescentes, Los 2-11-76:38
Adolescents, The (See: Fleur de
L'Age, ou les Adolescentes,
La)
Adolf & Marlene 6-01-77:17
Adolphe, ou L'Age Tendre 7-24-
68:25
Adonis Is Robbed of His Clothes
11-27-09-13
Adopted Son, The 11-02-17:50
Adoption, L' 12-13-78:26
Adorable 5-23-33:19
Adorable Cheat, The 4-18-28:27
Adorable Creatures 1-18-56:6
Adorable Doctor, The 12-22-26:18
Adorable Julia 5-23-62:6
Adorable Menteuse 3-07-62:6
Adorable Outcast 2-13-29:30
Adorables Creatures 10-15-52:6
Adoration 1-16-29:14
Adoring an Ad 1-29-10:13
Adrienne Lecouvreur 11-09-38:17
Adrift 5-26-71:13
Adua e le Compagne 9-14-60:20
Adult Fun 12-06-72:20
Adulterio a Brasileira 12-21-69:6
Advance to the Rear 4-01-64:6
Adventuras de Juan Quin Quin, Las
8-02-67:6
Adventure 4-22-25:35
Adventure 12-19-45:18
Adventure en New York 10-25-32:
15
Adventure Girl 8-14-34:15
Adventure in Baltimore 3-23-49:8
Adventure in Blackmail 8-18-43:
26
Adventure in Bokhara 8-23-44:18

Adventure in Diamonds 1-24-40:14
Adventure in Hearts, An 1-09-20:
52
Adventure in Manhattan 10-28-36:14
Adventure in Sahara 12-21-38:15
Adventure in Washington 8-06-41:8
Adventure Island 8-13-47:15
Adventure Limited 3-20-29:13
Adventure Mad 5-09-28:17
Adventure of Fifine 7-24-09:11
Adventure of Salvador Rosa, An
9-25-40:18
Adventure Shop, The 1-03-19:38
Adventurer, The 10-26-17:29
Adventurers, The 3-21-51:7
Adventurers, The 3-25-70:18
Adventures de Rabbi Jacob, Les
11-14-73:14
Adventures de Till L'Espiegle 1-16-
57:20
Adventure's End 11-17-37:17
Adventures in Africa (s) 7-21-31:
12; 8-18-31:17 (Also see:
Man-Eaters, Buffalo Stampede,
The)
Adventures in Iraq 9-22-43:12
Adventures in Pygmy Island 3-07-
28:28
Adventures in the Far North 9-13-
23:30
Adventures in Warsaw 11-02-55:6
Adventures of a Beggar 2-22-08:11
Adventures of a Dentist 7-05-78:17
Adventures of a Newsreel Camera-
man (s) 10-03-33:15
Adventures of a Rookie 8-18-43:26
Adventures of a 10-Mark Bill 12-
29-26:15
Adventures of Barry McKenzie
10-25-72:26
Adventures of Bullwhip Griffin, The
3-01-67:6
Adventures of Captain Fabian 9-26-
51:6
Adventures of Captain Marvel 3-05-
41:24
Adventures of Carol, The 11-02-
17:49
Adventures of Casanova 2-18-48:8
Adventures of Chico 2-23-38:14
Adventures of Don Coyote 4-30-47:
10
Adventures of Don Juan 12-29-48:6
Adventures of Gallant Bess 7-28-
48:15
Adventures of Garel Hama 2-20-15:
25
Adventures of Giacomo Casanova
3-16-55:6

7 •

Africa Speaks English (s) 2-21-
33:14
Africa Squawks (s) 7-28-31:14
Africa-Texas Style 5-17-67:6
Africa Uncensored (See: Africa
Ama)
African Adventure, An 5-11-27:
24 and 8-10-27:20
African Boma (s) 6-23-31:18
African Diamond Conspiracy 5-
29-14:21
African Dodger (s) 3-18-31:14
African Elephant, The 10-20-71:
14
African Holiday 6-09-37:25
African Lion 8-10-55:6
African Queen, The 12-26-51:6
African Treasure 5-14-52:20
Africanus Sexualis (See: Black Is
Beautiful)
Afskedens Time 11-28-73:18
Aftenlandet 3-02-77:24
After a Million 5-14-24:28
After Business Hours 6-17-25:36
and 4-21-26:38
After Dark 1-07-25:55
After Five 2-06-15:23
After His Own Heart 5-02-19:59
After Mein Kampf? 9-18-40:16
After Mein Kampf 8-02-61:7
After Midnight 9-30-21:36
After Midnight 8-17-27:24
After Office Hours 3-13-35:15
After Petty Larceny Thieves 2-
06-20:53
After Seven (s) 5-29-29:14
After the Ball 3-26-24:44
After the Ball (s) 10-16-29:17
After the Ball 12-13-32:15 and
3-21-33:16
After the Ball 8-21-57:18
After the Dance 8-21-35:31
After the Fog 1-29-30:60
After the Fox 10-12-66:6
After the Show 1-01-30:15
After the Show 1-01-30:15
After the Storm 5-16-28:29
After the Thin Man 12-30-36:10
After Tomorrow 3-08-32:23
After Tonight 11-07-33:16
After You, Comrade 4-05-67:6
Aftermath 6-08-27:14 and 12-07-
27:20
Against a Crooked Sky 12-24-75:
18
Against All Flags 11-26-52:6
Against All Odds 8-13-24:21
Against the Law 12-18-34:13

Against the Rules (s) 7-07-31:25
Against the Wind 2-25-48:8
Agatha 2-14-79:23
Agaton Sax Och Bykoebings Gaesta-
bud 12-08-76:19
Age d'Or, L' 9-23-64:6
Age for Love 11-17-31:15
Age of Consent 9-06-32:21
Age of Consent 5-14-69:32
Age of Illusions (See: Almodzasok
Kora)
Age of Indiscretion 5-22-35:16
Age of Infidelity (See: Muerte de un
Ciclista
Age of Innocence 10-23-34:18
Agee 9-24-80:18
Agence Matrimoniale 6-18-52:20
Agent 69 Jensen I Skorpionens 7-
27-77:23
Agent 69 Jensen I Skyttens 8-02-78:
14
Agenzia Riccardo Finzi Praticamente
Detective 2-20-80:28
Aggie Appleby 10-24-33:17
Agilok und Blubbo 3-26-69:38
Agit 9-06-72:29
Agitator, The 8-24-49:22
Agnoula 11-05-41:8
Agonas 10-29-75:17
Agony and the Ecstasy, The 9-15-
65:6
Agony of Fear, The 10-18-15:22
Agony of the Eagles 5-12-22:33
Agostino 12-26-62:6
Agosto '68 9-10-69:46
Agraharathil Kazhuthai 1-31-79:22
Agression, L' 4-23-75:18
Agua en el Suelo, El 5-01-34:15
Aguas Bajan Turbias, Las 2-18-
53:18
Aguila 6-25-80:20
Aguila Blanca 5-07-41:20
Aguirre, Der Zorn Gottes 5-30-73:
26
Aguirre: The Wrath of God (See:
Aguirre, Der Zorn Gottes)
Agustina de Aragon 11-01-50:18
Ah! Afti I Yeeneka Mou 10-25-67:
20
Ah! Nomugi Toge 7-30-80:23
Ah, Wilderness 1-01-36:44
Ahi Viene Martin Corona 7-02-52:6
Ahora Seremos Felices 6-28-39:20
Ai Diavolo Con Celebrita 2-08-50:
22
Ai Kruie 2-23-77:16
Ai Kwai Legg 8-24-77:20
Ai No Borei 5-24-78:36

Ai No Corrida 2-25-76:22
Ai No Kawaki 8-10-66:6 and 3-15-
    67:26
Aida 10-13-54:6
Aido (Slave of Love) 7-09-69:26
Aigle et la Colombe, L' 3-23-77:
    24
Aiguille Rouge, L' 8-15-51:6
Aika Nyva Ihmiseksi 8-09-78:20
Aile et la Cuisse 11-10-76:22
Aililia 9-03-75:18
Aimez-Vous les Femmes? 5-13-
    64:19
Aimless Bullet, The 11-13-63:17
Aine des Ferchaux 10-02-63:28
Ainsi Finit la Nuit 1-25-50:18
Ain't Love Funny 7-06-27:23
Ain't Misbehavin' 5-25-55:6
Ain't She Sweet (s) 5-09-33:14
Air Cadet 2-21-51:6
Air Circus 9-05-28:14
Air Communique (s) (See: British
    War Docus)
Air de Paris, L' 9-22-54:6
Air Devils 5-11-38:16
Air Eagles 1-26-32:23
Air Force 2-03-43:14
Air Hawks 6-12-35:41
Air Hostess 1-21-33:21
Air Hostess 7-06-46:9
Air Legion 11-14-28:26
Air Mail, The 3-25-25:37
Air Mail 11-08-32:17
Air Mail Pilot 5-02-28:26
Air Maniacs (s) 6-05-34:12
Air Patrol, The 1-18-28:19
Air Police 4-29-31:50
Air Strike 7-13-55:20
Air Tight (s) 8-18-31:30
Airbourne 6-13-62:7
Airplane! 7-02-80:18
Airport 2-18-70:17
Airport 1975 10-16-74:14
Airport '77 3-23-77:22
Ajandek Ez A Nap 2-27-80:21
Ajuricaba 8-31-77:19
Akahige 9-08-65:6
Akai Satsui 11-18-64:7
Akai Tenshi 11-02-66:22
Akanegumo 10-18-67:18
Akasen Chitai 7-25-56:18
Akasen Tamanoi Nekeraremasu
    5-28-75:19
Akce Kalimantan 7-94-62:6
Akcija Stadion 8-17-77:20
Akee Bororo 7-25-73:6
Akenfield 7-26-75:16
Akras Al-Hob 11-20-68:40

Akibiori 7-26-78:21
Akiket a Pas Cirta Elkisert 9-16-
    59:16
Akitsu Onsen 11-19-80:21
Akjica 8-10-60:6
Akramana 2-06-80:24
Akran 12-03-69:16
Aktenskapsleken 12-25-35:25
Aktorzy Prowincjonaini 5-21-80:20
Al Abbott (s) 2-06-29:18
Al Aswar 1-25-79:20
Al Boustagui 11-20-68:40
Al Capone 2-11-59:6
Al Chet 9-15-37:15
Al Diablo Con Este Cura 5-31-67:6
Al Diavolo Con Celebrita 2-08-50
Al Fahd 8-16-72:14
Al-Haress 11-06-68:26
Al Hayatt Al Yawmiyah Fi Quariah
    Suriyah 7-07-76:16
Al Herman (s) 8-15-28:17
Al Jennings of Oklahoma 1-17-51:
    11
Al Kautsar 12-14-77:14
Al Moutmarred 11-13-68:26
Al Rass 2-06-80:22
Al Servicio de la Mujer Espanola
    10-04-78:22
Al Tariq 2-12-75:36
Al Tarik 8-04-65:28
Al Tejruba 2-06-80:22
Al Tish Ali Im Ani Ohev 4-18-79:
    22
Al Toque de Clarin 8-13-41:18
Al Wohlman (s) 10-16-29:17
Al-Yemen 1-14-31:19
Al Zouga Talattshar 7-04-62:63
Alabok Magbabalik 9-29-76:90
Aladdin 9-28-17:38
Aladdin and His Lamp 2-06-52:20
Aladdin from Broadway 3-23-17:21
Aladdin's Other Lamp 7-13-17:26
Alakazam the Great! 7-12-61:6
Alakdang Gubat 6-23-76:17
Alambrista 5-24-78:38
Alamo, The 10-26-60:6
Alarm Clock Andy 3-19-20:53
Alaska Highway 6-23-43:24 and 10-
    27-43:10
Alaska Passage 2-04-59:6
Alaska Patrol 1-19-49:10
Alaska Seas 1-27-54:6
Alaskan, The 9-17-24:28
Alaskan Adventures 3-02-27:17
Alat 10-15-75:26
Alaztosan Jelentem 9-07-60:6
Alba Regia 11-22-61:6
Albaniles, Los 7-06-77:17

9 •

Albany Night Boat 9-26-28:14
Albatros, L' 9-22-71:18
Albeniz 8-13-47:22
Albero Degli Zoccoli, L' 5-24-78:34
Albero di Adamo, L' 1-20-37:14
Albert, R. N. 10-21-53:6
Albert Schweitzer 2-06-57:6
Albert Spalding 8-22-28:14
Albert--Warum? 1-17-79:24
Albuquerque 1-21-48:8
Alcatraz Island 10-13-37:16
Alcoholiday--The Story of a
      Thirst, An 6-04-24:27
Alcool 9-24-80:22
Alderman's Picnic, The 1-15-10:
      13
Aldevaran 11-05-75:34
Alejandra 9-08-43:16
Aleko 1-12-55:6
Aleluia, Gretchen 6-15-77:21
Alerte Au Sud 2-10-54:20
Alerte En Mediterranee 11-02-38:
      22
Aleska Dundie 8-20-58:6
Alex and the Gypsy 9-29-76:30
Alex in Wonderland 12-23-70:6
Alex the Great 3-21-28:22
Alexander Graham Bell 4-05-39:
      15
Alexander Hamilton 9-22-31:22
Alexander Nevsky 3-29-39:16
Alexander the Great 4-04-56:6
Alexander's Ragtime Band (s) 3-
      11-31:14
Alexander's Ragtime Band 6-01-
      38:12
Alexandre le Bienheureux 2-28-68:
      22
Alfie 3-30-66:6
Alfie Darling 3-19-75:32
Alfred the Great 7-23-69:6
Alfredo, Alfredo 12-19-73:12
Alf's Button 4-09-30:39
Algiers 6-29-38:12
Algo Flota Sobre El Agua 9-29-
      48:18
Ali and Wolfi (s) 6-23-31:18
Ali-Baba 1-19-55:6
Ali Baba and the Forty Thieves
      3-21-08:15
Ali Baba and the Forty Thieves
      1-17-19:53
Ali Baba and the Forty Thieves
      1-12-44:24
Ali Baba Goes to Town 10-20-
      37:12
Ali: Fear Eats the Soul (See:
      Angst Essen Seele Auf)

Ali the Man: Ali the Fighter 7-
      30-75:24
Alias a Gentleman 1-28-48:11
Alias Bad Man 7-28-31:24
Alias Bulldog Drummond 9-11-35:
      17
Alias French Gertie 4-16-30:49
Alias Gardelito 5-30-62:22
Alias Jesse James 3-18-59:6
Alias Jimmy Valentine 4-16-20:43
Alias Julius Caesar 11-10-22:42
Alias Mary Brown 8-09-18:32
Alias Mary Dow 7-03-35:14
Alias Mary Smith 8-30-32:21
Alias Mrs. Jessop 12-14-17:43
Alias Nick Beal 1-19-49:10
Alias Night Wind 10-11-23:30
Alias the Champ 10-25-49:20
Alias the Deacon 6-22-27:30
Alias the Doctor 3-08-32:23
Alias the Dragon 5-15-40:16
Alias the Lone Wolf 10-05-27:25
Alibert 2-12-30:18
Alibi 4-10-29:16
Alibi 5-13-31:64
Alibi, L' (See: Alibi, The)
Alibi, The 4-19-39:23
Alibi, The 3-31-43:8
Alibi for Murder 10-07-36:31
Alice Adams 6-28-23:23
Alice Adams 8-21-35:21
Alice Boulden (s) 6-12-29:16
Alice Doesn't Live Here Anymore
      12-11-74:16
Alice Gentle (s) 2-19-30:21
Alice in der Stadten 10-19-74:36
Alice in the Cities (See: Alice in
      der Stadten)
Alice in Wonderland 1-23-15:25
Alice in Wonderland 12-26-33:10
Alice in Wonderland 7-04-51:8
Alice in Wonderland 8-01-51:6
Alice in Wonderland 9-08-76:20
Alice Ou la Derniere Fugue 1-12-
      77:45
Alice's Adventures in Wonderland
      9-17-10:12
Alice's Adventures in Wonderland
      11-15-72:24
Alice's Restaurant 8-13-69:18
Alicia 10-16-74:18
Alicia en la Espana de las Mara-
      villas 5-24-78:38
Alien, The 6-04-15:18
Alien 5-23-79:22
Alien, The 3-36-80:26
Alien Enemy, An 4-19-18:41
Alien Souls 5-05-16:23

Alieskine Liubov 10-11-61:7
Aliki-My Love 12-18-63:7
Alimony 6-15-49:13
Alimony Aches (s) 7-24-35:21
Alimony Madness 5-09-33:15
Alise et Chloe 11-18-70:67
Alison's Birthday 10-17-79:10
Alive and Kicking 6-24-59:6
Alkeste--Die Bedeutung, Protek-
    tion Zu Haben 4-22-70:28
Alksande Par 5-26-65:7
All Aboard 5-11-27:17
All About Alice 5-10-72:24
All About Dogs (s) 6-24-42:8
All About Eve 9-13-50:6
All-American, The 10-04-32:15
All-American, The 7-22-53:20
All-American Boy, The 11-07-73:
    19
All-American Co-Ed 10-18-41:9
All-American Drawback 12-11-35:
    19
All-American Sweetheart 12-08-
    37:16
All American Tramp 11-04-36:19
All Ashore 2-11-53:6
All at Sea 12-25-57:6
All by Myself 6-02-43:8
All Dolled Up 3-25-21:43
All Fall Down 3-28-62:6
All for a Nickle 10-02-09:13
All for a Woman 12-09-21:36
All for Fun 1-09-29:10
All for Mabel 11-26-30:18
All for Mary 1-11-56:22
All for Old Ireland 7-16-15:18
All for One 9-04-35:14
All Girl Revue (s) 6-12-29:16
All Gummed Up 5-20-31:16
All Hands on Deck 4-05-61:6
All I Desire 6-24-53:6
All in a Night's Work 3-22-61:15
All Kinds to Make a World (s)
    3-07-28:28
All Man 11-24-16:28
All Man 8-02-18:39
All Men Are Apes 11-24-65:6
All Men Are Enemies 5-29-34:12
All Mine to Give 11-06-57:6
All Mixed Up 11-11-64:6
All My Sons 2-25-48:8
All Neat in Black Stockings 4-09-
    69:28
All Night 12-06-18:39
All Night Long 2-14-62:6
All Nudity Shall Be Punished (See:
    Toda Nudez Sera Castigada)
All of a Sudden Norma 12-20-18:36

All of Me 2-06-34:14
All on Account of a Letter 9-25-
    09:20
All on Account of a Lie 10-08-10:
    12
All on Account of the Milk 1-22-
    10:14
All on Account of the Milk 7-31-
    14:16
All on Deck 4-03-34:17
All Over the Town 3-09-49:20
All Over Town 9-22-37:18
All Quiet on the Canine Front (s)
    12-24-30:21
All Quiet on the Western Front
    5-07-30:21 (Also see: A
    L'Ouest Rien de Nouveau)
All Screwed Up (See: Tutto A Posto
    E Niente In Ordine)
All Soul's Eve 2-18-21:41
All Steamed Up (s) 10-02-29:19
All Teed Up (s) 5-07-30:20
All That Heaven Allows 10-26-
    55:6
All That Jazz 12-12-79:22
All the Advantages 5-24-72:26
All the Brothers Were Valiant 1-
    19-23:47
All the Brothers Were Valiant 10-
    21-53:6
All the Fine Young Cannibals 7-
    20-60:6
All the King's Horses 3-13-35:15
All the King's Men 11-09-49:6
All the Loving Couples 4-09-69:8
All the Other Girls Do 11-02-66:
    22
All the President's Men 3-31-76:
    15
All the Way Home 9-18-63:6
All the Way Up 6-17-70:24
All the World for Nothing 11-22-
    18:44
All the Young Men 8-03-60:6
All These Women (See: For Att
    Inte Tala Om Alla Dessa
    Kvinnor)
All This and Heaven Too 6-12-40:
    14
All This and Rabbit Stew (s) 10-
    01-41:9
All This and World War II 11-17-
    76:18
All Through the Night 12-03-41:
    8
All Woman 5-24-18:34
All Women Have Secrets 11-22-39:
    16

All Wrong 5-16-19:56 and 6-13-19:48
Alla en el Rancho Grande 10-21-36:17 and 12-02-36:38
Alla en el Rancho Grande 2-16-49:16
Alle Jahre Wieder 7-12-67:6
Alle Menschen Werden 4-11-73:20
Allegheny Uprising 11-08-39:14
Allegri Masnadieri 10-20-37:27
Allegro Cantante, L' 4-27-38:23
Allegro Non Troppo 12-08-76:18
Alleman 1-15-64:22
Aller Retour 8-16-78:19
Aller Simple, Un 6-30-71:29
Allergic to Love 5-03-44:23
Alles-Um Eine Frau 1-01-36:58
Allez France 11-18-64:7
Alliance, L' 9-16-70:14
Alligator 11-19-80:18
Alligator Named Daisy 12-28-55:6
Alligator People, The 7-15-59:6
Alljon Meg a Menet 7-03-74:22
Allo, Allo, Carnaval 12-12-36:18
Allonsafan 10-22-75:34
Allotment Wives, Inc. 1-02-46:16
Allotria 7-22-36:17
All's Fair in Love 11-06-09-13
All's Fair in Love 1-14-11:18
Allseitig Reduzierte Persoen Lickkeit Redupers 6-28-78:28
Alluring Goal 5-07-30:21
Allvarsamme Leken, Den 8-31-77:36
Almafuerte 2-08-50:22
Almatlan Evek 9-16-59:16
Almighty Dollar, The 8-25-16:24
Almobo Ifjusag 10-09-74:36
Almodozasok Kora 8-04-65:32
Almost a Divorce 9-01-31:34
Almost a Gentleman 3-22-39:20
Almost a Honeymoon 10-08-30:23 and 1-14-31:19
Almost a Husband 10-17-19:63
Almost a Lady 9-29-26:18
Almost Angels 8-29-62:20
Almost Human 3-14-28:28
Almost Human 7-30-80:26
Almost Married 7-26-32:17
Almost Perfect Affair, An 4-11-79:20
Almost Summer 4-26-78:10
Aloha 4-29-31:37
Aloha, Bobby and Rose 4-16-75:22
Aloha Hooey (s) 3-25-42:18
Aloha Joe 11-12-15:22
Aloise 4-16-75:22
Aloma of the South Seas 5-19-26:16

Aloma of the South Seas 8-27-41:8
Alona of the Sarong Seas (s) 9-16-42:20
Alone in London 6-25-15:21
Alone in New York 1-09-15:23
Along Came Jones 6-13-45:17
Along Came Love 1-13-37:13
Along Came Ruth 7-30-24:26
Along Came Ruth (s) 5-16-33:17
Along Came Sally 6-19-34:27
Along Came Youth 1-14-31:19
Along the Great Divide 5-02-51:6
Along the Navajo Trail 12-12-45:12
Along the Oregon Trail 9-10-47:17
Along the Rio Grande 1-29-41:18
Alpageur, L' 3-31-76:15
Alpen Melodien (s) 4-29-31:37
Alpenbaringen 1-10-79:56
Alpha Beta 11-21-73:12
Alphabet Murders, The 3-16-66:6
Alphaville (See: Alphaville, Une Etrange Adventure de Lemmy Caution)
Alphaville, Une Etrange Adventure de Lemmy Caution 5-05-65:26
Alpine Antics (s) 4-24-29:13
Alraune 5-02-28:14 and 12-24-30:29
Altar Stairs 12-08-22:34
Alpine Echo, An 9-18-09:13
Alpine Echoes (s) 12-10-30:15
Alpine Echoes (s) 12-01-31:15
Alpine Retreat, An 11-19-10:13
Alranne 12-10-52:18
Als Twee Druppels Water 5-08-63:26
Alskarinnan 7-10-63:6
Also Es War So ... 6-01-77:17
Alson de la Marimba 8-25-43:10
Alster Case, The 12-10-15:21
Alt Paa et Braet 3-02-77:22
Alta Infedelta 2-26-64:6
Altars, Ancestors and Incense 11-09-55:6
Altars of Desire 4-27-27:20
Altars of the World 1-21-76:32
  (Also see: Lew Ayres Religious Docus)
Alte Burscherherlichkeit 6-21-32:15
Alte Fritz, Der 5-02-28:14
Alte Kleider (s) 8-11-31:30
Alte, Lied, Das 9-15-31:28
Alte und Junge Kaiser 12-11-35:19
Alter Kultur in Java (s) 1-05-32:19

● 12

Amici Miei 12-17-75:23
Amici Per la Pelle 9-28-55:9
Amico, Un 10-19-68:26
Amies de la Pension 3-04-31:14
Amis, Les 6-09-71:17
Amities Particulieres, Les 9-09-64:24
Amityville Horror, The 8-01-79:20
Amlash Enchanted Forest, The 6-05-74:16
Amleto di Meno, Un 5-30-73:12
Amo Non Amo 3-07-79:22
Amo Te Sola 7-22-36:34
Amok 10-28-46:10
Among Human Wolves 11-27-40:16
Among the Cannibal Isles 7-26-18:31
Among the Clouds 6-05-34:12
Among the Living 9-03-41:8
Among the Missing 11-06-34:17
Amor Brujo, El 7-26-67:24
Amor, Carnaval E Sonho 2-28-73:20
Amor de Captain Brando, El 7-03-74:16
Amor Der Perdicao 10-15-80:74
Amor en el Aire 10-02-68:28
Amor Solfeando, El 12-08-31:15
Amor Ultimo Modelo 1-20-43:20
Amore 2-20-74:15
Amore Amaro 12-04-74:22
Amore Che Canta, L' 4-07-34:15
Amore Difficile, L' 1-16-63:20
Amore e Chiacchere 2-26-58:6
Amore e Morte 10-04-32:27
Amore e Rabbia 7-23-69:26
Amore e Veleni 4-26-50:22
Amore in Citta 3-10-54:6
Amore in 4 Dimensioni 4-15-64:22
Amore Mio Aiutami 12-17-69:22
Amori e Veleni 4-26-50:22
Amorous Adventures of Don Quixote and Sancho Panza 4-21-76:23
Amorous Adventures of Moll Flanders, The 5-26-65:6
Amorous Prawn, The 11-21-62:12
Amour, L' 7-22-70:22
Amour 8-19-70:16
Amour, L' 8-23-72:24
Amour a la Mer, L' 8-04-65:28
Amour a Vingt Ans, L' 5-30-62:6
Amour, Amour 10-11-32:33
Amour Autour de la Maison, L' (See: Love Locked Out)

Amour C'est Gai, l'Amour, L' 11-26-69:28
Amour Chante, L' 12-03-30:15
Amour D'Une Femme, L' 6-30-54:6
Amour de la Vie: Artur Rubinstein 6-04-69:36
Amour de Pluie, Un 4-24-74:18
Amour de Poche 3-26-58:14
Amour en Fuite, L' 1-24-79:23
Amour en Herbe, L' 7-27-77:23
Amour en Question, L' 11-01-78:40
Amour Est En Jeu, L' 10-09-57:6
Amour Fou, L' 8-07-68:6
Amour Humain, L' 6-09-71:17
Amour, L'Apres-Midi, L' 8-30-72:18
Amour Madame 4-02-52:22
Amour Toujours L'Amour, L' 9-03-52:12
Amoureux du France, Les 6-03-64:6
Amoureuse, L' 11-01-72:30
Amours Celebres, Les 11-08-61:6
Amours de Paris, Les 3-08-61:7
Amours de Toni, Les 11-18-36:13
Ampelopede, L' 3-06-74:26
Amphibious Man, The 7-24-63:6
Amphytrion 3-31-37:19
Amsterdam Affair 6-12-68:26
Amsterdam Kill 5-11-77:79
An 01, L' 3-21-73:26
Ana y Los Lobos 5-28-73:36
Anacoreta, El 1-12-77:45
Analfabeto, El 10-11-61:7
Anaparastasis 11-11-70:27 and 12-12-73:20
Anastasia 12-19-56:6
Anata All'Arancia, L' 1-14-76:21
Anatahan 7-15-53:6 (Also see: Devil's Pitchfork, The)
Anatoliki Periferia 11-28-79:17
Anatomie d'un Rapport 9-29-76:90
Anatomie des Liebesakts 2-25-70:15
Anatomy of a Marriage: My Days with Jean-Marc and My Nights with Francoise (See: Francoise ou la Vie Conjugale et Jean-Marc ou la Vie Conjugale)
Anatomy of a Murder 7-01-59:6
Anchors Aweigh 7-18-45:34
Ancient Highway 11-11-25:41
Ancient Mariner, The 1-20-26:41
And a Still Small Voice 12-13-18:40

And Baby Makes Three 11-30-49:6
And Baby Makes Three 12-06-72:16
And Death Is Dead (See: Et, Morte la Nuit)
And Hope to Die (See: Course du Lievre a Travers les Champs, La)
And How (s) 12-11-29:35
... And Justice for All 9-19-79: 18
And Now for Something Completely Different 10-13-71:16
And Now, Miguel 5-18-66:18
And Now My Love (See: Toute Une Vie)
And Now the Screaming Starts 5-09-73:6
And Now Tomorrow 10-18-44:10
And One Was Beautiful 4-03-40:16
And Quiet Flows the Don 6-01-60:6 (Also see: Tichy Don)
And Satan Calls the Turns (See: Et Satan Conduit le Bal)
And So They Were Married 5-20-36:23
And So to Bed (See: Das Grosse Liebespiel)
And Soon the Darkness 7-22-70:20
And Sudden Death 7-22-36:17
And the Angels Sing 4-26-44:12
And the Villainess Still Pursued Him 11-13-09:13
... And the Wild, Wild Women (See: Nella Citta L'Inferno)
And Then There Were None 7-11-45:14
And There Came a Man (See: E Venne un Uomo)
... And Wife (s) 6-18-30:37
Andalousie 5-02-51:27
Andalusische Naechte 7-20-38:13
Andere, Der 1-19-32:29 (Also see: Other, The)
Andere Laechein, Das 6-21-78:19
Anderson Tapes, The 5-12-71:19
Andre Gide 4-09-52:22
Andrei Roublov 6-04-69:36
Androcles and the Lion 10-29-52:6
Andromeda Strain, The 3-10-71:16
Andy Clyde (s) 9-12-33:17
Andy Hardy Comes Home 7-30-58:6
Andy Hardy Gets Spring Fever 7-12-39:12
Andy Hardy Meets Debutante

7-03-40:18
Andy Hardy's Blonde Trouble 4-05-44:14
Andy Hardy's Double Life 12-02-42:8
Andy Hardy's Private Secretary 2-26-41:16
Andy Panda's Victory Garden (s) 10-07-42:25
Andy Warhol's Women 1-12-72:26
Anemone 5-01-68:26
Ang Boyfriend King Badoy 4-01-76:26
Ang Leon at Ang Daga 5-05-76:18
Ang Nobya Kong Sexy 3-12-75:20
Ang Pinakamagandany Hayop Sa Balat Ng Lupa 12-12-75:36
Ange Rouge, L' (See: Red Angel)
Angaaende Lone 7-08-70:14
Ange et la Femme, L' 2-01-78: 24
Ange Gardien, L' 1-31-79:22
Angel 9-15-37:13
Angel and Sinner 2-26-47:11
Angel and the Badman 2-12-47:14
Angel, Angel, Down We Go 8-13-69:18
Angel Baby 5-10-61:19
Angel Cake (s) 3-04-31:14
Angel Child 9-13-18:41
Angel Comes to Brooklyn, An 12-95-45:16
Angel Exterminador, El 5-23-62: 6
Angel Face 12-03-52:6
Angel from Texas, An 5-08-40:12
Angel in Exile 12-29-48:6
Angel in My Pocket 12-04-68:6
Angel Levine, The 7-15-70:20
Angel Mine 1-10-79:54
Angel Number Nine 11-27-74:16
Angel of Broadway, The 11-02-27: 18
Angel of Crooked Street 5-26-22: 34
Angel of Dawson's Camp, The 4-30-10:16
Angel of the Amazon 12-22-48:6
Angel of the House 1-30-14:17
Angel on My Shoulder 9-18-46:16
Angel Paso Sobre Brooklyn 9-25-57:26
Angel Passed over Brooklyn, An (See: Angel Paso Sobre Brooklyn)
Angel Unchained 8-19-70:16
Angel Who Pawned Her Harp 9-15-54:6

Angel with a Trumpet 2-22-50:6
Angel Wore Red 8-31-60:6
Angela 5-11-55:8
Angela 7-04-73:18
Angela Davis, L'Enchainement 12-28-77:14
Angela Davis: Portrait of a Revolutionary 1-26-72:16
Angele 11-13-34:15
Angeli del Quartiere, Gli 9-03-52:12
Angelika 10-06-54:22
Angelina 4-07-48:20
Angelique et le Roi 3-16-66:7
Angelique et le Sultan 9-25-68:6
Angelo 12-13-50:25
Angelo in the Crowd 9-17-52:22
Angels 4-07-76:26
Angels Alley 1-28-48:11
Angels Die Hard 6-24-70:22
Angels from Hell 7-17-68:6
Angels Hard as They Come 8-18-71:15
Angel's Holiday 5-26-37:15
Angels in the Outfield 8-29-51:6
Angels of the Streets 1-18-50:6
Angels One Five 4-02-52:22
Angels over Broadway 10-09-40:16
Angels Wash Their Faces 9-06-39:14
Angels with Broken Wings 6-04-41:15
Angels with Dirty Faces 10-26-38:13
Angels y Querubines 8-16-72:26
Anges, Les 3-21-73:26
Angi Vera 2-28-79:22
Anglar, Finns Donn? (See: Love Mates)
Angles of Angling (s) 6-09-31:18
Angry Breed 12-25-68:18
Angry God, The 10-27-48:9
Angry Hills, The 2-18-59:6 and 6-10-59:6
Angry Red Planet, The 12-02-59:6
Angry Sea, The (See: Chi No Hate Ni Ikiru Mono)
Angry Silence, The 3-23-60:6
Angst 3-16-55:24
Angst 8-25-76:68
Angst Essen Seele Auf 5-22-74:26
Angst Haben Und Angst Machen 9-22-76:30
Angst Vor der Angst (See: Fear of Fear)
Anguilla da 300 Milioni, Un' 9-01-71:22
Ani Imouto 1-26-77:30

Ani Obev Otach Rosa 5-17-72:20
Ani Yerushalmi 5-19-71:26
Aniakehak 11-14-33:17
Anima Persa 1-26-77:56
Animal, L' 10-19-77:26
Animal Crackers 9-03-30:19
Animal Fair, The (s) 2-18-31:14
Animal Farm 1-26-55:6
Animal Kingdom 1-03-33:19
Animal World, The 4-18-56:6
Animal World of Make-Believe 8-04-31:18
Animals, The 10-20-71:20
Animals of the Amazon (s) 6-02-31:14
Animas Trujano 9-13-61:28
Animated Doll, An 6-20-08:13
Animated Snowballs 3-21-08:15
Animaux, Les 6-24-64:7
Anita Droegemoeller Ruhe Die Puhe An der Ruhr 4-27-77:22
Anita, Swedish Nymphet 8-20-75:73
Anjos e Demonios 4-22-70:17
Ankles 7-23-30:19
Ankles Preferred 4-20-27:20
Ankur 7-03-74:16
Ann and Eve 8-12-70:15
Ann Carver's Profession 6-13-33:15
Ann Grey and Orch. (s) 9-19-28:12
Ann Seymour (s) 7-16-30:15
Anna 7-22-36:34
Anna 3-05-52:22
Anna 11-11-70:24
Anna and the King of Siam 6-05-46:13
Anna Ascends 11-17-22:41
Anna Christie 12-06-23:23
Anna Christie 3-19-30:34
Anna Cross 10-27-54:6
Anna Karenina 4-16-15:19
Anna Karenina 9-04-35:14
Anna Karenina 1-28-48:11
Anna Karenina 7-17-68:6
Anna Karenina 10-22-75:34
Anna Lucasta 7-13-49:16
Anna Lucasta 11-19-58:6
Anna Na Ulee 7-20-60:20
Anna of Rhodes 3-29-50:11
Anna und Elisabeth 5-02-33:22 and 7-01-36:23
Annabel Lee 6-16-22:42
Annabel Takes a Tour 10-19-38:12
Annabelle's Affairs 6-30-31:15
Annapolis 2-06-29:18

Apres L'Amour 1-12-32:28
Apres L'Amour 3-17-48:18
Apres Mein Kampf Mes Crimes
   4-24-40:16
April Blossoms 2-03-37:14
April 1, 2000 5-20-53:16
April Fool 11-03-26:17
April Fools, The 5-28-69:6
April Hat 30 Tage, Ein 7-30-
April in Paris 11-19-52:6
April Love 11-20-57:6
April Showers 11-22-23:27
April Showers 3-10-48:10
Apur Sanshar 9-23-59:18
Aqua Antics (s) 2-04-42:8
Aquatic Champions (s) 8-22-33:22
Aquella Casa En Las Afueras 11-
   19-80:21
Aquella Largo Noche 9-26-79:20
Aquellos Anos Locos 9-30-70:20
Arab, The 6-18-15:17
Arab, The 7-16-24:22
Arabella 9-03-69:29
Arabesque 5-04-66:6
Arabian Adventure 5-30-79:17
Arabian Knight, An 8-13-20:36
Arabian Knights (s) 3-25-31:16
Arabian Love 5-19-22:41
Arabian Nights 12-23-42:8
Arabian Nights (See: Fiore Della
   Mille e Una Notte, Il)
Arabian Shrieks, The (s) 1-26-32:
   21
Arabian Tights (s) 7-11-33:15
Arabische Naechte 6-04-80:22
Aragnee D'Eau, L' 3-17-71:26
Aran 9-05-79:30
Aranyer Din Ratri 7-08-70:15
Arashi 7-31-57:6
Araya 5-20-59:6
Arbe de Guernica, L' 12-10-
   75:26
Arc 8-12-70:15
Arcadians, The 12-14-27:23
Arch, The 11-13-68:6
Arch of Triumph 2-18-48:8
Arche de Noe, L' 2-26-47:11
Archie's Archery 10-29-10:14
Archimede le Chochard 5-13-59:6
Arctic Antics (s) 6-30-31:15
Arctic Flight 7-30-52:6
Arctic Fury 5-11-49:18
Arctic Giant, The (s) 3-11-42:20
Arctic Manhunt 8-24-49:22
Ard, El 5-13-70:26
Arde 9-08-71:26
Ardoise, L' 1-28-71:26
Are All Men Alike? 1-21-21:41

Are Husbands Necessary? 6-17-
   42:8
Are Passions Inherited 3-02-17:25
Are the Children to Blame 12-01-
   22:35
Are These Our Children 11-17-
   31:15
Are These Our Parents 8-30-44:10
Are They Born or Made? 12-25-
   14:42
Are We Civilized 6-19-34:27
Are You a Failure? 4-26-23:26
Are You a Mason? 3-26-15:24
Are You a Mason? 11-06-34:17
Are You Fit to Marry? (See:
   Black Stork, The)
Are You Legally Married? 7-18-
   19:43
Are You Listening? 4-26-32:25
Are You Positive 8-07-57:6
Are You There? 7-14-31:22
Are You With It? 3-17-48:8
Arena 6-24-53:6
Aren't Men Beasts? 2-03-37:15
Aren't We All? 7-05-32:14
Argent de Poche, L' 3-24-76:21
Argent des Autres, L' 2-06-78:24
Argentina--the Rich 11-02-27:25
Argentine Horses (s) 9-02-42:34
Argentine Love 12-24-24:32
Argentine Nights 9-04-40:18
Argentine Question, The 3-11-42:
   20
Argine, L' 10-26-38:15
Argonauts, The 1-07-11:13
Argyle Case, The 2-09-17:29
Argyle Case, The 9-04-29:13
Argyle Secrets, The 4-21-48:18
Ari No Machi No Maria 8-12-59:
   19
Aria Dia Atlety 6-25-80:20
Ariane 3-18-31:38
Ariane, Jeune Fille Russe 3-15-
   32:21
Ariel Gunner 4-24-43:20
Arise, My Love 10-23-40:14
Aristide Maillol 10-06-48:11
Aristocats, The 11-25-70:13
Aristocracy 11-21-14:27
Aristocrates, Les 11-23-55:6
Arizona 12-20-18:36
Arizona 11-20-40:16
Arizona Bound 4-13-27:22
Arizona Bound 9-10-41:16
Arizona Bushwackers 2-14-68:16
Arizona Cat Claw, The 11-21-19:
   55
Arizona Cowboy 4-26-50:16

Arizona Cyclone 5-09-28:41
Arizona Cyclone 3-11-42:8
Arizona Days 5-08-29:29
Arizona Days 4-14-37:33
Arizona Express 4-23-24:20
Arizona Gunfighter 9-29-37:15
Arizona Kid, The 5-21-30:25
Arizona Kid, The 10-11-39:13
Arizona Legion 7-05-39:16
Arizona Mahoney 2-24-37:19
Arizona Manhunt 9-19-51:6
Arizona Raiders, The 9-16-36:31
Arizona Raiders 7-21-65:7
Arizona Ranger, The 3-24-48:8
Arizona Romeo 5-13-25:38
Arizona Sweepstakes 1-20-26:40
Arizona Territory 10-04-50:22
Arizona Terror 9-29-31:22
Arizona Terrors 4-01-42:8
Arizona to Broadway 7-25-33:35
Arizona Trail 5-03-44:23
Arizona Whirlwind 4-05-44:14
Arizona Wildcat 1-25-28:12
Arizona Wildcat 11-09-38:17
Arizonian, The 7-31-35:19
Arkadas 8-02-78:16
Arkansas Judge 7-23-41:30
Arkansas Traveler 10-05-38:14
Arm of the Law 7-05-32:19
Arma, L' 8-09-78:20
Armaguedon 3-23-77:24
Armata Brancaleone, L' 6-01-
    66:6
Arme a Gauche, L' 7-21-65:7
Armee der Liebenden Oder Auf-
    stand der Perversen 3-21-
    79:28
Armee des Ombres, L' 9-24-69:
    15
Armino Negro 10-14-53:6
Armored Car 7-28-37:31
Armored Car Robbery 6-14-50:22
Armored Command 8-02-61:6
Armored Vault 11-14-28:26
Armorer's Daughter 10-15-10:12
Arms and the Girl 10-12-17:41
    and 10-19-17:32
Arms and the Woman 12-03-10:14
Arms and the Woman 11-10-16:29
Armstrong-Ambers Fight (s) 8-
    30-39:14
Armstrong-Jenkins Fight (s) 7-24-
    40:16
Armstrong's Wife 12-03-15:21
Army Bound 10-29-52:24
Army Chaplain (s) 1-06-43:50
Army Companions (s) 10-01-41:9
Army Game, The (See: Tire-Au-
    Flac)

Army Girl 7-20-38:12
Army Mascot, The (s) 6-03-42:24
Army Surgeon 11-11-42:8
Army Wives 11-22-44:10
Arnaud, Les 11-01-67:20
Arnaut Bros. (s) 6-27-28:14
Arnelo Affair 2-12-47:14
Arnold 10-24-73:17
Around Paris (s) 12-19-28:23
Around Peking 10-22-10:14
Around the Samovar (s) 2-18-31:
    14
Around the World 11-24-43:18
Around the World in 80 Days 10-
    24-56:6
Around the World in 80 Minutes
    11-24-31:21
Around the World Under the Sea
    4-06-66:24
Around the World Via Graf Zep-
    pelin 11-06-29:31
Aroused 8-28-68:6
Arp Statue, The 9-15-71:6
Arpenteurs, Les 5-10-72:21
Arrangement, The 11-19-69:22
Arrangiatevi! 11-11-59:6
Arrebato 10-15-80:220
Arrest Bulldog Drummond 11-23-
    38:14
Arrest of the Duchess de Berry
    3-19-10:17
Arretez les Tambours 2-22-61:6
Arriba Hazana 6-21-78:23
Arrival of Josie, The 7-31-14:16
Arrival of Perpetua, The 3-26-
    15:24
Arrival of the Lusitania 10-12-07:
    12
Arrivederci, Baby 12-21-66:7
Arrivederci, Papa 7-20-49:20
Arriviste, L' 2-09-77:24
Arrivistes, Les 5-04-60:6
Arrow in the Dust 4-21-54:6
Arrowhead 6-17-53:6
Arrowsmith 12-15-31:14
Arroz Con Leche 12-13-50:25
Arruza 6-16-71:22
Arsene Lupin 2-16-17:25
Arsene Lupin 3-01-32:20
Arsene Lupin Contre Arsene Lupin
    10-03-62:6
Arsene Lupin Returns 2-23-38:14
Arsenic and Old Lace 9-06-44:10
Arshin Mal Alan 3-10-37:15
Arshin Takes a Wife 8-02-50:16
Arson for Hire 3-18-59:23
Arson Gang Busters 6-01-38:13
Arson, Inc. 5-04-49:18

Arson Squad 9-26-45:14
Art of Killing 11-22-78:22
Art of Love, The 5-12-65:6
Art of Self-Defense, The (s) 2-
04-42:8
Art Trouble (s) 9-18-34:11
Arte de Vivir, El 8-04-65:32
Arte di Arrangiarsi 4-06-55:6
Arthur 1-21-31:30 and 6-09-31:19
Arthur and Garon (s) 8-14-29:18
Arthur and Morton Havel (s) 6-
12-29:16
Arthur Miller on Home Ground
9-05-79:27
Arthur Penn, 1922--Themes and
Variants 5-27-70:22
Arthur Takes Over 4-07-48:20
Arthur Tracy 6-14-32:16
Arthur Tracy-Nick Kenny (s) 1-
17-33:14
Art. 519, Codice Penale 7-08-
53:18
Artie, the Millionaire Kid 4-14-16:
24
Artillery Sergeant Kalen 4-11-62:6
Artisten in der Zirkuskuppel: Rat-
los, Die 9-11-68:106
Artistic Temper (s) 7-19-32:24
Artists and Models 8-04-37:18
Artists and Models 11-09-55:6
Artists and Models Abroad 11-02-
58:15
Artists Pay Day 1-07-11:13
Artist's Reverie 7-23-30:19
Arturo Tose-Anni 5-03-44:26
Arturo's Island (See: Isola di Ar-
turo, L')
Arvacska 5-26-76:20
Arven 5-23-79:22
Aryan, The 3-24-16:28
Arzt Stellt Fest, Der 5-18-66:18
Arzt Von St. Pauli, Der 6-11-69:
40
Arzt Von Stalingrad, Der 8-27-
58:6
As a Man Lives 12-15-22:41
As a Man Thinks 4-25-19:82
As a Woman Sows 1-28-16:23
As Amorosas 7-02-69:24
As Armas 2-18-70:21
As Deusas 3-07-73:24
As Du Turf, Les 4-19-32:25 and
5-22-35:17
As Good as Married 5-26-37:14
As Horas de Maria 10-10-79:34
As Husbands Go 1-30-34:12
As in a Looking Glass 3-03-16:
21

As Long as They're Happy 4-06-
55:6
As Man Desires 2-11-25:32
As Man Made Her 3-16-17:35
As Men Love 5-11-17:34A
As the Devil Commands 10-17-
33:27
As the Earth Turns 4-17-34:18
As the Sea Rages 8-24-60:6
As the Sun Went Down 2-21-19:
68
As Time Goes By 7-31-74:18
As Ye Sow 12-19-14:26
As You Desire Me 6-07-32:21
As You Like It 9-16-36:16 and
11-11-36:14
As You Mike It (s) 10-16-29:17
As Young as You Feel 6-06-51:6
As Young as We Are 9-24-58:6
Asa-Hanna 5-15-46:8
Asa-Nisse I Kronans Kläder 1-14-
59:16
Asayake No Uta 7-10-74:18
Ascenseur Pour L'Echafaud 5-07-
58:22
Asea on the Shore (s) 7-29-36:14
Asessino de Pediables, El 10-11-
78:48
Ash Wednesday 11-21-73:6
Ashani Sanket 8-01-73:18
Ashanti 2-07-79:20
Ashes and Diamonds (See: Popiol
I Diament)
Ashes of Embers 9-29-16:26
Ashes of Hope 10-05-17:43
Ashes of Vengeance 8-30-23:26
Asi Era Pancho Villa 8-05-59:6
Asi Se Quiere en Jalisco 8-18-
43:28
Asia's Desert 7-03-29:30
Asignatina Pendiente 8-17-77:20
Ask a Policeman 4-26-39:12
Ask Any Girl 5-13-59:6
Asleep in the Feet (s) 7-11-33:15
Asphalt 4-10-29:25 and 5-07-30:39
Asphalt Jungle, The 5-10-50:6
Asphalte 8-19-59:16
Asphaltnacht 10-08-80:22
Asphyx, The 9-20-72:14
Assassin Connait la Musique, L'
10-30-63:6
Assassin Est Dans L'Annuaire, L'
4-18-62:6
Assassin Musicien, L' 5-14-75:27
Assassin N'Est Pas Coupable 11-
06-46:18
Assassinat du Pere Noel, L' (See:
Who Killed Santa Claus?)

Authentique Proces de Carl-
Emmanuel Jung, L' 8-07-
68:6
Author, The (s) 8-22-28:14
Auto Hero, The 11-21-08:13
Auto und Kein Gold, Ein 8-12-
36:19
Autobiography of a Flea 2-09-77:
26
Autobiography of a Princess 10-
08-75:6
Autobuyography (s) 3-27:34:12
Autopsie d'un Complot 8-02-78:
18
Autopsy 11-28-73:26
Autopsy 10-04-78:18
Autour de Votre Main, Madame
6-18-30:37
Autre Homme, Une Autre Chance,
Un (See: Another Man, An-
other Chance)
Autres, Les 5-22-74:26
Autumn Afternoon, An (See: Samma
No Aji)
Autumn Crocus 11-06-34:17
Autumn Leaves 4-18-56:6
Autumn Love 10-31-28:31
Autumn Sonata 9-13-78:21
Aux Jardins de Murcie (See: Heri-
tage)
Aux Urnes, Citoyens 4-12-32:29
Aux Urnes, Citoyens 10-11-72:18
Aux Yeux du Souvenir 12-15-48:6
Avalanche, The 7-04-19:43
Avalanche 12-12-28:28
Avalanche 7-10-46:8
Avalanche 9-06-78:22
Avalanche Express 7-25-79:17
Avant le Deluge 4-07-54:24
Avantaszh 2-22-78:19
Avanti! 12-27-72:6
Avare, L' 3-26-80:20
Ave Maria 8-14-14:22
Ave Maria (s) 1-01-30:15
Ave Maria 9-16-36:17
Avec Des Si 11-27-63:6
Avec la Peau des Autres 9-21-
66:6
Avec L'Assurance 6-28-32:15
Avec le Sourire 2-08-39:19
Avenged by the Sea 3-14-08:13
Avenger 4-22-31:19
Avenger, The 10-10-33:23
Avengers, The 11-04-42:8
Avengers, The 6-14-50:22
Avenging Conscience, The 8-07-
14:18
Avenging Dentist, The 1-08-10:13

Avenging Fangs 6-01-27:24
Avenging Rider 11-14-28:30
Avenging Rider, The 9-29-43:8
Avenging Shadow 6-13-28:27
Avenging Trail, The 1-11-18:43
Adventuras de Joselito y Pulgar-
cito 10-26-60:6
Aventure, C'est L'Aventure, L'
5-17-72:30
Aventure Commence Demain, L'
3-24-48:22
Aventure de Billy le Kid, Un 3-
17-71:18
Aventures d'Arsene Lupin, Les
5-22-57:6
Aventures de Salavin 12-30-64:6
Aventurier de Seville, L' 6-09-
54:21
Aventuriers, Les 3-29-67:26
Average Husband (s) 9-03-30:19
Average Woman 4-02-24:23
Aveu, L' 5-06-70:15
Aveux les Plus Doux, Les 6-30-
71:29
Aviateur, L' 2-18-31:25 (Also
see: Aviator, The)
Aviation at L.A. 2-26-10:15
Aviation Contests at Rheims 9-
25-09:12
Aviation Craze, The 10-22-10:14
Aviator, The 1-15-30:22 (Also
see: Aviateur, L')
Avivato 11-30-49:6
Avocate D'Amour 9-14-38:23
Avodah 2-19-36:32
Avoir 20 Ans Dans les Aures 5-
10-72:34
Avventura, L' 5-25-60:7
Awakening, The 10-09-09:20
Awakening, The 11-23-17:46
Awakening 1-09-29:11
Awakening, The 9-17-80:18
Awakening Giant--China, The 5-
30-73:26
Awakening of Jim Burke 5-22-35:16
Awans 8-25-76:68
Awara 4-11-56:7
Away All Boats 5-16-56:6
Away Goes Prudence 7-09-20:26
Awful Truth, The 7-08-25:38
Awful Truth, The 10-20-37:12
Axel Munthe, Der Arzt Von San
Michele 10-24-62:20
Ay, Jalisco No te Rajes 12-31-
41:16
Ay, Pena, Penita, Pena 12-02-
53:6
Ayudeme Ud, Compadra 11-20-68:38

25 •

● B ●

B. F. 's Daughter 2-18-48:8
B. S. , I Love You 3-03-71:22
Baara 6-23-78:30 and 2-07-79:22
Baba Yaga 7-25-73:6
Babae, Hndi Ka Dapat Nilalang 4-23-75:24
Babatu 5-26-76:20
Babbitt 7-16-24:22
Babbitt 12-18-34:13
Babbling Brook (s) 3-01-32:20
Babbling Tongues 8-17-17:24
Babe Comes Home 6-01-27:21
Babe Ruth Story, The 7-21-48:10
Babek 7-02-80:20
Babes in Arms 9-20-39:15
Babes in Bagdad 12-10-52:6
Babes in the Woods (s) 11-22-32:16
Babes in Toyland 12-18-34:12
Babes in Toyland 12-06-61:18
Babes on Broadway 12-03-41:8
Babes on Swing Street 9-20-44:10
Babette S'en Va-T-En Guerre 9-09-39:6
Babies for Sale 6-12-40:16
Bab's Burglar 11-02-17:52
Bab's Candidate 7-09-20:28
Bab's Diary 9-28-17:40
Baby and the Battleship, The 8-01-56:6
Baby Blue Marine 4-28-76:28
Baby Blues (s) 9-11-34:11
Baby Carriage, The (See: Barnvagnen)
Baby Cyclone, The 10-17-28:24
Baby Doll 12-05-56:6
Baby Face 6-27-33:15
Baby Face Harrington 6-26-35:23
Baby Face Morgan 10-21-42:24
Baby Face Nelson 11-06-57:6
Baby Love 3-12-69:6
Baby Maker, The 9-30-70:15
Baby Mine 9-28-17:37
Baby Mine 1-11-28:27
Baby Rose Marie (s) 9-04-29:13
    (Also see: Child Wonder, The)
Baby Rosemary 8-11-76:19
Baby Sitter, La 11-05-75:38

Baby Snakes 12-26-79:13
Baby Swallows a Nickel 12-04-09:13
Baby Take a Bow 7-03-34:26
Baby Talks (s) 9-18-29:15
Baby Vickie 3-05-69:6
Babykins (s) 7-21-31:12
Babylon 5-14-80:14
Babylone-XX 9-03-80:26
Babysitter, The 10-08-69:28
Baccara 2-19-36:32
Bacchanale 7-01-70:13
Bach: H Moll Messe 4-25-79:22
Bachelor, The 11-12-10:16
Bachelor and the Bobby Soxer, The 6-04-47:16
Bachelor Apartment 5-20-31:17
Bachelor Bair 12-25-34:12
Bachelor Brides 5-19-26:16
Bachelor Daddy 4-28-22:42
Bachelor Father 2-04-31:16
Bachelor Flat 11-29-61:6
Bachelor Girl, The 7-24-29:39
Bachelor in Paradise 11-01-61:6
Bachelor Lady 7-02-41:12
Bachelor Mother 2-21-33:21
Bachelor Mother 7-05-39:14
Bachelor of Arts 4-17-35:15
Bachelor of Hearts 12-24-58:6
Bachelor Party, The 3-06-57:6
Bachelor's Affairs 6-28-32:14
Bachelor's Baby 10-08-10:12
Bachelor's Baby, A 7-07-22:60
Bachelor's Baby 5-11-27:17
Bachelors' Club 9-04-29:24
Bachelor's Daughters, The 9-11-46:10
Bachelor's Love, A 11-06-09:13
Bachelors' Paradise 7-18-28:31
Bachelor's Romance, The 4-02-15:21
Bachelor's Visit 9-25-09:20
Bachelor's Wife, A 5-16-19:51
Bacio di una Morta, Il 11-30-49:20
Back Among the Old Folks 3-05-10:13
Back at the Front 10-01-52:6
Back Door to Heaven 4-12-39:13
Back from Abroad (s) 3-27-29:12
Back from Eternity 8-29-56:6
Back from Shanghai 3-26-30:42
Back from the Dead 8-14-57:6
Back Home 6-18-30:37
Back Home and Broke 1-05-23:41
Back in Circulation 7-28-37:27
Back in the Saddle 3-26-41:18
Back of the Man 3-02-17:29
Back Pay 2-17-22:40

Bako L'Antre Rive 8-23-78:36
Bakuso 3-29-67:26
Bal, Le 11-10-31:15 and 10-04-
32:19 (Also see: Ball, Der)
Bal Cupidon, Le 6-22-49:20
Bal de Samedi Soir, Le 6-19-68:39
Bal des Voyous, Le 8-21-68:26
Bal du Comte D'Orgel, Le 5-13-
70:26
Bal Tabarin 6-18-52:6
Balaclava 4-30-30:38
Balada O Trubi I Oblaku 8-09-61:6
Balalaika 12-20-39:14
Balance (s) 6-20-33:11
Balaoo or the Demon Ape 10-03-
14:21
Balarrasa 5-09-51:6
Balcony, The 3-20-63:6
Bald-Headed Betty 9-10-75:20
Baleine Qui Avait Mal Aux Dents,
Une 4-17-74:16
Baleydier 2-02-32:19
Bali 5-23-33:15
Bali 1-13-71:24
Balinese Love 12-08-31:15
Ball, Der 9-29-31:22 (Also see:
Le Bal)
Ball of Fire 12-03-41:8
Ballad for a Hoodlum (See: Ballade
Pour un Voyou)
Ball of Fire 12-03-41:8
Ballad in Blue 3-03-65:6
Ballad of a Hussar 7-31-63:6
Ballad of Cable Hogue 3-11-70:17
Ballad of Cossack Golota 3-09-38:
14
Ballad of Josie, The 12-27-67:7
Ballad of Narayama (See: Narayama
Bushi-Ko)
Ballad of Tara 5-28-80:44
Ballada O Soldatie 5-18-60:7
Ballade des Daltons, La 9-27-78:
22
Ballade Om Carl-Henning 5-07-69:
6
Ballade Pour un Chien 3-27-68:6
Ballade Pour un Voyou 3-20-63:18
Balle Au Coeur, Une 3-16-66:7
Balle Dans le Canon, Une 12-17-
58:6
Ballerina 10-04-50:22
Ballerina e Buon Dio 10-01-58:6
Ballet Girl, The 1-28-16:22
Ballet Gayane 12-27-78:14
Ballo Al Castello 11-01-39:18
Ballon Rouge, Le 5-16-56:6
Ballongen 12-04-46:13
Baltagul 9-17-69:23

Baltic Deputy 9-08-37:19
Baltimore Bullet, The 2-27-80:20
Baltutlaminingen 11-25-70:13
Bambi 5-27-42:8
Bambina (See: Faro da Padre, Le)
Bambole, Le 2-03-65:6
Bambolona, La 1-15-69:39
Bamboo Blonde, The 6-19-46:8
Bamboo Gods and Iron Men 1-23-
74:14
Bamboo Prison 12-15-54:6
Bamboo Saucer, The 11-06-68:24
Bamse 2-11-70:16
Banana Peal (See: Peau de Banane)
Bananas 4-28-71:6
Banco a Bangkok 7-22-64:6
Band Concert, The (s) 3-06-35:20
Band Master, The (s) 7-07-31:25
Band of Angels 7-10-57:6
Band of Outsiders (See: Bande a
Part)
Band Plays On, The 12-25-34:12
Band Wagon, The 7-08-53:6
Bandbox, The 12-05-19:61
Bande a Bonnot, La 11-13-68:26
Bande a Bouboule, La 1-12-32:28
Bande a Part 4-29-64:6
Bandera, La 10-02-35:17
Bandera Rota 9-05-79:22
Bandida, La 9-05-62:16
Bandidi 8-12-64:22
Bandido 8-15-56:6
Bandidos de Rio Frio 3-28-56:6
Bandit, The 2-12-10:17
Bandit, The 6-01-49:20
Bandit, The (See: Bandida, La)
Bandit King of Texas 10-05-49:8
Bandit of Sherwood Forest, The
2-20-46:8
Bandit of Zhobe, The 3-11-59:6
Bandit Queen 11-29-50:22
Bandit Trail, The 9-10-41:18
Banditi a Milano 5-22-68:6
Banditi a Orgosolo 8-30-61:6
Bandit's Baby, The 6-17-25:37
Bandits of Corsica, The 3-18-53:17
Bandits of Dark Canyon 12-10-47:
12
Bandits of Death Valley, The 2-
12-15:23
Bandits of El Dorado 6-27-51:9
Bandits of Orgosolo (See: Banditi
a Orgosolo)
Bandits on the West 8-19-53:6
Bandits on the Wind 9-26-62:6
Bandit's Son, The 2-08-28:24
Bandolero, The 10-29-24:27
Bandolero 6-05-68:6

29 •

Battle Circus 1-28-53:6
Battle Cry 2-02-55:6
Battle Cry of Peace, The 8-13-15:17
Battle Flame 5-13-59:6
Battle for Kiev 1-08-36:13
Battle for Paris 9-18-29:25
Battle for the Planet of the Apes 5-23-73:28
Battle Hymn 12-19-56:7
Battle Hymn of the Republic (s) 9-19-28:12
Battle in Outer Space 6-15-60:18
Battle of Algiers (See: Batta Glia di Algeri, La)
Battle of Blood Island 5-18-60:6
Battle of Britain 9-15-43:10
Battle of Britain 9-17-69:13
Battle of Broadway 4-27-38:22
Battle of Chile II: Coup D'Etat, The (See: Batalla de Chile, II: El Golpe de Estado)
Battle of Gallipoli 12-08-31:15
Battle of Gettysburg 6-27-13:16
Battle of Greed 5-18-38:13
Battle of Hearts 5-26-16:22
Battle of Life, The 12-15-16:37
Battle of Love, The 8-06-15:18
Battle of Love's Return 6-23-71:46
Battle of Midway, The (s) 9-16-42:20
Battle of Mons 3-20-29:13
Battle of Neretva (See: Bitka Na Neretva)
Battle of Oil, The (s) 3-18-42:25
Battle of Paris 2-12-30:19
Battle of Przemysl 8-06-15:17
Battle of River Plate 11-14-56:6
Battle of Rogue River 3-03-54:6
Battle of Russia 10-06-43:8
Battle of Somme 12-05-28:19
Battle of the Amazons 12-05-73:20
Battle of the Bulge 12-22-65:6
Battle of the Bulge--The Brave Rifles, The 2-09-66:6
Battle of the Centuries (s) 12-06-32:15 and 3-21-33:16
Battle of the Clouds, The 1-08-10:12
Battle of the Coral Sea 10-14-59:6
Battle of the Rails 12-14-49:22
Battle of the Sexes 4-17-14:21
Battle of the Sexes, The 10-17-28:16
Battle of the Sexes, The 12-30-59:6
Battle of the Somme, The

10-06-16:27
Battle of the Worlds (See: Pianeta Degli Uomini, Il)
Battle of Torreon 5-15-14:22
Battle of Villa Fiorita, The 5-26-65:14
Battle Stations 1-01-56:6
Battle Taxi 1-12-55:6
Battle Zone 10-15-52:6
Battleground 9-28-49:6
Battlements de Coeur 3-20-40:16
Battles of a Nation 11-26-15:23
Battles of Chief Pontiac 12-17-52:18
Battles of Coronel and Falkland Islands, The 2-16-28:24 (Also see: Battles of Falkland Island)
Battles of Falkland Island 2-29-28:27
Battleship Potemkin (See: Cruiser Potemkin and Potemkin, The)
Battlestar Galactica 9-20-78:52
Battling Bunyan 3-25-25:36
Battling Butler 8-25-26:18
Battling Fool, The 7-16-24:23
Battling Jane 10-04-18:49
Battling Mason 3-04-25:39
Battling Orioles, The 11-05-24:32
Batu-Bato Sa Langit 11-05-75:38
Bavu 5-17-23:23
Bawbs O' Blue Ridge 11-17-16:26
Bawdy Adventures of Tom Jones 9-08-76:20
Baxter 1-31-73:18
Baxter, Vera Baxter 6-22-77:17
Bay of the Angels, The (See: Baie des Anges, Le)
Bayou 6-05-57:6
Bbicot 7-31-57:6
Be a Little Sport 7-04-19:43
Be Big (s) 3-18-31:14
Be Careful Ladies (See: Mefiez-Vous Mesdames)
Be Mine Tonight 4-18-33:21
Be My Guest 4-21-65:7
Be Reasonable 3-17-22:42
Be Yourself 3-12-30:21
Beach Babies (s) 7-10-29:13 and 8-21-29:18
Beach Ball 9-29-65:6
Beach Blanket Bingo 4-07-65:6
Beach Girls and the Monster 9-22-65:6
Beach of Dreams 6-03-21:41
Beach Party 7-17-63:6
Beach Red 8-02-67:6
Beachcomber, The 11-30-38:12

(Also see: Vessel of Wrath)
Beachcomber, The 8-18-54:6
Beachhead 2-03-54:6
Beans 9-27-18:42
Bear, The 9-21-18:42
Bear and the Tiger, The (s)
    4-22-42:18
Bear Cat 3-31-22:40
Bear Country 1-28-53:6
Bear Hunt in Russia, A 12-18-09:
    15
Bear Hunt in the Rockies 1-15-
    10:13
Bear Island 1-23-80:26
Bear Shooters, The (s) 8-06-30:31
Bearded Lady, The (s) 5-21-30:19
Bears and I, The 10-16-74:14
Bear's Wedding, The 8-01-28:22
Beast, The 1-16-20:62
Beast, The (s) 7-04-28:16
Beast, The 12-24-80:15
Beast from Haunted Cave 3-23-
    60:6
Beast from 20,000 Fathoms, The
    6-17-53:6
Beast Must Die, The 4-24-74:18
Beast of Budapest 2-12-58:6
Beast of Hollow Mountain, The
    8-29-56:6
Beast of the City 3-15-32:14
Beast of Yucca Flats, The 5-24-
    61:6
Beast with Five Fingers, The
    12-25-46:12
Beast with 1,000,000 Eyes 12-14-
    55:6
Beasts of Berlin 11-22-39:16
Beat Generation, The 7-01-59:6
"Beat" Girl 11-16-60:6
Beat the Band 2-26-47:10
Beat the Devil 12-02-53:6
Beating the Game 9-23-21:42
Beating the Odds 5-16-19:53
Beatrice Fairfax 8-11-16:26 and
    8-25-16:25
Beatrice Lillie (s) 5-23-28:21
Beau and Arrows (s) 5-03-32:14
Beau Bandit 6-18-30:37
Beau Broadway 8-01-28:18
Beau Brummell 4-04-24:22
Beau Brummell 10-06-54:6
Beau Geste 9-01-26:14
Beau Geste 7-26-39:15
Beau Geste 7-20-66:6
Beau Ideal 1-21-31:17
Beau James 6-12-57:6
Beau Masque 12-27-72:20
Beau Monstre, Un 2-24-71:26

Beau Night (s) 6-05-29:15
Beau Revel 3-18-21:34
Beau Sabreur 1-25-28:12
Beau Serge, Le 6-04-58:6
Beau Voyage, Le 2-18-48:9
Beaujolais Nouveau est Arrive, Le
    4-26-78:18
Beaute du Diable, La 4-19-50:8
Beauties, The (s) 4-01-31:16
Beauties of the Night (See: Les
    Belles de Nuit)
Beautiful Adventure, The 10-26-
    17:32
Beautiful Adventure 9-27-32:29
Beautiful and the Damned, The
    12-15-22:40
Beautiful Blonde from Bashful Bend,
    The 5-25-49:8
Beautiful Blue Danube 2-27-29:95
Beautiful Blue Danube (s) 9-29-
    31:14
Beautiful but Nice 3-01-44:20
Beautiful but Dumb 9-12-28:27
Beautiful Cheat, The 4-21-26:34
Beautiful Cheat, The 7-18-45:34
Beautiful City, The 11-25-25:38
Beautiful Gambler, The 8-12-21:
    35
Beautiful Ippolita, The (See: Bel-
    lezza Ippolita, La)
Beautiful Liar 12-16-21:35
Beautiful Lie, The 6-02-17:22
Beautiful Mrs. Reynolds, The 1-
    11-18:43
Beautiful People 11-27-74:16
Beautiful Stranger 7-21-54:6
Beautiful Swindlers, The 11-01-
    67:7
Beautifully Trimmed 12-10-20:35
Beauty and Bullets 1-23-29:43
Beauty and the Bad Man 6-24-25:
    84
Beauty and the Beast 12-24-47:13
    (Also see: Belle et la Bete,
    La)
Beauty and the Beast 2-07-79:22
Beauty and the Boss 4-05-32:14
Beauty and the Bullfighter (See:
    Sang et Lumieres)
Beauty and the Rogue 2-08-18:39
Beauty for Sale 9-19-33:13
Beauty for the Asking 2-15-39:13
Beauty in Chains 3-08-18:41
Beauty Jungle, The 9-02-64:6
Beauty Market 1-23-20:60
Beauty on Broadway (s) 5-30-33:
    15
Beauty on Parade 7-26-50:10

33 •

Beauty Parlor, The (s) 7-27-27: 21

Beauty Parlor 10-04-32:19

Beauty Prize, The 12-31-24:26

Beauty Proof 7-25-19:44

Beauty Shop 5-12-22:32

Beauty Shoppers 7-13-27:23

Beauty's Worth 3-31-22:40

Beaux Dimanches, Les 10-30-74:42

Beaux Jours, Les 10-23-35:13

Beaux Verités, Les 7-30-52:18

Beaver Valley 7-05-50:10

Bebert et L'Omnibus 12-25-63:16

Bebo's Girl (See: Ragazza di Bube, La)

Because 9-11-29:33

Because He Loved Her 1-21-16: 27

Because of Eve 12-15-48:6

Because of Him 1-09-46:79

Because of You 10-08-52:12

Because They're Young 3-09-60:6

Because You're Mine 9-03-52:12

Becket 3-04-64:6

Beckoning Flame, The 12-17-15:18

Beckoning Trail, The 8-04-16:28

Becky 10-26-27:24

Becky Sharp 6-19-35:21

Bed and Board (See: Domicile Conjugal)

Bed and Breakfast 1-07-31:36

Bed of Roses 7-04-33:16

Bed Sitting Room, The 7-16-69:6

Bed Time (s) 11-13-29:12

Bedazzled 12-13-67:6

Bedelia 6-05-46:13

Bedevilled 4-13-55:8

Bedford Incident, The 10-13-65:6

Bedknobs and Broomsticks 10-13-71:16

Bedlam 4-24-46:8

Bedniyat Louka 7-18-79:14

Bedroom Blunder, A 9-28-17:39

Bedroom Window 6-11-24:28

Bedside 3-13-34:16

Bedside Manner 6-13-45:17

Bedtime for Bonzo 1-17-51:11

Bedtime Story, A 4-25-33:15

Bedtime Story 12-10-41:8

Bedtime Story 6-03-64:6

Bedtime Worries (s) 1-16-34:15

Bedzie Lepiej 4-07-37:29

Been Down So Long It Looks Like Up To Me 9-08-71:6

Beer Is Here (s) 4-11-33:17

Bees, The 11-15-78:18

Bees Buzz (s) 4-16-30:21

Beethoven Concerto 3-31-37:19

Beethoven "Fidelio" 3-21-79:28

Beethoven--Tage Aus Einem Leben 12-15-76:22

Beetle, The 1-02-20:75

Before and After 2-19-10:15

Before Dawn 10-24-33:17

Before Him All Rome Trembled 2-09-47:9

Before Hindsight 11-16-77:20

Before I Hang 10-02-40:12

Before Midnight 8-26-25:57

Before Midnight 1-16-34:54

Before Morning 11-21-33:37

Before Silence Came 2-28-79:26

Before the Bar (s) 10-09-29:23

Before the Dawn 8-28-09:13

Before the Mountain Was Moved 3-11-70:17

Before the Revolution (See: Prima Della Rivoluzione)

Before Winter Comes 1-15-69:6

Beg, Borrow or Steal 12-01-37: 14

Begar 12-18-46:14

Beggar of Cawnpore, The 4-28-16:29

Beggar on Horseback 6-10-25:37

Beggar Student, The (See: Der Bettelstudent)

Beggar Woman, The 3-01-18:43

Beggars, The 8-07-63:20

Beggars in Ermine 5-01-34:15

Beggars of Life 9-26-28:14

Beggars Opera, The 6-17-53:16

Begging the Ring 3-21-79:28

Beginners' Luck (s) 5-29-35:14

Beginning of the Road 7-03-57:6

Beginning or the End 2-19-47:8

Beguiled, The 3-10-71:16

Beguin de la Garnison 5-09-33:15

Behave Yourself 9-12-51:6

Behemoth, Sea Monster 11-04-59:7

Behind a Mask 12-03-10:14

Behind City Lights 9-19-45:12

Behind Closed Doors 1-28-16:23

Behind Closed Doors 4-24-29:26

Behind Closed Shutters 6-11-52: 18

Behind Green Lights 4-24-35:13

Behind Green Lights 1-16-46:18

Behind Jury Doors 3-28-33:27

Behind Locked Doors 9-08-48:10

Behind Office Doors 3-25-31:24

Behind Prison Gates 8-23-39:20

Behind Prison Walls 5-26-43:8

Behind Show-Window 4-24-57:6

Behind Stone Walls 4-19-32:25

Behind That Curtain 7-03-29:17
Behind the Altar 2-06-29:19
Behind the Curtain 7-23-24:26
Behind the Door 1-31-20:56
Behind the 8 Ball 12-09-42:16
Behind the Enemy Lines 4-11-45:20
Behind the Evidence 2-05-35:31
Behind the Front 2-10-36:40
Behind the German Lines 12-05-28:19
Behind the Great Wall 12-16-59:6
Behind the Green Door 8-16-72:30
Behind the Headlines 6-09-37:25
Behind the High Wall 6-13-56:6
Behind the Lines 9-15-16:25
Behind the Makeup 1-15-30:22
Behind the Mask 5-03-32:15
Behind the Mask 4-03-46:12
Behind the Mask 11-12-58:6
Behind the Microphone (s) 11-03-31:17
Behind the Mike 11-03-37:14
Behind the News 12-25-40:18
Behind the Rising Sun 7-14-43:18
Behind the Scenes 10-31-14:27
Behind the Screen 11-17-16:26
Behinderte Liebe 3-30-79:16
Behold a Pale Horse 8-19-64:6
Behold My Wife 10-15-20:41
Behold My Wife 2-20-35:15
Behold the Man! 1-28-20:41
Beiderseits der Rollbahn 8-12-53:6
Being Respectable 8-06-24:24
Being There 12-19-79:19
Being Two Isn't Easy 11-20-63:6
Beiss Mich, Liebling 10-14-70:32
Bejleren 8-20-75:73
Bekenntnisse des Hochstaplers Felix Krull, Die 6-12-57:18
Bekotott 3-12-75:20
Bel Age, Le 10-28-59:6
Bel Ami 3-19-47:12
Bel Ami 4-09-58:20
Bel Ami 2000 Oder: Wie Verfuehrt Man Einen Playboy 12-07-66:22
Bel Amour 7-18-51:20
Bel Ordure 5-23-73:34
Bela Lugosi Meets a Brooklyn Gorilla 9-10-52:6
Belated Flowers 11-29-72:26
Belated Meal 5-01-09:15
Belated Weddings, The 10-23-09:13
Belfer 1-10-79:54
Belgian, The 11-02-17:51

Belgian War Pictures 12-05-14:24
Belgian Army, The 9-17-10:12
Beli Bim--Chornoye Ukho 7-05-78:17
Believe in Me 9-08-71:16
Believe It or Not (s) 5-07-30:20; 8-20-30:14; 1-28-31:14; 3-94-31:14; 5-20-31:16; 11-10-31:14; 12-08-31:14; 12-29-31:166; 3-08-32:14; 3-22-32:13; 5-24-32:29; 7-12-32:16; 7-19-32:24; 8-30-32:14
Believe Me, Xantippe 6-07-18:33
Beliye Nochi 10-11-61:7
Bell, The 5-03-67:24
Bell' Antonio, Il 4-20-60:8
Bell, Book and Candle 10-22-58:6
Bell Boy, The 3-22-18:52
Bell Boy 13 3-29-23:36
Bell for Adano, A 6-20-45:11
Bell Jar, The 3-21-79:24
Bell of the Night 3-26-30:20
Bella di Giorno (See: Belle de Jour)
Bella Donna 11-19-15:23
Bella Donna 4-19-23:35
Bella Donna 8-14-34:15 and 3-06-35:21
Bella Grita, Una 7-14-65:6
Belladonna 7-04-73:30
Bellamy Trial 1-30-29:22
Bellboy, The 7-13-60:6
Belle 5-30-73:12
Belle Americaine, La 10-18-61:22
Belle de Jour 4-19-67:58
Belle Equipe, La 10-07-36:15
Belle et la Bete, La 12-04-46:13 (Also see: Beauty and the Beast)
Belle Fille Comme Moi, Une 9-27-72:6
Belle Image, La 7-18-51:20
Belle le Grand 2-28-51:18
Belle Ma Povere 3-19-58:18
Belle Mentalite 11-04-53:6
Belle Meuniere, La 2-05-49:58
Belle of New York, The 2-28-19:57
Belle of New York, The 2-20-52:6
Belle of Old Mexico 2-08-50:18
Belle of Samoa (s) 4-24-29:13
Belle of the Harvest 11-27-09:13
Belle of the 90's 9-25-34:13
Belle of the Season, The 8-01-19:52
Belle of the Yukon 11-29-44:18
Belle Otero, La 12-22-54:22
Belle Que Voila, La 5-10-50:16
Belle Russe, La 7-10-14:20

Belle Starr 8-27-41:8
Belle Starr's Daughter 10-27-48:9
Belle Trave 8-25-76:27
Belle Vie, La 9-04-63:6
Belles and Ballets 7-27-60:6
Belles de Nuit, Les 10-15-52:6
Belles Manieres, Les 5-16-79:44
Belles of Bali (s) 4-05-32:14
Belles of Capistrano 9-16-42:8
Belles of St. Trinians, The 10-13-54:6
Belles on Their Toes 4-09-52:6
Bellezza Ippolita, La 7-18-62:16
Bellezze di Hollywood, Le (s) 3-25-41:16
Bellissima 4-09-52:22
Bellissima Novembre, Un (See: That Splendid November)
Bellman, The 9-09-47:16
Bello O Brutte Si Sposen Tutte (See: Pretty or Plain, They All Get Married)
Bello Onesto Emigrato Australia Sposerebbe Compaesana Illibata 1-19-72:6
Bells, The 9-20-18:44
Bells Are Ringing 6-08-60:6
Bells Go Down, The 5-12-43:8
Bells of Autumn 3-26-80:26
Bells of Coronado, The 1-18-50:6
Bells of Old Town 1-22-47:17
Bells of Rosarita 5-16-45:8
Bells of St. Mary's, The 11-28-45:10
Bells of San Angelo, The 5-28-47:20
Bells of San Fernando 4-02-47:16
Beloved 1-30-34:12
Beloved Adventuress, The 7-06-17:23
Beloved Bachelor, The 10-20-31:27
Beloved Blackmailer, The 8-02-18:29
Beloved Brute, The 11-12-24:25
Beloved Cheater, The 3-19-20:54
Beloved Enemy, The 12-30-36:10
Beloved Imposter, The 12-13-19:40
Beloved Infidel 11-18-59:6
Beloved Jim 12-14-17:44
Beloved Rogue, The 3-16-27:17
Beloved Traitor, The 3-01-18:41
Beloved Vagabond, The 9-09-36:17 and 2-10-37:15
Below the Belt 12-17-80:17
Below the Border 2-25-42:8

Below the Deadline 6-10-36:18
Below the Deadline 10-02-46:8
Below the Hill 9-01-65:24
Below the Line 9-23-25:39
Below the Rio 10-18-23:23
Below the Sahara 6-03-53:18
Below the Sea 6-06-33:14
Below the Surface 6-11-20:34
Below Zero (s) 10-15-30:25 and 10-29-30:17
Beloy and the Kid 6-23-76:34
Belphegor 5-13-21:42
Belstone Fox, The 11-28-73:18
Belyazani Atomi 7-25-79:42
Belyi Parohod 7-14-76:25
Ben 6-14-72:24
Ben Bernie and Orch. (s) 7-04-28:16 and 4-09-30:22
Ben Blair 3-03-16:22
Ben et Benedict 4-27-77:20
Ben-Gurion Remembers 12-13-72:15
Ben-Hur 1-06-26:38
Ben-Hur 11-18-59:6
Ben Pollock Orch. (s) 9-11-29:18
Bend of the River 1-23-52:6
Beneath the Car 5-08-14:20
Beneath the Planet of the Apes 5-06-70:15
Beneath the Sea 11-29-32:19
Beneath the 12-Mile Reef 12-16-53:6
Beneath the Valley of the Ultra-vixens 4-18-79:22
Beneath Western Skies 5-17-44:20
Benedict Arnold and Major Andre 11-20-09:13
Benefactor, El 6-06-73:30
Beneficiary, The 3-12-80:17
Benefit, The (s) 2-05-30:19
Benefit on the Doubt, The 10-04-67:14
Bengal Brigade 10-20-54:6
Bengal Tiger 8-05-36:16
Bengal Tiger 8-02-72:24
Bengazi 9-21-55:6
Bengelchen Liebt Kruez und Quer 3-05-69:6
Beniamino Gigli (s) 7-11-28:13 and 12-05-28:12
Beniamino Gigli and Marion Talley (s) 5-23-28:21
Benito Cereno 8-27-69:18
Benitou 3-21-22:40
Benjamin (See: Benjamin, ou les Memoires d'Un Puceau)
Benjamin 1-10-73:18
Benjamin ou les Memoires d'Un

Puceau 1-24-68:6
Benji 11-13-74:19
Benny Goodman Story, The 12-21-55:6
Benson Murder Case, The 4-16-30:49
Benvenuto, Reverendo! 6-28-50:18
Beregis Automobilyi (See: Uncommon Thief, The)
Bereketli Topraklar Uzerinde 9-03-80:25
Berenice 4-05-67:20
Berg, Ruft, Der 2-16-38:25
Bergado 5-05-76:22
Berge in Flammen 10-13-31:29
Bergere et le Ramoneur, La 10-08-52:12
Bergslagsfolk 3-23-38:17
Berkeley Square 9-19-33:13
Berlin 6-13-28:27
Berlin After Dark 5-29-29:26
Berlin Alexanderplatz 10-27-31:25 (Also see: Sur le Pave de Berlin)
Berlin Alexanderplatz 9-17-80:23
Berlin Correspondent 8-12-42:20
Berlin--Dein Filmgesicht 8-20-80:20
Berlin Express 4-07-48:10
Berlin Ist Eine Suende Wert 4-13-66:20
Berlin Medley (s) 11-15-32:19
Berlin Today (s) 8-30-32:14
Berlin Via America 8-02-18:39
Berliner Ballade 9-28-49:15
Berliner Bettwurst 2-16-77:26
Berlinger 7-14-76:25
Bermuda Mystery 4-19-44:12
Bermuda Triangle, The 1-17-79:21
Bernadette of Lourdes (See: Suffit d'Aimer, Il)
Bernadine 7-03-57:6
Bernardo de Pace (s) 6-13-28:12 and 5-22-29:16
Bernice Bobs Her Hair 10-13-76:22
Bernie Cummins (s) 3-20-29:12
Beroringen (See: Touch, The)
Berserk 12-27-67:20
Bert Lahr (s) 1-01-30:15
Bert Swor and Co. (s) 7-04-28:16
Bertha (the Sewing Machine Girl) 1-05-27:16
Bertie's Elopement 9-24-10:12
Bertlevyettes 1-01-15:29
Beru et Ces Dames 11-20-68:36
Beschreibung Einer Insel 8-15-79:24
Besserer Herr, Ein 1-14-28:17

Best Bad Man, The 12-02-25:40
Best Boy 9-19-79:18
Best Foot Forward 6-30-43:8
Best Friends 11-19-75:18
Best House in London, The 7-30-69:6
Best Man, The 5-02-19:58
Best Man, The 4-01-64:6
Best Man Wins 1-08-35:18
Best Man Wins 5-19-48:13
Best of Benny Hill 4-02-75:30
Best of Cinerama, The 12-25-63:6
Best of Enemies 7-18-33:37
Best of Enemies, The 12-20-61:7
Best of Everything, The 10-14-59:6
Best of Luck, The 7-09-20:26
Best of the Badman 5-02-51:6
Best of Walt Disney's True-Life Adventures, The 10-15-75:26
Best People, The 10-21-25:35
Best Things in Life Are Free, The 9-25-56:6
Best Years of Our Lives, The 11-27-46:14
Bestiaire D'Amour, Le 1-12-66:28
Bestije 8-17-77:22
Bestione, Il 10-16-74:18
Besuch Beim Wettermacher (s) 2-02-32:15
Beszallasolas 12-14-38:15
Bete, La 8-27-75:16
Bete a L'Auffut, La 7-01-59:6
Bete Errante, La 9-06-32:21
Bete Humaine, La 2-15-39:13
Bete Mais Discipline 9-26-79:34
Bethlehem to Jerusalem (s) 12-27-32:14
Betia, La 1-12-72:14
Betrayal 8-31-17:29
Betrayal 5-08-29:20
Betrayal, The 5-08-29:17
Betrayal 9-20-39:27
Betrayal from the East 4-25-45:14
Betrayed 7-21-54:6
Betrayed Women 2-01-56:18
Betrogen Bis Zum Juengsten Tag 5-15-57:7
Betsy, The 2-15-78:19
Betsy Ross 9-07-17:33
Betsy's Burglar 3-09-17:24
Bettelstudent, Der 12-16-36:15 and 12-30-36:11

Bettelstudent, Der 1-29-58:6
Better Bowling (s) 2-04-42:22
Better Man, The 8-14-14:21
Better N.Y.C., A (s) 11-25-36: 14
Better 'Ole The 2-28-19:58
Better 'Ole, The 10-13-26:17
Better Than Gold 2-26-10:15
Better Times 7-11-19:61
Better Way, The 7-13-27:22
Better Wife 7-11-19:57
Better Woman, The 10-29-15:23
Bettie's Choice 10-09-09:22
Bettina Loved a Soldier 8-04-16: 28
Betty Blokk--Buster Follies 8-18-76:22
Betty Boop and Bimbo (s) 9-22-31:22
Betty Boop for President (s) 9-20-32:14
Betty Boop, M.D. (s) 11-01-32:12
Betty Co-Ed (s) 5-13-31:36
Betty Co-Ed 11-27-46:28
Betty Compton (s) 5-23-28:21
Betty Is Punished 10-15-10:12
Betty Is Still at Her Old Tricks 10-08-10:12
Betty of Graystone 3-24-16:25
Betty Takes a Hand 1-04-18:44
Betty to the Rescue 3-02-17:25
Between Fighting Men 2-14-33:44
Between Friends 5-14-24:27
Between Heaven and Hell 10-10-56:7
Between Men 12-03-15:21
Between Men 1-29-36:16
Between Men 5-23-79:27
Between Midnight and Dawn 9-27-50:8
Between Tears and Smiles 10-28-64:6
Between the Acts (s) 7-04-28:16
Between the Lines 4-20-77:73
Between Two Husbands 8-20-24: 22
Between Two Women 8-11-37:19
Between Two Women 12-20-44:17
Between Two Worlds 5-10-44:10
Between Us Girls 9-02-42:18
Between Wars 12-18-74:12
Between Worlds 7-09-24:24
Beulah 5-14-15:20
Beverly Hills Call Boys, The 11-11-70:22
Beverly of Graustark 4-21-26:34
Beware 6-19-46:8
Beware, My Lovely 7-30-52:6

Beware of Bachelors 2-06-29:19
Beware of Blondes 8-22-28:16
Beware of Blondes 12-16-36:14
Beware of Blondie 4-05-50:6
Beware of Ladies 1-13-37:13
Beware of Married Men 4-11-28: 13
Beware of Pity 6-26-46:11
Beware of Widows 5-25-27:20
Beware Spooks! 10-25-39:11
Beware the Blob 6-07-72:18
Beware the Holy Whore (See: Warnung Vor Einer Heligen Nutte)
Bewitched 6-20-45:11
Beyond 9-09-21:44
Beyond a Reasonable Doubt 9-12-56:6
Beyond All Limits (See: Flor de Mayo)
Beyond and Back 2-08-78:18
Beyond Bengal 5-22-34:29
Beyond Evil 5-07-80:10
Beyond Glory 6-16-48:8
Beyond Good and Evil (See: Oltre il Bene e il Male)
Beyond London's Lights 4-11-28: 13
Beyond Love and Evil 3-17-71:26
Beyond Mombasa 10-17-56:6
Beyond Our Own 11-05-47:8
Beyond Price 6-24-21:36
Beyond Reasonable Doubt 10-01-80:26
Beyond the Blue Horizon (s) 4-26-32:13 and 5-17-32:14
Beyond the Blue Horizon 5-06-42:8
Beyond the Crossroads 1-27-22:40
Beyond the Door 8-06-75:16
Beyond the Forest 10-19-49:8
Beyond the Last Frontier 11-03-43:16
Beyond the Law 4-11-19:56
Beyond the Law 11-06-34:17
Beyond the Law 10-02-68:24
Beyond the Line of Duty (s) 9-30-42:20
Beyond the Poseidon Adventure 5-30-79:16
Beyond the Purple Hills 7-19-50:6
Beyond the Rainbow 3-03-22:41
Beyond the Rio Grande 5-28-30: 38
Beyond the Rockies 9-20-32:15
Beyond the Rocks 5-12-22:32
Beyond the Sacramento 5-07-41: 12
Beyond the Shadows 8-09-18:33

Beyond the Sierras 12-12-28:31
Beyond the Time Barrier 9-14-60:18
Beyond the Valley of the Dolls 6-24-70:20
Beyond This Place 5-06-59:6
Beyond Tomorrow 4-03-40:14
Beyond Victory 4-08-31:19
Bez Milosci 10-01-80:28
Bez Znieczulenia 2-07-79:26
Bharat Mata 8-27-58:6
Bhowani Junction 5-09-56:6
Bhumika 11-15-78:37
Bhuvan Shome 9-03-69:30
Bialata Staia 7-01-70:13
Biancanere e i Sett Lavri 1-25-50:20
Bianco, Il Giallo, Il Nero, Il 2-05-75:26
Bianco, Rosso e ... (See: White Sister)
Bible, The 9-28-66:6
Bible 3-20-74:18
Bible Pictures 12-22-22:33
Bice Skoro Propast Sveta 5-14-69:34
Biches, Les 4-10-68:24
Biciklisti 8-12-70:14
Bicycle Thief, The (See: Ladri Di Biciclette)
Bicycling to the Moon 3-06-63:6
Bidasses en Folie, Les 1-12-72:14
Bidasses S'En Vont, Les 1-01-75:16
Bidone, Il 11-02-55:18
Bielaya Ptitsa S Tchornem Piatnom 11-10-71:16
Bierkampf 7-12-77:18
Biff and Bang (s) 10-24-28:24
Big Ambition, The (s) 9-10-30:17
Big Bad Mama 9-04-74:20
Big Bad Sis 10-27-76:46
Big Banana Feet 12-08-76:18
Big Benefit, The (s) 12-12-33:19
Big Bird Cage, The 7-12-72:24
Big Blockade, The 2-18-42:8
Big Bluff, The 10-24-31:22
Big Bluff 7-13-55:20
Big Bonanza, The 2-28-45:15
Big Boodle, The 1-30-57:6
Big Boss, The 5-21-41:15
Big Bounce, The 2-12-69:6
Big Boy 9-17-30:21
Big Brain, The 8-08-33:19
Big Brawl, The 8-27-80:20
Big Broadcast, The 10-18-32:14
Big Broadcast of 1936, The 9-18-35:15

Big Broadcast of 1937, The 10-28-36:14
Big Broadcast of 1938, The 2-09-38:14
Big Brother Cheng 8-27-75:15
Big Brothers 12-27-23:26
Big Brown Eyes 5-06-36:18
Big Build-Up, The (s) 9-16-42:20
Big Bus, The 6-23-76:17
Big Business 6-02-37:23
Big Business Girl 6-16-31:34
Big Cage, The 5-16-33:17
Big Caper, The 4-03-57:6
Big Cat, The 4-27-49:11
Big Chance, The 9-05-33:19
Big Cheese, The (s) 12-03-30:15
Big Circus, The 7-08-59:6
Big City, The 3-28-28:30
Big City, The 9-15-37:13
Big City, The 3-24-48:8
Big City Blues 9-13-32:29
Big Clock, The 2-18-48:8
Big Combo 2-16-55:16
Big Country, The 8-13-58:6
Big Cube, The 3-12-69:6
Big Dame Hunting (s) 6-28-32:14
Big Dan 12-20-23:26
Big Day, The (See: Jour de Fete)
Big Dog House (s) 8-25-31:24
Big Executive 10-03-33:15
Big Family, A 6-08-55:6
Big Fella 7-07-37:25
Big Fisherman, The 7-01-59:7
Big Fix, The 10-04-78:18
Big Flash, The (s) 10-25-32:15
Big Frame, The 3-18-53:6
Big Gamble, The 9-22-31:26
Big Gamble, The 8-16-61:6
Big Game 8-26-21:35
Big Game (s) 9-01-31:21
Big Game, The 10-28-36:14
Big Game of the Sea (s) 2-02-32:15
Big Gundown, The 8-14-68:28
Big Guns 9-26-73:18
Big Gusher, The 7-18-51:6
Big Guy, The 11-29-39:14
Big Hand for the Little Lady, A 4-27-66:6
Big Hangover 3-15-50:12
Big Happiness 9-03-20:44
Big Hearted (s) 7-30-30:16
Big Hearted Herbert 11-20-34:17
Big Heat, The 9-23-53:6
Big Heat, The 2-05-58:6
Big Holdup 11-05-75:18
Big Hop, The 1-09-29:45
Big House, The 7-02-30:25

Big House Party (s) 9-22-31:22
Big House, U.S.A. 3-02-55:9
Big Idea, The (s) 9-11-34:11
Big Jack 4-13-49:11
Big Jake 5-26-71:20
Big Jewel Case, The (s) 2-12-30:18
Big Jim Garrity 4-21-16:29
Big Jim McLain 8-27-52:6
Big Job, The 10-13-65:18
Big Kick, The (s) 1-29-30:21
Big Killing, The 7-04-28:16
Big Knife, The 9-21-55:6
Big Land, The 1-30-57:6
Big Leaguer, The 7-15-53:6
Big Lift, The 4-12-50:6
Big Medicine 9-24-10:12
Big Money (s) 5-07-30:20
Big Money 11-26-30:19
Big Money 6-18-58:16
Big Mouth, The 6-28-67:6
Big News 10-09-29:41
Big Night, The 11-07-51:6
Big Noise, The 5-09-28:17
Big Noise, The 7-08-36:15
Big Noise, The 9-20-44:10
Big Operator, The 8-05-59:6
Big Pal, The 2-03-26:43
Big Palooka, The (s) 6-26-29:12
Big Parade, The 11-11-25:36 and 12-02-25:40
Big Parade of 1935, The 1-01-35:18
Big Paraders, The (s) 8-28-29:18
Big Party, The 4-16-30:49
Big Payoff, The 1-24-33:19
Big Pond, The 5-21-30:25 (Also see: Grande Mare, La)
Big Punch, The 3-25-21:43
Big Punch, The 5-26-48:8
Big Race, The 3-06-34:27
Big Red 4-18-62:6
Big Red One, The 5-14-80:14
Big Request Concert 8-02-61:7
Big Rush, The (See: Classe Tour Risques)
Big Shakedown, The 2-13-34:14
Big Shot, The 1-05-32:23
Big Shot, The 8-11-37:19
Big Shot, The 6-03-42:9
Big Show, The 7-14-26:18
Big Show, The 3-03-37:15
Big Show, The 5-10-61:7
Big Show-Off, The 5-16-45:8
Big Sister, The 9-15-16:26
Big Sky, The 7-09-52:6
Big Sleep, The 8-14-46:10
Big Sleep, The 3-15-78:20

Big Sombrero, The 2-02-49:12 and 4-13-49:11
Big Steal, The 6-15-49:13
Big Store, The 6-18-41:16
Big Street, The 8-05-42:27
Big T-N-T Show, The 1-19-66:28
Big Thumbs 4-17-77:22
Big Timber 6-22-17:26
Big Timber 10-25-50:6
Big Time 9-11-29:18
Big Time Charlie (s) 10-16-29:17
Big Time or Bust 1-16-34:54
Big Tip Off 4-27-55:6
Big Town 12-27-32:54
Big Town 2-19-47:9
Big Town After Dark 11-19-47:8
Big Town Czar 4-26-39:12
Big Town Girl 11-10-37:19
Big Town Ideas 6-10-21:35
Big Town Scandal 5-26-48:18
Big Trail, The 10-29-30:17 (Also see: Grosse Fahrt, Die)
Big Trees, The 2-06-52:6
Big Tremaine 12-01-16:28
Big Wednesday 5-24-78:40
Big Wheel, The 11-09-49:6
Bigamist, The 12-04-09:13
Bigamist 9-09-21:45
Bigamist, The 3-31-22:40
Bigamist, The 10-28-53:6
Bigger Man, The 10-08-15:23
Bigger Splash, A 5-15-74:28
Bigger Than Barnum's 7-14-26:14
Bigger Than Life 8-15-56:6
Bigger They Are, The (s) 6-30-31:15
Biggest Bundle of Them All, The 1-17-68:24
Biggest Show on Earth, The 5-03-18:39
Bigorne, Caporal de France, La 9-03-58:16
Bij de Besten Af (See: Ape and Superape)
Bijou 10-18-72:18
Bijoutiers du Clair de Lune, Les 5-07-58:23
Bijoux de Famille, Les 3-19-75:36
Bijutaril de Familie 8-06-58:6
Bike Boy 10-11-67:22
Bikini Beach 7-08-64:6
Biladi, une Revolution 10-14-70:30
Bilans Kwartalny 7-09-75:24
Bilbao 5-24-78:38

Bilder Aus Einem Fremden Land 6-21-72:24

Bildnis Einer Trinkerin 3-12-80: 26

Bilitis 4-06-77:26

Bill 12-13-23:23

Bill 9-07-27:24

Bill and Coo 12-24-27:13

Bill Apperson's Boy 7-18-19:43

Bill Cracks Down 5-19-37:22

Bill Cunningham's Sports (s) 6-14-32:16

Bill Henry 8-22-19:77

Bill of Divorcement, A 9-01-22: 41 and 4-19-23:35

Bill of Divorcement, A 10-04-32: 15

Bill of Divorcement, A 3-13-40: 16

Bill Peters' Kid 1-28-16:23

Bill, the Billposter 11-13-09:13

Bille de Logement, Le 10-18-32: 15

Billie 9-08-65:6

Billiken 10-09-09:20

Billion Dollar Scandal 1-10-33:15

Billion Dollar Brain 11-22-67:6

Billion Dollar Hobo 6-21-78:18

Billion Dollar Limited (s) 2-04-42:8

Billionaire, The 5-29-14:21

Billions 12-10-20:35

Billposter's Trials 9-04-09:13

Billy and Elsa Maxwell (s) 7-04-28:16

Billy in the Lowlands 1-17-79:21

Billy Jack 5-05-71:22

Billy Jack Goes to Washington 4-20-77:24

Billy Jim 2-03-22:42

Billy Liar 8-21-63:6

Billy Rose's Jumbo 12-05-62:6

Billy the Kid 10-22-30:23

Billy the Kid 5-28-41:16

Billy the Kid in Texas 11-20-40: 18

Billy the Kid Returns 9-21-38:13

Billy the Kid Trapped 4-22-42:18

Billy the Kid Wanted 11-26-41:9

Billy the Kid's Fighting Pals 6-25-41:18

Billy the Kid's Range War 3-12-41:16

Billy the Kid's Roundup 1-07-42:45

Billy Two-Hats 11-07-73:19

Biltmore Trio (s) 10-09-29:23

Bim 3-31-76:17

Bimbo and Betty (s) 8-11-31:30

Bimbo the Great 5-03-61:26

Bimbo's Express (s) 9-01-31:21

Binghi, or The Cockeyed Animal World 7-19-32:34

Bingo Long Traveling All-Stars and Motor Kings, The 5-19-76:19

Bio-Graphia 11-05-75:19

Biography of a Bachelor 3-06-35: 20

Biophone Talkers 9-18-14:19

Biotaxia 6-26-68:22

Birch Interval 3-24-76:20

Bird in Hand, A (s) 2-06-29:18

Bird in the Hand, A (s) 5-22-29: 16

Bird Islands of Peru (s) 11-12-30: 21

Bird of Paradise 9-13-32:19

Bird of Paradise 3-14-51:6

Bird of Prey, The 3-31-16:24

Bird of Prey, The 8-30-18:37

Bird Store, The (s) 5-10-32:18

Bird with the Crystal Plumage, The 7-29-70:15

Birdman of Alcatraz 6-20-62:6

Birds, The 3-27-63:6

Birds and the Bees, The 3-28-56:6

Birds Do It 8-03-66:6

Birds Do It, Bees Do It 5-22-74: 19

Birds in Peru (See: Oiseaux Vont Mourir Au Peru, Les)

Birds of a Feather (s) 4-15-31:20

Birds of a Feather 11-13-35:17

Birds of a Feather (See: Cage Aux Folles, La)

Birds of Prey 11-02-27:25

Birds of Prey 12-03-30:14

Birds of the Sea (a) 9-15-31:20

Birds, the Bees, and the Italians, The (See: Signore e Signori)

Biribi 6-30-71:29

Birjuk 3-01-78:22

Birobidjian 10-21-36:23

Birth Control 4-13-17:27

Birth of a Baby, The 3-09-38:14

Birth of a Man, The 5-12-16:19

Birth of a Nation, The 3-12-15: 23; 12-08-22:24; 1-06-26:39; 12-24-30:21

Birth of a Race, The 12-06-18: 38 and 4-25-19:82

Birth of a Soul 2-27-20:46

Birth of Democracy, The 1-11-18:42

Birth of the Blues 9-03-41:8

Birthday Affair, A 10-09-09:13
Birthday Party, The 12-18-68:26
Birthday Present, The 11-13-57:6
Birthright 2-13-52:18
Biruma No Tategoto 9-19-56:6
Bis Dass Das Geld Euch Scheidet
     11-09-60:19
Bis Dass Der Tod Euch Scheidet
     7-30-80:28
Bis Fuenf Minuten Nach Zwolf 12-
     09-58:6
Bis Zum Happy End 10-30:68:28
Bischen Liebe, Ein 3-22-32:61
Biscuit Eater, The 4-10-40:14
Biscuit Eater, The 3-15-72:6
Bishop Misbehaves, The 10-02-
     35:16
Bishop Murder Case, The 2-05-
     30:24
Bishop's Emeralds, The 6-13-19:49
Bishop's Wife, The 11-19-47:8
Bisturi: La Mafia Bianca 5-30-
     73:12
Bit of Jade, A 4-05-18:45
Bitch, The 10-03-79:14
Bite the Bullet 4-30-75:19
Bitka Na Neretva 12-10-69:20
Bits of Broadway (s) 11-06-29:19
Bits of Life 10-21-21:35
Bitter Apples 4-27-27:21
Bitter Creek 3-17-54:22
Bitter Friends (s) 4-16-30:21
Bitter Harvest 12-18-63:7
Bitter Springs 7-12-50:6
Bitter Sweet 9-26-28:27
Bitter Sweet 8-29-33:14
Bitter Sweet 11-20-40:16
Bitter Tea of General Yen, The
     1-17-33:14
Bitter Truth 1-19-17:25
Bitter Victory 9-04-57:26
Bitteren Traenen der Petra von
     Kant, Die 7-12-72:17
Bittersweet Love 10-27-76:26
Bitter Tears of Petra von Kant
     (See: Bitteren Traenen der
     Petra von Kant, Die)
Bizalom 2-20-80:22
Bizarre, Bizarre 3-29-39:14
Bizyo to Tozoku 10-15-52:6
Bjelorusski Voksal 11-01-71:16
Black Aces 8-25-37:23
Black Age, The 9-05-28:31
Black and Tan (s) 11-06-29:19
Black and White in Color (See:
     Victoire en Chantant, La)
Black Angel 8-07-46:15
Black Arrow, The 6-30-48:10

Black Bag 6-12-22:40
Black Banana 12-07-77:20
Black Bandit 9-21-38:13
Black Bart 2-04-48:13
Black Beauty 5-11-07:13
Black Beauty 2-25-21:42
Black Beauty 8-29-33:15
Black Beauty 7-17-46:8
Black Beauty 9-29-71:22
Black Belly of the Tarantula 5-
     10-72:48
Black Belt Jones 1-30-74:11
Black Bird, The 12-24-75:18
Black Bird Descending: Tense
     Alignment 11-16-77:21
Black Butterflies 10-17-28:27
Black Butterfly 12-08-16:28
Black Caesar 2-07-73:18
Black Camel, The 7-07-31:34
Black Cargoes of the South Seas
     6-12-29:35
Black Castle, The 10-22-52:6
Black Cat, The 5-22-34:15
Black Cat, The 4-30-41:16
Black Cat, The (See: Kuroneko)
Black Chariot 7-14-71:20
Black Christmas 10-16-74:16
Black Circle, The 10-24-19:60
Black Coffee 9-01-31:31
Black Crook, The 1-14-16:19
Black Cyclone 5-20-25:47
Black Dakotas 9-08-54:6
Black Diamond Express 6-22-27:34
Black Diamonds 9-11-40:14
Black Doll, The 2-09-38:14
Black Dragons 4-29-42:8
Black Eagle 10-27-48:9
Black Envelope, The 7-09-15:18
     and 12-03-15:21
Black Eye 4-24-74:18
Black Eyes 4-19-39:12
Black Fantasy 9-20-72:14
Black Fear 12-31-15:25
Black Fox 9-12-62:6
Black Friday 3-13-40:16
Black Fury 4-17-35:14
Black Gestapo, The 4-16-75:23
Black Girl (See: Noire de..., La)
Black Girl 11-08-72:18
Black Godfather 11-06-74:20
Black Gold 6-25-47:8
Black Gold 5-22-63:6
Black, Gunn 12-27-72:6
Black Hand, The 1-25-50:18
Black Hand Gang, The 11-12-30:
     21
Black Heart 11-19-10:13
Black Hills 7-03-29:32

Black Hills 1-28-48:11
Black Hills Ambush 6-18-52:6
Black Hills Express 9-22-43:12
Black Hole, The 12-19-79:20
Black Horse Canyon 5-19-54:6
Black Is Beautiful 4-29-70:18
Black Is White 3-12-20:53
Black Jack 12-07-27:23
Black Jack 1-31-51:6
Black Jack 12-12-73:16
Black Jack 12-12-79:20
Black Jesus (See: Seduta Alla Sua D'Estra)
Black Joy 6-01-77:17
Black King 7-19-32:25
Black Klansman, The 6-08-66:18
Black Knight 9-08-54:6
Black Lash, The 4-23-52:6
Black Legion, The 1-20-37:14
Black Lightning 12-10-24:35
Black Like Me 5-20-64:6
Black Magic 9-04-29:31
Black Magic 8-24-49:18
Black Magic 2 12-14-77:14
Black Mama, White Mama 1-31-73:28
Black Marble, The 2-27-80:20
Black Market Babies 4-03-46:12
Black Market Rustlers 9-01-43:20
Black Midnight 11-09-49:16
Black Moon 7-03-34:26
Black Moon 9-24-75:22
Black Narcissus (s) 11-20-29:12
Black Narcissus 5-07-47:18
Black Natchez 9-27-67:6
Black Network (s) 4-01-36:17
Black Nissen 6-12-14:22
Black Oak Conspiracy, The 4-13-77:20
Black on White 10-15-69:15
Black Orchid, The 1-28-59:6
Black Orchids 12-29-16:22
Black Orpheus (See: Orfeu Negro)
Black Oxen 1-03-24:23 and 1-10-24:26
Black Panther, The 12-21-77:20
Black Panther's Club 3-06-21:40
Black Parachute, The 5-24-44:10
Black Paradise 6-23-26:18
Black Pearl 3-20-29:28
Black Peter (See: Cerny Petr)
Black Pirate, The 3-10-26:40
Black Raven, The 6-30-43:8
Black Ridinghood 3-20-29:13
Black Rodeo 6-28-72:18
Black Room, The 8-21-35:21
Black Rose 8-09-50:8

Black Roses 5-13-21:43
Black Samson 8-07-74:18
Black Scorpion, The 9-15-57:26
Black Sea Fighters 8-18-43:26
Black Sea Mutiny 6-23-31:19
Black Shadows 3-19-20:53
Black Shadows 6-21-23:25***
Black Shadows 10-05-49:8
Black Shampoo 6-02-76:17
Black Sheep, A 10-18-15:22
Black Sheep 7-03-35:15
Black Sheep of Whitehall 2-18-42:8
Black Shield of Falworth 8-04-54:6
Black Silk 7-12-61:7
Black Six 3-20-74:18
Black Sleep, The 6-13-56:6
Black Spurs 5-05-65:26
Black Stallion, The 10-17-79:10
Black Stork, The 3-02-17:29
Black Sun (See: Soleil Noir)
Black Sun 3-31-78:28
Black Sunday 12-29-26:15
Black Sunday 2-22-61:6
Black Sunday 3-30-77:19
Black Swan, The 10-21-42:8
Black Tent, The 3-28-56:6 and 6-12-57:6
Black 13 11-24-54:6
Black Torment, The 10-21-64:6
Black Triangle, The 10-10-14:25
Black Tuesday 12-22-54:6
Black Trail, The 8-06-24:25
Black Tulip, The (See: Tulipe Noire, La)
Black Veil for Lisa, A 7-16-69:28
Black Watch, The 5-15-29:20
Black Waters 7-10-29:24
Black Whip, The 1-02-57:6
Black Widow 10-27-54:6
Black Windmill, The 5-08-74:37
Black Wings 8-07-63:6
Black Zoo 5-08-63:6
Blackbeard, the Pirate 12-03-52:6
Blackbeard's Ghost 1-17-68:6
Blackbird, The 2-03-26:37
Blackbirds 10-22-15:24
Blackbirds 12-10-20:35
Blackboard Jungle, The 3-02-55:8
Blackguard, The 5-27-25:42 and 4-07-26:39
Blackhawk 8-13-52:6
Blackie's Redemption 4-25-19:81
Blackjack Ketchum, Desperado 4-04-56:6
Blacklist, The 2-18-16:21

Blackmail 10-22-20:39
Blackmail 7-10-29:24 and 10-09-29:34
Blackmail 9-13-39:12
Blackmail 8-06-47:12
Blackmailed 2-07-51:6
Blackmailer 7-29-36:14
Blackout 5-05-54:6
Black-Out 10-21-70:22
Blackout 3-31-78:26
Blacks Britannica 3-28-79:22
Blackwell's Island 3-08-39:18
Blacula 8-02-72:18
Blade 12-05-73:20
Blades of Musketeers 9-02-53:6
Blaise Pascal 3-26-75:22
Blajackor 3-27-46:12
Blame the Woman 11-01-32:13
Blanc et le Noir, Le 6-02-31:19
Blanche 6-30-71:20
Blanche Fury 3-03-48:8
Blarney 10-20-26:62
Blarney Kiss 8-22-33:22
Blarney Stone, The 3-28-33:27
Blast of Silence 4-12-61:6
Blasted Event, A (s) 10-02-34:37
Blau Licht, Das 4-29-32:25
Blaze O' Glory 1-01-30:15 and
    1-15-30:37 (Also see: Sombras
    de Gloria)
Blaze of Noon 3-05-47:8
Blazing Arrows 10-27-22:41
Blazing Days 6-08-27:17
Blazing Forest, The 10-01-52:6
Blazing Frontier 4-19-44:12
Blazing Guns 10-20-43:12
Blazing Love 5-05-16:26
Blazing Saddles 2-13-74:18
Blazing Six Shooters 2-13-40:18
Blazing Sixes 8-04-37:25
Blazing Sun, The 11-08-50:18
Blazing Trail, The 5-13-21:43
Blazing Trail, The 11-16-49:16
Ble en Herbe, Le 3-24-54:24
Bleak Moments 8-23-72:24
Blechtrommel, Die 5-16-79:27
Bled, Le 7-17-29:57
Bless the Beasts and Children 7-14-71:16
Blessed Event 9-06-32:15
Blessed Miracle, The 4-16-15:19
Blessings of the Land 11-24-65:6
Blessington's Bonnie Babies 10-23-09:13
Blight of Sin 9-11-09:13
Blimp Mystery (s) 8-27-30:21
Blind Adventure, The 1-18-18:42
Blind Adventure 11-07-33:16

Blind Alibi 5-25-38:13
Blind Alley 4-26-39:12
Blind Alleys 3-02-27:16
Blind Bargain, A 12-08-22:33
Blind Beast, The 4-23-69:6
Blind Bird, The 4-28-65:6
Blind Circumstances 9-15-22:43
Blind Date 9-04-34:19
Blind Date 8-26-59:6
Blind Desire 6-09-48:12
Blind Goddess, The 4-07-26:36
Blind Goddess, The 9-29-48:18
Blind Hearts 10-14-21:43
Blind Husbands 12-12-19:46
Blind Justice 9-22-16:37
Blind Makker 9-15-76:17
Blind Man's Eyes 3-14-19:46
Blind Passagiere 3-24-37:17
Blind Youth 6-25-20:35
Blind Youth (s) 7-09-30:19
Blindfold 2-20-29:17
Blindfold 5-18-66:6
Blindfolded 5-03-18:40
Blinding Trail, The 4-11-19:55
Blindman 4-12-72:16
Blindness of Courage, The 8-20-15:20
Blindness of Devotion, The 11-12-15:22
Blindness of Divorce, The 5-31-18:31
Blindness of Love, The 3-17-16:32
Blindness of Virtue, The 8-27-15:19
Blinky 8-30-23:27
Bliss of Mrs. Blossom, The 10-09-68:6
Bliss on Earth 1-30-57:7
Blithe Spirit 4-25-45:14
Blitz Wolf (s) 9-02-42:34
Blizna 2-12-77:24
Blizzard, The 3-19-24:27
Blob, The 9-10-58:6
Block Busters 8-16-44:16
Block Signal, The 9-29-26:14 and
    10-27-26:68
Blockade 6-08-38:17
Blockade 10-20-65:26
Blockade, The 5-22-29:47 and
    7-31-29:27
Block-Heads 8-31-38:18
Blockhouse, The 7-04-73:30
Blod Och Eid 3-27-46:12
Bloko 5-11-66:6
Blomstrande Tider 2-20-80:22
Blonde Alibi 3-20-46:26
Blonde Bait 10-10-56:7

Blonde Bandit   1-11-50:6
Blonde Buzzell (s)   11-10-31:14
Blonde by Choice   5-09-28:41
Blonde Captive   3-01-32:21
Blonde Comet   12-31-41:8
Blonde Comme Ca!, Une   2-27-63:7
Blonde Crazy   12-08-31:15
Blonde de Pekin, La   1-31-68:6
Blonde Dynamite   3-01-50:16
Blonde Fever   11-22-44:10
Blonde for a Day   7-31-46:16
Blonde for a Night   11-14-28:26
Blonde from Brooklyn   6-27-45:16
Blonde from Singapore   9-03-41:8
Blonde Ice   7-28-48:15
Blonde Inspiration   2-19-41:16
Blonde Like That, A (See: Blonde Comme Ca!, Une)
Blonde Nachtigall   8-25-31:20
Blonde or Brunette   1-12-27:14
Blonde Ransom   5-30-45:16
Blonde Saint, The   11-24-26:15
Blonde Savage   10-08-47:8
Blonde Trouble   8-04-37:19
Blonde Vampire   9-15-22:42
Blonde Venus   9-27-32:17
Blonder Traum, Ein   10-18-32:19
Blondes Are Dangerous   11-10-37:19
Blondes at Work   3-16-38:17
Blondes by Proxy (s)   6-21-32:14
Blondes for Danger   3-16-38:17
Blondes Prefer Bonds (s)   7-14-31:17
Blondes That Gentlemen Prefer (s)   2-20-29:14
Blondie   11-02-38:22
Blondie Brings Up Baby   11-08-39:14
Blondie for Victory   10-14-42:8
Blondie Goes Latin   2-19-41:16
Blondie Goes to College   2-11-42:8
Blondie Has Servant Trouble   8-07-40:16
Blondie Hits the Jackpot   9-14-49:8
Blondie in Society   7-02-41:12
Blondie Johnson   2-28-33:15
Blondie Knows Best   9-18-46:16
Blondie Meets the Boss   3-08-39:18
Blondie of the Follies   9-13-32:19
Blondie on a Budget   2-28-40:16
Blondie Plays Cupid   10-30-40:15
Blondie Takes a Vacation   7-19-39:12
Blondie's Big Deal   3-16-49:11

Blondie's Holiday   3-05-47:8
Blondie's Number One   6-23-71:46
Blondie's Reward   8-18-48:11
Blondie's Secret   1-26-49:11
Blondy   1-28-76:15
Blood Alley   9-21-55:6
Blood and Black Lace   6-23-65:6
Blood and Guts   9-20-78:24
Blood and Lace   3-17-71:18
Blood and Roses (See: Et Mourir de Plaisir)
Blood and Sand   8-11-22:32
Blood and Sand   5-21-41:15
Blood and Steel   3-11-25:43
Blood and Steel   12-16-59:6
Blood Arrow   5-07-58:23
Blood Bath   3-09-66:6
Blood Beast from Outer Space   11-08-67:6
Blood Brothers   2-25-53:18
Blood Feast   5-06-64:17
Blood Feud (See: Revenge)
Blood for Dracula   2-20-74:16
Blood from the Mummy's Tomb   10-27-71:18
Blood in the Streets   1-14-76:21
Blood Money   11-21-33:20
Blood of a Poet (See: Sang D'Un Poete)
Blood of Hussain, The   5-14-80:15
Blood of the Vampire   9-03-58:6
Blood on the Moon   11-10-48:15
Blood on the Sun   5-02-45:27
Blood Ship, The   7-20-27:16
Blood Will Tell   5-29-14:21
Blood Will Tell   3-09-17:22
Blood Will Tell   1-25-28:13
Bloodbrothers   9-20-78:26
Bloodeaters   10-29-80:18
Bloodhounds of Broadway   10-29-52:6
Bloodless Duel, A   9-04-08:12
Bloodline   7-04-79:25
Bloody Brood, The   11-04-59:7
Bloody Mama   3-18-70:18
Bloomfield   7-07-71:18
Blooming Angel   2-13-20:45
Blossom Time   7-24-34:14
Blossoms in the Dust   6-25-41:16
Blossoms on Broadway   11-17-37:16
Blot, The   8-19-21:35
Blotto (s)   3-19-30:20
Bloudeni   8-03-66:7
Blow Your Own Horn   1-10-54:27
Blowdry   11-10-76:20

Blowing Wild 9-16-53:6
Blow-Up 12-21-66:7
Bludgeon, The 10-15-15:21
Blue 4-24-68:6
Blue and Grey, or the Days of '61, The 6-20-08:13
Blue Angel, The 4-30-30:35 and 12-10-30:15
Blue Angel, The 8-26-59:6
Blue Beard 12-04-09:13
Blue Bird, The 4-05-18:43
Blue Bird, The 1-24-40:14
Blue Bird, The 5-12-76:34
Blue Blazes 4-21-26:34
Blue Blazes (s) 10-21-36:15
Blue Blazes Rawden 2-22-18:46
Blue Blood 6-21-18:27
Blue Blood 1-27-26:39
Blue Blood 1-17-51:11
Blue Blood and Red 4-07-16:21
Blue Bonnet, The 10-31-19:61
Blue Boy, The (s) 10-06-26:54
Blue Collar 2-08-78:18
Blue Dahlia, The 1-30-46:12
Blue Danube, The 5-02-28:14
Blue Danube, The 11-20-34:17
Blue Denim 7-29-59:6
Blue Envelope Mystery, The 10-13-16:28
Blue Fin 11-15-78:18
Blue Fire Lady 5-10-78:22
Blue Gardenia, The 3-18-53:6
Blue Grass of Kentucky 1-18-50:6
Blue Hawaii 11-29-61:6
Blue Idol, The 10-13-31:29
Blue Jeans 3-22-18:50
Blue Lagoon, The 3-09-49:20
Blue Lagoon, The 6-11-80:20
Blue Lamp, The 1-25-50:18
Blue Max, The 6-22-66:6
Blue Montana Skies 5-03-39:20
Blue Movie, or "Fuck" 6-25-69:18
Blue Movie 10-13-71:20
Blue Pearl 3-05-20:62
Blue Rhythm (s) 3-08-32:14
Blue Sextet 5-24-72:24
Blue Sierra 5-08-46:8
Blue Skies 7-17-29:53
Blue Skies 9-25-46:10
Blue Steel 7-17-34:15
Blue Streak, The 3-30-17:29
Blue Streak, The 3-03-26:35
Blue Streak M'Coy 9-03-20:45
Blue Suede Shoes 2-13-80:16
Blue Summer 11-21-73:6
Blue Veil, The 10-22-47:12
Blue Veil, The 9-12-51:6

Blue Velvet 4-29-70:173
Blue Water, White Death 5-12-71:19
Blue, White and Perfect 12-24-41:16
Bluebeard 1-31-45:10
Bluebeard (See: Landru)
Bluebeard 8-23-72:6
Bluebeard, Jr. 6-16-22:41
Bluebeard's Eighth Wife 8-09-23:26
Bluebeard's Eighth Wife 3-23-38:16
Bluebeard's Seven Wives 1-13-26:42
Bluebeard's Ten Honeymoons 3-30-60:22
Blueprint for Murder, A 7-29-53:6
Blueprint for Robbery 1-18-61:20
Blues (s) 6-30-31:15
Blues Brothers, The 6-18-80:22
Blues Buster 10-25-50:6
Blues in the Night 11-05-41:8
Blues Under the Skin 2-21-73:24
Bluff 10-20-16:26
Bluff 4-30-24:19
Bluff Stop 3-29-78:24
Bluffer, The (s) 12-17-30:13
Blum 8-26-70:22
Blume in Love 5-23-73:19
Blume von Hawaii, Die 4-25-33:27
Blumenfrau von Lindeau, Die 5-13-31:64 and 7-12-32:17
Blushing Brides 8-06-30:21
Boarder Raiders, The 10-04-18:47
Boarder Wireless, The 10-11-18:46
Boardwalk 11-14-79:22
Boatniks, The 5-27-70:20
Bob & Carol & Ted & Alice 7-02-69:6
Bob & Daryl & Ted & Alex 6-21-72:18
Bob Hampton of Placer 5-06-21:41
Bob le Flambeur 11-07-56:6
Bob Mathias Story, The 10-06-54:6
Bob Nelson (s) 3-27-29:12 and 10-23-29:17
Bob, Son of Battle 6-11-47:8
Bob White (s) 3-01-32:20
Bobbe Arnst and Peggy Ellis (s) 5-05-30:21
Bobbed Hair 3-21-22:40
Bobbed Hair 11-04-25:42
Bobbie Jo and the Outlaw 4-07-76:28

Bobbie of the Ballet   6-02-16:17
Bobbikins   8-05-59:6
Bobby Deerfield   9-14-77:16
Bobby Folsom (s)   2-20-29:14 and
   7-03-29:17
Bobby Geht Los   12-22-31:21
Bobby's Krig   7-03-74:24
Bobo, The   5-31-67:6
Bobo, Jacco   11-21-79:25
Bobosse   4-08-59:6
Bob's Electric Theatre   10-23-09:
   13
Boby, the Gasoline Boy   10-02-29:
   31
Boccaccio   9-16-36:17
Boccaccio '70   5-16-62:6
Bockbierfest   4-08-31:19
Body, The   (See: Ratai)
Body, The   11-11-70:22
Body and Soul   11-05-20:41
Body and Soul   11-09-27:24
Body and Soul   3-18-31:14
Body and Soul   8-13-47:15
Body Building (s)   12-11-29:35
Body Disappears, The   12-03-41:
   18
Body Punch, The   9-05-28:28
Body Slam, The   7-16-30:15
Body Snatcher, The   2-21-45:8
Bodyguard   9-01-48:14
Bodyguard, The   7-30-80:30
Boeing, Boeing   12-01-65:6
Bof ... Anatomie D'Un Livreur
   4-07-71:18
Bofors Gun   8-21-68:6
Bogus Uncle   1-18-18:42
Boheme, La   3-03-26:34
Boheme, La   10-13-65:18
Bohemian Dancer   12-12-28:31
Bohemian Girl, The   2-08-23:41
Bohemian Girl, The   2-19-36:12
Bohemian Rapture   2-04-48:22
Bohoc a Falon   1-31-68:22
Bohrloch Oder Bayern Ist Nicht
   Texas, Das   4-13-66:6
Boiling Point, The   11-08-32:17
Boina Blanca   11-19-41:20
Bois des Amants, Le   8-31-60:16
Bois Sacre, Le   12-27-39:12
Boite de Nuit   8-08-51:18
Bokyo   7-09-75:24
Bold and the Brave, The   3-21-
   56:6
Bold Caballero, The   3-17-37:15
Bold Dragon   11-14-28:17
Bold Emmet, Ireland's Martyr
   8-30-15:21
Bold Frontiersman, The   4-28-48:8

Bold Impersonation, A   8-27-15:20
Bolek and Lolek   12-16-36:21
Bolero   2-20-34:25
Bolibar   8-29-28:31
Boliche   7-31-34:14
Bolshaia Doroga   9-11-63:22
Bolshevism on Trial   5-02-19:60
Bolshoi Ballet, The   10-30-57:6
Bolshoi Ballet 67   9-28-66:24
Bolted Door, The   9-11-14:22
Bolted Door, The   4-05-23:37
Bomb Throwers, The   5-14-15:20
Bomba and the Hidden City   10-18-
   50:6
Bomba on Panther Island   1-11-
   50:6
Bomba, the Jungle Boy   3-02-49:20
Bombardier   5-12-43:8
Bombay Buddha, The   7-02-15:16
Bombay Clipper, The   1-14-42:8
Bombay Mail   1-09-34:16
Bombay Talkie   11-25-70:13
Bomben Auf Monte Carlo   9-15-
   31:28
Bomber und Paganini   2-02-77:24
Bomber's Moon   7-14-43:18
Bombers B-52   10-30-57:6
Bombs over Burma   8-12-42:22
Bombshell   10-24-33:17
Bomsalva   3-27-78:24
Bon Baisers A Lundi   12-11-74:18
Bon Baisers de Hong Kong   12-31-
   75:14
Bon Bast   7-27-77:32
Bon Dieu Sans Confession, Le
   10-14-53:6
Bon et les Merchants, Le   2-04-76:
   16
Bon Voyage   5-09-62:6
Bon Voyage, Charlie Brown (And
   Don't Come Back!)   5-28-
   80:14
Bonanza Town   7-18-51:20
Bonaparte et la Revolution   9-22-
   71:6 (Also see: Napoleon and
   Napoleon Bonaparte)
Bond Between, The   4-06-17:23
Bond Boy   10-13-22:43
Bond of Fear, The   9-21-17:43
Bond Street   6-02-48:12
Bondage   10-19-17:33
Bondage   11-07-28:34
Bondage   4-25-33:15
Bondage of Fear   1-12-17:24
Bonded Woman, The   8-04-22:36
Bonditis   5-10-67:21
Bondman, The   3-24-16:24
Bondman, The   6-05-29:26

Border Sheriff, The 4-21-26:35
Border Street 4-05-50:22
Border Tale, A 12-03-10:14
Border Treasure 8-30-50:6
Border Vengeance 8-12-25:33
Border Vigilantes 4-02-41:16
Border Wildcat 4-24-29:26
Border Wolves 3-02-38:25
Border Woman 8-27-24:25
Borderland 7-28-22:33
Borderland 4-14-37:33
Borderline 1-11-50:6
Borderline 7-23-80:22
Bordertown 1-29-35:14
Bordertown Gun Fighters 10-06-
    43:8
Bored of Education (s) 9-02-36:
    18
Boreno 9-08-37:19
Borghese Piccolo Piccolo, Un
    8-31-77:30
Boris Godunov 1-25-56:6
Born Again 9-06-78:22
Born for Glory 10-23-35:31
Born Free 3-23-66:6
Born Losers 7-12-67:22
Born Reckless 6-11-30:19
Born Reckless 7-21-37:18
Born Reckless 4-01-59:6
Born to Be Bad 6-05-34:12
Born to Be Bad 8-23-50:8
Born to Be Loved 6-10-59:6
Born to Be Wild 2-23-38:14
Born to Boogie 12-20-72:18
Born to Dance 12-09-36:12
Born to Fight 5-25-38:13
Born to Gamble 10-09-35:15
Born to Kill 4-16-47:20
Born to Kill 6-04-75:19
Born to Love 4-29-31:37
Born to Raise Hell 10-15-75:26
Born to Sing 1-21-42:8
Born to Speed 1-22-47:17
Born to the West 6-30-26:12
Born to the West 3-16-38:17
Born to Win 10-13-71:16
Born Yesterday 11-22-50:8
Borrah Minevitch and His Har-
    monica School (s) 1-06-43:
    50
Borrowed Clothes 8-28-09:13
Borrowed Clothes 11-22-18:44
Borrowed Finery 1-20-26:41
Borrowed Hero 12-17-41:8
Borrowed Plumage 7-06-17:28
Borrowed Trouble 11-17-48:13
Borrowed Wives 10-29-30:27
Borrowing Trouble 10-27-37:18

and 11-17-37:16
Borsalino 4-01-70:14
Borsalino & Co. 11-06-74:20
Bosko at the Beach (s) 8-09-32:
    17
Bosko Buha 8-15-79:28
Bosko in Dutch (s) 2-07-33:12
Bosko's Fox Hunt (s) 11-24-31:17
Bosko's Holiday (s) 9-01-31:21
Bosom Friends (s) 10-21-34:17
Bosque de Ancines, El 5-06-70:
    26
Boss, The 5-14-15:19
Boss, The 8-22-56:6
Boss of Big Town 1-13-43:8
Boss of Camp Four 1-05-23:43
Boss of Hangtown Mesa 9-16-42:8
Boss of Lone Valley 12-22-37:25
Boss of the Lazy Y 4-12-18:45
Boss of the Rawhide 9-13-44:10
Boss Rider of Gun Creek 12-16-
    36:15
Boss' Son, The 9-20-78:26
Bossu, Le 3-02-60:6
Boston Blackie and the Law 11-20-
    46:38
Boston Blackie's Little Pal 9-06-
    18:39
Boston Blackie's Rendezvous 8-
    22-45:20
Boston Strangler, The 10-16-68:6
Boszka Ema 7-23-80:20
Botany Bay 9-30-53:6
Botschaft der Goetter 5-26-76:36
Botta e Risposta 4-26-50:22
Bottle, The 6-11-15:19
Bottom of the Bottle 2-01-56:6
Bottom of the World, The 7-16-30:
    29
Bottoms Up 3-27-34:12
Bottoms Up 3-03-60:22
Bou Posleden 11-17-76:19
Boucher, Le 3-11-70:22
Boucher, la Star et L'Orpheline,
    Le 3-12-75:20
Boudoir Diplomat, The 12-10-30:
    15 (Also see: Don Juan Dip-
    lomatico and Liebe Auf Befehl)
Boudu: Saved from Drowning 3-01-
    67:6
Bouffon, Le 5-15-09:15
Bought 8-18-31:17
Bought and Paid For 11-03-16:25
Bought and Paid For 3-17-22:41
Bougnoul, Le 5-14-75:31
Boulanger de Valorgue, Le 3-25-
    53:78
Boulder Dam (s) 11-15-32:19

Boulder Dam 4-01-36:17
Boule de Suif 12-12-45:12
Boulevard 12-14-60:6
Boulevard du Rhum 10-27-71:24
Boulevard Nights 3-21-79:24
Boum Sur Paris 4-07-54:24
Bouncing Babies (s) 1-29-30:21
Bound for Glory 10-27-76:26
Bound in Morocco 8-02-18:37
Bound on the Wheel 7-30-15:20
Boundary Rider, The 9-11-14:22
Bounty Hunters 8-25-54:6
Bounty Killer, The 6-23-65:7
Bouquet, The 10-29-10:14
Bourgeois Gentilhomme, Le 9-17-58:18
Bourlive Vino 7-28-76:24
Bowery, The 10-10-33:17
Bowery Batallion 2-14-51:13
Bowery Bimbos (s) 4-09-30:22
Bowery Blitzkrieg 10-08-41:9
Bowery Bombshell 7-24-46:26
Bowery Boy 1-01-41:14
Bowery Boys Meet the Monsters 7-07-54:6
Bowery Buckaroos 10-15-47:10
Bowery Champs 11-08-44:23
Bowery Cinderella, A 1-25-28:13 and 2-22-28:25
Bowery to Broadway 10-25-44:12
Box, The 8-20-75:19
Box Car Blues (s) 3-11-31:14
Boxcar Bertha 5-31-72:6
Boxer, The 11-13-63:17
Boxer, The 11-16-77:24
Boy 12-11-40:25
Boy (See: Shonen)
Boy ... A Girl, A 5-14-69:32
Boy, A Girl, and a Bike, A 6-01-49:20
Boy, A Girl, and a Dog, A 6-26-46:11
Boy Across the Street, The 8-10-66:18
Boy and a Camel, A 8-07-68:6
Boy and His Dog, A 3-26-75:32
Boy and the Bridge, The 8-05-59:6
Boy and the Law, A 4-03-14:21
Boy and the Pirates 4-06-60:6
Boy, Did I Get the Wrong Number! 6-08-66:6
Boy Friend, The 8-25-26:18
Boy Friend 6-21-39:16
Boy Friend, The 12-22-71:6
Boy Friends (s) 2-04-31:16
Boy from Indiana 3-29-50:11
Boy from Oklahoma 1-20-54:6

Boy Girl, The 2-23-17:22
Boy in the Tree (See: Pojken I Tradet)
Boy Kumasenu, The 7-15-53:6
Boy Meets Girl 8-31-38:18
Boy Named Charlie Brown, A 12-93-69:16
Boy of Flanders, A 4-16-24:23
Boy of Mine 12-27-23:26
Boy of the Streets 11-30-27:23
Boy of the Streets 12-01-37:14
Boy, Oh Boy (s) 9-02-36:18
Boy on a Dolphin 4-17-57:6
Boy Rider, The 11-02-27:21
Boy Slaves 1-18-39:12
Boy Trouble 4-05-39:19
Boy! What a Girl 2-05-47:20
Boy Who Caught a Crook 10-18-61:6
Boy Who Cried Wolf, The 5-25-17:23
Boy Who Cried Wolf, The 8-01-73:18
Boy Who Stole a Million, The 9-21-60:6
Boy Who Stole a Million, The 7-05-61:6
Boy with Green Hair, The 11-17-48:13
Boy Woodburn 5-19-22:40
Boyce Combe 9-04-29:13
Boyhood Days (s) 1-16-29:14
Boys, The 10-03-62:7
Boys, The 7-24-63:8
Boys and Girls 7-23-69:26
Boys from Brazil, The 9-27-78:20
Boys from Syracuse 7-17-40:16
Boys from the Streets 3-15-50:12
Boys in Company C., The 1-25-78:24
Boys in the Band, The 3-18-70:18
Boys in the Sand 12-22-71:6
Boys' Night Out 6-13-62:7
Boys of Paul Street, The 3-19-69:6
Boys of the City 8-21-40:20
Boys' Ranch 5-01-46:8
Boys' Reformatory 5-10-39:3
Boys Town 9-07-38:12
Boys Will Be Boys 5-20-21:41
Boys Will Be Girls (s) 11-30-27:23
Brabanconne, La 2-23-32:19
Brace Dei Biassoli, La 9-24-80:22
Brace Up 3-15-18:42

Braddock-Farr Fight (s) 1-26-38: 15
Braddock-Louis Fight (s) 6-30-37:21
Brain Eaters 11-05-58:7
Brainstorm 5-12-65:28
Brainwashed 7-05-61:7
Bramble Bush, The 8-22-19:76
Bramble Bush, The 1-20-60:6
Brancaleone Alle Crociate 8-04-71:18
Brand, The 2-28-19:56
Brand-Boerge Rykker Ud 3-03-76: 21
Brand in der Oper 11-12-30:42 and 7-19-32:25
Brand of Cowardice, The 11-03-16:30
Brand of Cowardice 7-29-25:36
Brand of Lopey 4-02-20:95
Brand of Satan, The 6-29-17:31
Brand X 6-03-70:20
Branded 11-10-31:23
Branded 11-15-50:6
Branded a Coward 10-23-35:31
Branded a Thief 3-25-25:36
Branded Man 6-06-28:25
Branded Men 12-15-31:21
Branded Sombrero 3-21-28:23
Brandenburg Arch 7-03-29:30
Branding Broadway 11-29-18:40
Branding Iron 11-12-20:36
Brandstellen 1-28-78:22
Brandy for the Parson 6-04-52:6
Brannigan 3-19-75:29
Branquinol 1-18-50:6
Bras de la Nuit, Les 12-20-61:7
Brasher Doubloon 2-05-47:12
Brasil Ano 2000 6-03-70:20
Brass 3-15-23:31
Brass Bottle, The 2-12-64:6
Brass Buttons 3-14-19:46
Brass Check, The 3-15-18:42
Brass Knuckles 12-21-27:25 and 2-22-28:25
Brass Legend, The 12-26-56:6
Brass Target 12-13-78:24
Brassie, The (s) 8-11-31:19
Brat, The 11-07-19:98
Brat, The 6-18-30:53
Brat, The 8-25-31:20
Brats (s) 4-30-30:17 (Also see: Glueckliche Kindheit)
Bratya Karamazov 7-30-69:36
Bravados, The 6-04-58:6
Brave and Gold 5-24-18:34
Brave Bulls, The 4-18-51:6
Brave Don't Cry, The 8-27-52:6

Brave Little Bat, The (s) 1-07-42:45
Brave One, The 9-19-56:6
Brave Soldat Schwejk, Der 1-18-61:20
Brave Suender, Der 11-10-31:23 and 4-04-33:15
Brave Warrior 5-14-52:6
Brave Women of '76 11-06-09:13
Bravest Way, The 6-07-18:32
Brave Maestro 6-07-78:28
Brawn of the North 4-05-23:37
Brazen Beauty, The 9-20-18:46
Brazen Women of Balzac, The 7-21-71:24
Brazil 10-25-44:12
Brazil 3-06-74:20
Brazo Fuerte, El 8-02-61:6
Breach of Promise 10-02-09:13
Breach of Promise 11-22-32:62
Bread 8-09-18:34
Bread 7-23-24:26
Bread and Chocolate (See: Pane e Cioccolata)
Break in the Circle 5-08-57:6
Break of Day 1-12-77:44
Break of Hearts 5-22-35:16
Break the News 1-08-41:24
Break the News to Mother 5-30-19:76
Break Up, The 8-06-30:38
Breakdown 7-16-52:6
Breaker, The 12-01-16:28
Breaker, Breaker 4-27-77:22
Breaker Morant 4-23-80:18
Breakfast at Sunrise 11-16-27:21
Breakfast at Tiffany's 10-11-61:7
Breakfast for Two 11-24-37:16
Breakfast in Bed (s) 2-18-31:14
Breakfast in Bed 4-12-78:27
Breakfast in Hollywood 1-16-46: 18
Breakheart Pass 2-04-76:16
Breaking Away 7-11-79:19
Breaking Chains 3-30-27:15
Breaking Glass 5-28-80:42
Breaking Home Ties 5-17-23:26
Breaking into Society 10-03-08:11
Breaking into Society 12-20-23:26
Breaking Point, The 2-04-21:43
Breaking Point, The 4-09-24:18
Breaking Point, The 9-13-50:6
Breaking Point, The 6-02-76:17
Breaking the Bank 10-09-09:22
Breaking the Ice 9-07-38:12
Breaking the Sound Barrier (See: Sound Barrier)
Breaking with Old Ideas 7-07-76:16

Breakout 11-01-50:6
Breakout 5-07-75:52
Breakthrough 3-21-79:24
Breath of Scandal 11-26-24:62
Breath of Scandal, A 10-26-60:
17
Breath of the Gods 10-29-20:42
Breathing Together: Revolution
of the Electric Family 5-
19-71:24
Breathless (See: A Bout du Souffle)
Bred in Old Kentucky 1-12-27:16
Bred in the Bone 10-22-15:24
Breed of Courage 11-02-27:25
Breed of Men 2-07-19:61
Breed of the Border 5-16-33:25
Breed of the Sunset 6-13-28:27
Breezing Home 3-24-37:17
Breezy 11-07-73:19
Breezy Jim 2-14-19:52
Brelan D'As 10-29-52:24
Brenn, Hexe, Brenn 5-20-70:26
Brennende Geheimnis 4-25-33:27
Brennende Herz, Das (See: Burn-
ing Heart, The)
Brennender Sand 6-01-60:6
Brent Jord 7-30-69:36
Breve Cielo 4-02-69:28
Breve Vacanza, Une 8-22-73:19
Brevet Fra Afdode 3-19-47:12
Brewster McCloud 11-18-70:67
and 12-09-70:14
Brewster's Millions 5-01-14:21
Brewster's Millions 1-28-21:39
Brewster's Millions 2-05-35:31
and 4-10-35:17
Brewster's Millions 3-14-45:16
Briarcliff Auto Races 5-02-08:11
Bribe, The 2-09-49:13
Bric-a-Brac (s) 3-27-35:15
Bridal Couple Dodging Cameras
5-09-08:11
Bridal Night (s) 8-25-31:24
Bridal Path, The 8-05-59:20
Bridal Suite 5-24-39:14
Bride, The 8-08-73:14
Bride and Groom's Visit to the
New York Zoological Gardens,
A 11-13-09:13
Bride and the Beast 2-12-58:6
Bride by Mistake 8-02-44:20
Bride Came C.O.D., The 7-02-
41:12
Bride Comes Home 1-01-36:44
Bride for a Night, A 10-08-24:
31
Bride for Henry, A 9-29-37:14
Bride for Sale 10-19-49:8

Bride Goes Wild, The 2-25-48:8
Bride of Buddha 4-16-41:18
Bride of Fear, The 4-19-18:42
Bride of Frankenstein 5-15-35:19
Bride of Hate, The 12-29-16:20
Bride of Samoa (s) 3-25-34:16
Bride of the Andes 9-14-66:24
Bride of the Atom (Monster) 6-
01-55:22
Bride of the Desert 11-20-29:33
Bride of the Gorilla 11-07-51:18
Bride of the Lake 9-25-34:14
Bride of the Regiment 5-28-30:21
Bride of the Storm 4-07-26:38
Bride of Time, The 10-22-15:26
Bride of Vengeance 3-30-49:13
Bride 68 4-16-30:49
Bride Sur le Cou, La 5-10-61:6
Bride with a Dowry 9-01-54:22
Bride Wore Black, The (See:
Mariee Etait en Noire, La)
Bride Wore Boots, The 3-20-46:8
Bride Wore Crutches, The 7-24-
40:14
Bride Wore Red, The 9-29-37:14
Bride's Awakening, The 9-29-37:
14
Bride's Relations (s) 3-06-29:12
Bride's Silence, The 9-21-17:42
Bridegroom for Two 3-08-32:23
Bridegroom's Joke, The 12-04-
09:13
Brides Are Like That 3-25-36:15
Brides of Dracula 5-18-60:6
Brides of Fu Manchu 12-14-66:6
Bridge, The (See: Bruecke, Die)
Bridge at Remagen, The 6-25-
69:18
Bridge in the Jungle, The 11-04-
70:26
Bridge of San Luis Ray, The 5-
22-29:16
Bridge of San Luis Rey, The 2-
02-44:18
Bridge of Shadows 10-17-13:44
Bridge of Sighs, The 5-28-15:17
Bridge of Sighs, The 11-17-22:42
Bridge of Sighs, The 5-06-36:18
Bridge over the River Kwai, The
11-20-57:6
Bridge That Failed, The 1-30-
15:24
Bridge to the Sun 8-16-61:6
Bridge Too Far, A 6-08-77:23
Bridges Burned 2-02-17:25
Bridges of Toko-Ri, The 12-29-
54:6
Brief, Der 12-07-66:6

Brief Encounter 11-28-45:17
Brief Moment 10-03-33:15
Brief Rapture 3-05-52:6
Brief Vacation, A (See: Breve Vacanza, Una)
Briegtraeger Mueller 11-11-73: 22
Brig, The 9-09-64:24
Brigade 10-10-66:6
Brigade, La 8-28-74:18
Brigade Mondaine 9-20-78:26
Brigadista, El 3-15-78:21
Brigadoon 8-11-54:6
Brigand, The 6-04-52:6
Brigand of Kandahar, The 8-18-65:18
Brigante, Il 9-06-61:6
Brigante di Tacca del Lupo, Il 10-29-52:24
Brigante Musolino, Il 6-06-51:18
Brigham Young 8-28-40:16
Bright College Years 6-02-71:15
Bright Eyes 7-02-30:42
Bright Eyes 12-25-34:12
Bright Leaf 5-24-50:6
Bright Lights, The 3-03-16:21
Bright Lights 11-18-25:44
Bright Lights 8-21-35:21
Bright Lights of Broadway 10-18-23:23
Bright Road 4-08-53:6
Bright Shawl 4-26-23:25
Bright Skies 4-30-20:44
Bright Victory 7-25-51:6
Brighton Rock 2-04-48:20
Brighton Strangler, The 5-02-45: 27
Brigitte et Brigitte 5-04-66:6
Brilliant Marriage 9-23-36:16
Brimstone 8-17-49:22
Bring 'Em Back Alive 6-21-32:14
Bring Him In 10-28-21:35
Bring Me the Head of Alfredo Garcia 8-07-74:18
Bring On the Bride (s) 8-14-29:18
Bring On the Girls 2-21-45:8
Bring Your Smile Along 6-22-55:6
Bringing Home Father 6-02-17:22
Bringing Home the Bacon (s) 9-03-41:7
Bringing Up Baby 2-16-38:15
Bringing Up Betty 7-25-19:43
Bringing Up Father 3-21-28:19
Bringing Up Father 11-27-46:28
Brink of Life (See: Nara Livet)
Brinks Job, The 12-13-78:24
Britain's Far Flung Battle Line 8-09-18:33

Britannia Mews 3-09-49:6
British Agent 9-25-34:13
British Intelligence 2-14-40:18
British North Sea Fleet 10-06-16: 27
British War Docus 6-11-41:14
British War Pictures 5-18-17:26 and 8-17-17:24
Britt Wood (s) 12-05-28:12
Brittany Lassies 3-12-10:39
Britton of the Seventh 5-05-16:23
Broad Coalition, The 1-26-72:24
Broad Daylight 11-17-22:43
Broadminded 7-07-31:34
Broadway 1-18-18:42
Broadway 5-29-29:14
Broadway 5-06-42:8
Broadway After Dark 5-21-24:26
Broadway and Home 1-21-21:40
Broadway Arizona 9-28-17:39
Broadway Babies 6-26-29:22
Broadway Bad 3-07-33:14
Broadway Big Shot 1-14-42:8
Broadway Bill 2-15-18:50
Broadway Bill 12-04-34:12
Broadway Broke 12-27-23:27
Broadway Bubble 11-19-20:34
Broadway Butterfly 5-20-25:47
Broadway by Day (s) 8-23-32:15
Broadway Cowboy, A 7-02-20:28
Broadway Daddies 6-06-28:25
Broadway Drifter, The 6-29-27: 26
Broadway Fever 2-20-29:17
Broadway Folly (s) 5-28-30:21
Broadway Gallant, The 6-16-26: 18
Broadway Gold 8-02-23:23
Broadway Gondolier 7-24-35:21
Broadway Gossip (s) 12-13-32:14
Broadway Highlights (s) 5-15-35: 19
Broadway Hoofer, The 12-18-29:22
Broadway Hostess 12-18-35:12
Broadway Jones 2-23-17:22
Broadway Light 10-27-22:41
Broadway Limited (s) 6-04-30:24
Broadway Limited 6-18-41:16
Broadway Madness 1-18-28:19
Broadway Melody, The 2-13-29:13
Broadway Melody of 1936, The 9-25-35:12
Broadway Melody of 1938, The 8-18-37:27
Broadway Melody of 1940, The 2-07-40:14
Broadway Musketeers 10-19-38:12
Broadway Nights 6-29-27:22

Broadway or Bust 7-16-24:23
Broadway Peacock 3-24-22:42
Broadway Rhythm 1-19-44:30
Broadway Rose 9-22-22:41
Broadway Saint, A 7-25-19:43
Broadway Scandal, A 5-31-18:29
Broadway Scandals 10-30-29:30
Broadway Serenade 4-05-39:15
Broadway Sport, The 7-06-17:28
Broadway Thru a Keyhole 11-07-33:16
Broadway to Cheyenne 9-27-32:21
Broadway to Hollywood 9-05-33:19
Broadway's Like That (See: Ruth Etting)
Broder Carl 5-19-71:26
Broederna Lejonhjaerta 10-05-77:28
Broken Arrow 6-14-50:8
Broken Barriers 2-13-29:30
Broken Blossoms 5-16-19:50
Broken Blossoms 6-10-36:18 and 1-20-37:27
Broken Chains 12-01-16:28
Broken Chains 12-15-22:40
Broken Commandments 10-24-19:60
Broken Doll, The 10-22-10:14
Broken Doll, A 7-22-21:36
Broken Dreams 11-28-33:43
Broken Fetters 6-23-16:20
Broken Gate, The 3-30-27:19
Broken Hearts of Broadway 7-19-23:34
Broken Hearts of Hollywood 10-20-26:60
Broken Journey 4-21-48:13
Broken Lance 7-28-54:6
Broken Law, The 12-03-15:21
Broken Laws 2-04-25:39
Broken Locket 9-25-09:20
Broken Love 10-23-46:10
Broken Mask 3-21-28:26
Broken Melody, A 10-30-09:11
Broken Melody 7-20-38:13
Broken Road 7-22-21:35
Broken Rose, The 6-05-14:19
Broken Shoes 4-03-34:17
Broken Spell, A 4-02-10:17
Broken Star, The 2-01-56:18
Broken Ties 8-28-09:13
Broken Ties 2-22-18:45
Broken Treaty at Battle Mountain 1-22-75:32
Broken Violin 7-04-23:23
Broken Wedding Bells (s) 9-24-30:23

Broken Wing 10-11-23:27
Broken Wing, The 3-29-32:34
Brokiga Blad 12-08-31:15
Brollopet Pa Solo 11-13-46:16
Brollopsbesvar 9-30-64:22
Brollopsnatten 4-23-47:18
Bronco Billy 6-11-80:20
Bronco Bullfrog 10-28-70:30
Bronco Buster 4-16-52:6
Bronco Twister 3-20-27:18 and 5-18-27:24
Bronte 7-12-72:24
Bronze Bell 7-08-21:27
Bronze Bracelet, The 7-24-74:22
Bronzes, Les 12-06-78:32
Brood, The 6-06-79:20
Brooding Eyes 4-28-26:49
Brooklyn Orchid 1-28-26:49
Brot der Fruehen Jahre, Das 5-30-62:22
Brot des Baeckers, Das 4-27-77:22
Brot und Rosen 8-09-67:6
Brot und Spiele 8-19-64:6
Brot und Steine 5-30-79:26
Brother, Can You Spare a Dime? 3-19-75:32
Brother John 3-24-71:19
Brother Man 10-15-10:12
Brother Officers 3-05-15:21
Brother Orchid 5-29-40:14
Brother Rat 10-19-38:12
Brother Rat and a Baby 1-10-40:14
Brother Sun, Sister Moon 3-21-73:18
Brotherhood, The 11-20-68:6
Brotherhood 8-18-76:22
Brotherhood of Satan, The 4-28-71:6
Brotherly Love 4-01-70:24
Brothers, The 10-09-09:20
Brothers 7-24-29:39
Brothers 11-19-30:21
Brothers, The 5-14-47:15
Brothers 3-23-77:22
Brother's Devotion, A 3-19-10:17
Brothers and Sisters 9-17-80:42
Brothers in Law 3-13-57:6
Brothers in the Saddle 2-09-49:13
Brothers Karamozov, The 2-19-58:6
Brothers Karamazov (See: Bratya Karamozov)
Brothers of the West 12-07-38:13
Brothers Rico, The 8-21-57:18
Brother's Wrong, A 10-30-09:11
Brott I Sol 2-04-48:22

Brought to Terms 12-04-09:13
Brown Derby, The 5-26-26:19
Brown of Harvard 2-01-18:43
Brown of Harvard 5-05-26:18
Brown on Resolution 5-29-35:34
Browne and La Velle 12-12-28:14
Browning Version, The 3-21-51:7
Brox Sisters (s) 8-01-28:12 and
   10-03-28:17
Brubaker 6-18-80:22
Bruce Bowers (s) 3-27-29:12
Bruce Lee and I 1-28-76:15
Bruce Lee--True Story 12-08-
   76:18
Bruecke, Die 2-03-60:20
Brueder, Die 12-15-76:18
Brune Que Voila, La 6-15-60:18
Bruno--Der Schqarze, es Blies ein
   Jager Wohl in Sein Horn 11-
   03-71:24
Bruno, L'Enfant du Dimanche 7-
   09-69:6
Brushfire 2-07-62:6
Brussels-Transit 12-17-80:20
Brute, The 5-08-14:21
Brute, The 4-20-27:20
Brute and the Beast, The 12-04-
   68:6
Brute Breaker, The 11-07-19:97
Brute Force 6-18-47:8
Brute Man, The 10-23-46:10
Brute Master, The 12-17-20:40
Brutes and Savages 11-22-78:26
Bruto, El 9-02-53:6
Brutti, Sporchi e Cattivi 6-02-76:
   16
Brutus 5-26-76:18
Brzezin 2-16-72:24
Bubasinter 8-25-71:23
Bubble, The 12-28-66:6
Bubble Party, The (s) 8-13-30:15
Bubbling Over (s) 1-09-34:16
Bube U Glavi 8-19-70:24
Buccaneer, The 1-12-38:14
Buccaneer, The 12-17-58:6
Buccaneer's Girl, The 3-01-50:6
Buchannan Rides Again 8-06-58:7
Buchenwald Orientation Film 1-
   16-74:20
Buck 2-28-79:22
Buck and the Preacher 4-19-72:
   18
Buck Benny Rides Again 4-17-40:
   13
Buck Privates 2-01-28:22
Buck Privates 2-05-41:12
Buck Privates Come Home 3-12-
   47:12

Buck Rogers 4-04-79:20
Buckaroo from Powder River 4-
   07-48:20
Buckaroo Kid, The 11-24-26:18
Buckaroo Sheriff of Texas 12-27-
   50:6
Bucket of Blood, A 10-28-59:6
Bucking Broadway 12-07-17:47
Bucking Society 5-05-16:26
Bucking the Barrier 6-14-23:26
Bucking the Tiger 5-06-21:41
Bucking the Truth 8-25-26:22
Bucklige von Soho, Der 12-07-66:6
Buckshot John 1-30-15:24
Buckskin 4-03-68:22
Buckskin Frontier 3-17-43:23
Buckskin Lady, The 7-03-57:6
Bucktown 7-09-75:25
Budai Cukraszda 1-15-36:19
Budapesti Mesek 3-02-77:26
Buddha 7-03-63:6
Buddy Holly Story, The 5-17-78:
   54
Buddy, the Little Guardian 1-21-
   11:12
Buddy Traps (s) 4-30-30:17
Budjenje Pacova 7-12-67:24
Buebchen 10-16-68:28
Buechse der Pandora (See: Pan-
   dora's Box)
Buchne Frei Fuer Marika 1-04-
   59:16
Buen Amor, El 5-22-63:19
Buenos Aires Today (s) 10-01-
   41:9 (Also see: Screen Snap-
   shots)
Buffalo Bill 3-15-44:32
Buffalo Bill and the Indians, or
   Sitting Bull's History Lesson
   6-30-76:20
Buffalo Bill in Tomahawk Territory
   1-20-52:6
Buffalo Bill Rides Again 4-02-47:
   16
Buffalo Fight 11-05-10:14
Buffalo Racing in Madeira 11-06-
   09:13
Buffalo Stampede, The (s) 8-04-31:
   18 (Also see: Adventures in
   Africa)
Buffet Froid 1-02-80:12
Bug 6-11-75:19
Bugle Call, The 5-05-16:23
Bugle Call, The 10-05-27:24
Bugle Sounds, The 12-17-41:8
Bugler of Algiers, The 11-24-16:
   29
Bugles in the Afternoon 2-06-52:6

Bugs Bunny Gets the Bird (s) 9-02-42:34
Bugs in Love (s) 12-13-32:14
Bugsy Malone 6-09-76:22
Buhay at Pag-Ibig Ni Boy Zapanta 8-25-76:20
Builder of Bridges, The 6-11-15:18
Builders of Castles 4-13-17:24
Builders of Socialism 1-29-36:16
Building a Nation 6-28-39:20
Building a Railroad in Africa 9-28-07:11
Buildup, The (s) 1-17-33:14
Bull Fight in Mexico, A 3-26-10:15
Bulldog Breed, The 12-21-60:6
Bulldog Courage 9-08-22:42
Bulldog Drummond 12-15-22:41
Bulldog Drummond 5-08-29:20
Bulldog Drummond 8-21-34:17
Bulldog Drummond Comes Back 9-08-37:18
Bulldog Drummond Escapes (See: Drummond Escapes)
Bulldog Drummond in Africa 8-31-38:40
Bulldog Drummond's Bride 7-05-39:14
Bulldog Drummond's Peril (See: Drummond's Peril)
Bulldog Drummond's Secret Police 4-05-39:15
Bulldog Edition 10-14-36:54
Bulldog Jack 5-22-35:17
Bulldog Pluck 9-21-27:24 and 10-26-27:25
Bulldogs of the Trail, The 4-30-15:18
Bulle, La 4-28-76:28
Bullet Code 2-28-40:16
Bullet for Joey, A 4-06-55:6
Bullet for Pretty Boy, A 7-15-70:20
Bullet for Sandoval, A 6-03-70:17
Bullet for Stefano, A 11-01-50:6
Bullet Is Waiting, A 9-01-54:6
Bullet Proof 4-30-20:44
Bullet Scars 3-04-42:8
Bullet Train 7-30-75:24
Bulleteers, The (s) 4-15-42:18
Bullets and Ballots 6-03-36:15
Bullets and Brown Eyes 2-25-16:22
Bullets for O'Hara 7-30-41:20
Bullets for Rustlers 2-14-40:20
Bullfight 7-11-56:6
Bullfighter and the Lady 5-02-51:6

Bullfighters, The 4-11-45:14
Bullin' the Bullsheviki 10-24-19:61
Bullitt 10-16-68:6
Bullwhip 6-04-58:6
Bully, The 4-23-10:16
Bully 10-04-78:18
Bum Voyage (s) 5-15-35:19
Bumerang 5-04-60:6
Bumptious as a Fireman 9-24-10:12
Buna Seara, Irini 7-23-80:24
Bunco Squad 8-16-50:11
Bundle of Joy 12-12-56:6
Bungalow 13 11-24-48:6
Bungalowing 6-08-17:25
Bunker Bean 7-01-36:12
Bunny Lake Is Missing 10-06-65:6
Bunny O'Hare 6-30-71:22
Buona Sera, Mrs. Campbell 12-18-68:6
Buone Notize 12-19-79:36
Buongiorno, Elefante! 8-20-52:22
Buona, Il Brutto, Il Cattivo, Il (See: Good, the Bad, and the Ugly, The)
Buque Maldito, El 9-25-74:16
Buraikan 5-27-70:22
Burden of Proof 9-13-18:43
Burdush 8-19-70:22
Burg Theatre 12-02-36:38
Burglar, The 10-05-17:42
Burglar, The (s) 8-07-29:201
Burglar, The 5-01-57:7
Burglar and the Lady, The 12-31-15:24
Burglar by Proxy 8-29-19:68 and 10-17-19:63
Burglar for a Night, A 9-06-18:39
Burglar in the Trunk 11-06-09:13
Burglars, The (See: Casse, Le)
Buried Alive 11-06-09:13
Buried Alive 1-10-40:16
Buried Alive 1-17-51:20 (Also see: Sepolta Viva, La)
Buried Loot (s) 4-17-35:15
Buried Treasure 2-18-21:40
Burma Cowboy 10-01-41:9
Burma Victory 12-19-45:18
Burmese Harp, The (See: Biruma No Tategoto)
Burn! 10-21-70:14
Burn 'Em Up Barnes 8-26-21:36
Burn 'Em Up O'Connor 3-01-39:15
Burning Court, The (See: Chambre Ardent, La)
Burning Cross, The 8-13-47:15

Burning Gold 5-27-36:15
Burning Heart, The 5-14-30:39
Burning Sands 9-08-22:41
Burning the Candle 3-30-17:30
Burning Trail, The 4-29-25:36
Burning Up 2-12-30:19
Burning Up Broadway 2-29-28:27
Burning Words 6-07-23:25
Burning Daylight 7-02-20:29
Burning Daylight 4-25-28:29
Burning Gold 2-23-27:19
Burning Hills, The 8-08-56:6
Burning Wind 10-31-28:31
Burns and Allen 5-21-30:19
Burns and Kisser (s) 11-28-28:15
Burns-Moir Fight 12-21-07:11
Burns-Palmer Fight 2-29-08:12
Burnt Fingers 3-30-27:19
Burnt Offerings 8-25-76:20
Burnt Wings 3-26-20:50
Bury Me Dead 9-24-47:11
Burschenlied Aus Heidelberg, Ein
    9-15-31:24
Bus, The 4-14-65:6
Bus, The 8-25-76:22
Bus Did Not Stop, The (See: Nem
    Alt Meg Az Autobusz)
Bus Is Coming, The 7-21-71:24
Bus Riley's Back in Town 3-17-
    65:7
Bus Stop 8-15-56:6
Busca de la Muerte, En 7-26-61:
    13
Busea, La 9-07-66:18
Bush Christmas 6-04-47:16 and
    11-26-47:11
Bush Leaguer, The 8-31-27:24
Bushbaby, The 10-21-70:23
Busher, The 5-30-19:77
Bushido 7-03-63:6
Bushido Zankoku Monogatari (See:
    Bushido)
Bushman 10-20-71:22
Bushman, The 6-01-27:24
Bushkhugin Ulger 7-30-80:28
Bushranger 2-06-29:19
Bushwhackers, The 12-19-51:18
Business and Pleasure 2-16-32:24
Business in Great Waters 4-02-30:
    19
Business Is a Pleasure (s) 2-06-
    34:14
Business Is Business 9-10-15:22
Business of Life, The 4-05-18:45
Busman's Honeymoon 8-07-40:14
Busses Roar 8-19-42:8
Buster, The 5-17-23:26
Buster and Billie 6-12-74:18

Buster Keaton Story, The 4-17-
    57:6
Busting 1-30-74:13
Busy Beavers, The (s) 7-14-31:
    17
Busy Body, The 2-01-67:6
Busy Fingers (s) 3-05-30:21
Busy Inn, The 4-12-18:43
But the Flesh Is Weak 4-19-32:15
But Where Is Daniel Vax? 4-13-
    66:6
Butasagom Tortenete 4-13-66:6
Butch and Sundance--The Early
    Years 6-06-79:20
Butch Cassidy and the Sundance
    Kid 9-10-69:36
Butch Minds the Baby 3-25-42:8
Butcher Boy, The 4-20-17:24
Butley 1-23-74:14
Butter, Egg Man 8-29-28:28
Buttercup Chain, The 10-07-70:14
Butterfield 8 10-26-60:6
Butterflies 3-14-13:14
Butterflies Are Free 7-05-72:16
Butterflies in the Rain 12-29-26:
    17
Butterfly 1-21-25:36
Butterfly Man, The 5-21-20:34
Butterfly Murders, The 8-01-79:
    42
Butterfly on the Wheel, A 11-19-
    15:23
Butterfly Ranch 12-22-22:34
Buttons 2-22-28:24
Buy Me That Town 7-30-41:18
Buying a Gun (s) 8-20-30:14
Buying an Automobile 12-05-08:
    13
Buzzin' Around (s) 2-28-33:14
Bwana Devil 12-02-52:6
Bwana Toshi 9-08-65:68
By Appointment Only 11-21-33:20
By Candlelight 1-09-34:17
By Divine Right 4-02-24:23
By Hook or Crook 9-20-18:46
By Love Possessed 6-14-61:6
By Love Redeemed 1-28-16:23
By Power of Mystery; or, The
    Mystery of Jack Hilton 5-
    08-14:20
By Proxy 7-26-18:31
By Right of Possession 8-17-17:
    30
By Right of Purchase 3-22-18:49
By Rocket to the Moon 2-11-31:
    29 (Also see: Woman in the
    Moon, The and Girl in the
    Moon, The)

By the Blood of Others (See: <u>Par</u>
   <u>le Sang des Autres</u>)
By the Campfire (s) 6-20-28:14
By the Light of the Silvery Moon
   3-25-53:6
By the World Forgot 10-04-18:47
By Whose Hand? 4-14-16:26
By Whose Hand? 11-23-27:27
By Whose Hand? 8-16-32:15
By Your Leave 1-01-35:146
Bye, Bye Birdie 4-10-63:6
Bye, Bye Braverman 2-07-68:6
Bye-Bye Brasil 12-19-79:36
   (Also see: Bye-Bye Brazil)
Bye-Bye Brazil 5-02-80:18 (Also
   see: Bye-Bye Brasil)
Bye-Bye Monkey 5-24-78:34
Bygones (s) 3-21-33:16
Byron Nelson (s) 6-03-42:24
Byuga! Obicham Te 7-25-79:38
Byways 11-14-28:17
Bzlet 9-05-79:26

Calcutta 5-14-69:35
Calcutta 71 9-06-72:18
Calda Vita, La 4-22-64:102
Caleb Piper's Girl 5-09-19:53
Caleb Powers Trials 3-28-08:13
Calender, The 11-10-31:15
Calendar, The 6-02-48:12
Calendar Girl 2-12-47:14
Calibre .38 3-28-19:93
Caliche Sangriento 11-05-69:15
Califfa, La 3-17-71:28
California 6-29-27:23
California 12-18-46:14
California Conquest 6-11-52:6
California Dreaming 4-04-79:24
California Firebrand 4-21-48:13
California Frontier 12-14-38:14
California in '49 3-30-27:19
California Joe 3-15-44:32
California Junior Symphony (s)
   4-22-42:18
California Mail 5-08-29:27
California Mail 1-27-37:24
California or Bust 6-01-27:24
California Passage 12-27-50:6
California Reich, The 3-31-76:14
California Romance, A 5-17-23:
   26
California Split 8-07-74:18
California Straight Ahead 7-14-
   37:21
California Suite 12-13-78:24
California Trail, The 8-01-33:14
Californian, The 7-07-37:13
Caligula 11-21-79:24
Call, The 1-29-10:13
Call, The 3-30-38:15
Call a Messenger 11-15-39:18
Call at Midnight 5-22-29:24
Call from the Wild 8-12-21:34
Call Her Savage 11-29-32:18
Call Him Mr. Shatter 1-14-76:21
Call It a Day 5-12-37:12
Call It Luck 7-17-34:29
Call Me Bwana 4-10-63:6
Call Me Madam 3-04-53:6
Call Me Sister 1-24-51:6
Call Northside 777 1-21-48:8
Call of Courage 11-11-25:43
Call of Her People 6-02-17:23
Call of the Blood 3-07-13:14
Call of the Blood 2-25-48:8
Call of the Canyon 12-20-23:22
Call of the Canyon 8-19-42:8
Call of the Circus 1-29-30:62
Call of the Cumberlands, The
   2-04-16:28
Call of the Dance, The

9-24-15:20
Call of the East 11-17-22:42
Call of the Flesh 9-17-30:30
   (Also see: Chanteur de
   Seville, Le)
Call of the Heart 4-23-10:16
Call of the Heart 1-25-28:13
Call of the Jungle 8-30-44:10
Call of the Klondike 12-20-50:6
Call of the Mate 8-06-24:25
Call of the Mesquiteers 3-02-38:
   25
Call of the North, The 8-14-14:21
Call of the North 12-02-21:43
Call of the North Seas 7-19-44:
   20
Call of the Prairie 12-02-36:38
Call of the Rockies 6-15-38:15
Call of the Sea 5-27-42:8
Call of the Soul, The 2-07-19:61
Call of the Wild 9-27-23:24
Call of the Wild 8-21-35:21
Call of the Wild 3-07-73:26
Call of the Yukon 4-27-38:22
Call of Youth, The 12-17-20:42
Call Out the Marines 1-14-42:8
Callahans and Murphys 7-13-27:22
Callaway Went Thataway 11-14-
   51:6
Calle Corrientes 8-18-43:26
Calle Grita, La (See: Street Calls,
   The)
Calle Mayor 9-12-56:18 and 10-
   03-56:26
Called Back 1-23-15:26
Called to the Front 11-28-14:25
Calling All Girls (s) 2-04-42:22
Calling All Husbands 11-06-40:16
Calling All Marines 9-27-39:12
Calling All Pa's (s) 12-02-42:8
Calling All Stars 3-17-37:15
Calling Bulldog Drummond 7-11-
   51:6
Calling Dr. Death 12-15-43:8
Calling Dr. Gillespie 6-17-42:8
Calling Dr. Kildare 5-17-39:12
Calling Homicide 10-17-56:6
Calling On Cairo (s) 8-18-31:17
Calling Philo Vance 2-14-40:20
Calliope 11-24-71:16
Calm, The 11-04-64:6
Calm Yourself 7-31-35:19
Calmos 2-11-76:21
Calypso 5-27-59:6
Calypso Heat Wave 6-05-57:6
Calypso Joe 5-15-57:7
Calzonzin Inspector 6-12-74:24
Cama, La 10-30-68:26

Camada Negra 5-11-77:95
Cambio, El 5-23-73:34
Cambio de Sexo 6-01-77:17
Came the Pawn (s) 1-28-31:14
Camelot 10-25-67:6
Cameo Kirby 1-01-15:29
Cameo Kirby 2-12-30:19
Camera Thrills (s) 1-28-31:14
Cameraing in Borneo (s) 10-25-32:15
Cameraman, The 9-19-28:12
Cameriera Bella Presenza Offresi 11-28-51:6
Cameron of the Mounted 2-17-22:40
Camicie Rosse 11-12-52:6
Camille 1-22-10:14
Camille 1-07-16:23
Camille 10-12-17:42
Camille 9-16-21:35
Camille 4-27-27:16
Camille 1-27-37:12
Camille 2000 7-16-69:6
Camino de la Vida, El 7-25-56:18
Camino de las Llamas, El 5-20-42:8
Camino de los Gatos, El 2-07-45:20
Camion, Le 5-18-77:20
Camisards, Les 3-01-72:24
Cammino Della Speranza, Il 1-10-51:13
Camouflage Kiss, The 4-12-18:44
Camp Meeting (s) 11-11-36:15
Camp on Blood Island 4-23-58:7
Campagada, La 4-16-80:28
Campana Del Infierno, La 9-26-73:18
Campanadas a Medianoche 5-18-66:7
Campbell's Kingdom 9-11-57:6
Campbells Are Coming, The 10-01-15:19
Camping Out (s) 1-05-32:19
Campo di Maggio 9-16-36:17
Campo Mamula 8-19-59:16
Campus Champs (s) 4-01-31:16
Campus Confessions 9-14-38:15
Campus Crushes (s) 7-30-30:16
Campus Flirt, The 9-22-26:14
Campus Honeymoon 1-28-48:11
Campus Hoofer (s) 1-08-35:18
Campus Knights 9-11-29:33
Campus Mystery, The (s) 7-05-32:14
Campus Rhythm 10-06-43:8
Campus Romeos (s) 7-06-27:23

Campus Sleuths 5-12-48:20
Campus Spirit (s) 9-06-32:15
Can a Woman Love Twice? 4-05-23:36
Can-Can 3-09-60:6
Can Heironymus Merkin Ever Forget Mercy Humppe and Find True Happiness? 3-12-69:6
Can I Do It ... Till I Need Glasses? 11-14-79:22
Can This Be Dixie 11-18-36:13
Canadian Pacific 3-09-49:6
Canadian Patrol (s) 10-07-42:25
Canadians, The 3-08-61:6
Canal Zone 4-01-42:8
Canal Zone 12-07-77:20
Canannes 10-01-80:26
Canaries Sometimes Sing 9-24-30:30
Canaris 3-02-55:9
Canary Murder Case, The 3-13-29:28
Canasta de Cuentos Mexicanos 12-19-56:7
Cancel My Reservation 9-20-72:14
Cancelled Head 10-26-27:24
Cancion de Cuna 11-05-41:8
Cancion de Los Barrios 4-02-41:16
Cancion Para Recordar, Una 10-05-60:6
Canciones Para Despues de Una Guerra 6-23-71:20
Candida la Mujer Del Ano 4-14-43:10
Candida Millonaria 10-08-41:20
Candidate, The 6-21-72:18
Candidate for Murder 9-25-68:6
Candide 2-01-61:22
Candlelight in Prison 3-22-44-18
Candles at 9 6-14-44:10
Candleshoe 12-21-77:20
Candy 12-18-68:26
Candy Girl, The 6-08-17:24
Candytuft--I Mean Veronica 7-22-21:35
Caniche 5-16-79:44
Canillita y la Dama, El 8-03-38:15
Canine Champs (s) 12-01-31:15
Canker of Jealousy, The 3-19-15:21
Cannabis 9-30-70:22
Cannibal Attack 11-10-54:6
Cannibal Girls 4-18-73:30
Cannibali, I 9-30-70:24
Cannon and the Nightingale, The 10-22-69:30

61 •

Cannon for Cordoba 9-30-70:15
Cannonball 7-21-76:22
Cannonball Express (s) 9-08-31: 15
Cannonball Express 3-15-32:21
Canoa 7-14-76:24
Canonity 6-23-78:6
Can't Help Singing 12-20-44:8
Can't Stop the Music 6-04-80:20
Cantata (See: Oldas es Kotes)
Cantata de Chile 7-28-76:22
Canterbury Tale, A 5-31-44:20
Canterbury Tales, The 7-12-72: 30
Canterini di Romagna (s) 11-24-31:17
Canterville Ghost, The 5-31-44: 20
Cantico 8-05-70:16
Cantiga da Rua 3-29-50:22
Canto del Cisne, El 7-04-45:8
Cantor, El 8-09-78:20
Cantor Rosenblatt and Choir (s) 1-16-29:14
Cantor's Son, The 12-29-37:19
Canvas Cut-Ups (s) 9-09-42:14
Canvas Kisser, The 6-17-25:37
Canyon City 12-15-43:20
Canyon Crossroads 3-16-55:6
Canyon Hawks 10-15-30:29
Canyon of Adventure 3-21-28:23
Canyon of Fools 3-15-23:32
Canyon of Light 1-26-27:21
Canyon of Missing Men 3-26-30: 42
Canyon Passage 7-24-46:14
Canyon River 8-22-56:6
Canzone del Sole, La 5-13-36:14
Canzone dell'Amore, La 3-18-31: 38
Canzoni di Mezzo Secolo 11-03-54: 11
Canzonieri--McLarnin Fight (s) 5-13-36:15
Cap de L'Esperance, Le 1-02-52: 68
Cape Fear 3-07-62:6
Cape Forlorn 1-28-31:40
Caper of the Golden Bulls 5-17-67:6
Caperucita Roja, La 6-15-60:18
Caperucita y Pulgarcito Contra los Monstruos 10-31-62:20
Caperucita y Sus Tres Amigos 6-28-61:6
Capital Punishment 9-03-15:24
Capital Punishment 2-04-25:33
Capitan Veneno 5-12-43:20

Capitane, Le 4-17-46:16
Capitane, Le 11-09-60:19
Capitane Ardant 8-20-52:22
Capitane Fracasse, Le 3-20-29: 22
Capitane Fracasse, Le 6-07-61: 20
Capitol 1-31-20:54
Capitu 10-30-68:28
Capone 4-16-75:22
Caporal Epingle, Le 5-30-62:22
Cappello a Tre Punte, Il 9-30-36:29
Cappotto, Il 6-04-52:18
Cappotto di Astrakhan, Il 8-06-80:22
Cappy Ricks 8-26-21:36
Cappy Ricks Returns 12-04-35:15
Caprice 5-17-67:6
Caprice de Caroline Chérie, Un 5-13-53:22
Caprice of the Mountains 7-14-16: 17
Caprices de Marie, Les 3-11-70: 24
Caprices of Kitty, The 2-27-15: 25
Capricious Summer (See: Rozmarne Leto)
Capricorn One 6-07-78:25
Captain Apache 10-20-71:22
Captain Blood 9-10-24:27
Captain Blood 1-01-36:44
Captain Blue Blood (s) 3-24-37: 16
Captain Boycott 9-10-47:17
Captain Calamity 12-23-36:18
Captain Careless 10-17-28:27
Captain Carey 2-22-50:6
Captain Caution 8-07-40:16
Captain China 11-02-49:10
Captain City, The (See: Citta Prigioniera, La)
Captain Courtesy 4-16-15:19
Captain Eddie 6-20-45:11
Captain Fly-by-Night 2-08-23:41
Captain from Castile 11-26-47:11
Captain from Koepenick, The (See: Der Hauptmann Von Koepenick)
Captain Fury 5-10-39:14
Captain Grant's Children 1-25-39: 15
Captain Hates the Sea, The 12-04-34:12
Captain Horatio Hornblower 4-18-51:6 and 6-20-51:6
Captain Hurricane 7-03-35:15
Captain January 7-09-24:24

Captain January 4-29-36:15
Captain John Smith and Pocahontas 11-18-53:6
Captain Kidd 8-01-45:16
Captain Kidd, Jr. 4-25-19:83
Captain Kidd's Kiddies (s) 12-28-27:22
Captain Kronos: Vampire Hunter 6-26, 74:22
Captain Lash 2-06-29:18
Captain Lightfoot 2-16-55:16
Captain Lust 3-30-77:18
Captain Milkshake 12-09-70:14
Captain Moonlight 5-15-40:18
Captain Nemo and the Underwater City 12-17-69:24
Captain Newman, M. D. 10-23-63:6
Captain of Grey Horse Troop 5-18-17:23
Captain of His Soul, The 2-08-18:39
Captain of the Guard 4-02-30:19
Captain Pirate 7-23-52:6
Captain Salvation 6-29-27:19
Captain Scarlett 9-23-53:24
Captain Sinbad 6-26-63:6
Captain Swagger 12-26-28:27
Captain Swift 9-26-14:22
Captain Thunder 5-13-31:64
Captain Tugboat Annie 3-06-46:12
Captain Was a Lady, The 6-26-40:16
Captain's Captain, The 1-03-19:37
Captains Courageous 5-19-37:22
Captain's Kid, The 1-20-37:15
Captains of the Clouds 1-21-42:8
Captain's Paradise, The 6-24-53:22
Captain's Table, The 1-14-59:16
Captivation 6-02-31:31 and 9-29-31:22
Captive, The 3-26-10:15
Captive, The 4-30-15:18
Captive City, The 3-26-52:6
Captive Girl 4-19-50:8
Captive God, The 7-07-16:24
Captive Heart, The 4-10-46:16
Captive of Billy the Kid 1-16-52:6
Captive of Nazi Germany 8-05-36:17
Captive Wild Woman 4-28-43:8
Captive Women 10-01-52:22
Capture, The 4-05-50:6
Capture That Capsule 5-24-61:6
Captured 8-22-33:22
Car, The 5-11-77:79

Car 99 2-27-35:26
Car of Dreams 9-18-35:32
Car Shy 2-23-27:19
Car Wash 9-01-76:22
Cara a Cara 10-30-68:28
Cara Sposa 10-12-77:16
Carabiniers, Les 6-19-63:6
Carambolages 5-22-63:19
Carapate, La 11-01-78:22
Caraque Blonde, La 4-07-54:24
Caravan 10-02-34:37
Caravan 4-17-46:32
Caravan to Russia 10-28-59:6
Caravan to Vaccares 8-21-74:20
Caravan Trail, The 3-27-46:12
Caravans 11-08-78:78
Carbine Williams 4-16-52:6
Carcel de Cananea, La 1-25-61:6 and 8-02-61:7
Card, The 3-05-52:6
Cardboard Cavalier 4-06-49:8
Cardena Perpetu 7-30-80:28
Cardigan 2-24-22:34
Cardillac 9-10-69:36
Cardinal, The 4-08-36:16
Cardinal, The 10-16-63:6
Career 7-12-39:12
Career 9-30-59:6
Career Girl 3-08-44:14
Career of Katherine Bush, The 8-08-19:49
Career Woman 12-16-36:21
Careers 6-12-29:31
Carefree 8-31-38:18
Careful, Soft Shoulders 8-12-42:
Careless Age 9-25-29:17
Careless Lady 4-19-32:15
Careless Tramp 10-02-09:13
Careless Years, The 9-04-57:6
Caretaker, The 7-03-63:6
Carevo Novo Ruho 8-09-61:6
Carey Treatment, The 3-29-72:30
Cargaison Blanche 3-17-37:15
Cargaison Blanche 5-07-58:22
Cargo to Capetown 4-05-50:6
Caribbean 8-06-52:6
Caribbean Mystery, The 7-18-45:34
Cariboo Trail 7-05-50:10
Carica Eroica 12-24-52:14
Carillons Sans Joie 5-16-62:19
Carinito (s) 5-14-30:19
Carl Emmy and Pals (s) 2-20-29:14
Carl Hagenbeck's Menagerie at Hamburg 1-11-08:17
Carl Hoff and Orch. (s) 1-07-42:45

Carlos and Elisabeth   4-16-24:27
Carlotta   7-21-71:24
Carlton-Browne of the F.O.   3-18-59:23
Carmela   5-18-49:20
Carmen   11-05-15:22
Carmen   11-05-15:22
Carmen   4-14-16:24
Carmen   6-15-17:27
Carmen   5-16-28:13
Carmen   12-01-43:10
Carmen   12-04-46:13
Carmen   12-28-49:6
Carmen   8-05-70:20
Carmen, Baby   10-11-67:6
Carmen Comes Home   1-13-60:7
Carmen Jones   10-06-54:6
Carmen la de Ronda   10-07-59:6
Carmen of the Klondike   3-08-18:41
Carmen of the North   5-14-20:35
Carnal Knowledge   6-30-71:22
Carnation Kid   2-27-29:86
Carne   12-04-68:6
Carnegie Hall   3-05-47:8
Carnera-Baer Fight   6-19-34:27
Carnera-Schaaf (s)   2-21-33:14
Carnet du Bal, Un   10-20-37:27
      (Also see: Life Dances On)
Carnets du Major Thompson, Les   1-11-56:22
Carnival   7-01-21:29 and 8-05-21:26
Carnival (s)   4-15-31:20
Carnival   11-17-31:26
Carnival   2-20-35:75
Carnival   10-30-46:14
Carnival   10-21-53:18
Carnival Boat   3-22-32:61
Carnival Day (s)   2-26-36:15
Carnival Girl, The   12-29-26:17
Carnival in Brazil (s)   3-11-42:20
Carnival in Ceylon   3-21-14:13
Carnival in Costa Rica   3-26-47:12
Carnival in Flanders (See: Kermesse Heroique, La)
Carnival King   2-20-29:17
Carnival Man (s)   3-13-29:14
Carnival Man (s)   9-03-30:19
Carnival Night   10-23-57:18
Carnival of Crime   7-10-29:13
Carnival of Japanese Firemen in Tokyo   1-07-11:13
Carnival of Rhythm (s)   9-03-41:17
Carnival of Sinners   4-02-47:16
      (Also see: Main du Diable, Le)
Carnival of Souls   10-03-67:7

Carnival Queen   11-03-37:14
Carnival Rock   10-09-57:6
Carnival Story   3-24-54:6
Carny   5-21-80:20
Caro Michele   7-14-76:24
Caro Papa   5-23-79:22
Carolina   2-20-34:14
Carolina Blues   12-13-44:8
Carolina Cannonball   1-26-55:20
Carolina Moon   7-17-40:18
Caroline Cherie   3-21-51:7
Caroline Cherie   2-28-68:22
Carolyn of the Corners   2-21-19:67
Carolynne Snowden Co. (s)   10-31-28:24
Carom Shots (See: Carambolages)
Carosello Napoletano   5-05-54:21
Carousel   2-22-56:6
Carpet from Bagdad, The   5-14-15:19
Carpetbaggers, The   4-15-64:6
Carrefour   11-30-38:13
Carrie   6-11-52:6
Carrie   11-03-76:27
Carrie Jacobs Bond (s)   1-16-34:15
Carrington V.C.   12-15-54:28
Carrosse D'Or, La   3-11-53:18
Carry It On   7-29-70:15
Carry On!   12-28-27:20
Carry On Admiral   5-22-57:20
Carry On Again, Doctor   12-10-69:28
Carry On Cabby   8-28-63:6
Carry On Camping   8-24-66:6
Carry On Camping   6-04-69:38
Carry On Cleo   2-16-64:17
Carry On Constable   3-02-60:6
Carry On Cowboy   4-06-66:24
Carry On Cruising   4-18-62:6
Carry On Doctor   3-27-68:20
Carry On Emmanuelle   12-06-78:32
Carry On England   11-03-76:26
Carry On Jack   2-26-64:6
Carry On Loving   11-11-70:22
Carry On Nurse   3-18-59:23
Carry On Regardless   4-12-61:6
Carry On, Sergeant   12-05-28:19
Carry On, Sergeant   9-24-58:18
Carry On Spying   7-22-64:6
Carry On, Teacher   9-02-59:6
Carry On, the Khyber   12-25-68:18
Carry On Up the Jungle   4-22-70:17
Cars That Ate Paris, The   6-26-74:20

Carson City 5-07-52:6
Carson City Cyclone 5-26-43:8
Carson City Kid 7-24-40:16
Carson City Raiders 6-02-48:12
Carta de Amor, Una 7-26-44:10
Carter Case, The 2-25-42:8
Carthage in Flames 1-25-61:6
Cartouche 5-09-62:17
Carve Her Name with Pride 2-26-58:6
Caryl of the Mountains 9-30-36:17
Cas de Malheur, En 9-17-58:18
Cas du Dr. Laurent, Le 4-17-57:6 (Also see: Case of Dr. Laurent, The)
Casa Chica, La 5-10-50:16
Casa de la Troya, La 11-04-59:6
Casa de la Zorra, La 9-03-47:16
Casa de las Palomas, La 3-01-72:20
Casa de las Cuervos, La 5-28-41:18
Casa de Munecas 11-17-43:20
Casa del Angel, La 5-15-57:7
Casa del Sur, La 7-30-75:22
Casa en Que Vivimos, La 8-12-70:22
Casa Estra Vacia, La 7-25-45:20
Casa Manana 7-11-51:6
Casa Sin Fronteras, La 5-03-72:20
Casablan 12-09-64:6
Casablanca 12-02-42:8
Casanova 12-22-76:20
Casanova and Co. 3-09-77:24
Casanova Brown 8-02-44:10
Casanova in Burlesque 1-26-44:12
Casanova '70 7-21-65:7
Casanova's Big Night 3-03-54:6
Casbah 3-10-48:10
Cascabel 8-31-77:30
Cascarrabias 10-22-30:35 (Also see: Grumpy)
Case Against Brooklyn, The 5-14-58:6
Case Against Mrs. Ames, The 6-03-36:15
Case at Law, A 11-16-17:53
Case for the Defence, The 7-25-19:43
Case of Becky, The 10-14-21:42
Case of Clara Deane, The 5-10-32:19
Case of the Curious Bride, The 4-10-35:17
Case of Dr. Laurent, The 7-02-58:6 (Also see: Cas du Dr. Laurent, Le)
Case of Jonathan Drew, The

6-13-28:12
Case of Lena Smith, The 1-16-29:14
Case of the Lucky Legs, The 11-13-35:17
Case of Sergeant Grischa, The 3-12-30:21
Case of the Stuttering Bishop, The 6-02-37:23
Case of the Baby Sitter, The 9-17-47:16
Case of the Black Cat, The 12-30-36:11
Case of the Black Parrot, The 1-15-41:14
Case of the 44's, The 9-09-64:6
Case of the Frightened Lady, The 7-10-40:14
Case of the Full Moon Murders, The 11-28-73:18
Case of the Howling Dog, The 10-23-34:18
Case of the Missing Hare, The (s) 1-06-43:50
Case of the Missing Man, The 11-27-35:14
Case of the Red Monkey, The 8-17-55:6
Case of the Velvet Claws 9-02-36:21
Case of Tom Mooney (s) 7-25-33:14
Case of Tomatoes, A 9-18-09:13
Case Van Geldern 9-27-32:21
Casey at the Bat 6-23-16:20
Casey at the Bat 4-06-27:24
Casey Jones 12-28-27:20
Casey's Shadow 3-08-78:35
Cash? Cash! 6-11-69:42
Cash McCall 12-09-59:6
Cash on Delivery 2-01-56:18
Casi Casados 10-18-61:22
Casi un Sueno 5-19-43:8
Casino de Paris 11-27-57:6
Casino Murder Case 4-17-35:15
Casino Royale 4-19-67:6
Casino to Korea 9-27-50:20
Caso Mattei, Il 2-16-72:24
Casotto, Il 10-22-80:25
Casque D'Or 5-28-52:24
Cass Timberlane 11-05-47:8
Cassandra Crossing, The 2-02-77:24
Casse, Le 11-03-71:24
Cassidy 10-19-17:32
Cassidy of Bar 20 3-30-38:15
Cast a Dark Shadow 9-28-55:9
Cast a Giant Shadow 3-30-66:6
Cast into the Flames 11-26-10:18

Casta Diva 5-22-35:17
Casta Susana, La 12-06-44:14
Castagne Sono Buone, Le 2-17-71:28
Castaway Cowboy, The 7-24-74:20
Caste 7-20-17:30
Castelul Condamnatilor 8-05-70:16
Castiglione, La 8-17-55:6
Castigo Al Traidor 3-23-66:6
Castillo de la Pureza, El 4-24-74:20
Castle in Sweden (See: Chateau en Suede)
Castle in the Desert 2-04-42:8
Castle Keep 7-23-69:6
Castle of Blood (See: Danse Macabre)
Castle of Crimes 4-04-45:10
Castle of Evil 10-11-67:22
Castles in the Air 5-16-19:50
Castles in the Air 7-16-52:20
Cast-Off, The 2-15-18:52
Castrati, I (See: Voci Bianche, Le)
Cat, The 7-06-66:6
Cat and Mouse (See: Chat et la Souris, Le)
Cat and Mouse (See: Katz und Mans)
Cat and the Canary, The 9-14-17:22
Cat and the Canary, The 11-01-39:14
Cat and the Canary, The 11-22-78:26
Cat and the Fiddle 2-20-34:14
Cat Ate the Parakeet, The 1-26-72:24
Cat Ballou 5-12-65:6
Cat Creeps, The 11-12-30:32
Cat Creeps, The 4-10-46:16
Cat from Outer Space, The 6-21-78:18
Cat Girl 9-04-57:28
Cat in the Sack, The (See: Chat Dans le Sac, Le)
Cat Meets Mouse (s) 4-08-42:20
Cat Murkell and the Silks 6-16-76:18
Cat o' Nine Tails 6-09-71:17
Cat on a Hot Tin Roof 8-13-58:6
Cat People, The 11-18-42:8
Cat-Women of the Moon 12-16-53:6
Catalan, the Minstrel 1-07-11:13
Catalina Caper, The 12-20-67:15
Catamount Killing, The 12-18-74:12

Catch As Catch Can 7-13-27:23
Catch As Catch Can 1-31-68:6
Catch Me a Spy 9-22-71:14
Catch My Soul 3-27-74:14
Catch-22 6-10-70:18
Catching Up 8-27-75:15
Catered Affair, The 4-25-56:6
Catherine et Cie 10-29-75:17
Catherine il Suffit D'Un Amour 6-04-69:6
Catherine the Great 1-30-34:12 and 2-20-34:14
Cathy's Child 5-02-79:26
Catlow 10-13-71:20
Catman of Paris, The 2-20-46:8
Cats, The 12-25-68:18
Cat's Nightmare, The (s) 10-27-31:19
Cat's Pajamas, The 9-01-26:15
Cat's Paw, The (s) 4-15-31:20
Cat's Paw, The 8-21-34:17
Catskill Honeymoon 2-01-50:20
Catspaw, The 1-14-16:19
Cattle Drive 7-18-51:6
Cattle Empire 2-12-58:6
Cattle King 6-19-63:21
Cattle Queen 10-10-51:6
Cattle Queen of Montana 11-17-54:6
Cattle Raiders 5-04-38:25
Cattle Stampede 12-29-43:8
Cattle Thief, The 5-27-36:14
Cattle Thieves 11-13-09:13
Cattle Town 11-26-52:6
Cattleman's Daughter, The 3-04-11:18
Caucasian Customs 10-02-09:13
Cauchemars 5-14-80:15
Caudillo 7-06-77:17
Caught 4-04-08:13
Caught 10-06-31:29
Caught 2-23-49:10
Caught Cheating 3-11-31:15
Caught in the Act 2-12-41:18
Caught in the Draft 5-28-41:16
Caught in the Fog 12-05-28:12
Caught Plastered 9-15-31:24
Caught Short 6-25-30:109
Causa Kralik 5-28-80:42
Cause for Alarm 1-31-51:6
Cause for Divorce 1-31-24:24
Cause Toujours Mon Lapin 12-20-61:6
Cavalcade 1-10-33:15
Cavalcade d'Amour 2-14-40:25
Cavalcade des Heures, La (See: Love Around the Clock)
Cavalcade of Academy Awards 4-17-40:16

Cavalcade of Aviation (s) 1-07-42:45
Cavalcade of the West 9-30-36:29
Cavale, La 10-27-71:18
Cavaleur, Le 1-24-79:23
Cavalier, The 11-07-28:15
Cavalier of the West 2-09-32:19
Cavaliere Inesistente, Il 11-18-
70:40 and 9-01-71:22
Cavalieri della Montagna 1-25-50:20
Cavalleria Rusticana 12-24-47:22
Calvary Captain Wronski 1-26-55:20
Cavalry Scout 4-18-51:24
Cavanaugh of Rangers 2-22-18:43
Cave, Un 7-12-72:28
Cave Club, The (s) 5-14-30:19
Cave Man, The 12-03-15:21
Cave Man, The 3-03-26:35
Cave of Outlaws 10-31-51:6
Cave Se Rebiffe, Le 10-18-61:6
Cavern, The 11-10-65:6
Caves du Majestic, Les 11-21-45:18
Caviar (s) 2-19-30:21
Cayman Triangle, The 12-97-77:20
Caza, La 7-06-66:6
Ce Cher Victor 5-14-75:30
Ce Corps Tant Desire 6-10-59:6
Ce Joli Monde 12-04-57:22
Ce Repondeur Ne Prend Pas De
Message 7-25-79:42
Ce Sacre Grand-Pere 5-15-68:28
Ce Siecle a 50 Ans 4-26-50:22
Ce Soir les Jupons Volent 7-11-56:
10
Ce Soir ou Jamais 10-25-61:6
Cease Fire 11-25-53:6
Cecil Lean and Cleo May Field (s)
11-27-29:21
Cecilia 11-19-75:26
Cecilia of the Pink Roses 6-07-
18:34
Ceddo 6-01-79:17
Ceiling Zero 1-22-36:14
Cela S'Appelle L'Aurore 5-16-56:6
Celebrated Case, A 5-08-14:21
Celebration at Big Sur 5-07-71:18
Celebrity 12-12-28:31
Celebrul 702 6-27-62:6
Celeste 12-23-70:6
Celeste Aide (s) 4-30-30:17
Celestial Brothers, The 7-24-63:6
Celestina, La 7-30-69:6
Celestina 8-11-76:19
Celine and Julie Go Boating (See:
Celine et Julie Vont en
Bateau)
Celine et Julie Vont en Bateau
8-21-74:22
Cell 2455, Death Row 4-13-55:9

Celui Qui Doit Mourir 5-15-57:7
Cena Grada 8-12-70:14
Cenerentola 6-01-49:20
Ceneri Della Memoria 9-14-60:20
Ceniza Al Viento 10-28-42:8
122 Rue de Provence 5-10-78:27
125 Rue Montmartre 10-28-59:6
Centennial Summer 5-29-46:10
Cento Piccoloe Mamme 7-30-52:22
Central Airport 5-09-33:14
Centroforward Murio Al Amanecer,
El 5-24-61:17
C'era una Volta Il West (See:
Once Upon a Time in the
West)
C'eravama Tanti Amati 1-15-75:26
Cercle Rouge, La 11-11-70:15
Ceremony, The 12-18-63:7
Cerf-Volant du Bout du Monde
5-07-58:22
Cerniti Angueli 8-05-70:22
Cerny Petr 8-12-64:6
Cerny Prador 9-03-58:6
Cerromaior 10-15-80:66
Certain Rich Man, A 2-03-22:42
Certain Smile, A 7-30-58:6
Certain Young Man 6-13-28:12
Certo, Certissimo, Anzi ... Pro-
babile 7-22-70:16
Certo Girono, Un 10-08-69:15
Cerveau, Le 3-19-69:6
Ces Dames Preferent le Mambo
3-12-58:7
Cesar 11-25-36:19
Cesar and Rosalie (See: Cesar
et Rosalie)
Cesar et Rosalie 11-15-72:24
C'est La Vie 9-03-80:26
C'est Pas Moi, C'est Lui 2-27-
80:26
Cest a Slava 7-16-69:6
C'est Arrive a Oden 12-05-56:6
C'est Arrive a Paris 3-11-53:6
C'est Arrive a Trente-Six Chan-
delles 12-04-57:22
C'est Dur Pour Tout le Monde
7-09-75:25
C'est la Faute D'Adam 5-07-58:22
C'est la Vie Parisienne (See: It's
the Paris Life)
C'est la Vie Rose 3-02-77:22
C'est Paree (s) 7-26-32:17
Cesta Duga Godinu Dana 8-06-58:
6 and 8-20-58:6
Cesty Muzu 8-16-72:26
Cet Age Sans Pitie 5-14-80:15
Cet Homme Est Dangereux 3-17-
54:22

Cet Obscure Objet du Desir 8-31-77:18
Cetiri Dana Do Smitl 8-25-76:27
Cette Nuit, La 10-01-58:6
Cette Sacree Gamine 4-18-56:7
Cette Vielle Canaille 12-12-33:29
Ceux du "Viking" 3-15-32:60
Cha-Cha-Cha Boom 9-26-59:16
Chac 3-12-75:34
Chacal de Nahueltoro, El 6-10-70:18
Chacun Sa Chance 1-07-31:23
Chad Hanna 12-18-40:16
Chafed Elbows 3-15-67:26
Chagrin et la Pitie, Le 6-16-71:22
Chaika 11-28-73:16
Chain Gang, The 10-29-30:17
Chain Gang 10-04-50:6
Chain Lightning 9-08-22:42
Chain Lightning 2-08-50:11
Chain of Circumstance 8-15-51:6
Chain of Evidence 5-08-57:6
Chain Reaction 4-23-80:19
Chained 10-26-27:22
Chained 9-04-34:19
Chains of the Past 8-07-14:18
Chair de L'Orchidee, La 2-19-75:22
Chair de Poule 11-27-63:6
Chair et le Diable, La 8-04-54:6
Chairman, The 6-18-69:6
Chaise Vide, La 1-01-75:14
Chajrchan Ondor Chaana Bajna 8-16-78:19
Chaleur du Sien 11-30-38:13
Chalice of Courage, The 7-30-15:19
Chalice of Sorrow, The 9-29-16:26
Chalk Garden, The 4-08-64:6
Challenge, The 12-29-16:21
Challenge, The 10-04-39:47
Challenge, The 2-18-48:8
Challenge, The 5-25-60:7
Challenge Accepted, The 12-13-18:40
Challenge for Robin Hood, A 7-31-68:6
Challenge of Chance, The 6-27-19:46
Challenge of Greatness 9-15-76:17
Challenge of the Law, The 12-17-20:40
Challenge of the Range 6-22-49:6
Challenge of the Wind 6-09-54:6
Challenge to Be Free 1-15-75:26
Challenge to Lassie 11-02-49:11

Challenge to Live 3-07-62:6
Chalutzim 4-10-34:13
Chamade, La 11-20-68:36
Chamber of Horrors 8-31-66:6
Chambre Ardent, La 4-25-62:6
Chambre Blanche, La 5-20-70:28
Chambre Rouge, La 2-21-73:24
Chambre Verte, La 3-29-78:22
Chameleon 9-20-78:26
Chamloey Sawat 4-30-75:23
Champ, The 11-17-31:14
Champ, The 3-28-79:20
Champ for a Day 9-16-53:6
Champagne 9-05-28:28
Champagne 7-03-29:30
Champagne a Martello 1-25-50:18
Champagne Charlie 5-13-36:14
Champagne Charlie 9-13-44:10
Champagne for Breakfast 7-10-35:19
Champagne for Caesar 2-08-50:11
Champagne Murders, The (See: Scandale, Le)
Champagne Waltz 2-10-37:14
Champignon, Le 4-22-70:17
Champion 3-16-49:11
Champion du Regiment 9-27-32:21
Champ's a Chump, The (s) 8-12-36:19
Chan at Monte Carlo 12-22-37:17
Chan at the Olympics 5-26-37:14
Chan at Treasure Island 8-23-39:20
Chan on Broadway 9-22-37:18
Chance, La 1-12-32:28 and 5-31-32:62
Chance at Heaven 12-26-33:26
Chance of a Lifetime, The 12-22-43:12
Chance of a Lifetime 5-03-50:20
Chance of a Night Time 6-02-31:31
Chances 6-16-31:21
Chandler 12-08-71:20
Chandu the Magician 10-04-32:19
Chang 5-04-27:20
Chang Kun Ui Su Yum 7-02-69:24
Change of Habit 10-22-69:16
Change of Heart, A 10-23-09:13
Change of Heart, A 10-03-14:21
Change of Heart, A 1-25-28:12
Change of Heart 5-15-34:14
Change of Heart 1-05-38:16
Change of Mind 10-08-69:28
Change of Seasons, A 12-24-80:14
Change Pas de Main 7-09-75:25
Changeling, The 2-20-80:12
Changes 2-05-69:30
Changing Husbands 6-25-24:26
Changing of the Guard (s) 8-12-36:19

Charlie Is My Darling 10-26-66:6
Charlie McCarthy, Detective 12-20-39:47
Charlie, the Lonesome Cougar 10-11-67:6
Charlots Font L'Espagne, Les 12-27-72:20
Charlotte Corday 3-27-14:20
Charlotte Corday 1-16-15:27
Charlotte Lowenskoeld 2-23-32:19
Charlotte Lowenskoeld 12-26-79:12
Charlotte's Web 2-21-73:18
Charly 7-03-68:6
Charly Og Steffen 12-26-79:13
Charm of La Boheme 3-13-38:15
Charm School, The 8-06-20:25
Charmants Garcons 1-15-58:7
Charme Discreet de la Bourgeoisie, Le 9-27-72:6
Charmer, The 8-31-17:31
Charmer, The 4-08-25:38
Charming Deceiver 4-08-21:40
Charming Deceiver 12-12-33:19
Charming Sisters 7-10-29:13
Charrette Fantome, La 3-20-40:24
Charro! 3-12-69:26
Charter Pilot 11-27-40:16 and 12-25-40:16
Charulata 7-07-65:16
Chase, The 7-04-23:22
Chase, The 10-16-46:8
Chase, The 2-02-66:6
Chase a Crooked Shadow 1-29-58:6
Chased into Love 12-15-16:35
Chaser, The 4-11-28:12
Chaser, The 8-10-38:12
Chasing a Sea Lion 9-18-09:13
Chasing Danger 5-17-39:14
Chasing Rainbows 8-22-19:75
Chasing Rainbows 2-26-30:35
Chasing the Moon 3-03-22:40
Chasing Through Europe 9-18-29:29
Chasing Trouble (s) 6-02-31:14
Chasing Trouble 1-31-40:26
Chasing Yesterday 10-23-35:13
Chasse a l'Homme, La 10-28-64:6
Chasse au Lion a l'Arc, La 9-15-65:95
Chasseur de Chez Maxims, Le 3-28-33:27 and 1-03-40:40
Chastity 4-30-24:19
Chastity 6-25-69:24
Chastity Belt, The 1-31-68:23
Chat, Le 6-16-71:15

Chat Dans le Sac, Le 9-30-64:22 and 5-19-65:31
Chat et la Souris, Le 9-24-75:24
Chateau de Verre, Le 1-10-51:20
Chateau en Suede 12-18-63:17
Chateaux en Espagne 10-06-54:22
Chatelaine du Liban, La 11-07-56:6
Chato's Land 5-17-72:28
Chatte, La 5-28-58:6
Chatte Sort Ses Griffes, La 7-27-60:6
Chattel, The 9-08-16:21
Chatterbox 2-19-36:12
Chatterbox 4-14-43:10
Chatterbox 2-23-77:18
Chaud Lapin, Le 11-13-74:19
Chauffer's Dream 8-08-08:11
Chauffeur de Mlle, Le 3-14-28:28
Chaussette Surprise 6-21-78:23
Che! 6-04-69:6
Che? 1-10-73:18
Che Gioia Vivere 5-24-61:17
Che Tempi! 6-16-48:20
Cheap 7-17-74:16
Cheap Detective, The 6-07-78:25
Cheap Kisses 12-31-24:26
Cheaper by the Dozen 3-29-50:11
Cheaper To Keep Her 9-24-80:14
Cheaper to Marry 2-04-25:33
Cheat, The 10-29-10:14
Cheat, The 12-17-15:18
Cheat, The 8-30-23:26
Cheat, The 12-15-31:14
Cheated Hearts 12-23-21:36
Cheater, The 7-30-20:33
Cheater Reformed, The 3-04-21:40
Cheaters 6-01-27:21
Cheaters 5-15-34:30
Cheaters, The 7-04-45:8
Cheaters, The (See: Tricheurs, Les)
Cheaters at Play 3-01-32:21
Cheating Blondes 5-23-33:15
Cheating Cheaters 1-25-19:46
Cheating Cheaters 12-07-27:20
Cheating Herself 8-15-19:71
Cheating the Public 1-25-18:43
Chechahcos, The 5-07-24:25
Check and Double Check 10-08-30:22
Check and Rubber Check (s) 10-20-31:21

71 •

Chiedo Asilo 1-16-80:31
Chief, The 12-05-33:17
Chief Caupolican (s) 10-31-28:24
Chief Cook, The 9-21-17:42
Chief Crazy Horse 2-23-55:8
Chieko-Sho (See: Portrait of Chieko)
Chien de Pique, Le 2-08-61:103
Chien Fou, Le 9-28-66:6
Chien Jaune, Le 7-19-32:25
Chienne, La 1-12-32:28
Chiens, Les 5-02-79:26
Chiens Perdus Sans Colliers 11-02-55:18
Chiffonniers D'Emmaus, Les 4-13-55:9
Chijin No Ai 9-06-67:20
Chikamatsu Monogartari 5-11-55:9
Chikita 1-24-62:22
Chikuzan Hitori Tabi 7-27-77:22
Child for Sale 3-26-20:51
Child in Judgement, A 12-10-15:21
Child in the House 8-22-56:6
Child Is a Wild Thing, A 9-15-76:17
Child Is Born, A 1-17-40:14
Child Is Waiting, A 1-16-63:6
Child of Divorce 10-16-46:8
Child of Manhattan 2-14-33:21
Child of M'sieu 2-14-19:51
Child of Mystery, A 12-29-16:21
Child of Paris Secrets, A 5-19-16:19
Child of the West, A 3-10-16:30
Child of the Wild, A 2-23-17:23
Child Shall Lead Them, A 9-08-22:41
Child Wonder, The (s) 6-05-29:15
Childhood of Maxim Gorky 9-28-28:21
Childhood II 5-24-72:26
Childish Things 7-02-69:6
Children, The 12-28-49:16
Children, The 7-09-80:18
Children in the House, The 4-21-16:30
Children Must Laugh 4-06-38:15
Children of Abraham 11-09-55:6
Children of Babylon 10-08-80:20
Children of Banishment 3-07-19:67
Children of Chance 1-28-31:40
Children of Chaos 4-26-50:22
Children of Divorce 4-20-27:21
Children of Dreams 7-21-31:34
Children of Dust 8-30-23:26
Children of Eve 11-12-15:23

Children of Jazz 7-12-23:29
Children of Labor 9-28-77:22
Children of Metropolis 7-03-29:30
Children of No Importance 4-04-28:28
Children of Paradise (See: Enfants du Paradis, Les)
Children of Pleasure 8-06-30:39
Children of Rage 1-22-75:34
Children of Sanchez, The 9-20-78:26
Children of the Damned 1-22-64:19
Children of the Feud 11-24-16:28
Children of the Ghetto 2-12-15:23
Children of the Night 7-22-21:36
Children of the Nile (s) 1-09-34:16
Children of the Revolution 4-08-36:17
Children of the Ritz 4-03-29:23
Children of the Sea 11-20-09:13
Children of the Stars (s) 3-18-42:25
Children of the Sun (s) 1-12-32:15
Children of Theatre Street, The 4-27-77:20
Children Pay, The 11-17-16:23
Children's Friend 9-18-09:13
Children's Games 9-17-69:22
Children's Hour, The 12-13-61:6
Child's Play 12-06-72:20
Child's Prayer, A 9-18-09:13
Chileno en Espana, Un 2-20-63:6
Chills and Fever (s) 6-25-30:109
Chiltern Hundreds, The 10-05-49:8
Chimes, The 9-18-14:19
Chimes at Midnight (See: Campanadas a Medianoche)
Chimimorya 6-02-71:15
Chimmie Fadden 7-02-15:16
Chimmie Fadden Out West 11-26-15:23
Chin Chin El Teporocho 8-25-76:22
Chin Nu Yu Haru 11-02-60:6
China 3-24-43:20
China 5-26-65:14
China Behind 11-13-74:36
China Bound 6-05-29:26
China Clipper 8-19-36:16
China Corsair 6-06-51:6
China Doll 8-20-58:6
China Express 3-12-30:33
China Gate 5-22-57:6

China Girl 12-09-42:8
China Is Near 9-20-67:20
China 9, Liberty 37 8-23-78:30
China Passage 4-21-37:15
China Plate, The (s) 6-30-31:15
China Poblana 10-25-44:12
China Seas 8-14-35:15
China Sky 5-30-45:16
China Slayer, The 5-22-29:24
China Speaks 2-16-32:33
China Syndrome, The 3-07-79:20
China Venture 8-26-53:6
China's Old Man River (s) 4-08-
31:18
Chinatown 6-19-74:16
Chinatown After Dark 11-24-31:
21
Chinatown After Midnight 11-23-
49:25
Chinatown Charlie 6-13-28:13
Chinatown Fantasy (s) 5-21-30:19
Chinatown Kid 12-07-77:20
Chinatown Nights 4-03-29:20
Chinatown Squad 6-05-35:54
Chinese Blue 6-25-75:24
Chinese Bungalow, A 1-18-28:19
Chinese Bungalow, The 10.08-30:
23
Chinese Bungalow, The 1-31-40:
26
Chinese Jinks (s) 8-02-32:15
Chinese Parrot 1-11-28:27
Chinese Ring, The 12-17-47:20
Chinesische Wunder, Das 2-09-
77:24
Chinesisches Roulett 12-01-76:19
Chinmoku 5-17-72:20
Chinois A Paris, Les 2-20-74:14
Chinois, Encore un Effort Pour
Etre Revolutionaires 11-16-
77:20
Chinoise, La 9-13-67:6
Chip of the Flying U 5-26-26:19
Chip of the Flying U 1-24-40:22
Chip Off the Old Block 2-16-44:
10
Chips from the Old Block (s) 8-
25-26:23
Chisum 6-24-70:20
Chitegu Chinte 1-31-79:22
Chitty Chitty, Bang Bang 11-20-
68:6
Chivalrous 12-02-21:43
Chiwit Batsop 6-22-77:17
Chkid Republic, The 9-27-67:26
Chloe in the Afternoon (See:
Amour, L'Apres-Midi, L')
Chobizenesse 11-05-75:38

Choca, La 7-24-74:22
Chocolate Soldier, The 10-15-41:8
Choirboys, The 12-21-77:20
Choix, Le 1-28-76:14
Choix d'Assassins, Un 8-30-67:8
Chomana Dudi 7-28-76:24
Chomeur de Clockemerle, Le
1-22-58:24
Chomps 12-26-79:13
Choo-Choo (s) 8-23-32:15
Choose Life 7-10-63:6
Choosing a Husband 1-08-10:12
Choosing a Wife 8-15-19:71
Chopin 8-25-26:23
Chorus 3-26-75:32
Chorus Girl's Romance, A 8-13-
20:35
Chorus Kid, The 5-23-28:39 (2)
and 5-30-28:30
Chorus Lady, The 10-22-15:23
Chorus Lady, The 2-04-25:39
Chosen Survivors 5-29-74:14
Choses De La Vie, Les 1-28-
70:22
Chotisi Baat 1-19-77:22
Chouans, Les 12-04-46:13
Chouchou and the Million 7-31-
63:12
Chris-Crossed (s) 8-18-31:17
Chrissomaloussa 5-23-79:23
Christa 5-26-71:22
Christian, The 5-22-14:22
Christian, The 1-25-23:41
Christian Licorice Store, The 12-
01-71:16
Christian the Lion 12-15-76:18
Christiania 6-01-77:16
Christina 4-03-29:11 and 12-25-
29:32
Christina 2-20-46:8
Christina 1-17-51:20
Christina 4-03-74:24
Christine 1-28-59:16
Christine Jorgenson Story, The
6-10-70:18
Christine of Hungry Heart 12-
10-24:35
Christine of the Big Tops 9-01-
26:18
Christmas Carol, A 12-14-38:14
Christmas Carol, A 11-14-51:16
Christmas Cheer (s) 12-25-29:20
Christmas Eve 10-29-47:15
Christmas Eve Tragedy 4-18-08:
13
Christmas Holiday 6-07-44:19
Christmas in Connecticut 7-18-45:
34

City That Stopped Hitler--Heroic
   Stalingrad, The 9-01-43:20
City's Child, A 7-21-71:16
Ciudad Cremada, La 10-27-76:28
Ciulinii Baraganului 5-21-58:16
Civil War 2-12-10:16
Civilian Clothes 9-10-20:35
Civilization 6-09-16:23
Civilization's Child 4-21-16:31
Claim, The 3-22-18:51
Clair de Femme 9-26-79:20
Clair de Terre 4-01-70:24
Claire's Knee (See: Genou de
   Claire, Le)
Clairboyant 6-12-35:41
Clambake 10-18-67:6
Clan Des Siciliens, Le 12-10-69:
   28
Clan of the White Lotus 6-11-80:
   24
Clancy 1-07-11:13
Clancy in Wall St. 5-07-30:21
Clancy Street Boys 5-05-43:16
Clancy's Kosher Wedding 9-07-
   27:21
Clandestine 6-02-48:14 (Also see:
   Clandestins, Les)
Clandestines, Les 4-20-55:6
Clandestins, Les 5-22-46:10
   (Also see: Clandestine)
Clans of Intrigue 4-20-77:24
Clara de Montargis 7-04-51:24
Clarence 10-20-22:40
Clarence 3-10-37:15
Clarence and Angel 8-20-80:21
Clarence, the Cross-Eyed Lion
   2-10-65:7
Clarence Tisdale (s) 5-22-29:16
Clarines del Miedo, Los 9-17-
   58:18
Clarion, The 3-10-61:31
Clark 9-21-77:16
Clark and Ulis (s) 1-16-29:14
Clash by Night 5-14-52:6
Class of '44 4-04-73:26
Class of Miss MacMichael 9-13-
   78:21
Classe Operaia Va in Paradiso, La
   2-09-72:18
Classe Tous Risques 7-27-60:6
Classified 11-11-25:39
Classmates 2-27-14:23
Classmates 12-31-24:26
Claude Duval 5-07-24:25
Claude Francois: Le Film de Sa
   Vie 5-30-79:17
Claude Hopkins and Orch. (s) 9-
   12-33:17 and 12-18-35:13

Claudelle Inglish 8-30-61:6
Claudia 8-18-43:10
Claudia and David 7-24-46:14
Claudine 4-03-40:16
Claudine 4-10-74:24
Clavo, El 6-22-49:20
Claw, The 6-14-18:31
Claw, The 5-11-27:16
Claws of the Hun, The 7-05-18:
   29
Clay 12-23-64:7 and 5-26-65:6
Clay Dollars 10-28-21:35
Clay Pigeon, The 2-09-49:13
Clay Pigeon 7-21-71:24
Cle Sur la Porte, La 12-13-78:
   26
Clean Heart, The 9-17-24:28
Clean Up, The 8-10-17:27
Clean Up 10-04-23:26
Clean-Up Man, The 3-21-28:23
Clean-Up on the Curb, A (s) 6-09-
   31:18
Cleaning Up (s) 12-10-30:15
Clear All Wires 3-07-33:14
Clear Skies 7-26-61:13
Clear the Decks 4-03-29:23
Clearing the Range 5-27-31:57
Clearing the Trail 9-26-28:58
Clemenceau Case, The 4-23-15:
   18
Cleo de 5 a 7 12-20-61:7
Cleo from 5 to 7 (See: Cleo de
   5 a 7)
Cleopatra 8-21-34:17
Cleopatra 6-19-63:6
Cleopatra Jones 7-04-73:18
Cleopatra Jones and the Casino
   of Gold 6-18-75:19
Cleopatra, Queen of Sex 5-10-
   72:48
Clerambard 10-22-69:31
Clever Mrs. Carfax, The 11-09-
   17:55
Client de la Morte Saison 2-04-
   70:18
Cliff Edwards (s) 12-05-28:12/
   12-11-29:35
Cliff Nazarro and 2 Marjories (s)
   8-22-28:14
Cliff of Sin, The 11-26-52:18
Climate Chasers (s) 7-07-31:25
Climax, The 2-26-30:39
Climax, The 9-27-44:14
Climax, The (See: Immorale, L')
Climax, 9-01-71:26
Climbers, The 8-27-15:20
Climbers, The 10-31-19:57
Climbers, The 5-04-27:22

Terror, The 2-27-14:23
Cocco di Mamma, Il 3-19-58:18
Cochecito, El 9-07-60:6
Cock o' the Walk 4-16-30:46
Cock of the Air 1-26-32:23
Cockeyed Cavaliers 7-31-34:14
Cockeyed Cowboys of Calico
    Country 4-15-70:17
Cockeyed Miracle, The 7-17-
    46:8
Cockeyed News (s) 7-09-30:19
Cockeyed World, The 8-07-29:
    208
Cockleshell Heroes 11-23-55:6
Cocktail Hour 6-06-33:14
Cocktail Molotov 2-27-80:20
Cocktails 12-26-28:42
Coco la Fleur, Candidat 2-28-79:
    20
Cocoanut Grove 5-18-38:12
Cocoanuts, The 5-29-29:14
Code of Honor, The 12-17-30:63
Code of Marcia Gray, The 3-10-
    16:30
Code of Scotland Yard 9-01-48:
    14
Code of the Air 12-19-28:23
Code of the Cow Country 6-15-
    27:25
Code of the Outlaw 2-18-42:19
Code of the Range 5-11-27:20
Code of the Range 2-03-37:15
Code of the Rangers 4-13-38:15
Code of the Scarlet 7-11-28:39
Code of the Sea 5-28-24:27
Code of the Secret Service 5-17-
    39:14
Code of the Silver Sage 4-12-50:
    22
Code of the Streets 4-19-39:22
Code of the West 4-15-25:36
Code of the West 2-26-47:11
Code of the Wilderness 7-02-24:
    26
Code of the Yukon 12-20-18:37
Code 7, Victim 5 11-18-64:6
Code 2 3-11-53:6
Codine 5-22-63:19
Coeur a l'Envers, Le 11-05-80:
    22
Coeur de Lilas 3-01-32:21
Coeur Ebloui, Le 6-15-38:15
Coeur Fou, Le 4-01-70:14
Coeur Gros Comme Ca!, Un 1-24-
    62:22
Coeur Vert, Le 4-27-66:19
Coffee and Aspirin (s) 10-18-32:
    14

Coffee and Love (s) 8-16-32:15
Coffee Culture 2-05-10:35
Coffey-Flynn Fight Picture 6-11-
    15:19
Coffins on Wheels (s) 9-03-41:17
Coffret de Laque, Le 8-02-32:17
Coffy 5-16-73:32
Cognasse 9-13-32:29
Cohabitation 6-11-75:18
Cohen on the Telephone (s) 4-09-
    30:22
Cohens and the Kellys, The 2-
    24-26:42
Cohens and the Kellys in Africa,
    The 12-24-30:21
Cohens and the Kellys in Atlantic
    City, The 3-20-29:12
Cohens and the Kellys in Holly-
    wood, The 4-26-32:54
Cohens and the Kellys in Paris,
    The 2-08-28:16
Cohens and the Kellys in Scotland,
    The 3-12-30:33
Cohens and the Kellys in Trouble,
    The 4-18-33:4
Coiffeur Pour Dames 6-07-32:
    25 and 11-08-32:17
Coiffure Pour Dames (See: French
    Touch)
Coincidence 7-22-21:36
Cold Deck, The 11-09-17:54
Cold Journey 6-04-75:18
Cold Storage Romance, A 10-08-
    10:12
Cold Sweat (See: De la Part des
    Copains)
Cold Tracks 7-24-63:6
Cold Turkey (s) 7-14-31:17 and
    10-13-31:14
Cold Turkey 12-05-33:16
Cold Turkey 2-03-71:17
Cold Wind in August, A 8-02-
    61:6
Colditz Story, The 2-09-55:11
Cole Case, The 4-05-32:14
Cole Younger, Gunfighter 4-02-
    58:16
Colera Del Viento, La 4-14-71:
    22
Colleagues 4-03-63:7
Collectionneuse, La 3-08-67:6
Collections Privees 7-11-79:19
Collective Marriage 7-21-71:24
Collector, The 5-26-65:6
Colleen 3-11-36:15
Colleen Bawn, The 2-07-24:23
College 9-14-27:22
College Champions (s) 2-18-42:8

College Chums 2-29-08:12
College Coach 11-14-33:30
College Coquette 8-28-29:31
College Cuties (s) 12-31-30:19
College Dads (s) 4-22-36:14
College Days 10-27-26:68
College Hero 11-23-27:24
College Holiday 12-30-36:10
College Hounds (s) 7-02-30:25
and 11-12-30:21
College Humor 6-27-33:14
College Love 8-07-29:201
College Lovers 12-03-30:14
College of Capers (s) 11-05-30: 23
College Orphan, The 10-22-15: 26
College Racket, A (s) 11-17-31:14
College Rhythm 11-27-34:15
College Romeos (s) 1-29-30:21
College Scandal 7-17-35:27
College Sweethearts 1-21-42:18
College Swing 4-27-38:22
College Vamp, The (s) 1-28-31: 14
College Widow, The 11-09-27:25
Collegiate 1-29-36:16
Collegiate Model, The (s) 7-16- 31:15
Collier de Chanvre, La 6-04-41: 15
Collier de la Reine, La 2-11-31: 29
Colombes, Les 9-27-72:6
Colombo and Its Environs 10-01- 10:18
Colonel Bontemps 5-28-15:17
Colonel Bridau 7-04-19:43
Colonel Chabert 6-11-47:8
Colonel Effingham's Raid 10-03- 45:20
Colonel Wolodyjowski 7-02-69:6
Colonel's Wife, The 1-23-15:26
Color Me Dead 1-14-70:38
Color Scales (s) 7-19-32:24
Color Sgt.'s Horse, The 12-24- 10:16
Colorado 11-05-15:22
Colorado 7-04-40:18
Colorado Ambush 5-09-51:6
Colorado Kid 1-12-38:15
Colorado Ranger 6-07-50:8
Colorado Serenade 6-12-46:6
Colorado Sundown 2-13-52:6
Colorado Sunset 8-02-39:25
Colorado Territory 5-18-49:8
Colorado Trail 11-02-38:22
Colorful North Carolina (s)

2-25-42:8
Colorful Sermon, A (s) 8-29-28: 15
Colorin, Colorado 9-29-76:34
Colossus of New York 6-25-58:6
Colossus of Rhodes, The 12-13- 61:6
Colt Comrades 6-23-43:24
Colt .45 5-03-50:6
Coltelli Dei Vendicatori, I
(See: Knives of the Avenger)
Columbia Revolt, The 11-06-68: 24
Columbus Entdeckt Kraehwinkel 9-15-54:6
Columbus of Sex 5-13-70:14
Column, The 11-06-68:6
Column South 5-13-53:18
Columnist Newsreel (s) 11-19- 32:18
Coma 1-25-78:24
Comanche 3-07-56:6
Comanche, Der 9-19-79:19
Comancheros, The 11-01-61:6
Combat, The 9-22-16:49
Combat Dans L'Ile, Le 9-26-62:6
Combat Squad 9-30-53:6
Come Across 7-17-29:57 and 7- 31-29:27
Come and Get It 11-18-36:12
Come and Meet My Wife (See: Romanzo Popolave)
Come Back, The 4-21-16:29
Come Back Africa 9-16-59:16
Come Back, All Is Forgiven 10- 02-29:31
Come Back Baby 6-19-68:37
Come Back Charleston Blue 7- 05-72:16
Come Back, Little Sheba 12-03- 52:6
Come Back Peter 2-17-71:18
Come Blow Your Horn 5-22-63:6
Come Clean (s) 11-17-31:14
Come Closer, Folks 11-25-36:15
Come Fill the Cup 9-26-51:6
Come Fly with Me 4-03-63:7
Come L'Amore 7-03-68:28
Come Live with Me 1-22-41:16
Come Next Spring 2-08-56:6
Come On, The 2-15-56:6
Come On Children 4-11-73:61
Come On, Cowboys 6-16-37:13
Come On Danger 12-31-41:8
Cone On In 9-27-18:44
Come On, Leathernecks 8-24-38: 15

Come On, Marines 3-27-34:12
Come On Over 3-17-22:41
Come On, Rangers 1-04-39:14
Come On Tarzan 1-17-33:15
Come One, Come All 10-28-70: 17
Come Out Fighting 9-05-45:15
Come Out of the Kitchen 5-16-19: 54
Come Out of the Pantry 12-11- 35:34
Come Perdere Una Moglie e Trovare Un' Amante 12-13-78: 26
Come Persi la Guerra 2-04-48: 22
Come, Quando, Con Chi 12-31- 69:6
Come September 6-28-61:6
Come Spy with Me 1-18-67:6
Come Through 6-22-17:24
Come to Dinner (s) 2-20-34:14
Come to My House 1-18-28:16
Come to Papa (s) 2-11-31:14
Come to the Stable 6-22-49:6
Come to Your Senses 10-20-71: 20
Comeback--Arthur Rubinstein in Poland, The 11-19-75:26
Comedia Rota 10-10-79:34
Comedians, The 11-01-67:6
Comedie Fantastica 8-06-75:17
Comedien Harmonists, Die 4-27- 77:22
Comedy and Tragedy 11-06-09:13
Comedy-Graph, The 2-26-10:15
Comedy Man, The 9-09-64:22
Comedy of Terrors, The 1-29- 64:6
Comes a Horseman 10-11-78:31
Comet over Broadway 12-21-38: 15
Cometogether 9-29-71:22
Comic, The 11-12-69:84
Comin' Round the Mountain 4-29- 36:15
Comin' Round the Mountain 8-14- 40:14
Comin' Round the Mountain 6-20- 51:6
Comin' Thro' the Rye 12-31-24: 26
Comin' Thro' the Rye 11-12-47:24
Coming Apart 10-08-69:28
Coming Home 2-15-78:19
Coming of Amos 9-16-25:41
Coming of the Law, The 5-30- 19:75

Coming Out Party 3-20-34:16
Coming Through 2-11-25:32
Comisar Acuza 7-17-74:16
Comizi D'Amore 8-05-64:7
Commanche Station 2-24-60:6
Commanche Territory 4-05-50:6
Command, The 1-20-54:6
Command Decision 12-29-48:6
Command Performance 3-18-31: 24
Command Performance 9-08-37: 19
Commanding Officer, The 4-02- 15:21
Commandos Strike at Dawn, The 12-16-42:16
Commare Secca, La 9-05-62:16
Comme la Lune 9-14-77:17
Comme Sur des Roulettes 4-20- 77:24
Comme un Boomerang 9-01-76: 22
Comme un Pot des Fraises 9-18- 74:22
Comment Qu'elle Est! 10-12-60:6
Comment Reussir en Amor 11-28- 62:6
Comment Reussir Quand ou Est Con et Pleurnichard 7-03- 74:12
Comment Trouvez-Vous Ma Soeur? 3-18-64:7
Comment Yukong Deplace les Moutagnes 3-17-76:23
Commissario, Il 5-30-62:23
Commissario Pepe, Il 10-22-69: 33
Commitment, The 2-04-76:24
Committee, The 1-01-69:6
Common Clay 3-07-19:67
Common Clay 8-06-30:21
Common Fascism, The 12-01- 65:6
Common Ground 7-28-16:24
Common Law, The 9-29-16:24
Common Law 11-01-23:27
Common Law, The 7-21-31:34
Common Level, A 7-16-20:33
Common Property 11-14-19:59
Common Sense 6-11-20:35
Comment Qu'elle Est! 10-12-60:6
Communale, La 11-03-65:6
Communion 9-21-77:16
Communion Solennelle, La 2-09- 77:29
Community Sing (s) 2-17-37:14; 5-06-42:27; 5-27-42:8
Commuting 6-22-17:24

Confessions of Amans 12-08-76: 18
Confessions of Boston Blackie 12-10-41:18
Confessions of Winifred Wagner (See: Winifred Wagner Und Die Geschichte des Hauses Wahnfried 1914-1975)
Confessor 5-30-73:26
Confetti 1-25-28:12
Confidence Girl 6-04-52:6
Confidence Man 4-16-24:23
Confidence Pour Confidences 12-27-78:14
Confident de Ces Dames, Le 9-09-59:6
Confidential 11-20-35:39
Confidential Agent 10-07-45:25
Confidential File 5-15-56:6 (Also see: Confidential Report and Mr. Arkadin)
Confidential Report (See: Confidential File and Mr. Arkadin)
Confidentially Connie 1-21-53:6
Confirm or Deny 11-19-41:9
Conflict, The 6-30-16:21
Conflict 10-28-21:36
Conflict 1-27-37:24
Conflict 2-08-39:19
Conflict 6-13-45:17
Conflict of Wings 4-07-54:6
Conformist, The (See: Il Conformista)
Conformista, Il 7-08-70:15
Confounded Interest (s) 2-18-31: 14
Confusione 9-17-80:23
Congehovdingen 8-08-62:6
Congiuntura, La 4-21-65:6
Congiura, La 9-06-72:18
Congo Crossing 6-13-56:6
Congo Jazz (s) 8-20-30:14
Congo Maisie 1-17-40:14
Congo Vivo 5-16-52:19
Congolaise 5-10-50:16
Congorilla 7-26-32:17
Congress Dances 5-17-32:14 (Also see: Kongress Tanzt, Der)
Conigliaccio, Il 7-05-67:6
Conjugal Pleasures (See: Placeces Conjugales)
Connecticut Yankee, A 4-15-31: 20
Connecticut Yankee in King Arthur's Court, A 1-28-21:40
Connecticut Yankee in King Arthur's Court, A 2-23-49:10

Connection, The 5-10-61:7
Conquer by the Clock (s) 1-06-43:50
Conquerants Solitaires, Les 10-01-52:6
Conquered City (See: Clandestines, Les)
Conquered Hearts 11-08-18:41
Conquering Hero 9-25-09:12
Conquering Horde, The 4-01-31:17
Conquering Power 7-08-21:27
Conquering the Woman 12-15-22: 41
Conqueror, The 12-31-15:25
Conqueror, The 9-21-17:44
Conqueror, The 2-22-56:6
Conqueror Worm 5-15-68:6
Conquerors, The 11-22-32:17
Conquerors of the Arctic 3-30-38:15
Conquest, A 4-02-10:17
Conquest 2-13-29:24
Conquest 10-01-30:34
Conquest 10-27-37:18
Conquest of Canaan, The 9-29-16: 24
Conquest of Canaan, The 7-15-21: 29
Conquest of Cascades (s) 6-30-31: 15
Conquest of Cochise 8-26-53:6
Conquest of Everest, The 11-11-53:22
Conquest of Space 4-13-55:8
Conquest of the Holy Land 9-04-29:31
Conquest of the Planet of the Apes 6-14-72:18
Conquest Picture Program 8-24-17:24
Conquests of Peter the Great 8-30-39:19
Conquistadores, Les 3-17-76:36
Conrack 2-20-74:14
Conrad in Quest 11-12-20:35
Conrad the Sailor (s) 3-25-42:18
Conscience 8-22-13:14
Conscience Fund, The 10-10-13: 14
Conseguenze, Le 12-30-64:6
Consequence, The (See: Die Konsequenz)
Consigliori, Il 11-21-73:12
Consolation Marriage 11-03-31:27
Conspiracy, The 12-12-14:27
Conspiracy 10-15-30:29
Conspiracy 8-30-39:14
Conspiracy Circus--Chicago '70,

Cops and Robbers 8-15-73:12
Cops on Strike 11-13-09:13
Copy (s) 12-03-30:15
Coquecigrole 1-12-32:28
Coqueluche, La 4-01-70:26
Coquette, The 1-29-10:13
Coquette 4-10-29:25
Coquto, La 2-10-78:24
Cora Green (s) 8-28-29:18
Corajo del Pueblo, El 5-08-74:
  41
Corazon del Bosque, El 3-14-
  79:24
Corazon Solitario 5-30-73:24
Corbeau, Le (See: Raven, The)
Corde Raide, La 5-04-60:6
Corde, un Colt, Une 4-02-69:30
Cordelia 2-27-80:27
Cordella the Magnificent 6-14-
  23:23
Cordon Bleu, Le 1-26-32:27
Corky 3-22-72:36
Corky of Gasoline Alley 9-12-51:
  18
Corleone 12-06-78:32
Corn Is Green, The 4-04-45:10
Corn on the Cop (s) 6-12-34:19
Cornbread, Earl & Me 5-14-75:
  31
Corner, The 12-10-15:21
Corner Grocer, The 9-28-17:37
Corner in Colleens, A 10-06-16:
  27
Corner in Cotton, A 2-25-16:24
Corner Store (s) 4-03-29:11
Cornered 10-22-24:26
Cornered 11-14-45:12
Corniaud, Le 4-07-65:30
Cornonado 12-25-35:15
Corona di Ferro (See: Iron Crown,
  The)
Coroner Creek 6-09-48:12
Corpo D'Amore 7-12-72:26
Corporal Kate 12-15-26:14
Corps a Coeur 7-25-79:16
Corps Celestes, Les 10-24-73:17
Corps de Diane, Le 7-02-69:26
Corps de Mon Enemi, Le 10-27-
  76:46
Corpse Came C.O.D., The 7-16-
  47:20
Corpse Grinders, The 1-12-72:
  14
Corpse of Beverly Hills, The (See
  Tote Von Beverly Hills, Die)
Corpse Vanishes, The 6-03-42:9
Corpus 7-25-79:20
Corregidor 6-02-43:8

Correo Del Norte, El 1-11-61:6
Corrida Pour un Espion 10-27-
  65:6
Corridor of Mirrors 3-17-48:8
Corrupcion de Chris Miller, La
  8-08-73:14
Corrupt Ones, The 2-22-67:6
Corruption 7-13-17:26
Corruption 6-27-33:15
Corruption 12-11-68:6
Corruzione, La 12-18-63:6
Corruzione al Palazzo di Giustizia
  1-22-75:32
Corsair 11-24-31:21
Corsaires du Bois de Boulogne,
  Les 11-03-54:11
Corsaro Nero, Il 1-13-37:30 and
  5-10-39:23
Corsaro Nero, Il 1-19-77:23
Corsician Brothers, The 12-24-
  41:18
Corsician's Revenge, A 2-26-10:
  15
Corvette K-225 9-29-43:8
Corvette Summer 5-24-78:27
Cosas de Mujer 8-01-51:18
Coscia and Verdi (s) 6-20-28:27
Cosecha, La (See: Harvest, and
  So Ye Shall Reap)
Cosette 10-30-09:11
Cosh Boy 3-11-53:18
Cosi Come Sei 12-20-78:30
Cosi e la Vita 12-01-31:21
Cosmic Man, The 1-21-59:6
Cossacchi, I (See: Cossacks, The)
Cossack Whip, The 11-17-16:26
Cossacks, The 6-27-28:31
Cossacks, The 4-06-60:6
Cossack's Bride, The (s) 2-19-
  30:21
Cossacks in Exile 2-15-39:13
  (Also see: Zaporosets Za
  Dunayem)
Cossacks of the Don 3-22-32:61
Cossacks of the Kuban 11-01-50:6
Costa Azzurra 11-04-59:7
Costal Command 4-19-44:12
Costello Case, The 11-12-30:45
Cote D'Azur 7-19-32:37
Cottage to Let 9-10-41:16
Cotton Comes to Harlem 6-10-
  70:18
Cotton King, The 9-03-15:21
Couch, The 2-21-62:6
Cougar 5-30-33:54
Cougar's Mistake, The (s) 5-02-
  33:12
Counsel for Crime 10-06-37:13

● 84

Cowboys, The 1-12-72:14
Cowboys and the Bachelor Girls,
    The 12-03-10:14
Cowboys from Texas 12-06-39:
    16
Cowboy's Vindication, A 12-14-
    10:16
Coyote Nights 9-17-24:29
Crab, The 2-16-17:22
Crabe Tambour, Le 4-06-77:26
Crack in the Mirror 5-11-60:6
Crack in the World 2-10-65:7
Crack o' dawn 10-21-35:38
Cracked Nuts 4-08-31:18
Crackerjack, The 5-13-25:37
Cracker's Bride 3-27-09:13
Cracking Up 7-27-77:25
Cracks, Les 3-20-68:26
Cracksman, The 8-07-63:20
Crack-Up 1-13-37:13
Crackup 6-19-46:8
Cradle, The 3-24-22:41
Cradle Buster 6-09-22:58
Cradle of Courage 9-24-20:42
Cradle Snatchers 6-01-27:16
Cradle Song 11-21-33:20
Cradles of Creed (s) 8-09-32:17
Craig's Wife 12-05-28:19
Craig's Wife 10-07-36:15
Crainquebille 8-04-54:6
Cran D'Arret 1-28-70:22
Crane Poison Case (s) 7-12-32:
    16
Cranes Are Flying, The (See:
    Letiat Jouravly)
Crap Game (s) 9-17-30:21
Crash, The 11-07-28:26
Crash, The 9-13-32:19
Crash Dive 4-21-43:8
Crash Donovan 8-12-36:19
Crash Landing 2-05-58:20
Crashin' Thru Danger 10-05-38:
    21
Crashing Hollywood 12-29-37:17
Crashing Reno (s) 7-21-31:12
Crashing Through to Berlin 8-16-
    18:36
Crashing Thru 4-19-23:36
Crashing Thru 12-27-39:12
Crashout 5-18-55:8
Cravache, La 5-10-72:48
Craving, The 9-27-18:42
Crawling Hand, The 11-25-64:6
Craze 6-12-74:18
Crazies, The 1-24-73:18
Crazy Desire (See: Voglia Matta,
    La)
Crazy-Horse Paris-France 11-02-
    77:17

Crazy House (s) 4-15-31:20
Crazy House 10-20-43:12
Crazy Inventions (s) 1-17-33:14
Crazy Joe 2-06-74:18
Crazy Mama 7-16-75:21
Crazy Nut, A (s) 7-24-29:29
Crazy Outfit, The 10-27-65:6
Crazy over Horses 11-28-51:6
Crazy Paradise 8-11-65:6
Crazy Sea (See: Mare Matto)
Crazy Sex 8-04-76:20
Crazy That Way 4-30-30:26
Crazy to Marry 8-05-21:27
Crazy World of Julius Vrooder,
    The 9-25-74:16
Crazy World of Laurel and Hardy,
    The 12-27-67:20
Crazylegs, All-American 9-30-
    53:6
Creation 9-08-22:42
Creation du Monde, La 1-16-63:
    20
Creation of the World (See: Crea-
    tion du Monde, La)
Creatore and Band (s) 4-16-30:
    21
Creature from the Black Lagoon
    2-10-54:7
Creature Walks Among Us, The
    3-14-56:22
Creature with the Atom Brain 6-
    22-55:6
Creatures, Les 9-07-66:18
Creatures the World Forgot 4-
    07-71:18
Crecer de Golpe 9-28-77:24
Creeper, The 10-06-48:11
Creeping Flesh, The 3-14-73:21
Creeping Unknown, The 6-27-56:
    10
Creole Fashion Plate (s) 9-26-28:
    14
Crescendo 11-01-72:20
Crest of the Wave 7-21-54:6
Cresus 10-05-60:6
Crew Cut 11-26-80:15
Cri du Coeur, Le 9-04-74:28
Cri du Cormoran le Soir Au-
    Dessus des Jonques, Le
    3-03-71:17
Cria! (See: Cria Cuervos)
Cria Cuervos 2-04-76:24
Criatura, La 2-01-78:24
Cricket, The 11-16-17:50
Cricket on the Hearth 3-12-24:27
Cries and Whispers 12-20-72:18
Criez-le Sur les Toits 8-30-32:
    23

Crusader, The   10-11-32:20
Crusades, The   8-28-35:12
Crush Proof   7-12-72:24
Cruvena Zamlja   8-20-75:72
Crveno Klasje   7-14-71:24
Cry Baby Killer, The   6-18-58:6
Cry Danger   2-07-51:6
Cry Dr. Chicago   7-21-71:16
Cry for Cindy   5-26-76:19
Cry for Happy   1-11-61:6
Cry Freedom   5-03-61:7
Cry Havoc   11-10-43:34
Cry in the Night, A   5-08-14:20
Cry in the Night, A   8-15-56:18
Cry in the Streets, A   8-13-58:6
Cry in the Wind   10-04-67:16
Cry Murder   2-01-50:20
Cry of Battle   10-16-63:16
Cry of the Banshee   8-05-70:20
Cry of the City   9-15-48:15
Cry of the Hunted   3-11-53:6
Cry of the Weak   4-25-19:81
Cry of the Werewolf   8-16-44:16
Cry of the World   5-10-32:19
Cry Terror   4-16-58:6
Cry, the Beloved Country   1-23-52:6
Cry Tough   7-29-59:6
Cry Uncle   3-17-71:18
Cry Vengeance   11-24-56:6
Cry Wolf   7-02-47:13
Crystal Ball, The   1-20-43:9
Crystal Cafe Revue (s)   11-14-28:17
Crystal Champions (s)   10-16-29:17
Crystal Cup, The   10-26-27:19
Crystal Gazer, The   8-03-17:24
Crystal Gazer, The (s)   12-03-30:15
Crystal Submarine, The   7-25-28:28
Csaladi Potlek   1-19-38:19
Csampeszek   8-06-58:6
Csardasfuerstin, Die   5-01-35:17
Csend es Kialttas   1-31-68:22
Cseplo Gyuri   8-23-78:30
Csillagosok, Katonak   11-22-67:18
Csipetke   12-26-33:26
Csokolj Meg Edes   4-12-32:15 and 11-29-32:19
Cu Minile Cunate   6-14-78:20
Cuando Canta el Corazón   9-03-41:17
Cuando Canta la Ley   5-31-39:14
Cuando el Amor Rie   4-22-31:19
Cuando Estallo la Paz   9-05-62:6
Cuando Florezca el Naranjo

5-12-43:20
Cuando Hijos Se Van   5-26-43:8
Cuando Regrese Mama   3-22-61:15
Cuanto Vale Tu Hijo?   1-31-62:6
Cub, The   7-23-15:18
Cub Reporter   9-22-22:42
Cuba   12-19-79:18
Cuba Baila   8-09-61:16
Cuba-Crossing   2-13-80:17
Cuba No Koibito (See: Kyuba No Koibito)
Cuba Va   9-29-71:22
Cuban Fireball   3-14-51:7
Cuban Love Song   12-08-31:15
Cuban Pete   7-24-46:26
Cucaracha, La (s)   7-17-34:15 and 9-04-34:18
Cucaracha, La   5-27-59:6
Cuccagna, La   11-14-62:6
Cuckoo Clock, The   12-14-38:15
Cuckoo Murder Case (s)   10-29-30:17
Cuckoos, The   4-30-30:17
Cudna Devojka   8-08-62:6
Cuerpo y la Sangre, El   7-04-62:6
Cuisine Au Beurre, La   1-29-64:6
Cul-De-Sac   6-08-66:6
Culottes Rouges, Les   1-16-63:6
Culpable   8-03-60:6
Culpepper Cattle Company, The   4-12-72:16
Cult of the Cobra   3-30-55:8
Culte Vaudou au Dahomey, Le   11-22-72:26
Cumberland Romance   8-13-20:36
Cumbite   6-29-66:6
Cumparsita, La   10-01-47:14
Cunning vs. Cunning   5-28-15:17
Cuore di Cane   3-17-76:23
Cuore di Mamma   2-26-69:30
Cuore Infranto (See: Broken Love)
Cup of Life   10-28-21:34
Cupid by Proxy   7-12-18:34
Cupid, Cow-puncher   7-30-20:33
Cupid's Firemen   4-30-24:19
Cupid's Round Up   2-01-18:43
Cupid's Understudy   7-25-19:44
Cupola   5-23-62:16
Cura Gaucho, El   7-23-41:30
Cure, The (s)   4-13-17:23 and 1-10-33:15
Cure de Village, Le   11-30-49:6
Cure for Love, The   1-11-50:16
Cure for Rheumatism, A   3-27-09:13
Cure It with Music (s)   6-26-35:23
Curee, La   7-27-66:6

Curing a Masher 10-01-10:18
Curiosities (s) 1-09-29:10;
2-11-31:14; 4-15-31:20;
8-18-31:30; 2-02-32:15;
3-01-32:20; 3-22-32:13;
3-29-32:24; 4-26-32:13;
5-10-32:18; 5-24-32:29;
6-14-32:16; 7-26-32:17
Curly Top 8-07-35:21
Curlytop 4-22-25:35
Curore Semplice, Un 10-25-78:20
Cursa 6-14-78:20
Curse of Creed, The 5-08-14:20
Curse of Dri 9-15-22:42
Curse of Frankenstein, The 5-15-57:22
Curse of Iku 3-22-18:49
Curse of the Cat People, The 2-23-44:10
Curse of the Demon 2-26-58:6
Curse of the Faceless Man 8-20-58:6
Curse of the Mummy's Tomb, The 9-02-64:6
Curse of the Speejacks 5-02-38:36
Curse of the Undead 7-01-59:6
Curse of the Voodoo 12-22-65:17
Curse of the Werewolf 5-03-61:7
Curses (s) 2-11-31:14
Curso En Qu Amamos A Kim Novak, El 10-29-80:26
Curtain 10-08-20:41
Curtain at Eight 2-13-34:34
Curtain Call 4-10-40:14
Curtain Call at Cactus Creek 5-24-50:6
Curtain Falls, The 5-22-35:17
Curtain Up 5-14-52:20
Curucu, Beast of the Amazon 10-31-56:6
Custard Cup 4-26-23:26
Custer of the West 11-15-67:6
Customs Agent 4-19-50:8
Cut Yourself a Piece of Cake (s) 4-10-29:16
Cuvare Plaze u Zimskom Periodu 7-07-76:16
Cycle of Adversity 1-16-14:12
Cycle Savages 5-06-70:26
Cycles South 5-12-71:19
Cyclone 2-27-20:46
Cyclone Fury 8-15-51:6
Cyclone Kid 11-24-31:21
Cyclone Kid, The 8-12-42:20
Cyclone of the Rouge 5-04-27:24
Cyclone on Horseback 6-18-41:18
Cyclone Ranger 5-22-35:17
Cyclops 8-21-57:6
Cyclops 11-10-76:22

Cynara 1-03-33:19
Cynthia 5-14-47:15
Cynthia of the Minute 7-16-20:32
Cyprus 10-27-76:30
Cyrano de Bergerac 7-08-25:37
Cyrano de Bergerac 11-15-50:6
Cyrano et D'Artagnan 6-03-64:6
Cytherea 5-28-24:27
Czar and the Shepherd, The 5-29-35:34
Czar I General 7-20-66:7
Czar Ivan, the Terrible 3-14-28:23
Czar of Broadway, The 7-02-30:25
Czar Wants to Sleep, The 12-18-34:13
Czas Przeszly 11-14-62:7
Czerwone I Zlote 12-31-69:18
Czifra Nyomorusag 10-26-38:15
Czikos Baroness 4-12-32:15
Czlowiek z Marmuru 6-01-77:16
Czomtvary 2-27-80:21
Czudaki 12-18-74:12

91 •

• D •

DAAG 2-20-77:34
D-Day the 6th of June 5-30-56:6
DM-Killer 2-24-65:6
D.I., The 5-29-57:6
D.O.A. 12-28-49:6
Da Bancarella a Bancarotta (See: Peddlin' in Society)
Da Lang Lao Sha 1-10-79:27
Da Svante Forsvandt 1-14-76:21
Dabbelte Mand, Un 4-07-75:28
Dablova Past 7-04-62:63
Dad and Dave Come to Town 11-2-38:22
Dad Knows Best (s) 5-07-30:20
Dad Rudd, M.P. 8-21-40:20
Dadathes 10-31-79:20
Daddies 2-14-24:26
Daddy 4-19-23:35
Daddy Knows Best (s) 5-23-33:15
Daddy Long Legs 5-16-19:54
Daddy Long Legs 5-04-55:6
Daddy Long Legs 6-09-31:18
Daddy's Gone A-Hunting 2-25-25:31
Daddy's Gone A-Hunting 5-28-69:36
Daddy's Lullaby (s) 2-12-30:18
Dad's Army 3-24-71:19
Dad's Day (s) 11-27-29:21
Daffy Duckaroo (s) 12-02-42:8
Daffydill (s) 9-08-26:20
Daffy's Southern Adventure (s) 4-22-42:18
Dage I Min Fars Hus 4-24-68:26
Dagfin 3-23-27:16
Dagmar's Hot Pants, Inc. 10-27-71:18
Dagny 6-01-77:17
Dahana-Aranja 7-28-76:22
Dai Kyoju Gappa 4-19-67:58
Dai Majin Gyakushu 1-25-67:58
Dai Tatsumaki (See: Whirlwind)
Daibosatsu Toge (See: Sword of Doom, The)
Daisies (See: Sedmikrasky)
Daisy Bell (s) 5-29-29:14
Daisy Kenyon 11-26-47:11
Daisy Miller 5-22-74:18

Daitozoku (See: Lost World of Sinbad, The)
Daj Sto Das 8-27-80:21
Dakota 11-07-45:25
Dakota 10-16-74:18
Dakota Incident 7-25-56:18
Dakota Kid, The 7-04-51:24
Dakota Lil 2-01-50:14
Dal Sabato Al Lunedi 4-03-63:6
Daleks Invade Earth 2150 A.D. 8-10-66:6
Dalia and the Sailors 9-16-64:19
Dallas 11-22-50:8
Dalle Ardenne All'Inferno (See: Dirty Heroes)
Dalton Gang, The 11-30-49:6
Dalton Girls, The 12-11-57:6
Daltons Ride Again, The 11-21-45:10
Daluyong at Habagat 6-23-76:34
Dam Busters 6-01-55:6
Dama de Beirut, La 11-24-65:19
Dama de la Muerte, La 9-11-46:10
Dama de las Camellias, La 10-04-44:8
Dama Duende, La 6-27-45:48
Dama Na Kolejich 8-03-66:6
Dama S Sobatchkoi 5-25-60:7
Dama Spathi 1-11-67:6
Damaged Goods 9-26-14:22
Damaged Goods 10-01-15:18
Damaged Goods 6-23-37:12
Damaged Hearts 2-28-24:22
Damaged Lives 6-16-37:13
Damaged Love 1-28-31:15
Dame Aux Camellias, La 12-04-34:12 and 3-27-35:31
Dame Aux Camellias, La 12-30-53:18
Dame Chance 10-27-26:64
Dame Dans l'Auto Avec des Lunettes et un Fusil, La 11-11-70:22
Dame de Chez Maxims 4-25-33:18
Dame de Pique, La 8-25-37:23
Dame de Pique, La 2-16-66:18
Dame in Schwarz, Die (See: Lady in Black)
Dame Mit der Maske, Die 11-14-28:17
Damernes Ven 9-10-69:48
Dames 8-21-34:17
Dames Ahoy 4-02-30:35
Dames du Bois du Boulogne, Les 3-11-64:6
Damien--Omen II 6-07-78:28

Damm, Der 10-28-64:6
Damn Citizen 1-22-58:6
Damn Yankees 9-17-58:6
Damnation Alley 10-26-77:20
Damned, The 6-25-69:6
Damned Be Those Who Cry 9-05-79:26
Damned Don't Cry, The 4-12-50:6
Damon and Pythias 12-12-14:28
Damon and Pythias 9-12-62:6
D'Amore Si Muore 2-14-73:92
Damsel in Distress, A 10-17-19:63
Damsel in Distress 11-24-37:16
Dan 9-04-14:13
Dan Cetrnaesti 5-17-61:7
Dan Matthews 1-29-36:16
Dance Band 6-12-35:12 and 1-08-36:12
Dance, Charlie, Dance 9-01-37:22
Dance Fever 9-26-28:27
Dance, Fools, Dance 3-25-31:24
Dance, Girl, Dance 10-31-33:25
Dance, Girl, Dance 8-28-40:16
Dance Hall 12-18-29:28
Dance Hall 7-23-41:8
Dance Hall 6-14-50:34
Dance Hall Marge (s) 1-21-31:17
Dance Little Lady 7-28-54:6
Dance Madness 1-27-26:39
Dance Magic 7-13-27:22
Dance Music 9-04-35:31 (Also see: Tanzmusik)
Dance of Death, The 9-29-71:18
Dance of Life, The 8-21-29:18
Dance of the Paper Dolls, The (s) 11-13-29:12 and 1-01-30:15
Dance Team 1-19-32:25
Dance with Me, Henry 12-12-56:6
Dance with Me into the Morning (See: Tanze Mit Mir in Den Morgen)
Dancer and the King, The 11-21-14:27
Dancer of Barcelona 11-27-29:31
Dancer of Paris, The 3-31-26:42
Dancers, The 1-07-25:38
Dancers, The 11-19-30:21
Dancers in the Dark 3-22-32:13
Dancers of the Various Nations 8-28-09:13
Dancer's Peril 3-02-17:29
Danceur Inconnu, Le (See: Unknown Dancer)
Dancin' Fool 5-07-20:34
Dancing Cheat, The 4-16-24:23
Dancing Co-Ed 9-27-39:12

Dancing Days 12-29-26:17
Dancing Dynamite 8-25-31:20
Dancing Feet 4-01-36:16
Dancing Girl, The 1-23-15:25
Dancing Girl of Butte, The 1-15-10:13
Dancing Heart, The 12-28-55:6
Dancing in Manhattan 1-24-45:10
Dancing in the Dark 11-09-49:6
Dancing Lady 12-05-33:16
Dancing Man 7-24-34:31
Dancing Masters, The 10-27-43:10
Dancing Mothers 2-17-26:40
Dancing on a Dime 10-16-40:31
Dancing Pirate 6-24-36:29
Dancing Sweeties 8-20-30:15
Dancing W Kwaterze Hitlera 6-19-68:39
Dancing with Crime 7-02-47:22
Dancing Years, The 4-26-50:22
Dandy Dick 3-06-35:21
Dandy in Aspic, A 4-03-68:22
Dandy--The All-American Girl 5-26-76:26
Danger (s) 5-21-30:19
Danger Ahead 3-20-40:16
Danger: Diabolik 5-15-68:28
Danger Flight 12-06-39:16
Danger Game, The 4-26-18:43
Danger! Go Slow! 12-13-18:40
Danger in the Pacific 8-05-42:27
Danger Is a Woman 4-23-52:6
Danger Lights 11-29-30:21
Danger--Love at Work 12-01-37:14
Danger Mark, The 7-12-18:34
Danger on the Air 7-20-38:12
Danger on Wheels 4-17-40:13
Danger Patrol 6-20-28:19
Danger Patrol 11-24-37:16
Danger Points 12-22-22:34
Danger Quest, The 4-07-26:39
Danger Rider 12-12-28:31
Danger Route 1-31-68:6
Danger Signal, The 12-19-15:23
Danger Signal, The 7-22-25:32
Danger Signal, The 11-14-45:12
Danger Street 9-26-28:27
Danger Street 2-26-47:10
Danger Trail, The 5-04-17:24
Danger Valley 6-03-21:41
Danger Valley 2-23-38:14
Danger Within 2-25-59:6
Danger Woman 7-10-46:8
Danger Zone, The 1-17-19:52
Danger Zone 6-13-51:16
Dangerous 1-01-36:44
Dangerous Adventure, A 9-15-37:13

Dangerous Age 2-08-23:41
Dangerous Blonde 5-21-24:27
Dangerous Blondes 10-13-43:10
Dangerous Business 12-03-20:32
Dangerous Charter 9-26-62:6
Dangerous Corner 2-05-35:31
Dangerous Coward 10-08-24:31
Dangerous Crossing 7-22-53:20
Dangerous Curve Ahead 10-07-21: 44
Dangerous Curves 7-17-29:53
Dangerous Dan McGrew 6-25-30: 115
Dangerous Days 3-19-20:53
Dangerous Dude, A 8-25-26:19
Dangerous Exile 11-27-57:6
Dangerous Females (s) 12-11-29: 35
Dangerous Flirt 12-17-24:37
Dangerous Friends 11-10-26:15
Dangerous Game, A 12-22-22:34
Dangerous Game, A 3-05-41:16
Dangerous Holiday 7-07-37:13
Dangerous Hour 12-20-23:26
Dangerous Hours 2-06-20:53
Dangerous Innocence 6-10-25:49
Dangerous Intrigue 1-22-36:15
Dangerous Intruder 11-21-45:18
Dangerous Journey 8-09-44:12
Dangerous Lady 10-29-41:9
Dangerous Little Demon 3-24-22: 42
Dangerous Love 8-25-22:35
Dangerous Maid 12-13-23:22
Dangerous Medicine 8-17-38:23
Dangerous Millions 12-04-46:13
Dangerous Mission 2-24-55:6
Dangerous Money 10-15-24:30
Dangerous Moonlight 7-30-41:20
Dangerous Number 3-10-37:15
Dangerous Occupations (s) 3-21- 33:16
Dangerous Pair, A 9-11-09:12
Dangerous Paradise 11-12-20:36
Dangerous Paradise 2-19-30:33
    (Also see: Tropen Nachte)
Dangerous Partners 8-08-45:22
Dangerous Passage 12-20-44:17
Dangerous Paths 9-30-21:37
Dangerous Profession, A 10-26- 38:13
Dangerous Talent 3-05-20:62
Dangerous to Know 3-16-38:15
Dangerous to Men 6-11-20:35
Dangerous Toys 6-17-21:35
Dangerous Trails 3-26-24:27
Dangerous Trails (s) 9-15-31:14
Dangerous Venture 2-19-31:14

Dangerous Virtue 11-03-26:20
Dangerous Waters 1-29-36:16
Dangerous When Wet 5-13-53:6
Dangerous Woman 5-22-29:16
Dangerous Years 12-17-47:8
Dangerous Youth (s) 3-25-31:16
Dangerous Youth 6-11-58:6
Dangerously They Live 4-15-42:8
Dangerously Yours 2-28-33:39
Dangerously Yours 10-20-37:12
Dangers of the Arctic 7-12-32:25
Dani 6-30-65:6
Dani Od Snova 5-28-80:45
Daniel Boone 10-28-36:14
Daniel Boone, Trail Blazer 2-13- 57:6
Danmark er Lukket 10-15-80:74
Danny Boy 5-28-41:18
Danny Boy 3-27-46:12
Dans L'Ombre du Harem 4-25-28: 28
Dans la Rue (s) 1-28-31:14
Dans les Rues 8-30-39:19
Dans une Ile Perdue 2-18-31:78
Danse Macabre 8-06-58:6
Dante, Akta're Fore Hajen 1-10- 79:27
Dante's Inferno 10-01-24:22
Dante's Inferno 8-07-35:21
Danton 6-17-21:35
Danton 2-18-31:78 and 9-01-31:33
Danza de Fuego 3-01-50:16
Dao Ruang 5-23-79:27
Daosawan Chan Rak Ter 4-09-75: 30
Daphne, The (See: Jinchoge)
Daphne and the Pirate 2-18-16:23
Daphnis Ke Chloe '66 11-02-66:22
Daraku Suru Onna 8-02-67:7
Darby O'Gill and the Little People 4-29-59:6
Darby's Rangers 1-22-58:6
Darclee 5-24-61:17
Dare Devil Circus Queen, The 7- 02-15:21
Daredevil Drivers 3-02-38:15
Daredevil in the Castle 3-05-69:28
Daredevil Kate 8-25-16:24
Daredevil Rodman Law 5-22-14: 23
Daredevils of Earth 1-22-36:15
Daredevils of the Clouds 7-21-48: 10
Daredevils of the Red Circle (s) 7-05-39:16
Daredevil's Reward 1-25-28:13
Daring Caballero, The 6-29-49: 20 and 7-27-49:12

Daring Chances   9-03-24:25
Daring Danger   6-28-32:15
Daring Daughters   3-28-33:27
Daring Deeds   1-25-28:13
Daring Game   5-01-68:26
Daring Love   9-17-24:28
Daring of Diana, The   7-21-16:23
Daring Years, The   3-19-24:26
Daring Young Men, The   7-24-35: 56
Daring Youth   5-28-24:29
Dark, The   5-02-79:26
Dark Alleys   10-11-23:25****
Dark Angel, The   10-14-25:42
Dark Angel   9-11-35:17
Dark at the Top of the Stairs, The 9-14-60:6
Dark Avenger   5-11-55:8
Dark City   8-09-50:8
Dark Command, The   4-10-40:14
Dark Corner, The   4-03-46:12
Dark Delusion   4-09-47:16
Dark Dreams   6-02-71:22
Dark Eyes   4-27-38:23
Dark Hazard   2-27-34:17
Dark Horse, The   6-14-32:17
Dark Horse, The   7-17-46:8
Dark Hour, The   8-05-36:17
Dark Intruder   7-28-65:6
Dark Is the Night   3-20-46:26
Dark Journey   3-17-37:23
Dark Lantern, A   8-13-20:35
Dark Man, The   1-31-51:6
Dark Manhattan   3-17-37:15
Dark Mirror   5-14-20:34
Dark Mirror, The   10-02-46:8
Dark Mountain, The   9-06-44:10
Dark Passage   9-03-47:16
Dark Past, The   12-29-48:6
Dark Places   5-22-74:18
Dark Purpose   1-29-64:6
Dark Rapture   10-12-38:15
Dark Red Roses   3-05-30:33
Dark River   3-07-56:18
Dark Road, The   3-23-17:20
Dark Room of Damocles, The (See: Als Twee Druppels Water)
Dark Sands   8-24-38:12
Dark Secrets   1-25-23:41
Dark Side of Tomorrow   7-08-70: 14
Dark Silence, The   9-22-16:40
Dark Skies   12-25-29:32
Dark Spring   10-21-70:23
Dark Stairways   7-16-24:23
Dark Star   5-01-74:18
Dark Streets   10-09-29:34

Dark Streets of Cairo   12-04-40: 12
Dark Swan, The   11-26-24:62
Dark Tower, The   6-23-43:24
Dark Victory   3-15-39:16
Dark Waters   11-01-44:10
Darkened Rooms   12-18-29:28
Darkening Trail, The   6-11-15:19
Darker Than Amber   8-19-70:16
Darkest Russia   4-13-17:25
Darkness to Dawn   5-01-14:21
Darktown Follies (s)   2-19-30:21
Darktown Strutters   10-15-75:26
Darlin' Mine   9-03-20:45
Darling   7-21-65:6
Darling (See: Rakas)
Darling Enemy (s)   6-05-34:12
Darling, How Could You   8-08-51:6
Darling Lili   6-24-70:17
Darling of New York   1-24-24:27
Darling of Paris, The   1-26-17:25
Darling of the Rich   1-12-23:34
Darn Tootin' (s)   12-08-31:14
Daro un Milione   4-07-37:29
Darshan   5-08-74:37
D'Artagnan   2-04-16:24 (Also see: Three Musketeers, The)
Dartmouth Days (s)   10-30-34:16
Darwin Adventure, The   10-11-72: 18
Das Hab'ich von Papa Gelernt   11-18-64:7
Dash of Courage, A   5-26-16:20
Dash of Death, A   9-04-09:13
Dassan--Isle of Penguins (s)   12-26-33:10
Date with Judy, A   6-23-48:6
Date with the Fellow, A   11-12-41:9
Dateline Diamonds   4-06-66:24
Daughter Angele   8-30-18:37
Daughter of Destiny   1-04-18:43
Daughter of Destiny, A   7-18-28: 15
Daughter of Devil Dan   7-22-21:36
Daughter of Dr. Jekyll   8-28-57:18
Daughter of Eve   10-03-19:56
Daughter of Israel   5-23-28:39
Daughter of Luxury   12-08-22:34
Daughter of MacGregor, The   9-22-16:37
Daughter of Maryland, A   11-09-17:55
Daughter of Mine   5-02-19:59
Daughter of Regiment   7-10-29:24
Daughter of Rosie O'Grady (s)   6-03-42:24
Daughter of Rosie O'Grady   3-29-50:11

Decade Prodigieuse, La 12-15-71:22

Decameron, The (See: Decamerone, Il)

Decameron Nights 9-17-24:29 and 5-30-28:30

Decameron Nights 1-21-53:6

Decamerone, Il 7-07-71:14

Deceiver, The 11-24-31:21

Deception 4-22-21:40

Deception 1-17-33:14

Deception 10-23-46:10

Decima Vittima, La (See: Tenth Victim, The)

Decision Against Time 7-10-57:6

Decision at Showdown 11-06-57:6

Decision Before Dawn 12-19-51:6

Decision of Christopher Blake, The 12-01-48:11

Decks Ran Red, The 9-24-58:6

Declasse 3-25-25:36

Decline and Fall 7-17-68:6

Decorated by the Emperor 1-22-10:15

Decoy, The 7-21-16:19

Decoy 11-06-46:18

Dedee 4-13-49:11

Dedee D'Anvers (See: Dedee)

Dedicatoria 5-28-80:15

Dee Kraft Phun Leben 5-04-38:25

Deemster, The 2-16-17:24

Deep, The 6-22-77:16

Deep Blue Sea, The 8-31-55:6

Deep End 9-16-70:14

Deep in My Heart 12-01-54:6

Deep in the Heart of Texas 9-09-42:14

Deep Jaws 5-05-76:22

Deep Knees (s) 10-27-31:19

Deep Purple, The 1-09-15:23

Deep Purple 5-07-20:34

Deep Red 6-23-76:16

Deep Six 1-01-58:6

Deep Throat 6-28-72:26

Deep Throat--Part II 2-13-74:18

Deep Thrust--The Hand of Death 5-23-73:28

Deep Valley 7-30-47:8

Deep Waters 6-30-48:10

Deer Hunter, The 11-29-78:24

Deer Hunting in the Celebes Islands 9-10-10:12

Deerslayer 11-10-43:35

Deerslayer, The 9-18-57:6

Deewar 1-19-77:22

Defector, The 11-16-66:6

Defector, The (See: Espions, Les)

Defenders of the Law 5-27-31:57

Defense de Savoir 11-28-73:26

Defense or Tribute 1-28-16:23

Defense Rests, The 8-21-34:25

Defiance 11-27-74:16

Defiance 3-12-80:22

Defiant Ones, The 8-06-58:6

Defroque, Le 3-17-54:22

Defying Destiny 1-10-24:27

Defying the Law 6-11-24:31

Degree of Murder, A (See: Mord und Totschlag)

Dein Frau--Das Unbekannte Wesan 3-12-69:26

Dein Kind, Das Unbekannte Wesen 10-14-70:32

Deiro (s) 6-12-29:16

Deja Que los Perros Ladren 9-27-61:7

Deja S'Envole la Fleur Maigre 5-15-63:6

Dejeuner Sur L'Herbe, Le 12-02-59:6

Del Amor y Otras Soledades 9-03-69:19

Del Brazo y Por la Calle 9-14-66:26

Del Rosa ... Al Amarillo 4-28-65:7

Delay in Marienborn 7-03-63:6

Delfini, I 9-07-60:6

Delicate Balance, A 10-31-73:26

Delicate Delinquent, The 5-29-57:6

Delicatessen Kid, The 2-05-30:19

Deliciosamente Amoral 3-19-69:6

Delicious 12-29-31:166

Delicious Little Devil, The 4-18-19:53 and 4-25-19:80

Delightful Rogue, The 10-23-29:17

Delightfully Dangerous 2-28-45:15

Delije 8-14-68:6

Delinquent Daughters 11-08-44:23

Delinquent Parents 7-06-38:15

Delinquents, The 2-27-57:6

Delirium 7-25-79:20

Delit de Fuite 4-29-59:20

Delitto A Porta Romana 12-17-80:16

Delitto D'Amore 5-29-74:16

Delitto di Mastrovanni, El 7-31-35:19

Delitto di Giovani Episcopo, Il (See: Flesh Will Surrender, The)

Deliverance 8-22-19:76

Deliverance 7-19-72:14

103 •

Dimitri Gorin's Career 9-13-61: 28
Dimples 2-11-16:21
Dimples 10-14-36:15
Dimri i Fundit 1-17-79:26
Dinah (s) 3-21-33:16
Dinah East 12-30-70:16
Dincolo de Pod 6-02-76:30
Dindon, Le 1-02-52:68
Diner Lassen Bitten 9-09-36:17
Dinero ed Amore 3-24-37:31
Ding Dog Daddy (s) 1-06-43:50
Ding Dong Williams 4-17-46:16
Dingaka 5-19-65:6
Dingen die Niet Voorbijgaan 10-28-70:28
Dinky 7-03-35:15
Dinner at 8 8-29-33:14
Dinner at the Ritz 11-10-37:19
Dinner Time (s) 8-22-28:14
Dino 6-12-57:6
Dinosaurus 6-15-60:6
Dinty 11-26-20:34
Dio Mio Come Sono Caduita In Basso 12-11-74:18
Dio Perdona ... Io No (See: God Forgives, I Don't)
Dionne Quintuplets (s) 2-05-35:14
Dionysus in '69 3-11-70:24
Dios Bendiga Cada Rincon de Esta Casa 9-28-77:24
Dip of Death, The 1-14-11:18
Diplomacy 3-03-16:23
Diplomacy 9-15-26:16
Diplomaniacs 5-04-33:12
Diplomatic Courier 6-11-52:6
Diplomats, The 12-26-28:11
Diplopenies 7-20-66:7
Diputado, El 2-07-79:27
Directed by John Ford 9-15-71:6
Directoire Gown 7-25-08:13
Dirigible 4-08-31:18
Dirigible Balloons at St. Louis 12-04-09:13
Dirt 3-21-79:28
Dirty Dingus Magee 7-29-70:15 and 11-04-70:24
Dirty Dozen, The 6-21-67:6
Dirty Game, The (See: Guerre Secret)
Dirty Harry 12-22-71:6
Dirty Heroes 11-24-71:16
Dirty Little Billy 5-17-72:28
Dirty Mary, Crazy Larry 5-15-74:24
Dirty O'Neil 6-26-74:18
Dirty Outlaws, The 6-30-71:29
Dirty Western, A 5-07-75:48

Dirty Work (s) 4-10-34:13
Dirty Work 12-25-34:12
Dirtymouth 6-17-70:22
Dis-Moi Que Tu M'Aimes 12-25-74:16
Dis-Moi Qui Tuer 12-29-65:6
Disappearance 9-28-77:22
Disappearing Enemies (s) 6-23-31: 18
Disaster 10-20-48:16
Disastrous Flirtation, A 8-29-08: 13
Disbarred 1-11-39:13
Disc Jockey 9-05-51:6
Discard, The 3-24-16:25
Discarded Lovers 2-09-32:19
Disciple, The 10-22-15:24
Disco Volante, Il 2-10-65:6
Discoteca Del Amor, La 8-27-80:21
Discontented Canary, The (s) 9-04-34:19
Discontented Husbands 3-12-24:27
Discord 7-18-28:28
Discovered (s) 1-14-31:12
Discovery 6-25-47:8
Discovery of America, The 6-17-70:24
Discreet Charm of the Bourgeoisie, The (See: Charme Discreet de la Bourgeoisie, Le)
Disembodies, The 8-28-57:6
Disgraced 7-18-33:37
Dishonest Bright 10-07-36:31
Dishonest Steward, The 10-08-10: 12
Dishonored 3-11-31:14
Dishonored 12-13-50:25
Dishonored Lady 4-23-47:8
Dishonored Medal, The 5-08-14: 20
Disillusion 11-02-49:22
Diskret Ophold 11-27-46:28
Diskretion--Ehrensache 3-15-39:18
Disorder (See: Disordine, Il)
Disorder in the Court (s) 8-12-36: 19
Disorderly Conduct 4-12-32:14
Disorderly Orderly, The 12-16-64:17
Disordine, Il 5-16-62:19
Disparue, La (s) 1-28-31:14
Disparus de Saint-Agil, Les 5-25-38:13
Dispatch from Reuters, A 9-25-40:15
Disputed Passage 10-18-39:14
Disque 413 8-19-36:17

Disraeli 8-26-21:36
Disraeli 10-09-29:46
Dissolution of Parliament 7-03-09:13
Distance 9-24-75:22
Distant Drums 12-05-51:6
Distant Thunder (See: Ashani Sanket)
Distant Trumpet, A 5-27-64:6
Distimto Amamecer 6-28-44:16
Distrait, Le 12-23-70:6
District Attorney, The 3-05-10: 13 and 9-03-10:21
Dit Vindarna Bar 11-24-48:14
Dita Saxova 7-24-68:24
Dites-le Avec les Fleurs 9-11-74:18
Dites Lui Que Je L'Aime 10-05-77:28
Dive Bomber 8-13-41:8
Dive In (s) 12-15-31:14
Diver's Honor, A 10-08-10:12
Diversion 11-07-13:14
Diversions 3-17-76:23
Divide and Conquer (s) 7-22-42:8
(Also see: Why We Fight Films)
Divided Heart 11-24-54:16
Dividend, The 6-16-16:24
Divina Creatura 9-14-76:27
Divine 6-25-75:23
Divine Cruise, The 5-22-29:27
Divine Lady 3-27-29:12
Divine Madness 9-17-80:18
Divine Nymph, The (See: Divina Creatura)
Divine Obsession, The 11-05-75: 19
Divine Sacrifice, The 1-28-18:43
Divine Sinner, The 9-26-28:15
Divine Woman, The 1-18-28:16
Division Brandenberg 12-28-60:6 and 1-28-61:20
Divka's Trema Velbloudy (See: Girl with Three Camels)
Divorce 6-28-23:22
Divorce 10-17-45:8
Divorce American Style 6-07-67:6
Divorce Among Friends 4-08-31:18
Divorce and the Daughter 11-17-16:24
Divorce Game, The 6-15-17:25
Divorce Heureux, Un 5-14-75:27
Divorce in the Family 11-01-32:13
Divorce Italian Style (See: Divorzio All'Italiana)
Divorce of Lady X, The 1-19-38:19
Divorce Trap, The 5-30-19:77

Divorcee, The 5-14-30:19
Divorced 10-29-15:22
Divorced Sweethearts (s) 12-24-30:21
Divorcee, The 1-25-19:46
Divorcement, Le 8-22-79:20
Divorzio All'Italiana 12-27-61:6
Divota Prasine 8-20-75:72
Dixiana 9-10-30:17
Dixie 6-30-43:8
Dixie Days (s) 5-21-30:19
Dixie Dugan 3-10-43:15
Dixie Flyer, The 10-06-26:50
Dixie Handicap 12-31-24:26
Dixie Jamboree 1-10-45:10
Dixieme Symphonie, La 10-04-67:14
17e Parallele le Vietnam en Guerre 3-13-68:24
17eme Ciel, Le 5-11-66:28
Dizengoff 99 6-13-79:15
Dizzy Dames 7-22-36:17
Dizzy Dishes (s) 7-23-30:19
Dizzy Doings (s) 9-08-41:17
Dizzy Heights 12-31-15:24
Djavulens Oga 11-09-60:19
Djevojka I Hrast 8-10-55:15
Djungelaeventyret Campa Campa 6-09-76:22
Djungelsaga, En 5-21-58:16
Djurgardskvallar 4-02-47:16
Dnevnye Zvezdy 9-03-69:19
Dny Zrady 6-19-74:18
Do and Dare 10-27-22:40
Do Ankhen Barah Haath 9-03-58:6
Do It Now 11-28-08:10
Do It Now (s) 2-26-30:24
Do Not Disturb 12-22-65:17
Do Not Throw Cushions into the Ring 6-17-70:22
Do You Keep a Lion at Home? (See: Mate Donna Liva?)
Do You Love Me? 4-17-46:16
Do Your Duty 11-07-28:26
Dobio Poshalovat 7-05-75:52
Dobri Stari Pianino 8-19-59:6
Dobro Morje 8-06-58:6
Dobro Poshalovat 7-05-78:16
Doc 8-11-71:16
Doc Savage 5-07-75:52
Dock Brief, The 10-03-62:7
Docks of Hamburg 7-09-30:35
Docks of New Orleans 3-17-48:8
Docks of New York 9-19-28:12
Docks of New York 2-28-45:15
Docks of San Francisco 3-15-32:60
Docteur Francois Gailland 12-31-75:15
Docteur Laennec 7-13-49:16

Docteur Popoul 10-04-72:18
Doctor and the Girl, The 9-14-49:8
Doctor and the Woman, The 4-26-18:40
Doctor at Large 4-03-57:6
Doctor at Sea 8-03-55:6
Doctor Beware 5-02-51:12
Doctor Black, Mr. Hyde 1-21-76:32
Dr. Blood's Coffin 5-03-61:7
Dr. Broadway 5-06-42:8
Dr. Bull 10-10-33:17
Dr. Christian Meets the Women 6-26-40:18
Dr. Crippen 8-21-63:17
Dr. Cyclops 3-06-40:16
Dr. Cyclops 4-10-68:6
Doctor Death: Seeker of Souls 11-14-73:16
Doctor Dolittle 12-20-67:6
Dr. Epameinondas 4-06-38:15
Dr. Erlich's Magic Bullet 2-07-40:14
Dr. Fabian--Lachen Ist Die Best Medizin 11-19-69:14
Doctor Faustua 10-25-67:20
Dr. Fu Manchu 7-24-29:29 and 5-07-30:38
Dr. Gillespie's Criminal Case 5-05-43:16
Dr. Gillespie's New Assistant 11-11-42:8
Doctor Glas (See: Doktor Glas)
Dr. Goldfoot and the Bikini Machine 11-10-65:6
Dr. Goldfoot and the Girl Bombs 11-16-66:6
Dr. Heckyl & Mr. Hype 7-02-80:18
Doctor in Clover 3-16-66:7
Doctor in Distress 8-07-63:20
Doctor in Love 7-20-60:6
Doctor in the House 4-07-54:6
Doctor in Trouble 6-24-70:22
Dr. Jack 1-05-23:41
Dr. Jekyll and Mr. Hyde 4-02-20:93
Dr. Jekyll and Mr. Hyde 1-05-32:19
Dr. Jekyll and Mr. Hyde 7-23-41:8
Dr. Jekyll and Sister Hyde 10-27-71:18
Dr. Jim 12-02-21:43
Doctor Judym 7-28-76:24
Doctor Kildare Goes Home 9-04-40:18

Dr. Kildare's Crisis 12-04-40:12
Dr. Kildare's Strange Case 4-17-40:13
Dr. Kildare's Victory 12-03-41:8
Dr. Kildare's Wedding Day 8-20-41:9
Dr. Knock 5-05-37:16
Dr. Mabuse 8-10-27:24
Dr. Mabuse, Der Spieler (See: Dr. Mabuse and Dr. Mabuse, the Gambler)
Dr. Mabuse, King of Crime (See: Dr. Mabuse)
Dr. Mabuse, the Gambler 6-02-22:34
Dr. Med. Sommer II 10-14-70:32
Doctor Monica 6-26-34:16
Dr. No 10-17-62:6
Dr. Norman Bethune 6-06-79:24
Dr. O'Dowd 2-14-40:20
Dr. Phibes Rises Again 7-19-72:14
Doctor Poenaru 6-14-78:20
Dr. Rameau 7-23-15:18
Dr. Renault's Secret 10-21-42:8
Dr. Rhythm 4-27-38:22
Doctor Says, The (See: Arzt Stellt Fest, Der)
Dr. Sigmund Spaeth (s) 3-06-29:12
Dr. Socrates 10-09-35:14
Dr. Strangelove; or, How I Learned to Stop Worrying and Love the Bomb 1-22-64:6
Doctor Syn 9-08-37:18
Doctor Takes a Wife 5-01-40:18
Dr. Terror's House of Horrors 3-03-65:7
Doctor Vlimmen 3-22-78:24 and 8-09-78:22
Dr. Who and the Daleks 7-07-65:6
Doctor X 8-09-32:17
Doctor, You've Got to Be Kidding 3-08-67:6
Doctor Zhivago 12-29-65:6
Doctora Quiere Tangos, La 8-24-49:22
Doctor's Bride 9-04-09:13
Doctor's Diary, A 2-24-37:17
Doctor's Dilemma 12-03-58:6
Doctor's Lunch 7-25-08:13
Doctor's Secret 2-06-29:18
Doctor's Secretary 1-07-11:13
Doctor's Wife, The (s) 11-26-30:18
Doctor's Wives 4-29-31:37
Doctor's Wives 1-27-71:17

Doctor's Women 6-05-29:26
Doda Clara 8-31-77:30
Dodeska-Den 12-09-70:14
Dodge City 4-12-39:13
Dodge City Trail 5-26-37:14
Dodging a Million 2-01-18:44
Dodsworth 9-30-36:17
Doeden Kommer Til Middag 10-14-64:6
Does It Pay? 12-13-23:23
Dog Catcher's Love, A 6-29-17:29
Dog Circus Rehearsal 8-28-09:13
Dog Dag Afternoon 8-27-75:15
Dog Doctor, The (s) 3-04-31:14
Dog Heaven (s) 3-07-28:28
Dog Law 10-10-28:26
Dog Meets Dog (s) 4-15-42:18
Dog of Flanders, A 9-25-35:42
Dog of Flanders, A 12-23-59:6
Dog of the Regiment 11-02-27:24
Dog on Business, A 9-10-10:14
Dog Pickpockets 10-16-09:12
Dog Trouble (s) 4-22-42:18
Dogadaj 8-20-69:17
Dogging It (s) 4-09-30:22
Dog-Gone Babies (s) 9-11-34:11
Dogora 8-04-65:7
Dog's Best Friend 1-20-60:7
Dog's Life, A 4-19-18:45
Dogs of Solitude (s) 9-15-30:14
Dogs of War, The 12-10-80:32
Dog's Pal, A (s) 5-11-27:24
Dogway Melody (s) 10-29-30:17
    and 4-29-31:37
Doigts dans le Tete, Les 12-25-74:16
Doing Phil a Favor (s) 5-28-30:21
Doing Their Bit 8-23-19:42
Dok Jinnung Nurguni 12-31-69:18
Dokter Pulden Zaalt Papavers 7-07-76:16
Doktor Glas 6-19-68:6
Dokuritsu Kikanjutai Imada Shagek-
    ichu 10-07-64:6
Dolce Vita, La 2-17-60:6
Dolci Notti, Le 11-14-62:7
Dolemite 8-06-75:17
Doll, The (See: Pupa, La)
Doll, The (See: Vaxdockan)
Doll Face 12-19-45:18
Doll Merchant 8-17-55:7
Doll Shop, The (s) 12-18-29:22
Doll That Took the Town, The
    (See: Donne del Giorno, La)
Dollar and the Law, The 11-24-16:29

Dollar Devils 4-19-23:36
Dollar Dizzy (s) 4-08-31:18
Dollar Down 8-12-25:33
Dollar Mark, The 9-11-14:22
Dollars ($) 12-15-71:18
Dollars and Sense 6-25-20:35
Dollars and the Woman 3-24-16:24
Doll's House, A 6-15-17:26
Doll's House, A 5-31-18:29
Doll's House, A 2-17-22:40
Doll's House, A 5-09-73:6
Doll's House, A 5-23-73:18
Dolly 12-02-28:31
Dolly Connolly and Percy Wenrich
    (s) 9-05-28:14
Dolly Macht Karriere 11-12-30:45 and 7-21-31:12
Dolly Sisters 9-26-45:14
Dolly's Vacation 12-20-18:36
Dolores 11-16-49:16
Dolores de Aradia 4-24-14:21
Dolphin 7-04-79:25
Dolyna Miru 5-15-57:7
Dom Bez Okien 5-23-62:16
Dom S Mezzaninom (See: House
    with an Attic)
Dom V A Kotorom la Sivou 7-02-58:6
Domani e Troppo Tardi 11-01-50:18
Domani e un Altro Giorno 2-28-51:18
Domaren 5-17-61:7
Dombey and Son 7-11-19:60
Domencia 4-02-52:22
Domencia D'Agosto 5-03-50:20
Domenica e Sempre Domineca 7-02-58:6
Domestic Meddlers 12-05-28:24
Domestic Relations 6-09-22:57
Domestic Trouble 6-20-28:15
Domicile Conjugal 8-26-70:16
Dominant Sex, The 2-10-37:15
Domingo a Tarde 9-08-65:68
Domino Kid 8-21-57:6
Domino Principle, The 3-23-77:22
Don Camillo 5-28-52:22
Don Camillo e L'on. Peppone 12-07-55:8
Don Cossack Chorus (s) 4-22-42:18
Don Desperado 5-11-27:20
Don Giovanni 9-16-70:14
Don Giovanni 10-24-79:17
Don Giovanni in Sicilia 7-26-67:22
Don Is Dead, The 11-14-73:16

Don Juan   8-11-26:11
Don Juan   3-14-56:22
Don Juan   7-18-56:6
Don Juan Diplomatico   4-22-31:19
   (Also see: Boudoir Diplomat,
   The and Liebe Auf Befehl)
Don Juan 1973 ou Si Don Juan Etait
   une Femme   3-07-73:18
Don Juan Quilligan   6-06-45:12
Don Juan's 3 Nights   9-08-26:17
Don Mike   2-23-27:16
Don Q, Son of Zorro   6-17-25:35
Don Quichotte   10-17-28:24
Don Quichotte   4-11-33:20 (Also
   see: Don Quixote)
Don Quixote   11-06-09:13
Don Quixote   6-06-33:14 (Also see:
   Don Quichotte)
Don Quixote   1-08-35:18
Don Quixote   5-29-57:6
Don Quixote   8-01-73:18
Don Quixote de la Mancha   5-11-
   49:18
Don Segundo Sombra   9-17-69:24
Don Winslow of the Coast Guard
   (s)   3-31:43:14
Dona Barbara   2-21-45:17
Dona Flor e Seurs Dois Maridos
   9-14-77:17
Dona Flora and Her 2 Husbands
   (See: Dona Flor e Seurs Dois
   Maridos)
Dona Mentiras   1-14-31:34
Dona Perfecta   11-09-77:16
Donald Brian (s)   2-06-29:18
Donald Meek Co. (s)   10-20-31:21
Donatella   10-24-56:6
Donde Estas Corazen?   9-06-61:6
Donde Meuren las Palabras   6-05-
   46:13 (Also see: Where
   Words Fail)
Done in Oil (s)   7-16-30:15
Done in Oil (s)   3-06-35:20
Donna Bella Domenica, La   1-28-
   76:15
Donna del Fiume, La   11-16-55:6
Donna del Lago, La   8-04-65:28
Donna D'Una Notte   3-14-33:15
Donna e Bello   11-20-74:16
Donna e una Cosa Meravigliosa,
   La   9-16-64:17
Donna Juana   5-02-28:14
Donna Nel Mondo, La   2-27-63:7
Donna Scimmia, La   5-06-64:6
Donne Alla Fonte (s)   11-03-31:17
Donne del Giorno   7-31-57:6
Donne e Briganti   7-04-51:24
Donne Sole   7-11-56:10

Donner, Glitz und Regen (s)   10-
   20-31:21
Donnez-Moi Dix Hommes Desperes
   5-09-62:17
Donnez-Moi Ma Chance   2-12-58:18
Donogoo Tonka   4-22-36:29 and
   7-29-36:15
Donovan Affair, The   5-01-29:29
Donovan's Brain   10-07-53:6
Donovan's Reef   6-19-63:6
Don's Party   10-06-76:21
Don't   2-17-26:41
Don't Answer the Phone   4-16-
   80:28
Don't Be a Sucker (s)   5-08-46:8
Don't Be Jealous (s)   8-01-28:12
Don't Bet on Blondes   7-24-35:21
Don't Bet on Love   8-01-33:57
Don't Bet on Women   3-11-31:15
Don't Bite Your Dentist (s)   1-21-
   31:17
Don't Bother to Knock   7-16-52:6
Don't Bother to Knock   6-07-61:20
Don't Call Me Little Girl   6-24-
   21:36
Don't Cry with Your Mouth Full
   (See: Pleure Pas la Bouche
   Pleine)
Don't Doubt Your Wife   3-24-22:
   41
Don't Drink the Water   11-12-69:21
Don't Ever Die, Mother (See:
   Kaachan Shiguno Iyada)
Don't Ever Leave Me   7-27-49:22
Don't Ever Marry   4-16-20:44
Don't Fence Me In   10-24-45:12
Don't Gamble with Love   3-04-36:
   27
Don't Gamble with Strangers   5-
   29-46:10
Don't Get Excited (s)   9-11-29:18
Don't Get Excited (s)   12-18-29:
   22
Don't Get Nervous (s)   7-31-29:17
Don't Get Personal   1-20-22:35
Don't Get Personal   2-26-36:37
Don't Get Personal   12-31-41:8
Don't Give Up the Ship   6-03-59:6
Don't Go in the House   6-11-80:
   22
Don't Go Near the Water   11-13-
   57:6
Don't Just Lie There   5-13-70:14
Don't Just Stand There   3-27-68:6
Don't Knock the Rock   12-26-56:6
Don't Knock the Twist   4-11-62:
   26
Don't Leave Home (s)   1-07-31:23

Drei Maenner im Schnee 7-27-55:6
Drei Tage Liebe 3-25-31:71
Drei Tage Mitelarest 5-23-33:21
Drei um Christine, Die 7-15-36:55
Drei Von der Tankstelle, Die (See: From the Gas Station)
Drei Wenschen 12-29-37:17
Dreigroschenoper, Die 5-20-31:16 (Also see: Threepenny Opera, The)
Dreiklang 8-03-38:21
Dreimaedelhaus, Das 1-21-59:6
Drenge 3-09-77:17
Dresden Doll, The (s) 3-26-30:25
Dress Parade 11-02-27:18
Dressed to Kill 3-14-28:23
Dressed to Kill 11-27-35:30
Dressed to Kill 7-23-41:8
Dressed to Kill 5-22-46:10
Dressed to Kill 7-23-80:18
Dressmaker from Paris 3-18-25:40
Drevo Jelania 6-21-78:19
Dreyfus Case, The 9-01-31:31
Dreyfus ou L'Intolerable Verite 2-05-75:20
Drift Fence 3-11-36:27 (Also see: Nevada)
Drifter, The 2-11-16:24
Drifter, The 3-20-29:28
Drifter, The 3-15-32:29
Drifter, The 5-24-44:10
Drifter, The 9-07-66:18
Drifter 9-24-75:24
Drifters, The 12-27-18:182
Drifting 8-23-23:23
Drifting 8-02-32:17
Drifting Along 2-20-46:8
Drifting Thru 5-05-26:20
Drifting Westward 2-15-39:13
Driftwood 3-24-16:25
Driftwood 12-12-28:31
Driftwood 11-05-47:20
Driller Killer 7-04-79:24
Drink 10-30-09:11
Dritte, Der 8-16-72:26
Dritte Generation, Die 5-23-79:26
Drive a Crooked Road 3-17-54:6
Drive, He Said 6-02-71:15
Drive-In 5-28-76:26
Driven 12-01-22:35
Driven by Fate 8-20-15:20
Driven from Home 5-25-27:21
Driven to Steel 4-09-10:15
Driver, The (s) 8-25-31:14
Driver, The 7-26-78:20

Driver Dagg Faller Regn 3-19-47:12
Driver's Remorse 10-23-09:13
Drivin' Fool 11-01-23:27
Droem om Frihet, En 11-11-70:27
Droemme Stoejer Ikke Naar De Doer 5-16-79:44
Droemmen Om Amerika 12-08-76:19
Droit D'Aimer, Le 8-30-72:18
Drole de Colonel, Un 5-15-68:30
Drole de Dimanche, Un 12-31-58:6
Drole de Jeu 3-13-68:24
Drolesse, La 5-09-79:80
Drop Kick, The 9-21-27:21
Dropped from the Clouds 9-15-09:12
Drowning Pool, The 6-18-75:18
Drug Connection 3-24-76:21
Drug Moi, Kol'ka 11-15-61:6
Drug Pretsednik Centafor 8-10-60:6
Drug Traffic, The 4-26-23:26
Druga Mlodosc 10-18-39:20
Drugarcine 8-15-79:28
Drum, The 4-20-38:25
Drum 8-04-76:20
Drum Beat 11-03-54:6
Drum Taps 5-02-33:22
Drumming It In (s) 1-15-30:22
Drummond at Bay 8-04-37:19
Drummond's Peril 3-23-38:16
Drummond's Revenge 12-22-37:17
Drums Across the River 5-19-54:6
Drums Along the Mohawk 11-08-39:14
Drums in the Deep South 10-03-51:6
Drums o' Voodoo 5-15-34:27
Drums of Africa 4-24-63:15
Drums of Destiny 11-10-37:19
Drums of Fate 1-19-23:46
Drums of Fear (s) 7-23-30:19
Drums of Fu Manchu (serial) 2-14-40:20 (feature) 11-10-43:35
Drums of Jeopardy 3-19-24:26
Drums of Jeopardy 4-15-31:53
Drums of Love 2-01-28:22
Drums of Tabu, The 6-07-67:6
Drums of Tahiti 1-13-54:6
Drums of the Congo 7-22-42:8
Drums of the Desert 8-10-27:26
Drums of the Desert 11-06-40:18

• 114

Drumsticks, A Thanksgiving Story 11-26-10:18
Drunkard's Fate 10-09-09:13
Drunken Angel 2-03-60:20
Drunken Monkey in a Tiger's Eye 11-29:78:24
Drunker, The (s) 6-07-32:20
Drunter und Drieber 12-20-32:16
Drusilla with a Million 5-27-25:40
Drvo Bez Koren 7-31-74:19
Dry Martini 11-07-28:24
Dry Summer (See: Susuz Yaz)
Drylanders 10-02-63:28
Drzwi in Murze 9-25-74:18
Du 1-15-69:38
Du aer inte Klok, Madicken 1-02-80:12
Du Bist die Welt Fuer 1-27-54:26
Du Bist Mein Glueck 11-18-36:29
Du Bist Mein--Ein Deutsches Tagebuch 7-30-69:36
Du Bout des Levies 1-28-76:14
Du Cote D'Orouet 9-01-71:16
Du Cote des Tennis 11-10-76:22
Du er Ikke Alene 3-08-78:35
Du Gamia Du Fria 9-13-72:23
Du Grabuge Chez les Veuves 5-13-64:19
Du Mouron Pour les Petits Oiseaux 2-27:63:7
Du Rififi a Paname 4-06-66:6
Du Rififi Chez les Femmes 6-10-59:6
Du Rififi Chez les Hommes 6-08-55:6
Du Soleil Plein les Yeux 6-10-70:26
Dual Alibi 6-18-47:8
Dub, The 1-17-19:52
Du Barry Was a Lady 5-05-43:8
Du Barry, Woman of Passion 11-05-30:30
Dublin in Brass (s) 11-06-35:20
Dubrovsky 4-01-36:16
Dubrovsky 8-12-59:19
Duchess and the Dirtwater Fox, The 3-17-76:22
Duchess of Buffalo 8-18-26:60
Duchess of Doubt 6-08-17:25
Duchess of Idaho 6-14-50:8
Duci de Kerekjarto (s) 4-09-30:22
Duck Soup 11-28-33:20
Duck, You Sucker! 6-21-72:18
Ducks and Deducts (s) 6-20-28:14
Ducks and Drakes 4-01-21:42
Ducks and Drakes (s) 1-05-32:19

Ducktator, The (s) 9-02-42:34
Ducky, Dear (s) 8-22-33:22
Dud, The 3-19-20:53
Duda, La 7-26-72:22
Dude Bandit, The 6-27-33:15
Dude Cowboy 9-10-41:16
Dude Goes West, The 4-28-48:8
Dude Ranch 4-29-31:37
Dude Ranger, The 10-02-34:37
Dude Wrangler, The 7-23-30:31
Dudes Are Pretty People 4-15-42:18
Due Colonnelli, I 1-16-63:20
Due Dezzi di Pane 3-28-79:20
Du Kennedy, I 10-29-69:17
Due Madri, Le 5-22-40:33
Due Marines e un Generale, Due (See: War Italian Style)
Due Misantropi, I 10-29-69:17
Due Pezzi di Pane 3-28-79:20
Due Soldi di Speranza 6-94-52:18
Duel, The 7-04-62:6
Duel 11-17-71:70
Duel at Apache Wells 2-20-57:6
Duel at Diablo 5-18-66:6
Duel at Silver Creek 7-16-52:6
Duel in Mid Air, A 11-13-09:13
Duel in the Jungle 7-07-54:6
Duel in the Sun 1-01-47:14
Duel of the Titans 3-27-63:6
Duel of the Mississippi 9-21-55:6
Duelle 6-02-76:30
Duellists, The 6-01-77:17
Duello Senza Onore 4-16-50:22
Duerme, Duerme, Mi Amor 2-19-75:22
Duet for Cannibals (See: Duett for Kannibaler)
Duett fur Kannibaler 5-21-69:18
Duffer Swings (s) 4-15-31:20
Duffy 9-18-68:6
Duffy of San Quentin 2-17-54:6
Duffy's Tavern 8-22-45:20
Dugan of the Bad Lands 9-15-31:24
Duggan of the Dugouts 8-22-28:34
Dugun 8-02-78:16
Duios Anastasia Trecea 7-30-80:28
Duke Comes Back 12-08-37:16
Duke Is Tops, The 7-20-38:12
Duke of Chicago 3-30-49:13
Duke of the Navy 2-11-42:8
Duke of West Point 12-21-38:14
Duke Wore Jeans, The 4-02-58:16
Duke's Plan, The 2-19-10:15
Dulcie's Adventure 10-06-16:26

Dulcima 7-07-71:14
Dulcinea 9-12-62:16
Dulcy 9-20-23:36
Dulcy 10-02-40:12
Dull Razor, The 11-26-10:18
Dulscy 4-21-76:26
Dumb Belles (s) 5-11-27:24
Dumb Girl of Portici, The 4-07-16:21
Dumbbell Letters (s) 9-04-34:19
Dumbbells in Derbies (s) 10-13-31:14
Dumbbells in Ermine 7-30-30:17
Dumbo 10-01-41:9
Duminica la Ora 6 7-20-66:6
Dummy, The 3-23-17:25
Dummy, The 3-06-29:21
Dummy Ache (s) 7-22-36:17
Dummy in Disguise 9-24-10:12
Dunaparti Randevu 2-03-37:31
   and 3-31-37:19
Dunce Cap, The 10-15-10:12
Dunder Klumpen 10-16-74:16
Dunkirk 3-26-58:6
Dunkle Gassen (See: Dark Alleys)
Dunkle Stern, Der 8-10-55:15
Dunwich Horror, The 1-21-70:18
Dupe, The 6-30-16:19
Duped 2-26-10:15
Dupes, The 6-23-72:26
Dupont-Barbes 3-05-52:22
Dupont Lajoie 2-26-75:20
Duquesa de Benameji, La 4-26-75:20
Durango Kid, The 8-28-40:20
Durango Valley Raiders 11-02-38:22
Durante L'Estate 9-08-71:26
Durchdreher, Der 5-23-79:26
Durs a Cuire, Les 6-24-64:20
Dusk to Dawn 9-08-22:41
Dusman 3-19-80:28
Dust 7-28-16:24
Dust Be My Destiny 8-16-39:14
Dust Flower 7-07-22:59
Dust of Desire 7-11-19:61
Dusty and Sweets McGee 6-16-71:22
Dusty Ermine 9-23-36:16
Dutch Guiana (s) 2-04-42:22
Dutch Kids 1-07-11:13
Dutch Types 11-19-10:13
Dutchman 12-28-66:6
Duty's Reward 6-15-27:25
Duvad 5-24-61:17
Duvidha 11-19-75:18
Dva Musketyri (See: Jester's Tale, A)

Dvenates 11-24-71:22
Dvoboj Za Juznu Prugu 8-16-78:18
Dvoje 8-23-61:6
Dvorianckoe Gnezdo 7-23-69:6
Dvoynikat 7-30-80:30
Dybbuk, The 2-02-38:17
Dybbuk, The 11-20-68:34
Dym Bramborove Nate 3-09-77:26
Dymky 5-25-66:24
Dyn Amo 7-12-72:26
Dynamit 4-30-47:26
Dynamite 1-01-30:24
Dynamite 11-17-48:13
Dynamite 8-16-72:28
Dynamite Dan 10-08-24:39
Dynamite Delaney 1-26-38:15
Dynamite Denny 9-20-32:15
Dynamite Jack 11-22-61:6
Dynamite Pass 3-22-50:6
Dynamite Ranch 12-27-32:54
Dynamiters, The 6-27-56:6
Dynasty 9-07-77:24
Dyrlaegens Plejeboern 1-15-69:38
Dyspeptic and His Double, The 9-04-09:13
Dziege Grzechu 5-28-75:19
Dzien Wisly 10-01-80:28
Dziura W Zlemi 8-05-70:16
D-Zug 13 Hat Verspaetung 6-02-31:26

• E •

E Atit de Aproape Feucirea 8-09-78:22
E Comincio il Viaggio Nelle Vertigini 1-26-77:50
E Flat Man (s) 11-13-35:16
E Poi lo Cohiamakono il Magnifico 10-11-72:28
E Primavera 3-15-50:12
E Simonal 8-19-70:22
E Tornato Carnevale 1-13-37:13
E Venne un Uomo 9-08-65:6
Each Dawn I Die 7-19-39:12
Each Day I Cry 7-24-63:6
Each Pearl a Tear 9-08-16:21
Each to His Kind 2-09-17:29
Eadweard Muybridge, Zoopraxographer 9-22-76:19
Eager Lips 8-17-27:24
Eagle, The 6-28-18:29
Eagle, The 11-11-25:36
Eagle and the Hawk, The 5-16-33:21
Eagle and the Hawk, The 2-08-50:11
Eagle Has Landed, The 12-22-76:22
Eagle in a Cage 12-22-71:66
Eagle of the Sea 11-17-26:14
Eagle Squadron 6-17-42:8
Eagle with Two Heads 9-29-48:18
Eagle's Blood, The 1-29-36:16
Eagle's Feather 10-11-23:26
Eagle's Mate, The 7-10-14:20
Eagle's Wing 8-01-79:42
Eagle's Wings, The 11-24-16:29
Eakins 11-28-73:16
Earl and Bell (s) 11-20-29:12
Earl Burnett and the Biltmore Orch. (s) 5-12-28:21 and 9-26-28:14
Earl Carroll Sketchbook 8-14-46:10
Earl Carroll's Vanities 3-07-45:20
Earl of Chicago, The 1-03-40:40
Earl of Pawtucket, The 7-16-15:18
Earl of Puddlestone 8-14-40:14

Early Autumn (See: Samma No Aji)
Early Bird, The 12-17-24:37
Early Bird (s) 9-30-36:17
Early Bird, The 12-08-65:6
Early Bird Gets It, The (s) 9-02-42:34
Early Cranes 6-25-80:21
Early Morning (s) 6-26-29:12
Early Mornings (See: Petits Matins, Le)
Early to Bed 7-22-36:17
Early to Wed 6-23-26:18
Earrings of Madame De... , The 7-21-54:6 (Also see: Madame De)
Earth (See: Zimlia)
Earth Entranced (See: Terra Em Transe)
Earth Is Mine, The 4-22-59:6
Earth vs. the Flying Saucers 6-06-56:6
Earth Woman, The 6-23-26:14
Earthbound 8-13-20:34
Earthbound 6-05-40:14
Earthling, The 7-30-80:26
Earthquake 11-13-74:18
Earthworm Tractors 7-29-36:14
Easiest Way, The 4-13-17:26
Easiest Way, The 3-04-31:22
East by North 4-30-47:10
East Is East 11-10-16:29
East Is West 10-20-22:40
East Is West 11-05-30:30
East Lynne 7-18-13:8
East Lynne 6-23-16:21
East Lynne 2-25-31:12
East Lynne on the Western Front 7-28-31:24
East Meets West 9-16-36:17 and 11-04-36:18
East of Borneo 9-29-31:22
East of Broadway 11-12-24:25
East of Eden 2-16-55:6
East of 5th Ave. 12-26-33:11
East of Java 12-18-35:12
East of Piccadilly 2-26-41:18
East of Sudan 8-12-64:6
East of Suez 1-07-25:37
East of Sumatra 9-16-53:6
East of the River 10-30-40:14
East Side Kids 2-21-40:12
East Side of Heaven 4-12-39:13
East Side Sadie 5-22-29:16
East Side, West Side 10-19-27:28
East Side, West Side 12-14-49:8
Easter Parade 5-26-48:8
Easterner, The 11-02-07:11
Easy Aces (s) 12-12-33:19

Easy Come, Easy Go 2-05-47:12
Easy Come, Easy Go 3-22-67:6
Easy Life, The (See: Sorpasso, Il)
Easy Living 7-07-37:12
Easy Living 8-10-49:8
Easy Millions 9-26-33:20
Easy Money 11-09-17:55
Easy Money 7-15-36:31
Easy Money 2-04-48:22
Easy Pickings 3-23-27:22 and 4-13-27:19
Easy Pickins (s) 5-13-36:15
Easy Rider 5-14-69:6
Easy Road, The 2-18-21:40
Easy Road, The 8-15-79:24
Easy Street 2-02-17:24
Easy to Get 2-27-20:46
Easy to Look At 8-01-45:16
Easy to Love 1-16-34:15
Easy to Love 11-11-53:6
Easy to Make Money 8-08-19:49
Easy to Take 12-23-36:18
Easy to Wed 4-10-46:16
Eat 'em Alive 11-07-33:17
Eat Me Kitty 8 to the Bar (s) 4-08-42:20
Eat My Dust 4-28-76:30
Eat Your Soup 11-06-09:13
Eating on the Cuff (s) 9-02-42:34
Eau a la Bouche, L' 3-02-60:6
Eau Vive, L' 5-21-58:16
Eavesdropper, The 9-21-66:6
Ebb Tide 7-16-15:19
Ebb Tide 10-13-37:16
Ebeo Errante, L' 4-14-48:8
Eboli (See: Cristo Si e Fermato a Eboli)
Ebon Lundin 11-06-74:22
Ebreo Fascista, L' 10-15-80:74
Ecce Bombo 5-24-78:36
Ecce Homo Homolka 7-22-70:22
Ecclisse, L' 5-09-62:7
Ech Burdjin Domog 7-28-76:20
Echappement Libre 10-07-64:6
Echec au Porteur 3-19-58:6
Echec au Roc 3-25-31:71
Echo 8-19-64:6
Echo Murders, The 9-05-45:15
Echoes of a Summer 2-04-76:17
Echoes of Silence 12-14-66:19
Echoes--Pink Floyd 11-15-72:24
Echtiger Amerikaner, Ein 1-01-30:15
Eclair au Chocolat 2-21-79:21
Eclipse, The (See: Ecclisse, L')
Eclipse de Sol 8-04-43:16

Ecole Buissonniere, L' 6-22-49:20
Ecoute Voir 10-25-78:42
Ecstasy 1-08-41:24 (Also see: Extase)
Ecstatic Stigmatic 3-12-80:27
Ecume des Jours, L' 3-20-68:6
Ed and Lou Miller (s) 12-18-29:22
Ed Lowry (s) 7-04-28:16; 7-18-28:15; 8-15-28:17
Eddie Cantor Story, The 12-23-53:6
Eddie Conrad and Marion Eddy (s) 8-29-28:15 and 10-17-28:16
Eddie Lambert (s) 5-08-29:20
Eddie Miller (s) 11-13-29:12
Eddie Nelson (s) 10-31-28:44
Eddie Peabody and Jimmy Maisel (s) 5-23-28:21 and 10-10-28:15
Eddie White (s) 12-05-28:12
Eddy Duchin Story, The 5-30-56:6
Eden et Apres, L' 5-06-70:26
Edera, L' 2-18-53:18
Edes Anna 5-13-59:7
Edes Mostoha 11-20-35:16 and 12-16-36:21
Edgar and Teacher's Wit 4-02-20:93
Edge of Doom 8-09-50:8
Edge of Eternity 11-04-59:7
Edge of Fury 5-07-58:6
Edge of the Abyss, The 11-26-15:23
Edge of the City, The 1-02-57:6
Edge of the World, The 7-21-37:13 and 9-14-38:15
Edinstvennaja 7-14-76:24
Edipo Re 9-13-67:6
Edison and Gregory (s) 8-14-29:18
Edison, the Man 5-22-40:14
Editie Speciala 6-28-78:28
Edouard et Caroline 5-16-51:18
Eduardo the Healer 2-07-79:20
Educated Abroad 3-27-09:13
Educating Father 6-24-36:45
Education Amoureuse de Valentin, L' 3-26-75:22
Education de Prince 11-02-38:22
Education du Prince (See: Barge-Keeper's Daughter)
Education of Elizabeth 2-18-21:40
Education of Love 9-13-61:28
Education of Mr. Pipp 11-21-14:27
Education of Sonny Carson, The 7-17-74:16

Education Sentimentale 10-03-62:6

Educatore Autoizzato 6-11-80:29

Edvard Munch 4-14-76:27

Edward, My Son 3-09-49:6

Een Koninkrijk Voor een Huis 3-30-49:13

Een Ochtend Van Zess Weken 7-13-66:14

Een Vrouw Als Eva (See: Woman Like Eva, A)

Een Vrouw Tussen Hond en Wolf 5-16-79:27

Effect of Gamma Rays on Man-in-the-Moon Marigolds, The 12-13-72:20

Effects 9-19-79:19

Effeuillant la Marguerite, En 10-31-56:6

Effi Briest 7-10-74:18

Efficiency Edgar's Courtship 9-07-17:32

Egg and I, The 3-26-47:12

Egg Crate Wallop, The 10-03-19:57

Egged On (s) 6-02-26:15

Egi Barany 7-14-71:16

Eglantine 2-23-72:6

Egouts du Paradis, Les 4-25-79:22

Egri Csillagok 2-26-69:32

Egy Erkolcsos Ejszaka 5-10-78:26

Egy Lany Elindul 2-23-38:15

Egy Oervelt Ejszaka 3-11-70:22

Egy Pikolo Vilagos 8-01-56:6

Egy Szerelem Harom Ejszakaja 9-20-67:20

Egypt by 3 4-08-53:6

Egypte, Terre du Pyramide (s) 5-27-31:56

Egyptian, The 8-25-54:6

Ehe, Eine 10-23-68:24

Ehe der Maria Bruan, Die 2-28-79:24

Ehe mit Beschraenkter Haftung 2-09-32:19

Ehe des Herr Mississippi, Die 9-13-61:28

Eheinstitut Aurora 3-21-62:6

Ehrliche Interview, Das 12-15-71:22

Eichmann and the Third Reich 6-07-61:6

Eien No Hito 7-18-62:6

Eierdiebe 5-11-77:79

Eifelkor 7-02-58:6

Eiger Sanction, The 5-14-75:26

$8\frac{1}{2}$ 4-03-63:6

Eight Bells 5-15-35:19

Eight Girls in a Boat 1-16-34:15

813 1-28-21:40

800 Heroes 1-10-76:22

800 Leguas Por el Amazonas 8-12-59:6

Eight Iron Men 10-22-52:6

Eight O'Clock Walk 3-24-54:6

Eight on the Lam 4-26-67:6

8 x 8 8-20-57:6

Eighth Commandment, The 6-25-15:20

Eighth Day of the Week 9-03-58:6

Eighteen and Anxious 11-13-57:20

Eighteen Minutes 4-24-35:13

1812 9-13-44:10

80 Blocks from Tiffany's 3-26-80:27

80 Huszar 5-24-78:40

80 Steps to Jonah 10-22-69:30

80,000 Suspects 8-21-63:6

81st Blow, The 4-30-75:19

Ein Compagnie de Max Linder 9-11-63:22

Einbrecher 1-07-31:23

Eine Von Uns 11-29-32:19

Einer Von Uns Beiden 1-24-79:22

Einmaleins der Liebe, Das 1-06-37:41

Eins 12-08-71:16

Einstein Theory 2-08-23:41

Eiste Waltzer, Der 1-17-79:16

Eiszeit 8-06-75:16

Ekdin Pratidin 2-06-80:24

Ekdromi 11-23-66:26

Ekel, Das 6-23-31:19 and 2-16-32:33

Ekino To Kalokeri 11-17-71:22

Ekko af et Skud 4-01-70:24

El 5-13-53:22

El Alamein 12-16-53:6

Elastic Transformation 8-28-09:13

El Cid 12-06-61:6

El Condor 6-24-70:20

Eldfagein 8-27-52:6

El Dorado 12-18-63:7

El Dorado 6-14-67:7

El Dorado Pass 5-04-49:18

Eldridge Cleaver 9-02-70:32

Eleanor Painter (s) 3-13-29:14

Eleanor Roosevelt Story, The 10-20-65:6

Electra 5-30-62:6 and 9-05-62:6

Electric Horseman, The 12-05-79:22

Electric Insoles 1-22-10:14

Electric Monster, The 5-25-60:7
Electric Ship (s) 11-05-30:23
Eleftherios Venizelos 1910-1927
4-02-80:24
Elegido, El 2-23-77:16
Elegy, The (s) 6-15-27:25
Elena et les Hommes 10-03-56:
26
Elephant Boy 2-24-37:17 and 4-
07-37:14
Elephant Ca Trompe Enormement,
Un 10-06-76:20
Elephant Man, The 10-01-80:20
Elephant Stampede 10-24-51:6
Elephant Walk 3-31-54:6
Eletbetancoltatott Lany 5-26-65:7
11 Harrowhouse 6-26-74:22
11 x 14 5-25-77:20
11 Who Were Loyal 5-22-29:16
Eleventh Commandment 10-22-14:
27
Eleventh Hour, The 7-26-23:27
Eleventh Hour Redemption, An 12-
03-10:14
Elf Jahre und ein Tag 10-02-63:
28
El Greco 10-19-66:20
El Hayat Kifar 11-20-68:40
Eli Eli 10-09-40:18
Eligible Mr. Bangs (s) 6-12-29:
16
Elika Katappa 10-29-69:30
Elinor Norton 3-06-35:21
Elisa 5-15-57:7
Elisa, Vida Mia 5-11-77:79
Elisabeth Von Oesterreich 8-11-
31:22 and 12-15-31:21
Elise ou la Vraie Vie 5-20-70:30
Elisir d'Amore, L' (See: This
Wine of Love)
Elixir of Dreams 3-27-09:13
Elixir of Love 10-29-47:15
Elixir of Strength 3-21-08:15
Elixier des Teufels, Des 7-27-77:
30
Eliza Comes to Stay 4-22-36:29
Eliza Fraser 12-29-76:18
Elizabeth of Ladymead 1-05-49:
58
Eliza's Horoscope 10-01-75:26
Ella Cinders 6-09-26:16
Elle Boit Pas, Elle Fume Pas,
Elle Drague Pas, Mais ...
Elle Cause! 5-13-70:24
Elle Cause Plus Elle Flinque
9-20-72:14
Elle Court, Elle Court la Banlique
5-02-73:6

El Leila El Akhira 5-20-64:20
Ellery Queen and the Murder Ring
9-24-41:8
Ellery Queen and the Perfect
Crime 8-13-41:18
Ellery Queen, Master Detective
12-25-40:18
Ellery Queen's Penthouse Mystery
3-12-41:14
Elles Etaient Douze Femmes 6-
05-40:14
El Less Wal Kilab 7-10-63:6
Elmer and Elsie 8-07-34:12
Elmer Gantry 6-29-60:8
Elmer Steps Out (s) 5-08-34:14
Elmer the Great 5-30-33:15
Elnok Kisasszony (See: Miss
President)
Elokuu 7-24-57:6
Elope, if You Can 4-14-22:39
Elopement 11-07-51:6
Eloy 3-12-69:26
El Paso Stampede 10-14-53:6
El Paso Wrecking Corp. 1-25-
78:24
Elsa Ersi and Nat Ayres (s) 11-
27-29:21
El Shaytan El Saheir 8-12-64:6
Elstree Calling 2-26-30:42 (Also
see: Hello, Everybody)
Elstree Story, The 2-25-53:18
Eltavozott Nap 1-31-68:22
Elusive Corporal, The (See:
Caporal Epingle, Le)
Elusive Isabel 5-05-16:26
Elusive Pimpernel, The 11-15-
50:18
Elve Vagy Halva 2-27-80:26
Elveszett Paradicsom 7-15-64:22
Elvira Fernandez (s) 7-29-42:8
Elvira Madigan 5-10-67:6
Elvis! Elvis! 7-27-77:22
Elvis on Tour 11-08-72:18
Elvis: That's the Way It Is (See:
That's the Way It Is)
Elyazerly 8-28-74:43
Embarrassing Moments 3-12-30:36
Embarrassing Moments 11-20-
34:17
Embarrassment of Riches, The
9-27-18:42
Embassy 3-08-72:24
Ember a Hid Alatt 5-06-36:19 and
12-02-36:38
Embraceable You 7-28-48:15
Embrassez-Moi 11-15-32:23
Embrujo 7-23-41:30
Embryo 1-17-68:6

Embryo 5-26-76:26
Emden Geht Nach USA: Wir Koennen So Viel 9-15-76:17
Emergency Call 6-27-33:14
Emergency Call 5-28-52:22
Emergency Case, The (s) 9-24-30:23
Emergency Hospital 3-21-56:6
Emergency Landing 6-18-41:16
Emergency Squad 4-17-40:13
Emergency Wedding 11-15-50:6
Emigrantes 1-26-49:22
Emigrants, The (See: Utvandrarna)
Emil 4-27-38:22
Emil and the Detectives (See: Emil und die Detektive)
Emil and the Detectives 3-27-35:26
Emil and the Detectives (See: Emil)
Emil and the Detectives 10-14-64:6
Emil Boreo 9-18-29:15
Emil Coleman (s) 9-30-36:17 and 5-13-42:16
Emil to Tanteitachi 9-12-56:18
Emil und die Detektive 12-22-31:21
Emilienne 6-25-75:24
Emily 12-15-76:22
Emitai 7-12-72:28
Emma 2-09-32:15
Emma Mae 12-29-76:14
Emmanuelle 7-31-74:18
Emmanuelle: The Joys of a Woman (See: Emmanuelle 2)
Emmanuelle 2 1-21-76:32
Emmenez-Moi Au Ritz 10-12-77:16
Emmerdeur, L' 9-12-73:36
Emmy of Stork's Nest 10-08-15:22
Emperor Chien Lung and the Beauty 4-02-80:26
Emperor and the Golem, The 1-12-55:6
Emperor Jones, The 9-26-33:15
Emperor Lee 2-21-68:6
Emperor Meiji and the Great Russo-Japanese War 1-29-58:6
Emperor of the North Pole, The 5-23-73:19
Emperor Waltz, The 5-05-48:8
Emperor's Candlesticks 6-30-37:21
Emperor's Nightingale 5-16-51:6
Empire de la Nuit, L' 1-16-63:20

Empire of the Ants 7-06-77:32
Empire of the Night, The (See: Empire de la Nuit, L')
Empire Strikes Back, The 5-14-80:14
Employee's Entrance 1-24-33:12
Empreinte des Geants, L' 4-23-80:19
Empress Dowager, The 4-02-75:16
Empressa Perdona un Momento de Locima, La 5-30-79:24
Empty Canvas, The 3-18-64:7
Empty Cradle 7-26-23:29
Empty Hands 8-20-24:22
Empty Holsters 10-20-37:27
Empty Saddles 2-03-37:15
Empty Star, The (See: Estrella Vacia, La)
En El Balcon Vacio 8-08-62:18
En Este Pueblo No Hay Ladrones 8-04-65:28
En la Ardiente Obscuriadad 9-02-59:6
En la Luz de Una Estrella 6-18-41:18
En Moremita Clara 6-28-44:16
En Och En 3-22-78:24
Enamorada 12-07-49:20
Encercles, Les 4-24-68:6
Enchanted April 3-13-35:15
Enchanted Barn, The 1-17-19:51
Enchanted Cottage, The 4-16-24:23
Enchanted Cottage, The 2-14-45:14
Enchanted Forest, The 9-19-45:12
Enchanted Forest, The 7-26-67:24
Enchanted Hill, The 1-20-26:41
Enchanted Island 6-15-27:17
Enchanted Island 11-05-58:6
Enchanted Mirror, The 7-22-59:6
Enchanted Valley, The 3-24-48:22
Enchanting Shadow, The (See: Chin Nu Yu Haru)
Enchantment 11-04-21:43
Enchantment 12-08-48:10
Enclos, L' 3-15-61:6
Encore 10-29-80:20
Encore 11-21-51:6
Encounter in Salzburg 10-28-64:7
Encrucijada, La 9-16-59:16
Encrucyada Para Una Monja (See: Nun at the Crossroads, A)
End, The 5-03-78:26
End of a Priest (See: Fararuv Konec)

End of August at the Hotel Ozone, The 7-05-67:24
End of St. Petersburg, The 4-25-28:28 and 6-06-28:12
End of Summer, The (See: Kohayagawake No Aki)
End of the Affair 3-02-55:8
End of the Game, The 3-21-19:53
End of the River 11-12-47:24
End of the Road, The 11-19-15:24
End of the Road 11-11-28:15
End of the Road 11-15-44:8
End of the Road 11-24-54:6
End of the Road 1-28-70:22
End of the Shadow, The 11-03-16:29
End of the Tour, The 2-09-17:25
End of the Trail, The 8-11-16:25
End of the Trail 11-04-36:19
End of the World, The (See: Fin du Monde, La)
End of the World in Our Usual Bed on a Night Full of Rain, The 2-01-78:40
End Play 12-24-75:16
Endless Summer, The 6-22-66:20
Endstation 7-03-35:15
Enemies of Children 12-20-23:26
Enemies of Progress 1-16-34:15
Enemies of the Law 7-14-31:17
Enemies of Women 4-05-23:35
Enemies of Youth 6-24-25:84
Enemy, The 1-11-28:16
Enemy Agent 4-24-40:16
Enemy Agents Meet Ellery Queen 8-26-52:18
Enemy Below, The 11-27-57:6
Enemy from Space 9-04-57:28
Enemy General, The 8-17-60:6
Enemy of the People, An 8-30-78:28
Enemy of Women 8-30-44:10
Enemy to the King, An 11-17-16:24
Enfance Nue, L' 9-04-68:6
Enfant dans la Foule, Un 6-02-76:30
Enfant de la Nuit, L' 11-22-78:22
Enfant de L'Amour, L' 9-10-30:29
Enfant du Miracle, L' 6-21-32:15
Enfant Sauvage, L' 2-18-70:21
Enfants de L'Amour, Les 12-09-53:6

• 122

Enfants de L'Oubli, Les 2-21-79:21
Enfants du Paradis, Les 2-26-47:11
Enfants du Placard, Les 5-18-77:21
Enfants du Soleil, Les 5-23-62:16
Enfants Terribles, Les 5-24-50:20
Enforcer, The 1-24-51:6
Enforcer, The 12-22-76:22
Engel Mit der Posaune, Der 11-24-48:14
Engel Mit Kleinen Fehlern 4-29-36:27
Engelchen 3-27-68:6
Engineer's Daughter (s) 6-21-32:14
Engineer's Romance, The 1-15-10:13
England Made Me 6-06-73:18
English Program 12-27-23:27
English Without Tears 8-16-44:16
Englishman and the Girl, The 2-26-10:15
Englishman's Home, An 10-18-39:20
Enigmatique Monsieur Parkes, L' 9-03-30:41 and 11-12-30:45
Enjeu de la Vie 9-19-56:22
Enjo 9-16-59:6
Enkel Melodi, En 9-04-74:28
Enlebement des Sabines, L' 1-03-62:6
Enlevez-Moi 11-15-32:52
Enlighten Thy Daughter 12-29-16:23
Enlighten Thy Daughter 2-20-34:25
Ennemi Public No. 1, L' 1-20-54:18
Ennemis, Les 2-21-62:6
Enough Rope (See: Meurtrier, Le)
Enrico Caruso, Leggenda di una Voce 11-21-51:18
Ensayo de un Crimen 11-07-56:6
Ensign Pulver 2-26-64:6
Enslaved, The 2-20-29:17
Ente Klingelt Um 1/2 7, Die 1-15-69:34
Entente Cordiale 5-17-39:14
Enter Arsene Lupin 11-15-44:8
Enter Laughing 8-02-67:7
Enter Madame 12-22-22:33
Enter Madame 1-15-35:63
Enter the Dragon 8-22-73:12
Enterprising Clerk, An 2-19-10:15

Eternal Retour, L' (See: Eternal Return, The)
Eternal Return, The 12-17-47:8
Eternal Sappho, The 5-12-16:19
Eternal Sea 4-06-55:6
Eternal Sin, The 3-23-17:21
Eternal Struggle 10-18-23:23
Eternal Temptress, The 12-14-17:45
Eternal Three 10-04-23:23
Eternal Woman 5-22-29:16
Eternally Yours 10-04-39:12
Etes Vous Fiancee a un Marin Grec ou a un Pilote de Ligne? 11-25-70:22
Ethel's Luncheon 9-11-09:13
Ethiopians, The 10-06-71:22
Etoile Disparait, Une 9-06-32:21 and 2-20-35:15
Etoile du Sud, L' 3-05-69:28
Etoile Sans Lumiere 4-24-46:8
Etoiles de Midi, Les 7-13-60:6
Etoiles Ne Meurent Jamais, Les 6-12-57:18
Etrange Desir de Monsieur Bard, L' 4-07-54:24
Etrange Destin 6-19-46:8
Etrange Madame X, L' 7-04-51:24
Etrange Monsieur Steve, L' 7-10-57:6
Etrange Monsieur Victor, L' 6-01-38:13
Etrangere, L' 2-18-31:35
Etrangere, L' 2-14-68:16
Etrangers, Les 7-16-69:28
Etrangleur, L' 3-17-71:18
Etre Libre 12-04-68:6
Etreinte, L' 5-20-70:15
Etrusco Uccidi Encore, L' (See: Dead Are Alive, The)
Ett Anstaendigt Liv 4-18-79:23
Eucharistic Congress 11-10-26:12
Eugen Heisst Wohlgeboren 9-18-68:26
Eugene Aram 7-16-15:19
Eugene Aram 4-16-24:27
Eugene Grandet 11-06-46:18
Eugenie--The Story of Her Journey into Perversion 8-12-70:15
Eugenio 11-19-80:21
Eunuch, The 5-10-72:48
Eureka Stockade 2-02-49:12
Europa di Notte 4-29-59:20
Europa's Letzte Pelikane (s) 6-02-31:14
Europe '51 9-24-52:6

European Nights (See: Europa di Notte)
Europeans, The 5-16-79:27
Euthanasia di un Amore 10-25-78:42
Eva 1-12-38:27
Eva 2-02-49:12
Eva 10-17-62:17
Eva a 5116 7-15-64:22
Eva and the Grasshopper 11-28-28:20
Eva Erbt das Paradies 10-17-51:6
Eva Peron Story, The 9-10-52:6
Evades, Les 7-13-55:20
Evadidos, Los 7-08-64:16
Evangeline 1-30-14:17
Evangeline 8-15-19:71 and 8-22-19:77
Evangeline 7-31-29:17
Eve and the Handyman 5-10-61:6
Eve Knew Her Apples 4-25-45:14
Eve of St. Mark, The 5-17-44:10
Eve Wants to Sleep Also 11-05-58:7 (Also see: Ewa Chce Spac)
Evel Knievel 7-07-71:20
Evelyn Prentice 11-13-34:15
Even as I. O. U. (s) 10-07-42:25
Even as You and I 4-06-17:22
Even Break, An 7-27-14:27
Even Dwarfs Started Small (See: Auch Zwerge Haben Klein Angefangen)
Even unto Death 2-06-15:23
Even Up (s) 1-19-27:18
Evenement le Plus Important Depuis Que L'Homme a Marche Sur la Lune, L' 10-17-73:14
Evening Clothes 3-23-27:15
Evening on the Don (s) 8-22-28:14
Evening with the Royal Ballet, An 11-11-64:6
Evenings for Sale 11-15-32:19
Evensong 9-25-34:13 and 11-20-34:15
Event, An (See: Dogadaj)
Events 6-03-70:17
Eventually but Not Now (s) 4-16-30:21
Ever in My Heart 10-17-33:19
Ever Since Eve 10-28-21:35
Ever Since Eve 4-03-34:27
Ever Since Eve 6-30-37:20
Ever Since Venus 11-01-44:10

Everest Symphony 7-21-71:16
Evergreen 5-08-34:14 and 1-15-35:13
Evergreen Playland (s) 2-04-42:8
Everlasting Glory, The 8-20-75:73
Everlasting Whisper, The 10-14-25:40
Every Bastard a King 7-31-68:6
Every Day Is a Holiday 7-06-66:6
Every Day's a Holiday 12-22-37:16
Every Day's a Holiday 12-02-64:6
Every Girl Should Be Married 11-10-48:15
Every Girl's Dream 9-07-17:34
Every Home Should Have One 3-11-70:26
Every Inch a Lady 9-10-75:20
Every Little Crook and Nanny 6-14-72:18
Every Man for Himself (See: Sauve Qui Peut la Vie)
Every Man for Himself and God Against All (See: Jeder Fur Sich und Gott Gegen Alle)
Every Night at Eight 8-07-35:21
Every Saturday Night 3-18-36:29
Every Sunday (s) 2-03-37:14
Every Which Way but Loose 12-20-78:30
Everybody Does It 8-31-49:8
Everybody Go Home 11-21-62:6
Everybody Sing 1-26-38:14
Everybody's Acting 11-10-26:12
Everybody's Baby 11-30-38:12
Everybody's Dancin' 4-12-50:22
Everybody's Doing It 1-12-38:15
Everybody's Girl 10-18-18:39
Everybody's Hobby 9-27-39:12
Everybody's Old Man 4-01-36:16
Everybody's Sweetheart 10-08-20:41
Everyman's Law 9-14-38:15
Everyman's Price 10-14-21:42
Everyman's Wife 8-26-25:58
Everything but the Truth 11-07-56:6
Everything for Sale 10-14-21:43
Everything Happens at Night 12-30-39:47
Everything Happens to Me (s) 10-01-30:19
Everything I Have Is Yours 9-24-52:6
Everything Is Rhythm 8-14-40:14
Everything Is Thunder 8-05-36:17

and 11-25-36:14
Everything You Always Wanted to Know About Sex but Were Afraid to Ask 8-09-72:20
Everything's Ducky 11-08-61:6
Everything's on Ice 9-06-39:14
Everything's Rosie 5-27-31:56
Everywoman 12-19-19:45
Everywoman's Husband 7-12-18:35
Eve's Daughter 3-01-18:41
Eve's Fall 3-05-30:21
Eve's Leaves 6-30-26:13
Eve's Lover 7-29-25:34
Eve's Secret 6-10-25:47
Evictors, The 4-18-79:22
Evidence 9-10-15:21
Evidence 1-18-18:42
Evidence 6-16-22:43 and 6-23-22:35
Evidence 10-09-29:46
Evig a Lankar 4-02-47:16
Evil, The 3-29-78:28
Evil of Frankenstein, The 4-22-64:6
Evil Eye, The 3-19-20:56
Evil Thereof, The 6-09-16:23
Evil Women Do, The 9-22-16:40
Evils of Betting, The 1-14-11:18
Evolution (s) 4-30-30:17
Evolution of Dance (s) 2-19-30:21
Evolution of Snuff, The 3-30-77:18
Evordulo 2-03-77:31
Evridkiki B. A. 2037 11-05-75:19
Ewa Chce Spac 8-27-58:6 (Also see: Eve Wants to Sleep Also)
Ewige Maske, Die 4-01-36:17
Ex-Bad Boy 9-29-31:22
Ex-Champ 5-17-39:12
Ex-Convict, The 10-10-14:25
Ex-Flame 1-28-31:15
Ex-Lady 5-16-33:21
Ex-Mrs. Bradford, The 6-03-36:15
Ex und Hopp 3-16-77:24
Exalted Flapper 8-14-29:44
Examination Day at School 10-08-10:12
Excess Baggage 9-26-28:14
Exchange of Wives 10-07-25:44
Exciters 6-07-23:24
Exciting Honeymoon, An 1-19-07:15 and 12-31-30:18
Exclusive 7-21-37:13
Exclusive Rights 1-12-27:18

Exclusive Story 1-22-36:14
Excuse Me 1-28-25:34
Excuse My Dust 3-26-20:51
Excuse My Dust 5-23-51:6
Excuse My Love (s) 6-19-35:21
Excuse the Pardon (s) 12-03-30: 15
Executioner, The (See: Verdugo, El)
Executioner, The 5-06-70:26
Executioners, The 2-01-61:6
Executioners from Shaolin 3-09-77:24
Executive Action 11-07-73:19
Executive Suite 2-24-54:6
Exhibition 7-09-75:25
Exhibition 2 11-10-76:22
Exile 9-21-17:43
Exile, The 5-27-31:57
Exile, The 10-15-47:10
Exile Express 8-23-39:20
Exiled 4-16-15:19
Exiled to Shanghai 12-15-37:17
Exiles, The 12-06-23:26
Exiles, The 8-30-61:6
Exit ... Nur Keine Panik 8-20-80:21
Exit Smiling 11-10-26:14
Exit Sunset Boulevard 3-12-80:26
Exit the Vamp 1-27-22:39
Exodus 12-14-60:6
Exorcist, The 12-26-73:12
Exorcist II: The Heretic 6-22-77: 16
Exorcistos Stin Kentriki Leoforo 11-14-79:22
Exotic Mexico (s) 6-17-42:20
Expensive Husbands 1-12-38:15
Expensive Kisses (s) 1-21-31:17
Expensive Women 11-17-31:26
Experience 8-12-21:35
Experiment, The 2-21-73:24
Experiment Alcatraz 11-22-50:8
Experiment in Terror 3-21-62:6
Experiment Perilous 12-13-44:8
Experimental Marriage 3-28-19: 92
Expert, The 3-01-32:20
Expert Glass Blowers 10-16-09: 12
Exploits of a Cowboy 12-18-09: 15
Explorer, The 9-24-15:21
Explorer Peary at Home 10-09-09:13
Explorers of the World 12-22-31:19
Explosia 6-28-78:28

Explosion 12-24-69:20
Explosion, L' 8-11-71:16
Explosive Generation, The 9-13-61:6
Exploszia 6-28-78:28
Expose Me, Lovely 3-03-76:21
Exposed 9-27-32:21
Exposed 11-23-38:14
Exposed 9-17-47:16
Express 13 8-11-31:34
Expresso Bongo 12-02-59:6
Expropiacion 7-14-76:21
Exquisite Sinner, The 4-28-26:49
Exquisite Thief, The 4-04-19:67
Extase 4-11-33:20 (Also see: Ecstasy)
Exterieur Nuit 8-13-80:26
Exterminating Angel, The (See: Angel Exterminador, El)
Exterminator, The 9-17-80:20
Extortion 5-04-38:15
Extra, El 10-24-62:20
Extra Day, The 4-04-56:16
Extra, Extra (s) 4-12-32:14
Extra Girl, The 1-24-24:26
Extraconjugale 2-24-65:6
Extraordinary Seaman, The 1-22-69:6
Extras, The 12-27-78:14
Extravagance 8-27-15:20
Extravagance 11-10-16:29
Extravagance 4-04-19:65
Extravagance 12-10-30:26
Extravagnte Mission, The 10-24-45:33
Extreme Close-Up 6-13-73:16
Eye for an Eye, An 3-05-10:13
Eye for an Eye, An 11-22-18:44
Eye for an Eye, An (See: Oeil Pour Oeil)
Eye for an Eye, An 5-25-66:6
Eye of a God, The 3-28-13:14
Eye of God, The 5-26-16:21
Eye of the Cat 6-11-69:6
Eye of the Devil 9-13-67:6
Eye of the Needle, The 6-23-65: 26
Eyeball 11-01-78:40
Eyes Have It, The (s) 11-10-31: 14
Eyes in the Night 9-09-42:14
Eyes of Envy 8-31-17:31
Eyes of Julia Deep, The 8-09-18:33
Eyes of Laura Mars 8-02-78:14
Eyes of Mystery, The 1-24-18: 41
Eyes of Texas 7-21-48:10

Fagyongyok 8-22-79:20
Fah Larng Fon 8-02-78:14
Faham, El 5-16-73:18
Fahrenheit 451 9-14-66:6
Fahrt Ins Abenteuer, Die 6-16-66:19
Fai Lui Ching Chuen 6-11-69:42
Faible Femme, Une 4-04-33:38
Faibles Femmes 3-11-59:22
Fail Safe 9-16-64:6
Faille, La 6-11-75:18
Faint Heart and Fair Lady 11-02-17:50
Fair and Square Ways (s) 6-16-31:21
Fair and Warmer 11-28-19:58
Fair Barbarian, The 12-21-17:44
Fair Cheat 11-15-23:33
Fair Co-Ed, The 10-26-27:18
Fair Days (s) 8-21-29:18
Fair Deceiver, The (s) 3-26-30:25
Fair Enough 12-20-18:36
Fair Exchange, A 9-25-09:12
Fair Lady 3-24-22:41
Fair People 9-03-30:41 (Also see: Vom Rummelplatz, Die)
Fair Play 7-15-25:35
Fair Pretender, The 5-31-18:29
Fair Warning 2-11-31:42
Fair Warning 3-24-37:17
Fair Week 6-04-24:26
Fair Wind to Java 4-29-53:6
Fairbanks and Foul (s) 12-11-29:35
Faites Sauter la Banque 4-01-64:23
Faith 2-07-19:59
Faith 3-05-20:62
Faith Endurin' 3-22-18:52
Faith Healer, The 3-18-21:34
Faith, Hope and Witchcraft 7-27-60:6
Faith of a Child, The 6-25-15:21
Faith of the Strong 10-03-19:57
Faithful City 4-02-52:6
Faithful Heart 9-01-22:42
Faithful Heart 8-22-33:22
Faithful in My Fashion 6-12-46:6
Faithful until Death 6-12-14:22
Faithful Wives 2-23-27:17
Faithless 11-22-32:17
Faithless Lover 3-14-28:28
Faits Divers a Paris 8-09-50:9
Faja Lobbi 7-06-60:6
Fake, The 10-12-27:24
Fake, The 10-28-53:6

Fake, The 6-24-53:22
Faking of a President 1974 5-19-76:19
Falak 1-31-68:22
Falcon and the Co-eds, The 11-10-43:35
Falcon in Danger, The 7-14-43:18
Falcon in Hollywood, The 12-13-44:8
Falcon in Mexico, The 7-26-44:10 and 8-09-44:12
Falcon in San Francisco, The 7-25-45:20
Falcon Out West, The 3-08-44:14
Falcon Strikes Back, The 3-17-43:23
Falcon Takes Over, The 5-06-42:27
Falcon's Adventure, The 12-11-46:8
Falcon's Alibi, The 4-17-46:16
Falcon's Brother, The 9-30-42:8
Fall, The 10-29-69:30
Fall, Der 5-03-72:22
Fall des General-Stabs-Oberst Redl, Der 3-18-31:34 (Also see: Fall des Oberst Redl, Der)
Fall des Oberst Redl, Der 8-30-32:21 (Also see: Fall des General-Stabs-Oberst Redl, Der)
Fall Guy, The 5-28-30:35
Fall In 5-19-43:8
Fall of a Nation, The 6-09-16:23
Fall of a Saint 9-24-20:42
Fall of an Empress 4-23-24:20
Fall of Babylon, The 4-02-10:17
Fall of Babylon, The 7-25-19:45 (Also see: Intolerance)
Fall of Berlin, The 9-12-45:16 and 6-18-52:20
Fall of Constantinople, The 1-30-15:24
Fall of Eve, The 6-19-29:30
Fall of the House of Usher 5-21-52:6
Fall of the Roman Empire, The 3-25-64:6
Fall of the Romanoffs, The 9-14-17:35
Fall Roberts, Der 5-23-33:19
Fallen Arches (s) 1-17-33:14
Fallen Angel 10-24-45:12
Fallen Idol, The 5-22-14:23
Fallen Idol, The 5-23-19:57

Fangschuss, Der 8-25-76:22
Fanny 1-21-48:20
Fanny 6-21-61:6
Fanny by Gaslight 6-07-44:19
Fanny Elssler 12-08-37:17
Fanny Foley Herself 10-27-31:19
Fanny Hawthorn 11-13-29:59
Fanny Hill 10-08-69:15
Fanny Hill: Memoirs of a Woman
    of Pleasure 3-17-65:6
Fanny Rice (s) 7-18-28:15
Fan's Notes, A 5-31-72:6
Fanstrecht der Freiheit 5-28-75:
    19
Fantabulous Inc. 10-30-68:28
Fantasia 11-13-40:16
Fantasia Chez les Ploucs 2-10-
    71:17
Fantasies Behind the Pearly Cur-
    tain 11-26-75:20
Fantasm 8-04-76:22
Fantasm Comes Again 5-10-79:
    23
Fantasma de la Opereta, El 2-
    22-61:7
Fantasmas en Buenos Aires 8-12-
    42:20
Fantasmi a Roma 8-09-61:16
Fantasterne 12-20-67:15
Fantastic Invasion of Planet Earth
    (See: Bubble, The)
Fantastic Night 10-12-49:20
Fantastic Planet (See: Planete
    Sauvage, La)
Fantastic Plastic Machine, The
    4-02-69:28
Fantastic Voyage 7-27-66:6
Fantastica 5-14-80:14
Fantastico Mundo del Dr. Coppelius,
    El (See: Dr. Cyclops)
Fanthom 7-26-67:6
Fantine 10-02-09:13
Fantiques, Les 3-19-58:18
Fantomas 3-27-14:20 (Also see:
    False Magistrate, The)
Fantomas 3-20-34:16
Fantomas 12-02-64:6
Fantomas Contre Scotland Yard
    4-12-67:19
Fantomas Se Dechaine 1-19-66:6
Fantome de la Liberte, Le 8-28-
    74:20
Fantozzi 6-18-75:28
Fantozzi Contro Tutti 12-17-80:
    17
Far Country, The 1-26-55:6
Far Cry, The 4-07-26:38
Far East Command (s) 2-11-42:21

Far from Dallas 12-20-72:18
Far from Moscow 7-04-51:24
Far from the Madding Crowd 6-
    30-16:21
Far from the Madding Crowd 9-
    27-67:6
Far from Vietnam 10-04-67:12
Far Frontier, The 1-19-49:10
Far Horizons 5-25-55:6
Far Jag Lana Din Fru? 7-15-59:
    12
Far Jag Lov, Magistern! 3-24-
    48:22
Far Out, Star Route 12-08-71:16
Far Shore, The 8-18-76:22
Far Til Fire I Hoejt Humoer 8-
    25-71:23
Far-West, Le 5-30-73:12
Fararuv Konec 5-21-69:6
Farbe des Himmels, Die 6-13-79:
    14
Farceur, Le 8-10-60:16
Fare Play (s) 11-01-32:12
Farewell 9-24-30:30
Farewell Again 5-19-37:22
Farewell, Doves! 8-15-62:6
Farewell, My Beautiful Naples
    10-08-47:18
Farewell, My Lovely 8-13-75:16
Farewell, Scarlett 2-04-76:24
Farewell to Arms, A 12-13-32:
    14
Farewell to Arms, A 12-25-57:6
Farewell to Yesterday 9-13-50:6
Fargo Express 3-07-33:54
Fargo Kid 2-12-41:14
Farlig Kys 1-10-73:18
Farlig Sommer 4-23-69:6
Farmer, The 3-02-77:24
Farmer in the Dell, The 3-11-
    36:15
Farmer Takes a Wife 4-22-53:6
Farmer's Daughter, The 11-14-
    28:30
Farmer's Daughter, The 2-14-
    40:18
Farmer's Daughter, The 2-29-
    47:6
Farmer's Treasure 9-25-09:20
Farmer's Wife, The 3-21-28:19
    and 1-22-30:30
Farmer's Wife, The 2-19-41:18
Farming in a Flat 10-30-09:11
Faro da Padre, Le 7-31-74:18
Faro Nell (s) 10-02-29:19
Faroan 5-25-66:7
Farodokument 1979 11-05-80:22
    (Also see: Faaroedokument)

Fatty and Mabel Adrift 2-04-16: 24

Fatty and the Broadway Stars 12-10-15:21

Fatty Finn 7-23-80:24

Faubourg Montmartre 10-13-31: 15

Faust 11-17-26:16 and 12-08-26: 16

Faust (Act 1) (s) 10-09-29:23

Faust 11-23-60:6

Faust 7-15-64:6

Faust and the Devil 4-26-50:8

Faust in der Tasche, Die 5-23-79:25

Faust XX 8-03-66:7

Faustina 5-22-57:20

Faustina 11-20-68:38

Faustrecht der Freiheit 5-28-75: 19

Faut Aller Parmi le Monde Pour le Savoir 6-09-71:22

Faut-il les Marier? 7-19-32:25

Faut Pas Prendre les Enfants du Bon Dieu Pour des Canards Sauvages 9-25-68:30

Faut Vivre Dangereusement, Il 9-10-75:20

Faute de L'Abbe Mouret, La 11-11-70:27

Fautine et le Bel Ete 1-19-72:6

Fauve Est Lache, Le 3-11-59:6

Faux-Cul, Le 10-29-75:16

Faux Pas de Deux 10-2-76:39

Favor to a Friend, A 8-15-19:71

Favorite Fool, A 10-08-15:22

Favorite of Schoenbrunn, The 12-11-29:35

Fazil 6-06-28:13

Fear 9-26-28:15

Fear 4-03-46:12

Fear (See: La Paura)

Fear and Desire 4-01-53:6

Fear Fighter, The 9-30-25:43

Fear in the Night 2-19-47:9

Fear Is the Key 1-17-73:20

Fear Market 1-09-20:52

Fear No Evil 4-06-49:8

Fear Not 12-07-17:49

Fear of Fear 10-20-76:39

Fear of Power 7-09-58:6

Fear Strikes Out 2-06-57:6

Fear Woman, The 7-11-19:61

Fearless Fagan 7-09-52:6

Fearless Lover 7-15-25:35

Fearless Rider, The 2-08-28:24

Fearless Vampire Killers (or, Pardon Me, but Your Teeth

Are in My Neck), The 11-15-67:6

Fearmakers, The 9-24-58:6

Feast of Friends 10-08-69:30

Feast of Life, The 4-28-16:29

Feather, The 12-11-29:39

Feather in Her Hat 10-30-35:14

Feathertop 4-14-16:25

Fecdundity 7-17-29:57

Fedelta 9-08-65:6

Federal Agent 4-15-36:23

Federal Agent at Large 3-22-50:6

Federal Bullets 10-27-37:19

Federal Fugitives 5-07-41:20

Federal Man 6-28-50:6

Federal Man-Hunt 1-11-39:13

Federale, Il (See: Fascist, The)

Fedora 3-12-15:23

Fedora 8-09-18:34

Fedora 2-06-46:12

Fedora 8-23-78:30

Feedback 3-28-79:20

Feel My Pulse 3-07-28:28

Feeling of Hostility, The 10-06-48:11

Feelings 8-17-77:20

Feerie du Jazz 1-07-31:36 (Also see: King of Jazz)

Feet First 11-05-30:23

Feet of Clay 9-24-24:26

Fegefeuer 4-21-71:22 and 10-27-71:18

Fehischuss 2-16-77:26

Fejloves 2-26-69:6

Fekete Gyemantok 5-13-38:13

Fekete Gyemantok 3-23-77:24

Feldherrnhuegel, Der 11-04-53:6

Feldobott Ko 2-26-69:6

Felices 60, Los (See: Happy Sixties, The)

Felicidad 7-24-57:7 and 9-30-59:6

Felicite 5-23-79:25

Feline Fighter, The (s) 3-26-30: 25

Felines, Les 3-17-76:22

Felins, Les 6-24-64:20

Felix and Otilia 9-06-72:16

Felix Ferdinand (s) 5-21-30:19 and 6-11-30:18

Felix O'Day 9-17-20:35

Fellini Satyricon (See: Satyricon)

Fellini's Casanova (See: Casanova)

Fellini's Roma (See: Roma)

Felmegyek a Ministerhez 6-27-62:6

Female, The 9-03-24:25

Female 11-07-33:16

Female, The (See: Femme et le Pantin)

Fever in the Blood, A 1-11-61:6
Few Days in the Life of I. I.
    Oblomov, A 5-28-80:43
ffolkes 4-23-80:18
Fiaca, La 4-02-69:6
Fiacre N.13, Il 7-07-48:6
Fiammata, La 2-18-53:18
Fiancée du Pirate, La 9-17-69:
    22
Fiat Volutans Dei 7-15-36:55
Fibbers, The 10-26-17:32
Fickle Finger of Fate, The 6-14-
    67:6
Fickle Women 8-20-20:34
Fico d'India 11-19-80:20
Fidanzati, I 5-29-63:6
Fiddle and the Fan 9-08-09:13
Fiddler on the Roof 11-03-71:16
Fiddlin' Buckaroo 1-09-34:16
Fiddling Around (s) 7-09-30:19
Fidele Bauer, Der 10-17-51:20
Fidelio 7-29-70:20 and 4-14-71:
    23
Fidlovacka 7-07-31:25
Fiebre 10-13-76:22
Fields and Johnston (s) 10-17-28:
    16
Fields of Honor 1-18-18:42
Fiend Who Walked the West 8-06-
    58:7
Field Without a Face 5-28-58:6
Fiendish Plot of Dr. Fu Manchu,
    The 8-13-80:23
Fiercest Heart, The 3-29-61:6
Fiesta 12-31-41:8
Fiesta 6-18-47:8
Fiesta, La (s) 6-20-28:14
Fiesta de Santa Barbara, La 4-
    22-36:14
Fietsen Naar de Maan 2-27-63:7
Fievre Monte a El Pao, La 2-03-
    60:6
Fifi 6-20-33:11
Fifi la Plume 6-02-65:22
Fifteen Maiden Lane 10-14-36:15
Fifteen Wives 9-25-34:14
15 Yok Yok 2-15-78:19
Fifth Avenue Girl 8-23-39:14
Fifth Avenue Models 5-06-25:47
Fifth Floor, The 3-12-80:27
Fifth Musketeer, The 4-11-79:21
Fifth Rider Is Fear, The (See: A
    Paty Jezdec de Strach)
Fifty Candles 1-06-22:43
Fifty Fathoms Deep 9-22-31:26
Fifty-Fifty Girl, The 5-16-28:13
55 Days at Peking 5-01-63:6
50 Miles from Broadway (s)

3-12-30:21
50 Million Frenchmen 4-01-31:16
50 Million Husbands (s) 5-07-30:20
50 Roads to Town 6-09-37:15
52nd Street 10-06-37:12
$50,000 Climax Show, The 6-04-
    75:8
50 Years Before Your Eyes 6-
    21-50:8
Fig Leaves 7-07-26:16
Figaro 11-27-29:31
Figaro e la Sua Grande Giornata
    11-07-33:17
Fight, The 1-23-15:25
Fight, The (s) 8-20-30:14
Fight, The (s) 3-27-71:18
Fight for a Million, A 4-16-15:
    19
Fight for Freedom 2-03-43:14
Fight for Life, A 5-15-14:23
Fight for Life, The (s) 8-25-26:
    23
Fight for Life, The 3-06-40:18
Fight for Love, A 2-22-08:11
Fight for Love, A 3-21-19:55
Fight for Matterhorn 7-31-29:23
Fight for Peace, The 5-18-38:13
Fight for Your Lady 10-20-37:12
Fight for Your Life 12-21-77:30
Fight of the Age 5-20-21:41
Fight Pictures 5-17-23:22
Fight Pictures 6-19-35:21
Fight to the Finish, A 7-07-37:25
Fighter, The 8-19-21:35
Fighter, The 5-07-52:6
Fighter Attack 11-25-53:24
Fighter Squadron 11-24-48:6
Fighters, The 1-23-74:14
Fighters' Paradise 9-24-24:26
Fightin' Fish (s) 9-04-35:14
Fightin' Mad 11-25-21:43
Fightin' Through 2-21-19:67
Fightin' Strain 9-27-23:30
Fighting American 6-04-24:26
Fighting Back 8-04-48:11
Fighting Bill Fargo 5-20-42:8
Fighting Blade 10-18-23:23
Fighting Blood 10-18-23:23
Fighting Bob 6-04-15:18
Fighting Boob, The 6-23-26:18
Fighting Caravans 1-28-31:15
Fighting Champ 3-14-33:15
Fighting Chance 7-23-20:33
Fighting Coast Guard 5-02-51:6
Fighting Code, The 1-16-34:54
Fighting Coward 3-19-24:26
Fighting Cub, The 7-29-25:34
Fighting Demon 7-29-25:36

137 •

Fire Down Below 5-29-57:6
Fire Flingers, The 3-28-19:93
Fire in the Middle 5-31-78:22
Fire in the Straw 7-07-43:8 (Also
    see: Feu de Paille, Le)
Fire over Africa 10-06-54:6
Fire over England 1-27-37:12
    and 3-10-37:14
Fire Patrol, The 5-21-24:24
Fire Sale 6-08-77:30
Fire Within, The (See: Feu Follet,
    Le)
Fire Worshippers (s) 9-24-30:23
Fireball 8-16-50:11
Fireball 500 6-15-66:6
Firebird, The 11-20-34:17
Firebrand Johnson 9-10-30:29
Firecreek 1-24-68:6
Firefly, The 7-28-37:16
Firefly of France, The 6-14-18:
    31
Firefly of Tough Luck, The 10-
    19-17:31
Firehouse Honeymoon (s) 11-22-
    32:16
Fireman, The 6-16-16:24
Fireman, The (s) 6-02-31:14
Fireman, Save My Child 8-31-
    27:24
Fireman, Save My Child 2-23-
    32:19
Fireman, Save My Child 4-28-
    54:6
Firemen's Ball (See: Hori, Ma
    Panenko)
Firepower 4-11-79:20
Fires of Conscience 9-29-16:27
Fires of Faith 5-09-19:52
Fires of Fate 8-09-23:41
Fires of Fate 4-04-33:15
Fires of Innocence 9-29-22:42
Fires of Youth, The 8-30-18:39
Fireworks Woman 8-06-75:16
Firing Line, The 7-11-79:61
Fire of Girdlestone, The 9-29-
    16:27
Firm Man, The 4-23-75:18
Firma Heiratet, Die 7-12-32:25
Firmaskovturen 3-01-78:27
Firpo-Brennan Fight (s) 3-29-23:
    36
First a Girl 11-20-35:39 and
    1-08-36:12
First Aid 10-13-31:29
First Aid (s) 2-03-43:14
First Airship Crossing the English
    Channel 9-11-09:12
First Auto, The 6-29-27:18

First Baby, The 5-27-36:14
First Barn, The 2-04-21:21
First Circle, The 1-17-73:20
First Comes Courage 9-08-43:16
First Deadly Sin 10-22-80:24
First Degree 2-01-23:42
First Family 12-31-80:20
First Film Concert 11-15-39:20
First Forty Days 10-04-50:22
First Error Step, The 7-25-79:
    24
First Fries, The (See: Uzavreli
    Grad)
First Front, The 11-16-49:16
First Gentleman, The 3-31-48:
    15
First Gray Hair, The 10-29-10:
    14
First Great Train Robbery, The
    1-17-79:21
First 100 Years, The 3-16-38:15
First in War (s) 8-30-32:14
First Kiss, The 8-22-28:16
First Lady 9-01-37:22
First Law, The 7-26-18:32
First Law of Nature, The 4-23-
    15:18
First Legion, The 4-11-51:6
First Love 1-06-22:42
First Love 11-08-39:14
First Love 7-22-70:16
First Love 11-02-77:17
First Mama Nicht Fabelhaft? 4-
    15-59:6
First Man into Space 2-18-59:6
First Mein Mann Nicht Fabelhaft?
    12-09-36:13
First Men in the Moon 8-05-64:6
First Night 2-09-27:16
First Nudie Musical, The 3-10-
    76:22
First of the Few, The 9-02-42:
    18
First Offenders 5-17-39:14
First Opera Film Festival 6-02-
    48:14
First Position 11-08-72:18
First Seven Years (s) 6-11-30:18
First Spaceship on Venus 12-19-
    62:7
First Start 2-18-53:18
First Step, The 12-17-75:23
First Swallow, The (s) 3-25-42:
    18
First Taste of Love (See: Nymph-
    ettes, Les)
First Texan, The 6-13-56:6
First Time, The 1-30-52:6

First Time, The 4-02-69:6
First Time Round 8-16-72:28
First to Fight, The 8-18-31:17
First to Fight 1-25-67:21
First Traveling Saleslady, The
  8-15-56:6
First Woman 4-21-22:41
First World War, The 11-13-34:
  15
First Yank into Tokyo 9-05-45:
  15
First Year, The 3-10-26:40
Fischio Al Naso, Il 7-12-67:24
Fish Feathers (s) 1-10-33:15
Fish, Fowl and Fun (s) 7-30-30:
  16
Fish from Hell (s) 5-01-35:17
Fish Hawk 9-05-79:22
Fish-Hooky (s) 1-17-33:14
Fish That Saved Pittsburgh, The
  11-07-79:18
Fisherman, The 9-11-09:12
Fisherman's Bride 11-27-09:13
Fisherman's Granddaughter, The
  2-26-10:15
Fisherman's Holiday (s) 9-05-33:
  19
Fisherman's Luck (s) 6-16-31:21
Fisherman's Luck (s) 3-01-32:20
Fisherman's Paradise (s) 4-29-
  31:12
Fisherman's Wharf 2-08-39:17
Fishing Boats on the Ocean 8-08-
  08:11
Fishing for Trouble (s) 9-04-34:
  19
Fishing Smack, The 11-12-10:16
F. I. S. T. 4-19-78:26
Fist of Fear Touch of Death 9-
  24-80:18
Fist of Fury 11-01-72:20 (Also
  see: Fists of Fury)
Fistful of Dollars, A (See: Per un
  Pugno Di Dollari)
Fists in the Pocket (See: Pugni In
  Tasca, I)
Fists of Fury 6-27-73:34 (Also
  see: Fist of Fury)
Fit for a King 9-01-37:29
Fit to Fight (s) 5-27-42:8
Fitzwilly 12-20-67:15
Five 4-25-51:6
Five Against the House 5-18-55:8
Five and Ten 7-14-31:22
Five Branded Women 4-06-60:6
Five Came Back 6-21-39:16
Five Card Stud 7-17-68:6
Five-Day Lover, The (See: Amant

de Cinq Jours, L')
Five Days from Home 4-19-78:
  26
Five Days to Live 1-13-22:42
Five Dollar Baby, The 6-30-22:
  33
Five Easy Pieces 9-16-70:15
Five Finger Exercise 4-18-62:6
Five Fingers 2-13-52:6
Five Fingers of Death 3-21-73:
  18
Five from Barska Street 3-16-
  55:6
Five Gates to Hell 9-23-59:6
Five Gents' Trick Book 12-29-
  65:6
Five Golden Hours 3-08-61:7
Five Graves to Cairo 5-05-43:8
Five Guns to Tombstone 3-08-
  61:6
Five Guns West 4-20-55:6
Five Little Peppers 9-06-39:14
Five Little Peppers at Home 3-
  06-40:16
Five Little Peppers in Trouble
  9-18-40:14
Five-Man Army 3-04-70:18
Five Miles to Midnight (See: Con-
  teau dans la Plaie, Le)
$5, 000, 000 Counterfeit Plot 8-14-
  14:21
Five Million Years to Earth 1-31-
  68:6
Five Minutes from the Station (s)
  3-11-31:14
Five Minutes to Twelve 1-29-10:
  13
Five of a Kind 10-12-38:15
Five on the Black Hand Side 10-
  24-73:16
Five out of a Million 11-18-59:6
Five Pennies, The 5-06-59:6
5% de Risque 7-30-80:26
5 + 5 4-02-80:26
Five Star Final 9-15-31:14
Five Steps to Danger 1-23-57:6
Five the Hard Way 4-16-69:30
$5, 000 an Hour 12-06-18:39
$5, 000 Reward 5-10-18:40
5, 000 Fingers of Dr. T., The
  6-17-53:6
Five Times Five (s) 7-26-39:27
Five Weeks in a Balloon 8-15-62:6
Five-Year Plan, The 6-02-31:31
Fixed Bayonets 11-21-51:6
Fixer, The 11-20-68:34
Fixer Dugan 5-10-39:14
Fizessen Nagysad 4-14-37:33

Fjanagan 4-07-76:32
Flaaden's Friske Fyre 9-22-65:6
Flag, The (s) 8-10-27:20 and
    11-09-27:25
Flag Lieutenant, The 7-06-27:20
Flag Lieutenant, The 11-08-32:
    17
Flag of Mercy (s) 2-25-42:8
Flagermusen 11-06-68:24
Flagrant Delit 4-01-31:17
Flame, The 1-14-48:10
Flame 2-19-75:22
Flame and the Arrow, The 6-21-
    50:8
Flame and the Fire 3-09-66:6
Flame and the Flesh 4-28-54:6
Flame in the Streets 6-28-61:6
Flame of Araby 11-21-51:6
Flame of the Barbary Coast 4-18-
    45:12
Flame of Calcutta 6-24-53:22
Flame of Love, The 11-05-30:30
Flame of New Orleans 4-30-41:16
Flame of Passion 11-05-15:22
Flame of Stamboul 2-28-51:13
Flame of the Argentine 7-21-26:
    15
Flame of the Desert 10-31-19:61
Flame of the Pacific (s) 5-09-33:
    14
Flame of the West 9-26-45:14
Flame of the Yukon 7-13-17:26
Flame of Youth 1-28-21:39
Flame of Youth 9-28-49:6
Flame of Zoroaster, The (s) 11-
    09-55:6
Flame Within, The 6-05-35:15
Flamenco 5-26-54:6
Flames 11-17-26:17
Flames 8-30-32:21
Flames of Chance 1-18-18:41
Flames of Desire 6-17-25:38
Flames of Johannis, The 4-14-
    16:25
Flames of Justice 5-01-14:21
Flames of Passion 12-15-22:41
Flames of the Flesh 2-13-20:44
Flaming Barriers 1-31-24:23
Flaming Feather 12-19-51:6
Flaming Forest 11-24-26:14
Flaming Forties 3-11-25:42
Flaming Frontier, The 4-07-26:
    36
Flaming Frontier 2-14-68:6
Flaming Fury 6-15-49:13
Flaming Gold 2-20-34:14
Flaming Hearts 3-01-23:32
Flaming Hour 12-15-22:42

Flaming Jungles (s) 9-08-31:15
Flaming Lead 11-15-39:20
Flaming Love 1-21-25:34
Flaming Omen, The 10-26-17:32
Flaming Star 12-21-60:6
Flaming Teen-Age, The 10-17-
    56:6
Flaming Waters 1-27-26:39
Flamingo Road 4-06-49:8
Flamme Empor 6-06-79:22
Flammende Herzen 3-29-78:26
Flammes Sur L'Adriatique 8-28-
    68:24
Flanagan 4-07-76:32
Flanders and Alcott Report on Sex
    Response, The 3-17-71:28
Flap 10-28-70:17
Flapper, The 5-21-20:34
Flareup 11-12-69:21
Flare-Up Sal 2-01-18:43
Flash, The 1-25-23:41
Flash Gordon (serial) 3-11-36:27
Flash Gordon 12-03-80:22
Flash Gordon's Trip to Mars
    (serial) 2-16-38:17 (Also see:
    Mars Attacks the World)
Flash of an Emerald, The 10-15-
    15:21
Flashback 6-04-69:38
Flashbacks 10-12-38:19
Flashing Blades (s) 2-25-42:8
Flashing Fangs 12-01-26:34
Flashing Guns 8-27-47:16
Flashlight, The 5-18-17:23
Flat Next Door, The 12-03-10:14
Flat Top 11-19-52:16
Flattery 12-31-24:26
Flavor of Green Tea over Rice,
    The 1-17-73:20
Flaxy Martin 1-19-49:10
Flea in Her Ear, A 10-23-68:24
Fledermaus, Die 1-19-32:29
Fledermaus, Die 11-24-37:17
Fledermaus, Die 3-17-48:8
Fledermaus, Die (See: Flagermusen)
Fleet's In, The 10-03-28:17
Fleet's In, The 1-21-42:8
Fleets of Strength (s) 4-15-42:18
Fleetwing 7-25-28:28
Fleisch 12-05-79:22
Flemish Farm, The 8-25-43:10
Flesh 12-13-32:14
Flesh 10-02-68:26
Flesh and Blood 3-21-51:7
Flesh and Fantasy 9-22-43:12
Flesh and Fury 3-12-52:16
Flesh and the Devil 1-12-27:14
Flesh and the Fiend 2-10-60:23

Flesh for Frankenstein 2-27-74:
18
Flesh Gordon 7-31-74:19
Flesh Is Weak, The 8-14-57:20
Flesh Will Surrender, The 11-
01-50:6
Fleshpot on 42nd Street 7-12-72:
24
Fleshy Devils (s) 11-30-27:23
Fleur Bleue 6-09-71:17
Fleur D'Oranger, La 11-08-32:
17
Fleur D'Oseille 10-25-67:6
Fleur de L'age ou les Adolescentes,
La 9-09-64:24
Fleurs du Miel, Les 3-17-76:23
Flic, Un 2-04-48:22
Flic, Un 11-15-72:24
Flic Ou Voyou 6-27-79:34
Flic Story 10-08-75:22
Flick 4-22-70:17
Flicka Och Hyacinter 2-03-71:26
Flickan Fran Fjallbyn 4-06-49:
22
Flickan Fran Tredje Raden 11-
16-49:29
Flickan I Frack 7-24-57:6
Flickorna 10-02-68:28
Flickorna I Smaland 10-22-47:13
Flickornas Alfred 9-18-35:32
Fliers 5-29-35:34
Flight 9-18-29:15
Flight 11-02-60:6
Flight, The 5-26-71:22
Flight Angels 5-15-40:16
Flight at Midnight 8-30-39:14
Flight Command 12-18-40:16
Flight Commander, The 10-12-
27:16 and 5-09-28:17
Flight from Ashiya 4-01-64:23
Flight from Destiny 1-01-41:14
Flight from Glory 8-11-37:19
Flight into Nowhere 5-04-38:15
Flight Lieutenant 9-05-42:27
Flight Nurse 11-04-53:6
Flight of Monsieur Valette, The
11-13-09:13
Flight of the Doves 3-31-71:6
Flight of the Duchess, The 3-10-
16:29
Flight of the Lost Balloon 11-01-
61:16
Flight of the Phoenix 12-15-65:
65:6
Flight of the White Heron 5-26-
54:6
Flight That Disappeared, The 9-
20-61:6

Flight to Fame 12-14-38:15
Flight to Hong Kong 10-03-56:6
Flight to Mars 11-07-51:18
Flight to Tangiers 10-14-53:6
Flight to the Last 12-28-38:13
Flim-Flam Man, The 7-12-67:6
Flinging Feet (s) 11-13-29:12
Flipper 5-01-63:6
Flipper's New Adventure 5-27-
64:24
Flirt, The 3-31-16:24
Flirt, The 1-05-23:44
Flirtation Walk 12-04-34:12
Flirting Widow, The 8-06-30:38
Flirting with Danger 3-06-35:21
Flirting with Death 9-28-17:40
Flirting with Fate 6-30-16:20
Flirting with Fate 12-14-38:15
Flirting with Love 9-03-24:25
Flirto-Maniac, The 2-05-10:16
Flirty Affliction, A 9-24-10:12
Flitterwochen 7-01-36:25
Flivvering 3-09-17:23
Floating College 12-12-28:28
Floating Mine, The 3-19-15:21
Floch 9-20-72:14
Floetenkonzert 1-07-31:36 (Also
see: Floetenkonzert Von
Sanssouci)
Floetenkonzert Von Sanssouci 10-
20-31:27 (Also see: Floeten-
konzert)
Flood, The 4-19-31:37
Flood Arena, The (See: Inundos,
Los)
Flood Tide 1-22-58:24
Floodgates 3-26-24:45
Floods of Fear 11-26-58:22
Floodtide 3-30-49:13
Floor Above, The 4-10-14:22
Floor Below, The 3-08-18:41
Floor Show 11-08-78:18
Floorwalker, The (s) 5-19-16:18
and 2-28-33:14
Flor de Durazno 12-12-45:12
Flor de Mayo 7-15-59:6
Flor de Santidad 4-18-73:32
Flor Del Mal (s) 6-13-28:12
Flor Sylvestre 1-24-45:10
Flora 4 Flush 10-31-14:27
Floradora Girl 6-04-30:25
Florence Brady (s) 11-28-28:15
Florence Moore (s) 6-20-28:14
Florence Nightingale 4-09-15:20
Florentine Choir (s) 5-23-28:21
Florentine Dagger, The 5-01-35:
17
Flores de Papel 3-15-78:18

Florian 4-03-40:14
Florida Enchantment, A 8-14-14:
21
Florida Special 6-03-36:15
Florrie le Vere and Lou Handman
(s) 10-24-28:24
Flottans Kavaljerer 4-13-49:20
Flower Drum Song 11-08-61:6
Flower Garden (s) 10-15-30:25
Flower Market, The 7-21-65:6
Flower of Faith, The 12-19-14:
25
Flower of Faith, The 9-22-16:40
Flower of No Man's Land, The 6-
23-16:19
Flower of the Night 10-21-25:34
Flower of the North 1-20-22:35
Flower of Youth 2-15-08:11
Flower Parade of Pasadena 1-29-
10:13
Flower Thief 6-04-69:6
Flowers and Trees (s) 9-06-32:15
Flowing Gold 3-12-24:26
Flowing Gold 8-28-40:16
Floyd Gibbons (s) 8-11-31:19
Flucht, Die 3-24-78:38 and 7-02-
80:20
Flucht Ins Schilf 3-25-53:24
Flucht Nach Berlin 3-15-61:7
Fluchtgefahr 8-27-75:14
Fluechtling Aus Chicago, Der 3-
18-36:29
Fluffy 4-07-65:30
Fluga Gor Ingen Sommar, En 11-
26-47:20
Flugten 5-02-73:6
Fly, The 7-16-58:6
Fly by Night 1-21-42:8
Fly Cop, The 9-21-17:42
Fly God, The 7-05-18:30
Fly Guy, The (s) 6-02-31:14 and
11-03-31:17
Fly Hi (s) 9-15-31:14
Fly in the Ointment, A 3-02-55:9
Fly-Away Baby 7-14-37:21
Flygniva 450 4-30-80:36
Flyin' Cowboy, The 5-16-28:29
Flying Blind 8-20-41:9
Flying Cadets 10-15-41:8
Flying Cadonas (s) 5-24-32:29
Flying Colors 9-14-17:35
Flying Deuces, The 10-11-39:13
Flying Devils 8-29-33:14
Flying Doctor, The 10-21-36:23
Flying Down to Rio 12-26-33:10
Flying Fever (s) 2-04-42:22
Flying Fists 8-27-24:25
Flying Fists 3-02-38:25

Flying Fleet 2-13-29:13
Flying Fontaines, The 12-23-59:6
Flying Fool 8-28-29:31
Flying Fool 10-20-31:27
Flying Fortress 7-15-42:9
Flying G-Men (serial) 3-22-39:
30
Flying Guillotine 3-19-75:36
Flying High 2-23-27:17
Flying High 12-15-31:14
Flying Hunters (s) 5-29-34:13
Flying Hoofs 3-04-25:38
Flying Horseman, The 9-22-26:
16
Flying Hostess 12-16-36:14
Flying Irishman, The 3-08-39:18
Flying Leathernecks 7-25-51:6
Flying Luck 3-21-28:26
Flying Mail, The 6-29-27:26
Flying Marine, The 8-07-29:208
Flying Matchmaker, The 11-01-
67:20
Flying Missile, The 12-27-50:6
Flying Pat 12-17-20:40
Flying Romeos 4-04-28:28
Flying Saucer 1-11-50:6
Flying Serpent, The 1-23-46:12
Flying Spikes (s) 8-09-32:17
Flying Squad 8-02-32:17
Flying Tigers 9-23-42:8
Flying Torpedo, The 3-17-16:32
Flying "U" Ranch, The 11-02-
27:25
Flying Wild 4-16-41:16
Flying with the Marines 6-18-18:
30
Foersterchristel, Die 3-04-31:22
and 4-29-31:50
Foersterchristel, Die 10-29-52:
24
Fog, The 7-26-23:28
Fog 1-09-34:16
Fog 11-24-65:6
Fog, The 1-16-80:31
Fog Bound 5-30-23:24
Fog Island 4-11-45:20
Fog over Frisco 6-12-34:19
Fogo Morto 7-14-76:24
Foiled 11-27-09:13
Foiled Again, or Souls Adrift (s)
5-31-32:14
Foiled by a Cigarette, or The
Stolen Plans of the Fortress
10-15-10:12
Foire aux Cancres, La 11-27-
63:6
Foire aux Chimeres, La 10-09-
46:14

Folie des Grandeurs, La 12-22-71:66
Folies Bergere 2-27-35:12 and 4-22-36:19
Folies-Bergere 3-06-57:6
Folies Bourgeoises 7-21-76:22
Folket I Simlangs-Dalen 6-16-48:20
Folks at Red Wolf Inn, The 11-22-72:14
Folks from Way Down East, The 4-24-14:21
Folle a Tuer 9-03-75:20
Folle di Toujane, La 5-01-74:18
Folle Nuit, La 5-03-32:15
Follies Girl, The 4-25-19:83
Follies Girl 8-25-43:10
Follow a Star 12-23-59:6
Follow Me 5-07-69:258
Follow Me, Boys! 10-12-66:6
Follow Me Quietly 7-13-49:16
Follow That Camel 12-20-67:15
Follow That Dream 3-28-62:6
Follow That Horse 7-20-60:6
Follow That Woman 8-22-45:20
Follow the Band 4-28-43:8
Follow the Boy 2-27-63:6
Follow the Boys 3-29-44:21
Follow the Fleet 2-26-36:15
Follow the Girl 8-03-17:24
Follow the Leader 12-10-30:26
Follow the Leader 6-07-44:19
Follow the Star 3-01-78:27
Follow the Sun 3-21-51:6
Follow the Swallow (s) 4-16-30:21
Follow Thru 9-17-30:30
Follow Your Heart 10-28-36:14
Following in Father's Footsteps 4-13-07:11
Following the Flag to France 6-28-18:30
Folly of Revenge, The 7-28-16:25
Folly to Be Wise 12-10-52:18
Fome de Amor 6-16-68:6
Fond de L'Air Est Rouge, Le 11-16-77:24
Foney Fables (s) 9-02-42:34
Fonissa, I 10-30-74:42
Fontamara 9-03-80:25
Food for Scandal 11-05-20:41
Food for Thought (s) 2-04-31:16
Food Gamblers, The 8-10-17:23
Food of the Gods 6-09-76:23
Food--Weapon of Conquest (s) 5-27-42:8

Fool, The 4-15-25:36
Fool About Women, A (s) 1-10-33:15
Fool and His Money, A 4-16-20:44
Fool and His Money, A 7-15-25:35
Fool and His Money, A (s) 11-30-27:23
Fool Killer, The 4-28-65:6
Fool of Love 9-18-29:25
Fool There Was, A 3-12-15:24
Fool There Was, A 7-21-22:33
Foolin' Around 4-23-80:18
Foolish Age, The 11-11-21:35
Foolish Follies (s) 5-07-30:20
Foolish 40s (s) 8-18-31:30
Foolish Happiness 5-08-29:24
Foolish Husbands 10-20-48:16
Foolish Maiden 1-16-29:25
Foolish Matrons 8-26-21:36
Foolish Parents 11-08-23:28
Foolish Virgin 12-10-24:35
Foolish Wives 1-20-22:35
Fools 12-23-70:6
Fools and Riches 5-30-23:32
Fools and Their Money 6-20-19:52
Fool's Awakening 3-19-24:26
Fools First 8-04-22:35
Fools for Scandal 3-30-38:15
Fools for Luck 9-28-17:38
Fools for Luck 6-13-28:13
Fool's Gold 5-09-19:49
Fool's Gold 10-09-46:17
Fool's Highway 4-02-24:23
Fools in the Dark 8-20-24:22
Fools of Desire 3-26-41:18
Fools of Fashion 10-20-26:62
Fools of Fate 10-16-09:12
Fools of Fortune 12-22-22:35
Fool's Parade 6-23-71:20
Fool's Paradise 12-16-21:35
Fool's Revenge, The 2-18-16:23
Fools Rush In 5-15-49:8
Foot Notes (s) 4-02-30:18
Football Daft 7-07-22:60
Football Footwork (s) 11-08-32:16
Footfalls 9-16-21:35
Foothills of Savoy, The 3-26-10:15
Footlight Fever 3-26-41:16
Footlight Glamour 11-10-43:34
Footlight Parade 10-10-33:17
Footlight Ranger 4-05-23:36
Footlight Serenade 7-08-42:8
Footlight Varieties 3-28-51:16

Footlights 10-07-21:44
Footlights (s) 12-29-31:166
Footlights and Fools 11-13-29:
12
Footlights and Shadows 2-13-20:
44
Footlights of Fate, The 8-25-16:
25
Footlights or the Farm 10-01-10:
18
Footloose Heiress 10-13-37:16
Footloose Widows 6-23-26:14
Footsteps in the Dark 3-05-41:16
Footsteps in the Fog 8-24-55:6
Footsteps in the Night 5-16-33:
21
Footsteps in the Night 7-24-57:7
Footsteps of Aztecs 6-16-26:19
For a Few Dollars More (See:
Per Qualche Dollaro In Piu)
For a Woman's Fair Name 3-10-
16:25
For a Woman's Honor 10-03-19:
56 and 11-14-19:59
For Alimony Only 9-22-26:14
For Another Woman 6-24-25:84
For Art's Sake (s) 9-24-30:23
For Att Inte Tala Om Alla Dessa
Kvinnor 7-01-64:22
For Beauty's Sake 6-25-41:16
For Better, For Worse 5-02-19:
60
For Better For Worse 10-13-54:6
For Big Stakes 6-30-22:33
For France 9-28-17:40
For Heaven's Sake 4-07-26:36
For Heaven's Sake 12-06-50:15
For Hennes Skull (See: For Her
Sake)
For Her Country's Sake 10-15-
10:12
For Her Sake 8-27-30:45 and
11-12-30:32
For Home and Country 11-28-14:
24
For Husbands Only 9-06-18:38
For King and Country 11-07-14:
23
For King or Kaiser 2-06-15:23
For Ladies Only 10-26-27:25
For Love of Ivy 7-10-68:6
For Love or Money (s) 7-16-30:
15
For Love or Money 7-31-34:27
For Love or Money 6-21-39:16
For Love or Money 6-26-63:6
For Me and My Gal 9-09-42:14
For Men Only 1-16-52:6

For Napoleon and France 4-17-
14:22
For Pete's Sake (s) 6-12-34:19
For Pete's Sake 6-26-74:20
For Sale 7-16-24:22
For Sale (s) 6-11-30:18
For Sale--A Baby 11-06-09:13
For Singles Only 6-19-68:37
For the Defense 3-10-16:28
For the Defense 7-23-30:31
For the Freedom of the World
9-14-17:38
For the King 4-01-10:17
For the Love o' Lil 12-17-30:26
For the Love of Benji 6-15-77:
31
For the Love of Fanny (s) 12-19-
31:166
For the Love of Ludwig (s) 7-19-
32:34
For the Love of Mary 9-01-48:
14
For the Love of Mike 8-24-27:
26
For the Love of Mike 1-03-33:
27
For the Love of Mike 8-03-60:6
For the Love of Pete (s) 4-01-
36:17
For the Love of Rusty 7-02-47:
13
For the Service 6-03-36:54
For the Soul of Rafael 10-08-20:
43
For the Term of His Natural Life
6-12-29:31
For Them That Trespass 5-18-
49:8
For Those Two in Peril 5-10-
44:10
For Those We Love 12-02-21:43
For Those Who Think Young 5-
20-64:6
For Two Cents (s) 6-02-31:14
For Valor 4-07-37:13
For Valour 11-23-17:43
For Whom the Bell Tolls 7-21-
43:22
For Whom to Be Murdered 12-
20-78:27
For Wives Only 12-08-26:20
For You I Die 12-24-47:13
For You, My Boy 4-26-23:25
Foraarsdag I Helvede, En 3-09-
77:24
Forbid Them Not 9-27-61:7
Forbidden 1-12-32:24
Forbidden 11-25-53:6

Forsaking Others 12-22-22:33
Forsummad Av Sin Fru 12-10-47: 12
Forsvundne Fuldmaegtig, Den 11-10-71:24
Fort Algiers 7-22-53:20
Fort Apache 3-10-48:10
Fort Bowie 2-05-58:20
Fort Defiance 10-31-51:18
Fort Dobbs 1-22-58:6
Fort Dodge Stampede 9-05-51:6
Fort du Fou 2-27-63:6
Fort Massacre 4-30-58:6
Fort of the Mad (See: Fort du Fou)
Fort Osage 1-23-52:22
Fort Savage Riders 3-14-51:7
Fort Ti 5-13-53:6
Fort Utah 6-07-67:6
Fort Vengeance 4-01-53:6
Fort Worth 5-16-51:6
Fort Yuma 9-28-55:9
Forteresse, La 5-07-47:18
40th Door, The 8-20-24:22
Fortress on the Volga 1-06-43:54
Fortunat 11-30-60:6
Fortunata y Jacinta 4-08-70:24
Fortunate Misfortune, A 1-05-10: 14
Fortunate Youth, The 3-24-16:25
Fortune, The 5-21-75:19
Fortune and Men's Eyes 6-09-71:17
Fortune Carree 4-27-55:6
Fortune Cookie, The 10-19-66:6
Fortune Follows the Brave 12-04-09:4
Fortune Hunter, The 10-10-14: 25
Fortune Hunter (2 reviews) 1-18-28:13
Fortune Hunters 9-25-09:20
Fortune Is a Woman 3-20-57:7
Fortune of Christian McNab, The 6-10-21:37
Fortune Teller 5-14-20:34
Fortune's Child 1-31-19:52
Fortune's Fool 8-22-28:16
Fortune's Mask 10-06-22:40
Fortunes of Captain Blood 5-15-50:6
Fortunes of Fifi, The 3-02-17: 29
40 Anos Sin Sexo 2-21-79:18
Forty Boys and a Song (s) 10-01-41:9
Forty Carats 6-27-73:20
45 Fathers 12-15-37:17
45 Minutes from Broadway

10-22-10:14
45 Minutes from Broadway 9-03-20:44
Forty Guns 9-18-57:15
Forty-Horse Hawkins 7-02-24:26
40 Little Mothers 4-17-40:13
40 Naughty Girls 9-08-37:18
Forty-Niners 12-20-32:16
Fortyniners 4-28-54:6
49th Man, The 5-13-53:18
49th Parallel 11-05-41:8
40 Pounds of Trouble 12-12-62:6
42nd Street 3-14-33:14
Forty Thieves (s) 12-06-32:15
Forty Winks 2-04-25:39
40 Winks (s) 9-17-30:21
40,000 Horsemen 2-05-41:12
Forvandlingen 3-08-75:18
Forward Pass 12-04-29:23
Forza del Pecado, La 6-07-50: 10
Fossa Degli Angeli, La 12-29-37:19
Foto Haber 7-15-64:22
Fotografia 4-24-74:20
Fou, Le 10-14-70:32
Fou du Labo 4, Le 1-17-68:6
Foul Play 7-12-78:18
Foule Hurle, La 10-25-32:54
Found Alive 4-17-34:32
Found in Morocco (s) 3-08-32: 14
Foundling, The 1-14-16:19
Fountain, The 9-04-34:19
Fountain of Love, The 10-22-69: 30
Fountainhead, The 6-29-49:14
Four Aces 1-17-33:15
4 Aristocrats, The (s) 6-06-28: 12
4 Boys and a Cow 1-30-57:6
Four Clowns 7-01-70:13
4D Man 10-07-59:6
Four Daughters 8-17-38:22
Four Days in November 10-07-64:6
Four Days Leave (See: Swiss Tour)
4 Days in Naples, The 11-28-62:6
4 Days Wonder 12-23-36:62
Four Devils, The 10-10-28:15 and 6-19-29:24
4 Faces West 5-12-48:8
4 Fast Guns 11-25-59:6
Four Feathers, The 6-19-29:24
Four Feathers, The 4-26-39:12
4 Features 5-28-15:17
4 Flights to Love 4-15-42:18
4 Flusher, The 1-18-28:13

147 •

4 Footed Ranger 4-04-28:29
Four for Texas 12-25-63:6
Four Frightened People 1-30-34: 12
Four Girls in Town 12-05-56:6
Four Girls in White 1-25-39:11
Four Guns to the Border 9-22-54:6
Four Hearts 2-27-46:8
Four Horsemen of the Apocalypse, The 2-18-21:40
Four Horsemen of the Apocalypse, The 2-14-62:6
Four Hours to Kill 4-17-35:14
400 Blows, The (See: Quatre Cents Coups, Les)
400 Million, The 3-15-39:18
Four in a Jeep 4-11-51:22
Four in the Morning 8-04-65:6
Four Infantry Men 6-18-30:55
Four Jacks and a Jill 11-12-41:9
Four Jills in a Jeep 3-15-44:32
Four Just Men, The 6-21-39:26
Four Leaved Clover, The 7-09-15:17
Four Men and a Prayer 4-27-38: 22
Four Moods 10-25-72:22
Four Mothers 1-15-41:14
Four Musketeers, The 3-12-75: 18
Four Nights of a Dreamer (See: Quatre Nuits d'un Reveur)
491 1-22-64:19
Four Poster, The 10-08-52:12
Four-Sided Triangle 5-20-53:16
Four Skulls of Jonathan Drake, The 5-13-59:7
Four Sons 2-15-28:24 (Reprinted: 2-22-28:17)
Four Sons 4-29-40:14
4-Star Boarder (s) 3-04-36:27
Four Star Broadcast (s) 4-18-33: 21
Four-Star Organlog (s) 3-07-33: 14
Four Stars (****) 12-27-67:6 (Also see: Loves of Ondine, The)
4 Steps in the Clouds 11-03-48: 14
4 x 4 7-21-65:6
413 9-11-14:22
Four Truths, The (See: Quatres Verites, Les)
4 Walls 8-22-28:16
Four Ways Out 12-08-54:6
Four Wives 11-22-39:14

Fourchambault 8-28-29:34
Fourgers Bleues, Les 6-15-77: 21
Four's a Crowd 8-17-38:22
14, The 7-11-73:18
14-18 4-03-63:6
Fourteen Hours 2-28-51:13
14,000 Witnesses 7-12-61:7
Fourteenth Lover, The 2-27-22: 40
XIVth Olympiad--The Glory of Sport 9-08-48:18
Fourth Alarm, The 12-17-30:63
Fourth Commandment, The 4-06-27:24
Fourth Estate, The 1-21-16:27
Fourth Horseman, The 1-31-33: 29
Fourth Musketeer 4-05-23:37
Fous du Stade, Les 11-01-72:30
Fowl Ball (s) 5-06-31:22
Fowler's Studio Varieties (s) 4-09-30:22
Fox, The 12-23-21:36
Fox, The 12-13-67:6
Fox and Curtis (s) 9-11-29:18
Fox Farm 8-11-22:34
Fox Grandeur News/Extra Wide Film on Extra Wide Screen 9-25-29:17
Fox in the Chicken Coop, The 6-28-78:22
Fox Movietone Follies of 1929 5-29-29:14
Fox Movietone Follies of 1930 (See: Movietone Follies of 1930)
Fox Movietone Newsreels (s)

11-02-27:21	1-16-29:14
5-30-28:14	1-23-29:18
6-06-28:12	1-30-29:14
6-20-28:14	2-06-29:18
6-27-28:14	2-13-29:13
7-11-28:13	2-20-29:14
8-15-28:17	2-27-29:80
8-22-28:14	3-06-29:12
8-29-28:15	3-13-29:14
9-05-28:14	3-20-29:12
9-12-28:12	3-27-29:12
9-19-28:12	4-03-29:11
10-03-28:17	5-01-29:17
10-10-28:15	5-15-29:20
10-17-28:16	5-22-29:16
10-24-28:24	5-29-29:14
10-31-28:24	6-05-29:15
11-07-28:15	6-12-29:24
11-14-28:17	6-19-29:24
11-21-28:13	6-28-29:12

Fratelli Castiglioni, I 10-13-37: 17

Fratelli Dinamite, I 9-28-49:15

Fratelli Karamazoff, I 4-14-48: 18

Fraternelle Amazone 8-04-65:16

Fraternity Row 2-23-77:16

Frau Cheney's Ende 10-02-63:28

Frau, Die Weiss, Was Sie Will, Eine 7-22-36:34

Frau Gegenuber, Die 5-24-78:38

Frau Genuegt Nicht?, Eine 8-31-55:6

Frau Hat Etwas, Eine 6-16-31: 62 (Also see: Cherie and Honey)

Frau Mit Verantwortung, Eine 3-14-79:24

Frau Ohne Bedeutung, Eine 11-18-36:29

Frau Sucht Liebe, Eine 2-05-69: 30

Frau Sorge 5-02-28:14

Frau Von der Man Spricht 5-02-33:13

Frau Warren's Gewerbe 4-20-60:8

Frau Wirtin Blaest Auch Gern Trompete 5-13-70:24

Frau Wirtin Hat Auch Eine Nichte 6-11-69:42

Frau Wirtin Hat Auch Einen Grafen 1-15-69:36

Frau Wirtin Treibt es Jetzt Noch Toller 11-18-70:40

Frauds and Frenzies 11-01-18:38

Frauenparadies, Das 11-25-36:19

Fraulein 5-07-58:6

Fraulein Doktor 4-09-69:8

Fraulein Else (See: Miss Else)

Frauendiplomat, Der 4-12-32:15

Freak, The 12-03-10:14

Freaks 7-12-32:16

Freaks of the Seas (s) 8-16-32: 15

Freaky Friday 12-22-76:22

Freche Husar, Der 11-14-28:17

Freckled Rascal 7-24-29:39

Freckles 6-08-17:21

Freckles 1-25-28:13

Freckles 10-30-35:14

Freckles 9-28-60:6

Freckles Comes Home 4-08-42:8

Fred Ardath and Co. (s) 12-19-28:12

Fred Waring and Pennsylvanians (s) 2-28-33:14

Freda and Palace (s) 12-05-28:12

Freddie Rich Orch. (s) 1-27-37:12

Freddy the Freshman (s) 3-08-32:14

Free 3-14-73:20

Free Air 6-16-22:43

Free and Easy 4-23-30:36 (Also see: Metteur en Scene, Le)

Free and Easy (s) 11-03-31:17

Free and Easy 3-19-41:16

Free and Equal 4-22-25:34

Free, Blonde and Twenty One 4-10-40:14

Free Booters 9-18-09:13

Free for All 11-02-49:22

Free Lips 1-16-29:25

Free Love 7-07-26:17

Free Love 12-17-30:13

Free Soul, A 6-09-31:18

Freebie and the Bean 11-13-74: 36

Freedom 1-14-31:19

Freedom 7-24-57:27

Freedom for Ghana 7-24-57:7

Freedom of the Press 9-26-28: 15

Freedom Radio 2-05-41:12

Freeman Sisters (s) 1-30-29:14

Freewheelin' 11-17-76:19

Freeze-Out, The 4-29-21:41

Freighters of Destiny 4-12-32: 15

Fremd Bin Ich Eigezogah 5-16-79:31

Fremde Stadt 5-31-72:6

Fremmed Banke Paa, En 11-02-60:6

French Blue 12-18-74:36

French Can-Can 6-01-55:22

French Connection, The 10-06-71: 16

French Connection II 5-14-75:26

French Doll 9-06-23:23

French Dressing 12-14-27:21

French Dressing 5-27-64:6

French Foreign Legion, The (s) 11-10-31:14

French Heels 3-03-22:41

French Key, The 5-22-46:10

French Kisses (s) 6-04-30:24

French Leave (s) 7-22-28:14

French Leave 9-03-30:19 and 12-08-31:21

French Leave 4-21-48:13

French Line, The (s) 3-11-31:14

French Line, The 1-06-54:52

French Mistress 9-14-60:21

French Postcards 9-12-79:18

French They Are a Funny Race, The (See: Carnets du Major Thompson, Les)

French Touch 9-08-54:22
French War Reel (s) 3-25-36:15
French Way, The 9-10-52:6
French Without Tears 11-15-39:
20
Frenchie 11-29-50:14
Frenchman Finish, A (s) 4-12-
32:14
Frenchman's Creek 9-20-44:10
Frenesia D'Estate 4-15-64:22
Frente Marchen!, Die 4-22-31:
19 (Also see: Dough Boys)
Frenzied Flames 12-08-26:17
Frenzy 7-24-46:26
Frenzy 5-31-72:6
Fresh from the Fleet (s) 5-27-
36:15
Freshie, The 12-22-22:34
Freshman, The 7-15-25:34
Freshman Love (s) 4-15-31:20
Freshman Love 1-29-36:16
Freshman Year 9-21-38:12
Freud 12-19-62:6
Freudenhaus, Das 3-17-71:28
Freudlose Gasse, Die (See: Streets
of Sorrow)
Freundin So Goldig Wie Du, Eine
10-27-31:25
Fric, Le 8-05-59:6
Fric Frac 8-02-39:18
Frida's Visor 10-20-31:27
Friday on My Mind 9-30-70:20
Friday the 13th 9-08-16:20
Friday the 13th 5-22-33:15 and
12-05-33:7
Friday the 13th 5-14-80:14
Friday the 13th--The Orphan 12-
12-79:23
Fridericus 3-24-37:17
Fried Chicken (s) 9-29-31:14
Frieda 6-25-47:8 and 8-20-47:16
Friederike 2-28-33:15
Friedland's Ritz Review (s) 7-18-
28:15
Friend from India 1-25-28:13
Friend Husband 8-09-18:33
Friend of Fathers, A (s) 11-21-
28:13
Friend Will Come Tonight, A 7-
14-48:12 (Also see: Ami
Viendra Ce Soir, Un)
Friendly Enemies 5-06-25:46
Friendly Enemies 6-24-42:8
Friendly Husband, A 6-14-23:23
Friendly Neighbors 11-13-40:20
Friendly Persuasion, The 9-26-
56:6
Friends 3-24-71:26

Friends and Lovers 11-10-31:15
Friends Are As Friends Go 7-
14-65:7
Friends for Life (See: Amici Per
la Pelle)
Friends of Eddie Coyle, The 6-
13-73:22
Friends of Mr. Sweeney 7-31-34:
14
Friendship (s) 3-06-29:12
Friendship in Full Bloom 1-15-
75:26
Friesennot 10-28-36:29
Fright 10-27-71:18
Frightened City, The 9-20-61:6
Frightened Lady 11-12-41:9
Frihetens Murar 4-11-79:20
Fringe Benefits 2-20-74:15
Fringe of Society, The 10-05-
17:40
Frisco Jenny 1-10-33:15
Frisco Kid, The 11-27-35:14
Frisco Kid, The 7-04-79:24
Frisco Lil 2-18-42:8
Frisco Sal 2-14-45:14
Frisco Sally Levy 4-13-27:18
Frisco Tornado 9-13-50:6
Frisco Waterfront 12-25-35:25
Fritz the Cat 4-05-72:16
Frock Coat 8-28-09:13
Froeken April 3-11-59:22
Frog, The 4-07-37:15
Frogmen, The 6-13-51:6
Frogs 3-29-72:30
Froken Julie 5-16-51:18
Frolicking Fish (s) 9-24-30:23
From Beyond the Seas 3-12-10:
39
From Cabin Boy to King 11-13-
09:13
From Ear to Ear 1-20-71:22
From Headquarters 7-17-29:57
From Headquarters 11-21-33:20
From Hell It Came 9-04-57:26
From Hell to Heaven 3-21-33:16
From Hell to Texas 5-14-58:6
From Hell to Victory 9-12-79:18
From Here to Eternity 7-29-53:6
From Lumiere to Langlois 9-23-
70:13
From Noon Till 3 8-04-76:20
From Now On 10-22-20:41
From Out of the Big Snows 8-13-
15:18
From Russia with Love 10-16-
63:6
From Saturday to Monday (See:
Dal Sabato al Lunedi)

● 152

Gambling Terror 3-10-37:15
Gambling Wives 4-16-24:26
Game, The 11-13-09:13
Game Chicken, A 3-10-22:41
Game Is Over, The (See: Curee, La)
Game Is Sex, The 7-30-69:38
Game of Death, A 11-28-45:10
Game of Death, The 6-13-79:34
Game of Jai Alai, The 3-18-36: 17
Game of Life, The 7-23-24:27
Game of Love, A 2-20-74:15
Game of Poker/Father's Choice, A 3-28-13:14
Game Old Knight, A 10-22-15:23
Game That Kills 9-22-37:18
Game with Fate, A 6-14-18:29
Gamekeeper, The 9-24-80:18
Gamera Tai Gyaos 4-19-67:58
Gamera Tai Uchu Kaiju Bairusu 5-22-68:28
Games 9-20-67:6
Games, The 4-08-70:16
Games of the XXI Olympaid Montreal 1976 6-08-77:23
Games That Lovers Play 2-17-71:18
Gamesters, The 11-05-20:41
Gamin 6-21-78:23 and 10-03-79: 18
Gamin de Paris 9-20-32:15
Gamma People, The 9-12-56:6
Gammera the Invincible 12-27-67:20
Gammera vs. Monster X (See: Gamera Tai Uchi Kaiju Bairusu)
Gander Goose in the Outpost (s) 6-24-42:8
Gang, The 12-28-38:13
Gang, Le 2-09-77:22
Gang Bullets 12-28-38:13
Gang Buster 1-28-31:15
Gang Busters (serial) 2-18-42:8
Gang Busters 3-23-55:6
Gang des Otages, Le 3-07-73:18
Gang That Couldn't Shoot Straight, The 12-15-71:18
Gang War 11-21-28:30
Gang War 4-03-40:16
Gang War 4-30-58:6
Ganga 9-13-61:28
Ganga Zumba 1-26-72:24
Ganges at Benares, The 3-14-13: 14
Gang's All Here, The 3-15-39:18
Gang's All Here, The 6-25-41:18

Gang's All Here, The 12-01-43: 10
Gangs of Chicago 5-22-40:33
Gangs of New York 5-25-38:13
Gangs of Sonora 7-16-41:22
Gangs of the Waterfront 8-08-45: 22
Gangster, The 10-01-47:14
Gangsterens Laerling 8-04-76:20
Gangsterfilmen 12-04-74:22
Gangsters, The 3-13-14:23
Gangster's Boy 11-09-38:16
Gangway (s) 8-11-31:19
Gangway 8-18-37:27
Gangway for Tomorrow 11-03-43: 16 and 12-22-43:12
Ganja and Hess 4-18-73:30
Ganovenehre 4-27-66:19
Gans-Herman Fight 1-26-07:11 (Reprinted on 12-31-30:18)
Gans-Nelson Fight 9-26-08:12
Gants Blancs du Diable, Les 5-23-73:28
Ganzer Kerl, Ein 4-29-36:15
Garage, The 1-16-20-62
Garage Sale 12-08-76:19
Garaget 10-08-75:18
Garakuta (See: Rabble, The)
Garbage of Paris, The 10-09-09: 13
Garcon Sauvage, Le 9-19-51:6
Garconne, La 6-19-57:7
Garden, The 6-01-77:16
Garden Murder Case, The 3-04-36:27
Garden of Allah, The 9-07-27:20
Garden of Allah, The 11-14-28: 26
Garden of Allah, The 11-25-36: 14
Garden of Allie, The 1-18-18:43
Garden of Eden 3-21-28:18
Garden of Eden 9-01-54:22
Garden of Evil 6-30-54:6
Garden of Knowledge, The 1-12-17:25
Garden of Lies, The 7-23-15:18
Garden of the Finzi-Continis, The (See: Giardino del Finzi-Continis, Il)
Garden of the Moon 8-17-38:12
Garden of Weeds 1-05-24:30
Garm Hava 6-19-76:18
Garment Jungle, The 4-24-57:6
Garno Italian Marionettes (s) 4-17-29:20
Garofano Rosso, Il 9-29-76:30
Garrincha--Allegria Do Povo 7-03-63:18

Gentleman of Quality, A 3-07-19:
66
Gentleman of Quality, A 11-03-
26:17
Gentleman Preferred, A 6-13-
28:13
Gentleman Tramp, The 3-12-75:
18
Gentleman's Agreement 11-12-
47:8
Gentleman's Fate 6-30-31:15
Gentleman's Gentleman 11-14-28:
17
Gentlemen Are Born 11-27-34:15
Gentlemen from America 3-15-23:
32
Gentleman Marry Brunettes 9-14-
55:6
Gentlemen of the Evening (s) 10-
02-29:19
Gentlemen of the Press 5-15-29:
23
Gentlemen Prefer Blondes 1-18-
28:13
Gentlemen Prefer Blondes 7-01-
53:6
Gentlemen with Guns 3-13-46:10
Gentlemen's Agreement, A 8-02-
18:37
Gents of Leisure (s) 8-18-31:30
Geordie 9-28-55:9
Georg 9-25-68:6
George and Margaret 4-17-40:16
George Bernard Shaw (s) 6-27-
28:14
George Dewey Washington (s) 11-
21-28:13
George Frideric Handel (s) 5-11-
27:24
George Givot and Leonard Hinds
(s) 12-05-28:12; 8-21-29:18
George Hall (s) 11-25-36:14
George Jessel (s) 6-13-28:12;
8-08-28:12; 2-25-31:12
George Lyons and Harp Vocafilm
(s) 5-30-28:14
George Raft Story, The 12-06-
61:18
George VI Coronation (s) 7-21-
37:19
George Washington Carver 4-17-
40:16
George Washington Cohen 5-22-
29:16
George Washington, Jr. 3-26-
24:27
George Washington Slept Here
9-23-42:8

George White's 1935 Scandals 5-
01-35:17
George White's Scandals 8-01-
45:16
Georges Bizet (s) 1-29-30:21
George's False Alarm (s) 2-08-
28:24
Georges Qui? 4-11-73:61
Georgia, Georgia 3-08-72:24
Georgia 'Possum Hunt, A 2-05-
10:35
Georgia Price (s) 12-18-29:22
and 12-25-29:20
Georgia Tech (s) 6-27-33:14
Georgy Girl 7-13-66:6
Gerald Cramson's Lady 3-11-25:
41
Geraldine 3-06-29:26
Geraldine 12-30-53:6
German Side of the War, The 10-
08-15:21
Germania 7-03-14:21
Germania Anno Zero 6-09-48:12
German's Side of War 9-26-28:
15
Germans Strike Again, The 5-18-
49:20
Germany at War 12-24-15:24
Germany in 15 Minutes (s) 9-29-
31:14
Germinal 10-16-63:16
Geronimo 11-22-39:14
Geronimo 4-25-62:6
Gertie 12-19-14:26
Gertie the Dinosaur (See: Gertie)
Gertrude Lawrence (s) 1-09-29:
10
Gervaise 9-19-56:6
Geschichten aus dem Wienerwald
7-07-37:13
Geschichten aus dem Wienerwald
11-21-79:25
Geschichtsunterricht 10-03-73:
15
Geschminkte Jugend (See: Painted
Youth)
Gesicht im Dunkeln, Das 8-20-
69:16
Gestaendnis Unter Vier Augen
10-13-54:6
Gestapo 6-05-40:14
Gesuzza la Sposa Garibaldina 11-
18-36:29
Get Back 7-04-73:30
Get Carter 1-20-71:13
Get Charlie Tully 7-28-76:18
Get Going 6-23-43:24

Giants of the Jungle (s) 4-22-31:
  18 and 5-30-33:15
Giants-White Sox 4-17-14:21
Giardino del Finzi-Continis, Il
  12-23-70:6
Gibbi West Germany 5-28-80:18
Gibraltar 2-08-39:17
Gideon of Scotland Yard (See:
  Gideon's Day)
Gideon's Day 4-02-58:6
Gidget 3-18-59:6
Gidget 3-18-59:6
Gidget Goes Hawaiian 5-31-61:6
Gidget Goes to Rome 7-31-63:6
Gifle, La 10-23-74:30
Gift 11-16-66:6
Gift Girl, The 3-09-17:22
Gift Horse 7-23-52:6
Gift of Gab 10-02-34:37
Gift of Love 2-12-58:6
Gift Supreme 4-16-20:44
Gifts of an Eagle 12-24-75:16
Gifts of Rhythm (s) 2-10-37:14
Gigantis 5-27-59:6
Giggle Water (s) 4-19-32:14
Gigi 11-02-49:22
Gigi 5-21-58:6
Gigolette 5-15-35:19
Gigolettes of Paris 10-17-33:27
Gigolo 10-13-26:21
Gigolo Racket, The (s) 6-16-31:
  21
Gigot 6-20-62:6
Gil Wells (s) 3-20-29:12
Gilbert-Sullivan (s) 12-18-29:22
Gilda 3-20-46:8
Gilda Live 3-26-80:20
Gilded Butterfly, The 3-03-26:38
Gilded Cage, The 9-29-16:27
Gilded Dream, The 11-12-20:36
Gilded Highway, The 3-31-26:42
Gilded Lily, The 3-11-21:32
Gilded Lily, The 2-12-35:19
Gilded Spider, The 4-28-16:29
Gilded Youth 12-31-15:24
Gildersleeve on Broadway 10-27-
  43:10
Gildersleeve's Bad Day 5-05-43:
  16
Gildersleeve's Ghost 6-21-44:12
Giliap 12-24-75:18
Gili-Bili Starik So Staroukhoi 6-
  02-65:6
Gimme 1-19-23:46
Gimme Shelter 11-25-70:13
Gina (See: Mort en Ce Jardin, La)
Ginger 4-25-19:83
Ginger 7-24-35:21

Ginger 3-17-71:28
Gingham Girl, The 7-20-27:18
Ginsberg from Nowhere (s) 7-30-
  30:16
Ginzberg the Great 1-25-28:13
Giordano Bruno 11-28-73:16
Giornata Balorda, La 2-22-61:7
Giornata Speciale, Una 5-18-77:
  20
Giorni Cantati, I 3-07-62:6
Giorni Contati, I 9-05-79:30
Giorni D'Amore 12-22-54:22
Giorni Dell'Ira, I (See: Day of
  Anger)
Giorno Della Civetta, Il 2-28-68:6
Giorno Per Giorno, Disperatamente
  1-17-62:6
Giovane Attila, Il 8-25-71:16
Giovane Normale, Il 12-31-69:6
Giovani Mariti 5-07-58:23
Giovani Tigri, I 3-13-68:6
Giovanna D'Arco Al Rogo 11-03-
  54:11
Giovanni Lupo, King of the Black-
  hands 5-14-15:19
Giovanni Martinelli (s) 7-11-28:
  13; 8-29-28:15; 2-13-29:13;
  12-25-29:20; 4-02-30:18; 5-
  06-31:22
Gioventu Perduta 4-14-48:8
Giovinezza Giovinezza 1-14-70:20
Gipfelstuermer, Der 4-14-37:33
Girl, A Guy and a Gob, A 3-05-
  41:16
Girl Alaska, The 8-22-19:77
Girl and the Bugler, The 10-18-
  67:6
Girl and the Gambler, The 6-07-
  39:12
Girl and the General, The (See:
  Ragazza e il Generale, La)
Girl and the Judge, The 2-05-10:
  16
Girl at Home, The 5-04-17:26
Girl at the Lock, The 10-17-14:
  24
Girl Can't Help It, The 12-19-
  56:7
Girl Crazy 3-29-32:25
Girl Dodger, The 2-28-19:57
Girl Downstairs, The 12-28-38:
  13
Girl Friend, The 10-02-35:16
Girl from Alaska, The 4-29-42:8
Girl from Avenue A, The 10-16-
  40:16
Girl from Bohemia, The 8-16-18:
  38

Girl from Calgary, The 11-22-32:36

Girl from Chicago 12-21-27:22

Girl from Coney Island, The 12-15-26:16

Girl from Gay Paree 12-07-27:21

Girl from God's Country 11-18-21:42

Girl from God's Country 8-07-40:16

Girl from Hanoi, The 8-06-75:17

Girl from Havana, The 9-04-29:13

Girl from Havana, The 9-11-40:14

Girl from His Town, The 8-13-15:18

Girl from Jones Beach, The 6-22-49:6

Girl from Leningrad, The 12-31-41:16

Girl from Mandalay, The 5-13-36:14

Girl from Manhattan, The 9-15-48:15

Girl from Maxim's 9-23-36:17

Girl from Mellons, The 2-12-10:16

Girl from Mexico, The 5-24-39:14

Girl from Missouri, The 8-07-34:12

Girl from Monterey, The 1-05-44:26

Girl from Montmartre, The 2-24-26:43

Girl from Outside, The 11-14-19:61

Girl from Paris, The 1-06-37:40 (Also see: Girl from Poltavka and Natalka Poltavka)

Girl from Petrovka, The 8-14-74:16

Girl from Poltavka 2-27-37:23 (also see: Girl from Paris, The and Natalka Poltavka)

Girl from Porcupine 11-24-22:35

Girl from Rio, The 10-12-27:25

Girl from Rio, The 9-06-39:19

Girl from Rocky Point 3-03-22:40

Girl from San Lorenzo, The 3-08-50:6

Girl from Scotland Yard, The 6-02-37:23

Girl from Tenth Avenue, The 5-29-35:14

Girl from the Revue, The 9-05-28:31

Girl from Woolworth's, The 12-25-29:26

Girl Grief (s) 12-27-32:14

Girl Habit 7-07-31:25

Girl He Didn't Buy, The 6-20-28:19

Girl He Left Behind, The 10-31-56:6

Girl Hunters, The 6-12-63:6

Girl I Abandoned, The (See: Watashi Ga Suteta Onna)

Girl I Left Behind Me, The 1-30-15:24

Girl I Loved, The 5-24-23:23 and 3-29-23:36

Girl in a Glass Cage 9-18-29:55

Girl in a Million, A 6-05-46:13

Girl in Black Stockings 10-02-57:6

Girl in Bohemia, A 11-07-19:100

Girl in Danger 11-06-34:26

Girl in Every Pot, A 2-22-28:20

Girl in Every Pot, A 12-26-51:6

Girl in 419 5-23-33:15

Girl in His House, The 6-21-18:29

Girl in His Room 6-16-22:43

Girl in No. 29, The 5-14-20:37

Girl in Possession 3-20-34:16

Girl in the Case 10-02-40:25

Girl in the Case 5-24-44:10

Girl in the Checkered Coat 4-06-17:20

Girl in the Dark, The 3-01-18:41

Girl in the Headlines 11-20-63:14

Girl in the Kremlin, The 4-24-57:6

Girl in the Limousine 10-08-24:30

Girl in the Mist, A 1-30-57:7

Girl in the Moon, The 8-06-30:38 (Also see: By Rocket to the Moon and Woman in the Moon)

Girl in the News 1-01-41:14

Girl in the Pullman 11-02-27:20

Girl in the Rain, The 7-23-20:34

Girl in the Rain 3-02-27:17

Girl in the Red Velvet Swing 10-12-55:6

Girl in the Show 10-09-29:46

Girl in the Taxi 9-15-37:15

Girl in the Tonneau (s) 1-19-32:25

Girl in the Tuxedo 1-16-29:25

Girl in the Web, The 7-23-20:33

Girl in the Woods 6-18-58:16
Girl in White, The 3-19-52:6
Girl Like That, A 3-09-17:22
Girl Loves Boy 4-28-37:15
Girl Missing 3-21-33:27
Girl Most Likely, The 12-18-57:6
Girl Must Live, A 5-10-39:23 and 10-08-41:9
Girl Named Mary, A 1-31-20:54
Girl Named Tamiko, A 12-05-62:6
Girl Next Door, The 5-13-53:6
Girl Nihilist 7-25-08:13
Girl No. 217 9-05-45:15
Girl of Dixon's, The 3-05-10:13
Girl of Limberlost 5-14-24:28
Girl of Lost Lake, The 8-18-16:26
Girl of My Dreams, The 12-06-18:39
Girl of My Dreams 3-20-35:17
Girl of My Heart 2-18-21:41
Girl of the Dance Hall, The 10-29-15:22
Girl of the Golden West, The 1-09-15:23
Girl of the Golden West 5-24-23:23
Girl of the Golden West 10-29-30:27
Girl of the Golden West 3-16-38:15
Girl of the Limberlost, The 11-13-34:15
Girl of the Limberlost, The 9-19-45:12
Girl of the Night 10-05-60:93
Girl of the Ozarks 8-12-36:18
Girl of the Port 7-16-30:29
Girl of the Rio 1-12-32:15
Girl of the Sea, The 7-09-20:28
Girl of the Time Lands 1-26-17:25
Girl of Yesterday, A 10-15-15:21
Girl on a Motorcycle, The (See: Motocyclette, La)
Girl on the Barge 2-27-29:86
Girl on the Bridge, The 12-12-51:6
Girl on the Front Page 11-11-36:14
Girl on the Stairs 3-04-25:38
Girl Overboard 8-14-29:31
Girl Overboard 3-03-37:14
Girl Philippa, The 1-05-17:27
Girl Problem, The 2-21-19:67

Girl Rush 10-25-44:12
Girl Rush 8-10-55:6
Girl Said No, The 4-09-30:22
Girl Scout, The 11-06-09:13
Girl Shock (s) 8-20-30:14
Girl Shy 4-02-24:23
Girl Spy Before Vicksburg, The 1-07-11:13
Girl Stroke Bay 8-18-71:22
Girl Thief, The 3-12-10:39
Girl Thief 1-12-38:15
Girl Trouble (s) 12-05-33:16
Girl Trouble 9-23-42:8
Girl Who Came Back, The 5-17-23:26
Girl Who Came Back, The 9-18-35:32
Girl Who Dared, The 8-13-20:34
Girl Who Didn't Think, The 2-02-17:24
Girl Who Doesn't Know, The 12-15-16:37
Girl Who Had Everything, The 3-04-53:6
Girl Who Knew Too Much, The 11-26-69:26
Girl Who Ran Wild, The 9-29-22:42
Girl Who Stayed at Home, The 3-28-19:93
Girl Who Wouldn't Quit, The 3-29-18:46
Girl Who Wouldn't Work, The 8-12-25:33
Girl with a Million 4-01-21:42
Girl with a Suitcase (See: Ragazza Con la Valigia, La)
Girl with Green Eyes, The 5-20-64:6
Girl with Ideas, A 11-03-37:14
Girl with No Regrets, The 1-31-19:53
Girl with the Golden Eyes, The (See: Fille Aux Yeux D'Or, La)
Girl with the Green Eyes, The 7-07-16:24
Girl with the Long Hair, The 12-31-75:15
Girl with Three Camels 7-31-68:6
Girl Without a Room 12-12-33:19
Girl Without a Sail, The 8-24-17:26
Girl Woman, The 8-08-19:48
Girl Worth Having, A 3-14-13:14
Girlfriends 5-10-78:23
Girls 7-04-19:43
Girls, The (See: Flickorna)

Girls About Town 11-03-31:17
Girls' Apartment (See: Appartement des Filles, L')
Girls Are for Loving 5-30-73:24
Girls at Sea 11-26-58:22
Girls Behind Bars 5-17-59:16
Girls Can Play 6-23-37:33
Girls Demand Excitement 2-11-31:29
Girl's Desire, A 9-08-22:42
Girls Don't Gamble 3-04-21:40
Girl's Folly, A 2-16-17:22
Girls' Dormitory 9-02-36:18
Girls for Sale 10-27-76:28
Girls! Girls! Girls! 11-07-62:6
Girls Gone Wild 4-24-29:22
Girls in Chains 9-01-43:20
Girls in Prison 9-12-56:6
Girls in the Night 1-14-53:6
Girls Marked Danger 5-26-54:18
(Also see: Tratta Delle Blanche, La)
Girls Men Forget 11-26-24:62
Girls of Pleasure Island 2-25-53:6
Girls of the Big House 11-14-45:22
Girls of the Night (See: Filles de la Nuit)
Girls of the Range 2-26-10:15
Girls of the Road 7-24-40:14
Girls on Probation 1-12-38:15 and 10-26-38:13
Girls on the Beach 5-19-65:30
Girls on the Loose 4-02-58:6
Girls Said No, The 6-23-37:33
Girls' School 9-28-38:14
Girls School 2-08-50:11
Girls' Town 4-15-42:8
Girls Town 9-30-59:6
Girls Under 21 11-13-40:16
Girls Who Dare 5-22-29:27 and 7-24-29:39
Girls Will Be Boys (s) 3-04-31:14
Girls Will Be Boys 10-02-34:37
Girolimoni, Il Mostro di Roma 1-10-73:18
Giron 6-19-74:16
Giselle 5-03-78:26
Gishiki 7-14-71:16
Git Along Little Doggies 12-08-37:17
Gitan, Le 12-31-75:14
Gitta Entdeckt Ihr Herz 10-04-32:19
Giudizio Universale, Il 9-13-61:6
Giulietta de Gli Spiriti 11-03-65:6

Giulietta e Romeo (See: Romeo and Juliet)
Giumenta Verde, La (See: Green Mare, The)
Giuseppe Verdi 11-30-38:13
Give a Girl a Break 12-02-53:6
Give and Take 1-09-29:11
Give Becky a Chance 7-27-17:27
Give 'Em Air (s) 7-15-36:31
Give 'Em Hell, Harry 9-03-75:18
Give Gud en Chance Om Soendagen 5-13-70:24
Give Her a Ring 8-12-36:19
Give Her Anything 1-13-22:41
Give Her the Moon (See: Caprices de Marie, Les)
Give Me a Job (s) 9-05-33:4
Give Me a Sailor 7-27-38:17
Give My My Son 3-03-22:40
Give Me Your Heart 9-16-36:16
Give My Regards to Broadway 5-26-48:8
Give Out, Sisters 9-02-42:18
Give Us a Life (s) 2-13-29:13
Give Us the Moon 8-02-44:20
Give Us This Day 10-19-49:8
Give Us This Night 4-08-36:16
Give Us Wings 11-13-40:16
Giving In (s) 1-09-29:10
Givoi Troup 7-23-69:28
Gizmo! 7-27-77:23
Glacier Fox, The 1-31-79:22
Glacier Park and Waterton Lakes (s) 4-22-42:18
Glacier's Secret, The (s) 6-04-30:24
Glad Rag Doll, The 6-05-29:26
Glada Paraden 6-16-48:20
Gladiator, The 8-31-38:18
Gladiatorerna 6-04-69:36
Gladiators, The (See: Gladiatorerna)
Gladiators 7 4-29-64:26
Gladiola 10-22-15:24
Glaeserne Zelle, Die 6-21-78:22
Glaive et la Balance, La 2-13-63:6
Glamour 6-16-31:34
Glamour 5-15-34:14
Glamour Boy 9-10-41:8
Glamour for Sale 10-23-40:14
Glamour Girl 12-31-47:10
Glamourous Night 5-19-37:23
Gland Parade, The (s) 10-20-31:21
Glas Wasser, Ein 5-17-23:27
Glas Wasser, Das 7-13-60:6
Glass Alibi, The 5-01-46:8

Glass Bottom Boat, The 4-20-66:6

Glass House 3-17-22:41

Glass Houses 4-29-70:19

Glass Key, The 6-19-35:21

Glass Menagerie, The 9-20-50:6

Glass Mountain, The 2-16-49:16

Glass of Water, A (See: Glas Wasser, Das)

Glass Slipper 2-16-55:6

Glass Wall, The 3-04-53:6

Glass Web, The 10-14-53:6

Gleam O'Dawn 5-19-22:41

Gleisdreick 2-24-37:19 and 6-22-38:23

Glen and Randa 6-02-71:22

Glen Gray and Casa Loma Orch. (s) 9-02-42:34

Glenn Miller Story, The 1-06-54:52

Glenrowan Affair, The 8-01-51:18

Glimpses of a Woman 7-23-21:44

Glimpses of Florida (s) 9-03-41:17

Glimpses of Germany (s) 3-25-31:16

Glimpses of Paris 9-11-09:12

Glimpses of the Moon 4-05-23:36

Glissements Progressifs du Plasir 3-27-74:14

Global Affair, A 2-05-64:6

Globero, El 4-05-61:6

Globe's War Films 1-21-16:27

Globo de Cantolla, El 7-12-44:20

Gloria 11-01-32:12

Gloria 10-05-77:28

Gloria 9-10-80:30

Gloria Mundi 12-03-75:22

Gloriana 11-03-16:28

Gloria's Romance (serial) episodes 1 & 2: 5-26-16:22; episodes 3 & 4: 6-02-16:16; episodes 5 & 6: 6-09-16:23

Glories of Nikko (s) 4-01-31:16

Glorifying the American Girl 1-15-30:22

Glorious Adventure, The 8-16-18:38

Glorious Fool, The 3-24-22:42

Glorious Lady, The 11-07-19:97

Glorious Trail, The 10-17-28:24

Glorious Vamps (s) 4-02-30:19

Glory 4-21-16:28

Glory 1-26-17:25

Glory 1-11-56:6

Glory Alley 5-21-52:6

Glory Boy 6-30-71:29

Glory Guns, The 7-14-65:6

Glory of Clementina 6-23-22:35

Glory of Faith 11-30-38:12

Glory of Yolanda, The 3-02-17:28

Glory Sky (See: Ouranos)

Glory Stompers, The 12-06-67:6

Glory Trail 4-21-37:15

Glos Z Tamtego Swiata 4-03-63:6

Glueckliche Kindheit (s) 2-18-31:14 (Also see: Brats)

Gluecklichen Minuten des Georg Hauser, Die 7-31-74:22

Gluecklichen Jahre der Thorwalds, Die 11-28-62:6

Glueckskinder 10-21-36:17 and 6-09-37:23

Gluehwuermschen, Das (s) 9-03-30:19

Gnezdo Na Vetru 7-23-80:24

Gnome-Mobile, The 5-31-67:18

Go Ahead and Eat (s) 12-10-30:15

Go and Get It 7-23-20:33

Go and Get It 2-20-29:17

Go Chase Yourself 4-20-38:15

Go For Broke 3-28-51:6

Go For It 7-28-76:18

Go Get 'Em Garringer 3-07-19:66

Go, Go, Go, World (See: Pelo Nel Mondo, Il)

Go Go Mania 5-26-65:15

Go into Your Dance 5-08-35:16

Go, Man, Go 1-20-54:18

Go Naked in the World 1-18-61:6

Go Straight 10-07-25:44

Go Tell the Spartans 6-14-78:20

Go to Blazes (s) 11-05-30:23

Go to Blazes 4-11-62:26

Go West 10-28-25:36

Go West 12-18-40:16

Go West, Young Lady 11-26-41:9

Go West, Young Man 1-31-19:54

Go West, Young Man 11-25-36:14

Goal! World Cup 1966 10-19-66:20

Goalie's Anxiety at the Penalty Kick, The 3-29-72:30

Goat, The 10-04-18:50

Goat, The (s) 4-07-22:41

Goat Getter, The 7-21-26:15

Go-Between, The 6-02-71:15

Gobs and Gals 4-30-52:6

Gobs of Fun (s) 9-12-33:17

Gobsek 7-21-37:19

Go-Daan 8-12-64:22

God Forgives, I Don't 5-21-69:6

God Gave Me 20¢   11-24-26:14
God Is My Co-Pilot   2-21-45:8
God Is My Partner   7-03-57:6
God, Man and the Devil   1-25-50:18
God of Little Children   1-19-17:24
God Told Me To   12-01-76:38
Goddess, The   4-23-58:7
Goddess of Lost Lake, The   10-18-18:38
Godelureaux, Les   4-05-61:6
Godfather, The   3-08-72:20
Godfather, Part II, The   12-11-74:16
Godfrey Ludlow (s)   8-07-29:201
Godisnja Doba   9-05-79:22
Godless Girl   4-03-29:11
Godless Men   2-04-21:43
God's Angels Are Everywhere   5-05-48:20
God's Country   6-09-31:28
God's Country   1-13-37:13
God's Country and the Law   7-07-22:59
God's Country and the Man   11-03-37:14
Cod's Country and the Woman   4-28-16:28
God's Crucible   1-19-17:25
God's Gift to Women   4-22-31:18
God's Gold   6-17-21:35
God's Good Man   8-29-19:67
God's Great Wilderness   9-07-27:24
God's Law and Man's   5-04-17:26
God's Little Acre   5-14-58:6
God's Man   4-06-17:24
Gods of Asia   6-16-22:40
God's Outlaw   7-11-19:61
Godsend, The   1-16-80:31
Godspell   3-28-73:18
Godzilla, King of the Monsters   4-25-56:6
Godzilla vs. Megalon   6-16-76:19
Godzilla vs. the Thing   9-23-64:6
Godzina Szczytu   1-01-75:16
Goetter der Pest   4-22-70:28
Goettliche Jette, Die   4-07-37:29
Gog   6-09-54:6
Go-Getter   4-12-23:30
Go-Getter, The   6-09-37:15
Gogo   4-17-63:6
Go-Go Bigbeat   5-19-65:30
Goha   5-21-58:18
Gohaku Muika   1-25-67:21
Goin' Coconuts   10-11-78:31
Goin' Down the Road   7-22-70:22
Goin' Home   12-29-76:14

Goin' South   10-04-78:18
Goin' to Town   5-15-35:19
Goin' to Town   9-17-44:14
Going Crooked   12-22-26:18
Going Highbrow   9-04-35:31
Going Hollywood   12-26-33:10
Going Home   11-24-71:16
Going Home   10-11-72:29
Going in Style   12-19-79:18
Going My Way   3-08-44:14
Going Places (s)   11-12-30:21
Going Places (s)   3-18-36:17
Going Places   1-11-39:12
Going Some   7-23-20:33
Going Spanish (s)   4-17-34:18 and 5-29-34:13
Going Steady   2-05-58:20
Going Straight   5-26-16:20
Going the Limit   8-26-25:26
Going to Press (s)   3-25-42:18
Going Up   10-11-23:27
Going Wild   1-28-41:15
Golapi Ekhon Trainey   9-05-79:26
Gold   10-11-32:20
Gold   10-02-74:22
Gold and the Girl   8-12-25:33
Gold and the Woman   3-17-16:31
Gold Bricks (s)   3-25-36:15
Gold Chevrons   11-23-27:25
Gold Cure, The   1-10-19:44
Gold Diggers, The   9-13-23:28
Gold Diggers in Paris   5-25-38:12
Gold Diggers of Broadway   9-04-29:13
Gold Diggers of 1933   6-13-33:15
Gold Diggers of 1935   3-20-35:17
Gold Diggers of 1937   12-30-36:10
Gold Dust Gertie   6-02-31:26
Gold Fever   7-23-52:18
Gold for the Caesars   6-17-64:6
Gold Ghost, The (s)   4-03-34:17
Gold Grabbers   11-24-22:34
Gold Madness   10-11-23:27
Gold Mine in the Sky   6-06-38:15
Gold News   12-03-47:11
Gold Nuggets (s)   1-30-34:12
Gold of the 7 Giants   2-08-61:8
Gold Racket, The   8-04-37:19
Gold Raiders   6-18-52:6
Gold Rush, The   7-01-25:32; 8-19-25:36; 3-04-42:8
Gold Rush Maisie   7-31-40:104
Gold Where You Find It   2-16-38:17
Goldbergs, The   11-22-50:8
Golden Apples of the Sun   6-09-71:22

Good Causes, The (See: Bonnes Causes, Les)
Good Companions, The 3-14-33:15 and 10-17-33:19
Good Companions, The 4-03-57: 24
Good Dame 3-20-34:16
Good Day for a Hanging, A 12-24-58:6
Good Die Young, The 3-17-54:7
Good Earth, The 2-10-37:14
Good Fairy, The 2-05-35:14
Good Fellows, The 8-11-43:10
Good for Nothing, The 6-12-14: 21
Good for Nothing, The 11-30-17: 45
Good Girls Beware (See: Mefiez-Vous Fillettes)
Good Girls Go to Paris 6-28-39: 14
Good Glue, A 9-17-10:12
Good Gracious Annabelle 4-04-19: 68
Good Guys and the Bad Guys, The 9-10-69:48
Good Guys Wear Black 6-28-78: 22
Good Humor Man 5-31-50:6
Good Intentions 7-30-30:17
Good Life, The (See: Belle Vie, La)
Good Little Devil, A 3-13-14:23
Good Loser, A 7-19-18:36
Good Love, The (See: Buen Amor, El)
Good Luck for the Coming Year 6-05-09:13
Good Luck, Mrs. Wyckoff 5-09-79: 80
Good Luck, Mr. Yates 7-21-43:22
Good Men and True 9-12-28:12
Good Morning (s) 8-18-31:17
Good Morning and Goodbye 12-20-67:14
Good Morning Boys 2-24-37:19
Good Morning Eve (s) 9-18-34:11
Good Morning, Judge 6-27-28:34
Good Morning, Judge 4-21-43:8
Good Morning, Miss Dove 11-16-55:6
Good Neighbor Sam 6-17-64:6
Good News 9-10-30:17
Good News 12-03-47:11
Good Night, Nurse 6-28-18:30
Good Night Paul 6-21-18:29
Good Old Days (s) 10-02-35:17
Good Old Days, The 6-28-39:20

Good Old Days (s) 4-02-30:18
Good Old Soak, The 4-28-37:15
Good Pie Forever (s) 7-21-31:12
Good Provider 4-14-22:39
Good References 9-24-20:43
Good Sam 7-28-48:15
Good Soldier Schweik, The (See: Brave Soldat Schwejk, Der)
Good Soup (See: Bonne Soupe, La)
Good, the Bad, and the Ugly, The 12-27-67:6
Good Time Charley 11-23-27:24
Good Time Girl 5-05-48:8 and 5-24-50:6
Good Times 4-26-67:6
Good Times Wonderful Times 9-01-65:6
Good Woman 5-20-21:41
Goodbye Again 9-05-33:23
Goodbye Again 7-05-61:6
Goodbye Broadway 5-18-38:12
Goodbye, Charlie 11-11-64:6
Goodbye, Columbus 3-19-69:6
Goodbye Emmanuelle 7-12-78:31
Goodbye Flickmania 12-19-79:34
Goodbye Gemini 8-12-70:22
Goodbye Girl, The 11-16-77:20
Goodbye Girls 5-03-23:23
Goodbye in the Mirror 8-05-64:7
Goodbye Love 4-03-34:27
Goodbye, Mr. Chips 5-17-39:12
Goodbye, Mr. Chips 10-15-69:15
Goodbye Mr. Moth (s) 4-01-42:8
Goodbye, My Fancy 4-11-56:6
Goodbye, My Lady 4-11-56:7
Goodbye, Norma Jean 1-28-76:15
Goodnight Sweetheart 6-14-44:10
Goofytone Newsreel (s) 9-26-33: 15
Goona-Goona 9-20-32:15
Goopy Gyne Bagha Byne 7-02-69:6
Goose and the Gander, The 9-18-35:15
Goose Boy, The 10-17-51:20
Goose Girl, The 1-30-15:24 and 11-29-18:41
Goose Hangs High, The 3-11-25: 40
Goose Woman, The 8-05-25:31
Goranssons Pojke 5-16-45:8
Gorath 5-20-64:6
Gordo de America, El 9-15-76: 16
Gordon's War 8-08-73:14
Gorechto Pladne 5-26-65:7
Gorgeous Hussy, The 9-09-36:16
Gorges of the Giants (s) 10-25-32:15

Gorgo 1-25-61:6
Gorgon, The 8-26-64:6
Gori, Gori Moja Zvezda 12-08-76:18
Gorilla, The 11-23-27:22
Gorilla, The 2-25-31:12
Gorilla, The 5-24-39:14
Gorilla at Large 5-05-54:6
Gorilla Hunt, The 11-24-26:18
Gorilla Man 12-09-42:8
Gorilla Ship, The 8-02-32:17
Gorilla von Soho, Der 10-25-72:22
Gorille Vous Salue Bien 10-08-58:6
Gorno Italian Marionettes (s) 7-24-35:21
Goroda I Gody 8-28-74:20
Gorp 5-07-80:576
Gosh 12-04-74:22
Gospel According to St. Matthew, The (See: Vangelo Secondo Matteo, Il)
Gospel Road, The 3-21-73:18
Gospodin Nuima 12-24-69:14
Gossip 5-17-23:26
Gossipy Plumber, The (s) 5-13-31:36
Gossipy Sex (s) 3-27-29:12
Got It Made 10-09-74:36
Got What She Wanted 12-31-30:19
Gotch-Hackenschmidt Wrestling Match 5-30-08:11
Gotham Rhythm Bosy (s) 10-09-29:23
Goto, L'ile D'Amour 10-30-68:26
Gotoma the Buddha 7-24-57:6
Gott Mit Uns 8-05-70:22
Gotterdammerung (See: Damned, The)
Gottes Engels Sind Ueberall (See: God's Angels Are Everywhere)
Goualeuse, La 11-30-38:13
Gout de la Violence, Le 9-20-61:6
Gouverneur, Der 6-14-39:14
Government Girl 11-10-43:35
Governor's Boss, The 6-18-15:17
Governor's Daughter, The 12-04-09:13
Governor's Lady, The 3-19-15:21
Gow 12-05-33:17
Goya 2-03-71:24
Goyokin 9-03-69:19
Goyescas 6-28-44:16
Gozencho No Jikanwari 1-02-74:15

Grabbes Letzter Sommer 12-17-80:20
Grace Johnston--Indiana 5 (s) 10-02-29:19
Grace's Place 11-14-73:14
Gracie Allen Murder Case, The 5-17-39:12
Gradiva 10-21-70:22
Graduate, The 12-20-67:6
Graduation in England (s) 2-25-31:12
Graduation Year (See: Annee du Bac, L')
Graefin von Monte Carlo 5-10-32:19
Graft 12-01-31:26
Grafter, The 2-02-07:11 (Reprinted on: 12-31-30:18)
Grafters 8-31-17:29
Grail, The 12-20-23:26
Grain de Beaute 3-22-32:61
Grain of Dust, The 1-25-18:44
Grain of Dust 9-26-28:27
Grajski Biki 11-01-67:6
Gramma Ston Nazim Hikmet 10-27-76:30
Gran Adventure, La 7-31-74:18
Gran Amor de Becquer, El 11-27-46:28
Gran Circo Chamorro, El 11-30-55:6
Gran Dia, El 9-11-57:6
Gran Mentiroso, El 12-30-53:18
Gran Rita, La 12-15-71:22
Gran Senora, La 10-21-59:23
Gran Varieta 4-27-55:6
Grand Amour, Le 4-02-69:28
Grand Bazar, Le 9-26-73:18
Grand Blond Avec une Chaussure Noire, Le 12-27-72:6
Grand Bluff, Le 7-24-57:6
Grand Canary 7-24-34:14
Grand Canyon 12-07-49:20
Grand Canyon (s) 1-21-59:6 (In review of Sleeping Beauty)
Grand Canyon Trail 11-24-48:14
Grand Central Murder 4-22-42:18
Grand Central Power House Explosion 12-24-10:16
Grand Ceremonial, Le 4-02-69:30
Grand Chef, Le 4-08-59:6
Grand Concert, The 9-10-52:6
Grand Dame, The (s) 4-29-31:12
Grand Delire, Le 4-23-75:24
Grand Depart, Le 12-20-72:18
Grand Duchess and the Waiter, The 2-10-26:40

Grand Escogiffe, Le 12-15-76:
22
Grand Hotel 4-19-32:14
Grand Illusion 9-14-38:23
Grand Jeu, Le 5-15-34:14
Grand Jeu, Le 5-26-54:18
Grand Jury 8-05-36:16
Grand Jury Secrets 7-05-39:16
Grand Larceny 3-03-22:41
Grand Maneuver, The 10-10-56:7
Grand Meulnes, Le 10-18-67:18
Grand National Night 4-29-53:18
Grand Old Girl 3-06-35:21
Grand Ole Opry 7-03-40:18
Grand Olympics, The (See: Grande
Olimpiade, La)
Grand Parade, The 2-05-30:24
Grand Passion, The 1-04-18:40
Grand Patron, Un 1-02-52:68
(Also see: Perfectionist, The)
Grand Pavois, Le 9-01-54:22
Grand Prix 12-28-66:6
Grand Rendezvous, Le 3-01-50:
16
Grand Restaurant, Le 10-12-66:
24
Grand Rock, Le 6-04-69:36
Grand Sabordage, Le 3-08-72:24
Grand Sauterelle, La 2-08-67:22
Grand Slam 2-28-33:15
Grand Slam 12-27-67:20
Grand Slam Opera (s) 3-25-36:15
Grand Soir, Le 8-25-76:68
Grand Substitution, The 11-24-
65:6
Grand Theft Auto 6-15-77:20
Grand Trouille, La 8-28-74:20
Grand Uproar (s) 7-16-30:15
Grandad Rudd 3-20-35:17
Grande Apello, Il 11-25-36:19
Grande Barriere de Corail, La
9-30-70:22
Grande Bouffe, La 5-16-73:6
Grande Bourgeoise, La (See: Fatti
di Gente Perbene)
Grande Colpo Dei Sette Uomini
D'Oro, Il 11-23-66:6
Grande Epreuve, La 6-13-28:27
(Also see: Soul of France)
Grande Fille Toute Simple, Une
(See: Just a Big, Simple
Girl)
Grande Frousse, La 12-02-64:6
Grande Guerre, La 9-16-59:6
Grande Illusion, La (See: Grand
Illusion)
Grande Lessive, La 12-11-68:6
Grande Maffia, La 10-06-71:22

Grande Mare, La 8-20-30:15
(Also see: Big Pond, The)
Grande Olimpiade, La 2-08-61:
103
Grande Speranza, La 11-03-54:6
Grande Strada Azzurra, La 3-26-
58:14
Grande Vadrouille, La 12-21-66:6
Grande Vie, La 8-31-60:6
Grandes Families, Les 12-17-58:6
Grandes Gueules, Les 11-24-65:19
Grandes Personnes, Les 2-22-
61:7
Grandeur et Decadence 6-02-37:
23
Grandeur Nature 6-05-74:16
Grandfather's Pills 7-18-08:10
Grandi Magazzini 11-15-39:20
Grandma's Boy 6-16-22:40
Grandmother's Plot 10-22-10:14
Grands Chemins, Les 7-31-63:6
Grands Sentiments Font les Bons
Gueuletons, Les 1-02-74:15
Grands Vacances, Les 12-20-67:
15
Granges Brulees, Les 6-20-73:20
Granny Get Your Gun 1-10-40:16
Granny's Birthday 3-05-10:13
Granpa Goes to Town 4-24-40:16
Granzone 8-22-79:52
Grapedealer's Daughter, The 2-
25-70:15
Grapes of Wrath, The 1-31-40:
14
Graphique de Boscop, Le 12-29-
76:14
Grasp of Greed, The 7-07-16:25
Grass Cutters, The (See: Kusa-O
Karu Musume)
Grass Eater, The 8-30-61:16
Grass Is Greener, The 11-30-
60:6
Grass Orphan, The 2-22-23:41
Grasshopper, The 5-20-70:15
Grasshopper and the Ants (s) 3-
27-34:12
Grateful Dead, The 6-08-77:23
Gratitude 9-25-09:12
Grausame Freundin, Die 8-09-
32:22
Graustark 9-09-25:35
Grauzone 8-22-79:52
Grave Disappointment, A 9-11-09:
12
Gravitcija 8-14-68:28
Gravy Train, The 6-26-74:18
Gray Dawn 6-09-22:58
Gray Lady Down 3-08-78:31

Great Yearning, The 9-17-30:34
  (Also see: Grosse Sehnsucht,
  Die)
Great Ziegfeld, The 4-15-36:16
Greater Claim, The 3-11-21:32
Greater Glory, The 5-05-26:18
Greater Law, The 7-20-17:31
Greater Love Hath No Man 7-16-
  15:18
Greater Profit 8-19-21:35
Greater Than a Clown 8-26-25:
  58
Greater Than Fame 1-16-20:61
Greater Will, The 12-17-15:18
Greatest, The 5-25-77:20
Greatest Gift, The (s) 9-02-42:
  34
Greatest Love, The 2-25-21:42
Greatest Love, The (See: Europa
  '51)
Greatest Love of All 11-12-24:
  24
Greatest Power, The 6-29-17:30
Greatest Question, The 1-02-20:
  74
Greatest Show on Earth, The 1-
  02-52:68
Greatest Story Ever Told, The
  2-17-65:7 and 6-14-67:7
Greatest Thing in Life, The 1-03-
  19:38
Greece on the March 4-09-41:18
Greece Without Ruins 10-20-65:
  26
Greed 2-02-17:22
Greed 12-10-24:34
Greek Tycoon, The 5-10-78:22
Greeks Had a Word for Them 2-
  09-32:15
Green Berets, The 6-19-68:6
Green Caravan 12-22-22:35
Green Cloak, The 10-22-15:26
Green Cockatoo, The 7-30-47:27
Green Dolphin Street 10-22-47:12
Green Eyes 8-16-18:35
Green Eyes 12-04-34:12
Green Fingers 2-19-47:9
Green Fire 12-29-54:6
Green for Danger 12-11-46:20
Green Glove, The 1-30-52:6
Green Goddess 8-16-23:27
Green Goddess 2-19-30:21
Green Grass of Wyoming 4-21-
  48:13
Green Grow the Rushes 11-21-51:
  18
Green Heart of Germany 2-21-
  33:14

Green Hell 1-24-40:22
Green Helmut, The 6-28-61:6
Green Horizons (See: Zalene
  Obzory)
Green Is the Heath 10-16-35:22
  (Also see: Gruen Ist die
  Heide)
Green Light 2-17-37:14
Green Magic 5-11-55:8
Green Man, The 9-26-56:15
Green Mansions 3-25-59:6
Green Mare, The 11-25-59:6
Green Pack, The 10-23-34:18
Green Parrot 1-09-29:45
Green Pastures 7-22-36:17
Green Promise, The 3-09-49:6
Green Room, The (See: Chambre
  Verte, La)
Green Scarf 9-08-54:7
Green Slime, The 5-28-69:6
Green Stockings 1-14-16:19
Green Swamp, The 1-07-16:23
Green Temptation 3-24-22:41
Green Wall, The (See: Muralla
  Verde, La)
Green Years, The 3-13-46:10
Greene Murder Case, The 8-14-
  29:18
Green-Eyed Blonde, The 12-11-
  57:6
Greengage Summer 4-12-61:6
Greenhorn and the Girl, The 10-
  01-10:18
Greenhorns, The 4-23-10:16
Greenie, The (s) 2-04-42:8
Greenwich Village 8-09-44:12
Greenwich Village Story 9-04-63:6
Greenwood Tree, The 12-17-30:
  26
Greetings 12-25-68:18
Greifer, Der (See: Copper, The)
Greifer, Der 9-03-58:6
Grell Mystery, The 11-23-17:45
Greluchon Delicat 10-23-34:25
Grenoble (See: 13 Jours en France)
Grenzfeuer 12-30-36:11
Gretchen, the Greenhorn 8-15-
  16:23
Grete Minde 5-25-77:26
Gretel und Liesel 1-28-31:42
Gretna Green 3-16-15:24
Greven Fran Grandel 11-16-49:
  29
Grey Devil, The 7-20-27:19
Grey Gardens 10-01-75:26
Grey Horizon, The 8-22-19:76
Greyfriars Bobby 7-19-61:6
Greyhound, The 6-05-14:19

Greyhound Ltd. 3-27-29:24
Grhana 2-13-80:17
Gri-Gri 4-11-56:7
Gribouille (See: Heart of Paris)
Gridiron Flash 1-22-35:15
Gridiron Glory (s) 11-27-29:21
Grido, Il 9-25-57:26
Grido Della Terra, Il 6-08-49:18
Grieche Sucht Griechin 11-30-66:
22
Griechische Felgen 6-01-77:17
Grief Street 10-13-31:15
Griffe et la Dent, La 5-26-76:36
Griffin and Phoenix 12-01-76:19
Grihapravesh 2-06-80:24
Grim Comedian 1-27-22:29
Grim Game, The 8-29-19:66
Grimaces 10-22-80:24
Grimm's Fairy Tales for Adults
1-27-71:17
Gringalet 10-02-46:16
Gringalet 10-21-59:23
Grinning Guns 8-03-27:18
Grip, The (s) 5-09-33:14
Grip of Iron 5-22-14:22
Grip of Jealousy, The 2-18-16:
22
Grip of the Strangler 10-15-58:6
Grip of the Yukon 7-11-28:25
Grips, Grunts and Groans (s) 2-
10-37:14
Gripsholm Castle, The (See:
Schloss Gripsholm)
Grisbi (See: Touchez Pas Au
Grisbi)
Grissly's Millions 1-17-45:14
Grissom Gang, The 5-26-71:13
Grit 3-05-24:23
Grit Wins 3-20-29:31
Grito Sagrado, El 8-04-54:6
Grizzly 5-26-76:18
Grocery Boy, The (s) 3-15-32:
14
Grock 3-18-31:34
Groenland 5-14-52:20
Groom Wore Spurs, The 2-07-51:
6
Groove Tube, The 5-15-74:30
Gros Bill, Le 10-19-49:18
Gross und Klein 7-02-80:20
Grosse Atlantik, Der 7-10-63:22
Grosse Attraktion, Die 9-15-31:
28
Grosse Caisse, La 8-18-65:6
Grosse Ekstase des Bildschitzer,
Die 9-03-75:20
Grosse Fahrt, Die 4-22-31:19
(Also see: Big Trail, The)

Grosse Liebe, Die 2-23-32:19
Grosse Liebespiel, Das 1-15-
64:6
Grosse Reinemachen, Das 6-29-
38:26
Grosse Sehnsucht, Die 10-13-31:
15 (Also see: Great Yearning,
The)
Grosse Tenor, Der 6-02-31:26
Grosse Tete, Une 7-25-62:6
Grosse Verhau, Der 9-22-71:14
Grosser Graublauer Vogel, Ein
7-14-71:20
Grosstadtschmetterling (See: City
Butterfly)
Grosstadtjugend (See: Children of
Metropolis)
Grouch, The 11-19-18:41
Ground Floor to the Left (See:
In Parteree Links)
Grounds of Marriage 12-13-50:8
Groundstar Conspiracy, The 5-10-
72:34
Group, The 3-02-66:6
Groupie Girl 10-07-70:22
Groupies 11-18-70:14
Grown-Up Children 4-17-63:6
Growth of Soil 10-02-29:22
Grozny Vek 1-16-77:24
Grudge, The 6-04-15:18
Gruen Ist die Heide 1-03-33:27
(Also see: Green Is the
Heath)
Gruene Kaiser, Der 3-15-39:18
Gruener Felder 10-27-37:19
Grumpy 3-29-23:36
Grumpy 8-06-30:21 (Also see:
Cascarrabias)
Gruppenbild mit Dame 5-18-77:
21
Gruss und Kuss, Veronika 3-04-
36:31
Grzeszny Zywot Franciszka Buly
9-24-80:20
Gsaladi Tuzfezek 2-28-79:22
Guadalajara 6-16-43:16
Guadalcanal Diary 10-27-43:
10
Guaglio 5-18-49:20
Guapo Del 900, Un 9-28-60:6
Guard That Girl 11-13-35:17
Guarded Lips 5-26-22:33
Guardian, The 8-17-17:25
Guardian of the Wilderness 3-02-
77:24
Guardians of Life (s) 11-09-55:6
Guardians of the Sea (s) 6-24-
42:8

175 ●

● H ●

H. C. Andersen: Italien 4-18-79: 23
H8 8-20-58:6
H. M. Pulham, Esq. 11-19-41:9
H-Man, The 6-03-59:6
Ha Gegjon Jozsef 7-28-76:24
Hababam Sinifi Tatilde 8-02-78: 20
Habanera, La 1-26-38:15
Haben Ha'oved 11-20-68:38
Habibeti--Ya Habba Atoot 9-05-79:27
Habit 9-09-21:45
Habit of Happiness, The 3-24-16: 29
Habla Mudita 7-04-73:18
Habricha el Hashemesh 8-16-72: 28
Hackenschmidt-Rogers Wrestling Match 2-29-08:12
Hadaka No Shima 11-15-61:6
Hadaka No Taisho 9-09-59:6
Hadaka No Taiyo 7-15-59:6
Hadashi No Gen 7-28-76:20
Hadjuk 3-12-75:76
Haek Kai Narok Dien Bien Phu 11-23-77:19
Haendeligt Unheld 2-10-71:17
Haendler der Vier Jahreszeiten, Der 4-12-72:16
Haervaerk 11-16-77:21
Haeschen in der Grube 1-01-69: 20
Hagenbeck's Menagerie 10-29-10: 14
Hagringen 8-03-60:7
Hai-Tang 10-08-30:23
Hail 5-24-72:26
Hail, Hero! 10-08-69:15
Hail! Mafia (See: Je Vous Salue, Mafia)
Hail the Conquering Hero 6-07-44:19
Hail the Woman 1-20-22:34
Hail to the Rangers 12-01-43:10
Haine 2-06-80:22
Hair 3-14-79:22
Hairpins 8-06-20:26

Hairy Ape, The 5-17-44:10
Haiti--Papa Doc Is Dead, Baby Doc Lives 6-14-72:18
Hajducka Vremena 3-02-77:24
Hajka 8-17-77:20
Hakuchu No Torima 8-10-66:6
Hakujitsumu 9-09-64:6
Halalos Tavasz 1-17-40:24
Halbe-Halbe 3-29-78:26
Halbstarken, Die 11-07-56:6
Halbzarte, Die 5-13-59:7
Haldane of the Secret Service 11-01-23:27
Half a Hero 7-29-53:6
Half a Sinner 6-26-34:16
Half a Sinner 6-05-40:14
Half a Sixpence 12-27-67:6
Half an Hour 1-28-21:39
Half Angel 6-03-36:54
Half Angel 4-11-51:6
Half Baked Relations (s) 6-12-34:19
Half Breed, The 7-14-16:19
Half Breed 7-21-22:35
Half-Breed, The 4-16-52:6
Half Dollar Bill 1-17-24:26
Half Marriage 8-14-29:31
Half Million Bribe, The 4-21-16: 31
Half Naked Truth, The 1-03-33: 27
Half Past Midnight 2-11-48:14
Half Pint 8-24-60:6
Half Shot at Sunrise 10-15-30:25
Half-Shot Shooters (s) 6-17-36: 23 and 7-15-36:31
Half-Way Girl 7-29-25:34
Half-Way Home 8-08-45:22
Half Way to Heaven 12-11-29:35
Half-Way to Hell 11-17-54:6
Half Way to Shanghai 9-09-42:14
Half Wit-Ness, The (s) 2-26-36: 15
Halfback, The 5-04-17:28
Halka 1-19-38:19
Hall Alla Doerrar Oeppna 11-21-73:6
Hall Johnson Singers (s) 3-10-37: 14
Hall of Injustice (s) 12-11-29:35
Hall Room Boys, The 7-18-19: 42
Hallelujah 8-28-29:18
Hallelujah, I'm a Bum 2-14-33: 12
Hallelujah the Hills 5-15-63:6
Hallelujah Trail, The 6-16-65:6
Halliday Brand, The 1-16-57:18

Hanover Street 5-16-79:21
Hans Christian Andersen 11-26-52:6
Hans le Marin 12-07-49:20
Hansel and Gretel 10-06-54:6
Hansuli Banker Upakatha 11-21-62:6
Happening, The 3-29-67:6
Happenings, The 5-07-80:576
Happiest Days of Your Life, The 3-15-50:12
Happiest Millionaire, The 6-28-67:6
Happiness 5-04-17:27
Happiness 3-12-24:26
Happiness Ahead 6-20-28:15
Happiness Ahead 10-16-34:12
Happiness Boys (s) 7-11-28:13; 11-21-28:13; 4-10-29:16
Happiness C.O.D. 12-25-35:15
Happiness Cage, The 7-12-72:24
Happiness of Three Dancers 11-10-54:6
Happiness of 3 Women 2-23-17:24
Happiness of Us Alone (See: Namonaku Mazushiku Utsu-kushiku)
Hapiness Remedy, The (s) 2-11-31:14
Happy 1-09-34:17
Happy Affair After 7-07-54:6
Happy Anniversary 11-04-59:6
Happy As Green Was Green 12-12-73:18
Happy Birthday (s) 7-10-29:13
Happy Birthday, Davy 4-01-70:14
Happy Birthday, Gemini 4-30-80:36
Happy Birthday, Wanda June 12-08-71:16
Happy Circus Days (s) 2-04-42:8
Happy Day 10-27-76:30
Happy Days 2-19-30:21
Happy Days 5-08-74:41
Happy Days in Tyrol (s) 6-16-31:21
Happy End 6-12-68:6
Happy Ending, The 3-04-25:39
Happy Ending, The 11-19-69:14
Happy Ever After 11-29-32:44
Happy Games 7-21-65:7
Happy Go Lovely 3-07-51:18
Happy-Go-Lucky 2-10-37:15
Happy Go Lucky 12-30-42:16
Happy Golf (s) 3-05-30:21
Happy Hooker, The 5-14-75:31
Happy Hooker Goes Hollywood,
    The 6-04-80:22
Happy Hooker Goes to Washington,
    The 9-07-77:24
Happy Hunting Ground (s) 5-31-32:14
Happy Is the Bride 3-12-58:6
Happy Land 11-10-43:34
Happy Landing 8-28-34:15
Happy Landing 1-26-38:14
Happy Little Honeymoon (s) 2-18-31:14 and 2-25-31:12
Happy Mother's Day ... Love, George 8-22-73:12
Happy New Year (See: Bonne Annee, La)
Happy Road, The 1-30-57:6
Happy Sixties, The 11-04-64:6
Happy Thieves, The 1-17-62:7
Happy Time, The 8-20-52:6
Happy Warrior, The 7-08-25:37
Happy Years, The 5-31-50:6
Ha'pritza Ha'gdola 3-11-70:22
Haps and Mishaps 10-23-09:13
Har Borjar Aventyret 12-15-65:15
Har Har Du Ditt Liv 7-12-67:24
Har Kommer Vi 11-26-47:20
Hara-Kari 12-05-28:24
Harakiri (See: Seppuku)
Harold Hondfaste 4-23-47:18
Harbor Lights 8-30-23:26
Harbor of Missing Men 4-19-50:8
Har modor 2-27-80:26
Hard Boiled 3-20-29:31
Hard Boiled Canary 2-26-41:16
Hard Boiled Haggerty 8-27-27:23
Hard Boiled Hampton (s) 6-05-29:15
Hard Boiled Yeggs (s) 11-12-30:21
Hard Cash 10-10-13:14
Hard Contract 4-16-69:6
Hard Day's Night, A 7-15-64:6
Hard, Fast and Beautiful 5-30-51:6
Hard Fists 6-01-27:24
Hard Guy, The (s) 9-03-30:19 and 9-10-30:17
Hard Guy, The 11-19-41:20
Hard Hombre, The 9-29-31:22
Hard Knocks 10-08-80:20
Hard Man, The 12-04-57:6
Hard Part Begins, The 11-14-73:14
Hard Ride, The 4-21-71:22
Hard Road, The 3-05-15:21
Hard Road, The 5-06-70:26
Hard Rock Breed, The 3-08-18:43

Hard Rock Harrigan   7-31-35:19
Hard Times   9-24-75:22
Hard to Get   10-02-29:22
Hard to Get   11-09-38:16
Hard to Handle   2-07-33:12
Hard Way, The   9-23-42:8
Hardcore   2-14-79:23
Harder They Come, The   9-06-72:16
Harder They Fall, The   3-28-56:6
Hardest Way, The   7-28-22:35
Hardi les Gars   11-17-31:26
Hardings' Heritage   4-24-14:22
Hardy's Ride High, The   4-19-39:22
Hare-Brained Hypnotist (s)   12-02-42:8
Harem, El   5-26-65:7
Harem   2-07-68:6
Harem Girl   1-16-52:6
Harem Scarem (s)   11-29-32:18
Harem Secrets (s)   12-15-31:14
Hari-Kari   5-15-14:23
Hark, Ye Hark (s)   6-19-35:21
Harlan County, U.S.A.   10-20-76:38
Harlem Globetrotters, The   10-17-51:20
Harlem Is Heaven   6-07-32:20
Harlem Knights (s)   12-04-29:15
Harlem on the Prairie   2-09-38:14
Harlem Sketches (s)   5-29-35:14
Harlequin   5-07-80:10
Harlis   2-07-73:18
Harlot   3-10-71:16
Harlow   5-19-65:6
Harlow   6-23-65:6
Harmon of Michigan   9-17-41:22
Harmonica Rascals (s)   12-12-33:19
Harmonic Sketch (s)   12-26-33:10
Harmony at Home   1-29-30:60
Harmony Boys (s)   6-26-29:12
Harmony Lane   10-30-35:14
Harmony Row   5-16-33:17
Harnessing a Horse   5-01-14:21
Haro   3-01-78:31
Harold and Maude   12-15-71:18
Harold Lloyd's Funny Side of Life   11-23-66:6
Harold Teen   8-15-28:17
Harold Teen   6-05-34:29
Harom Sarkany   11-25-36:19 and 12-30-36:11
Harp in Hock, A   11-02-27:20
Harp of Burns   1-30-57:7

Harper   2-16-66:6
Harper Valley, P.T.A.   6-07-78:25
Harpoon   11-24-48:6
Harrad Experiment, The   5-16-73:32
Harrad Summer, The   8-14-74:16
Harriet and the Piper   10-22-20:39 and 1-28-21:40
Harriet Craig   11-01-50:6
Harrigan's Kid   3-10-43:15
Harrington Sisters (s)   8-22-28:14
Harris and Howe (s)   12-12-28:14
Harry and Dan Downing (s)   10-24-28:24
Harry and Tonto   7-31-74:18
Harry and Walter Go to New York   6-16-76:18
Harry Black   7-30-58:6
Harry Bros., The   3-05-10:13
Harry Delf (s)   10-31-28:24
Harry Fox (s)   6-26-29:12 and 10-01-30:19
Harry Horlick and the A&P Gypsies (s)   6-05-29:15 and 2-05-35:14
Harry Horlick and Orchestra (See: Harry Horlick and A&P Gypsies)
Harry in Your Pocket   8-22-73:12
Harry Lauder Pictures   4-03-14:21
Harry Munster   1-14-70:20
Harry of Kammertjener   5-30-62:22
Harry Warren (s)   11-21-33:14
Harukanaru Yama No Yobigoe   5-28-80:14
Harum Scarum   10-27-65:6
Harvard, Here I Come   4-01-42:8
Harvest   10-11-39:13
Harvest, and So Ye Shall Reap   10-18-67:18
Harvest Melody   12-08-43:8
Harvest of Hate   2-13-29:30
Harvest: 3,000   4-07-76:32
Harvester, The   11-09-27:25
Harvester, The   7-08-36:15
Harvey   10-18-50:6
Harvey Girls, The   1-02-46:8
Harvey Middleman, Fireman   7-14-65:7
Has Anybody Seen My Gal   6-11-52:6
Has the World Gone Mad   4-19-23:36
Hasard et la Violence, Le   5-08-74:41
Hasards de la Gloire, Les   4-04-73:26

Haschish 10-23-68:22
Hasenklein 5-31-32:25
Hasereth Festival Hayeladim 8-06-80:36
Hashechuna Shelanu 1-01-69:6
Hashi No Nai Kawa 7-23-69:28
Hashinura Togo 8-17-17:25
Hashoter Azulai 7-28-71:14
Hassan Terro 11-06-68:26
Hasta Que El Matrimonio Nos Separe 3-23-77:24
Hasty Heart, The 9-21-49:8
Hasty Heart, The 12-07, 49:6
Haszakadas 7-31-74:22
Hat Check Girl 10-11-32:20
Hat Check Honey 3-08-44:14
Hat, Coat and Glove 7-31-34:14
Hat Juggler, The 8-28-09:13
Hatari! 5-23-62:6
Hatarnegol 3-31-71:6
Hatbox Mystery, The 8-27-47:16
Hatchet Man, The 2-09-32:15
Hate 6-22-17:25
Hate 6-30-22:32
Hate Ship, The 1-15-30:37 and 11-19-30:28
Hater of Men 6-22-17:27
Hatful of Rain, A 6-19-57:7
Hatred 1-29-41:18
Hats Off (s) 6-02-31:14 and 7-07-31:25
Hats Off 1-06-37:41
Hatter's Castle 12-24-41:16
Hatteras Honkers (s) 6-03-42:24
Haunted Bedroom, The 6-27-19:45
Haunted Castles 2-24-26:46
Haunted Gold 1-17-33:15
Haunted Hat 9-04-09:13
Haunted House, The 12-19-28:12
Haunted House 9-18-40:14
Haunted House, The (s) 2-12-30:18
Haunted Pajamas, The 6-22-17:22
Haunted Range, The 10-05-27:25
Haunted Ship, The 2-01-28:22
Haunted Ship, The (s) 7-02-30:25
Haunted Strangler, The 5-28-58:6
Haunting, The 8-21-63:6
Haunting Fear, The 6-18-15:18
Haunting of M., The 11-28-79:17
Haunts 7-20-77:18
Hauptdarsteller, Der 12-28-77:14
Hauptlehrer Hofer 2-09-77:24

Hauptmann Kreutzer 7-06-77:17
Hauptmann Trial 2-05-35:14
Hauptmann und Sein Held, Der 9-14-55:6
Hauptmann von Koeln, Der 12-21-60:6
Hauptmann von Koepenick, Der 1-12-32:28 and 1-24-33:19
Hauptmann von Koepenick, Der 9-12-56:18
Haupsache Ferien 9-27-72:6
Haus des Lebens 3-25-53:78
Haus in der Karpfengasse, Das 7-07-65:16
Hausfrauen-Report 8-25-71:23
Havana Casino Orchestra (s) 7-07-31:25 (Also see: Havana Orchestra)
Havana Cocktail (s) 10-06-31:23
Havana Orchestra 7-30-30:16 (Also see: Havana Casino Orchestra)
Havana Rose 9-19-51:6
Havana Widows 11-28-33:20
Have a Drink (s) 2-08-28:24
Have a Heart 10-23-34:18
Have a Nice Weekend 9-24-75:22
Have a 200 Fix 10-21-36:23
Have Rocket, Will Travel 7-29-59:6
Have You Heard of the San Francisco Mime Troup? 7-03-68:6
Having a Wild Weekend 6-23-65:7
Having Wonderful Crime 2-21-45:8
Having Wonderful Time 6-15-38:14
Havou Banot Le'eilat 6-30-65:6
Hawaii 10-05-66:6
Hawaii Calls 3-02-38:15
Hawaiian Buckaroo 2-02-38:17
Hawaiian Fantasy (s) 1-03-33:19
Hawaiian Nights (s) 9-05-28:14
Hawaiian Nights (s) 3-06-29:12
Hawaiian Nights 8-23-39:14
Hawaiian Pineapples (s) 5-28-30:21
Hawaiian Romance (s) 5-28-30:21
Hawaiians, The 6-17-70:16
Hawk, The 5-11-17:34b
Hawk of Powder River, The 3-03-48:8
Hawk of Wild River, The 2-12-52:18
Hawk the Slayer 12-24-80:14
Hawkin's Hat 10-29-10:14
Hawkins & Watkins (s) 7-12-32:16

Hawks and the Sparrows, The
(See: Uccellacci e Uccellini)
Hawk's Nest, The 6-27-28:34
Hawley's of High Street 6-06-33:
15
Hawmps 5-26-76:19
Hawthorne of the U.S.A. 11-21-
19:55
Hay Foot, Straw Foot 6-27-19:
45
Hay Que Caesar a Ernesto 9-17-
41:22
Hay Que Romper in Rutina 10-09-
74:18
Hay Tang 3-26-30:39
Hay Wire (s) 6-04-30:24
Hayam Ha'Acharon 5-07-80:574
Haz a Sziklak Alatt 9-17-58:18
Hazal 5-21-80:22
Hazard 3-17-48:8
Hazardous Valley 11-30-27:23
Hazel Green and Band (s) 9-12-
28:12
Hazel Kirke 2-04-16:25
Hazing, The 1-18-78:19
He 1-09-34:17 (Also see: Rosier
de Mme. Husson, Le)
He and She 6-24-70:17
He Comes Up Smiling 9-13-18:45
He Couldn't Help It 2-23-27:19
He Couldn't Take It 3-27-34:12
He Couldn't Say No 4-06-38:14
He Did and Didn't 2-04-16:29
He Did His Best (s) 10-02-29:19
He Fell in Love with His Wife
10-30-09:11
He Fell in Love with His Wife
3-10-16:29
He Found a Star 10-08-41:20
He Got Rid of the Moths 1-22-
10:15
He Got There After All 2-09-17:
25
He Hired the Boss 3-10-43:23
He Knew Women 4-23-30:36
He Knows You're Alone 8-27-80:
20
He Laughed Last 7-25-56:18
He Loved an Actress 5-25-38:13
He Man Jockey (s) 1-05-32:19
He Married His Wife 1-17-40:14
He Met the Champion 9-17-10:12
He Nacido en Buenos Aires 12-
30-59:6
He Never Gives Up 7-25-79:17
He Ran All the Way 6-06-51:6
He Rides Tall 2-26-64:6
He Stayed for Breakfast 8-14-40:14

He Tried On Handcuffs 9-11-09:
12
He Trumped Her Ace (s) 3-19-30:
20
He Walked by Night 11-10-48:15
He Was Her Man 5-22-34:15
He Was 25¢ Short of His Salary
5-29-09:11
He Who Laughs Last Laughs Best
11-28-08:10
He Who Gets Slapped 11-12-24:24
He Who Rides a Tiger 1-26-66:6
Head, The 10-18-61:22
Head 10-16-68:28
Head 11-13-68:6
Head Guy (s) 6-18-30:37
Head Hunters of Equador (s) 1-25-
28:13
Head Man, The 9-26-28:15
Head of a Tyrant 5-11-60:6
Head of the Family 12-19-28:23
Head of the Family 9-06-67:6
Head On 9-29-71:18
Head On 10-01-80:22
Head over Heels 10-24-79:17
Head over Heels in Love 2-17-
37:14
Head Work (s) 2-19-30:21
Headache, The (s) 6-02-31:14
Headache Man, The (s) 12-03-30:
15
Headin' East 12-29-37:19
Headin' for God's Country 7-28-
43:8
Headin' for the Rio Grande 2-24-
37:19
Headin' for Trouble 10-06-31:29
Headin' Home 9-24-20:42
Headin' North 9-22-22:42
Headin' South 3-01-18:43
Headin' West 2-10-22:35
Headin' Westward 7-24-29:35
Heading for Heaven 12-24-47:13
Headless Horseman, The 1-05-
23:42
Headless Horseman, The 6-25-
75:24
Headleys at Home, The 3-01-39:15
Headline 12-08-43:8
Headline Crasher 8-11-37:34
Headline Shooter 10-24-33:17
Headline Woman, The 6-26-35:26
Heads Up 4-21-26:35
Heads Up 10-15-30:25
Heads We Go 9-12-33:17
Headwaiter, The 7-03-29:17
Health 8-27-80:21
Health in War (s) (See: British War
Docus)

Hear 'Em and Weep (s) 5-23-33: 15
Hear Generous Way 12-04-09:13
Hear Me Good 10-16-57:6
Hear Ye Hear Ye (s) 2-12-35:19
Hearse, The 9-24-80:20
Hearst-Wiz Radio Kids (s) 6-20-28:14
Heart and Soul 5-25-17:23
Heart and Soul 6-28-50:18
Heart Bandit, The 1-31-24:23
Heart Beat 12-05-79:22
Heart Beat 12-05-79:22
Heart Burn (s) 3-25-42:18
Heart Buster, The 7-09-24:25
Heart in Pawn, A 2-28-19:56
Heart Is a Lonely Hunter, The 7-31-68:6
Heart Line, The 7-15-21:29
Heart of a Clown, The 12-04-09: 13
Heart of a Coward 5-11-27:21
Heart of a Follies Girl 3-14-28: 23
Heart of a Girl, The 6-21-18:28
Heart of a Gypsy, The 12-05-19: 61
Heart of a Hero, The 11-03-16: 30
Heart of a Lion, The 2-01-18:43
Heart of a Man, The 6-17-59:6
Heart of a Nation 3-17-43:8
Heart of a Painted Woman, The 4-23-15:18
Heart of a Race Trout 7-24-09: 11
Heart of a Siren 4-08-25:38
Heart of a Texan 8-04-22:36
Heart of a Woman, The 10-08-20:42
Heart of Arizona 4-20-38:15
Heart of Broadway 4-04-28:29
Heart of Ezra Greer, The 10-26-17:29
Heart of Glass (See: Herz Aus Glas)
Heart of Gold 1-17-19:53
Heart of Juanita, The 12-05-19: . 62
Heart of Lincoln, The 2-05-15: 21
Heart of Maryland, The 3-26-15:21
Heart of Mexico (s) 6-24-42:8
Heart of New York 3-08-32:23
Heart of Nora Flynn, The 4-21-16:28
Heart of Paris 1-18-39:12

Heart of Paula, The 4-07-16:22
Heart of Rachel, The 10-04-18: 47
Heart of Romance, The 2-08-18: 41
Heart of Salome, The 4-27-27:21 and 6-08-27:14
Heart of Tara, The 3-10-16:30
Heart of the Blue Ridge, The 10-29-15:23
Heart of the Golden West 11-18-42:8
Heart of the Hills 12-05-19:61
Heart of the Matter 11-11-53:22
Heart of the North 9-30-21:35
Heart of the North 12-14-38:14
Heart of the Rio Grande 3-11-42:20
Heart of the Rockies 9-22-37:19
Heart of the Sunset 7-12-18:34
Heart of Texas Ryan, The 2-23-17:24
Heart of the Hills, The 10-13-16:28
Heart of the Rockies 3-28-51:16
Heart of the West 2-17-37:23
Heart of the Wilds 8-23-18:42
Heart of the Yukon, The 5-18-27:24
Heart of 20 6-25-20:35
Heart of Virginia 5-05-48:8
Heart of Wetona, The 1-10-19:45
Heart Punch 12-13-32:15
Heart Raider 6-07-23:24
Heart Specialist, The 3-24-22:41
Heart Strings 1-26-17:28
Heart Thief, The 4-27-27:17
Heart to Heart 9-12-28:12
Heart to Let, A 8-05-21:27
Heart Trouble 10-10-28:26
Heartaches 7-02-47:13
Heartbeat 9-06-39:19
Heartbeat 4-24-46:8
Heartbreak 10-20-31:27
Heartbreak Kid, The 12-13-72: 20
Heartbreak Ridge 4-06-55:6
Heartbreakers, The 2-11-16:24
Heartland 3-12-80:23
Heartland Reggae 3-26-80:21
Heartless Husbands 8-25-26:22
Hearts Adrift 2-20-14:23
Hearts Aflame 2-08-23:41
Hearts and Hoofs (s) 5-28-30:21
Hearts and Masks 7-01-21:29
Hearts and Minds 5-15-74:28
Hearts and Spangles 7-14-26:18
Hearts and Sparks 7-07-16:25

Hearts and Spurs 7-15-25:35
Hearts Are Trumps 1-28-21:40
Hearts Asleep 3-28-19:92
Heart's Desire 9-04-35:31 and
  7-14-37:21
Hearts Divided 9-01-22:42
Hearts Divided 6-17-36:23
Heart's Heaven 11-24-22:35
Hearts in Bondage 10-21-36:17
Hearts in Dixie 3-06-29:15
Hearts in Exile 4-09-15:20
Hearts in Exile 12-04-29:23
Hearts of Humanity 9-27-32:21
Hearts of Men 11-12-15:22
Hearts of Men 4-11-19:55 and
  6-10-19:53
Hearts of Men 6-06-28:25
Hearts of Oak 5-15-14:22
Hearts of Oak 1-21-25:36
Hearts of the West 10-01-75:18
Hearts of the World 4-12-18:43
Hearts of Youth 5-20-21:41
Hearts That Are Human 11-19-
  15:24
Heartsease 8-29-19:68
Heartstrings 11-08-23:29
Heat 6-21-72:18
Heat Lightning 3-13-34:16
Heat Wave 5-22-35:17
Heat's On, The 12-01-43:10
Heave 2 (s) 6-20-33:11
Heaven Can Wait 7-21-43:22
Heaven Can Wait 6-28-78:20
Heaven Help the Working Girl (s)
  12-26-33:10
Heaven Is Around the Corner 3-
  08-44:14
Heaven Knows, Mr. Allison 3-
  20-57:6
Heaven on Earth 6-08-27:17
Heaven on Earth 12-22-31:19
Heaven on Earth 11-02-60:6
Heaven Only Knows 7-30-47:8
Heaven with a Gun 4-02-69:6
Heaven with Barbed Wire Fence
  12-06-39:14
Heavenly Body, The 12-29-43:8
Heavenly Days 8-02-44:10
Heaven's Gate 11-26-80:14
Heavy Load 5-28-75:18
Heavy Traffic 7-25-73:7
Hecho Violento, Un 10-07-59:6
Hectic Days 5-29-35:34
Hedda 11-26-75:20
Hedda Hopper's Hollywood (s)
  2-18-42:8; 6-24-42:8; 8-19-
  42:21; 9-16-42:20
Hedelmaton Puu 7-02-47:22

Heedless Moths 6-10-21:34
Hei Tiki 2-05-35:31
Heiden von Kummerow, Die 3-20-
  68:26
Heidi 11-10-37:18
Heidi 12-31-52:6
Heidi 4-03-68:22
Heidi and Peter 5-18-55:9
Heights of Hazard 11-12-15:23
Heilige Erbe, Das 5-01-57:7
Heimatland 10-05-55:6
Heimatsklange 2-18-31:14
Heimlich, Still und Leise 11-25-
  53:24
Heinrich 5-18-77:16
Heinrich Heine Revue 9-10-80:28
Heintje--Ein Herz Geht Auf Reisen
  12-03-69:20
Heintje--Einmal Wird die Sonne
  Wieder Scheinen 6-03-70:20
Heir of Clavencourt Castle, The
  12-18-09:15
Heir of the Ages 7-20-17:30
Heir of the Largarders, The 4-
  02-15:21
Heir Spricht Berlin 4-12-32:15
Heir to the Hoorah, The 11-03-
  16:30
Heir to Trouble 2-12-36:31
Heiratskandidaten 5-07-58:22
Heiress, The 1-10-13:14
Heiress, The 7-16-15:18
Heiress, The 9-07-49:11
Heiress at "Coffee Dan's," The
  12-15-16:37
Heiress for a Day 3-01-18:42
Heiser Sand auf Sylt (See: New
  Life Style, The)
Heisse Spur St. Pauli 12-29-71:
  14
Heisses Blut 6-24-36:45
Hej, Stine! 1-31-71:24
Held by the Enemy 10-01-20:34
Held by the Law 2-09-27:16
Held for Ransom 8-22-08:13
Held for Ransom (s) 6-05-34:12
Held for Ransom 7-20-38:12
Held to Answer 11-15-23:23
Helden 1-28-59:6
Heldorado 12-25-46:24
Helen Morgan Story, The 9-18-
  57:6
Helen of Troy 2-04-25:39 and
  12-14-27:18 (Reprinted: 1-
  04-28:38)
Helen of Troy 12-21-55:6
Helena 4-16-24:27
Helena Ritchie 12-29-16:20

Helene 1-26-38:15
Helen's Babies 1-21-25:36
Helga 1-17-68:24
Helga und Michael 10-30-68:26
Heliotrope 12-03-20:32
Hell and High Water 12-19-33:19
Hell and High Water 2-03-54:6
Hell Below 5-02-33:12
Hell Below Zero 6-30-31:20
Hell Below Zero 1-27-54:6
Hell Bent fer Heaven 5-05-26:21
Hell Bent for Frisco 8-11-31:22
Hell Bent for Leather 1-13-60:7
Hell Bent for Love 7-31-34:14
Hell Bound 5-13-31:64
Hell Bound 10-02-57:6
Hell Cat, The 11-29-18:41
Hell Cat, The 7-10-34:13
Hell Diggers, The 8-26-21:36
Hell Divers 12-29-31:166
Hell Divers 8-14-57:20
Hell Fire Austin 8-02-32:17
Hell Harbor 4-09-30:39
Hell in the Heavens 12-18-34:13
Hell in the Pacific 12-11-68:30
Hell Is a City 5-18-60:7
Hell Is for Heroes 5-30-62:6
Hell Morgan's Girl 3-02-17:28
Hell on Devil's Island 8-21-57:6
Hell on Earth 2-06-34:34 (Also
   see: Niemandsland)
Hell on Frisco Bay 12-28-55:6
Hell on Wheels 9-27-67:26
Hell Raiders of the Deep 6-09-
   54:20
Hell River (See: Partisani)
Hell Roarin' Reform 2-21-19:67
Hell Ship Bronson 6-20-28:15
Hell-Ship Morgan 3-11-36:27
Hell Squad 10-29-58:6
Hell to Eternity 8-03-60:7
Hell-to-Pay Austin 8-11-16:26
Hell Up in Harlem 1-02-74:6
Hell with Heroes, The 8-14-68:6
Hellbenders, The 9-06-67:6
Hellcats, The 6-18-69:6
Hellcats of the Navy 5-01-57:7
Helldorado 1-08-35:18
Helle 6-07-72:18
Helle for Lykke 7-23-69:26
Heller in Pink Tights 3-09-60:6
Hellfighters, The 11-27-68:6
Hellfire 6-01-49:11
Hellgate 9-10-52:6
Hellion, The 10-03-19:57
Hellions, The 11-15-61:6
Hello Baby (s) 4-30-30:17
Hello Budapest 11-13-35:17

Hello Cheyenne! 6-20-28:19
Hello, Dolly 12-24-69:14
Hello Down There 3-26-69:6
Hello, Everybody 12-24-30:21
   (Also see: Elstree Calling)
Hello, Everybody 1-31-33:12
Hello, Frisco, Hello 3-10-43:15
Hello Good Times (s) 2-02-32:15
Hello Goodbye 7-08-70:14
Hello Goodnight Goodbye 8-27-75:
   16
Hello, Lafayette (s) 7-21-26:19
Hello, Moscow 6-19-46:22
Hello Russia (s) 12-24-30:21
Hello Sister 3-05-30:33
Hello, Sister! 5-09-33:15
Hello, Sucker (s) 3-25-31:16
Hello Sucker 7-02-41:12
Hello Sunshine (s) 7-30-30:16
Hello Television (s) 10-15-30:25
Hello, Thar! (s) 4-02-30:18
Hello Trouble 10-18-32:19
Hell's Angels 6-04-30:25 and 1-
   17-40:14
Hell's Angels '69 7-30-69:38
Hell's Angels on Wheels 6-14-
   67:6
Hell's Belles 4-09-69:28
Hell's Bells (s) 3-05-30:21
Hell's Cargo 11-29-39:18
Hell's Crossroads 5-22-57:6
Hell's End 7-19-18:36
Hell's Five Hours 3-26-58:14
Hell's Half Acre 2-10-54:6
Hell's Headquarters 5-31-32:15
Hell's Heroes 1-01-30:28 (Also
   see: Galgenvoegel)
Hell's Highroad 10-07-25:46
Hell's Highway 9-27-32:21
Hell's Hinges 2-11-16:21
Hell's Hole 11-22-23:27
Hell's Holiday 7-18-33:37
Hell's Horizon 11-23-55:6
Hell's House 2-16-32:24
Hell's Island 7-23-30:31
Hell's Island 5-05-55:6
Hell's Kitchen 7-05-39:14
Hell's Outpost 3-09-55:6
Hellstrom Chronicle, The 6-16-
   71:22
Hellzapoppin' 12-24-41:8
Help! 8-04-65:7
Help! De Doktor Verzuipt 7-31-
   74:19
Help! Help! Police 5-02-19:59
Help Wanted 5-07-15:17
Help Wanted--Male! 8-20-20:35
Help Yourself 9-24-20:43

185 ●

Helping Grandma (s) 10-29-30:17
Helpmates (s) 4-19-32:14
Helyet Az Gregeknek 1-08-35:39
Hem Hayu Asara 12-07-60:22
Hemat I Natten 5-25-77:26 and
9-28-77:22
Hempas Bar 10-19-77:16
Hemsoborna 8-01-56:6
Hennes Melodi 2-18-42:19
Hennessy 7-23-75:20
Henri Le Bel (s) 12-12-28:14
Henry Aldrich, Boy Scout 1-05-
44:16
Henry Aldrich, Editor 9-30-42:8
Henry Aldrich for President 7-30-
41:8
Henry Aldrich Gets Glamour 12-
30-42:23
Henry Aldrich Haunts a House 11-
10-43:35
Henry Aldrich Plays Cupid 4-26-
44:19
Henry Aldrich Swings It 6-30-
43:8
Henry Aldrich's Little Secret 6-
14-44:10
Henry and Dizzy 3-18-42:25
Henry Brown, Farmer (s) 12-02-
42:22
Henry V 4-24-46:8
Henry IV 3-10-48:22
Henry VIII 10-17-33:19
Henry VIII and His Six Wives 8-
02-72:24
Henry Goes Arizona 12-13-39:11
Henry, King of Navarre 5-07-24:25
Henry King Orchestra (s) 1-27-37:
12
Henry Miller Odyssey, The 9-18-
74:19
Henry Santry (s) 2-25-31:12
Henry, the Rainmaker 1-26-49:11
Hep Cat, The (s) 9-30-42:20
Her Accidental Husband 4-19-23:
36
Her Adopted Parents 10-01-10:18
Her Adventurous Night 6-26-46:11
Her American Husband 1-25-18:
45
Her Beloved Villian 12-03-20:33
Her Better Half 11-15-18:45
Her Better Self 5-25-17:23
Her Big Night 12-29-26:16
Her Blue Black Eyes (s) 11-30-
27:23
Her Body in Bond 6-21-18:28
Her Bodyguard 8-08-33:19
Her Boy 2-01-18:44

Her Broken Promise 5-05-16:23
Her Busy Day 9-18-09:13
Her Cardboard Lover 9-05-28:14
Her Cardboard Lover 5-27-42:8
Her Code of Honor 3-07-19:66
Her Country First 11-01-18:38
Her Debt of Honor 2-04-16:25
Her Debt of Honor 3-29-18:47
Her Decision 5-17-18:46
Her Discretion 10-12-27:24
Her Double Life 9-29-16:26
Her Duplicate Husband 12-25-14:
42
Her Excellency, The Governor 7-
06-17:28
Her Family Jewels 1-21-76:32
Her Fatal Millions 7-12-23:30
Her Fatal Sin 1-09-15:23
Her Father Said No 12-29-26:16
Her Father's Gold 5-12-16:20
Her Father's Keeper 3-23-17:20
Her Father's Son 10-20-16:25
Her Fiance and the Dog 10-08-
10:12
Her Fighting Chance 5-18-17:25
Her Final Reckoning 6-28-18:31
Her First Affair 2-26-47:11
Her First Affaire 12-27-32:54
Her First Appearance 4-23-10:16
Her First Beau 5-07-41:12
Her First Biscuits 6-26-09:12
Her First Elopement 1-21-21:42
Her First Kiss 8-22-19:75
Her First Mate 9-05-33:19
Her First Romance 5-02-51:6
Her Five-Foot Highness 4-09-20:
60
Her Forgotten Past 11-07-33:17
Her Gilded Cage 8-04-22:36
Her Good Name 1-26-17:29
Her Great Chance 10-18-18:38
Her Great Hour 1-07-16:23
Her Great Price 3-17-16:32
Her Greater Love 4-06-17:22
Her Guilty Secret 2-13-14:24
Her Half Brother 12-15-22:42
Her Highness and the Bellboy 7-
11-45:14
Her Honor the Governor 7-21-26:
14
Her Hour 11-16-17:51
Her Husband Lies 3-24-37:17
Her Husband's Affairs 7-23-47:
10
Her Husband's Friend 11-22-18:
45
Her Husband's Secret 7-15-25:
34

Her Husband's Secretary 3-24-37: 17

Her Husband's Trademark 2-24-22:34

Her Husband's Women (s) 8-14-29: 18

Her Jungle Love 3-23-38:16

Her Kind of Man 4-24-46:8

Her Kingdom of Dreams 9-26-19: 60 and 10-17-19:63

Her Ladyship 5-01-14:21

Her Last Affaire 11-06-35:21

Her Life and His 2-02-17:22

Her Lord and Master 4-01-21:41

Her Mad Bargain 4-28-22:43

Her Mad Night 11-29-32:19

Her Majesty 8-18-22:41

Her Majesty Bunker Bean 4-12-18:42

Her Majesty Love 12-01-31:21

Her Man 8-23-18:40

Her Man 1-21-25:37

Her Man 9-17-30:30

Her Man o' War 9-15-26:17

Her Martyrdom 2-27-15:25

Her Master's Voice 2-26-36:37

Her Maternal Right 5-05-16:27

Her Mistake 4-05-18:44

Her Moment 8-16-18:37

Her Mother's Secret 12-17-15:18

Her Naked Soul 4-28-16:29

Her New Beau on His Wedding Day 3-28-13:14

Her New York 1-26-17:25

Her Official Fathers 4-13-17:24

Her One Mistake 5-17-18:46

Her Only Son 5-28-15:17

Her Only Way 8-23-18:42

Her Own Free Will 9-10-24:28

Her Own Money 2-24-22:34

Her Own Way 6-11-15:18

Her Painted Hero 10-29-15:23

Her Panelled Door 8-29-51:20

Her Price 8-02-18:39

Her Primitive Man 4-05-44:14

Her Private Affair 1-15-30:22

Her Purchase Price 2-11-21:41

Her Reckoning 11-05-15:22

Her Reputation 9-13-23:30 and 9-27-23:24

Her Resale Value 6-27-33:15

Her Right to Live 1-12-17:26

Her Screen Idol 6-21-18:29

Her Second Husband 1-11-18:44

Her Silent Sacrifice 11-30-17:44

Her Sister from Paris 8-26-25: 25

Her Sister's Rival 11-30-17:44

Her Sister's Secret 9-11-46:10

Her Sister's Sin 4-23-10:16

Her Social Value 2-17-22:10

Her Splendid Folly 11-14-33:30

Her Story 9-01-22:42

Her Strange Wedding 6-15-17:25

Her Sturdy Oak 8-12-21:34

Her Summer Hero 6-20-28:19

Her Sweet Revenge 4-30-10:16

Her Temporary Husband 1-03-24: 23

Her Terrible Ordeal 1-15-10:13

Her Triumph 2-12-15:23

Her Twelve Men 6-30-54:6

Her Unwilling Husband 12-10-20: 35

Her Vocation 7-23-15:18

Her Wedding Night 10-01-30:19

Her Wild Oat 2-08-28:16

Her Winning Way 9-23-21:42

Her Wonderful Lie 5-10-50:16

Herbie Goes Bananas 7-02-80:18

Herbie Goes to Monte Carlo 6-22-77:17

Herbie Rides Again 3-27-74:14

Herbst der Gammler 11-01-67:6

Hercule 4-13-38:23

Hercules 5-13-59:6 (Also see: Fatiche di Ercole, Le)

Hercules Unchained (See: Ercole e la Regina di Lidia)

Herd on Horseback 7-13-27:23

Here Come the Co-eds 1-31-45: 10

Here Come the Girls 10-21-53:6

Here Come the Huggetts 12-08-48:11

Here Come the Jets 6-03-59:6

Here Come the Marines 5-28-52: 22

Here Come the Nelsons 1-16-52:6

Here Come the Waves 12-20-44:8

Here Comes Carter 11-08-36:13

Here Comes Cookie 10-16-35:22

Here Comes Elmer 10-27-43:10

Here Comes Everybody 11-15-72: 24

Here Comes Flossie (s) 11-21-33: 14

Here Comes Happiness 5-14-41:18

Here Comes Kelley 8-04-43:16

Here Comes Mr. Jordan 7-30-41: 18

Here Comes Showboat (s) 5-08-29: 20

Here Comes the Band 9-25-35:12

Here Comes the Circus (s) 8-02-32:15

Here Comes the Groom 6-19-34: 27
Here Comes the Groom 7-11-51: 6
Here Comes the Navy 7-24-34: 14
Here Comes the Tigers 5-31-78: 22
Here Comes Trouble 4-08-36:17
Here Comes Trouble 4-14-48:8
Here I Am a Stranger 9-27-39: 12
Here Is Ireland 10-09-40:18
Here Is My Heart 12-25-34:12
Here We Go Again 8-26-42:18
Here We Go Round the Mulberry Bush 1-24-68:6
Herederos, Los 7-08-70:24
Hereditary Instinct 2-05-30:31
Heredity 7-26-18:31
Herencia, La 5-06-64:16
Here's Flash Casey 10-20-37:27
Here's Looking at You, Kid 10-08-80:22
Here's the Gang (s) 6-05-35:15
Here's to Romance 10-09-35:14
Here's Your Life (See: Har Har Du Ditt Liv)
Heretic Father, A 8-21-09:17
Herfra Min Verden Gaar 2-18-76: 38
Heritage 10-01-20:34
Heritage 5-29-35:34
Heritage 11-06-40:16
Heritage, L' 8-27-75:15
Heritage of France, The 11-14-19:6
Heritage of the Desert 1-24-24: 27
Heritage of the Desert 3-14-33: 15
Heritage of the Desert 3-22-39: 20
Heritier, L' 4-11-73:61
Heritier de Mon Desir, L' 6-05-40:14
Heritiers, Les 3-30-60:6
Herkulesfurdoi Emlek 3-02-77:26
Hermana Blanca, La 12-28-60:6
Hermanas Karambazo, Las 7-06-60:22
Hermano Jose, El 11-19-41:20
Hermanos, Los 7-04-62:6
Hermanos del Hierro, Los 12-27-61:6
Hermine und die 7 Aufrechten 9-25-35:42
Hermit of Bird Island, The

3-12-15:24
Hero, The 3-08-23:31
Hero Ain't Nothin' but a Sandwich, A 12-14-77:12
Hero at Large 2-06-80:20
Hero for a Day 9-13-39:12
Hero for a Night, A 12-28-27:16
Hero of All Girls' Dreams, The 4-24-29:22
Hero of Submarine D-2, The 3-10-16:31
Hero of the Circus 12-19-28:23
Hero Worship (s) 6-03-42:24
Herod the Great 12-14-60:6
Heroes 11-02-77:17
Heroes All 11-17-31:26
Heroes and Husbands 9-01-22:42
Heroes Are Made 3-22-44:18
Heroes de la Marne 1-11-39:13
Heroes for Sale 7-25-33:14
Heroes in Blue 2-08-28:24
Heroes in Blue 12-06-39:14
Heroes of Shipka 9-12-56:6
Heroes of Telemark, The 11-03-65:6
Heroes of the Alamo 4-06-38:14
Heroes of the Hills 8-03-38:15
Heroes of the Night 6-29-27:26
Heroes of the Range 8-19-36:16
Heroes of the Saddle 1-17-40:24
Heroes of the Sea 4-30-41:18
Heroes of the Street 12-22-22:33
Heroic Somnambulist 5-22-09:14
Heroina 9-06-72:20
Hero's Island 9-19-62:6
Heros N' Ont Pas Froid Aux Oreilles, Les 1-10-79:27
Heros Sont Fatigues, Les 9-28-55:9
Hero's Wife, The (See: Eshet Ha'Gibor)
Herostratus 1-17-68:6
Herounes du Mal, Les 5-23-79: 37
Herr Buerovorsteher, Der 6-28-32:15
Herr der Welt, Der 12-18-35:13
Herr Finanzdirektor, Der 10-13-31:15
Herr Kobin Geht Auf Abenteuer 12-04-35:21
Herr Mit der Schwarzen Melone, Der 8-03-60:7
Herr Puntila und Sein Knecht Matti 12-11-57:14
Herr Ueber Leben und Tod 6-22-55:6
Herre Og Hans Tjener 7-22-59:6

Herren Machen Das Selber, Dass Ihnen Der Arme Mann Feyndt Wird, Die 3-26-80:27
Herren mit der Weissen Weste, Die 4-01-70:24
Herren von Maxim, Die 4-07-37:15
Herrenpartie 7-15-64:22
Herrliche Zeiten im Spessart 11-08-67:6
Herrscher, Der 4-07-37:14
Hers to Hold 7-14-43:18
Herschel Henlere (s) 1-01-30:15
Hertha's Erwachen 3-14-33:14
Herz Aus Glas 12-01-76:19
Herz Spielt Falsch, Ein 7-15-53:6
Herzblatt--Wie Sag Ich's Meiner Tochter 10-22-69:30
He's a Cockeyed Wonder 10-25-50:6
He's My Guy 3-17-43:8
Hesitating Love (s) 1-24-33:12
Hesper of the Mountains 8-04-16:28
Hester Street 5-14-75:27
Het Afscheid 9-14-66:24
Het Dwaallicht 5-30-73:24
Het Gangstermeisje 7-05-67:6
Het Mes 4-26-61:21
Het Verloren Paradise 9-27-78:22
Hetenkint Egyszer Lathatom 4-07-37:15
Hetzi-Hetzi 12-08-71:20
Heung 8-10-77:16
Heureux Qui Comme Ulysse 8-12-70:22
Heute Nacht Oder Nie 9-13-72:20
Hex 9-19-73:16
Hexer, Der 8-30-32:23
Hexer, Der 4-28-65:7
Hey Boy, Hey Girl 4-15-59:6
Hey Hey Cowboy 4-06-27:25
Hey! Hey! U.S.A. 10-05-38:21
Hey, Let's Twist! 12-20-61:6
Hey, Pop (s) 12-13-32:14
Hey, Rookie 4-12-44:10
Hey, Rube 3-20-29:13
Hey There, It's Yogi Bear 5-27-64:24
Heym Hayu Assara (See: They Were Ten)
Hi Beautiful 11-29-44:18
Hi, Buddy 2-17-43:14
Hi de Ho (s) 8-21-34:17

Hi-De-Ho 5-14-47:15
Hi Diddle Diddle 8-04-43:16
Hi Gaucho 4-29-36:27
Hi Good-Lookin' 3-15-44:32
Hi, Mom! 4-15-70:17
Hi, Nellie 2-06-34:14
Hi'Ya Chum 2-10-43:8
Hi'Ya, Sailor 10-06-43:8
Hi-Yo Silver 4-17-40:16
Hiawatha 12-10-52:6
Hibernatus 9-24-69:15
Hickey and Boggs 8-30-72:18
Hidden Aces 8-31-27:25
Hidden Children, The 4-06-17:25
Hidden Code, The 7-23-20:34
Hidden Danger 3-02-49:20
Hidden Enemy 4-03-40:14
Hidden Eye, The 7-25-45:20
Hidden Fear 7-17-57:6
Hidden Fires 11-08-18:41
Hidden Fortress, The (See: Kakushitoride No Sanakunin)
Hidden Gold 3-28-33:27
Hidden Gold 5-22-40:14
Hidden Guns 3-07-56:6
Hidden Hand, The 9-23-42:18
Hidden Light 11-19-20:34
Hidden Menace, The 4-10-40:18
Hidden Power 8-02-39:18
Hidden River 12-13-50:25
Hidden Scar, The 10-06-16:26
Hidden Spring, The 7-27-17:26
Hidden Truth, The 1-25-19:45
Hidden Valley 10-27-16:28
Hidden Way, The 12-08-26:20
Hide and Seek 6-24-64:6
Hide and Seek 9-15-76:16
Hide in Plain Sight 3-19-80:28
Hideaway 7-21-37:13
Hideaway Girls 1-20-37:15
Hideg Napok 7-27-66:7
Hide-Out, The 4-23-30:36
Hide-Out 8-28-34:15
Hideout, The (See: Planque, La)
Hideout 3-30-49:13
Hideout in the Alps 4-27-38:23
Hiding Place, The 5-14-75:31
Hidir 8-02-78:16
Hiev Up 6-26-78:22
Higgins Family, The 9-07-38:13
High 7-10-68:6
High and Handsome 9-02-25:37
High and Low (See: Tengoku To-Jigoku)
High and the Mighty, The 5-26-54:6
High Anxiety 12-21-77:20

High Barbaree   3-12-47:12
High Blood Pressure (s)   5-13-36:15
High Bright Sun, The   2-10-65:7
High C (s)   12-24-30:21
High Command   7-27-38:17
High Conquest   3-12-47:12
High Cost of Living   3-12-58:7
High Explosive   3-24-43:20
High Finance   4-13-17:22
High Flier, The   10-20-26:66
High Flight   9-25-57:6 and 3-19-58:6
High Flyers   11-10-37:19
High Fury   11-03-48:11
High Gear (s)   3-18-31:14
High Gear   4-18-33:41
High Hand, The   9-15-26:19
High Hat   4-27-27:17
High Hat   3-16-38:17
High Hats and Low Brows (s)   5-17-32:14
High Heels   10-28-21:34
High Hell   4-02-58:16
High Infidelity (See: Alta Infedelta)
High Lonesome   8-16-50:11
High Nests (s)   9-15-31:20
High Noon   4-30-52:6
High Plains Drifter   3-28-73:24
High Powered   2-21-45:8
High Powered Rifle, The   8-03-60:7
High Pressure   2-02-32:15
High Priestess of Sexual Witch-craft   6-20-73:20
High Rise   1-17-73:28
High Rolling   7-06-77:32
High Royal Highness   3-01-18:43
High School   1-10-40:16
High School   5-21-69:19
High School Confidential   5-28-58:6
High School Girl   3-20-35:17
High School Hellcats   8-27-58:6
High School Hero   10-26-27:18
High School Hero   10-23-46:10
High School Hoofer (s)   12-08-31:14 and 12-29-31:166
High Sierra   1-22-41:16
High Sign, The (s)   3-24-22:42
High Society   5-11-55:8
High Society   7-18-56:6
High Society Blues   4-23-30:26
High Speed   7-27-17:28
High Speed   5-28-24:29
High Speed   4-12-32:15
High Speed Biker, A   10-08-10:12

High Spots of Far East (s)   9-06-32:15
High Stakes   5-31-18:29
High Steppers (s)   6-02-31:14
High Tension   7-15-36:55
High Terrace   3-20-57:7
High Tide   8-30-18:37
High Tide   8-06-47:12
High Tide at Noon   5-15-57:6
High Time   9-21-60:6
High Toned (s)   4-02-30:18
High Treason   10-02-29:22
High Treason   11-21-51:18
High Velocity   9-28-77:22
High Wall   12-17-47:8
High Waters (s)   6-12-29:16
High, Wide, Handsome   7-28-38:16
High, Wild and Free   3-13-68:6
High Wind in Jamaica, A   5-26-65:6
High-Ballin'   6-07-78:25
Higher and Higher   12-15-43:8
Highest Bid, The   6-30-16:19
Highest Bidder, The   4-15-21:40
Highest Trump, The   1-25-19:46
Highlander's Defiance, The   1-15-10:13
Highlowbrow (s)   1-30-29:14
Highly Dangerous   12-13-50:25
Highway Dragnet   1-27-54:6
Highway of Hope, The   6-22-17:25
Highway Patrol   8-10-38:12
Highway 13   12-29-48:16
Highway 301   11-29-50:14
Highway West   8-06-41:8
Highwayman, The   8-22-51:10
Highways by Night   8-12-42:20
Hija del Ministro, La   4-07-43:8
Hi-Jacked   6-28-50:18
Hijo de Pistolero, El (See: Son of a Gunfighter)
Hijos Artificiales, Los   8-04-43:16
Hikinge   4-27-66:6
Hiko Shojo (See: Each Day I Cry)
Hilda (s)   10-09-29:23
Hilda Crane   5-02-56:6
Hilfe--Ich Liebe Zwillinge!   2-25-70:20
Hilfe, Meine Frau Klaut   8-26-64:6
Hill, The   6-09-65:6
Hill in Korea, A   10-10-56:7
Hill 24 Doesn't Answer   5-11-55:9
Hillbilly Blitzkrieg   9-16-42:8
Hillcrest Mystery, The   4-05-18:43

Hitler's Children 12-30-42:16
Hitler's Hangman 6-09-43:8
Hitler's Reign of Terror 5-01-
34:14
Hittin' the Trail 9-29-37:15
Hitting a New High 12-01-37:14
Hitting the High C's (s) 3-25-31:
16
Hitting the Trail 11-22-18:45
Hizzoner (s) 1-30-34:12
Hjartats Rost 6-30-31:20 (Also
see: Richiamo Del Cuore,
Sarah and Son, Toute Sa Vie,
and Wiegenlied)
Hjerter er Trumf 4-07-76:32
Hlidac 8-19-70:22
Ho 11-13-68:26
Ho Perduto Mio Marito 3-24-37:
31
Ho Scelto L'Amore 5-13-53:22
Ho Sognato il Paradiso 7-12-50:6
Hoa Binh 4-01-70:24
Hoarded Assets 12-20-18:35
Hoax, The 12-06-72:16
Hoaxters, The 12-10-52:6
Hobbies (s) 10-01-41:9
Hobbs in a Hurry 10-04-18:49
Hoboes' Christmas 12-24-10:16
Hoboes in Paradise 10-18-50:18
Hoboken Hokum (s) 9-25-29:17
Hoboken to Hollywood (s) 6-30-
26:16 and 10-06-26:54
Hobson's Choice 10-13-31:15
Hobson's Choice 3-03-54:6
Hochzeitsreise, Der 10-15-69:26
Hochzeitsreise Zu Dritt 3-21-33:
27
Hochzeitstraum, Ein 10-28-36:15
Hocus Focus (s) 5-02-33:12
Hocus Pocus (s) 4-01-31:16
Hocuspocus 10-12-66:24
Hodge Podge (s) 6-30-31:15
Hodina Pravdy 8-02-78:20
Hoedown 6-21-50:18
Hoehere Befehl, Der 4-15-36:23
Hoelle von Manitoba, Die 12-29-
65:6
Hoellische Liebe 12-14-49:22
Hoer, Var der Okke en Som Lo?
9-20-78:26
Hoffman 7-22-70:20
Hofkonzert 4-07-37:15
Hofrat Geiger 2-18-48:9
Hog Wild (s) 7-23-30:19
Hog Wild 6-11-80:24
Hogan's Alley 11-25-25:39
Hogy Szaladnak a Fak 11-15-67:
20
Hoitu Rabu 3-05-80:22

Hoitu Rabu 3-05-80:22
Hokuspokus 7-30-30:38
Hold Back the Dawn 7-30-41:8
Hold Back the Night 7-25-56:18
Hold Back Tomorrow 9-21-55:6
Hold 'Em Jail 8-23-32:46
Hold 'Em Navy! 11-10-37:19
Hold 'Em Yale 5-01-35:17
Hold Everything 3-26-30:25
Hold It (s) 2-24-37:15
Hold Me Tight 5-23-33:19
Hold On 3-16-66:7
Hold That Baby! 7-06-49:9
Hold That Blonde 11-14-45:12
Hold That Co-ed 9-28-38:14
Hold That Ghost 7-30-41:18
Hold That Girl 3-27-34:12
Hold That Kiss 5-11-38:16
Hold That Line 4-02-52:6
Hold That Lion 9-08-26:16
Hold That Woman 11-20-40:18
Hold the Press 12-05-33:17
Hold Your Horses 1-28-21:39
Hold Your Man 10-16-20:17
Hold Your Man 7-04-33:16
Hold Your Temper (s) 3-20-34:16
Holdudvar 2-26-69:32
Hold-Up, The (s) 4-11-33:17
Hold-Up in Calabria, A 2-29-08:
12
Hole in the Head, A 5-20-59:6
Hold in the Wall 1-06-22:43
Holiday 7-09-30:19
Holiday 5-18-38:12
Holiday Affair 11-16-49:16
Holiday Camp 8-13-47:15
Holiday for Lovers 7-15-59:6
Holiday for Sinners 6-25-52:6
Holiday in Havana 10-05-49:8
Holiday in Mexico 7-24-46:14
Holiday in Storyland (s) 4-02-
30:18
Holiday Inn 6-17-42:8
Holiday Rhythm 10-04-50:6
Holka Na Zabiti 7-28-76:22
Holland (s) 5-28-30:21
Holland in Tulip Time (s) 11-06-
34:16
Holland Mosaics (s) 2-28-33:14
Hollow Triumph 8-11-48:8
Holly and the Ivy, The 2-10-54:6
Hollywood 7-26-23:27
Hollywood and Vine 4-11-45:20
Hollywood at Home (s) 6-03-42:
24
Hollywood Babylon 2-16-72:18
Hollywood Barn Dance 6-04-47:
16

Home Sweet Home 3-29-72:30 and 11-21-73:12
Home Sweet Homicide 7-17-46:8
Home Town Girl, The 6-13-19: 50
Home Town Story 5-09-51:6
Home Wanted 6-27-19:44
Home Without Children, A 10-23-09:13
Home Work (s) 11-13-35:16
Home Work (s) 2-04-42:22
Homebodies 9-04-74:20
Homebreaker, The 7-11-19:57
Homecoming 7-31-29:23 (Also see: Home Coming)
Homecoming 4-07-48:10
Homecoming, The 10-31-73:26
Homeland of the Danes (s) 6-30-31:15
Homenaje a la Hora de la Siesta 8-29-62:6
Homer 9-30-70:15
Homer Come Home 7-02-20:27
Homes for All (s) 9-25-46:10
Homesick 2-06-29:19
Homespun Folks 10-08-20:41
Homespun Vamp 2-17-22:40
Homesteaders, The 3-25-53:6
Hometown, U.S.A. 7-04-79:24
Homeward Bound 8-02-23:23
Homicidal 6-21-61:20
Homicide 3-09-49:6
Homicide Bureau 2-08-39:19
Homicide for 3 11-17-48:13
Homicide Squad 10-20-31:27
Homicides: The Criminals, Part II 9-01-76:22
Homme a Abattre, Un 11-22-67:6
Homme a L'Hispano, L' 5-09-33: 17
Homme a L'Impermeable, L' 4-03-57:24
Homme a L'Oreille Cassee 4-24-35:13
Homme A Tout Faire, L' 4-02-80:26
Homme au Cerveau Greffe, L' 4-19-72:18
Homme au Chapeau Rond, L' 7-10-46:8
Homme aux Cles D'Or, L' 1-16-57:18
Homme d'Istanbul, L' 10-13-65:6
Homme de Desir, L' 4-22-70:26
Homme de Ma Vie, L' 5-28-52:24
Homme de Marrakech, L' 5-04-66:22
Homme de Rio, L' 3-11-64:6

Homme de Trop, Un 4-19-67:6
Homme du Jour, L' (See: Man of the Hour)
Homme du Niger, L' 3-20-40:16
Homme en Colere, L' 4-11-79: 21
Homme en Fuite, Un 6-11-80: 24
Homme en Habit, Un 7-14-31:55
Homme est Mort, Un 2-14-73:18
Homme et l'Enfant, L' 1-16-57: 20
Homme et Sa Femme, Un (See: Man and His Wife, A)
Homme et Son Peche, Un 2-23-49:6
Homme et une Femme, Un 5-18-66:7
Homme Marche Dans la Ville, Un 5-17-50:16
Homme Libre, Un 5-16-73:6
Homme Orchestre, L' 9-30-70: 22
Homme Presse, L' 8-31-77:19
Homme Que J'Ai Tue, L' 11-08-32:17
Homme Que Revient de Loin, L' 8-02-50:16
Homme Qui Aimait les Femmes, L' 4-27-77:24
Homme Qui Cherche la Verite, L' 4-10-40:18 (Also see: Man Who Seeks the Truth, The)
Homme Qui Dort, Un 4-10-74:20
Homme Qui Me Plait, Un 12-31-69:18
Homme Qui Ment, L' 4-10-68:22
Homme Qui Trahit la Mafia, L' 5-31-67:6
Homme Qui Valait des Milliards, L' 9-27-67:26
Homme Sans Nom, Un 11-15-32: 23 (Also see: Mensch Ohne Namen)
Homme Sans Visage, L' 6-26-74: 20
Hommes, Les 4-04-73:26
Hommes a Femmes, L' 12-07-60: 22
Hommes en Blanc, Les 11-23-55:6
Hommes Ne Pensent Qu'a Ca, Les 8-11-54:6
Hommes Veulent Vivre, Les 1-30-63:6
Homo Eroticus 11-24-71:16
Hon Dansade en Sommar 3-05-52:22

Hondo 11-25-53:6
Honest Crooks (s) 5-07-30:20
Honest Man, An 5-10-18:42
Honesty-Best Policy 8-25-26:19
Honey 4-02-30:19 (Also see:
Frau Hat Etwas, Eine and
Cherie)
Honey Pot, The 3-22-67:6
Honeybaby, Honeybaby 10-09-74:
19
Honeychile 11-14-51:16
Honeyless Honeymoon, The 2-02-
17:22
Honeymoon, The 12-07-17:49
Honeymoon 4-16-47:8
Honeymoon at Niagara Falls 3-
02-07:10
Honeymoon Beach (s) 10-18-32:
14
Honeymoon Deferred 2-21-40:
12
Honeymoon Express, The 9-08-
26:17 and 10-06-26:51
Honeymoon Flats 11-28-28:20
Honeymoon for Three, A 3-19-
15:21
Honeymoon for Three 2-12-41:14
Honeymoon Hate 12-14-27:21
Honeymoon Hotel (s) 2-27-34:17
Honeymoon Hotel 6-03-64:6
Honeymoon in Bali 9-13-39:12
Honeymoon Killers, The 9-10-
69:36
Honeymoon Land (s) 6-30-31:15
Honeymoon Lane 8-04-31-21
Honeymoon Limited 8-05-36:17
Honeymoon Lodge 7-28-43:8
Honeymoon Machine, The 7-05-
61:22
Honeymoon Ranch 10-22-20:41
Honeymoon Trail (s) 7-28-31:14
Honeymoon's Over, The 12-20-
39:47
Honeysuckle Rose 7-16-80:23
Hong Kong 11-14-51:6
Hong Kong Affair 4-16-58:6
Hong Kong Confidential 10-01-58:6
Hong Kong Emmanuelle 4-06-77:26
Hong Kong Tycoon, The 8-01-79:
42
Hong Thong 9-14-77:16
Hongyboly 8-16-72:26
Honjin Satsujin Jiken 7-14-76:21
Honk Your Horn (s) 6-25-30:109
Honkers, The 3-01-72:20
Honky 11-17-71:14
Honky Donkey (s) 10-23-34:18
Honky Tonk 6-12-29:29

Honky Tonk 9-17-41:9
Honneurs de la Guerre, Les 7-
26-61:13
Honning Maane 8-30-78:28 (Also
see: Honningmane)
Honningmane 11-05-80:22 (Also
see: Honning Maane)
Honno (See: Lost Sex)
Honolulu 2-01-39:13
Honolulu to Havana (s) 4-29-31:37
Honolulu-Tokyo-Hong Kong 12-18-
63:17
Honolulu Wiles (s) 10-01-30:19
Honoo to Onna 5-01-68:26
Honor 9-11-29:33
Honor Among Lovers 3-04-31:14
Honor Among Men 12-10-24:36
Honor Bound 5-09-28:17
Honor of His Family, The 1-29-
10:13
Honor of Mary Blake, The 12-
15-16:36
Honor of Old Glory 7-03-14:21
Honor of the Family 10-20-31:21
Honor of the Mounted 10-04-32:27
Honor of the Press 7-19-32:25
Honor of the Range 5-01-34:15
Honor of the West 7-26-39:27
Honor System, The 2-16-17:24
Honor System, The (s) 8-01-28:
12
Honor Thy Name 8-04-16:30
Honorable Algy 11-03-16:29
Honorable Catherine, The 8-25-
48:18
Honorable Friend, The 8-25-16:
25
Honor's Altar 3-17-16:32
Honor's Cross 6-28-18:28
Honors Easy 8-14-35:15
Hoodlum, The 9-05-19:61
Hoodlum, The 6-06-51:18
Hoodlum Empire 2-20-52:6
Hoodlum Priest 2-22-61:6
Hoodlum Saint, The 2-06-46:12
Hoodman Blind 3-26-24:44
Hoodoo, The 10-01-10:18
Hoodoo Ann 4-07-16:22
Hoofbeats of Vengeance 6-12-29:
35
Hook, The 1-16-63:6
Hook and Ladder No. 9 12-21-27:
25
Hook, Line and Sinker 12-31-30:
19
Hook, Line and Sinker 3-16-69:
30
Hook Line Melody (s) 9-25-29:17

Hooked (s) 7-02-30:25
Hooked Generation 4-16-69: 30
Hooper 7-26-78:20
Hoopla 12-05-33:17
Hooray for Love 7-17-35:27
Hoose Gow, The (s) 2-26-30:24
Hoosier Holiday 8-25-43:10
Hoosier Schoolboy 6-30-37:21
Hoosier Schoolmaster, The 11-14-14:25
Hoosier Schoolmaster, The 3-19-24:26
Hoosier Schoolmaster, The 9-25-35:12
Hoot Gibson Trio (s) 7-11-28:13
Hootenanny Hoot 8-28-63:6
Hop, the Devil's Brew 2-04-16: 29
Hopalong Cassidy 10-02-35:16
Hopalong Cassidy Returns 1-06-37:40
Hopalong Rides Again 11-17-37: 17
Hope, The 9-24-20:41
Hope 7-21-22:35
Hope, The (See: Nadeje)
Hope Chest, The 1-10-19:44
Hope Hamptom (s) 3-20-29:12
Hopeless Ones, The 2-23-66:6
Hopla Paa Sengekanten 2-04-76: 17
Hopper, The 2-01-18:45
Hoppla, Jetzt Kommt Eddie 5-13-59:6
Hoppy Serves a Writ 3-17-43:23 and 4-28-43:8
Hoppy's Holiday 5-07-47:18
Hopscotch 7-23-80:20
Hor Balevana 5-19-65:31
Hora de las Sorpresas, La 11-05-41:24
Hora de los Hornos, La 6-26-68: 22
Hora de los Ninos, La 10-14-70: 30
Hora de Maria y el Pajaro de Oro, La 4-07-76:30
Horace Heidt Orchestra (s) 10-09-29:23; 2-12-30:18; 12-01-31:15
Horace 62 2-14-62:6
Hordubal 10-29-80:20
Hori, Ma Panenko 12-06-67:6
Horizon 5-16-33:21
Horizon, L' 5-03-67:30
Horizons Sans Fin 7-15-53:6
Horizons West 9-24-52:6

Horizont 11-22-32:62
Horizont 9-08-71:27
Horizonte Te Hapura 1-24-79:22
Horloger de Saint-Paul, L' 1-30-74:16
Horn Blows at Midnight, The 4-04-45:10
Hornet's Nest 9-02-70:40
Horoki (See: Lonely Lane)
Horoskop 8-20-69:28
Horoskop der Familie Hesselbach, Das 2-15-56:6
Horror Castle 4-21-65:6
Horror House 4-29-70:18
Horror Island 4-02-41:16
Horror of Dracula 7-05-58:22
Horror of Frankenstein 10-21-70: 22
Horror of It All, The 9-16-64:19
Horror on Snape Island 4-26-72:6
Horrors of the Black Museum 4-22-59:6 and 5-06-59:6
Horrors of War 2-14-40:20
Horse, La 3-11-70:24
Horse and the Haystack, The 9-04-09:13
Horse Ate the Hat, The 9-08-31:50
Horse Feathers 8-16-32:15
Horse in the Gray Flannel Suit, The 10-16-68:6
Horse of Another Color, A 6-22-07:13
Horse Play 3-13-34:16
Horse Sense (s) 11-12-30:21
Horse Sense (s) 1-10-33:18
Horse Shoes 5-25-27:21
Horse Soldiers, The 6-10-59:6
Horse with the Flying Tail, The 1-25-61:6
Horseman of the Plains 5-02-28:26
Horsemen, The 2-07-51:18
Horsemen, The 6-23-71:20
Horsemen of the Sierras 3-08-50:6
Horses, Horses, Horses (s) 1-06-43:50
Horse's Mouth, The 9-17-58:6
Horseshoe, The 4-02-10:17
Horseshoes (s) 12-31-30:19
Horton Hatches the Egg (s) 4-22-42:18
Hose, Die (See: Royal Scandal, The)
Hosekraemmeren 12-29-71:6
Hoshizora No Marionette 8-23-78: 34
Hospital, The 12-08-71:16

Hospitality 11-08-23:26 (Also see:
    Our Hospitality)
Hostage, The 1-25-08:11
Hostage, The 9-14-17:36
Hostage, The 8-17-66:6
Hostages 8-11-43:10
Hostile Country 5-17-50:16
Hostile Guns 7-26-67:22
Hot Air Merchant (s) 8-20-30:
    14
Hot and Bothered (s) 11-12-30:
    21
Hot--and How (s) 1-15-30:22
Hot Angel 12-10-58:6
Hot Blood 2-29-56:6
Hot Bridge (s) 3-12-30:21
Hot Car Girl 6-18-58:6
Hot Cargo 3-13-46:10
Hot Cars 8-08-56:6
Hot Channels 5-23-73:28
Hot Circuit 3-22-72:20
Hot Curves 7-09-30:35
Hot Dog (s) 5-11-27:24
Hot Dog (s) 3-12-30:21
Hot Dog (s) 4-16-30:21
Hot Enough for June 3-11-64:6
Hot for Hollywood (s) 6-25-30:
    109
Hot for Paris 1-08-30:89
Hot from Petrograd (s) 9-26-33:
    15
Hot Heels 5-23-28:21
Hot Heiress 3-18-31:24
Hot Lead 10-24-51:6
Hot Lead and Cold Feet 7-12-76:
    30
Hot Lemonade (s) 9-18-29:15
Hot Millions 9-04-68:6
Hot Money 7-29-36:15
Hot New Margie (s) 11-24-31:17
Hot News 7-25-28:14
Hot News 11-25-53:24
Hot Paprika (s) 3-18-36:17
Hot Pepper 1-24-33:12
Hot Potato 4-07-76:30
Hot Rhythm 4-19-44:12
Hot Rock, The 1-26-72:16
Hot Rod 10-25-50:6
Hot Rod Gang 8-27-58:6
Hot Rod Girl 9-05-56:6
Hot Rod Rumble 5-15-57:22
Hot Rods to Hell 2-01-67:34
Hot Saturday 11-08-32:16
Hot Shots (s) 4-03-29:11
Hot Spell 5-14-58:6
Hot Spot 10-22-41:8
Hot Steel 6-26-40:18
Hot Stuff 5-15-29:49

Hot Stuff 6-06-79:20
Hot Summer Night 1-23-57:6
Hot Times 12-18-74:36
Hot Tip 10-23:35:12
Hot Tips (s) 11-20-29:12
Hot Tomorrows 5-03-78:22
Hot Water 9-10-24:26
Hot Water 11-03-37:14
Hot Wires (s) 4-01-31:16
Hotbed of Sin (See: Boite de Nuit)
Hotel 1-18-67:6
Hotel Alojamiento 4-27-66:19
Hotel Anchovy (s) 5-01-34:14
Hotel Berlin 3-07-45:20
Hotel Continental 3-22-32:13
Hotel de la Plage, L' 2-08-78:
    34
Hotel de Verano 5-10-44:10
Hotel des Etudiants 10-04-32:19
Hotel Du Nord 2-01-39:18
Hotel for Women 8-02-39:18
Hotel Haywire 6-16-37:13
Hotel Imperial 1-05-27:16
Hotel Imperial 5-10-39:14
Hotel Kikelet 9-22-37:18
Hotel La Swing (s) 3-24-37:16
Hotel Mysteries 4-10-29:23
Hotel Pacific 12-31-75:15
Hotel Paradiso 9-07-66:6
Hotel Pro Cizince 5-10-67:6
Hotel Reserve 6-28-44:16
Hotel Sahara 7-18-51:20
Hotel Variety 1-10-33:17
Hotelgeheimnisse (See: Hotel
    Mysteries)
H. O. T. S. 9-12-79:18
Hotsy Totsy (s) 12-25-29:20
Hottentot, The 2-22-23:41
Hottentot, The 9-11-29:18
Hotter Than Haiti (s) 10-27-31:
    19
Hottest Show in Town, The 11-20-
    74:16
Hou Halach Ba'Sadot 1-31-68:23
Houdini 5-20-53:6
Houkutuslintu 4-02-47:16
Hound-Dog Man 11-04-59:6
Hound of Silver Creek 9-05-28:
    31
Hound of the Baskervilles 9-15-
    22:42
Hound of the Baskervilles, The
    10-02-29:31
Hound of the Baskervilles, The
    4-19-32:15
Hound of the Baskervilles, The
    3-29-39:14
Hound of the Baskervilles, The

4-01-59:6
Hound of the Baskervilles, The
11-08-78:28
Hound That Thought He Was a
Racoon, The 8-10-60:6
Hounds of Notre Dame, The 10-
22-80:25
Houp-La 7-25-28:28
Hour Before Dawn 7-16-20:32
Hour Before the Dawn 3-08-44:14
Hour of Reckoning, The 11-30-27:
23 and 1-25-28:13
Hour of the Gun 10-04-67:16
Hour of the Wolf 2-28-68:22
Hour of 13, The 10-01-52:6
Hours of Love, The (See: Ore
Dell'Amore, Le)
House 9-21-77:18
House Across the Bay 2-28-40:
16
House Across the Street, The 8-
17-49:8
House Built on Sand, A 12-29-16:
23
House by the Lake, The 3-23-77:
22
House by the River 3-29-50:11
House Calls 5-15-78:21
House Divided, A 1-12-32:28
House I Live In, The (s) 10-10-
45:8
House in Naples 9-30-70:20
House in the Sun 5-29-29:26
House Is Not a Home, A 8-05-64:
6
House Next Door, The 7-23-15:19
House of a Thousand Candles 4-
08-36:16
House of 1,000 Dolls 11-08-67:6
House of Bamboo 7-06-55:6
House of Cards, The 12-18-09:15
House of Cards 10-23-68:6
House of Dark Shadows 9-02-70:
40
House of Death 8-16-32:15
House of Dracula 12-05-45:16
House of Fear, The 1-30-15:24
House of Fear, The 6-14-39:14
House of Frankenstein 12-20-44:
17
House of Fright 5-17-61:6
House of Glass, The 3-01-18:41
House of Gold, The 6-28-18:29
House of Greed 8-14-34:15
House of Horror 6-19-29:32
House of Intrigue, The 11-18-
59:6
House of Lies, The 9-22-16:34

House of Mirrors, The 8-11-16:
25
House of Mirth, The 8-16-18:38
House of Mystery, The 7-10-14:
21
House of Mystery 6-04-41:15
House of Numbers 6-26-57:6
House of Pleasure (See: Plaisir,
Le)
House of Rothschild 3-20-34:16
House of Sand, A 6-13-62:6
House of Scandal, The 6-06-28:
13
House of Secrets 10-23-29:17
House of Secrets 2-24-37:17
House of Secrets 10-31-56:6
House of Shame 8-29-28:31
House of Silence, The 4-26-18:41
House of Strangers 6-15-49:13
House of Tears, The 12-10-15:21
House of Temperley, The 5-15-
14:23
House of the Lost Court, The 5-
14-15:19
House of the Lute 8-08-79:22
House of the Seven Gables 3-13-
40:16
House of the Seven Hawks, The
1-11-59:6
House of the Sleeping Virgins 5-
08-68:36
House of Tolling Bells 9-17-20:
35
House of Toys, The 4-28-20:42
House of Usher 6-29-60:8
House of Wax 4-15-53:6
House of Whispers 10-15-20:42
House of Women 4-11-62:26
House of Youth 12-03-24:30
House on Chelouche Street, The
11-14-73:14
House on 56th Street 12-05-33:16
House on Haunted Hill 12-03-58:6
House on 92nd Street, The 9-12-
45:16
House on Skull Mountain, The 10-
16-74:16
House on Telegraph Hill, The 3-
07-51:6
House on the Front Line, The
(See: Na Semi Vetrach)
House on the Square, The 10-17-
51:20
House on the Waterfront, The (See:
Port de Desir)
House That Dripped Blood, The
3-03-71:17
House Under the Rocks 11-12-58:6

Hunchback, The 12-26-13:12
Hunchback of Notre Dame, The 9-06-23:22
Hunchback of Notre Dame, The 12-20-39:14
Hunchback of Notre Dame, The 11-06-57:6
Hunchback of the Morgue, The 5-16-73:32
Hunchback's Night (s) 4-16-30: 46
Hunde, Wollt Ihr Ewig Leben 9-09-59:6
Hundred Pound Window, The 12-08-43:8
Hundson-Fulton Land Parade 10-09-09:13
Hundson-Fulter Military Parade 10-09-09:20
Hungarian Goulash (s) 7-09-30: 19
Hungarian Nights 6-25-30:109
Hungarian Rhapsodie (s) 7-16-30:15
Hungarian Rhapsody 8-07-29:201
Hungary 3-10-37:15
Hungerjahre 3-05-80:26
Hungnam Story, The (s) 3-21-51:7
Hungry Actor 8-21-09:17
Hungry Arms 8-25-26:19
Hungry Eyes 3-08-18:44
Hungry Heart, A 1-26-17:29
Hungry Heart, The 11-30-17:43
Hungry Hearts 12-01-22:34
Hungry Hill 1-15-47:12
Hungry Wives 4-18-73:32
Hungry Wolf, The (s) 2-25-42:8
Hunt, The 12-31-15:24
Hunt, The (See: Caza, La)
Hunt the Man Down 12-27-50:6
Hunted, The 2-04-48:20
Hunted 3-05-52:6
Hunted Men 5-18-38:12
Hunted People 10-17-28:27
Hunted Samurai, The 7-21-71:24
Hunted Woman, The 3-03-16:22
Hunter, The 7-30-80:26
Hunters, The 8-06-58:6
Hunters of the Deep 12-15-54:28
Hunting Big Game 12-08-22:33 and 1-12-23:34
Hunting Dogs at Work (s) 3-25-42:18
Hunting Jack Rabbits in Hungary 10-23-09:13
Hunting of the Hawk, The 4-06-17:22

Hunting Party 5-26-71:20
Hunting Scenes from Bavaria (See: Jagdszene aus Niederbayern)
Hunting Sea Lions in Tasmania 12-14-10:16
Hunting the Hunters (s) 11-06-29:19
Hunting the Panther 9-17-10:12
Hunting Thrills (s) 5-20-31:16
Hunting Tigers in India 12-11-29:42
Hunting Tigers in India (s) 2-18-31:14 and 3-11-31:14
Hunting Tower 3-21-28:19
Huntress 10-11-23:30
Hurdy Gurdy (s) 6-26-29:12
Hurley, Putnam and Snell (s) 10-03-28:17
Hurling (s) 1-06-37:40
Hurra, die Schule Brennt 3-11-70:22
Hurra--Ein Junge 11-10-31:23 and 6-28-32:15
Hurra fuer de Blau Husarer 12-09-70:14
Hurra, Unsere Eltern Sind Nicht Da 9-30-70:22
Hurra, Wir Sind Mal Wieder Junggesellen 2-17-71:28
Hurricane 4-16-24:27
Hurricane 5-12-26:16
Hurricane 10-30-29:37
Hurricane, The 11-10-37:18
Hurricane 4-04-79:20
Hurricane Horseman 11-17-31:26
Hurricane Island 7-11-51:6
Hurricane Islands (s) 6-09-31:18
Hurricane Kid, The 1-07-25:55
Hurricane Smith 2-04-42:8
Hurricane Smith 9-17-52:6
Hurricane's Gal 7-28-22:33
Hurry Call, A (s) 4-05-32:14
Hurry, Charlie, Hurry 7-09-41: 14
Hurry Doctor (s) 3-11-31:14
Hurry Sundown 2-25-67:6
Hurry Tomorrow 12-03-75:22
Hurry Up, Or I'll Be 30 11-14-73:14
Husband by Proxy 6-13-28:27
Husband-Hunter, The 11-12-20: 36
Husband Hunters 2-23-27:19
Husbands 11-04-70:26
Husbands and Lovers 12-10-24: 35
Husbands and Lovers 11-23-27: 22

I Killed Wild Bill Hickok 1-18-56:6
I Kiss Your Hand 8-30-32:21
I Know Everybody and Everybody's Racket (s) 2-28-33:14
I Know Where I'm Going 11-14-45:12 and 8-06-47:12
I Like It That Way 4-24-34:14
I Like Mike 1-18-61:6
I Like Your Nerve 9-15-31:24
I Live As I Please 1-29-47:8
I Live for Love 10-23-35:12
I Live for You 10-02-29:31
I Live in Danger 6-17-42:8
I Live in Fear (See: Ikimono No Kiroku)
I Live in Grosvenor Square 5-30-45:16
I Live My Life 10-16-35:22
I Lived with You 6-27-33:15
I Loevens Tegn 8-04-76:22
I Love a Bandleader 8-15-45:14
I Love a Lassie (s) 5-31-32:14
I Love a Mystery 2-28-45:15
I Love a Parade (s) 8-02-32:15
I Love a Parade (s) 9-20-32:14
I Love a Soldier 11-08-44:23
I Love Melvin 2-04-53:6
I Love My Wife 12-16-70:28
I Love That Man 7-11-33:15
I Love Trouble 12-24-47:13
I Love You 1-11-18:40
I Love You Again 8-07-40:14
I Love You, Alice B. Toklas 8-28-68:6
I Loved a Woman 9-26-33:15
I Loved You Wednesday 6-20-33:11
I Married a Communist 9-21-49:8
I Married a Doctor 4-22-36:14
I Married a Monster from Outer Space 9-17-58:7
I Married a Spy 7-13-38:15
I Married a Witch 10-21-42:8
I Married a Woman 5-07-58:6
I Married Adventure 9-25-40:15
I Married an Angel 5-20-42:8
I, Maureen 9-20-78:24
I Met a Murderer 3-15-39:18
I Met Him in Paris 6-09-37:15
I Met My Love Again 1-12-38:14
I Miss You, Hugs and Kisses 5-31-78:26
I, Mobster 1-14-59:16
I Morgen, Min Elske 5-12-71:19
I Never Promised You a Rose Garden 7-20-77:18
I Never Sang for My Father 10-21-70:14

I Only Asked 11-19-58:26
I Ora Tou Lykon 11-21-79:24
I Passed for White 3-02-60:6
I Promise to Pay 3-03-37:15
I Remember Mama 3-10-48:10
I Ring Doorbells 1-02-46:16
I-Ro-Ha-Ni-Ho-He-To 9-14-60:20
I Sao Untarai 1-19-77:38
I Saw What You Did 5-12-65:28
I Scream (s) 4-03-34:17
I See a Dark Stranger 7-10-46:8
I See Ice 2-23-38:14
I Sell Anything 1-01-35:18
I Shot Billy the Kid 8-02-50:6
I Shot Jesse James 2-02-49:12
I Sing, I Cry 12-12-79:22
I Sing, I Cry 12-12-79:22
I Slik en Natt 8-06-58:6
I Spheres Den Yeerizoun Pisso 11-01-67:7
I Spy 8-29-33:14
I Stand Accused 11-02-38:15
I Stand Condemned 7-08-36:15
I Start Counting 11-18-70:14
I Stole a Million 7-19-39:12
I Sua 5-11-77:95
I Surrender Dear (s) 11-10-31:14
I Surrender Dear 8-25-48:8
I Take This Family 6-16-31:62
I Take This Oath 6-19-40:14
I Take This Woman 1-31-40:14
I Tembelides Tis Eforis Kiladas 8-23-78:20
I Thank a Fool 7-25-62:6
I Thank You 10-08-41:20
I, the Jury 7-22-53:6
I Told You So (s) 5-02-28:36
I, Too, Am Only a Woman (See: Ich Bin Auch Nur Eine Frau)
I Tvillingermes Tegn 7-30-75:24
I Tyrens Tegn 9-18-74:19
I Walk Alone 12-17-47:8
I Walk in Moscow 5-27-64:6
I Walk the Line 10-14-70:17
I Walked with a Zombie 3-17-43:23
I Wanna Hold Your Hand 4-19-78:26
I Want a Divorce 9-04-40:18
I Want My Man 4-08-25:38
I Want to Be a Mother 3-03-37:15
I Want to Forget 12-20-18:35
I Want to Live 10-29-58:6
I Want What I Want 3-01-72:20
I Want You 10-31-51:6

I Wanted Wings 3-26-41:16
I Was a Communist for the FBI 4-25-51:6
I Was a Convict 3-08-39:18
I Was a Male War Bride 8-10-49:8
I Was a Prisoner in Siberia 9-24-52:20
I Was a Prisoner on Devil's Island 7-30-41:20
I Was a Shoplifter 4-12-50:22
I Was a Spy 9-19-33:13 and 1-16-34:15
I Was a Teenage Frankenstein 1-01-58:6
I Was a Teenage Werewolf 7-10-57:6
I Was an Adventuress 5-01-40:18
I Was an American Spy 3-28-51:6
I Was Framed 4-08-42:8
I Was Happy Here 7-13-66:6
I Was Monty's Double 11-05-58:7
I Will, I Will ... For Now 2-11-76:21
I Will Repay 11-23-17:44
I Will Repay 3-12-24:27
I Wonder Who's Kissing Her Now (s) 12-08-31:14
I Wonder Who's Kissing Her Now 6-11-47:8
I Wouldn't Be in Your Shoes 5-05-48:20
Ia Wa Kokyo O Koite 2-08-67:22
Ibis Rouge L' 6-11-75:19
Ibo Kyodai 9-03-58:16
Ice 5-06-70:20
Ice Castles 12-20-78:27
Ice Cold in Alex 7-09-58:16
Ice Flood, The 10-27-26:64
Ice Follies of 1939 3-08-39:18
Ice Palace 6-15-60:6
Ice Station Zebra 10-23-68:6
Icebound 3-05-24:22
Ice-Capades 8-20-41:9
Ice-Capades Revue 12-16-42:16
Iced Bullet, The 1-05-17:27
Iceland 8-12-42:8
Iceman Cometh, The 10-24-73:16
Iceman's Ball (s) 12-27-32:14
Ich Bei Tag, Du Bei Nacht 1-03-33:27
Ich Bin Auch Nur eine Frau 1-02-63:6
Ich Bin ein Antistar 4-27-77:20
Ich Bin ein Elefant, Madame 4-09-69:40
Ich Dachte, Ich Waere Tot 7-02-75:28

Ich Gen'Aus (Du Bleibst Da) 4-29-31:50 and 11-29-32:19
Ich Glaub Nie Mehr An eine Frau 10-24-33:22 (Also see: I Have No Faith in Women)
Ich Liebe Dich, Ich Toete Dich 5-19-71:24
Ich Sehne Mich Nach Dir 9-09-36:17
Ich Suche einen Mann 3-16-66:68
Ich und die Kaiserin 4-04-33:38
Ich und Du 3-10-54:6
Ich und Meine Frau 9-23-53:24
Ich War 19 6-19-68:39
Ich Werde Dich Auf Haenden Tragen 4-01-59:6
Ich Will Leben 7-27-77:22
Ich Will Nicht Wissen (Wer Du Bist) 10-18-32:26 and 2-21-33:14
Ich Zwing Dich Zu Leben 6-28-78:26
Ichijo Sayuri: Nureta Yokujo 1-16-74:40
Ickle Meets Pickle (s) 12-02-42:8
Iconoclast, The 10-08-10:12
Iconoclast, The 3-14-13:14
Iconostasis 10-14-70:30
Icy Breasts (See: Seins de Glace, Les)
I'd Climb the Highest Mountain (s) 6-02-31:14
I'd Climb the Highest Mountain 1-17-51:11
I'd Give My Life 8-19-36:16
I'd Rather Be Rich 7-29-64:8
Ida Regenye 4-24-34:25
Idaho 2-17-43:14
Idaho Kid 8-04-37:25
Idaho Red 4-24-29:26
Idaho Transfer 3-26-75:32
Idea Girl 2-06-46:12
Ideal Husband, An 11-26-47:11
Ideal Woman, The 6-12-29:35
Ideale Frau, Die 9-23-59:18
Ideale Frau Gesucht 11-05-52:18
Idealer Gatte, Ein 1-13-37:13
Idealist 8-18-76:24
Identikit 5-29-74:16
Identite Judiciaire 5-09-51:18
Identity Unknown 4-04-45:10
Idi Amin Dada (See: General Idi Amin Dada)
Idiot, L' 6-26-46:11 and 2-04-48:20
Idiot, The (See: Makuchi)

Idiot, The 8-05-59:20
Idiot, The (See: Idiot, L')
Idiot a Paris, Un 4-05-67:20
Idiot's Delight 1-25-39:11
Idle Chatter (s) 4-09-30:22
Idle Class, The 9-30-21-36
Idle Hands 6-10-21:35
Idle on Parade 4-01-59:6
Idle Rich, The 2-17-22:41
Idle Rich, The 6-19-29:30
Idle Roomer, An (s) 7-18-33:36
Idle Roomers (s) 7-26-32:17
Idle Tongues 3-11-25:42
Idle Wives 9-22-16:36
Idler, The 1-01-15:29
Ido Zero Daisakusen 9-17-69:23
Idol, The 11-05-15:23
Idol, The 8-03-66:6
Idol Dancer 3-26-20:51
Idol of Millions, The (s) 2-05-36:12
Idol of Paris 3-10-48:22
Idol of the Crowds 12-08-37:16
Idol of the North 5-20-21:41
Idol of the Stage, The 2-11-16:23
Idolaters 9-07-17:32
Idolmaker, The 11-05-80:22
Idols, Les 5-08-68:5
Idols of Clay 11-19-20:34
Idu Dani 8-12-70:14
Idylle Au Caire 7-25-33:34
If ... 12-11-68:30
If a Man Answers 8-29-62:20
If Ever I See You Again 5-17-78:54
If He Hollers, Let Him Go 10-02-68:26
If I Had a Million 12-06-32:14
If I Had a Million Rubles 4-24-74:18
If I Had My Way 5-01-40:18
If I Marry Again 1-14-25:43
If I Were a Queen 11-17-22:41
If I Were Free 1-09-34:16
If I Were King 7-30-15:20
If I Were King 7-02-20:28
If I Were King 9-21-38:12
If I Were Single 12-28-27:20 and 3-07-28:28
If I'm Elected (s) 8-09-32:17 and 12-26-33:10
If I'm Lucky 8-28-46:14
If It's Tuesday, This Must Be Belgium 4-09-69:8
If Marriage Fails 6-03-25:43
If Men Played Cards As Women Do (s) 2-27-29:80

If Moscow Strikes 5-07-52:6
If Only Jim 3-18-21:34
If This Be Sin 6-28-50:6
If War Comes Tomorrow 7-20-38:13
If Winter Comes 3-08-23:30
If Winter Comes 12-24-47:13
If You Believe It It's So 7-14-22:40
If You Could Only Cook 1-01-36:44
If You Knew Susie 2-04-48:13
Igen 7-15-64:6
Igloi Diakok 4-03-35:17
Igloo 7-26-32:17
Igy Joettem 8-31-66:6 and 11-30-66:22
Ihr Schoenster Tag 5-09-62:17
Ihre Hoheit Befiehlt 3-25-31:71 and 11-10-31:15
Ihre Majestaet die Liebe 1-28-31:40
Ija Ominara 9-05-79:22
Ikari No Koto 8-06-58:6
Ikarie XB1 7-24-63:6
Ikarus 6-13-79:15
Ikimono No Kiroku 9-18-63:6
Ikiru 5-15-57:22
Il ... Bel Paese 1-18-78:19
Il Est Charmant 3-15-32:21 and 4-12-32:15
Il Est Minuit Dr. Schweitzer 12-10-52:18
Il Ne Faut Pas Mourir Pour Ca 7-17-68:24
Il n'y a Pas de Fumee 5-30-73:24
Il y a Longtemps Que J'taime 9-05-79:27
Il y a un Train Toutes les Heures 7-04-62:6
Ile du Bout du Monde 3-25-59:22
Ile Mysterieuse, L' 11-28-73:14
Ileksen 3-28-79:22
Iles Enchantees, Les 5-12-65:6
I'll Be Seeing You 12-20-44:8
I'll Be Suing You (s) 11-20-44:15
I'll Be Your Sweetheart 7-11-45:14
I'll Be Yours 1-22-47:17
I'll Cry Tomorrow 12-21-55:6
I'll Fix It 11-20-34:15
I'll Get By 9-27-50:8
I'll Get Him Yet 5-23-19:59
I'll Get You 2-04-53:6
I'll Give a Million 7-13-38:15
I'll Love You Always 4-03-35:17
Ill Met by Moonlight 3-20-57:7
I'll Never Forget You 12-12-51:6

Inside Jennifer Welles 8-10-77: 16
Inside Job 6-19-46:8
Inside Looking Out (s) 9-01-31: 21
Inside Looking Out 6-15-77:21
Inside Marilyn Chambers 2-11-76:21
Inside Moves 12-10-80:32
Inside North Vietnam 12-27-67:6
Inside of the Cup, The 1-14-21: 41
Inside of the White Slave Traffic, The 1-02-14:12
Inside Out 10-08-75:18
Inside Story 4-19-39:22
Inside Story, The 3-24-48:8
Inside Straight 3-07-51:6
Inside the Lines 8-16-18:35
Inside the Lines 7-09-30:31
Inside the Mafia 9-30-59:6
Inside the Walls of Folsom Prison 5-23-51:6
Insoumis, L' 10-21-64:28
Inspecteur la Bavure 12-31-80:20
Inspecteur Sergil, L' 2-26-47:11
Inspector Calls, An 3-23-54:24
Inspector Clouseau 5-22-68:6
Inspector General 12-01-37:14
Inspector General 11-23-49:8
Inspector Hornleigh 6-21-39:16 and 10-25-39:23
Inspiration 11-05-15:23
Inspiration 6-06-28:25
Inspiration 2-11-31:14
Installment Collector (s) 5-29-29:14
Insurance (s) 6-25-30:109
Insurance Investigator 3-21-51:6
Insurrection, The 7-30-15:20
Intelligence Man, The 4-21-65:6
Intent to Kill 7-23-58:6
Interdit au Public 1-25-50:18
Interference 11-21-28:13
Interiors 8-02-78:14
Interloper, The 5-24-18:34
Interlude 5-08-57:6
Interlude 6-26-68:6
Intermezzo 11-25-36:15
Intermezzo 12-29-37:19
Intermezzo 10-04-39:12
Intermittent Alarm Clock 2-01-08:11 and 4-04-08:13
Internado Para Senoritas 5-10-44: 10
International Burlesque 11-29-50: 22
International Crime 5-18-38:12

International Forum (s) 2-26-41: 18
International House 5-30-33:15
International Lady 10-15-41:8
International Police 4-10-57:6
International Settlement 1-26-38:14
International Squadron 8-13-41:8
International Velvet 6-28-78:20
Internecine Project, The 10-02-74:24
Internes Can't Take Money 5-12-37:12
Interno D'Un Convento 8-02-78:14
Interns, The 6-13-62:7
Interpol Calling Lima 3-19-69:6
Interrupted Honeymoon, An 3-19-10:17
Interrupted Journey, The 10-19-49:18
Interrupted Melody 3-30-55:8
Interval 6-20-73:28
Interview, The (s) 6-06-28:12
Interview, The (s) 10-02-29:19
Interview, The 8-16-72:26
Intill Helvetets Portar 12-15-48:6
Intimate Lighting (See: Intimi Osvetlani)
Intimate Relations 3-25-53:24
Intimi Osvetlani 8-03-66:6
Into Her Kingdom 8-11-26:14
Into the Blue 1-19-51:13
Into the Primitive 5-26-16:20
Into the Shadow 11-13-09:13
Into the Straight 1-18-50:6
Into the Unknown (s) 6-02-31:14
Intoarcerea Lui Voda Lupusneanu 10-15-80:188
Intoccabili, Gli 5-28-69:34
Intolerance 9-08-16:20 (Also see: Fall of Babylon, The)
Intramuros 7-29-64:8
Intrigantes, Les 5-19-54:6
Intrigue, An 1-14-11:18
Intrigue, The 10-13-16:29
Intrigue, The 4-07-22:41
Intrigue 12-24-47:13
Introduce Me 3-11-25:41
Introduction to Live (See: Vstup-lenjie)
Introduction to the Enemy 3-12-75:18
Intruder, The 4-25-33:27
Intruder, The 11-04-53:6
Intruder, The 5-23-62:16
Intruder in the Dust 10-12-49:6
Intrus, Les 3-01-72:24
Intrusion of Isabel 4-04-19:66
Intruso, El 4-18-45:12

It Shouldn't Happen to a Vet 4-
14-76:26
It Started in Naples 7-06-60:6
It Started in Paradise 11-12-52:6
It Started with a Kiss 8-19-59:6
It Started with Eve 10-01-41:9
It Takes All Kinds 8-13-69:18
It! The Terror from Beyond Space
8-06-58:6
Italian, The 1-01-15:29
Italian-Austrian War Film 10-08-
15:21
Italian Barber, The 1-21-11:12
Italian Battle Front, The 8-17-
17:24
Italian Connection, The 10-31-73:
26
Italian Graffiti 6-19-74:16
Italian in America, An 1-10-68:6
Italian Mob, The 6-11-69:38
Italian Secret Service 3-06-68:6
Italian Straw Hat, The (See:
Horse Ate the Hat, The)
Italiani Brava Gente 10-14-64:22
Italien des Roses, L' 9-13-72:
34
Italienreise-Liebe Inbegriffen 5-
07-58:22
Itching Palms 9-13-23:34
Itchy Fingers 2-21-79:21
Itel a Balaton 3-28-33:27
Itelet 8-05-70:22
Ithele Na Guini Vassilias 10-25-
67:20
Itim 3-21-79:26
It's a Bear 3-07-19:66
It's a Bet 3-13-35:27
It's a Big Country 11-28-51:6
It's a Boy 6-27-33:15 and 6-12-
34:19
It's a Date 3-27-40:17
It's a Dog's Life (s) 8-12-42:
20
It's a Funny, Funny World 7-29-
78:20
It's a Gift 1-08-35:18
It's a Great Feeling 7-27-49:12
It's a Great Life 9-03-20:44
It's a Great Life 1-22-30:17
It's a Great Life 2-05-36:33
It's a Great Life 6-16-43:16
It's a Hap-Hap-Happy Day (s)
9-03-41:17
It's a Joke, Son! 1-22-47:17
It's a King 1-17-33:17
It's a Mad, Mad, Mad, Mad
World 11-06-63:6
It's a Pipe (s) 6-30-26:16

It's a Pleasure 2-28-45:15
It's a Small World 6-26-35:26
It's a Small World 5-17-50:6
It's a Trade, Dad! 5-02-62:6
It's a Wise Child 5-20-31:16
It's a Wonderful Life 12-25-46:
12
It's a Wonderful World 9-05-56:6
It's Alive 10-16-74:16
It's Alive 2 (See: It Lives Again)
It's All Happening 6-19-63:7
It's All Over Now (s) 3-24-37:16
It's All Yours 1-12-38:14
It's Always Fair Weather 8-24-
55:6
It's Easy to Become a Father 7-
03-29:30
It's Forever Springtime (See:
E Primavera)
It's Great to Be Alive 7-11-33:15
It's Great to Be Young 9-18-46:
22
It's Great to Be Young 6-13-56:6
It's Hard to Be Good 11-24-48:
14
It's Hits and a Miss (s) 12-02-
42:22
It's in the Air 12-11-40:16
It's in the Bag 2-14-45:14
It's Love Again 5-20-36:23 and
5-27-36:14
It's Love I'm After 7-21-37:13
It's Me 3-21-79:26
It's My Turn 10-22-80:24
It's Never Too Late 1-10-13:14
It's No Laughing Matter 1-23-15:
25
It's Not the Size That Counts 4-
04-79:20
It's Only Money 11-21-62:6
It's Showtime 4-07-76:26
It's the Law 12-02-42:22
It's the Old Army Game 7-07-
26:16
It's the Paris Life 7-14-54:24
It's Tough to Be a Bird (s) 4-01-
70:26
It's Turned Out Nice Again 6-25-
41:8
Itsu Itsu Made Mo 12-10-52:18
It's You I Want 10-21-36:23
It's Your Thing 8-26-70:16
Itto 2-27-35:26
Ivan 11-29-32:18 and 3-07-33:54
Ivan Grozny (See: Ivan the Terri-
ble, Pts. I & II)
Ivan Pavlov 2-15-50:55
Ivan the Great 7-04-23:22

Jailbreak 8-12-36:18
Jailhouse Rock 10-16-57:6
Jak Byc Kochana 5-29-63:6
Jake the Plumber 11-02-27:24
Jakob der Luegner 7-16-75:20
Jakobli und Meyeli 4-26-61:21
Jakten 5-18-60:7 and 7-06-66:6
Jakub 3-16-77:24
Jalma la Double 3-21-28:22
Jalna 9-18-35:15
Jalopy 3-25-53:6
Jalsaghar 12-07-60:6
Jam Session 5-03-44:26
Jamaica Inn 5-31-39:14
Jamaica Run 4-08-53:6
Jamais Plus Toujours 4-07-76: 30
Jambon D'Ardenne 5-04-77:23
Jamboree 3-29-44:21
Jamboree 11-27-57:6
James Boys in Missouri 4-25-08:13
James Dean, the First American Teenager 10-01-75:28
James Ou Pas 10-28-70:28
Jamilya 7-12-72:26
Jan Garber and Band (s) 10-16-29:17
Jan Garber Orch. (s) 7-10-29:13
Jan Rubini Co. (s) 2-06-29:18
Jan Savitt's Serenade in Swing (s) 10-07-42:25
Jana 6-24-36:45
Jane Austen in Manhattan 7-30-80:22
Jane Bleibt Jane 4-26-78:19
Jane Eyre 2-17-22:40
Jane Eyre 2-20-35:15
Jane Eyre 2-02-44:18
Jane Eyre 3-24-71:19
Jane Goes A-Wooing 1-10-19:45
Jane Green (s) 2-13-29:13
Jane Is Unwilling to Work 10-09-09:20
Jane Shore 6-04-15:18
Jane Steps Out 5-25-38:13
Jangmeae Sung 10-01-69:30
Janice Meredith 8-13-24:19
Janie 7-26-44:10
Janie Gets Married 6-05-46:13
Janiksen Vuosi 3-28-79:20
Janis 10-23-74:30
Janken 8-05-70:16
Janne Wangmans Bravader 12-15-48:6
Janosik 12-18-74:36
Japan 9-19-13:15
Japanese Bowl (s) 6-11-30:18

Japanese Nightingale, A 8-23-18: 38
Japanese Scenes (s) 5-29-29:14
Japanese War Bride 1-09-52:6
Japoteurs (s) 9-16-42:20
Jaque a la Dama 10-04-78:22
Jardin de las Delicias, El 9-16-70:15
Jardin des Supplices, Le 10-20-76:39
Jardin Qui Bascule, Le 5-21-75: 22
Jardinier D'Argenteuil, Le 10-19-66:6
Jarha Fi Lhaite 5-24-78:38
Jaroslaw Dabrowski 7-28-76:20
Jason and the Argonauts 6-05-63:6
Jasper and the Choo-Choo (s) 2-03-43:14
Jasper and the Haunted House (s) 12-02-42:8
Jasper and the Watermelon (s) 2-04-42:8
Jassy 8-20-47:18
Jaula de los Leones, La 2-25-31:22
Java Head 2-08-23:41
Java Head 8-07-35:62
Javanese Journey (s) 1-12-32:15
Javoronok 5-26-65:15
Jaws 6-18-75:16
Jaws of Hell 1-07-31:23
Jaws of Steel 2-22-28:24
Jaws of the Jungle 4-15-36:16
Jaws 2 6-07-78:25
Jay C. Flippen (s) 7-18-28:15
Jay Velie (s) 4-03-29:11 (two reviews)
Jay Walker (s) 9-11-30:21
Jayhawkers, The 10-21-59:6
Jazz a la Cuba (s) 7-11-33:15
Jazz Boat 11-23-60:20
Jazz Cinderella 10-01-30:34
Jazz Girl, The 6-15-27:25
Jazz Heaven 11-06-29:19
Jazz Mad 7-18-28:28
Jazz on a Summer's Day 9-16-59:6
Jazz Preferred (s) 6-18-30:37
Jazz Rehearsal, The (s) 5-07-30:20
Jazz Reporters (s) 11-24-31:17
Jazz Rhythm (s) 11-12-30:21
Jazz Singer, The 10-12-27:16 (Reprinted on: 12-31-52:6) and 4-01-31:12
Jazz Singer, The 12-31-52:6

Jazz Singer, The 12-10-80:32
Jazz Time (s) 10-09-29:23
Jazzbo Singer, The (s) 1-12-32:
15
Jazzgossen 11-05-58:7
Jazzland 3-20-29:13
Jazzmania 3-15-23:31
Je L'Ai Ete Trois Fois 11-12-
52:6
Je Reviendrai a Kandara 4-03-
57:24
Je Sais Rein Mais Je Dirai Tout
1-02-74:6
Je Suis de la Revue 7-04-51:24
Je Suis Pierre Riviere 2-18-76:
38
Je Suis Timide: Mais Je Me Soigne
9-06-78:24
Je T'Adore ... Mais Pourquoi 9-
17-30:30
Je T'Aime 3-13-74:18
Je T'Aime, Je T'Aime 5-15-68:7
Je T'Aime Moi Non Plus 3-17-
76:23
Je Te Tiens Tu Me Tiens Pa Da
Barbichette 6-27-79:34
Je, Tu, Elles 9-03-69:30
Je Vais Craquer 5-21-80:24
Je Vous Aimerai Toujours 6-27-
33:15
Je Vous Salue, Mafia 10-13-65:
18
Jealous Lover, The (s) 1-31-33:
12
Jealousy 11-24-16:30
Jealousy 5-30-23:31
Jealousy 11-27-34:63
Jealousy 12-12-28:31 and 9-26-
28:27
Jealousy 9-18-29:29
Jealousy 7-25-45:20
Jean de la Lune 4-01-31:60 and
3-14-32:21
Jean Goes Foraging 10-29-10:14
Jean the Matchmaker 9-24-10:12
Jean Valjean 12-04-09:13
Jeanne Dore 1-11-39:13
Jeanne Eagels 7-24-57:6
Jeannie 8-27-41:20
Jedanaesta Zapovest 4-22-70:28
Jedda 6-15-55:6
Jede Frau Hat ein Geheimnis 3-
17-37:15
Jeden Stribny 8-04-76:22
Jeder Fuer Sich und Gott Gegen
Alle 5-14-75:30
Jeder Stirbt Fuer Sich Allein 2-
04-76:17

Jederman 1-17-62:7
Jed's Vacation (s) 9-11-29:18
Jeepers Creepers 11-01-39:14
Jefe, El 11-26-58:6
Jeff 6-11-69:40
Jeg Elsker Blat 7-03-68:26
Jeg--En Kvinde 9-29-65:6
Jeg--En Kvinde, II (See: I, A
Woman, Part II)
Jeg--En Kvinde, III (See: Daughter,
The)
Jeg Saa Jesus Doe 2-26-75:20
Jelenido 2-26-72:18
Jennie 3-19-41:16
Jennie Gerhardt 6-13-33:15
Jennifer 5-24-78:27
Jennifer on My Mind 10-13-71:20
Jenny 4-09-58:20
Jenny 12-24-69:14
Jenny Be Good 7-02-20:27
Jenny Lamour 1-14-48:10
Jens Mansson I Amerika 11-12-
47:8
Jenseits Von Oder Und Neisse--
Heute 5-05-65:26
Jeopardy 1-21-53:6
Jeremiah Johnson 5-10-72:21
Jeremy 5-23-73:18
Jericho 9-08-37:18
Jericho 3-27-46:12
Jerk, The 12-12-79:23
Jerry, the Giant (s) 6-30-26:16
Jerusalem, the Holy City (s) 9-
15-31:20
Jerusalem File, The 2-09-72:18
Jes' Call Me Jim 5-28-20:42
Jesli Mxz Serce Bijace 10-01-80:
28
Jesse James 10-19-27:28
Jesse James 1-11-39:12
Jesse James, Jr. 4-01-42:8
Jesse James vs. the Daltons 1-
27-54:6
Jesse James' Women 9-15-54:6
Jesse Stafford's Band (s) 10-31-
28:24
Jessica 3-21-62:6
Jest for a While (s) 4-02-30:18
Jester's Tale, A 10-28-64:7
Jesus 10-24-79:16
Jesus Christ, Superstar 6-27-73:
20
Jesus Trip, The 9-01-71:16
Jet Attack 3-26-58:6
Jet Generation 5-07-69:258
Jet Job 3-26-52:16
Jet Pilot 9-25-57:6
Jet Storm 9-02-59:6

Joe Palooka in the Big Fight
2-23-49:11
Joe Palooka in the Counterpunch
9-14-49:20
Joe Palooka in the Squared Circle
12-27-50: 6
Joe Palooka in Triple Cross   9-
12-51:18
Joe Palooka in Winner Take All
8-25-48: 8
Joe Palooka Meets Humphrey   2-
01-50:14
Joe Panther   11-03-76:27
Joe Smith, American   7-07-42:44
Joerg Ratgeb, Maier   3-29-78:28
Joey Boy   3-31-65:6
Johan   7-21-76:22
Johann Orth   12-06-32:15
Johanna Enlists   9-13-18:45
Johannes Brahms (s)   9-17-30:21
Johansson Och Vestman   10-16-
46:8
Johansson-Patterson (s)   7-01-59:7
John and Julie   8-03-55:6
John and Marsha   7-31-74:19
John and Mary   11-26-69:14
John Barleycorn   7-17-14:17
John Charles Thomas (s)   10-31-
28:24 and 11-21-28:13
John Dough and the Cherub   12-
24-10:16
John F. Kennedy: Years of Light-
ning, Day of Drums   6-23-
65:26
John Forrest Finds Himself   12-03-
20:32
John Glayde's Honor   10-22-15:23
John Glenn Story, The   2-27-63:6
John Glueckstadt   7-09-75:24
John Goldfarb, Please Come Home
11-18-64: 6
John Halifax, Gentleman   7-16-15:
19
John Heartfield, Fotomonteur   4-
27-77:24
John Loves Mary   1-26-49:11
John Meade's Woman   2-24-37:15
John Needham's Needle   3-31-16:
25
John P. Medbury (s)   11-10-31:14
and 3-01-32:20 (Also see:
Laughing in Africa, Laughing
in Reno, Laughing in Turkey,
Medbury in Hollywood, Med-
bury Travelaugh)
John Paul Jones   6-17-59:6
John Petticoats   11-07-19:97
John Smith   6-16-22:43

John Wesley   4-28-54:6
Johnny Allegro   6-01-49:11
Johnny Angel   8-01-45:16
Johnny Apollo   4-17-40:13
Johnny Belinda   9-15-48:15
Johnny Come Lately   9-01-43:20
Johnny Comes Flying Home   3-
20-46:8
Johnny Concho   7-11-56:6
Johnny Cool   10-09-63:6
Johnny Dark   6-02-54:6
Johnny Doesn't Live Here Any-
more   6-28-44:16
Johnny Doughboy   5-12-43:20
Johnny Eager   12-10-41:8
Johnny Farrell (s)   4-22-31:18
Johnny Frenchman   7-18-45:34
Johnny, Get Your Gun   3-21-19:
54
Johnny Got His Gun   5-19-71:17
Johnny Guitar   5-05-54:6
Johnny Hallyday Par Francois
Reichenbach   6-28-72:26
Johnny Hamlet   5-10-72:20
Johnny Holiday   12-14-49:8
Johnny Larsen   10-10-79:20
Johnny Marvin (s)   11-07-28:15;
11-21-28:13; 7-17-29:42
Johnny Minotaur   4-21-71:22
Johnny Nobody   12-01-65:6
Johnny O'Clock   2-05-47:12
Johnny on the Spot   2-21-19:68
Johnny One-Eye   6-14-50:8
Johnny Reno   3-02-66:6
Johnny Rocco   11-19-58:6
Johnny "Scat" Davis (s)   12-02-
42:8
Johnny Stool Pigeon   7-20-49:6
Johnny the Giant Killer   7-08-53:
16
Johnny Tiger   4-13-66:6
Johnny Tremain   5-01-57:6
Johnny Trouble   9-11-57:6
Johnny Unser   11-05-80:24
Johnny Vik   8-29-73:14
Johnny West   5-29-78:26
Johnny Yuma   9-13-67:6
Johnny's Pix of the Polar Region
4-23-10:16
Johnny's Weekend (s)   11-12-30:
21
Johnson-Ketchel Fight   10-30-09:
11
Johnstown Flood, The   3-17-26:
38
Joi Baba Felunath   12-12-79:23
Join the Marines   2-17-37:14
Joint Wipers (s)   4-05-32:14

Joy Ride 10-08-58:6
Joyas Del Pecad, Las 6-07-50:8
Joyenes Viejos, Los 4-11-62:6
Joyless Street, The (See: Streets of Sorrow)
Joyous Liar, The 11-14-19:59 and 12-19-19:44
Joyous Troublemakers, The 7-02-20:29
Joyride 6-01-77:16
Jua Arom 4-30-75:23
Juan Lamaglia y Sra 4-08-70:24
Juan Moreira 8-08-73:14
Juan Pedro, El Dallador 4-29-70:180
Juan Perez Jolote 10-08-75:22 and 3-09-77:24
Juan Vincente Gomez y Su Epoca 10-08-75:22
Juana Gallo 8-02-61:7
Juarez 4-26-39:12
Jubal 4-04-56:6
Jubilee 2-28-45:15
Jubilee 2-01-78:24
Jubilee Trail 1-20-54:6
Jubilo 12-19-19:44
Jucklins, The 12-17-20:40
Jud 9-01-71:16
Judendrichter, Der 8-03-60:6
Judex 12-18-63:17
Judge, The 2-23-49:11
Judge Hardy and Son 12-13-39:11
Judge Hardy's Children 4-06-38:14
Judge Not 3-05-15:22 and 3-26-15:25
Judge Not; or, The Woman of Mona Diggins 10-01-15:19
Judge Not That Ye Be Judged 8-28-09:13
Judge Priest 10-16-34:12
Judge Steps Out, The 5-11-49:6
Judgement 1-27-22:40
Judge's Ward 10-09-09:20
Judge's Whiskers 8-21-09:17
Judgment at Nuremberg 10-18-61:6
Judgment House, The 11-30-17:44 and 2-08-18:42
Judgment of an Assassin 12-14-77:14
Judgment of the Hills 8-03-27:16
Judgment of the Jungle 2-20-14:23
Judgment of the Storm 1-31-24:23

Judith 1-12-66:6
Judith of Bethulia 3-27-14:20
Judith of the Cumberlands 8-04-16:28
Judith Therpauve 10-18-78:72
Judo Showdown 8-21-68:26
Judoka Agent Secret, Le 3-22-67:6
Judy Forgot 8-20-15:21
Judy of Rogues' Harbor 2-13-20:44
Juego de la Oca, El 6-02-65:6
Jueves Milagro, Los 7-02-58:6
Juge et L'Assassin, Le 3-03-76:21
Juge Fayard Dit le Sheriff, Le 1-19-77:22
Jugement Dernier, Le 1-16-46:18
Jugend 6-01-38:13
Jugend der Welt 7-29-36:15
Jugend von Heute 11-09-38:19
Juggernaut, The 3-12-15:23
Juggernaut 9-23-36:17 and 7-21-37:19
Juggernaut 9-18-74:19
Juggler, The 2-19-10:15
Juggler, The 5-06-53:6
Juguemos en el Mundo 9-22-71:6
Juguetes Rotos 12-21-66:7
Juha 9-04-57:6
Juif Polonais, Le 9-29-37:27
Juk un Ja San Ja 6-29-66:6
Juke Box Jamboree (s) 6-17-42:20
Juke Box Rhythm 3-25-59:6
Juke Girl 4-08-42:8
Jukebox Jenny 3-25-42:8
Jukyu-Sai No Chizu 5-21-80:20
Jula Treekul 5-07-80:575
Julefrokosten 12-08-76:8
Jules and Jim (See: Jules et Jim)
Jules Bledsoe (s) 6-05-29:15
Jules et Jim 2-07-62:6
Jules le Magnifique 3-09-77:17
Jules of the Strong Heart 1-18-18:39
Julia 10-03-56:6
Julia (See: Lieberschuler, Der)
Julia 9-21-77:16
Julia Misbehaves 8-18-48:11
Julia Sanderson and Frank Crumit (s) 3-20-29:12
Juliana Do Amor Perdido 10-14-70:33
Julie de Carneilhan 5-24-50:20
Julie la Rousse 9-09-59:6
Julie Pot de Colle 4-20-77:24

Julie, the Redhead (See: Julie la Rousse)
Juliet of the Spirits (See: Giulietta de Gli Spiriti)
Julietta 11-18-53:6
Juliette de Sade 12-24-69:20
Juliette et Juliette 3-13-74:28
Juliette et L'Air du Temps 8-25-76:28
Juliette Ou le Clef des Songes 5-16-51:18
Julio Comienz en Julio 5-16-79:21
Julius Caesar 11-14-14:25
Julius Caesar 5-14-15:19
Julius Caesar 2-10-22:34
Julius Caesar 6-03-53:6
Julius Caesar 6-10-70:26
July 14 2-07-33:12 and 10-24-33:17
July 4, 1910 12-18-09:15
Jument Vapeur, La 4-05-78:40
Jump 7-14-71:24
Jump for Glory 3-24-37:31
Jump into Hell 3-30-55:8
Jumping Ash 9-15-76:17
Jumping for Joy 2-29-56:6
Jumping Jacks 6-04-52:6
Jun 5-16-79:31
Junction City 7-09-52:6
June (s) 7-10-29:13
June Bride 10-20-48:11
June Friday 8-27-15:20
June Madness 9-29-22:41
June Moon 3-18-31:24
Junge Graf, Der 12-16-36:21
Junge Liebe 6-12-34:63
Junge Lord, Der 8-05-70:20
Junge Moench, Der 1-17-79:26
Junge Suenderin, Der 12-28-60:6
Junge Toerless, Der 4-27-66:19
Junges Blut 5-13-36:14
Jungfrukallan 2-24-60:6
Jungfrun Pa Jungfrnsund 4-26-50:22
Jungle, The 6-26-14:19
Jungle, The 8-13-52:6
Jungle Adventures 9-16-21:35
Jungle Belles 5-18-27:25
Jungle Book, The 3-25-42:8
Jungle Book, The 10-04-67:6
Jungle Bride 5-16-33:21
Jungle Captive 6-13-45:17
Jungle Cat 8-10-60:6
Jungle Cavalcade 7-09-41:14 (Reprinted: 7-23-41:9)
Jungle Child, The 9-22-16:36
Jungle Drums (s) 12-25-29:20
Jungle Festival (s) 10-13-31:14

Jungle Flight 2-26-47:11
Jungle Girl (serial) 5-28-41:18
Jungle Goddess 11-03-48:14
Jungle Headhunters 5-02-51:12
Jungle Heat 7-31-57:6
Jungle Jaunt (s) 3-18-42:25
Jungle Jazz (s) 8-27-30:21
Jungle Jim 2-24-37:19
Jungle Jim 12-22-48:6
Jungle Jim in the Forbidden Land 3-05-52:6
Jungle Jumble, A (s) 8-16-32:15
Jungle Killer 11-29-32:19
Jungle Lovers, The 9-24-15:20
Jungle Man-Eaters 6-09-54:20
Jungle Manhunt 10-03-51:22
Jungle Menace (serial) 10-27-37:19
Jungle Moon-Men 3-30-55:9
Jungle Patrol 9-22-48:8
Jungle Princess, The 12-30-36:11
Jungle Stampede 8-02-50:16
Jungle Woman, The 6-23-26:19
Jungle Woman 5-24-44:10 and 7-19-44:13
Jungles of the Amazon (s) 1-25-28:13
Junior (s) 1-12-32:15
Junior Army 4-28-43:8
Junior Bonner 6-14-72:18
Junior G-Men of the Air (serial) 5-27-42:8
Junior Miss 6-13-45:17
Junior Prom 2-27-46:8
Juno and the Paycock 1-22-30:30
Junoon 1-31-79:24
Jupiter 11-05-52:6
Jupiter 3-31-71:6
Jupiter's Darling 1-26-55:6
Jury of Fate, The 8-17-17:28
Jury's Evidence 1-22-36:15
Jury's Secret, The 2-02-38:17
Jusqu'au Bout du Monde 2-27-63:7
Jusqu'au Coeur 6-04-69:36
Jusqu'au Dernier 5-22-57:6
Just a Bear (s) 3-25-31:16
Just a Big Simple Girl 11-02-49:22
Just a Gigolo (s) 6-02-31:14
Just a Gigolo 6-16-31:34
Just a Gigolo 2-21-79:20
Just a Pal (s) 6-02-31:14
Just a Song at Twilight 12-29-16:23
Just a Woman 12-21-17:45
Just a Woman 5-27-25:40

• 228

Karamazov 9-22-31:26
Karambol 7-15-64:6
Karami-Ai 6-27-62:6
Karamoja 11-17-54:6
Kard, A 3-09-77:16
Kare John 12-09-64:6
Karl For Sin Hatt 10-08-41:20
Karl Fredrik Regerer 2-16-38:
25
Karl May 3-31-76:14
Karlek Och Stortlopp 10-23-46:
10
Karlek 65 5-12-65:6
Karlek, Solsken Och Sang 5-12-
48:20
Karlekens Brod 5-05-54:21
Karlekens Sprak 7-08-70:15
Karlekshistoria, En 5-06-70:15
Karma 5-30-33:54
Karneval und Liebe 4-22-36:29
Karnival Kid, The (s) 11-12-30:
21
Karol Lir (See: King Lear)
Karosszek, A 11-15-39:20
Karugtong Ng Kahapon 11-12-75:
24
Karyl Norman (s) 8-22-28:14
Kaseki 3-26-75:20
Kashi To Kodomo 9-12-62:16
Kashima Paradise 5-16-73:18
Kashmir to Khyber (s) 10-18-32:
14
Kasper in de Onderwereld 2-07-
79:22
Kassbach 3-07-79:22
Kassen Stemmer 8-18-76:22
Katachrissis Exoussias 11-10-
71:24
Katawang Lupa 6-04-75:19
Kate 8-21-14:19
Katerina a Jeli Deti 7-28-76:22
Katerina Izmailova 5-17-67:18
Kathleen 1-26-38:14
Kathleen 11-12-41:9
Kathleen Mavourneen 8-22-19:76
Kathy O 4-23-58:7
Katia 11-16-38:15
Katia 2-24-60:6
Katie Did It 4-11-51:6
Katrina 11-30-49:6
Kat's Meow, The (s) 2-26-30:24
Kattorna (See: Cats, The)
Katu 12-16-64:17
Katz & Karasso 1-26-72:24
Katz und Maus 2-15-67:6
Katzelmacher 10-22-69:32
Katzensteg, Der 1-26-38:23
Kaufman Bros. (s) 7-25-28:14

Kazablan 8-22-73:19
Kazan 10-28-21:34
Kazan, The 6-16-43:16
Kazan 6-15-49:13
Kazdy Den Odvahu 5-11-66:28
Kazdy Mlady Muz 8-10-66:18
Kazoku 4-14-71:22
Kde Reky Maji Slunce 9-06-61:
18
Kdo Chce Zabot Jessii 8-03-66:7
Kdo Hleda Zlate Dno 7-16-75:20
Ke Ha See Dang 11-05-80:24
Ke Xana Pros Ti Doxa Trava 10-
29-80:22
Kean 2-26-30:7
Kean--The Madness of Genius 5-
21-24:24
Keby Som Mal Dievca 8-25-76:
20
Keby Som Mal Pushka 8-16-72:
26
Keep 'Em Flying 11-26-41:9
Keep 'Em Rolling 6-26-34:38
Keep 'Em Sailing (s) 12-02-42:8
Keep 'Em Slugging 3-03-43:18
and 4-21-43:8
Keep Moving 11-19-15:23
Keep Smiling 1-20-26:41
Keep Smiling 8-17-38:22
Keep to the Right 11-05-20:41
Keep Your Powder Dry 2-21-45:8
Keeper, The 5-26-76:19
Keeper of the Bees 10-28-25:37
Keeper of the Bees 8-21-35:21
Keeper of the Flame 12-16-42:
16
Keeping Circuit 1-01-41:14
Keeping Company (s) 4-09-30:22
Keeping in Shape (s) 6-24-42:8
Keeping Up with Lizzie 5-13-21:
43
Keetje Tippel 5-14-75:20
Kefauver Crime Probe Hearings
3-28-51:6
Keiko 9-12-79:20
Kein Tag Ohne Dich 3-14-33:15
Keine Feier Ohne Meier 11-01-
32:13
Keith of the Border 2-15-18:51
Kejsaren 3-07-79:22
Kelek 10-22-69:33
Keller Sisters and Lynch (s) 7-
10-29:13
Kelly and Me 1-16-57:18
Kelly Gang, The 9-03-24:25
Kelly of U.S.A. 12-18-34:13
Kelly the Second 10-07-36:15
Kelly's Heroes 6-17-70:22

229 •

Kid Rides Again, The 3-17-43:23
Kid Rodelo (s) 1-19-66:6
Kid Sister, The 10-12-27:25
Kid Sister, The 3-21-45:10
Kidder and Co. 7-19-18:37
Kiddie Kabaret (s) 4-16-30:21
Kid'n Hollywood (s) 8-22-33:22
Kidnapped 5-11-17:34c
Kidnapped 5-25-38:12
Kidnapped 9-08-48:10
Kidnapped 2-17-60:6
Kidnapped 12-15-71:18
Kidnappers, The 1-27-54:26
Kidnapping Gorillas 4-16-41:18
Kidnapping of the President, The
    8-13-80:22
Kids Are Alright, The 5-23-79:
    24
Kid's Clever, The 5-15-29:49
Kid's Last Ride 3-26-41:18
Kids of the Movies 7-03-14:21
Kierion 9-18-68:28
Kif Tebbi 5-22-29:16
Kiganjo No Boken 5-25-66:7
Kihajoini Veszelyes 5-24-78:40
Kiki 4-07-26:36
Kiki 3-11-31:14
Kiku and Isamu 9-16-59:16
Kilas 8-30-80:21 (Also see: Kilas,
    O Mau Da Fita)
Kilas, O Mau Da Fita 10-15-80:
    146 (Also see: Kilas)
Kildare of Storm 9-27-18:43
Kilenc Honap 10-26-77:20
Kilet Khon 6-15-77:21
Kill (See: Kiru)
Kill 12-15-71:22
Kill a Dragon 11-01-67:20
Kill, Baby, Kill 10-30-68:26
Kill Her Gently 9-17-58:6
Kill or Be Killed 6-14-50:22
Kill or Be Killed 5-21-80:16
Kill or Cure 11-14-62:6
Kill the Umpire 5-03-50:6
Kille Och En Tjej, En 8-20-75:
    73
Killer Ape 11-25-53:6
Killer at Large 10-28-36:15
Killer at Large 6-04-47:18
Killer Clans 4-07-76:32
Killer Dill 5-14-47:15
Killer Dog (s) 8-12-36:19
Killer Elite, The 12-24-75:14
Killer Fish 10-24-79:16
Killer Force 10-24-75:14
Killer Inside Me, The 10-20-
    76:38
Killer Is Loose, The 2-01-56:6

Killer McCoy 10-29-47:15
Killer Shark 4-12-50:22
Killer Shrews, The 7-01-59:22
Killer That Stalked New York,
    The 12-06-50:15
Killers, The 8-07-46:15
Killers, The 5-27-64:24
Killers from Space 1-27-54:6
Killer's Kiss 9-21-55:6
Killers of Kilimanjaro 4-13-60:6
Killers of the Sea 6-16-37:13
Killers of the Wild 4-03-40:16
Killers Three 11-20-68:34
Killing, The 5-23-56:6
Killing Kind, The 6-13-73:16
Killing of a Chinese Bookie, The
    2-18-76:35
Killing of Sister George, The 12-
    18-68:6
Killing to Live 12-22-31:21
Kilmeny 7-12-15:18
Kilroy Was Here 7-09-47:17
Kim 12-06-50:15
Kimberley Jim 5-05-65:6
Kimen 8-28-74:43
Kimiko 4-14-37:12
Kind, The 11-07-28:15
Kind der Donau, Das 9-06-50:8
Kind Hearts and Coronets 6-29-
    49:20
Kind Lady 1-01-36:58
Kind Lady 6-20-51:6
Kind of Loving, A 4-25-62:6
Kind Van de Zon 5-14-75:35
Kindaichi Kosuke no Boken 6-04-
    80:22
Kindan No Suna 4-06-60:6
Kinder aus No. 67, Die 2-27-80:
    27
Kinder, Mutter und ein General
    5-18-55:9
Kinder Vor Gericht 6-16-31:62
Kinderarzt Dr. Engel 9-29-37:27
Kindling 7-16-15:17
Kindling Courage 3-08-23:31
Kindred of the Dust 1-27-22:40
    and 9-01-22:41
Kinetic Art 3-11-70:26
King, The (s) 7-09-30:19
King: A Filmed Record ... Mont-
    gomery to Memphis 3-04-
    70:18
King and Country 9-16-64:6
King and Four Queens, The 12-
    19-56:6
King and I, The 7-04-56:6
King and the Chorus Girl, The
    3-31-37:17

● L ●

L. A. Plays Itself 4-12-72:16
L-Shaped Room, The 11-21-62: 12
La La Lucille 7-23-20:34
Labbra Rosse 11-02-60:6
Labor of Love, A 2-18-76:38
Labor's Holiday (s) 9-05-33:19
Labrytintus 8-25-76:68
Laburnum Grove 5-12-36:15
Labyrinth, The 12-10-15:21
Labyrinth 11-11-59:6
Labyrinth of Passion 5-22-29:27
Lac aux Dames 6-05-34:29
Lacemaker, The (See: Dentelliere, La)
Lachdoktor, Der 3-16-38:17
Lachende Dritte, Der 12-16-36: 15
Lachenite Obouvki Na Neznainiya Voin 7-25-79:38
Laches Vivent D'Espoir, Les 4-05-61:6
Lacombe 1-30-74:11
Lacombe, Lucien (See: Lacombe)
La Conga Nights 6-12-40:14
Lacrime e Sorrisi 12-30-36:11
Lad, The 3-19-35:27
Lad: A Dog 5-02-62:6
Lad and the Lion, The 5-18-17: 23
Lad from Old Ireland, The 12-03-10:14
Lad from Our Town 10-13-43:10
Ladden Jinx 10-20-22:41
Ladder of Lies, A 7-09-20:27
Laddie 10-09-09:13
Laddie 11-03-26:17
Laddie 5-08-35:16 and 9-18-40:14
Ladies and Gentlemen ... The Rolling Stones 4-17-74:16
Ladies at Ease 10-05-27:24
Ladies at Play 11-17-26:16
Ladies, Beware 9-07-27:24
Ladies' Choice (s) 3-12-30:21
Ladies Courageous 3-22-44:18
Ladies Crave Exictement 7-24-35:21
Ladies' Day 3-17-43:8

Ladies First (See: Femmes D'Abord, Les)
Ladies in Distress 6-15-38:14
Ladies in Love 6-18-30:53
Ladies in Love 11-04-36:18
Ladies in Retirement 9-10-41:8
Ladies in Washington 5-24-44:10
Ladies Like Hats (s) 12-18-35:13
Ladies Love Brutes 5-21-30:25
Ladies Love Danger 9-11-35:17
Ladies' Man, The (s) 10-17-28: 16
Ladies' Man 5-06-31:23
Ladies' Man, The 6-07-61:6
Ladies Must Live 11-25-21:43
Ladies Must Live 12-05-33:17
Ladies Must Live 9-04-40:18
Ladies Must Play 8-20-30:15
Ladies Must Press 12-14-27:21
Ladies Night 4-11-28:13
Ladies Not Allowed (s) 12-19-33: 19
Ladies of Leisure 3-17-26:41
Ladies of Leisure 5-28-30:35
Ladies of the Big House 1-05-32:19
Ladies of the Jury 4-05-32:14
Ladies of the Mob 6-20-28:15
Ladies of the Night Club 7-25-28: 14
Ladies Should Listen 7-31-34:14
Ladies They Talk About 2-28-33: 15
Ladies to Board 5-14-24:28
Ladies Who Do 2-05-64:16
Ladri Di Biciclette 12-15-48:6 and 12-07-49:6
Ladroes de Cinema 9-28-77:22
Ladrone, Il 4-02-80:26
Ladrones 1-15-30:22
Lady, The 1-28-25:32
Lady and Gent 7-19-32:24
Lady and the Bandit, The 8-08-51:18
Lady and the Mob, The 3-08-39: 18
Lady and the Monster, The 3-22-44:18
Lady and the Tramp 4-20-55:6
Lady at Midnight 7-21-48:10
Lady Audley's Secret 8-13-15:18
Lady Barber, The 11-12-10:16
Lady Barnacle 6-15-17:27
Lady Be Careful 10-14-36:15
Lady Be Good 5-30-28:14
Lady Be Good 7-16-41:8
Lady Behave 12-29-37:17
Lady Bodyguard 12-30-42:16

Lady by Choice 11-20-34:15
Lady Caroline Lamb 11-29-72: 26
Lady Chatterley's Lover (See: Amant de Lady Chatterley, L')
Lady Confesses, The 6-27-45:16
Lady Consents, The 2-12-36:18
Lady Doctor, The (See: Toto, Vittorio e la Dottoressa)
Lady Drummer, The 10-27-16:26
Lady Escapes, The 8-25-37:17
Lady Eve, The 2-26-41:16
Lady Fare, The (s) 10-02-29:19
Lady Fights Back, The 10-27-37: 18
Lady for a Day 9-15-33:17
Lady for a Night 12-31-41:8
Lady from Cheyenne 4-02-41:16
Lady from Chungking 1-20-43:20
Lady from Hell, The 3-31-26:43
Lady from Longacre 12-09-21: 36
Lady from Louisiana 5-21-41:18
Lady from Nowhere 9-01-31:34
Lady from Nowhere 12-23-36:18
Lady from Paris, A 10-12-27:21
Lady from Shanghai, The 4-14-48:8
Lady from Texas, The 9-26-51:6
Lady Gambles, The 5-11-49:6
Lady Gangster 4-08-42:8
Lady Godiva 5-12-22:32
Lady Godiva 9-28-55:8
Lady Godiva Rides Again 10-31-51:6
Lady Grey 10-22-80:24
Lady Hamilton 12-06-23:26
Lady Hamilton 2-05-69:6
Lady Has Plans, The 1-21-42:8
Lady Ice 8-08-73:14
Lady in a Cage 6-03-64:15
Lady in a Jam 7-01-42:8
Lady in Black 7-03-29:30
Lady in Cement 11-06-68:6
Lady in Danger 12-18-34:13
Lady in Distress 2-18-42:19
Lady in Ermine 1-05-27:16
Lady in Love, A 5-21-20:34
Lady in Question 8-07-40:14
Lady in Red, The 8-01-79:20
Lady in Scarlet 1-08-36:12
Lady in the Car with Glasses and a Gun (See: Dame Dans l'Auto Avec Des Lunettes et un Fusil)
Lady in the Dark 2-16-44:10
Lady in the Death House

4-05-44:14
Lady in the Iron Mask 6-11-52:18
Lady in the Lake 11-27-46:14
Lady in the Morgue 5-11-38:16
Lady Is a Square, The 2-11-59: 10
Lady Is Fickle, The 2-11-48:14
Lady Is Willing, The 1-23-34:21 and 8-14-34:15
Lady Is Willing, The 1-28-42:8
Lady Jane Grey 5-13-36:15
Lady Jane's Flight 7-25-08:13
Lady Killer 1-02-34:13
Lady L 12-01-65:6
Lady, Let's Dance 1-26-44:12
Lady Liberty (See: Mortadella, La)
Lady Lies, The 9-11-29:18
Lady Luck 7-17-46:8
Lady Lust 9-23-36:16
Lady Mackenzie's Pictures 6-11-15:18
Lady Objects, The 10-12-38:15
Lady of Burlesque 5-05-43:8
Lady of Chance 1-16-29:22
Lady of Monosreau 12-20-23:27
Lady of Quality 12-26-13:12
Lady of Quality, A 12-27-23:26
Lady of Scandal, The 6-18-30: 37
Lady of Secrets 2-26-36:37
Lady of the Dugout, The 8-08-19: 49
Lady of the Harem, The 8-25-26:18
Lady of the Law 8-20-75:73
Lady of the Night 3-04-25:37
Lady of the Pavements 3-13-29: 14
Lady of the Tropics 8-09-39:14
Lady of Vengeance 8-07-57:6
Lady on a Train 8-08-45:22
Lady on the Tracks, The (See: Dama Na Kolejich)
Lady or the Tiger, The (s) 4-22-42:18
Lady Oscar 12-19-79:34
Lady Paname 6-28-50:18
Lady Pays Off, The 10-24-51:6
Lady Possessed 2-20-52:6
Lady Robin Hood 8-26-25:26
Lady Rose's Daughter 9-03-20:44
Lady Says No, The 11-28-51:6
Lady Scarface 7-23-41:8
Lady Sings the Blues 10-18-72: 18
Lady Surrenders, A 10-08-30:23
Lady Surrenders, A 6-18-47:8
(Also see: Love Story)

Latest from Paris 2-29-28:23
Latin Lovers 7-22-53:6
Latin Quarter 5-08-29:29
Latin Quarter 10-31-45:17
Latitude Zero (See: Ido Zero
  Daisakusen)
Latuko 1-16-52:18
Laubenkolonie 6-06-33:14
Laugh and Get Rich 4-01-31:17
Laugh, Clown, Laugh 5-30-28:
  14
Laugh It Off (s) 4-29-31:12
Laugh, Pagliacci 2-04-48:20
Laugh Your Blues Away 2-17-43:
  14
Laugh-Back, The (s) 1-21-31:17
Laughing Anne 5-05-54:21
Laughing at Danger 1-28-25:43
Laughing at Danger 8-02-40:20
Laughing at Death 6-05-29:41
Laughing at Life 7-18-33:37
Laughing at Trouble 2-03-37:15
Laughing Bill Hyde 9-27-18:45
Laughing Boy 5-15-34:14
Laughing Gas 12-21-07:10
Laughing Gravy (s) 6-16-31:21
Laughing in Africa (s) 4-22-31:
  18 and 7-21-31:12
Laughing in Reno (s) 8-18-31:30
Laughing in Turkey (s) 9-22-31:
  22 (Also see: John P. Med-
  bury)
Laughing Irish Eyes 4-08-36:16
Laughing Lady, The 1-08-30:89
Laughing Lady 10-23-46:10
Laughing Policeman, The 11-28-
  73:14
Laughing Sinners 7-07-31:34
Laughing Woman, The (See: Femina
  Ridens)
Laughs in the Law 12-05-33:16
Laughter 10-08-30:23
Laughter in Hell 1-17-33:15
Laughter in Paradise 6-17-51:9
Laughter in the Dark 5-14-69:6
Laughter Through Tears 11-21-
  33:20
Launching of the Roma 11-14-08:
  13
Launching the Voltaire 9-11-09:12
Laundry Blues (s) 8-27-30:21
Laura 10-11-44:12
Laura: Les Ombres de L'Ete 1-
  23-80:104
Lauracha 11-27-46:28
Laurel and Hardy Murder Mystery,
  The (s) 7-30-30:16
Laurel and Hardy's Laughing 20's

8-11-65:6
Lausbubengeschichten 2-10-65:7
Lautare 8-02-72:24
Lavender Hill Mob, The 7-04-
  51:8
Law and Disorder 6-11-58:6
Law and Disorder 10-09-74:18
Law and Jack Wade 6-04-58:6
Law and Lead 4-21-37:15
Law and Order 3-01-32:21
Law and Order 11-27-40:16
Law and Order 10-21-42:24
Law and Order 4-08-53:6
Law and the Lady, The 7-18-
  51:6
Law and the Man, The 12-24-
  10:16
Law and the Man, The 2-08-28:
  16
Law and the Woman, The 1-20-
  22:35
Law Comes to Texas, The 5-17-
  39:14
Law Commands 8-17-38:23
Law Decides, The 4-21-16:29
Law for Tombstone 12-29-37:19
Law in Her Hands 7-29-36:15
Law Men 6-28-44:16
Law of Compensation, The 4-20-
  17:26
Law of Fear, The 3-21-28:23
Law of Life, The 2-04-16:29
Law of Men, The 5-16-19:50
Law of Nature, The 10-03-19:56
  and 10-31-19:56
Law of the Badlands 12-27-50:6
Law of the Barbary Coast 3-16-
  49:11
Law of the Golden West 5-18-49:8
Law of the Great Northwest, The
  4-19-18:45
Law of the Land, The 8-17-17:
  29
Law of the Lash 3-19-47:12
Law of the Lawless 6-21-23:22
Law of the Lawless 3-25-64:6
Law of the Mounted 7-03-29:32
  and 8-14-29:44
Law of the North, The 9-06-18:
  41
Law of the North 8-30-32:33
Law of the Northwest 7-07-43:8
Law of the Pampas 10-25-39:11
Law of the Panhandle 10-18-50:6
Law of the Plains 7-27-38:17
Law of the Range 6-27-28:34 and
  11-07-28:24
Law of the Range 7-16-41:22

Lenin in October 4-06-38:14
Lenin v Polche 5-25-66:7
Leningradsko Nebo 9-14-60:20
Lenny 11-13-74:19
Lenny Bruce 3-22-67:6
Lenny Bruce Performance Film 11-20-74:16
Lenny Bruce Without Tears 11-24-71:16
Lenz 5-26-71:20
Leo and Loree 5-07-80:10
Leo Beers (s) 12-12-28:14
Leo M. Frank and Gov. Slaton 7-30-15:19
Leo Reisman and the Hotel Brunswick Orchestra (s) 6-05-29:15
Leon Belasco Orch. (s) 7-18-33:36
Leon Morin, Pretre 9-13-61:6
Leon Navara (s) 3-06-29:12
Leonard-Tendler (s) 7-26-23:28
Leonardo da Vinci 11-26-52:18
Leone Have Sept Cabecas, Der 9-02-70:32
Leonor 9-10-75:20
Leopard, The 4-17-63:7
Leopard Lady, The 2-29-28:29
Leopard Man, The 5-05-43:16
Leopard Men of Africa 7-31-40:104
Leopard Woman 10-08-20:42
Leopardess 3-29-23:36 and 5-30-23:36
Leopard's Bride, The 4-21-16:29
Lepke 5-14-75:26
Leptirov Oblak 3-09-77:17
Les Girls 10-02-57:6
Less Than Kin 7-26-18:30
Less Than the Dust 11-10-16:25
Lesson in Love, A (s) 9-01-31:21
Lesson in Love, A (See: Lektion I Karlek, En)
Lesson in Palmistry, A 11-06-09:13
Lesson Number 1 (s) 7-24-29:29
Lessons in Love 6-10-21:35
Lest We Forget 2-01-18:46
Lest We Forget 4-17-35:15
Let Bygones Be Bygones 11-13-09:13
Let 'Em Have It 6-05-35:15
Let 'Er Buck (s) 8-27-30:21
Let 'Er Go Gallagher 1-18-28:16
Let Freedom Ring 2-22-39:12
Let George Do It 8-24-38:12

Let George Do It 10-16-40:31
Let It Be 5-20-70:15
Let It Rain 3-09-27:16
Let Joy Reign Supreme (See: Que La Fete Commence)
Let Katy Do It 12-10-15:21
Let Me Call You Sweetheart (s) 7-26-32:17
Let Me Explain, Dear 12-13-32:53
Let No Man Write My Epitaph 9-21-60:6
Let the Balloon Go 5-05-76:19
Let the Good Times Roll 5-30-73:13
Let the People Sing 4-22-42:18
Let Them Live 6-09-37:25
Let There Be Light 11-12-80:26
Let Us Be Gay 7-16-30:15
Let Us Live 2-22-39:12
Let Women Alone 1-28-25:43
Letaci Velikog Neba 8-17-77:22
Letiat Jouravly 5-21-58:16
Let's Be Famous 3-15-39:18
Let's Be Fashionable 6-18-20:33
Let's Be Happy 5-22-57:6
Let's Be Ritzy 7-10-34:13
Let's Dance (s) 4-18-33:21
Let's Dance 9-09-50:8
Let's Do It Again 6-17-53:6
Let's Do It Again 10-08-75:16
Let's Elope 5-23-19:59
Let's Face It 8-11-43:10
Let's Fall in Love 1-23-34:13
Let's Get a Divorce 4-26-18:40
Let's Get Married 3-03-26:34
Let's Get Married 3-30-60:6
Let's Go 12-13-23:22
Let's Go Collegiate 11-12-41:9
Let's Go Native 9-03-30:41
Let's Go Navy 8-01-51:6
Let's Go Places 3-05-30:21
Let's Go Steady 3-14-45:16
Let's Hope (s) 6-11-30:18
Let's Kill Uncle 9-21-66:6
Let's Live a Little 10-27-48:9
Let's Live Tonight 3-20-35:17
Let's Love and Laugh 5-27-31:57
Let's Make a Million 1-27-37:13
Let's Make a Night of It 7-07-37:25
Let's Make It Legal 11-14-51:6
Let's Make Love 8-24-60:6
Let's Make Music 12-11-40:16
Let's Play (s) 4-01-31:16
Let's Play Post Office (s) 4-24-34:14
Let's Rock 5-07-58:6

Lost Command, The 5-25-66:6
Lost Continent 7-25-51:6
Lost Continent 7-03-68:26
Lost Cord, The 4-29-25:36
Lost Empire, The 1-23-29:43
Lost Expedition, The 10-10-28:
26
Lost Gods 7-09-30:31 and 10-08-
30:23
Lost Happiness 3-03-48:8
Lost Honeymoon 3-12-47:12
Lost Honor of Katharine Blum,
The (See: Verlorene Ehre
der Katharina Blum, Die)
Lost Horizon 3-10-37:14
Lost Horizon 3-07-73:18
Lost in a Big City 4-19-23:36
Lost in a Harem 8-30-44:10
Lost in a Limehouse (s) 8-08-33:
19
Lost in Alaska 7-30-52:6
Lost in London 12-19-14:26
Lost in Mid-Ocean 7-10-14:21
Lost in Siberia 10-23-09:13
Lost in the Arctic 8-01-28:12
Lost in the Stars 2-06-74:18
Lost in the Stratosphere 3-06-35:
21
Lost in Transit 9-14-17:34
Lost Jungle, The 6-19-34:44
Lost Lady, A 1-21-25:34
Lost Lady, A 10-09-34:18
Lost Lagoon 2-05-58:20
Lost Limited, The 9-07-27:24
Lost, Lonely and Vicious 10-22-
58:6
Lost Man, The 5-14-69:30
Lost Missile 12-03-58:20
Lost Moment, The 10-15-47:10
Lost Money 1-23-20:61
Lost One, The 3-31-48:15
Lost Paradise, The 9-04-14:13
Lost Patrol, The 4-03-34:17
Lost People, The 9-07-49:18
Lost Princess, The 10-31-19:61
Lost Ranch, The 9-21-38:13
Lost Romance, The 5-13-21:42
Lost Sex 7-03-68:28
Lost Shadow, The 3-28-28:31
Lost Squadron, The 3-15-32:14
Lost, Strayed or Stolen 2-08-08:
11
Lost Trail, The 11-28-45:10
Lost Tribe, The 11-12-24:52
Lost Tribe, The 7-03-29:30
Lost Tribe, The 4-20-49:11
Lost Volcano, The 6-28-50:18
Lost Weekend, The 8-15-45:14

Lost World, The 2-11-25:31
Lost World, The 7-06-60:22
Lost World of Sinbad, The 3-17-
62:7
Lot in Sodom (s) 1-09-34:16
Lotna 5-20-64:20
Lots of Water (s) 5-19-26:20
Lotte in Weimar 5-21-75:22
Lottery Bride 12-03-30:14
Lottery Lover 2-20-35:15
Lottery Man, The 10-10-19:61
Lotus Eaters, The 1-02-21:43
Loud Mouth (s) 6-07-32:20
Loudspeaker, The 8-14-34:15
Louie 3-16-77:24
Louis-Baer Fight (s) 10-02-35:
17 and 5-28-41:18
Louis-Carnera Fight (s) 7-03-35:
15
Louis-Conn Fight (s) 6-25-41:18
Louis-Galento Fight (s) 7-05-39:
16
Louis-Godoy Fight (s) 2-14-40:18
and 6-26-40:16
Louis Pasteur 2-12-36:16
Louis-Pastor Fight (s) 2-03-37:
14 and 9-17-39:14
Louis-Schmeling Fight (s) 6-29-
38:12
Louisa 7-02-47:22
Louisa 5-31-50:6
Louisa, A World of Love 4-26-
72:6
Louise 6-21-39:26
Louisiana 7-25-19:45
Louisiana 3-13-47:15
Louisiana Hayride 8-23-44:18
Louisiana Purchase 11-26-41:9
Louisiana Story, The 9-22-48:8
Louisiana Territory 10-14-53:6
Loulou 5-28-80:15
Loulous, Les 3-30-77:18
Loup Chassent la Nuit, Les 3-19-
52:6
Louppo 7-29-70:15
Loups Dans la Bergerie, Les 7-
20-60:20
Loutre, La 9-16-64:22
Louve Solitaire, La 2-28-68:22
Louves, Les 6-21-57:18
Lovable Cheat, The 3-23-49:8
Lovagias Ugy 3-10-37:15
Love 12-07-27:18
Love a la Carte (See: Adua e la
Compagne)
Love a la Mode (s) 10-22-30:23
Love Affair 4-19-32:15
Love Affair 3-15-39:16

Love Affair; or, The Case of the Missing Switchboard Operator (See: Ljubavni Slucaj ou Tragedija Sluzbenice P. T. T.)
Love Aflame 1-19-17:24
Love Among the Millionaires 7-09-30:19
Love and Anarchy (See: Film d'Amore e d'Anarchia)
Love and Base Ball 10-31-14:27
Love and Bullets 3-28-79:20
Love and Death 6-11-75:18
Love and Faith (See: Wa Islamah)
Love and Glory 8-06-24:24
Love and Hate 11-03-16:30
Love and Hate 8-04-65:32
Love and Hisses (s) 7-10-34:13
Love and Hisses 12-22-37:17
Love and Kisses 8-11-65:6
Love and Larceny 2-27-63:7
Love and Learn 2-22-28:24
Love and Learn 3-26-47:12
Love and Marriage 8-10-66:6
Love and Pain 3-14-13:14
Love and Pain and the Whole Damn Thing 4-18-73:32
Love and the Frenchwoman (See: Francaise et L'Amour, La)
Love and the Midnight Auto Supply 6-07-78:28
Love and the Woman 6-20-19:51
Love and War 10-02-09:13
Love Around the Clock 12-07-49:20
Love at First Bite 4-11-79:20
Love at First Sight 11-19-10:13
Love at First Sight 2-05-30:31
Love at First Sight 7-20-77:18
Love at Twenty (See: Amour a Vingt Ans, L')
Love Auction, The 2-28-19:56
Love Bandit, The 2-14-24:27
Love Bargain, The (s) 1-21-31:17
Love Before Breakfast 3-18-36:17
Love Begins at 20 9-23-36:16
Love Birds 5-29-34:13
Love Boat, The 4-09-30:22
Love Bound 7-12-32:17
Love Brand 8-09-23:41
Love Brokers, The 4-05-18:45
Love Bug, The 12-11-68:6
Love Burglar, The 8-01-19:53
Love Business (s) 2-04-31:16
Love Call, The 5-02-19:60
Love Captive, The 6-19-34:44
Love Charm, The 12-16-21:35

Love Cheat, The 8-08-19:49
Love Comes Along 2-05-30:24
Love Commandment 12-26-28:42
Love Contract, The 8-09-32:22
Love Crazy 5-14-41:16
Love Cycles (See: Dama Spathi)
Love Defender, The 3-21-19:55
Love Department (s) 9-04-35:31
Love Doctor, The 10-05-17:43
Love Doctor, The 11-13-29:32
Love Drops 3-19-10:17
Love 'Em and Leave 'Em 12-08-26:17
Love Epidemic, The 1-15-75:26
Love Eterne, The 11-13-63:17
Love Expert 4-30-20:43
Love Fever (s) 3-18-31:14
Love Finds Andy Hardy 7-13-38:15
Love Flower, The 8-27-20:28
Love Follows Rain 1-26-77:50
Love from a Stranger 1-27-37:13 and 4-21-37:14
Love from a Stranger 11-05-47:8
Love Gamble, The 9-16-25:42
Love Gambler, The 3-15-23:31
Love Girl, The 6-30-16:19
Love God?, The 5-28-69:6
Love Goddesses, The 3-03-65:7
Love Habit, The 2-04-31:43 (Two reviews)
Love Happy 7-20-49:6
Love Has Many Faces 2-10-65:6
Love Hermit, The 11-03-16:29
Love, Honor, and ---- 10-03-19:56
Love, Honor and Behave 6-03-21:40
Love, Honor and Behave 2-16-38:17
Love, Honor and Goodbye 9-12-45:16
Love, Honor and Obey 9-17-20:36
Love, Honor, and Obey (s) 4-02-30:18
Love, Honor, Oh Baby! 10-31-33:17
Love Hour, The 9-02-25:37
Love Hungry 4-18-28:26
Love in a Bungalow 7-07-37:12
Love in a 4-Letter World 5-20-70:28
Love in a Goldfish Bowl 6-07-61:20
Love in a Hurry 1-03-19:36
Love in a Taxi 9-17-80:23
Love in Bloom 4-24-35:13

Love in Caucasus 12-11-29:42
Love in Exile 5-27-36:15 and
12-16-36:14
Love in 4 Dimensions (See: Amore
in 4 Dimensioni)
Love in Morocco 3-21-33:27
(Also see: Baroud)
Love in Pawn 10-28-53:6
Love in Quarantine 12-03-10:14
Love in the Afternoon 8-21-29:18
Love in the Afternoon 6-05-57:6
Love in the City (See: Amore in
Citta)
Love in the Dark 11-24-22:35
Love in the Desert 5-08-29:27
Love in the Ring 5-07-30:43
Love in the Rough 10-01-30:34
Love in the Suburbs (s) 4-08-31:
18
Love-Intrigue Passion 8-30-23:27
Love Is a Ball 3-06-63:6
Love Is a Headache 2-02-38:15
Love Is a Lie 7-04-28:23
Love Is a Many Splendored Thing
8-10-55:6
Love Is a Racket 6-14-32:16
Love Is an Awful Thing 9-08-22:
41
Love Is Better Than Ever 2-06-
52:6
Love Is Like That 5-09-33:15
Love Is Love 8-15-19:71
Love Is News 3-10-37:15
Love Is on the Air 9-15-37:13
Love Is War 7-14-71:24
Love Island 7-23-52:18
Love Laughs at Andy Hardy 12-04-
46:13
Love Letters 1-04-18:44
Love Letters 8-22-45:20
Love Letters of a Star 12-02-36:
38
Love Liar, The 3-31-16:25
Love, Life and Laughter 6-07-23:
25
Love Life of Adolf Hitler, The 3-
03-48:8
Love Light, The 1-14-21:41
Love, Live and Laugh 11-06-29:
19
Love Locked Out 12-14-49:22
Love Lottery 2-10-54:6
Love, Lust & Violence 7-02-75:
28
Love Machine, The 8-04-71:18
Love Madness 9-24-20:44
Love Makes 'Em Wild 3-09-27:
17

Love Makes Us Blind 8-24-27:26
and 5-02-28:15
Love Mart, The 12-28-27:18
Love Mask, The 4-14-16:24
Love Masquerade 5-08-29:29
Love Master, The 5-21-24:26
Love Mates 1-31-68:22
Love Me 3-22-18:49
Love Me and the World Is Mine
2-08-28:16
Love Me Forever 7-03-35:14
Love Me Like I Do 3-18-70:18
Love Me--Love My Wife 6-16-71:
15
Love Me or Leave Me 5-25-55:6
Love Me Tender 11-21-56:6
Love Me Tonight 8-23-32:15
Love Nest 10-17-51:6
Love Net, The 12-13-18:40
Love Never Dies 10-13-16:25
Love Never Dies 12-16-21:36
Love of a Clown 2-08-50:22
Love of Paquita 9-21-27:24
Love of the Rott Bros., The 7-
17-29:53
Love of the White Snake 8-23-78:
36
Love of Women 7-23-24:26
Love on a Bet 3-11-36:15
Love on a Budget 1-12-38:14
Love on a Ladder (s) 6-05-34:12
Love on a Pillow (See: Repos du
Guerrier, Le)
Love on Skis 11-14-33:30
Love on the Dole 4-30-41:16
Love on the Gallows (See: Am
Galgen Hangt Die Liebe)
Love on the Riviera (See: Femmes
D'un Ete)
Love on the Run 12-02-36:18
Love on the Run (See: Amour en
Fuite, L')
Love on Toast 12-22-37:17
Love on Wheels 8-09-32:22
Love or a Kingdom 12-08-37:17
Love or Justice 6-22-17:26
Love Over Night 12-19-28:12
Love Parade, The 11-27-29:21
Love Past Thirty 3-13-34:56
Love Piker 7-19-23:26
Love Pirate, The 7-25-28:36
Love Punch, The (s) 12-10-30:
15
Love Slave 8-04-22:36
Love Slaves of the Amazons 12-
04-57:6
Love Special, The 3-25-21:43
Love Specialist, The (See: Ragazza
Del Palio, La)

259 •

Loves of Salammbo, The 10-31-62:20
Love's Old Sweet Song 10-01-10: 18
Love's Old Sweet Song 2-22-23: 41
Love's Option 10-10-28:26
Love's Pay Day 11-29-18:40
Love's Penalty 5-27-21:35
Love's Prisoner 5-30-19:77
Love's Redemption 1-13-22:42
Love's Toll 5-05-16:26
Love's Whirlpool 3-12-24:27
Love's Wilderness 12-24-24:32
Lovetime 8-12-21:34
Lovey Mary 6-23-26:14
Lovin' Molly 3-13-74:18
Loving 2-18-70:21
Loving and Laughing 6-09-71:17 and 11-03-71:16
Loving Cousins 4-14-76:26
Loving Couples 9-10-80:34
Loving Hearts 2-19-10:15
Loving Lies 1-31-24:24
Loving the Ladies 3-26-30:39
Loving Touch, The 3-18-70:18
Loving You 7-03-57:6
Low Down (s) 2-26-30:24
Low-Priced Homes (s) 6-17-36: 23
Lower Depths, The 9-15-37:15
Lower Depths, The 3-19-58:6
Loyal Heart 3-06-46:12
Loyal Lives 8-30-23:26
Loyalties 7-25-33:35 and 10-30-34:28
Loyalty 6-05-14:19
Loyalty 11-30-17:46
Loyalty of Love 3-24-37:31
Loyola--The Soldier Saint 4-16-52:6
Lu Kur Yue Dau Kur 4-22-70:26
Lucertola Con la Pelle di Donna, Una 4-21-71:17
Luces de Buenos Aires 11-10-31:23
Luci Sommerse 7-01-36:23
Lucia 7-30-69:6
Lucia di Lammermoor 11-12-47: 24
Lucia McCartney 12-22-71:66
Luciano 7-31-63:12
Luciano Serra, Pilot 9-21-38:25
Lucie 9-19-79:22
Lucie a Zazraky 8-25-71:16
Luck 8-09-23:27
Luck and Pluck 2-07-19:59
Luck in Pawn 12-19-19:44

Luck of Ginger Coffey, The 9-23-64:6
Luck of Roaring Camp, The 1-29-10:13
Luck of Roaring Camp, The 12-22-37:24
Luck of the Irish 1-31-20:56
Luck of the Irish 1-20-37:15
Luck of the Irish, The 9-15-48:15
Luck of the Navy, The 12-21-27: 25
Luckiest Girl in the World, The 12-09-36:12
Lucky Boy 1-09-29:11
Lucky Bride, The 1-28-48:20
Lucky Cisco Kid 5-29-40:14
Lucky Dan 12-08-22:33
Lucky Devil, The 7-08-25:36
Lucky Devils 2-21-33:14
Lucky Devils 2-26-41:16
Lucky Horseshoe, The 8-19-25: 36
Lucky in Love (s) 6-20-28:27 and 9-12-28:12
Lucky in Love 12-18-29:28
Lucky Jim 9-25-57:26
Lucky Jo 12-02-64:6
Lucky Jordan 11-18-42:8
Lucky Lady, The 6-23-26:15
Lucky Lady 12-17-75:23
Lucky Larkin 3-12-30:36
Lucky Larrigan 3-28-33:27
Lucky Losers 5-31-50:6
Lucky Luciano (See: Re: Lucky Luciano)
Lucky Luke 12-22-71:6
Lucky Me 4-14-54:6
Lucky Nick Cain 2-07-51:6
Lucky Night 5-03-39:16
Lucky Number 6-06-33:15
Lucky Partners 8-21-40:18
Lucky Spurs 11-02-27:24
Lucky Star 7-24-29:29
Lucky Star, The 5-28-80:42
Lucky Stiff, The 1-19-49:10
Lucky Terror 4-08-36:17
Lucky Texan 2-13-34:14
Lucky 13 (s) 10-06-31:23
Lucrece Borgia 11-11-53:22
Lucrecia Borgia 12-26-28:27
Lucretia Lombard or ... Flaming Passion 12-20-23:22
Lucrezia Borgia 10-20-37:12
Lucy at Boarding School 9-17-10: 12
Lucy Gallant 10-05-55:6
Luda Kuca 8-27-80:21
Lude Godina 8-16-78:18

Mad Doctor of Market Street, The 1-07-42:44
Mad Dog 5-05-76:19
Mad Dog Coll 5-03-61:7
Mad Dogs and Englishmen (See: Joe Cocker: Mad Dogs and Englishmen)
Mad Empress, The 2-21-40:12
Mad Game, The 11-14-33:30
Mad Genius, The 10-27-31:19
Mad Ghoul, The 11-03-43:16
Mad Holiday 12-02-36:38
Mad Hour 4-18-28:26
Mad House, The (s) 12-18-29:22
Mad Love 3-08-23:30 (Also see: Sappho)
Mad Love 8-07-35:21
Mad Lover, The 7-27-17:28
Mad Magician, The 3-31-54:6
Mad Marriage, The 2-04-21:43
Mad Martindales 4-22-42:18
Mad Max 5-16-79:38
Mad Melody (s) 4-29-31:12
Mad Men of Europe 6-26-40:16
Mad Miner 4-10-09:13
Mad Miss Manton, The 10-12-38:15
Mad Monster, The 6-03-42:24
Mad Parade, The 9-22-31:22
Mad Queen, The 11-01-50:6
Mad Room, The 3-12-69:6
Mad Wheel, The 7-08-25:38
Mad Youth 5-22-40:33
Madalena 5-17-61:7
Madam Kitty (See: Salon Kitty)
Madam Satan 5-22-14:23
Madam White Snake 11-03-65:6
Madame Aki 11-27-63:6
Madame Bo-Peep 5-25-17:20
Madame Bovary 11-27-34:63
Madame Bovary 6-02-37:23
Madame Bovary 7-09-47:17
Madame Bovary 8-03-49:16
Madame Butterfly 11-12-15:22
Madame Butterfly 12-27-32:14
Madame Butterfly 4-27-55:6
Madame Claude 5-18-77:16
Madame Curie 11-24-43:18
Madame De 10-21-53:18 (Also see: Earrings of Madame De..., The)
Madame Du Barry 3-21-28:19
Mme. Du Barry 10-30-34:16
Madame Du Barry 11-10-54:6
Mme. Frances Alda (s) 2-12-30:18
Madame Guillotine 8-20-24:23
Madame Jealousy 2-08-18:41

Madame la Presidente 2-11-16:22
Mme. Marion Kurenko (s) 4-10-29:16
Mme. Ne Veux Pas d'Enfant 4-25-33:18
Madame of the Jury (s) 12-03-30:15
Madame Peacock 10-29-20:41
Mme. Pompadour 8-03-27:16
Madame Sans Gene 4-22-25:34
Madame Sans Gene 4-18-45:12
Madame Sans-Gene 6-20-62:18
Mme. Schumann-Heink (s) 8-29-28:15
Madame Sphinx 6-14-18:30
Madame Spy 2-13-34:14
Madame Spy 12-09-42:16
Mme. Wants No Children 4-13-27:23
Madame Who? 1-18-18:41
Madame Wuenscht Keine Kinder 3-23-27:16
Madame X 1-21-16:27
Madame X 10-01-20:34
Madame X 5-01-29:17
Madame X 9-29-37:14
Madame X 2-23-66:6
Madame Zenobia 12-12-73:18
Madamiegella di Maupin 3-16-66:7
Madarkak 11-10-71:16 and 8-30-72:26
Madcap Betty 6-18-15:17
Madcap Madge 6-22-17:22
Madcap of the House 12-13-50:25
Maddalena 8-17-55:6
Maddalena 11-17-71:14
Made 9-13-72:20
Made for Each Other 2-01-39:13
Made for Each Other 12-15-71:14
Made in Heaven 4-22-21:41
Made in Heaven 11-26-52:18
Made in Italy 3-30-66:28 and 5-03-67:30
Made in Paris 2-02-66:17
Made in Sweden 7-09-69:26
Made in U. S. A. 12-14-66:19
Made on Broadway 7-11-33:15
Madeline 2-22-50:6
Madeline Is 4-28-71:6
Madelon, La 1-25-56:6
Mademoiselle 5-18-66:7
Mademoiselle--Age 39 4-04-56:16
Mlle. Desiree 11-17-48:13
Mademoiselle Docteur 4-21-37:15
Mademoiselle Fifi 8-02-44:10
Mademoiselle from Armentieres 7-18-28:28

Mademoiselle Ma Mere 9-27-39: 14

Mmle. Midnight 5-28-24:28

Mademoiselle Modiste 4-28-26:48

Mlle. Paulette 5-17-18:44

Mademoiselle S'Amuse 3-24-48: 22

Maden 8-02-78:16

Madero of Mexico (s) 2-03-43:14

Madhouse, The (s) 2-12-30:18

Madhouse 3-27-74:24

Madhouse Movies (s) 9-05-33:19

Madigan 3-27-68:6

Madigan's Millions 2-04-70:26

Madison Avenue 8-01-62:6

Madison Square Garden 10-18-32: 15

Madly 12-30-70:16

Madmen of Mandoras 1-29-64:6

Madness of Helen, The 11-10-16: 25

Madness of the Heart 9-07-49:18

Mado 11-17-76:18

Madonna of Avenue A 8-14-29:31

Madonna of the Desert 3-10-48:22

Madonna of the Seven Moons 1-17-45:14

Madonna of the Sleeping Cars 10-16-29:33

Madonna of the Streets 10-29-24: 27

Madonna of the Streets 12-03-30: 15

Madonna, Wo Bist Du? 4-01-36: 16

Madonnas and Men 6-18-20:34

Madonna's Secret, The 2-20-46:8

Madrasta, La 5-07-75:48

Madre 4-25-28:28

Madre a la Fuerza 8-21-40:20

Madriguera, La 7-16-69:6

Madron 12-23-70:22

Madwoman of Chaillot, The 6-25-69:6

Maedchen Aus Zwelter, Ein 6-02-76:30

Maedchen Beim Frauenarzt 4-21-71:17

Maedchen in Uniform 9-27-32:17

Maedchen in Uniform 7-16-58:6

Maedchen in Weiss 10-07-36:31

Maedchen Irene, Das 11-18-36: 29

Maedchen, Maedchen 3-08-67:6

Maedchen mit Gewalt 4-01-70:26

Maedchen Pensionat 11-04-36:19

Maedchen von Gestern Nacht, Das 6-22-38:23

Maedchenjahre einer Koenigan 4-08-36:17

Maedchenkrieg, Der 9-14-77:17

Maedel der Strasse 4-11-33:20

Maedel vom Ballett, Ein 2-24-37:19

Maedel von der Reeperbahn, Das 2-18-31:35

Maenak America 1-14-76:21

Maenner Im Gefaehrlichen Alter 6-30-54:6

Maerchen von Glueck 10-05-49:8

Maes 10-27-76:30

Maestrita de los Obreros 4-01-42:8

Maestro di Vigerano, Il 1-15-64:6

Maestro e Margherita, Il 9-13-72:30

Maeva 9-06-61:18

Maffia, La 8-30-72:26

Mafiaen, Det er Osse Mig 10-02-74:24

Mafioso 11-21-62:12

Mafu Cage, The 5-24-78:38

Mag-ingat: Kapag Biyda Ang Umbig 7-30-75:24

Magandang Gabi Sa Inyong Lahat 6-23-76:16

Magasiskola 3-11-70:24

Magda 10-12-17:42

Magdalene of the Hills, A 4-20-17:26

Magdat Kicsapjak 4-13-38:23

Maggie, The 3-17-54:6

Maggie Pepper 2-14-19:51

Magic 11-01-78:22

Magic Adventure 12-19-73:12

Magic Blade, The 8-04-76:22

Magic Bow, The 9-25-46:10

Magic Box, The 9-26-51:6

Magic Boy 8-09-61:6

Magic Carpet, The 9-26-51:6

Magic Carpet Series (s) see: Alpine Echoes; Berlin Medley; Big Game of the Sea; Birds of the Sea; Broadway by Day; Desert Tripoli; Fisherman's Luck; French Foreign Legion, The; Gorges of the Giants; Here Comes the Circus; In the Guianas; In the South Seas; Incredible India; India Today; Lure of the Orient, The; Manhattan Medley; Mickey in Arabia; Over the Bounding Main; Paris on Parade; Pirate Isles; Rhineland Memories;

Man and His Woman 7-16-20:33
Man and Maid 4-08-25:38
Man and the Girl 10-23-09:13
Man and the Moment 1-05-23:43
Man and the Moment 8-07-29:201
Man and the Woman, A 3-23-17:
21
Man and Wife 6-28-23:23
Man and Woman 9-09-21:44
Man at Large 9-10-41:16
Man at Six, The 8-11-31:22
Man at the Gate 1-29-41:18
Man at the Top 11-28-73:18
Man-Bait 1-19-27:18
Man Bait 1-30-52:12
Man Beast 12-12-56:6
Man Behind the Curtain, The 6-
16-16:22
Man Behind the Door, The 11-28-
14:24
Man Behind the Gun, The 12-24-
52:14
Man Beneath, The 7-11-19:61
Man Betrayed, A 2-03-37:15
Man Betrayed, A 3-12-41:14
Man Between 10-04-23:26
Man Between, The 9-30-53:22
Man Called Adam, A 6-29-66:6
Man Called Back, The 8-02-32:15
Man Called Dagger, A 12-20-67:15
Man Called Demon, The 7-31-57:6
Man Called Flintstone, A 8-10-66:
18
Man Called Gannon, A 6-11-69:6
Man Called Horse, A 4-29-70:18
Man Called Noon, The 8-01-73:18
Man Called Peter 3-23-55:6
Man Called Sledge, A 3-03-71:17
Man Could Get Killed, A 3-16-
66:6
Man Crazy 12-21-27:22
Man Crazy 12-16-53:6
Man-Eater of Kumaon 6-23-48:6
Man-Eaters (s) 9-29-31:14
Man-Eating Sharks (s) 8-30-32:14
Man for All Seasons, A 12-14-
66:6
Man for Burning, A (See: Uomo da
Bruciare, Un)
Man Friday 5-14-75:27
Man from Beyond 4-07-22:41
Man from Bitter Ridge, The 4-20-
55:6
Man from Bitter Root, The 7-07-
16:24
Man from Black Hills, The 5-14-
52:20
Man from Blankley's, The 4-02-
30:19

Man from Brodney 12-20-23:22
Man from Cairo, The 12-02-53:6
Man from Cheyenne, The 1-28-
42:8
Man from Chicago, The 11-05-
30:45 and 1-21-31:30
Man from Colorado, The 11-24-
48:6
Man from Dakota, The 2-21-40:
12
Man from Death Valley, The 10-
13-31:29
Man from Del Rio, The 10-03-
56:26
Man from Down Under, The 8-
04-43:8
Man from Downing Street, The
4-14-22:39
Man from Frisco, The 4-26-44:
19
Man from Funeral Range, The
10-11-18:44
Man from Galveston, The 1-15-
64:6
Man from Glengarry, The 4-05-
23:37
Man from God's Country, The 10-
22-24:26
Man from God's Country, The 2-
26-58:6
Man from Gun Town, The 1-08-36:
13
Man from Hardpan, The 4-13-27:
23
Man from Headquarters, The 10-
17-28:27
Man from Headquarters, The 3-25-
42:8
Man from Hell, The 10-02-34:37
Man from Hell's Edge, The 8-02-
32:17
Man from Hell's River, The 6-
30-22:33
Man from Home, The 11-07-14:
23
Man from Home, The 5-05-22:33
Man from Hong Kong, The 6-11-
75:19
Man from Laramie, The 6-29-55:
6
Man from Lost River, The 1-20-
22:35
Man from Mexico, The 11-21-14:
27
Man from Montana, The 11-30-
17:45
Man from Montana, The 12-17-
41:8

Man Must Live, A 1-28-25:34
Man Next Door, The 3-14-13:14
Man Next Door, The 5-30-23:24
Man of a Thousand Faces 7-17-57:6
Man of Affairs 2-24-37:15
Man of Africa 10-24-56:6
Man of Aran 5-29-34:13 and 10-23-34:18
Man of Bronze, The 11-29-18:41
Man of Conflict 10-21-53:6
Man of Conquest 4-21-39:25
Man of Courage 4-21-22:41
Man of Courage 11-20-34:17
Man of Courage 3-31-43:8
Man of Iron, A 6-24-25:84
Man of Iron 12-11-35:19
Man of Iron 12-19-73:12
Man of La Mancha 12-06-72:16
Man of Marble (See: Czlowiek z Marmuru)
Man of Music 5-13-53:20
Man of Mystery, The 1-05-17:26
Man of Peace, A (s) 6-20-28:14
Man of Sentiment, A 11-14-33:30
Man of Shame, The 10-29-15:23
Man of Sorrow, A 4-28-16:28
Man of Stone 11-18-21:43
Man of the Forest 8-26-21:36
Man of the Forest 10-31-33:17
Man of the Hour, The 10-10-14:25
Man of the Hour 11-27-40:16
Man of the Moment 9-28-55:9
Man of the Music Mountain 12-21-17:47
Man of the People 3-03-37:14
Man of the West 9-17-58:6
Man of the World 3-25-31:17
Man of Two Worlds 1-16-34:15
Man of Violence 6-17-70:22
Man on a String 4-13-60:6
Man on a Swing 2-27-74:16
Man on a Tightrope 4-01-53:6
Man on Fire 6-05-57:6
Man on the Box, The 7-24-14:18
Man on the Box, The 9-30-25:42
Man on the Eiffel Tower, The 12-21-49:8
Man on the Flying Trapeze, The 8-07-35:21
Man on the Prowl 12-04-57:22
Man on the Roof (See: Mannen Pa Taget)
Man on the Run 6-01-49:20
Man Outside 6-20-33:46
Man Outside 5-08-68:36
Man Power 7-27-27:16

Man-Proof 12-15-37:17
Man Rustlin' 4-21-26:38
Man She Brought Back, The 10-13-22:43
Man Sku Vaere Noget Ved Musikken 7-12-72:30
Man Spricht Ueber Jacqueline 5-19-37:22
Man Tamer, The 5-27-21:35
Man That Married His Own Wife, The 4-28-22:43
Man They Could Not Hang, The 9-27-39:14
Man They Couldn't Arrest, The 8-11-31:22; 3-14-33:15; 10-31-33:17
Man to Man 3-31-22:40
Man to Man 1-07-31:23
Man to Men, The 11-24-48:14
Man to Remember, A 10-05-38:14 and 11-09-38:16
Man Trackers 8-12-21:34
Man Trail, The 9-17-15:25
Man Trailer 5-29-34:13
Man Trap, The 11-02-17:51
Man-Trap 11-01-61:6
Man Trouble 9-10-30:29
Man Unconquerable 7-21-22:33
Man Under Cover 4-07-22:41
Man Under the Bed, The 3-12-10:39
Man Upstairs, The 10-08-58:6
Man Wanted 4-19-32:14
Man Who, The 8-19-21:35
Man Who Broke the Bank at Monte Carlo, The 11-20-35:16
Man Who Came Back, The 6-11-15:19
Man Who Came Back, The 9-03-24:23
Man Who Came Back, The 1-07-31:22
Man Who Came to Dinner, The 7-07-42:44
Man Who Changed His Mind 3-20-34:31 and 9-23-36:16
Man Who Changed His Name, The 10-23-34:25
Man Who Changed the World, The (s) 9-03-41:17
Man Who Cheated Himself, The 12-20-50:6
Man Who Cheated Life, The 2-13-29:24
Man Who Could Cheat Death, The 6-24-59:6
Man Who Could Not Lose, The 11-21-14:27

271 •

Marie des Iles 3-09-60:6
Marie du Port, La 4-26-50:22
Marie Galante 11-27-34:15
Marie la Misere 10-17-45:8
Marie, Ltd. 4-04-19:65
Marie-Louise 11-14-45:12
Marie-Octobre 5-27-59:6
Marie-Poupee 9-15-76:16
Marie Pour Memoire 5-15-68:30
Marie Soleil 4-21-65:7
Marie Tudor 10-04-67:14
Mariee Est Trop Belle, La 1-23-57:6
Mariee Etait en Noire, La 4-24-68:26
Maries de l'An Deux, Les 5-05-71:22
Marigolds in August 3-12-80:26
Marihuana 11-08-50:18
Marika 3-23-38:16
Mariken von Nieumeghen 5-14-75:30
Marilyn 6-12-63:6
Marilyn and the Senator 4-16-75:23
Marine Raiders 6-21-44:12
Marines Are Coming, The 2-27-35:12
Marines Are Here 7-06-38:15
Marines Come Through, The 7-14-43:22
Marines Fly High 3-06-40:18
Marines in the Making (s) 2-03-43:14
Marines, Let's Go 8-16-61:6
Marion, Das Gehoert Sich Nicht 3-14-33:15
Marion Harris (s) 10-24-28:24 and 11-21-28:13
Marionettes, The 2-08-18:43
Marionettes (s) 12-04-29:15
Marionettes (s) 7-02-30:25
Marions-Nous 3-25-31:71
Marisa la Civetta 3-26-58:14
Marital Fulfillment 5-13-70:14
Marital Happiness 5-08-29:24
Mariti In Citta 3-19-58:18
Marito e Mio e L'Amazzo Quando Mi Piace, Il 3-13-68:24
Marito Per Anna Zaccheo, Un 12-30-53:18
Marius 10-27-31:25; 4-25-33:15; 6-02-33:14
Marja Pieni 8-16-72:26
Marjoe 5-10-72:21
Marjorie Beebe (s) 3-01-32:20
Marjorie Morningstar 3-12-58:6
Mark, The 2-01-61:6

Mark It Paid 1-24-33:21
Mark of Cain, The 1-14-48:22
Mark of the Beast 11-15-23:23
Mark of the Devil (See: Brenn, Hexe, Brenn)
Mark of the Gorilla 2-22-50:6
Mark of the Hawk 2-12-58:6
Mark of the Renegade 7-25-51:6
Mark of the Vampire 5-08-35:45
Mark of the Whistler 11-15-44:8
Mark of Zorro, The 12-03-20:32
Mark of Zorro, The 11-06-40:16
Marked Cards 7-26-18:32
Marked Cards 7-13-49:16
Marked Men 9-11-40:14
Marked Trails 10-11-44:12
Marked Woman, The 12-12-14:28
Marked Woman 4-14-37:12
Markers of Men 9-16-25:42
Markers, Staakt Uw Wild Geraas 7-12-61:7
Market of Souls, The 9-12-19:52
Market of Vain Desire, The 5-19-16:19
Marketa Lazarova 11-06-68:6
Markia 9-18-14:19
Marking Time (s) 11-06-29:19
Marknadsafton 10-06-48:18
Marlowe 10-08-69:30
Marmeladupporet 3-12-80:23
Marnie 6-10-64:6
Maroc 7 3-29-67:6
Marooned 11-19-69:14
Marooned Hearts 10-08-20:41
Marquis Preferred 1-23-29:34
Marquise d'O, La 5-19-76:23
Marquise von Pompadour, Die 1-28-31:15
Marquise von Pompadour, Die 2-19-36:32
Marriage 11-08-18:41
Marriage 5-18-27:21
Marriage 5-22-29:24
Marriage 2-28-45:15
Marriage 1-29-75:16
Marriage by Aeroplane 1-30-14:17
Marriage by Contract 11-14-28:17
Marriage Came Tumbling Down, The (See: Ce Sacre Grand-Pere)
Marriage Chance 1-19-23:46
Marriage Cheat, The 6-04-24:26
Marriage Circle, The 2-07-24:22
Marriage Circle 7-24-63:6
Marriage Clause, The 9-29-26:14
Marriage de Figaro, Le 5-08-63:26

Marriage de Ramuntcho, Le 9-17-47:16

Marriage Forbidden 7-20-38:12

Marriage-Go-Round, The 12-07-60:6

Marriage Humor (s) 8-08-33:19

Marriage in the Shadows 9-15-48:20

Marriage Is a Private Affair 8-16-44:16

Marriage--Italian Style 12-23-64:6

Marriage License 10-27-26:65

Marriage Maker 9-20-23:35

Marriage Market, The 8-31-17:30

Marriage Morals 8-16-23:27

Marriage of a Young Stockbroker, The 8-18-71:15

Marriage of Corbal 6-10-36:35

Marriage of Figaro, The 11-08-50:18

Marriage of Kitty, The 8-20-15:19

Marriage of Mr. Mississippi, The 7-05-61:7

Marriage of Molly-O, The 7-21-16:19

Marriage of the Cook, The 1-08-10:13

Marriage of the Nephew of the Maharajah of Tagore 11-20-09:13

Marriage of William Ashe 2-25-21:42

Marriage on Approval 1-09-34:17

Marriage on the Rocks 9-22-65:6

Marriage Pit, The 10-29-20:41

Marriage Playground, The 12-18-29:28

Marriage Price, The 3-21-19:53

Marriage Ring, The 9-27-18:42

Marriage Rows (s) 3-25-31:16

Marriage Whirl 7-15-25:32

Married 2-24-26:42 and 5-19-26:17

Married Alive 8-10-27:26

Married and in Love 2-07-40:16

Married Bachelor 9-10-41:8

Married Before Breakfast 7-28-37:27

Married Couple, A 11-12-69:84

Married Flirts 11-19-24:30

Married in Haste 4-18-19:53

Married in Hollywood 9-25-29:17

Married Life 6-25-20:33

Married or Single (s) 1-24-33:12

Married People 9-22-22:42

Married Woman, The (See: Femme Mariee, Une)

Marry in Haste 2-07-24:22

Marry Me 7-15-25:34

Marry Me 11-29-32:44

Marry Me! 6-15-49:13

Marry Me Again 9-23-53:24

Marry the Boss' Daughter 11-19-41:9

Marry the Girl 4-04-28:29

Marry the Girl 8-04-37:18

Marrying Kind, The 3-12-52:6

Marrying Widows 9-04-34:29

Mars Attacks the World 11-09-38:16 (Also see: Flash Gordon's Trip to Mars)

Marseillaise, La 3-16-38:17 and 11-15-39:20

Marshal of Amarillo 10-20-48:16

Marshal of Cedar Rock 2-25-53:18

Marshal of Cripple Creek 8-20-47:18

Marshal of Mesa City 12-27-39:12

Marshall of Heldorado 7-19-50:16

Marshal's Daughter, The 6-17-53:16

Marta 5-05-71:16

Marta of the Lowlands 10-10-14:25

Martes, Orquideas, Los 6-25-41:18

Martha 8-28-74:43

Martha's Vindication 3-24-16:29

Marthe Richard 5-12-37:13

Martien de Noel, Le 6-09-71:22

Martin 1-10-79:27

Martin et Lea 12-27-78:14

Martin Fierro 7-24-68:20

Martin Luther 5-13-53:6

Martin Soldat 10-12-66:24

Martin U Oblacima 8-09-61:6

Martlet's Tale, The 11-04-70:26

Marty 3-23-55:6

Martyr Sex, The 4-16-24:26

Martyr to His Duty, A 1-09-15:23

Martyrdom of Philip Strong 12-01-16:27

Martyre de L'Obese, Le 4-18-33:21

Martyrer, Der 8-28-74:18

Martyries 11-05-75:19

Martyrs of Love (See: Mucednici Lasky)

Martyrs of the Alamo, The 10-19-15:22

Master Mystery, The (serial) 11-15-18:45
Master of Ballantrae 7-22-53:6
Master of Bankdam 8-27-47:16
Master of His Home 8-03-17:25
Master of Men 12-05-33:17
Master of Merripit, The 4-02-15:21
Master of the House 10-08-15:22
Master of the World 5-03-61:6
Master Race, The 9-27-44:14
Master Rogues of Europe, The 5-28-15:17
Master Shakespeare 4-21-16:29
Master Spy 8-26-64:6
Master Stroke, A 7-09-20:27
Master Sweeper, The (s) 3-05-30:21
Master Touch, The 5-08-74:41
Master Will Shakespeare (s) 8-19-36:16
Masterdetektiven Blomkvist 3-24-48:22
Masterpiece 10-09-09:20
Masters of Men 5-17-23:22
Masters of the Congo 12-26-59:6
Masters of the Congo Jungle (See: Seigneurs de la Foret, Les)
Masters of the Deep 5-20-31:30
Masters of the Deep (s) 1-07-42:45
Masterson of Kansas 11-24-54:6
Mata-Hari 7-27-27:20 and 11-14-28:22
Mata Hari 1-05-32:19
Mata-Hari 2-17-65:6
Matatabi 12-12-73:20 and 12-26-73:17
Match King, The 12-13-32:15
Match Play (s) 5-21-30:19
Matchless 9-20-67:6
Matchless 10-09-74:19
Matchmaker, The 5-07-58:6
Mate Doma Liva? 8-18-65:6
Mater Amatisima 6-11-80:26
Maternal Spark, The 12-14-17:43
Maternale 4-19-78:26
Maternelle, La 9-26-33:56 and 10-23-35:12
Maternite 5-08-35:45 and 6-09-37:25
Maternity 5-18-17:22
Mathias Sandorf 3-20-63:18
Matilda 6-21-78:18
Matilda's Winning Ways 9-17-10:12
Matinee Idol, The 4-25-28:29
Matinee Idol (s) 6-11-30:18
Matinee Ladies 4-13-27:18

Mating, The 7-16-15:18
Mating, The 10-04-18:49
Mating Call 10-10-28:15
Mating Game, The 2-18-59:6
Mating of Millie, The 3-10-48:10
Mating Season, The 1-10-51:13
Matka Joanna Od Aniolow 5-17-61:7
Matomeno Heliovasilema 5-13-59:7
Matou a Familia e Foi Ao Cinema 4-22-70:17
Matriarca, La 1-15-69:38
Matriarkat 5-31-78:23
Matrimaniac, The 12-08-16:28
Matrimonial Bed, The 8-27-30:21
Matrimonial Martyr, A 7-07-16:25
Matrimony 10-29-15:22
Matrimony Blues (s) 7-28-26:19
Matsuri No Junbi 10-11-78:48
Mattanza 9-18-68:26
Mattatore, Il (See: Love and Larceny)
Matter of Days, A 5-21-69:19
Matter of Dignity, A 1-20-60:7
Matter of Fat, A 10-07-70:14
Matter of Life and Death, A 11-13-46:16
Matter of Morals, A 6-22-60:6
Matter of Time, A 10-06-76:20
Matter of Who, A 10-11-61:7
Matto Regiert 6-11-47:8
Matzor 5-28-69:34
Maude Muller 10-30-09:11
Maudite Galette, Une 5-10-72:20
Maudits, Les 11-12-47:24
Maudits Sauvages, Les 6-09-71:22
Maurie 7-25-73:6
Mauvais Coups, Les 5-24-61:17
Mauvais Fils, Un 11-19-80:21
Mauvaises Rencontres, Les 9-14-55:6
Maverick, The 8-27-20:28
Maverick, The 12-24-52:14
Maverick Queen, The 5-02-56:6
Mawas 5-28-30:38
Mawson's Antartic 3-12-15:23
Max Comes Across 2-09-17:25
Max et les Ferrailleurs 2-24-71:26
Max Havelaar 10-06-76:21
Max in a Dilemma 11-12-10:16
Max in the Alps 11-05-10:14
Max Makes Music 3-04-11:18
Max Schmeling (s) 3-20-29:12

Meet Boston Blackie 3-05-41:16
Meet Danny Wilson 1-16-52:6
Meet Dr. Christian 10-18-39:14
Meet John Doe 3-19-41:16
Meet Me After the Show 8-03-51:
6
Meet Me at Dawn 1-15-47:12
Meet Me at the Fair 12-10-52:6
Meet Me in Las Vegas 2-08-56:6
Meet Me in St. Louis 11-01-44:
10
Meet Me Tonight 9-17-52:6
Meet Miss Bobby Socks 11-15-
44:8
Meet Miss Mozart 12-01-37:29
Meet Mr. Lucifer 12-09-53:6
Meet My Sister 8-08-33:19
Meet Nero Wolfe 7-22-36:17
Meet the Baron 10-31-33:17
Meet the Boy Friend 7-21-37:19
Meet the Champ (s) 8-08-33:19
Meet the Chump 2-12-41:14
Meet the Girls 8-31-38:40
Meet the Mayor 10-12-38:15
Meet the Missus (s) 3-13-29:14
Meet the Missus 7-07-37:12
Meet the Missus 12-18-40:22
Meet the Mob 5-13-42:16
Meet the Navy 5-29-46:10
Meet the People 4-05-44:14
Meet the Stewarts 5-20-42:8
Meet the Wife (s) 2-20-29:14
Meet the Wife 6-23-31:19
Meet the Wildcat 10-30-40:15
Meetings with Remarkable Men
3-14-79:34
Mefiez-Vous Fillettes 12-04-57:
22
Mefiez-Vous Mesdames 11-20-63:
14
Meg Ker a Nep 5-24-72:19
Meg-O-Ruerda 7-30-69:36
Mega Lesz a Ferjem 3-16-38:17
Meglio Vedova 11-20-68:36
Megszallottak 9-12-62:16
Meguara 10-30-74:44
Megvedtem Egy Asszonyt 8-24-
38:12
Mei (See: Lost)
Meilleure Facon de Marcher, La
2-18-76:35
Meilleure Part, La 4-18-56:7
Mein Freund der Millionaer 2-02-
32:19
Mein Freund der Nicht Nein Sagen
Kann 1-11-50:16
Mein Herz Ruft Dich 4-17-34:32
Mein Kampf 11-30-60:6

Mein Leopold 1-05-32:23 and 4-
05-32:23
Mein Lieber Robinson 9-06-72:16
Mein Liebster Ist Ein Jaegersmann
9-16-36:17
Mein Schulfreund 8-03-60:7
Mein Vater, Der Affe und Ich 8-
18-71:15
Meine Frau, die Hochstaplerin
10-13-31:29 and 2-09-32:19
Meine Freundin Barbara 6-15-38:
15
Meine Kusine aux Warschau 9-15-
31:24
Meine Nicht Tut das Nicht 9-28-
60:6
Meine Sorgen Moecht Ich Haben
7-02-75:28
Meine Tochter Patricia 8-19-59:
16
Meineid (See: Perjury)
Meistersinger 12-25-29:30
Meistersinger von Nuernberg, Die
7-22-70:20
Mejor Papa Del Mundo, El 4-16-
41:18
Melancholy Baby 10-31-79:16
Melancholy Dame (s) 2-20-29:14
Melancolicas, Las 5-24-72:26
Melba 6-24-53:6
Melbourne Rendezvous 10-16-57:6
Melech Leyom Echad 8-06-80:36
Melinda 8-16-72:24
Melo 11-08-32:17 and 2-06-34:14
Melodias de America 2-11-42:8
Melodie, Le (s) 7-28-31:14
Melodie der Liebe 5-31-32:25
Melodie der Welt (See: Melody of
the World)
Melodie en Sous-Sol 4-17-63:7
Melodie Immortali 3-11-53:18
Melodies des Herzens 9-03-30:41
Melodies of Japan (s) 4-14-37:12
Melodies of the World 11-20-29:
12
Melodies Old and New (s) 2-25-
42:8
Melodii Veriiskogo Kvartala 8-28-
74:20
Melodrama? 8-20-80:21
Melodrama in a Bowery Theatre
5-11-07:12
Melodrame 5-19-76:27
Melody (s) 5-20-53:6
Melody 3-17-71:18
Melody and Moonlight 10-16-40:
31
Melody Cruise 6-27-33:14

Melody for Three 3-05-41:16
Melody for Two 5-26-37:14
Melody in Spring 4-03-34:17
Melody Lane 7-17-29:42
Melody Lingers On, The 11-13-35:17
Melody Makers Series (s) 12-06-32:15 and 4-25-33:15
Melody Man 2-26-30:29
Melody Man (s) 7-11-33:15
Melody of Love, The 10-17-28:24
Melody of Love 5-12-54:6
Melody of the Plains 7-07-37:25
Melody of the World 4-10-29:23 and 10-13-31:14
Melody Parade 8-18-43:26
Melody Ranch 1-01-41:14
Melody Time 5-19-48:13
Melody Trail 12-11-35:34
Melting Millions 3-02-17:25
Melting Pot, The 6-04-15:18
Meltosagos Kiasasszony 2-24-37:27
Melvin and Howard 9-10-80:30
Mem Ja 3-19-75:36
Member of Tattersalls, A 11-28-19:56
Member of the Wedding 12-17-52:6
Memetih 4-21-65:7
Memoire Courte, La 2-27-63:7
Memoire Courte, La 6-13-79:15
Memorandum 10-04-67:14
Memoria de Helena 10-14-70:30
Memorias de Letica Valle 9-26-79:20
Memorias de Um Gigolo 10-14-70:32
Memorias del Subdesarrollo 6-26-68:6
Memories (s) 8-10-27:26
Memories (s) 6-05-29:15
Memories (s) 11-12-30:21
Memories (s) 3-04-31:14
Memories of Underdevelopment (See: Memorias del Subdesarrollo)
Memories Within Miss Aggie 4-24-74:20
Memory Lane 2-03-26:42
Memory of Justice, The 6-09-76:22
Memory of Us 5-01-74:18
Memphis Belle 3-22-44:18
Men 5-24-18:36
Men 5-07-24:24
Men, The 5-24-50:6

Men Against the Sky 8-28-40:16
Men and Jobs 1-17-33:15
Men and the Beasts, The (See: Lyudi y Zvery)
Men and Women 4-01-25:31
Men Are Like That 8-06-30:38
Men Are Like That 8-18-31:30
Men Are Such Fools 3-14-33:15
Men Are Such Fools 6-22-38:14
Men Aren't Gods 12-09-36:13 and 1-20-37:14
Men Call It Love 6-23-31:18
Men for the Fleet (s) 2-04-42:8
Men from the Monastery 11-27-74:16
Men in Black (s) 11-20-34:15
Men in Exile 5-05-37:16
Men in Her Diary 9-12-45:16
Men in Her Life 12-01-31:15
Men in Her Life, The 11-05-41:8
Men in the Raw 10-18-23:23
Men in War 1-23-57:6
Men in Washington--1942 (s) 7-22-42:8
Men in White 5-01-34:14 and 6-12-34:19
Men Like These 11-17-31:26
Men Make Steel (s) 4-20-38:15
Men Must Fight 3-14-33:14
Men o' Sail (s) 6-20-33:11
Men o' War (s) 10-09-29:23
Men of America 2-28-33:39
Men of Boys Town 4-09-41:16
Men of Bronze 9-28-77:22
Men of Chance 1-05-32:23
Men of Daring 5-04-27:25
Men of Ireland 10-05-38:59
Men of Purpose 10-20-26:63
Men of Rio 7-06-60:6
Men of San Quentin 8-26-42:18
Men of Steel 7-14-26:14
Men of Texas 7-08-42:8
Men of the Desert 9-28-17:37
Men of the Fighting Lady 5-12-54:6
Men of the Hour, The 5-10-18:44
Men of the Hour 5-15-35:19
Men of the Night 7-28-26:19
Men of the Night 12-04-34:12
Men of the North 12-17-30:26
Men of the Plains 9-30-36:17
Men of the Sea 6-22-38:14
Men of the Sky 7-21-31:34
Men of Tomorrow 10-18-32:26 and 4-17-35:15
Men of Two Worlds 7-24-46:14
Men on Call 2-25-31:22

Men of West Point (s) 6-24-42:8
Men on Wings 6-12-35:41
Men She Married, The 11-17-16:
  23
Men Who Have Made Love to Me
  2-01-18:45
Men Who Tread on the Tiger's
  Tail, The 1-27-60:6 (Also
  see: Tora No O)
Men with Steel Faces 5-01-40:20
Men with Wings 10-26-38:13
Men Without a Profession 9-18-
  29:25
Men Without Names 7-03-35:14
Men Without Skirts (s) 8-27-30:
  21
Men Without Souls 5-15-40:16
Men Without Women 2-05-30:24
Menace, The 1-18-18:43
Menace, The 2-02-32:15
Menace 11-27-34:63
Menace, La 3-29-61:6
Menace, La 10-19-77:25
Menace in the Night 10-08-58:6
Menace of the Rising Sun (s) 4-15-
  42:18
Menaces 2-24-40:20
Menage All'Italiana 3-16-66:6
Menage Ultra Modernes (s) 1-26-
  32:21
Mendel Beilis 12-05-13:16
Mendiants et Orgeuilles 5-03-72:
  22
Menino de Engenho 7-20-66:7
Mennelsyden Varjo 7-24-46:26
Menneske Moed Og Soed Musik
  Opstaa I Hjertet 12-27-67:7
Mensch Ohne Namen 7-19-32:27
  and 11-15-32:23 (Also see:
  Homme Sans Nom, Un)
Mensch und Bestie 7-10-63:6
Menschen Im Hotel 2-03-60:20
Menschen Im Kaefig 12-10-30:26
Menschen Im Netz 9-16-59:16
Menschenfrauen 11-05-80:24
Mensonge de Nina Petrovna, Le
  4-06-38:15
Mentirosa, La 7-22-42:8
Mephisto of a Masquerade 4-23-10:
  16
Mephisto Waltz, The 2-03-71:17
Mepris, Le 1-01-64:6
Mer 8-19-59:6
Mercenaries, The 2-14-68:16
Mercenario, Il (See: Mercenary,
  The)
Mercenary, The 3-04-70:18
Merchant of Four Seasons, The

(See: Haendler der Vier
  Jahreszeiten)
Merchant of Slaves 8-24-49:22
Mercy Island 10-15-41:8
Mercy Plane 10-30-40:15
Merely Mary Ann 2-11-16:23
Merely Mary Ann 10-15-20:42
Merely Mary Ann 9-15-31:24
Merely Players 8-09-18:33
Merlusse 1-01-36:58 and 3-23-
  38:16
Mermaid, The 2-02-66:17
Mermaids of the South Seas (s)
  7-28-26:19
Mermaids of Tiburon 6-20-62:18
Merrill's Marauders 5-09-62:6
Merrily We Go to Hell 6-14-32:17
Merrily We Live 3-02-38:15
Merry Andrew 3-19-58:6
Merry Chase, The 9-22-48:8
Merry Comes to Town 6-02-37:
  23
Merry Dwarfs, The (s) 12-25-29:
  20
Merry Frinks, The 6-19-34:27
Merry-Go-Round 10-31-19:57
Merry-Go-Round 7-04-23:22
Merry-Go Round of 1938 10-27-
  37:18
Merry Madcaps (s) 3-18-42:23
Merry Monahans, The 8-16-44:16
Merry Widow, The 1-25-08:11
  (Reprinted on: 12-31-30:18)
Merry Widow, The 9-02-25:36
Merry Widow, The 10-16-34:12
Merry Widow, The 7-09-52:6
Merry Widow Takes Another, The
  4-23-10:16
Merry Widower, The 5-22-29:24
Merry Wives, The 11-13-40:20
Merry Wives of Reno, The 6-12-
  34:63
Merry Wives of Tobias Rourke,
  The 10-25-72:22
Merry Wives of Windsor, The 3-
  20-29:13
Merry Wives of Windsor, The
  (See: Lustigen Weiber von
  Windsor, Die)
Merry Wives of Windsor, The 10-
  01-52:22
Mersekelt Egov 10-21-70:22
Merton of the Movies 9-10-24:26
Merton of the Movies 7-23-47:10
Merveilleuse Angelique 8-18-65:6
Merveilleuse Journee, La 12-13-
  32:53
Merveilleuse Visite, La 12-18-74:
  13

Midnight Patrol, The 5-10-32:19
Midnight Patrol (s) 10-31-33:17
Midnight, Place Pigalle 9-05-28:
31
Midnight Romance, A 3-14-19:46
Midnight Sons 9-04-09:13
Midnight Special 1-21-31:58
Midnight Story, The 6-12-57:6
Midnight Sun, The 4-28-26:48
Midnight Taxi 10-31-28:27
Midnight Taxi, The 4-10-29:23
Midnight Taxi, The 4-08-37:15
Midnight Warning 3-14-33:15
Midnight Watch 3-09-27:17
Midshipmaid, The 12-27-32:54
Midshipman, The 10-14-25:40
Midshipman Jack 11-21-33:20
Midst Woodland Shadows 10-31-
14:27
Midstream 9-18-29:29
Midsummer Madness 12-10-20:35
Midsummer Night's Dream, A 5-
27-25:42
Midsummer Night's Dream, A 10-
16-35:22
Midsummer Night's Dream, A 11-
23-66:6
Midsummer Night's Dream, A 2-
05-69:6
Midt I en Jazztid 5-14-69:32
Midway 6-16-76:18
Miedos, Los 9-10-80:32
Miel, La 9-19-79:19
Miene Frau (s) 1-01-30:15
Miercoles de Ceniza 8-27-58:6
Miert Rosszak a Magyar Filmek
7-22-64:6
Mies es Mucha, La 6-01-49:20
Mif of Mafiaen 1-02-74:6
Mig Og Charly 3-29-78:22
Mig Og Dig 2-26-69:33
Might and the Man 5-18-17:26
Mighty, The 1-01-30:24
Mighty Crusaders, The 9-27-61:6
Mighty Joe Young 5-25-49:8
Mighty Lak' a Rose 3-22-23:28
Mighty Like a Moose (s) 6-23-26:
19
Mighty McGurk, The 11-20-46:22
Mighty Peking Man, The 8-31-77:
36
Mighty Treve, The 4-07-37:14
Mignon 1-23-15:25
Migove u Kibritena Boutiyka 7-25-
79:42
Miguelin 4-28-65:7
Mihai Viteazul 11-21-73:12
Mijn Vriend 4-18-79:23

Minn Nachten Met Susan, Olga,
Albert, Julie, Priet &
Sandra 5-21-75:19
Mikado, The 1-25-39:15
Mikado, The 2-22-67:6
Mike 1-13-26:40
Mike and Meyer 2-12-15:23
Mikey and Nicky 12-22-76:20
Mikkai 9-07-60:6
Milady 1-25-23:41
Milady 9-12-33:17
Milady o' the Beanstalk 11-15-18:
45
Milanese Story, A (See: Storia
Milanese, Una)
Milano Odisa: La Polizia non puo
Sparare (See: Almost Human)
Milarepa 4-17-74:20
Milczenie 9-04-63:20
Mild West, The (s) 11-21-33:14
Mildred Pierce 10-03-45:20
Mile-a-Minute Kendall 5-10-18:
41
Mile a Minute Man 9-15-26:22
and 7-27-27:21
Mile-a-Minute Morgan 3-19-24:
27
Mile a Minute Romeo 4-16-24:23
Milenci V Roce Jedna 8-07-74:18
Milestones 9-10-20:36
Milestones 5-14-75:27
Milieu de Monde, Le 8-21-74:22
Milionaro e Ze Rico na Estrada
da Vida 11-26-80:15
Military Academy 8-07-40:14
Military Academy 4-26-50:8
Military Cyclists of Belgium 12-
03-10:14
Military Kite Flying at Rheims 9-
10-10:14
Military Post, The (s) 5-07-30:20
Military Secret 8-08-45:51
Military Tournament 1-18-08:15
Milizia Territoriale 4-15-36:23
Milkman, The (s) 7-12-32:16
Milkman, The 10-11-50:8
Milky Way, The (s) 7-07-31:25
Milky Way, The 4-01-36:16
Milky Way, The (See: Voie Lactee,
La)
Mill on the Floss, The 11-22-39:
16
Mille et Deuxieme Nuit 5-30-33:
54
Mille et Une Mains 2-30-74:15
Miller and Farrell (s) 8-08-28:
12
Miller and Lyles (s) 4-10-29:16

Millhouse: A White Comedy 10-06-71:16
Milliard Dans un Billard, Un 1-12-66:6
Millie 2-11-31:29
Millieme Fenetre, La 6-15-60:18
Million, The 2-20-15:25
Million, Le 4-29-31:50 and 5-27-31:57
Million Bid, A 6-01-27:16 and 6-15-27:17
Million Dollar Baby 5-08-35:45
Million Dollar Baby 5-28-48:16
Million Dollar Collar 3-20-29:22
$1,000,000 Duck 6-16-71:15
Million Dollar Kid 2-23-44:10
Million Dollar Legs 6-12-32:17
Million Dollar Legs 7-12-39:12
Million Dollar Mermaid 11-05-52:6
Million Dollar Mystery 6-26-14:19 and 7-10-14:20
Million Dollar Pursuit 5-23-51:18
Million Dollar Ransom 9-25-34:13
Million Dollar Robbery 6-05-14:19
Million Dollar Weekend 10-13-48:11
Million for Love, A 6-06-28:25
Million for Mary, A 8-18-16:25
Million in Jewels, A 2-01-23:41
Million Pound Note, The 1-13-54:6
Million to Burn, A 11-01-23:27
Million to One, A 6-01-38:12
Millionaire, The 11-18-21:42
Millionaire, The 4-15-31:20
Millionaire for Christy, A 8-01-51:6
Millionaire in Trouble 7-19-78:20
Millionaire Orphan 1-25-28:13
Millionaire Playboy 3-06-40:16
Millionaire Policeman 7-14-26:18
Millionaire Vagrant, The 5-25-17:23
Millionaire's Double, The 5-11-17:34a
Millionaire's Son, The 4-28-16:29
Millionaires 5-04-27:24
Millionaires d'un Jour (See: Simple Case of Money, A)
Millionaires in Prison 7-17-40:18
Millionairess, The 10-26-60:17
Millions in the Air 12-18-35:12
Millions Like Us 11-17-43:20
Mills of the Gods 1-22-35:15

Milord l'Arsouille 2-29-56:6
Milton C. Work (s) 4-02-30:18
Mimi 4-17-35:15 and 6-05-35:15
Mimi, Metallurgico Ferito Nell' Onore 4-19-72:18
Mimi Pinson 9-24-58:6
Mimino 8-03-77:22
Min Aelskade 4-25-79:19
Min and Bill 11-26-30:18
Min Van Klock-Johan 9-17-41:22
Mina, La 3-19-58:18
Mina Droemmara Stad 11-24-76:19
Mina, Viento de Libertad 9-28-77:24
Minamata, the Victims of Their World 7-12-72:30
Mind Benders, The 2-27-63:6
Mind of Mr. Reeder 3-15-39:18
Mind of Mr. Soames, The 9-23-70:22
Mind Reader, The 4-11-33:17
Mind the Paint Girl 11-28-19:58
Mind Your Business (s) 10-09-29:23
Mind Your Business (s) 8-20-30:14 14
Mind Your Own Business 2-17-37:23
Mine Own Executioner 11-26-47:20
Mine Soestres Barn Naar de er Vaerst 10-27-71:24
Mine to Keep 8-30-23:27
Mine Warfare 3-27-74:24
Mine with the Iron Door, The 10-29-24:30
Mine with the Iron Door, The 7-15-36:31
Miner and Camille, The 4-30-10:16
Miner's Wife, The 4-03-74:24
Mines of Deauville, The 12-28-07:11
Minesweeper 11-10-43:35
Mingus 5-15-68:28
Mini Weekend 5-31-67:18
Miniature, The 2-26-10:15
Mini-Skirt Mob, The 5-29-68:20
Minister's Daughter, The 10-16-09:12
Ministro y Yo, El 8-04-76:20
Ministry of Fear 10-18-44:10
Miniver Story, The 8-30-50:6
Minne (See: Minne, l'Ingenue Libertine)
Minne, l'Ingenue Libertine 6-28-50:18
Minnesota Clay 2-10-65:6

Mr. Pratman 5-28-80:44
Mr. Quilp 10-22-75:34 (Reprinted on: 11-05-75:31)
Mr. Reckless 2-18-48:8
Mr. Ricco 1-29-75:16
Mister Roberts 5-25-55:6
Mr. Robinson Crusoe 9-27-32:17
Mr. Rock and Roll 10-23-57:6
Mr. Sardonicus 10-25-61:6
Mr. Scoutmaster 8-19-53:6
Mr. Skeffington 5-31-44:20
Mr. Skitch 12-26-33:11
Mr. Smarty (s) 10-07-36:15
Mr. Smith Goes to Washington 10-11-39:13
Mr. Soft Touch 7-27-49:12
Mr. Strauss Takes a Walk (s) 4-22-42:20
Mr. Sycamore 12-24-75:16
Mr. Topaze 4-21-61:6
Mr. Universe 1-17-51:11
Mr. W's Little Game (s) 5-01-34:14
Mr. Walkie Talkie 12-03-52:6
Mr. Washington Goes to Town 6-18-41:18
Mr. Winkle Goes to War 7-12-44:20
Mr. Wise Guy 3-11-42:20
Mr. Wong, Detective 11-23-38:14
Mr. Wong in Chinatown 8-02-39:18
Mr. Wu 4-20-27:17
Mr. X 9-08-26:20
Misteri di Roma, I 9-11-63:26
Mistero di Oberwald, Il 9-10-80:30
Mistigri 12-22-31:19 and 1-17-33:15
Mistress, The (See: Alskarinnan)
Mistress, The 11-04-59:7
Mistress Nell 2-06-15:23
Mistress of Shenstone 3-18-21:34
Mistress of the Summer, A (See: Fille Pour L'Ete, Une)
Mistress of the World 3-17-22:41 (Also see: City of Gold)
Misty 6-21-61:20
Mit Eichenlaub und Feigenblatt 8-28-68:24
Mit Himbeergeist Geht Alles Besser 12-07-60:22
Mitchell 9-10-75:20
Mitchell Ayres Orchestra (s) 2-03-43:14
Mitgift 5-26-76:36
Mitson 2-13-57:6
Mitt Hem Ar Copacabana 6-16-65:16

Mitternachtstaxi, Die (See: Midnight Taxi, The)
Mix in Masks, A 1-14-11:18
Mix Me a Person 8-15-62:6
Mixed Company 8-07-74:18
Mixed Facts 12-15-22:40
Mixed Magic (s) 12-16-36:14
Mixed-Up Letters 12-04-09:13
Mlad I Zadrav Kao Ruza 8-11-71:16
Mlady Muz A Bila Velryba 9-05-79:26
M'liss 5-10-18:41
M'liss 8-12-36:18
M'Lord of the High Road 11-22-23:27
Mne Dvatsat Let 9-08-65:6
Mo Hoozue Wa Tsukanai 9-10-80:32
Moan and Groan, Inc. (s) 4-23-30:24
Moana 2-10-26:40
Moartea Liu Ipu 8-16-72:26
Mob, The 9-05-51:6
Mob Town 10-08-41:9
Moby Dick 8-20-30:14
Moby Dick 6-27-56:6
Mockery 8-24-27:23
Model and the Marriage Broker, The 11-21-51:6
Model Shop, The 1-15-69:6
Model Wife 4-16-41:16
Modello 10-30-74:44
Models, Inc. 5-07-52:6
Moderato Cantabile 6-01-60:6
Modern Cinderella, A 1-12-17:24
Modern Commandments 7-13-27:20
Modern Daughters 7-29-27:23
Modern Enoch Arden, A 1-28-16:23
Modern Fairy Tales (s) 2-18-31:14
Modern Hero, A 4-24-34:14
Modern Highwayman, A 1-15-10:13
Modern Husbands 5-02-19:59
Modern Lorelei, A 12-06-18:39
Modern Love 9-20-18:44
Modern Love 7-24-29:35
Modern Marriage, A 4-05-50:6
Modern Matrimony 9-13-23:30 and 10-25-23:22
Modern Mephisto, A 3-20-14:24
Modern Monte Cristo, A 1-19-17:25
Modern Mothers 6-20-28:19
Modern Musketeer, A 1-04-18:40

Modern Thelma, A 4-21-16:28
Modern Times 2-12-36:16
Modern Youth, The 8-25-26:23
Modern Zeus, A 12-26-33:10 and
  1-09-34:16
Modesty Blaise 5-11-66:6
Modification, La 9-16-70:24
Moemoea 5-14-80:15
Moerderer, Der 3-11-31:39
Moerderspiel 2-07-62:6
Mogambo 9-16-53:6
Mogliamante 11-16-77:21
Moglie Americana, Una 8-04-65:6
Moglie Del Prete, La 1-20-71:22
Moglie e Buoi 2-06-57:6
Moglie Per Una Notte 11-05-52:6
Moglie Piu Bella 4-22-70:26
Mohawk 3-21-56:6
Mohawk's Way, A 9-17-10:12
Mohican's Daughter, The 9-22-
  22:42
Mohn Ist Auch eine Blume 5-18-66:
  18 (Also see: Poppy Is Also
  a Flower, The)
Moi et l'Imperatice 5-30-33:54
Moi et les Hommes de Quarante
  Ans 4-07-65:6
Moi, Fleur Bleue 11-16-77:25
Moi Laskoviy I Niejnie Zver 5-24-
  78:36
Moi Tinh Dau 8-09-78:20
Moi Tintin 11-24-76:19
Moi Y'en a Vouloir 3-14-73:20
Moine, Le 7-11-73:18
Mois de Plus Beau, Le 7-24-68:
  20
Moja Strana Svijeta 8-20-69:28
Moja Wojna--Moja Milosc 6-02-76:
  17
Mojave Kid, The 7-27-27:20
Mokey 3-25-42:8
Mokhtar 10-23-68:22
Mole People, The 10-31-56:6
Moliere 5-31-78:21
Molly and I 3-26-20:51
Molly and Lawless John 12-27-72:
  20
Molly and Me 6-19-29:32
Molly and Me 3-07-45:20
Molly Entangled 11-30-17:43
Molly Go-Get-Em 1-18-18:39
Molly Louvain 5-10-32:18
Molly Maguires, The 1-21-70:18
Molly Make Believe 4-21-16:30
Molly O 11-25-21:43
Molly of the Follies 1-31-19:53
Molly Picon (s) 3-05-30:21
Mollycoddle, The 6-18-20:33

Molo 7-02-69:6
Molokai 12-30-59:6
Molti Sogni Per la Strada (See:
  Woman Trouble)
Molucca Islands 10-08-10:12
Mome Vert de Gris, La 6-10-53:
  21
Moment Before, The 5-05-16:27
Moment by Moment 12-20-78:30
Moment d'Egarement, Un 12-21-
  77:21
Moment of Terror (See: Hikinge)
Moment of Truth, The (See:
  Momento Della Verita, Il)
Moment to Moment 1-26-66:6
Momento Della Verita, Il 3-31-
  65:6
Moments 9-25-74:18
Moments 5-16-79:31
Mon Ami Pierette 12-09-70:22
Mon Ami Tim 7-12-32:25
Mon Ami Victor 1-21-31:58
Mon Amour, Mon Amour 5-17-
  67:18
Mon Coeur Balance 11-08-32:17
Mon Coeur Est Rouge 3-09-77:24
Mon Coquin de Pere 9-03-58:6
Mon Grosse de Pere 5-21-30:19
Mon Grosse de Pere 8-05-53:6
Mon Mari Est Merveilleux 7-08-
  53:18
Mon Oncle 5-21-58:16
Mon Oncle Antoine 6-09-71:17
Mon Oncle Benjamin 11-12-69:21
Mon Oncle d'Amerique 5-21-80:
  22
Mon Phoque et Elles 5-02-51:27
Mon Premier Amour 9-27-78:20
Mona 2-24-71:18
Mona Lisa (s) 2-09-27:17
Monaca Santa 8-03-49:16
Monache Di Sant'Archangelo 3-14-
  73:21
Monarch 3-05-80:28
Monarchs of the Field (s) 1-07-
  31:23
Monastery 2-02-38:17
Monday's Child 5-10-67:20
Monde du Silence, Le 6-06-56:6
Monde Etait Plein de Couleurs, Le
  10-24-73:16
Monde Nouveau, Un 4-06-66:24
Monde Sans Arms, Le (See: World
  Unarmed, The)
Monde Sans Soleil, Le 11-04-64:
  18
Mondo Balordo 1-17-68:24
Mondo Cane 5-09-62:7

Mondo Cane No. 2 1-22-64:19
Mondo di Notte, Il 5-18-60:24
(Also see: World by Night
No. 2)
Mondo di Notte No. 3, Il 12-11-
63:6
Mondo Hollywood 8-02-67:7
Mondo Rocco 3-11-70:24
Mondo Trasho 2-11-70:16
Monelle 2-08-50:18
Money 2-13-29:30
Money, The 9-24-75:22
Money and the Woman 9-18-40:14
Money Corral, The 4-25-19:83
Money for Nothing 2-16-32:33
Money from Home 12-02-53:6
Money Isn't Everything 9-20-18:
45
Money Jungle, The 11-06-68:24
Money Madness 3-31-48:22
Money Maker, The 9-10-15:21
Money Makers of Manhattan (s) 11-
10-31:14
Money Magic 1-26-17:29
Money Means Nothing 7-24-34:14
Money-Money 10-23-68:22
Money, Money, Money 2-22-23:
41
Money, Money, Money 4-10-29:
25
Money, Money, Money (s) 4-02-
30:18
Money, Money, Money (See: Aven-
ture, C'est l'Aventure, L')
Money Monster 12-22-22:35
Money Movers 10-18-78:72
Money Talks 5-12-26:13
Money Talks 8-02-72:18
Money to Burn 4-21-22:41
Money to Burn 11-24-26:19
Money to Burn 1-03-40:40
Money Trap, The 1-19-66:6
Money, Women and Guns 10-08-
58:6
Mongols, The 12-26-73:14
Mongrel and Master 5-22-14:23
Monika (See: Sommaren Med
Monika)
Monique 4-01-70:14
Monique's Fault 11-07-28:24
Monismanien 1995 8-20-75:19
Monitors, The 10-15-69:15
Monkey Business (s) 5-19-26:20
Monkey Business (s) 4-08-31:18
Monkey Business 10-13-31:14
Monkey Business 9-10-52:6
Monkey Doodle Dandies (s) 12-
02-42:8

Monkey Hustle, The 12-29-76:18
Monkey in White, A (See: Singe en
Hiver, Un)
Monkey into Man 4-17-40:16
Monkey Meat (s) 4-08-31:18
Monkey Melodies (s) 10-15-30:25
Monkey on My Back 5-15-57:6
Monkey Talks, The 2-23-27:17
Monkey Whoopee (s) 8-18-31:17
Monkeynuts 6-13-28:13
Monkeys, Go Home 1-25-67:6
Monkey's Paw, The 11-08-23:28
Monkey's Paw, The 6-06-33:14
Monkey's Uncle, The 5-26-65:14
Monna Vanna 2-08-23:42
Monna Vanna 9-27-23:24
Monnaie de Singe 3-30-66:28
Monocle Noir, Le 9-27-61:7
Monocle Rit Jaune, Le 9-30-64:
22
Monolith Monsters, The 10-23-57:
18
Monolog 6-06-73:18
Monosabio, El 8-02-78:14
Monpti 10-23-57:18
Monseigneur 1-25-50:18
Monsieur 6-03-64:6
Monsieur Albert 7-12-32:25
Monsieur Albert 4-07-76:28
Monsieur Balboss 10-29-75:17
Monsieur Beaucaire 8-13-24:19
Monsieur Beaucaire 5-15-46:8
Monsieur Brotoneau 8-30-39:19
Monsieur de Compagnie, Un 11-
18-64:22
Monsieur de Minuit, La 9-01-31:
34
Monsieur de Pourceaugnac 11-08-
32:17
Monsieur Fabre 10-24-51:20
Monsieur Gregoire S'evade 6-12-
46:6
Monsieur Hawarden 10-23-68:24
Monsieur la Souris (See: Midnight
in Paris)
Monsieur, Madame et Bibi 4-05-
32:23
Monsieur Papa 9-14-77:16
Monsieur Ripois 5-05-54:21
Monsieur Taxi 10-01-52:22
Monsieur Verdoux 4-16-47:8
Monsieur Vincent 10-22-47:13
Monsoon 2-04-53:6
Monster, The 2-18-25:41
Monster and the Girl, The 3-26-
41:16
Monster from the Ocean Floor
6-09-54:6

293 •

Monster Maker, The 5-17-44:20
Monster of London City, The 8-02-67:22
Monster on the Campus 10-15-58:17
Monster That Challenged the World, The 5-22-57:6
Monster Walks, The 5-31-32:15
Monstri, I 11-27-63:6
Monstrosity 12-16-64:17
Monsu' Travet 4-17-46:16
Mont-Dragon 1-13-71:24
Montana 1-04-50:63
Montana Belle 10-29-52:6
Montana Desperado 11-14-51:16
Montana Kid, The 9-15-31:24
Montana Moon 4-16-30:46
Montana Schoolmarm, A 2-06-09:13
Montana Territory 6-04-52:6
Monte Carlo 4-21-26:35
Monte Carlo 9-03-30:19
Monte Carlo Madness 6-07-32:21
Monte Carlo Story, The 6-19-57:6
Monte Cassino 11-03-48:14
Monte-Charge, Le 6-20-62:18
Monte Cristo 8-18-22:41
Monte Cristo 7-10-29:24
Monte la Dessus (s) 5-03-32:14
Monte Walsh 10-07-70:14
Montecassino 10-30-46:14
Monterey Pop 9-18-68:28
Montevideo 12-05-64:16
Montmartre 7-09-24:25
Montmartre Rose 6-12-29:35
Montoneros, Los 7-29-70:15
Montparnasse 19 5-07-58:23
Montreal Main 2-27-74:26
Monty Python and the Holy Grail 3-19-75:32
Moods of Love 2-02-77:34
Mool-Dori Village 7-25-79:17
Moon and Sixpence, The 9-09-42:14
Moon and the Sledgehammer, The 12-01-71:16
Moon for Your Love 11-27-09:13
Moon in Taurus 9-10-80:28
Moon Is Blue, The 6-03-53:6
Moon Is Down, The 3-10-43:15
Moon of Israel 2-04-25:39
Moon of Israel 6-29-27:18
Moon over Burma 10-16-40:16
Moon over Las Vegas 4-12-44:10
Moon over Miami 6-18-41:16
Moon Over the Alley 10-01-80:22
Moon Pilot 1-17-62:6

Moon-Spinners, The 6-24-64:6
Moon Zero Two 10-29-69:28
Moon's Our Home 5-20-36:12
Moonbeam's Bride (s) 1-01-30:15
Moonfleet 5-11-55:8
Moonlight and Cactus (s) 1-05-32:19
Moonlight and Honeysuckle 8-05-21:27
Moonlight and Monkey Business (s) 11-12-30:21
Moonlight and Pretzels 8-29-33:14
Moonlight Fantasy (s) 4-18-33:21
Moonlight in Havana 10-14-42:8
Moonlight in Hawaii 10-15-41:8
Moonlight in Vermont 12-22-43:12
Moonlight Masquerade 6-24-42:8
Moonlight Murder 4-01-36:17
Moonlight on the Prairie 2-19-36:32
Moonlight on the Range 10-06-37:13
Moonlight Sonata 2-24-37:17
Moonlighters, The 9-09-53:6
Moonlighting Wives 9-28-66:6
Moonraker, The 5-28-58:6
Moonraker 6-27-79:18
Moonrise 9-15-48:20
Moonrunners 5-28-75:18
Moons of Love 2-02-77:34
Moonshine County Express 6-08-77:30
Moonshine Trail, The 10-24-19:61
Moonshine Valley 10-13-22:43
Moonshine War, The 7-01-70:13
Moonshiners, The 6-09-16:23
Moonshiner's Daughter, The (s) 10-10-33:17
Moonstone 6-19-09:11
Moonstone 6-11-15:18
Moonstone, The 9-18-34:11
Moonstone of Fez, The 7-10-14:21
Moonstruck 4-17-09:13
Moontide 4-22-42:8
Moonwalk One 11-15-72:32
Moorish Spain (s) 5-15-34:14
Moos Auf den Steinen 10-09-68:26
Moral 9-09-36:17
Moral Courage 5-04-17:25
Moral Deadline, The 2-14-19:52
Moral der Banditen, Die 7-28-76:22
Moral der Ruth Holbfass, Die 5-03-72:22

Moral Fabric, The 3-10-16:29
Moral Fibre 11-11-21:35
Moral Law, The 3-08-18:42
Moral of Lady Letty, The 2-10-22:34
Moral Sinners 4-09-24:34
Moral Suicide 3-22-18:51
Moralist, The (See: Moralista, Il)
Moralista, Il 10-28-59:6
Morals 1-06-22:42
Morals for Men 11-18-25:42
Morals for Women 11-17-31:15
Morals of Marcus, The 1-23-15:25
Morals of Marcus, The 4-10-35:17 and 1-15-36:19
Moran and Mack (s) 9-04-29:13
Moran of the Marines 10-17-28:17
Moranbong 5-25-60:7
Morbo 8-02-72:24
Mord und Totschlag 5-03-67:6
Mordi e Fuggi 3-28-73:18
Mordprozess Mary Dugan 3-04-31:22 (Also see: Trial of Mary Dugan, The)
Mords Pas on T'aime 5-05-76:18
Mor(d)skab 9-10-69:48
Mordus, Les 7-06-60:22
More 5-14-69:34
More American Graffiti 7-25-79:16
More Dead Than Alive 12-18-68:6
More Deadly Than the Male 12-12-19:45
More Excellent Way, The 4-06-17:24
More Gas (s) 10-06-31:23
More Pitted Than Scorned 10-20-22:41
More Precious Than Gold 11-06-09:13
More Sinned Against Than Usual (s) 2-19-30:21
More Than a Miracle 11-01-67:20
More Than a Queen 12-12-14:28
More Than a Secretary 12-16-36:14
More Than His Duty 10-08-10:12
More the Merrier, The 4-07-43:8
More Trouble 5-31-18:29
Morena Clara 7-01-36:23
Morgan! (A Suitable Case for Treatment) 4-13-66:6
Morgan and the Pirate 6-07-61:6
Morgane 6-26-29:29
Morgan's Last Stand 2-20-29:31

Morgan's Raiders 2-15-18:51
Morganson's Finish 7-21-26:15
Morgen Beginnt Leben 8-22-33:40
Morgen Gaat Het Beter 3-15-39:18
Morgenrot 2-28-33:39 and 5-23-33:19
Morgens Um 7 Ist die Welt Noch In Ordnung 1-15-69:38
Morgiana 8-09-72:20
Morianna--I, the Body 2-21-68:6
Morire Gratis 11-06-68:6
Morituri 7-28-65:6
Moritz Lieber Moritz 3-29-78:22
Moritz Macht Sein Glueck 1-17-33:17
Mormon Maid, A 2-16-17:23
Mormor og de atte Ungene i Byen 11-19-80:20
Morning 7-23-69:28
Morning After, The 4-19-72:18
Morning Departure 3-01-50:16
Morning Glory 8-22-33:22
Morning, Noon and Night 12-21-75:15
Morning Star 8-22-62:6
Morning Star, The 7-02-80:20
Moro Witch Doctor 12-02-64:6
Moroccan Nights (s) 3-27-34:12
Morocco 11-19-30:21
Morozko 1-28-31:40
Morris' War Film 12-10-15:22
Morrissey and Miller (s) 6-20-28:14
Mors Aux Dents, Le 11-21-79:24
Mors Hus 8-28-74:43
Morsiusseppele 4-07-54:24
Mort d'un Bucheron, La 2-21-73:18
Mort d'un Guide 10-22-75:34
Mort d'un Pourri 12-21-77:21
Mort d'un Tueur, La 4-22-64:102
Mort de Belle, La 4-05-61:6
Mort du Cygne, La 3-09-38:14
Mort en Ce Jardin, La 11-07-56:6
Mort en Fraude 7-24-57:26
Mort, Ou Est la Victoire? 2-05-64:6
Mort Trouble, La 3-18-70:26
Mortadella, La 1-12-72:14
Mortal Sin, The 3-16-17:35
Mortal Storm, The 6-12-40:14
Morte Al Lavoro, La 8-23-78:30
Morte Comanda O Cangaco, A 7-12-61:7

Morte Di un Amico 12-30-59:6
Morte Di un Operatore 7-25-79: 20
Morte Risale Aieri Sera, La 11-11-70:27
Morte-Saison Des Amours, La 9-27-61:7
Morte Viene a Cavaldo, La (See: Death Rides a Horse)
Mortgaged Wife, The 6-28-18:31
Mortman 9-03-15:21
Morton Downey (s) 3-28-33:15
Mosch 10-29-80:20
Moscow As It Laughs 9-05-28:28
Moscow, Heart of Soviet Russia 10-18-32:14
Moscow Laughs 3-27-35:15
Moscow Nights 11-20-35:39
Moscow-Shanghai 10-28-36:15
Moscow Skies 1-24-45:10
Moscow Strikes Back 8-19-42:8
Moses 2-25-76:22
Moses and Aaron 10-08-75:16
Moshi-Moshi, Hallo Japan 8-08-62:18
Moskwa Sljesam Nje Jerit 3-05-80:26
Mosquito Squadron 7-08-70:14
Moss Rose 5-21-47:15
Most Beautiful Age, The (See: Nejkrasnejsi Vek)
Most Dangerous Game, The 11-22-32:16
Most Dangerous Man Alive, The 6-14-61:6
Most Dangerous Sin, The (See: Crime et Chatinaut)
Most Immoral Lady, The 10-23-29:17
Most Precious Thing, The 12-04-34:12
Most Wanted Man in the World, The (See: Ennemi Public No. 1, L')
Motards, Les 4-15-59:24
Mote I Natten 11-13-46:16
Motel Hell 10-22-80:24
Moth, The 4-17-34:32
Moth and the Flame, The 5-21-15:18
Mother 9-18-14:19
Mother 1-04-18:42
Mother 5-04-27:20
Mother 5-18-27:24 and 6-12-34: 19
Mother and Daughter 8-27-75: 24
Mother and Son 9-01-31:34

Mother and Sons 9-21-38:25
Mother and the Law, The 10-31-19:56
Mother and the Whore, The (See: Maman et la Putain, La)
Mother Carey's Chickens 7-27-38:17
Mother Didn't Tell Me 2-01-50: 14
Mother Eternal 4-22-21:40
Mother Goose on the Loose (s) 4-01-42:8
Mother Heart, The 6-17-21:34
Mother Instinct, The 4-09-15:20
Mother Instinct, The 7-27-17:27
Mother Is a Freshman 3-02-49:8
Mother, Jugs and Speed 5-19-76: 19
Mother Knows Best 9-19-28:12
Mother Kusters Goes to Heaven (See: Mutter Kusters Fahrt Zum Himmel)
Mother Machree 3-07-28:23
Mother o' Mine 8-31-17:29
Mother o' Mine 8-05-21:26
Mother of His Children 5-21-20: 34
Mother of Mine 12-26-28:27
Mother Wore Tights 8-20-47:16
Mother's Atonement, A 10-22-15:26
Mother's Confession, A 8-27-15: 19
Mother's Crime, A 5-16-08:11
Mother's Cry, A 12-10-30:26
Mother's Day 9-24-80:18
Mother's Helper (s) 9-05-33:4
Mothers of France 3-16-17:36
Mothers of Men 3-05-20:63
Mother's Pride and Joy (s) 2-28-33:14
Mother's Roses 1-09-15:23
Mother's Sin, A 1-25-18:45
Mothers-in-Law 9-13-23:28
Mothra 5-16-62:19
Motive for Revenge 7-03-35:15
Motocyclette, La 7-24-68:20
Motor Madness 5-05-37:16
Motor Patrol 5-10-50:15
Motor Psycho 8-18-65:6
Motor Races at Monaco 11-07-08: 12
Motorboating 8-03-17:23
Motorcycle Gang 11-27-57:6
Motorcycle Mania (s) 1-24-33:12
Motoring Around the World 7-18-08:11
Motorvej Paassengekanten 10-04-72:18

Moucharde, La 9-24-58:6
Mouchette 4-05-67:6
Moulin Rouge 4-11-28:12 and 7-03-29:30
Moulin Rouge 2-13-34:14
Moulin Rouge 11-29-44:18
Moulin Rouge 12-24-52:6
Mount Hakkoda 7-27-77:30
Mount of Venus, The 4-23-75:18
Mount Venus 4-22-64:102
Mountain, The 10-03-56:6
Mountain Blizzard, A 3-19-10:18
Mountain Climbing Through a Telescope 1-26-07:11 (Reprinted: 12-31-30:18)
Mountain Dew 9-21-17:44
Mountain Family Robinson 10-24-79:16
Mountain Justice 5-21-30:27
Mountain Justice 5-19-37:22
Mountain Melodies (s) 3-19-30:20
Mountain Men, The 7-23-80:22
Mountain Music 6-30-37:20
Mountain Rat, The 5-22-14:22
Mountain Rhythm 7-12-39:12
Mountain Road, The 3-23-60:6
Mountain That Was God, The (s) 2-21-33:14
Mountains of Copper (s) 2-25-31:12 and 9-15-31:20
Mountains of Manhattan 5-11-27:20
Mountebank's Son 9-25-09:20
Mountebank's Watchcase 11-06-09:13
Mounted Fury 12-22-31:19
Mounted Stranger 2-12-30:35
Mourez ... Nous Ferons le Reste 11-17-54:6
Mourir a Madrid 3-20-63:18
Mourir a Tue-Tete 6-06-79:24
Mourir d'Aimer 12-23-70:22
Mourning Becomes Electra 11-19-47:8
Mourning Suit, The 9-03-75:20
Mouse and His Child, The 6-29-77:28
Mouse of Tomorrow (s) 12-02-42:8
Mouse on the Moon, The 5-15-63:6
Mouse That Roared, The 8-05-59:6
Mouse Trapper, The (s) 2-07-33:12
Moutarde Me Monte Au Nez, La 11-06-74:20
Mouth to Mouth 5-10-78:26
Mouthpiece, The 4-26-32:13

Mouton a Cinq Pattes, Le 8-11-54:6
Mouton Enrage, Le 3-27-74:24
Mouton Noire, Le 10-10-74:20
Moutonnet 8-12-36:18
Moutons de Panurge, Les 7-19-61:6
Move 8-05-70:16
Move Over, Darling 12-11-63:6
Move Over Her Shoulder 10-22-41:8
Movie Alarm (s) 3-15-32:14
Movie Crazy 9-20-32:14
Movie Man, The 6-20-28:14
Movie Memories (s) 11-26-30:18; 12-31-30:19; 1-14-31:12; 5-13-31:36; 11-06-34:16
Movie, Movie 11-15-78:18
Movie Star, American Style; or, LSD, I Hate You! 8-17-66:6
Movie Stuntmen 9-23-53:24
Movies March On, The 7-05-39:14 (Also see: March of Time Newsreels)
Movietone Follies of 1930 6-25-30:109
Movietone Newsreel (s) 11-02-27:21 (Also see: Fox Movietone Newsreels)
Moving 12-18-74:36
Moving Finger, The 11-20-63:6
Moving In (s) 6-09-31:18
Moving Violation 7-28-76:29
Mozart 10-09-40:18
Mozart 1-25-56:6 and 5-16-56:6
Mozart--Auf Zeichnungen einer Jugend 7-14-76:24
Mozart Story, The 11-17-48:13
Mozart's Last Requiem 9-18-09:13
Mozo No. 13, El 3-19-41:16
Mrigayaa 7-27-77:22
Mrs. Barrington 5-15-74:30
Mrs. Black Is Back 12-19-14:25
Mrs. Brown, You've Got a Lovely Daughter 5-22-68:6
Mrs. Dane's Confession 3-12-24:26
Mrs. Dane's Defense 1-11-18:44
Mrs. Fitzherbert 12-17-47:8
Mrs. Leffingwell's Boots 10-04-18:47
Mrs. Mike 12-21-49:8
Mrs. Miniver 5-13-42:8
Mrs. O'Malley and Mr. Malone 11-10-50:6
Mrs. Parkington 9-20-44:10
Mrs. Pollifax--Spy 3-03-71:17

297 ●

Music Box Kid, The 6-01-60:6
Music for Madame 9-15-37:13
Music for Millions 12-13-44:8
Music Goes Round, The 2-26-36:
15
Music Hath Charms (s) 9-11-29:18
Music in Manhattan 7-16-44:10
Music in My Heart 1-10-40:16
Music in the Air 12-18-34:12
Music Is Magic 11-20-35:16
Music Lesson 10-09-09:13
Music Lovers, The 1-27-71:17
Music Machine, The 6-20-79:18
Music Makers (s) 3-20-29:12
Music Man, The 4-11-62:6
Music Master, The 1-19-27:18
Music Masters (s) 4-10-29:16
Music Room, The (See: Jalsaghar)
Music Shop, The (s) 12-25-29:20
Music to My Ears (s) 4-18-33:21
Musica, La 3-01-67:6
Musical Beauty Shop, The (s) 7-
09-30:19
Musical Charmers (s) 12-02-36:
18
Musical Doctor, The (s) 9-20-32:
14
Musical Mystery (s) 10-27-31:19
Musical Poster No. -- (s) (See:
British War Docus)
Musical Queens (s) 10-02-34:37
Musical Story 11-05-41:8
Musicale, The (s) 3-19-30:20
Musicens du Ciel 4-03-40:16
Musician's Love Story, The 3-06-
09:13
Musicland (s) 10-23-35:13
Musik I Morker 4-14-48:18 and
7-29-59:6
Musik Im Blut 2-15-56:6
Muss 'Em Up 2-05-36:12
Mussolini (s) 9-21-27:20 (Also
see: Fox Movietone Newsreels)
Mussolini Speaks 3-14-33:14
Mussolini: Ultimo Atto 4-10-74:
20
Mussorgsky 8-22-51:24
Must We Marry? 3-20-29:28
Mustaa Valkoisella 5-29-68:22
Mustang 3-18-59:23
Mustang County 3-24-76:21
Mustang: The House That Joe Built
4-14-76:27
Mustergatte, Der 11-17-37:17
Mutation, The 5-29-74:24
Mutige Seefahrer, Der 11-25-36:
15
Mutineers, The 5-04-49:11

Mutiny 3-02-17:25
Mutiny 2-20-52:6
Mutiny in Outer Space 5-19-65:6
Mutiny in the Arctic 5-07-41:12
Mutiny in the Bighouse 11-01-39:
14
Mutiny of the Universe, The 8-
06-20:26
Mutiny on the Blackhawk 8-09-
39:14
Mutiny on the Bounty 11-13-35:
16
Mutiny on the Bounty 11-14-62:6
Mutiny on the Elsinore 9-22-37:
19
Mutt and Jeff 3-24-16:24
Mutt and Jeff (s) 4-10-29:16
Mutter Courage und Ihre Kinder
8-02-61:6
Mutter Kusters Fahrt Zum Himmel
5-12-76:34
Mutterliebe 2-18-31:14
Mutterlied 1-26-38:23
Muurahaispolku 7-08-70:24
Muz Z Prvniho Stoleti 5-16-62:6
Muzuki Vremena 5-31-78:23
My Ain Folk 11-20-74:14
My American Wife 1-05-23:44
My American Wife 8-26-36:20
My Baby Is Black! (See: Laches
Vivent d'Espoir, Les)
My Best Gal 4-12-44:10
My Best Girl 6-18-15:17
My Best Girl 11-09-27:20
My Bill 6-15-38:14
My Blood Runs Cold 3-17-65:7
My Blue Heaven 8-23-50:8
My Bodyguard 6-18-80:22
My Boy 1-06-22:43
My Brilliant Career 5-23-79:22
My Brother Jonathan 2-18-48:9
My Brother Talks to Horses 11-
20-46:22
My Brother, the Outlaw 2-07-
51:6
My Brother's Keeper 7-21-48:10
My Buddy 9-27-44:14
My Chauffeur 9-26-28:15
My Childhood 9-13-72:20
My Country First 5-19-16:18
My Cousin 11-29-18:41
My Cousin Rachel 12-24-52:6
My Dad 9-08-22:41
My Darling Clementine 10-09-46:
14
My Daughter Joy 6-28-50:18
My Dear Miss Aldrich 10-06-37:
12

My Dear Secretary 9-08-48:10
My Dog, Buddy 5-18-60:24
My Dog Rusty 6-09-48:12
My Dream Is Yours 3-16-49:11
My Enemy, the Sea 11-20-63:14
My Fair Baby 12-12-73:20
My Fair Lady 10-28-64:6
My Father's House 9-24-47:11
My Favorite Blonde 3-18-42:8
My Favorite Brunette 2-19-47:8
My Favorite Duck (s) 1-06-43:50
My Favorite Spy 5-06-42:8
My Favorite Spy 10-10-51:6
My Favorite Wife 5-01-40:18
My First Big Ship (s) 6-14-32:16
My First Love 6-13-51:16
My First Year 8-23-32:15
My Flag 11-29-18:40
My Foolish Heart 10-19-49:8
My Forbidden Past 3-28-51:6
My Four Years in Germany 3-15-
18:45
My Friend Flicka 4-07-43:8
My Friend Irma 8-17-49:8
My Friend Irma Goes West 5-31-
50:6
My Friend, the Chauffeur 3-17-
26:30
My Friend, the Doctor 10-08-
10:12
My Friends (See: Amici Miei)
My Gal Loves Music 11-22-44:
10
My Gal Sal 4-22-42:8
My Geisha 1-31-62:6
My Girl Tisa 1-21-48:8
My Girlfriend's Wedding 5-14-
69:34
My Gun Is Quick 8-07-57:6
My Hands Are Clay 7-21-48:20
My Heart Belongs to Daddy 11-
04-42:8
My Heart Is Calling 4-17-35:14
My Hero (s) 2-11-31:14
My Hobo 8-07-63:6
My Home Town 5-02-28:15
My Husband's Wives 12-31-24:
26"A"
My Hustler 7-12-67:6
My Irish Molly 10-02-40:25
My Kingdom for a Cook 10-20-
43:12
My Lady "Incog" 1-28-16:23
My Lady of Whims 6-30-26:13
My Lady's Garter 3-19-20:52
My Lady's Latchkey 3-18-21:34
My Lady's Past 8-21-29:27
My Lady's Slipper 1-28-16:22

My Last Mistress 1-26-49:22
My Learned Friend 10-13-43:10
My Life to Live (See: Vivre Sa
Vie, La)
My Life with Caroline 7-16-41:8
My Lips Betray 11-07-33:16
My Little Chickadee 2-14-40:18
My Love Came Back 6-26-40:16
My Lover, My Son 3-11-70:17
My Lucky Star 9-14-38:15
My Madonna 11-05-15:23
My Man 2-14-24:26
My Man 12-26-28:11
My Man and I 8-20-52:6
My Man Godfrey 9-23-36:16
My Margo 5-07-69:258
My Marriage 2-26-36:37
My Merry Oldsmobile (s) 3-11-
31:14
My Mother 2-21-33:21
My Mother-in-Law Is an Angel
11-30-07:10
My Name Is Ivan 6-26-63:6
My Name Is Julia Rosa 11-14-
45:12
My Name is Nobody (See: Mio
Nome e Nessino, Il)
My Native Land 3-28-33:15
My Neighbor's Wife 5-27-25:41
My Night at Maud's (See: Ma Nuit
Chez Maud)
My Official Wife 7-17-14:17
My Old Dutch 7-16-15:19
My Old Dutch 6-23-26:15
My Old Dutch 9-25-34:14
My Old Kentucky Home 4-28-22:
43
My Old Kentucky Home 2-09-38:
15
My Own Pal 3-17-26:38
My Own True Love 12-08-48:11
My Own United States 1-25-18:
42
My Pal Gus 11-12-52:6
My Pal the King 10-11-32:33
My Pal Trigger 6-19-46:8
My Pal, Wolf 9-20-44:10
My Partner 3-24-16:28
My Past 3-18-31:24
My People (s) 8-28-29:18
My Pony Boy (s) 9-18-29:15
My Reputation 1-09-46:79
My Side of the Mountain 2-26-69:
6
My Sin 9-15-31:24
My Sister and I 10-02-29:34
My Sister and I 6-26-48:8
My Sister Eileen 9-16-42:8

Naked Heart, The 1-213-50:25
Naked Hearts 5-19-16:20
Naked Hills, The 7-18-56:6
Naked Hours, The 10-21-64:6
Naked Jungle, The 2-17-54:6
Naked Maja, The 3-25-59:6
Naked Night, The 2-08-56:6
Naked Paradise 3-13-57:6
Naked Prey, The 3-16-66:6
Naked Runner, The 7-05-67:6
Naked Sea, The 10-26-55:6
Naked Soul, A 6-02-17:27
Naked Soul, A 6-02-17:27
Naked Spur, The 1-14-53:6
Naked Street, The 8-17-55:6
Naked Truth, The 6-12-14:21
Naked Truth, The 12-11-57:6
Naked Woman 1-25-50:18
Naked Zodiac 2-25-70:20
Nam Karng Yod Deo 12-06-78:
32
Namak Haram 7-17-74:16
Name of the Game Is Kill, The
4-03-68:22
Name of the Prince of Peace 4-
30-15:18
Name the Man 1-17-24:26
Name the Woman 7-25-28:28
Name the Woman 12-04-34:12
Nameless Men 3-21-28:19
Namensheirat 1-17-33:15
Namida o Shishi no Tategami 10-
29-80:18
Namonaku Mazushiku Utsukushiku
8-30-61:6
Namu, the Killer Whale 8-03-66:6
Nana 5-19-26:20
Nana 2-06-34:14
Nana 10-05-55:6
Nana 5-05-71:22
Nana, Mom and Me 1-15-75:26
Nancy Comes Home 3-29-18:44
Nancy Drew and the Hidden Stair-
case 11-08-39:14
Nancy Drew--Detective 12-07-38:
12
Nancy Drew--Reporter 3-01-39:
15
Nancy Drew, Trouble Shooter 9-
20-39:15
Nancy from Nowhere 2-03-22:42
Nancy Goes to Rio 2-01-50:14
Nancy Steele Is Missing 3-10-37:
14
Nancy's Birthright 6-02-16:16
Nanette of the Wilds 12-01-16:
27
Nanga Parbat 3-11-36:27

Nangsao Maliwan 5-21-75:19
Nankai No Dai Ketto 1-25-67:6
Nanny, The 10-13-65:6
Nanook of the North 6-16-22:40
and 9-01-48:14
Nantes and Its Surroundings 12-
03-10:14
Naomi 7-02-80:20
Naples Au Baiser de Feu 2-02-
38:27
Napoleon 4-27-27:20 and 1-23-
29:34 (Also see: Bonaparte
et la Revolution and Napoleon
Bonaparte)
Napoleon 2-26-41:18
Napoleon 4-13-55:8
Napoleon and Josephine 11-12-
24:52
Napoleon and Samantha 7-12-72:
17
Napoleon Bonaparte 5-29-35:14
and 3-30-55:9 (Also see:
Bonaparte et la Revolution
and Napoleon)
Napoleon on St. Helena 12-11-29:
42
Napoleon's Barber 11-28-28:20
Napoleon's Bust (s) 6-14-32:16
Napoletani a Milano 9-02-53:6
Napoli Che Non Muore 8-30-39:
19
Napoli D'Altri Tempi 1-26-38:15
Napoli Milionaria 7-18-51:20
Nappali Sotetseg 8-05-64:7
Naprawde Wczoraj (See: Yesterday
in Fact)
Napuli e Surrinto 9-29-31:22
Nar Rosorna Sla Ut 2-18-31:35
(Also see: Trou Dans le
Mur, Un)
Nara Livet 5-21-58:16
Narayama Bushi-Ko 9-17-58:7
Narco Men, The 11-24-71:16
Narcotics Story, The 3-05-58:6
Narko--En Film Om Kjaerlighed
9-01-71:16
Narrische Gluck, Das (See: Foolish
Happiness)
Narrow Corner, The 7-18-33:37
Narrow Margin, The 4-02-52:6
Narrow Path, The 11-29-18:41
Narrow Street 1-07-25:54
Narrow Trail, The 1-11-18:41
Nasa Lupa Ang Langit At Implyerno
5-05-76:19
Nashville 6-11-75:18
Nashville Rebel 11-30-66:6
Nasilje Na Trgu 8-23-61:6 (Also

see: Square of Violence, The)
Nasty Habits 10-27-76:26
Nasty Rabbit, The 12-09-64:6
Nasvidenje V. Naslednji Vojni 8-
13-80:27
Naszut Felaron 11-25-36:15
Nat Car (s) 6-06-28:12
Natale Al Campo 119 2-18-48:9
Natale Che Quasi Non Fu, Il (See:
Christmas That Almost
Wasn't, The)
Natalia 7-15-70:20
Natalka Poltavka 12-30-36:27
(Also see: Girl from Paris, The
and Girl from Poltavka, The
Nathalie Agent Secret 1-20-60:7
Nathalie Granger 9-06-72:16
Nation Aflame 4-07-37:15
Nation Dances, A (s) 9-30-42:20
Nation's Peril, The 11-19-15:23
National Barn Dance 9-06-44:10
National Health, or Nurse Norton's
Affair, The 3-14-73:21
National Lampoon's Animal House
6-28-78:20
National Velvet 12-06-44:14
Native Land 5-13-42:8
Native Son 4-25-51:14
Nativos Del Planeta Tierra 12-12-
73:20
Natsu No Omoto 9-06-72:20
Nattens Ljus 9-03-58:6
Nattlek 9-07-66:6
Nattvaktens Hustru 3-24-48:22
Nattvardsgaesterna 3-20-63:6
(Also see: Winter Light)
Natun Pata 10-29-69:28
Natural Enemies 10-31-79:14
Natural Gas Pipeline--Texas to
Chicago (s) 11-10-31:14
Natural Law, The 11-02-17:51
Natural Voice Talking Pictures
5-16-08:11
Nature's Fairyland 5-07-24:25
Nature's Half Acre 7-11-51:6
Naufrages de l'Ile de la Tortue,
Les 9-01-76:22
Naughty 10-12-27:21
Naughty Baby 2-06-29:18
Naughty but Nice 7-06-27:22
Naughty but Nice (s) 2-26-30:24
Naughty but Nice 6-28-39:14
Naughty Duchess 10-31-28:31
Naughty Flirt 4-15-31:33
Naughty Marietta 3-27-35:15
Naughty Martine 4-22-53:6
Naughty Nanette 4-20-27:25
Naughty, Naughty 3-22-18:52

Naughty Nineties, The 6-20-45:11
Naughty Victorians, The 11-19-75:
26
Naulahka, The 3-15-18:44
Navajo 1-30-52:6
Navajo Kid, The 1-30-46:12
Navajo Joe 11-01-67:6
Navajo Run 6-08-66:18
Navajo Trail Raiders 10-19-49:18
Navajo Witch (s) 8-25-31:14
Naval Academy 5-28-41:18
Naval Review 10-02-09:13
Nave Delle Donne Maledette, La
12-09-53:6
Navidad de Los Pobres, La 10-
01-47:14
Navigator, The 10-15-24:27
Navrat Ztraceneho Syna 8-09-67:6
Navy and Nation (s) 2-03-43:14
Navy Blue and Gold 11-17-37:16
Navy Blues 1-15-30:37
Navy Blues 5-12-37:13
Navy Blues 8-13-41:8
Navy Born 6-24-36:29
Navy Bound 2-21-51:6
Navy Comes Through, The 10-14-
42:8
Navy Lark, The 10-21-59:6
Navy Secrets 3-22-39:20
Navy Spy 3-24-37:17
Navy vs. the Night Monsters, The
11-23-66:6
Navy Way, The 3-01-44:20
Navy Wife 1-08-36:12
Navy Wife 6-13-56:6
Nay, Nay, Nero (s) 10-29-30:17
Nayak 7-13-66:14
Nazar Stodolya 8-18-37:42
Nazarene Cryz y el Lobo 6-18-75:
19
Nazarin 5-20-59:6
Nazi Spy Ring 6-10-42:8
Nazis Strike, The 5-05-43:2
(Also see: "Why We Fight"
Films)
N'Diangane 6-04-75:18
Ne Bolit Golowa U Djatia 9-08-
76:20
Ne de Pere Inconnu 5-16-51:18
Ne Diraj U Srecu 8-23-61:6
Ne Dokantchence Pismo 6-21-61:6
Ne'er Do Well, The 2-18-16:21
Ne'er Do Well 5-03-23:23
Ne'er to Return Road 9-30-21:36
Ne Fillim Te Veres 1-24-79:35
Ne Goryuy 4-08-70:24
Ne Jouez Pas Avec les Martians
4-10-68:6

Ne Naginji Se-Van 8-17-77:20
Ne Nous Fachons Pas 5-04-66:6
Ne Pleure Pas 4-05-78:23
Ne Si Otivai 11-17-76:19
Ne Sirj Edesanyam 11-25-36:19
Nea 9-01-76:22
Neal of the Navy (serial) 9-10-
    15:21; Part II: 9-17-15:25;
    Part III: 9-24-15:20; Part IV:
    10-01-15:18; Part V: 10-08-
    15:21; Part VI: 10-15-15:21;
    Part VII: 10-22-15:23; Part
    VIII: 10-29-15:22; Part IX:
    11-05-15:22; Part X: 11-12-
    15:22
Neapolitan Carousel (See: Carozello
    Napoletano)
Near Lady 12-06-23:26
Near the Trail's End 11-24-31:21
Nearly a King 2-18-16:22
Nearly a Lady 8-13-15:17
Nearly a Nasty Accident 5-24-61:6
Nearly Divorced (s) 4-24-29:13
Nearly Eighteen 10-20-43:12
Nearly Married 11-30-17:45
Nearly Naked (s) 10-17-33:19
Nearly Spliced 5-26-16:22
Neat and Tidy (s) 11-05-30:23
Neath the Arizona Skies 3-20-35:
    31
Neath the Lion's Paw 6-26-14:20
Nebraskan, The 11-04-53:6
Necesito Una Madre 6-29-66:6
Necessary Evil, The 7-08-25:39
Nechci Nic Slyset 2-28-79:26
Neck and Neck 11-17-31:26
Necromancy 10-11-72:18
Necronomicon--Getraeumte Suenden
    4-24-68:29
Necropolis 12-09-70:22
Ned Kelly 6-17-70:16
Ned McCobb's Daughter 2-20-29:
    14
Nedeini Matchove 8-25-76:68
Nedelia 8-20-69:16
Nedtur 11-19-80:20
Neem Annapurna 2-20-80:28
Negatives 10-16-68:6
Neglected Wives 6-25-20:35
Negresco 2-28-68:22
Negro Soldier, The 2-23-44:10
    (Also see: "Why We Fight"
    Films)
Neige a Fondu Sur la Manicouagan,
    La 8-18-65:6
Neige Etait Sale, La 4-07-54:24
Neighbor Trouble (s) 8-16-32:15
Neighborly Neighbors (s) 7-30-30:
    16

Neighbors 7-19-18:36
Neighbors (s) 11-20-34:15
Neighbors 1-04-39:14
Neighbor's Wives 10-17-33:27
Neighbours Under Fire (s) (See:
    British War Docus)
Neither by Day, Nor by Night 7-
    12-72:17
Neither the Sea Nor the Sand 1-
    30-74:23
Nejkrasnejsi Vek 7-16-69:28
Nell Gwyn 1-27-26:38
Nell Gwyn 6-26-35:23
Nell Gwynne 9-11-14:22
Nell of the Circus 11-28-14:25
Nell of the Dance Hall 11-12-15:
    23
Nell'anno Del Signore 11-26-69:28
Nella Citta L'Inferno 3-11-59:6
Nella Cita' Perduta Di Sarzana
    10-08-80:22
Nellie and Sara Kouns (s) 6-27-
    28:14
Nellie, Beautiful Cloak Model 4-
    16-24:23
Nelson 8-31-27:24
Nelson Affair, The 3-28-73:18
Nem Alt Meg Az Autobusz 11-13-
    63:6
Nemesio 11-12-69:21
Nemesis 11-23-27:24
Nemica, La 3-11-53:18
Nemu No Ki No Utu 7-24-74:22
Nemureru Bijo (See: House of the
    Sleeping Virgins)
Nene 12-14-77:13
Nenita Unit 3-21-54:6
Neola the Sioux 6-18-15:18
Neon Palace, The 11-11-70:24
Neprimirimite 10-14-64:6
Neptune Factor, The 5-23-73:19
Neptune's Daughter 4-10-14:22
Neptune's Daughter (s) 12-02-42:8
Neptune's Daughter 5-18-49:8
Nero 5-26-22:33
Nero's Mistress (See: Mio Figlio
    Nerone)
Nervous Wreck, The 10-13-26:20
Nes Ba'ayara 9-18-68:26
Neskolko Interwju Po Litschnym
    Woprosam 2-28-79:24
Nest, The 1-18-28:19
Nest of Vipers 9-05-79:20
Nestbruch 12-31-80:20
Nesting Habits (s) 5-06-31:22
Net, The 4-07-16:24
Net, The 2-18-53:6
Netepichnaja Istoria 7-06-78:21

New Spirit, The (s) 2-11-42:21
New Stenographer, The 3-04-11: 18
New Teacher, The 8-04-22:36
New Teacher, The 4-16-41:18
New Toys 2-18-25:34
New War Films 11-26-15:23
New Wine 7-30-41:18
New Year's Sacrifice 9-04-57:6
New York 8-15-08:11
New York 2-11-16:21
New York City--The Most 6-12-68:26
New York Confidential 2-16-55:6
New York Idea, The 12-03-20:33
New York Luck 1-04-18:43
New York, New York 6-22-77:16
New York Nights 2-05-30:24
New York Peacock, The 2-09-17: 30
New York Philharmonic (s) 8-28-29:18
New York Sur-Mer 8-05-64:7
New York Town 7-30-41:8
New York's Finest (s) 2-04-42:8
Newcomers, The 9-06-72:20
Newcomers, The 7-18-73:14
Newly Rich 7-07-31:34
Newlyweds, The (s) 2-12-30:18
Newlywed's Neighbors, The (s) 6-23-26:19
Newlywed's Surprise (s) 6-15-27: 25
Newman's Law 5-08-74:37
News Hounds (s) 4-24-34:14
News Hounds 6-18-47:8
News Is Made at Night 7-19-39: 12
News Parade, The 5-30-28:14
Newsboys' Harmonica Band (s) 3-20-29:12
Newsboys' Home 1-25-29:15
Newsfront 5-10-78:22
Newsreel Era--70 Years of Head-lines, The 5-24-72:24
Newsreels 7-15-36:55
Next 8-11-71:28
Next Corner, The 2-14-24:26
Next Man, The 11-03-76:26
Next of Kin, The 6-17-42:20
Next Stop, Greenwich Village 2-04-76:16
Next Time I Marry 12-07-38:12
Next Time We Love 2-05-36:12
Next to No Time 8-20-58:10
Next Voice You Hear, The 6-07-50:8
Nez de Cuir 4-23-52:6

Nezabybaemaya Osen 7-27-77:22
Nezha Nao Hai 5-28-80:42
Nguyen Van Troy 7-26-67:6
Ni Liv 5-21-58:16
Ni Ljuger 2-25-70:15
Ni Vu, Ni Connu 7-02-58:6
Niagara 1-21-53:6
Niagara Falls (s) 2-12-30:18
Niagara Falls (s) 4-12-32:14
Niagara Falls 9-24-41:8
Nianchan 7-13-60:6 and 11-02-60:6
Nibelungen, (Siegfrieds Tod), Die (See: Nibelungen (Siegfried), The)
Nibelungen (Siegfried), The 4-16-24:26 (Also see: Kriemhild's Revenge)
Nibelungen (Part I: Siegfried), Die 4-12-67:6
Nice Girl? 2-26-41:16
Nice Girl Like Me, A 11-12-69: 21
Nice People 8-18-22:41
Nice Woman 2-23-32:13
Nicholas and Alexandra 12-08-71: 16
Nicholas Nickleby 3-26-47:12
Nicht Alles Was Fliegt Ist Ein Vogel 4-25-79:25 (Also see: Not Everything That Flies Is a Bird)
Nicht Fummeln Liebling! 2-04-70: 26
Nicht Versoht 9-22-65:6
Nichts Als Aerger Mit der Liebe 12-19-56:6
Nick Carter et le Trefle Rouge 12-22-65:6
Nick Carter, Master Detective 12-13-39:11
Nickel Queen 6-30-71:22
Nickel Ride, The 5-22-74:19
Nickelette, The (s) 8-30-32:14
Nickelodeon 12-22-76:22
Nicole et Sa Vertu 1-19-32:29
Nidhanaya 9-20-72:18
Nido, El 10-08-80:22
Nie Na Moenych 12-25-74:16
Nie Wieder Liebe 8-18-31:30 and 1-19-32:29
Niedorajda 1-12-38:27
Niedziene Dzieci 5-18-77:16
Niejnosti 8-09-67:6
Niemandsland 12-29-31:169 (Also see: Hell on Earth)
Niet Voor de Poesen 4-11-73:61
Niewinni Czarodzieje 5-31-61:6

Nifty Numbers (s) 12-11-34:19
Night (s) 5-14-30:19
Night Affair (See: Desordre et la Nuit, Le)
Night After Night 11-01-32:12
Night Alarm 1-08-35:39
Night Alone 8-03-38:15
Night and Day 5-30-33:54
Night and Day 7-10-46:8
Night and Fog (See: Nuit et Brouillard)
Night and the City 5-24-50:6
Night Angel, The 6-16-31:21
Night at Coffee Dan's, A (s) 7-18-28:15
Night at Earl Carroll's, A 11-20-40:16
Night at the Crossroads (See: Nuit du Carrefour, La)
Night at the Opera, A 12-11-35:19
Night at the Ritz, A 5-22-35:16
Night Beat 1-19-32:29
Night Beat 2-04-48:22
Night Before, The 10-31-73:26
Night Before the Divorce, The 2-11-42:8
Night Bird, The 10-03-28:23
Night Birds 10-29-30:27 and 1-07-31:39 (Also see: Nacht Bummler)
Night Boat to Dublin 1-23-46:12
Night Bride, The 3-30-27:15
Night Club, The 5-06-25:46
Night Club 8-14-29:31
Night Club (s) 10-30-29:25
Night Club Girl 12-06-44:14
Night Club Lady 8-30-32:21
Night Club Queen 4-03-34:17
Night Club Revels (s) 4-01-31:16
Night Club Scandal 12-22-37:17
Night Court 5-31-32:14
Night Creatures 5-09-62:17
Night Creatures 10-03-79:14
Night Cry, The 4-07-26:36
Night Digger, The 5-19-71:17
Night Editor 4-03-46:12
Night Evelyn Came Out of the Grave, The 7-26-72:18
Night Fighters, The 9-14-60:18
Night Flight 10-10-33:23
Night Flowers 9-05-79:27
Night Flyer, The 3-14-28:25
Night for Crime 3-10-43:23
Night Freight 8-17-55:6
Night Games (See: Nattlek)
Night Games 1-30-80:28
Night Has a Thousand Eyes, The

7-14-48:12
Night Hawk 4-16-24:23
Night Hawk, The 10-05-38:21
Night Heaven Fell, The 7-16-58:6
Night Holds Terror, The 7-13-55:6
Night Horsemen, The 11-04-21:42
Night in a Dormitory, A (s) 1-01-30:19
Night in Bangkok, A (See: Bangkokuu No Yoru)
Night in Casablanca, A 4-17-46:16
Night in Montmartre, A 8-04-31:21
Night in New Orleans, A 5-06-42:8
Night in Paradise, A 4-10-46:16
Night in the Shooting Gallery, A (s) 10-01-30:19
Night into Morning 5-23-51:6
Night Is My Future (See: Musik I Morker)
Night Is Ours, The 2-05-30:28 (Also see: Nacht Gehort Uns, Die and Nuit Est a Nous, La)
Night Is Young, The 1-15-35:13
Night Key 4-21-37:15
Night Life 12-21-27:22
Night Life (s) 12-11-35:19
Night Life in Hollywood 3-08-23:31
Night Life in New York 7-15-25:32
Night Life in Reno 12-01-31:21
Night Life of the Gods 2-27-35:12
Night Mayor 11-29-32:19
Night Message, The 3-26-24:45
Night Monster 10-21-42:8
Night Moves 3-26-75:18
Night Must Fall 5-05-37:16
Night Must Fall 3-18-64:6
Night My Number Came Up, The 3-30-55:9
Night Nurse 7-21-31:12
Night of Adventure, A 6-07-44:19
Night of Cobra Woman 3-13-74:18
Night of Counting the Years, The 9-09-70:16
Night of Dark Shadows 8-11-71:16
Night of January 16th, The 9-10-41:8
Night of June 13th, The 9-20-32:15
Night of Love 1-26-27:20

Nina de Luto, La 5-13-64:19
Nina, The Flower Girl 1-12-17:
   24
Nincs Ido 7-31-74:22
Nincsenek Veletlenek 3-15-39:18
Nine Days a Queen 10-07-36:15
Nine Days of One Year (See:
   Devyat Dney Odnogo Goda)
Nine Girls 3-29-44:21
Nine Hours to Rama 2-20-63:6
Nine Lives Are Not Enough 9-03-
   41:8
Nine Lives of Fritz the Cat, The
   5-22-74:19
999--Aliza the Policeman 6-26-
   72:6
Nine O'Clock Town, A 8-02-18:39
Nine Seconds from Heaven 6-30-
   22:33
Nine-Tenths of the Law 4-26-18:
   41
9-30-55 8-31-77:18
Nine to Five 12-17-80:17
1900 6-02-76:16
1905 7-11-56:10
1914 2-11-31:42 and 9-06-32:21
1918--A Man and His Conscience
   7-24-57:26
1941 12-19-79:19
1984 3-14-56:22
9th Circle, The (See: Deveti Krug)
Ninth Configuration, The 2-06-80:
   20
Ninth Guest, The 3-06-34:39
Ninth Heart, The 10-22-80:20
90 Degrees in the Shade 7-07-65:6
90 Minuten Aufenthalt 10-14-36:54
99 6-11-20:34
99 and 44/100% Dead! 6-19-74:18
99 River Street 9-09-53:6
99 Women 2-05-69:30
99th Amendment, The (s) 6-19-29:
   24
91--An Karlsson 12-04-46:13
92 in the Shade 8-27-75:15
92 Minutter Af I Gaar 5-31-78:26
Ningen 9-11-63:22
Nini Tirabuscio 1-20-71:13
Ninja Bugelijo 1-25-67:6
Ninjutsu (See: Secret Scrolls [Part
   II])
Nino Es Nuestro, El 5-30-73:13
Nino Valiente 10-15-75:26
Nino y el Muro, El 9-22-65:6
Ninotchka 10-11-39:13
Niobe 4-09-15:20
Nippon Chinbotsu 5-22-74:19
Nippon No Don--Yabohen 1-18-78:
   38

Nippon No Ichiban Nagai Hi 9-13-
   67:6
Nippon O Shikaru 6-22-66:6
Nippon Sengoshi--Madam Onboro
   No Seikatsu 7-03-74:16
Nirjan Saikate 6-23-65:6
Nise Daigakusi 9-13-61:28
Nishant 5-26-76:36
Niskavuoren Naiset 11-30-38:13
Nissei Keiji 5-10-67:6
Nissuim Nosach Tel Aviv 12-26-
   79:13
Nitakayama Nobore 2-21-68:6
Nitra Sayan 1-15-75:26
Nitten Roede Roser 8-28-74:20
   and 12-18-74:12
Nittioettan Karlssons Permis 3-
   24-48:22
Nitwits, The 6-26-35:23
Nix on Dames 11-27-29:31
Nizvodno Od Sunca 8-20-69:28
Nje Udhetimi I Veshtire 6-13-79:
   34
No Babies Wanted 6-13-28:27
No Blade of Grass 11-04-70:24
No Boy Wanted (s) 10-30-29:25
No Control 7-06-27:23
No Defense 1-27-22:39
No Defense 7-10-29:24
No Deposit, No Return 1-28-76:
   14
No Down Payment 10-02-57:6
No Drums, No Bugles 8-11-71:16
No Escape 12-16-36:15
No Escape 8-05-53:6
No Exit 2-09-55:11
No Exit 7-11-62:6
No Funny Business 7-04-33:16 and
   3-13-34:16
No Greater Glory 5-08-34:14
No Greater Love 5-17-32:14
No Greater Love 3-01-44:20
No Greater Sin 9-03-41:17
No Gun Man, The 4-01-25:38
No Hands on the Clock 12-10-41:
   18
No Hay Que Aflojarle a la Vida
   8-27-75:16
No Highway 7-04-51:8
No Ho Tempo 5-16-73:18
No Holds Barred (s) 1-12-32:15
No Holds Barred 12-24-52:14
No, Il Caso e Felicemente Risolto
   9-05-73:6
No Kidding 12-21-60:6
No Lady 5-20-31:17
No Leave, No Love 8-28-46:14
No Limit 1-21-31:30
No Limit 11-13-35:17

1-24-79:23
Nosferatu the Vampire 12-25-29: 26
Nosferatu: The Vampire (See: Nosferatu: Phantom der Nacht)
Nosotros Dos 10-02-57:6
Nosotros Los Muchachos 12-25-40:18
Nostra Signora Dei Turchi 9-11-68:106
Not a Drum Was Heard 3-19-24: 27
Not as a Stranger 6-15-55:6
Not as Bad as It Seems 12-03-10: 14
Not Damaged 6-11-30:19
Not Everything That Flies Is a Bird 3-21-79:26 (Also see: Nicht Alles Was Fliegt Ist Ein Vogel)
Not for Publication 7-13-27:22
Not Guilty 11-26-15:23
Not Guilty 8-05-21:28
Not Just Another Woman 1-30-74: 16
Not My Sister 5-12-16:19
Not of This Earth 3-27-57:6
Not On Your Life (See: Verdugo, El)
Not Quite a Lady 9-05-28:31
Not Quite Decent 5-08-29:20
Not So Dumb 2-12-30:18
Not So Long Ago 7-29-25:34
Not the Type (s) 5-11-27:24
Not Tonight Henry 1-18-61:6
Not Wanted 6-22-49:6
Not Wanted on Voyage 2-23-38:14
Not Wanted on Voyage 11-13-57:6
Not with My Wife, You Don't! 9-21-66:6
Nothin' Doin' 7-27-27:21
Nothing but a Man 9-09-64:6
Nothing but Lies 9-03-20:45
Nothing but the Best 3-18-64:7
Nothing but the Truth 1-23-20:59
Nothing but the Truth 4-24-29:13
Nothing but the Truth 7-30-41:8
Nothing but Trouble 11-29-44:18
Nothing by Chance 1-29-75:17
Nothing Ever Happens (s) 2-28-33: 14
Nothing Personal 3-12-80:27
Nothing Sacred 12-01-37:14
Nothing to Wear 1-16-29:22
Notoriety 10-20-22:41
Notorious 7-24-46:14
Notorious Affair, A 4-30-30:35

Notorious but Nice 3-06-34:27
Notorious Lady, The 4-13-27:18
Notorious Landlady, The 6-27-62:6
Notorious Lone Wolf, The 3-13-46:10
Notorious Miss Lisle, The 8-20-20:34
Notorious Mrs. Sands, The 5-14-20:37
Notre-Dame de Paris 1-16-57:6
Notte, La 3-29-61:6
Notte Brava, La 1-27-60:6
Notte Che Evelyn Usca Dalla Tomba, La (See: Night Evelyn Came Out of the Grave, The)
Notte di San Juan, La 11-17-71:22
Notti Bianche, Le 9-25-57:26
Nouba Des Femmes du Mont Chenoua, La 9-19-79:22
Nous Etions Un Seul Homme 12-24-80:14
Nous Irons a Monte Carlo 2-27-52:16
Nous Irons a Paris 3-29-50:24
Nous Irons Tous au Paradis 11-23-77:19
Nous Maigrirons Ensemble 9-05-79:30
Nous N'irons Plus au Bois 4-16-69:30
Nous Ne Viellirons Pas Ensemble 5-10-72:21
Nous Sommes des Juifs Arabes En Israel 11-23-77:19
Nous Sommes Tous les Assassins 5-28-52:24
Nouveau Journal d'une Femme en Blanc 4-20-66:28
Nouveau Testament 3-04-36:31
Nouveau Venu, Le 8-22-79:20
Nouveaux Aristocrats, Les 1-17-62:6
Novia de Primavera, La 1-13-43:8
Novela de un Joven Pobre 5-27-42:8
Novela de un Joven Pobre, La 5-27-08-68:6
November 1828 7-25-79:17
Novia de Primavera, La 1-13-43:8
Novia En Apuros, Una 4-29-42:8
Novices, Les 11-18-70:14
Novinar 8-29-79:20
Novios Para las Muchachas 2-26-41:18
Now and Forever 10-16-34:12

Now and Forever 2-29-56:6
Now and Then (s) 2-27-29:80
Now Barabbas Was a Monster
6-01-49:11
Now I'll Tell 5-29-34:12
Now or Never 8-15-79:20
Now That April's Here 7-09-58:6
Now the Peace (s) 11-14-45:12
Now, Voyager 8-19-42:8
Now We're in the Air 12-14-27:
18
Now You See Him, Now You Don't
7-05-72:16
Nowhere to Go 12-03-58:6
Noz W Wodzie 9-12-62:16
'Nth Commandment 4-12-23:30
Nu Borjar Livet 9-15-48:20
Nu Comme un Ver 6-06-33:15
Nu Gaar Den Paa Dagmar 11-01-
72:30
Nuage Entre les Dents, Un 5-15-
74:24
Nuchia de Piatra 5-16-73:18
Nude Bomb, The 5-07-80:10
Nude Odyssey (See: Odissea Nuda)
Nude Restaurant, The 11-22-67:6
Nudist Paradise 2-25-59:6
Nuernberger Prozess, Der 12-10-
58:18
Nues vom Raeuber Hotzenplotz 5-
23-79:26
Nuestra Cosa (See: Our Latin
Thing)
Nuestros Odiosos Maridos 5-30-62:
23
Nueve Cartas a Berta 8-02-67:22
Nuevo Amanecer, Un 1-06-43:50
Nuevos, Los 11-28-73:16
Nuevos Espanoles, Los 1-15-75:
26
Nugel Bujan 7-29-64:8
Nugget Nell 8-01-19:53
Nuisance, The 5-30-33:54
Nuit a l'Hotel, La 5-31-32:25
Nuit Americaine, La 5-23-73:34
Nuit des Adieux, La 11-30-66:22
Nuit d'Or 12-15-76:22
Nuit de Noces, Une 6-28-50:18
Nuit de Saint-Germain des Pres,
La 5-18-77:20
Nuit des Bulgares, La 4-21-71:
22
Nuit du Carrefour, La 5-10-32:
19
Nuit Est a Nous, La 3-18-31:31
(Also see: Nacht Gehort
Uns, Die and Night Is Ours
The)

Nuit Est Mon Royaume, La 9-19-
51:24
Nuit et Brouillard 7-11-56:10
Nuit Infidele, La 10-02-68:6
Nuit Moscovites 12-11-34:19
Nuit Tous les Chats Sont Gris, La
11-16-77:24
Number 11 4-06-38:15 (Also see:
Number 111)
Number 96 5-22-74:26
Number One 8-06-69:6
Number One 6-13-73:16
Number 111 11-17-37:17 (Also
see: Number 11)
Number, Please (s) 3-18-31:14
Number, Please 7-14-31:55
Number 17 2-04-21:20
Number Seventeen 8-02-32:17
Numbered Men 6-11-30:19
Numbero Deux 10-08-75:20
Nun and the Sergeant, The 7-11-
62:27
Nun at the Crossroads, A 3-25-
70:22
Nunca Es Tarde 10-26-77:20
Nunca Pasa Nada 9-04-63:6
Nun's Story, The 5-06-59:6
Nunzio 4-26-78:18
Nuoruns Sumussa 7-24-46:26
Nuovi Angeli, I 2-28-62:6
Nur Am Rhein 9-29-31:22
Nur Du 1-12-32:28
Nuremberg 12-13-61:6
Nuremberg Trials, The 5-28-47:
20
Nurse Edith Cavell 8-23-39:14
Nurse from Brooklyn, The 4-13-
38:15
Nurse Marjorie 5-28-20:42
Nurse on Wheels 2-05-64:16
Nurse's Secret, The 6-11-41:16
Nursing a Viper 11-13-09:13
Nut, The 3-11-21:32
Nutcracker Fantasy 8-08-79:22
Nutty, Naughty Chateau (See:
Chateau en Suede)
Nutty Professor, The 5-22-63:6
Nutville (s) 2-12-36:16
N'y D'Oubli, Il 8-25-76:68
N'y de Fumee, Il 5-30-73:24
Nyar a Hegyen 11-15-67:20 and
1-31-68:27
Nybggarna 3-22-72:36
Nyckeln Och Ringen 12-10-47:12
Nymphettes, Les 2-22-61:7
Nyt Legetoej 5-18-77:21

Ocalenie 5-23-73:36
Ocalic Miasto 8-03-77:24
Ocana, Retrat Intermitent 5-24-78:40
Occasionally Yours 10-22-20:41
Occhio Selvaggio, L' 7-26-67:24
Occupe--Toi d'Amelie 10-19-49:18
Occupe--Toi d'Amelie 10-19-49:18
Oceano 8-04-71:18
Ocean's Eleven 8-10-60:6
Ochazuke No Aji (See: Flavor of Green Tea over Rice, The)
Octagon, The 8-13-80:26
October 1917 (See: Ten Days That Shook the World)
October Man, The 9-10-47:17
Octopus, The 7-23-15:18
Odd Angry Shot, The 4-25-79:18
Odd Couple, The 5-01-68:6
Odd Job, The 11-01-78:22
Odd Man Out 2-12-47:14
Odd Numbers 10-09-29:23
Odd Obsession (See: Kagi)
Odd Pairs of Limbs 5-23-08:12
Oddities of Fashion (s) 4-10-29:16
Odds Against Tomorrow 10-07-59:6
Odds On 10-17-28:27
Ode to Billy Joe 6-09-76:22
Oder Keine, Die 10-18-32:19
Odessa File, The 10-08-74:18
Odette 3-21-28:19
Odette 6-14-50:22
Odette Myrtil (s) 11-07-28:15
Odio a Mi Cuerpo 6-05-74:16
Odisca de los Andes, La 10-27-76:46
Odissea Nuda 5-10-61:6
Odongo 7-11-56:10
Odwiedziny Prezydenta 9-13-61:6
Odyssey 2-16-77:24
Odyssey of the North 9-18-14:19
Oedipus Rex 1-02-57:6
Oedipus Rex (See: Edipo Re)
Oedipus the King 7-03-68:6
Oeil du Maitre, L' 4-23-80:19
Oeil du Malin, L' 3-28-62:6
Oeil du Monocle, L' 11-28-62:6
Oeil Pour Oeil 9-25-57:26
Oejeblikket 10-15-80:74
Oelprinz, Der 11-10-65:6
O'er Crag and Torrent 4-09-10:15
Oese, Die 2-19-64:6
Oeuf, L' 4-26-72:6
Oeufs Brouilles, Les 4-07-76:30

Oeufs de l'Autruche, Les 10-23-57:18
Of All People (s) 11-17-31:14
Of Human Bondage 7-03-34:26
Of Human Bondage 7-03-46:10
Of Human Bondage 7-01-64:6
Of Human Hearts 7-01-64:6
Of Love and Desire 8-28-63:6
Of Love and Lust 11-30-60:6
Of Men and Demons 4-01-70:26
Of Men and Music 11-29-50:14
Of Mice and Men 1-03-40:40
Of Stars and Men 8-30-61:16
Of Wayward Love (See: Amore Difficile, L')
Off Limits 2-04-53:6
Off the Beat (s) 11-27-34:15
Off the Edge 3-16-77:24
Off the Highway 9-23-25:39
Off the Record 2-22-39:12
Off the Wall 4-06-77:26
Off the Peoria (s) 6-11-30:18
Off to the Races 2-03-37:29
Offbeat 3-01-61:15
Offender, The 11-12-24:25
Offense, The 5-16-73:32
Offering, The 12-07-66:6
Office Blues (s) 1-21-131:17
Office Girl 6-28-32:15
Office Picnic, The 8-02-74:20
Office Scandal, The 7-24-29:35
Office Scandal, The (s) 12-17-30:13
Office Steps (s) 5-28-30:21
Office Wife, The 10-01-30:19
Officer and the Lady, The 7-16-41:22
Officer Jim 6-19-14:22
Officer O'Brien 2-26-30:35
Officer 666 12-19-14:26
Officer 666 11-05-20:41
Officer 13 1-31-33:12
Officier de Police Sans Importance, Un 5-02-73:6
Offshore Pirate 3-04-21:40
Oficio de Tinieblas 10-29-80:22
O'Garry of the Mounted 3-12-15:24
Og Sa er der Bal Bagefter 12-30-70:16
Oggetti Smarriti 5-14-80:15
Oggi, Domani e Dopodomani 3-30-66:28 (Also see: Man with the Balloons)
Ogheya Ala el Mamar 8-09-72:20
Oginsaga 4-18-79:23
Ogon No Paatonaa 12-26-79:13
Ogro 9-19-79:18

O. H. M. S.   2-03-37:15
O'Henry's Full House   8-20-52:6
O'Henry's Stories   3-23-17:23
Oh, America   11-05-75:18
Oh Baby   8-11-26:16
Oh, Boy!   6-13-19:49
Oh Dad, Poor Dad, Mama's Hung
    You in the Closet and I'm
    Feeling So Sad   2-15-67:6
Oh, Daddy   4-03-35:17
Oh, Doctor   10-05-17:41
Oh, Doctor!   2-25-25:31
Oh, Doctor   6-23-37:33
Oh Dolci Baci e Languide Carezze
    2-04-70:26
Oh, Evaline (s)   11-13-35:16
Oh, For a Man   12-03-30:15
Oh, God!   10-05-77:28
Oh, God! Book II   10-01-80:20
Oh Heavenly Dog   7-16-80:23
Oh, Johnny!   1-25-19:46
Oh Johnny, How Can You Love?
    2-14-40:20
Oh Jonathan, Oh Jonathan   5-30-
    73:24
Oh Kay   8-29-28:28
Oh, Lady, Lady!   12-24-20:27
Oh, Men! Oh, Women!   2-20-57:6
Oh, Mr. Porter!   10-20-37:27
Oh, My Operation (s)   7-05-32:14
Oh, My Operation (s)   1-24-33:12
Oh, Oh, Cleopatra (s)   11-10-31:
    14
Oh Pop!   7-06-17:23
Oh Rosalinda   11-30-55:6
Oh! Que Mambo   6-10-59:24
Oh, Sailor, Behave (s)   10-16-34:
    12
Oh, Sarah (s)   4-09-30:22
Oh, Susanna   3-24-37:31
Oh! Susanna   3-14-51:6
Oh, Uncle   9-04-09:13
Oh Yeah!   12-25-29:30
Oh, You Women!   6-20-19:52
Oh! What a Lovely War!   4-16-
    69:6
Oh, What a Night   12-01-26:34
Oh, What a Night   9-06-44:10
Oh! What a Nurse   2-24-26:43
Oh, What Lungs!   8-22-08:13
Oh, You Beautiful Doll   9-21-49:8
Oh, You Doggie   1-08-10:12
Oh, You Skeleton   10-29-10:14
Ohlednuti   10-01-69:30
Ohne Datum   7-11-62:6
Oil for the Lamps of China   6-
    12-35:12
Oily Maniac   10-20-76:39

Oily Scoundrel, An   5-05-16:23
Oiseau de Paradis, L'   11-14-62:7
Oiseau Rare, Un   6-12-35:41
Oiseau Rare, L'   9-05-73:6
Oiseaux Vont Mourir Au Peru, Les
    7-24-68:24
Ojciec Krolowej   10-01-80:28
Ojo de la Cerradura, El (See:
    Eavesdropper, The)
Ojos Mas Lindosdel Mundo, Los
    9-08-43:16
Ojos Tapatios   4-19-61:6
Ojos Vendados, Los   5-31-78:22
Ok Ketten   11-16-77:24
Oka Oorie Katha   5-31-78:26
Okasan   1-26-55:20
Okasareta Byakui   7-14-71:20
Okay America   9-13-32:19
Okay Bill   2-24-71:18
Okay for Sound   5-12-37:13
Okay Toots (s)   5-01-35:17
Okinawa   2-27-52:6
Oklahoma!   10-12-55:6
Oklahoma Annie   4-09-52:6
Oklahoma Badlands   3-03-48:8
"Oklahoma Bob" Albright (s)   7-
    03-29:17
Oklahoma Crude   6-06-73:18
Oklahoma Frontier   12-06-39:14
Oklahoma Jim   12-29-31:169
Oklahoma Kid, The   3-15-39:16
Oklahoma Sheriff, The   7-16-30:
    29
Oklahoma Territory   2-10-60:6
Oklahoma Terror   9-06-39:14
Oklahoma Woman   7-04-56:6
Oklahoman, The   5-01-57:7
Okraina   5-16-33:21
Oksigen   8-12-70:14
Oktoberi Vasarnap   2-27-80:26
Okupacija U 26 Slika   8-09-78:22
Ol' Man Whoopee (s)   7-30-30:16
Ola & Julia   9-13-67:24
Old Acquaintance   11-03-43:16
Old Actor, The   7-25-08:13
Old Age Handicap   5-23-28:39
Old Age Pension (s)   4-10-35:17
Old and Modern New Orleans (s)
    10-07-42:25
Old and New   5-14-30:43
Old Barn, The (s)   5-01-29:17
Old Barn Dance   1-12-38:15
Old Bill (s)   3-28-28:30
Old Bill and Son   12-25-40:18
Old Bill Through the Ages   4-16-
    24:27
Old Bill's Christmas (s)   12-04-
    29:15

Olly, Olly, Oxen Free 8-16-78: 19
Olovna Brigada 8-13-80:27
Olsen-Banden Deruda 10-19-77: 26
Olsen-Banden Gaar Amok 10-24-73:22
Olsen-Banden Gaar I Krig 11-22-78:26
Olsen-Banden I Jylland 10-13-71: 20
Olsen-Banden Overgiver Sig Aldrig 12-26-79:13
Olsen-Banden Paa Spanden 10-15-69:15
Olsen-Banden Paa Sporet 10-01-75:24
Olsen-Banden Ser Roedt 10-13-76: 23
Olsen-Bandens Sidste Bedrifter 10-23-74:30
Olsen-Bandens Store Kup 10-18-72:18
Olsen's Night Out 1-09-34:17
Oltre Il Bene e Il Male 10-12-77:17
Olvidados, Los 5-16-51:18
Olyan Mint Otthon 5-24-78:31
Olympia 10-22-30:35 and 11-26-30:18 (Also see: His Glorious Night and Si l'Empereur Savait Ca)
Olympia-Olympia 7-12-72:30
Olympaid I Witt 5-12-48:20
Olympic Champ, The (s) 12-02-42:22
Olympic Elk, The 1-09-52:6
Olympic Hero, The 9-26-28:58
Olympics in Mexico 7-22-70:20
Olympische Winterspiele in Innsbruck 7-08-64:16
Om 7 Flickor 1-30-74:13
Omaha Trail, The 9-16-42:8
O'Mahoney-George Match (s) 8-21-35:21
O'Malley of the Mounted 2-11-21: 41
O'Malley of the Mounted 4-08-36: 17
O'Malley Rides Alone 2-05-30:31
Omar Gatlato 3-13-77:17 and 8-03-77:22
Omar Khayyam 8-07-57:6
Omar the Tent Maker 1-25-23:41
Ombre d'une Chance, L' 1-30-74:23
Ombre des Chateaux, L' 12-01-76:19

Ombre et Lumiere 7-11-51:25
Ombrellone, L' 3-30-66:6
Ombres et Mirages 8-09-67:6
Ombres Fuyantes 7-12-32:17
Omega Man, The 8-04-71:18
Omen, The 6-09-76:23
Omicron 9-11-63:22
Omina Vincit Amor 10-28-70:28
Omoo-Omoo 6-22-49:6
On 5-25-66:7
On a Clear Day You Can See Forever 6-17-70:16
On a Racket 1-22-10:15
On a Retrouve la 7e Compagnie 12-24-75:14
On a Vole la Cuisse de Jupiter 2-27-80:27
On a Vole la Joconde 6-08-66:6
On a Vole un Homme 4-03-34:27
On Again--Off Again 8-11-37:19
On Aime Qu'une Fois 6-28-50:18
On an Empty Balcony (See: En El Balcon Vacio)
On an Island with You 4-28-48:8
On and Off the Air (s) 11-21-33: 14
On Another Man's Pass 8-28-09: 13
On Any Sunday 7-21-71:16
On Approval 9-17-30:30
On Approval 3-22-44:18
On Aura Tout Vu 7-21-76:22
On Borrowed Time 7-05-39:14
On Company Business 3-12-80: 23
On Dangerous Ground 12-29-16: 23
On Dangerous Ground 12-05-51:6
On Dangerous Paths 7-30-15:19
On Demande Compagnon 6-06-33: 14
On Desert Sands 1-16-15:27
On Dress Parade 11-01-39:14
On Efface Tout! 8-23-78:30
On Est Toujours Trop Bon Avec les Femmes 7-07-71:14
On Fortune's Wheel 3-28-13:14
On Friday at Eleven 10-25-61:6
On Her Doorsteps 10-22-10:14
On Her Majesty's Secret Service 12-17-69:16
On Her Wedding Night 7-30-15: 19
On His Own 9-27-39:14
On Mission Trail (s) 4-11-33:17
On Moonlight Bay 7-11-51:6
On My Way to the Crusades I Met

321 •

a Girl Who ... (See: Chastity Belt, The)
On N'Arrete Pas le Printemps 9-22-71:14
On N'Enterre Pas le Dimanche 5-11-60:6
On N'Est Pas Serieux Quand On a 17 Ans 11-20-74:14
On Ne Meurt Pas Comme Ca 7-24-46:26
On Ne Roule Pas Antoinette 6-10-36:18
On Our Selection 8-02-32:17
On Peut le Dire Sans Se Facher 1-18-78:38
On Probation 5-27-25:41
On Record 4-06-17:25
On Stage Everybody 7-11-45:14
On Such a Night 8-18-37:27
On the Air (s) 7-25-28:14
On the Air 2-13-34:14
On the Air 3-03-37:14
On the Avenue 2-10-37:14
On the Bank of the River 1-15-10:13
On the Battle Line 10-31-14:28
On the Beach 12-02-59:6
On the Beat 12-19-62:6
On the Blue Pacific (s) 5-16-33:17
On the Border 11-27-09:13
On the Border 2-05-30:31
On the Bowery 9-12-56:18
On the Divide 1-09-29:45
On the Divide 2-13-29:30
On the Double 5-17-61:6
On the Fiddle 10-18-61:22
On the Great White Trail 8-10-38:27
On the High C's (s) 12-25-29:20
On the High Seas 10-06-22:40
On the Isle of Samoa 7-26-50:10
On the Job (s) 3-25-31:16
On the Jump 11-08-18:41
On the Level 7-09-30:19
On the Loose 7-25-51:6
On the Nickel 3-26-80:21
On the Night of the Fire 11-22-39:14
On the Old Spanish Trail 10-22-47:13
On the Other Side of the Street 11-13-29:38
On the Quiet 8-30-18:39
On the Reef 1-22-10:15
On the Riviera 4-25-51:6
On the Russian Frontier 10-08-15:21

On the Slopes of the Andes (s) 4-01-31:16
On the Spot 6-26-40:18
On the Steps of the Throne 8-21-14:19
On the Stroke of 3 1-21-25:36
On the Stroke of 12 1-25-28:13
On the Sunny Side 2-04-42:8
On the Third Day (s) 5-22-74:19
On the Threshold of Space 3-07-56:6
On the Town 12-07-49:6
On the U. P. Trail 7-20-27:19
On the Wagon (s) 12-18-35:13
On the Waterfront 7-14-54:6
On the White Trails (See: Na Bialym Szlaku)
On the Yard 11-15-78:19
On Their Own 6-12-40:14
On Thin Ice 3-11-25:41
On Time 6-15-27:25
On Top of Old Smokey 3-04-53:18
On Trial 6-15-17:25
On Trial 11-21-28:30
On Trial 3-29-39:14
On with the Show 6-05-29:15
On Your Back 9-17-30:30
On Your Toes 1-18-28:13
On Your Toes 10-25-39:11
On ze Boulevard 7-13-27:23
Onawanda 10-02-09:13
Once 10-03-73:15 and 12-18-74:12
Once a Crook 7-09-41:14
Once a Doctor 2-03-37:14
Once a Gentleman 10-08-30:22
Once a Jolly Swagman 1-12-49:8
Once a Lady 11-10-31:15
Once a Mason 3-14-19:44
Once a Plumber 9-24-20:44
Once a Sinner 1-21-31:30
Once a Sinner 2-20-52:18
Once a Thief 6-28-50:6
Once a Thief 8-25-65:6
Once in a Blue Moon 12-09-36:13
Once in a Lifetime 11-01-32:13
Once in a Million 4-01-36:17
Once in Paris 11-08-78:20
Once Is Not Enough 6-18-75:18
Once More My Darling 7-27-49:12
Once More with Feeling 2-10-60:6
Once Over Lightly (s) 5-13-31:36
Once There Was a Girl 12-26-45:14
Once to Every Bachelor 9-25-34:14
Once to Every Man 11-29-18:41

One Man Law 2-16-32:22
One Man Reunion (s) 4-16-30:21
One-Man Trail, The 5-13-21:43
One-Man Trail, The 5-11-27:21
One Man's Journey 9-05-33:19
One Man's Law 7-10-40:14
One Man's Way 2-05-64:6
One Mile from Heaven 7-21-37: 13
One Million B.C. 5-01-40:18
One Million Dollars 11-12-15:22
1,000,000 Eyes of Sumuru, The 6-14-67:22
One Million Years B.C. 12-28-66:18
One Minute to Play 9-01-26:14
One Minute to Zero 7-16-52:6
One More American 2-22-18:45
One More Chance (s) 12-22-31:15
One More River 8-14-34:15
One More Spring 2-27-35:12
One More Time 6-03-70:17
One More Tomorrow 5-15-46:8
One More Train to Rob 4-21-71: 17
One Mysterious Night 10-25-44:12
One New York Night 5-08-35:45
One Night 7-23-24:27
One Night and Then 2-19-10:15
One Night at Susie's 11-26-30:18
One Night in Lisbon 5-14-41:16
One Night in Paris 4-05-23:35
One Night in Paris 7-24-40:16
One Night in the Tropics 11-06-40: 16
One Night of Love 9-11-34:11
One Night Stand 8-25-76:20
One Night with You 4-28-48:8
One Nutty (s) 9-24-30:23
One of a Kind 5-26-76:18
One of Many 2-16-17:25
One of Our Aircraft Is Missing 4-29-42:8
One of Our Dinosaurs Is Missing 6-18-75:18
One of Our Girls 6-12-14:21
One of the Bravest 3-03-26:38
One of the Finest 6-06-19:49
One of the Millions 11-07-14:23
One of the Smiths (s) 6-30-31:15
One on Max 10-22-10:14
One on One 6-15-77:21
One on Top of the Other 1-19-72:6
One Plus One (Exploring the Kinsey Reports) 8-23-61:6
One Plus One 12-11-68:30
1 + 1 = 3 11-07-79:10
One Potato, Two Potato 5-06-64:6

One Rainy Afternoon 5-20-36:12
One Romantic Night 6-04-30:36
One Round Hogan 10-26-27:19
One Run Elmer (s) 3-27-35:15
One Shot Ross 10-12-17:39
One Silver Dollar 6-18-75:19
One Sings, the Other Doesn't (See: Une Chante, l'Autre Pas, L')
One Splendid Hour 5-29-29:58
One Spy Too Many 9-28-66:24
One Step Away 10-02-68:24
One Stolen Night 2-01-23:41
One Stolen Night 5-08-29:29
One Sunday Afternoon 9-05-33:19
One Sunday Afternoon 12-08-48:11
One That Got Away, The 10-23-57:18
One Third of the Nation 2-15-39: 12
1,000 Convicts and a Woman 10-27-71:24
1001 Arabian Nights 12-09-59:6
One Thousand Dollars 7-05-18:31
$1,000 a Minute 12-25-35:15
$1,000 a Touchdown 9-27-39:12
One Thrilling Night 7-01-42:8
One Too Many 11-22-50:18
One Touch of Venus 8-25-48:8
One Track Minds (s) 7-18-33:36
One-Trick Pony 10-01-80:20
One, Two, Three 11-29-61:6
1 2 3 Duan Mahadhai 6-22-77:16
1-2-3, Go! (s) 9-03-41:17
One Way Boogie Woogie 4-26-78: 18
One Way Out (s) 2-11-31:14 and 3-18-31:14
One Way Passage 10-18-32:15
One Way Street 4-12-50:6
One-Way Ticket 1-08-36:12
One Way to Leave 1-02-46:8
One Way Trail 5-14-20:37
One Way Trail 12-22-31:21
One Way Wahini 9-29-65:6
One Week of Life 5-23-19:59
One Week of Love 11-17-22:41
One Wild Night 4-11-38:16
One Wild Oat 5-30-51:6
One Wild Week 8-26-21:35
One Wish Too Many 4-28-65:6
One Woman, The 9-20-18:45
One-Woman Idea 6-12-29:31
One Woman to Another 9-21-27: 20
One Wonderful Night 8-14-14:22
One Wonderful Night 1-05-23:41
One Yard to Go (s) 2-11-31:14
One Year Later 11-21-33:20

One Year to Live 7-08-25:37
Oni Sra Jalis Za Rodwou 5-28-75:18
Onibaba 2-10-65:7
Onion Field, The 5-23-79:23
Onionhead 9-24-58:6
Onkel Aus Amerika, Der 2-18-53:18
Onkel Tom's Cabin 5-19-65:30
Onkraj 8-12-70:14
Only a Shop Girl 6-22-22:35
Only a Woman (See: Ich Bin Auch Nur eine Frau)
Only Angels Have Wings 5-17-39:12
Only Game in Town, The 1-28-70:17
Only Girl, The 7-04-33:16
Only God Knows 10-16-74:16
Only Once in a Lifetime 9-26-79:34
Only Saps Work 12-17-30:13
Only Son, The 6-19-14:21
Only the Brave 3-12-30:33
Only the Brave (s) 7-31-35:19
Only the French Can (See: French Can-Can)
Only the Valiant 3-07-51:6
Only Thing, The 11-25-25:39
Only Thing You Know, The 9-08-71:16
Only 38 6-14-23:26
Only Two Can Play 1-24-62:6
Only Way, The 9-23-25:40
Only Way, The 5-13-70:24
Only Way Home, The 9-27-72:6
Only Way Out, The 4-02-15:21
Only When I Larf 7-03-68:26
Only Woman, The 11-05-24:30
Only Yesterday 11-14-33:17
Only You Know and I Know 4-28-71:6
Onna Ga Kaidan O Agaru Toki 9-14-60:20
Onna No Rekishi 7-29-64:8
Onore Della Figlia Del Popola, L' 1-13-37:30
Onore e Sacrificio (See: Dishonored)
Onze Mille Verges, Les 11-05-75:18
Ooh-La-La (s) 12-31-30:19
Oom Pahpah (s) 6-11-30:18
Opa Schulz 5-18-77:21
Open All Night 9-10-24:27
Open All Night 11-06-34:17
Open City (See: Rome, Open City)
Open Eye Detectives (s) 11-17-31:14
Open Letter 10-23-68:22

Open Range 3-21-28:26
Open Road, The 10-09-40:18
Open Season 8-21-74:20
Open Secret (See: Yksityisalue)
Open Street 1-14-48:10
Open the Door and See All the People 12-11-63:6
Open Your Eyes 7-04-19:42
Opened by Mistake (s) 5-29-35:14
Opened by Mistake 5-08-40:12
Opened Shutters, The 11-21-14:27
Opened Shutters, The 8-26-21:35
Opening Night 2-15-28:27
Opening Night 12-28-77:14
Opening of Misty Beethoven, The 4-07-76:30
Opera de Paris (s) 11-11-36:15
Opera Prima 6-25-80:21
Opera Singer's Triumph, The 2-06-15:23
Operacion Alfa 12-06-72:20
Operacion Rosa Rosa 7-31-74:18
Operasjon Cobra 10-24-79:17
Operation, The (s) 2-12-30:18
Operation A-Bomb (s) 12-10-52:6
Operation Air Raid: Bed Muffler 4-13-66:20
Operation Amsterdam 1-15-59:6 and 4-06-60:6
Operation Bikini 4-10-63:6
Operation Bullshire 7-15-59:12
Operation Crossbow 4-07-65:6
Operation Dames 3-04-59:6
Operation Daybreak 3-03-76:21
Operation Eichmann 3-15-61:6
Operation Haylift 4-19-50:8
Operation Ivy (s) 4-07-54:6
Operation Kid Brother 10-11-67:22
Operation Lady Marlene 8-27-75:15
Operation Manhunt 10-27-54:6
Operation Pacific 1-10-51:13
Operation Petticoat 9-30-59:6
Operation Secret 10-15-52:6
Operation Thunderbolt 2-16-77:23
Operator 13 6-26-34:16
Operators Opera (s) 12-26-33:10
Operazione Goldman (See: Lightning Bolt)
Operazione Paura (See: Kill, Baby, Kill)
Operazione San Gennaro 12-28-66:18
Operetta 6-08-49:18
Opernball, Der 9-19-56:22

325 ●

Opernredoute 8-18-31:30 and 11-10-31:23
Ophelia 5-30-62:23
Opium Smoker, The 7-24-14:18
Opium Smugglers, The 5-08-14:21
Opium War, The (See: Lin Tse-hsu)
Opklada 8-11-71:16
Opname (See: In For Treatment)
Oppenheim Family, The 5-31-39:14
Opportunity 7-12-18:35
Opposite Sex, The 9-19-56:6
Oppressed, The 7-24-29:39
Opry House, The (s) 4-10-29:16 and 11-13-29:12
Optimistic Tragedy (See: Optimistit Cheskaia)
Optimistit Cheskaia 5-29-63:6
Optimists, The 10-17-73:14
Or, L' 6-19-34:44
Or du Cristobal, L' 5-15-40:18
Or et le Plomb, L' 3-16-66:7
Ora Ponciano 5-12-37:13
Oracle, The 6-10-53:6
Orage 3-23-38:17
Orage 8-11-54:6
Orage d'Ete 4-26-50:23
Orca 7-13-77:18
Orchestra Rehearsal (See: Prova d'Orchestra)
Orchestra Wives 8-12-42:8
Orchid Dancer, The 5-09-28:17
Orchids and Ermine 4-20-27:21
Orchids to You 8-14-35:15
Ordered to Love (See: Lebensborn)
Ordeal, The 9-25-09:12
Ordeal, The 10-24-14:22
Ordeal, The 6-02-22:34
Ordeal of Rosetta, The 7-19-18:36
Orders Is Orders 7-18-33:37 and 5-08-34:21
Orders to Kill 4-02-58:6
Ordet 9-07-55:6
Ordinary People 9-17-80:18
Ordinateur des Pompes Funebres, L' 4-21-76:26
Ordonnance, L' 9-12-33:17
Ordre et la Securite du Monde, L' 7-26-78:21
Ordres, Les 11-20-74:16 and 5-21-75:22
Ore Dell'Amore, Le 3-27-63:6
Ore Nude, Le (See: Naked Hours, The)
Oregon Passage 1-29-58:6
Oregon Trail Scouts 5-21-47:15

Orfeo, L' 10-18-78:72
Orfeu Negro 5-20-59:6
Organ, The 8-09-65:6
Organ Grinder, The 10-16-09:12
Organization, The 10-20-71:14
Organizer, The (See: Compagni, I)
Orgasmo (See: Paranoia)
Orgueilleux, Les 9-30-53:22
Orguismeni Guenia 11-15-72:32
Orid Halla 12-18-74:12
Orient 5-08-29:27
Orient Express 3-06-34:14
Oriental Blue 8-20-75:73
Oriental Playgirls 3-17-76:36
Original Cast Album: "Company" 9-23-70:13
Orloff and Tarakanova 5-04-38:25
Orm Ok Savan 11-14-62:7
Ornung 5-07-80:575
Oro di Roma, L' 1-17-62:6
Oro en la Mano 1-05-44:26
Oro Rojo 9-20-78:34
Orok Titok 4-06-38:15
Orokbefogadas 7-23-75:20
Orokseg 5-21-80:18
Orphan 4-30-20:42
Orphan of the Pecos 9-28-38:21
Orphan of the Wilderness 1-27-37:24
Orphans of the North 11-06-40:16
Orphans of the Storm 1-06-22:42
Orphans of the Street 2-01-39:18
Orphee 7-12-50:16
Orpheus (See: Orphee)
"Orpheus" Overture (s) 3-27-29:12
Orquesta de Senoritas 6-18-41:18
Orquidea, La 9-19-51:6
Ortliebschen, Die 3-05-80:26
O'Shaughnessy's Boy 10-09-35:14
Os Anos JK--Uma Trajetoria Politica 9-10-80:28
Os Bandeirantes 11-23-60:6
Os Cafajestes 7-11-62:6
Os Deuses e Os Mortos 7-08-70:15
Os Fuzis 7-08-64:6
Os Marginais 9-17-69:24
Os Mucker 3-05-80:23
Os Paqueras 12-31-69:18
Os Pastores da Noite 8-31-77:19
Os Verdes Anos 8-05-64:7
Osa Krivi I Nichta 10-14-64:6
Osaka--Io Monogatari (See: Daredevil in the Castle)
Osam Kila Srece 8-13-80:27
Oscar 11-01-67:6
Oscar, The 2-16-66:6

Oscar, Kina y el Laser 3-14-79:
24
Oscar Wilde 5-25-60:6
Osennie Svadjby 10-30-68:28
Osenny Maraphon 9-12-79:18
Osinda 7-27-77:22
Osma Vrata 8-19-59:6
Osmiat 10-07-70:14
Osmosis: Mysterious Passage (s)
4-30-47:10
Ospite, L' 9-22-71:14
Oss Emellan 4-08-70:24
Oss 117--Mission For a Killer
(See: Furia a Bahia Pour
Oss 117)
Oss 117 Prend des Vacances 2-
25-70:15
Ossessione 11-04-59:7
Ossudeni Doushi 1-14-76:20
Ostia 10-28-70:26
Ostre Sledovane Vlaky 10-26-66:
6
Ostrov Stribrnych Volavek 3-09-
77:26
Osvanje Slobode 9-05-79:27
Oswalt Kolle: Dein Mann, Das
Unbekannte Wesen 4-08-70:16
Oswalt Kolle--Zum Beispiel:
Ehebruch 8-27-69:18
Ot Nishto-Neshto 6-11-80:26
Otages, Les 5-03-39:20
Otalia de Bahia Putik Ka Man 9-
29-76:36
Otarova Vdova 9-10-58:6
Otchi Dom 5-20-59:6
Othchi Tchornia (See: Dark Eyes)
Othello 4-30-10:16
Othello 8-06-15:17
Othello 6-02-22:33 and 2-22-23:41
Othello 5-21-52:6
Othello 5-16-56:6 and 3-16-60:6
Othello 12-15-65:6
Other, The 9-10-30:29 (Also see:
Andere, Der)
Other, The 5-24-72:19
Other Half of the Note, The 5-15-
14:23
Other Half of the Sky: A China
Memoir, The 2-19-75:22
Other Kind of Love 8-20-24:22
Other Love, The 4-02-47:16
Other Man, The 2-01-18:44
Other Man's Wife, The 6-13-19:
50
Other Men's Daughters 7-26-18:
30
Other Men's Women 4-22-31:19
Other One, The 10-04-67:12

Other Peoples' Children 3-07-13:
14
Other Side of Joey, The 8-16-72:
28
Other Side of Midnight, The 6-08-
77:26
Other Side of the Door, The 1-
07-16:23
Other Side of the Mountain, The
3-19-75:29
Other Side of the Mountain, Part
II, The 2-08-78:18
Other Side of the Underneath, The
12-06-72:20
Other Voices 3-26-69:30
Other Way, The 11-26-10:18
Other Woman, The 4-22-21:40
Other Woman, The 12-15-54:6
Other Woman's Husbands, The
4-28-26:48
Other Woman's Story, The 3-31-
26:43
Other World of Winston Churchill
4-19-67:58
Otietz Sergii 10-25-78:42
Otley 1-22-69:6
Otoro Francisco, El 8-06-75:17
Ototo 5-17-61:7
Otra, La 1-01-47:14
Otro Cristobal, El 5-29-63:6
Ottokar Der Weltverbesserer 6-
28-78:20
Ou Est Passe Tom? 10-27-71:24
Ou Etes-Vous Donc ...? 10-29-
69:28
Ou S'Est Trompe d'Histoire
d'Amour 5-15-74:30
Ouchard 3-05-10:13
Our America at War (s) 1-07-42:
45
Our Betters 2-28-33:15
Our Blushing Brides (See: Blushing
Brides)
Our Bridge of Ships 8-23-18:42
Our Daily Bread 10-09-34:18
Our Daily Bread 10-18-50:6
Our Dancing Daughters 10-10-28:22
Our Fighting Forces 4-13-17:27
Our Fighting Navy 5-12-37:13
Our Girl Friday 12-30-53:6
Our Hearts Were Growing Up 3-
13-46:10
Our Hearts Were Young and Gay
9-06-44:10
Our Hitler: A Film from Germany
(See: Hitler, A Film from
Germany)
Our Hospitality 12-13-23:22 (Also
see: Hospitality)

329 •

331 •

Painting the Town 8-03-27:16
Pair of Cupids, A 8-09-18:32
Pair of Kings, A 6-16-22:41
Pair of Silk Stockings, A 7-19-18:
   38
Pair of Sixes, A 6-07-18:32
Pais, Lo 5-30-73:12
Pais Llamado Chile, Un 7-19-61:6
Pais Portatil 10-10-79:34
Pais S.A. 10-01-75:28
Paix Sur les Champs 4-21-71:22
Paisan 2-11-48:14
Pajama Game, The 8-07-57:6
Pajama Party (s) 11-03-31:17
Pajama Party 11-18-64:6
Pajamas 11-09-27:24
Pajarite Gomez 7-07-65:6
Pajaros de Baden-Baden, Los 2-
   25-76:22
Pal Joey 9-11-57:6
Pal o' Mine 6-04-24:26
Palabras de Max, La 3-15-78:21
Palac 10-15-80:66
Palace Hotel 5-14-52:20
Palace of Flame 5-29-14:21
Palace of the King 12-06-23:23
Palace Scandal 6-08-49:19
Palaces of a Queen 12-07-66:6
Palais de Danse 9-05-28:31
Palaver 7-23-69:28
Pale Face's Wooing 11-27-09:13
Pale Horseman, The 5-15-46:24
Palec Bozy 8-28-74:43
Paleface, The 7-21-22:35
Paleface, The 10-20-48:11
Paleface Pup (s) 7-14-31:17
Palermo--Wolfsburg 2-13-80:38
Palestine (s) 5-28-47:20
Pallieter 12-24-75:16
Palm Beach 5-23-79:24
Palm Beach Fours (s) 5-29-29:14
Palm Beach Girl 6-23-26:14
Palm Beach Story, The 11-04-
   42:8
Palm Springs 6-24-36:29
Palm Springs Weekend 11-06-63:6
Palmy Days 9-29-31:14
Paloma, La 10-28-36:15
Paloma, La 5-15-74:28
Paloma Brava 3-01-61:15
Palomino 2-01-50:20
Palooka 3-06-34:14
Palooka Flying School (s) 5-28-
   30:21
Palooka in Paducah (s) 1-29-35:15
Pals (s) 5-11-27:24
Pals (s) 8-01-28:12
Pals First 10-04-18:51

Pals First 8-25-26:18
Pals in Blue 6-18-15:18
Pals in Paradise 11-24-26:15
Pals of the Golden West 1-16-52:
   18
Pals of the Pecos 6-04-41:15
Pals of the Prairie 7-31-29:23
Pals of the Saddle 9-14-38:15
Pals of the Silver Sage 5-29-40:
   14
Pamela, Pamela You Are ... 12-
   18-68:6
Pampa Salvaje 7-27-66:7
Pampered Youth 3-04-25:38
Pan-American 2-21-45:8
Pan Redaktor Szaleje 6-29-38:26
Pan Twardowski 9-29-37:15
Panagulis Zei 10-15-80:66
Panama Flo 1-26-32:21
Panama Hattie 7-22-42:8
Panama Lady 6-07-39:12
Panama Patrol 8-16-39:16
Panama Sal 12-25-57:6
Panama Trails 8-16-39:16
Paname 3-21-28:22
Panamericana 1-15-69:39
Panamint's Bad Man 8-10-38:27
Panay Newsreels (s) 1-05-38:16
Pancho Villa Returns 10-25-50:6
Pancho Villa y la Valentina 9-14-
   60:18
Pandillero, El 5-10-61:19
Pandora and the Flying Dutchman
   10-10-51:6
Pandora's Box 12-11-29:39
Pane, Amore, e.... 3-28-56:6
Pane, Amore, e Fantasia 1-20-
   54:18
Pane, Amore, e Gelosia 1-26-55:
   20
Pane e Cioccolata 2-27-74:26
Panel Story 6-11-80:29
Panhandle 1-28-48:11
Panic Button 4-15-64:6
Panic in Chicago 7-14-31:22
Panic in Needle Park 5-26-71:13
Panic in the City 11-06-68:6
Panic in the Pullman (s) 8-19-
   36:16
Panic in the Streets 6-14-50:8
Panic in the Year Zero 7-04-62:6
Panic on the Air 4-22-36:29
Panicky-Picnic, The 2-26-10:15
Panico en el Transiberiano 10-25-
   72:22
Panier a Crabes, Le 7-13-60:6
Panique 12-11-46:8
Panische Zeiten 6-11-80:24

Panna Zazracnica 8-09-67:6
Panny z Wilka 7-25-79:20
Pano Ne Passera Pas 10-29-69:
17
Panorama Blue 2-27-74:26
Pantlaskas 2-03-60:6
Pantelei 5-31-78:23
Panthea 1-12-17:26
Panther's Claw, The 6-17-42:20
Panzer Gewoelbe, Das 3-23-27:
16
Paolo and Francesca 2-18-53:6
Paolo Barca, Maestro Elementare
Praticamente Nudista 6-18-
75:19
Paolo Il Caldo 11-28-73:16
Papa Corazon Se Quiere Casar
7-24-74:20
Papa les Petits Bateaux 12-29-71:6
Papa, Mama, the Maid and I 2-
09-55:11
Papa Sans le Savoir 5-03-32:19
Papa Tiene Novia 12-17-41:8
Papa's Delicate Condition 2-06-
63:6
Papa's First Outing 10-15-10:12
Papa's Hat 10-09-09:20
Papa's Honeymoon 10-16-09:12
Papa's Intrigues 8-09-39:18
Papa's Pest (s) 6-23-26:19
Papa's Vacation (s) 8-01-28:12
Papanicolis 11-17-71:22
Papaucshos 10-15-38:21
Paper Bullets 6-11-41:16
Paper Chase, The 9-12-73:36
Paper Gallows 2-22-50:6
Paper Hanging (s) 5-28-30:21
Paper Lion 10-02-68:28
Paper Moon 4-18-73:22
Paper Tiger 11-12-75:24
Paperback Hero 10-10-73:12
Papillon 12-12-73:16
Papillon Sur l'Epaule, Un 5-10-
78:27
Papinin's Diary 10-26-38:15
Pappi 5-27-36:15
Paprika 11-29-32:19 and 12-26-
33:26
Paprika--Kisasszony 12-27-32:54
Par le Sang des Autres 4-24-74:
18
Par Ordre Du Tsar 7-28-54:6
Par un Beau Matin d'Ete 3-17-
65:6
Parachute Athletes (s) 6-24-42:8
Parachute Battalion 7-16-41:8
Parachute Jumper 1-31-33:12
Parachute Nurse 7-29-42:8

Parade 5-22-74:19
Parade du Temps Perdu 12-22-
48:18
Parade of the West 2-05-30:28
Parades 5-24-72:24
Paradies 7-14-76:24
Paradies und Feuerhofen 7-08-
59:6 and 9-09-59:6
Paradiesgarten, Der 10-28-70:30
Paradine Case, The 12-31-47:10
Parading Pajamas (s) 6-09-31:18
Paradis de Satan, Le 10-05-38:21
Paradis Perdu 10-04-67:14
Paradis Retour 4-22-64:102
Paradis Terrestre 9-25-57:26
Paradise 10-06-26:50
Paradise 9-26-28:15 and 11-06-
29:31
Paradise 9-07-77:24
Paradise Alley 9-13-78:21
Paradise and Back (See: Paradis
Retour)
Paradise Canyon 9-18-35:32
Paradise Express 2-24-37:17
Paradise for Three 1-19-38:19
Paradise for Two 1-26-27:20
Paradise for Two 12-29-37:19
Paradise Garden 10-12-17:41
Paradise, Hawaiian Style 6-08-
66:6
Paradise Island 8-13-30:31
Paradise Isle (s) 5-29-26:20
Paradise Isle 7-28-37:27
Paradise Lost (See: Paradis Perdu)
Paradise Now 5-27-70:22
Paradiso Dell-Uomo 4-03-63:6
Paradistorg 3-30-77:19
Paragons, The (s) 2-20-29:14
Paragraph 173 11-13-29:32
Paraguelia 10-29-80:22
Parallax View, The 6-19-74:16
Parallels 10-15-80:66
Parallelstrasse, Die 1-22-64:6
Paramount en Parade 12-24-30:
21 (Also see: Paramount on
Parade)
Paramount Movietone (s) 11-21-
28:13
Paramount News (s) 8-03-27:16
Paramount on Parade 4-23-30:26
(Also see: Paramount en
Parade)
Paramount Pictorial (s) 3-25-31:
16; 4-08-31:18; 4-29-31:12;
7-14-31:17; 1-26-32:21; 5-17-
32:14; 8-02-32:15; 1-10-33:15
Paranoia 7-12-67:24
Paranoia 8-27-69:18

Paranoiac 4-10-63:6
Parapluies de Cherbourg, Les 1-29-64:20
Parash Pathar 5-21-58:16
Parashat Winchell 10-03-79:15
Parasite, The 2-18-25:41
Parasol Ant, The (s) 8-24-27:27
Parasuram 1-31-79:24
Paratroop Command 1-28-59:6
Parbeszed 7-15-64:22
Parce Plavog Neba 8-23-61:6
Parceiros de Aventura 8-20-80:21
Pardesi 5-21-58:16
Pardners 6-27-56:6
Pardon, The 8-06-15:17
Pardon My French 1-06-22:42
Pardon My French 8-22-51:10
Pardon My Gun 5-12-43:20
Pardon My Nerve 3-31-22:40
Pardon My Past 9-12-45:16
Pardon My Rhythm 5-03-44:23
Pardon My Sarong 8-05-42:8
Pardon My Stripes 4-22-42:18
Pardon Our Nerve 2-08-39:17
Pardon Us 8-25-31:14
Pardoned 10-15-15:21
Pardoned 7-18-28:31
Paree, Paree (s) 10-30-34:16
Parent Trap, The 5-03-61:26
Parentage 6-08-17:25
Parents on Trial 9-20-39:27
Parents Terribles, Les 1-19-49: 10
Parfum de la Dame en Noir 12-01-31:35
Parias de la Gloire 4-29-64:6
Parigi e Sempre Parigi 1-23-52:22
Parigi O Cara 9-12-62:16
Paris 11-13-29:38
Paris After Dark 10-06-43:8
Paris at Midnight 10-31-28:31
Paris au Mois d'Aout 1-26-66:6
Paris-Beguin 1-17-33:17
Paris Belongs to Us (See: Paris Nous Appartenir)
Paris Blues 9-27-61:7
Paris Bound 9-25-29:17
Paris Brule-t-Il (See: Is Paris Burning?)
Paris Calling 12-10-41:8
Paris Chante Toujours 2-27-52:16
Paris Commune 5-09-37:15
Paris Does Strange Things 3-06-57:6
Paris Fashions 3-07-13:14
Paris Fire Brigade 9-26-08:12
Paris Follies of 1956 12-28-55:6
Paris Girls 6-26-29:25

Paris Green 4-16-20:43
Paris Holiday 3-12-58:6
Paris Honeymoon 12-21-38:14
Paris in Spring 7-17-35:27
Paris Incident 8-18-54:7
Paris Interlude 7-31-34:14
Paris-Mediterranee 3-08-32:23
Paris Model 11-04-53:6
Paris N'Existe Pas 3-12-69:26
Paris--New York 5-15-40:18
Paris Nights (s) 9-08-31:15
Paris 1900 2-16-49:16 and 5-24-50:20
Paris Nous Appartenir 6-28-60:9
Paris of the Orient (s) 8-04-31:18
Paris on Parade (s) 1-10-33:15
Paris Orchestra du Conservatoire (s) 7-15-36:31
Paris Palace Hotel 11-07-56:6
Paris Playboys 3-10-54:6
Paris Secret 6-16-65:6
Paris Underground 8-22-45:20
Paris Vu Par 5-26-65:7
Paris When It Sizzles 3-18-64:6
Parisian, The 8-25-31:20
Parisian Gaieties (s) 5-27-31:56
Parisian Nights 6-03-25:34
Parisian Romance, A 1-14-16:19
Parisian Romance, A 12-16-21:36
Parisian Romance, A 10-18-32:26
Parisian Tigeress, The 4-04-19:67
Parisienne, Une 1-22-58:24
Parisiennes 4-11-28:12
Parisiennes, Les 1-31-62:6
Park Avenue Lodger 4-07-37:15
Park of Caserta, The 1-08-10:12
Park Row 8-06-52:6
Parked in Paree (s) 12-16-36:14
Parley Vous (s) 10-22-30:23
Parlez-Moi d'Amour 10-22-75:34
Parliamo di Donne 4-15-64:22
Parlor, Bedroom and Bath 7-30-20:32
Parlor, Bedroom and Bath 4-08-31:19
Parlor Pest, The 6-19-29:24
Parmi les Decombres 8-12-59:6
Parmigiana, La 4-17-63:7
Parnell 6-09-37:15
Parola di Ladro 4-03-57:24
Parole 7-01-36:12
Parole Fixer 2-07-40:16
Parole Girl 24-11-33:17
Parole, Inc. 1-05-49:58
Parole Racket 3-10-37:15

Paroled from the Big House 10-12-38:19
Paroled-to-Die 1-12-38:15
Parque de Madrid 6-03-59:6
Parranda 3-23-77:22
Parrish 3-22-61:15
Parson and the Outlaw 9-04-57:26
Parson of Panamint, The 9-15-16:26
Parson of Panamint, The 6-25-41:16
Parson's Prayer, The 12-04-09:13
Parson's Umbrella, The 1-22-10:14
Part de l'Ombre, La (See: Blind Desire)
Part des Lions, La 9-29-71:22
Part du Feu, La 1-11-78:27
Part of the Family 9-15-71:20
Part Time Wife, The 3-24-26:39
Part 2, Sounder 10-13-76:22
Part 2 Walking Tall 7-16-75:21
Parted (s) 9-08-26:20
Parted Curtains 10-07-21:44
Partie de Plaisir, La 1-01-75:14
Parting of the Trails, The 4-02-30:39
Partings (See: Pozegnania)
Partir 9-29-31:22
Partire 10-26-38:15
Partisami 8-21-74:24
Partizanske Price 8-10-60:6
Partner 9-18-68:6
Partners (s) 3-18-31:14
Partners 3-01-32:21
Partners 10-06-76:21
Partners Again 2-17-26:40
Partners in Crime 5-02-28:14
Partners in Crime 10-20-37:12
Partners in Time 4-24-46:8
Partners of the Night 3-05-20:63
Partners of the Plains 2-16-38:17
Partners of the Sunset 4-12-22:41
Partners of the Tide 4-08-21:40
Partners of the Trail 9-01-31:34
Partners of the Trail 3-29-44:21
Partners Three 4-11-19:54
Partners Two (s) 4-11-33:17
Parts the Clonus Horror 11-14-79:22
Party, The 3-20-68:6
Party Crashers, The 9-17-58:6
Party Girl 1-08-30:89
Party Girl 10-22-58:6
Party Husband 5-20-31:17

Party Wire 5-22-35:16
Party's Over, The 10-16-34:16
Party's Over, The 5-19-65:30
Parvi Urok 5-25-60:7
Pas de Pitie Pour les Femmes 5-02-51:12
Pas de Problems 7-23-75:20
Pas de Roses Pour Oss 117 8-21-68:26
Pas Folle la Guepe 12-13-72:20
Pas Koji Je Voleo Vozove 2-22-78:19
Pas Paa Ryggen Professor 8-31-77:19
Pas Perdus, Les 6-17-64:6
Pas Question le Samedi 2-24-65:6
Pas Si Mechant que Ca ... 2-05-75:26
Pas Sur la Bouche 10-30-31:29
Pasazerka 12-25-63:6
Pascual Duarte 5-19-76:23
Pasi 4-23-80:19
Pasion Desnuda, La 7-08-53:18
Pasja 8-02-78:18
Paskutine Atostogu Diena 8-04-65:6
Pasquale 5-26-16:20
Pasqualino: Settelbellezze 1-14-76:20
Passage, The 2-28-79:20
Passage du Rhin, Le 9-14-60:6
Passage to Marseilles 2-16-44:10
Passage West 5-30-51:6
Passager Clandestin, Le 9-03-58:6
Passagers, Les 3-09-77:17
Passante, La 7-18-51:20
Passaporto Rosso 9-09-36:17
Passaros de Asas Cartadas 7-31-63:12
Passatore, Il (See: Bullet for Stefano, A)
Passe du Diable, La 11-11-59:6
Passe Montagne 7-26-78:21
Passe Simple, Le 7-27-77:23
Passe Ton Bac d'Abord 10-03-79:14
Passeggiata, La 1-27-54:26
Passenger, The (See: Pasazerka)
Passenger, The 3-19-75:29
Passenger of the Rain 1-28-70:23
Passeport Pour le Monde 11-18-59:6
Passeport 13,444 7-21-31:62
Passers By 3-31-16:25

335 •

Passers-By 6-25-20:33
Passing Mr. Quinn 8-29-28:31
Passing of the Third Floor Back,
The 9-25-35:42 and 5-06-
36:19
Passing Shadow, The 2-12-10:17
Passing Through 8-31-77:30
Passing Thru 9-09-21:44
Passion 12-17-20:40
Passion 10-24-51:20
Passion 10-06-54:6
Passion, En 5-06-70:20
Passion Flower, The 4-08-21:40
Passion Flower, The 12-24-30:
20
Passion for Life (See: Ecole
Buissonniere, L')
Passion Island 12-21-27:22
Passion Island 5-12-43:20
Passion of Anna, The (See: Pas-
sion, En)
Passion of Joan of Arc, The 4-
10-29:25
Passion of St. Francis, The 12-
20-32:16
Passion of Slow Fire, The (See:
Mort de Belle, La)
Passion Song 3-20-29:28
Passionate Adventure, The 6-17-
25:37
Passionate Friends 12-06-23:26
Passionate Plumber, The 3-15-
32:14
Passionate Stranger, The 3-06-
57:6
Passionate Strangers 7-06-66:6
Passionate Summer, The 10-01-
58:6
Passionate Youth 7-08-25:38
Passione Secondo San Matteo, La
9-07-49:18
Passionment 10-18-32:15
Passionnelle 2-04-48:20
Passions of Carol, The 3-19-75:
36
Passion's Pathway 9-17-24:28
Passion's Playground 6-11-20:34
Passkey to Danger 8-14-46:10
Passover Plot, The 11-03-76:27
Passport Husband 7-27-38:17
Passport to Adventure 2-02-44:18
Passport to Alcatraz 6-19-40:16
Passport to Hell 8-30-32:21
Passport to Pimlico 5-18-49:8
Passport to Shame 11-26-58:6
Passport to Suez 8-18-43:26
Passport to Treason 9-19-56:22
Password Is Courage, The

10-17-62:6
Past of Mary Holmes 5-02-33:
13
Pasteboard Crown 5-19-22:41
Pasteur 11-13-35:17 and 2-12-
36:31
Pastor Hall 6-12-40:16 and 7-
31-40:104
Pastorale, La 3-18-31:14
Pastorale 6-28-78:22 and
8-02-78:18
Pat and Mike 5-14-52:6
Pat and Patachon 3-20-29:13
Pat Garrett and Billy the Kid 5-
30-73:13
Pat West and His Middies (s)
9-19-28:12
Patagonia Rebelde, La 7-10-74:
16
Patata Bollente, La 2-20-80:26
Patate 11-18-64:7
Patate 10-29-69:17
Patates, Les 12-10-69:28
Patayin Mo Sa Sindaksi Barbara
9-25-74:16
Patch of Blue, A 12-08-65:6
Patchwork Girl of Oz 9-26-14:
22
Patents Pending (s) 3-21-33:16
Path of Happiness, The 2-11-16:
21
Pathe Audio Review (s)
5-19-26:20   3-19-30:20
5-28-26:21   4-23-30:24
6-02-26:15   7-02-30:25
7-14-26:19   1-07-31:23
9-08-26:20   2-25-31:12
9-22-26:20   8-11-31:30
12-25-29:20   6-28-32:14
1-22-30:17
Pathe Sound News (s)
11-14-28:17   4-03-29:11
12-19-28:12   4-10-29:16
1-09-29:10   4-24-29:13
1-23-29:18   5-15-29:20
2-13-29:13   6-19-29:24
2-20-29:14   7-03-29:17
2-27-29:80   7-17-29:42
3-06-29:12   7-24-29:29
3-20-29:12   7-31-29:17
3-27-29:12
Pather Panchali 6-06-56:6
Pathetic Symphony 12-19-28:23
Pathfinder, The 12-17-52:6
Paths in Palestine (s) 5-31-32:14
Paths of Enemies 11-06-33:21
Paths of Glory 11-20-57:6
Paths of Paradise 7-01-25:32

• 336

Peacock Fan, The 5-22-29:27
Peacock Feathers 1-13-26:43
Peak of Fate, The 6-17-25:36
Peaks of Destiny 11-30-27:19
Peanut Vendor, The (s) 7-11-33: 15
Pearl, The 2-11-48:14
Pearl Fisher, The 12-21-07:10
Pearl of Death, The 8-30-44:10
Pearl of Paradise, The 11-10-16:24
Pearl of the Punjab, A 7-10-14: 21
Pearl of the South Pacific 7-13-55:20
Pearls of the Crown 4-13-38:15 (Also see: Perles de la Couronne, Les)
Peasants 5-29-35:34 and 9-04-35: 31
Peasants' Paradise (s) 1-12-32: 15
Peau d'Ane 12-30-70:16
Peau de Banane 11-13-63:17
Peau de Torpedo, La 6-24-70:22
Peau d'Espion 4-26-67:6
Peau Douce, La 5-13-64:6
Peau et les Os, Le 5-17-61:7
Peaux Noires 3-08-32:25
Pecado de Una Madre, El 4-25-62:6
Pecado Mortal 9-09-70:22
Peccati In Famiglia 4-09-75:30
Peccato Che Sia Una Canaglia 3-16-55:6
Peccato Veniale 2-13-74:14
Pecheur d'Islande 9-25-35: 42
Pecheur d'Islande 7-22-59:6
Pechmarie 4-24-35:13
Peck's Bad Boy 5-30-08:11
Peck's Bad Boy 4-29-21:41
Peck's Bad Boy 10-09-34:18
Peck's Bad Boy with the Circus 11-23-38:14
Peck's Bad Girl 9-20-18:46
Pecora Nera, La 11-27-68:26
Pecos River 11-28-51:6
Peddler and the Lady, The 10-12-49:20
Peddlin' in Society 5-18-49:20
Pedestrian, The 2-20-74:14
Pedro Paramo 5-17-67:18
Pedro Paramo 9-28-77:22
Pedro So 5-10-72:21
Peep in the Deep, A (s) 7-30-30:16
Peeper 10-01-75:24

Peeping Tom (s) 11-14-33:17
Peeping Tom 4-20-60:8
Peeping Toms 2-07-73:18
Peer Gynt 9-24-15:20
Peg Leg Pete (s) 5-03-32:14
Peg o' My Heart 1-25-23:41
Peg o' My Heart 5-23-33:19
Peg of Old Drury 9-11-35:17 and 4-15-36:23
Peg of the Pirates 5-31-18:30
Peggy 1-21-16:27
Peggy 6-14-50:8
Peking Blonde (See: Blonde de Pekin, La)
Peking Express 6-20-51:6
Peking Remembered 3-01-67:6
Pele 5-25-77:21
Pelea Cubana Contra los Demonios, Una 8-09-72:20
Pelican, The 3-06-74:26
Pelicula, La 10-01-75:28
Peligros de Juventud 11-23-60: 20
Pell Street Mystery, The 1-21-25:36
Pelle Viva, La 5-15-63:21
Pelnia 6-11-80:29
Pelo Nel Mondo, Il 4-22-64:102
Pelota de Trapo 9-22-48:8
Peloton d'Execution 12-05-45:16
Peluqueria de Senoras 12-17-41:8
Pelvis 3-09-77:16
Penal Code, The 3-07-33:54
Penalties (s) 10-13-31:14
Penalty, The 11-19-20:34
Penalty, The 3-12-41:14
Pendin Heng Kuam Rak 11-26-80: 14
Pendleton Roundup, The (s) 4-02-30:18 and 11-19-30:21
Pendulum 1-15-69:6
Penelope 11-09-66:6
Penguin Pool Murder, The 12-27-32:15
Penitentes, The 12-03-15:21
Penitentiary 1-26-38:15
Penitentiary 12-26-79:12
Penn of Pennsylvania 8-27-41:20
Pennies from Heaven 12-16-36: 14
Pennington's Choice 11-05-15:22
Penny of Top Hill 6-17-21:34
Penny Princess 7-23-52:18
Penny Serenade 4-16-41:16
Penon de las Animas, El 5-10-44:10
Penrod 2-24-22:34
Penrod and His Twin Brother

1-12-38:14
Penrod and Sam 6-28-23:22
Penrod and Sam 9-29-31:22
Penrod and Sam 3-17-37:14
Penrod's Double Trouble 7-27-38:17
Pensaci Giacomino 1-20-37:15
Pension Schoeller 9-20-32:15
Pensionnaire, La 10-06-54:22
Penthouse 9-12-33:17
Penthouse, The (See: Attico, L')
Penthouse, The 7-05-67:6
Penthouse Blues (s) 1-14-31:12
Penthouse Party 2-19-36:32
Penthouse Rhythm 6-06-45:12
Pentimento 3-26-80:21
Penultima Donzela 1-14-70:20
People Against O'Hara, The 8-22-51:10
People Are Funny 10-17-45:8
People Born in April (s) 4-09-30:22
People Born in August (s) 8-13-30:15
People Born in October (s) 10-15-30:25
People Meet and Sweet Music Fills the Air (See: Menneske Moed Og Saed Musik Opstaa I Hjertet)
People Next Door, The 8-05-70:20
People of France, The 12-08-37:17
People of Russia, The (s) 2-03-43:14
People of the Soul 4-24-29:22
People of the Wind 10-27-76:26
People on Wheels 11-02-66:6
People That Time Forgot, The 6-22-77:17
People vs. Dr. Kildare, The 5-07-41:12
People vs. John Doe, The 12-15-16:35
People Virus, The (s) 4-02-30:18
People Will Talk 6-19-35:21
People Will Talk 8-22-51:10
People's Avengers 6-21-44:12
People's Choice, The 3-27-46:12
People's Enemy, The 5-01-35:17
Pepe 12-21-60:6
Pepe Le Moko 3-24-37:17
Pepita Jimenez 6-25-75:24
Pepo 10-16-35:23
Pepote 7-25-56:6 and 12-19-56:6
Pepper 8-12-36:18
Peppermint Frappe 9-06-67:20

Peppery Salt (s) 9-02-36:18
Peppy Polly 4-11-19:56
Pequenda Madrecita, La 12-27-44:9
Per 1-29-75:16
Per Amare Ofelia 8-21-74:20
Per Grazia Ricevuta 3-31-71:6
Per Jom Phen 10-29-80:20
Per le Antiche Scale 8-27-75:14
Per Motivi di Gelosia 5-27-70:22
Per Qualche Dollaro In Piu 2-16-66:6
Per un Pugno Di Dollari 11-18-64:22
Per Uomini Soli 6-28-39:20
Perceval (see: Perceval Le Gallois)
Perceval Le Gallois 9-13-78:36
Perche Si Uccide Un Magistrato? 10-01-75:28
Percy 3-25-25:37
Percy 3-03-71:22
Pere Noel a les Yeux Bleus, Le 5-11-66:6
Pere Tranquille, Le 12-04-46:13
Perez Garcia, Los 3-08-50:20
Perfect Alibi, The 4-22-31:18
Perfect Clown, The 3-10-26:40
Perfect Clue, The 3-20-35:17
Perfect Couple, A 4-04-79:20
Perfect Crime, A 4-22-21:41
Perfect Crime, The 8-08-28:20
Perfect Day, A (s) 7-17-29:42
Perfect Flapper, The 6-25-24:26
Perfect Friday 10-07-70:14
Perfect Furlough, The 10-08-54:6
Perfect Gentleman, A 12-25-35:15
Perfect Lady, A 12-06-18:37
Perfect Lover, The 9-12-19:52
Perfect Marriage, The 11-20-46:22
Perfect Match, A (s) 4-02-30:18
Perfect Sap, The 1-12-27:16
Perfect Snob, The 11-19-41:9
Perfect Specimen, The 9-29-37:15
Perfect Strangers 9-05-45:15
Perfect Strangers 3-01-50:6
Perfect Suitor, The (s) 3-22-32:13
Perfect "36," The 12-12-14:27
Perfect Understanding 2-28-33:14
Perfect Woman, The 7-30-20:33
Perfect Woman, The 6-01-49:20
Perfectionist, The 4-30-52:18
(Also see: Grand Patron, Un)
Performance 8-05-70:20
Perilous Holiday 6-05-46:13
Perilous Journey, A 5-13-53:18

Perilous Waters 1-21-48:8
Perils of Divorce, The 6-16-16: 25
Perils of Pauline, The 4-10-14: 21
Perils of Pauline, The 5-28-47: 15
Perils of Pauline, The 5-10-67:6
Perils of the Jungle (serial) 7-27-27:21
Period of Adjustment 10-31-62:6
Periodista Turner, El 10-30-68: 28
Periplanissis 10-31-79:20
Perjury 8-19-21:35
Perjury 5-22-29:24
Perla W Koronie 5-17-72:30
Perlas Ng Silangan 8-27-69:18
Perle, La 8-09-32:22
Perles de la Couronne, Les 5-26-37:14 (Also see: Pearls of the Crown)
Perlicky Na Dne 8-04-65:28
Permanent Wave, The 8-03-27: 19
Permanent Wave (s) 9-25-29:17
Permette? Rocco Papaleo 12-01-71:22
Permission, La 11-08-67:24
Permission to Kill 12-03-75:22
Pero No Vas a Cambiar Nunca Margarita? 11-22-78:22
Perrak 5-27-70:22
Perri 8-21-57:6
Perro, El 8-17-77:20 and 9-07-77:44
Perro de Alambre 11-19-80:21
Persecution 11-13-74:56
Persecution and Assassination of Jean-Paul Marat As Performed by the Inmates of the Asylum of Charenton Under the Direction of the Marquis De Sade, The 2-08-67:6
Persecution Hasta Valencia (See: Narco Men, The)
Perseguidor, El 4-03-63:7
Pershing's Crusaders 5-31-18:29
Persiane Chiuse (See: Behind Closed Shutters)
Persona 11-30-66:6
Persona Honrada Se Necesita 9-03-41:17
Personal Affair 10-28-53:6
Personal Conduct of Henry, The 11-20-09:13
Personal Maid 9-08-31:15
Personal Maid's Secret 12-11-35:19

Personal Property 4-21-37:14
Personal Secretary 9-28-38:14
Personality 2-26-30:39
Personality Kid, The 8-07-34:12
Personality Kid, The 8-14-46:10
Personality Plus (s) 4-22-42:20
Personals 5-10-72:34
Personel 4-21-76:23
Persons in Hiding 1-25-39:11
Persuader, The 11-13-57:6
Persuasive Peggy 11-09-17:54
Peruvaziambalan 2-13-80:17
Pervy Den Mira 9-09-59:6
Pesma 8-23-61:6
Pest, The 4-25-19:80
Pest, The (s) 2-04-31:16
Pest, The (s) 5-31-32:14
Pest, The (s) 5-15-34:14
Pest of Honor (s) 5-30-31:16
Pest Pilot (s) 9-03-41:17
Pesti Mese 6-16-37:13
Pesti Szerelem 5-15-34:27
Pestuplenie I Nakazanie 9-02-70: 40
Pet Holek Na Krku 7-24-68:25
Pet Minuta Raja 8-19-59:6
Pet of the Big Horn Ranch 10-16-09:12
Pet Z Milionu 9-23-59:18
Petachki-Lawotschki 12-08-76:19
Petal on the Current, The 8-08-19:48
Pete and Repeat (s) 3-18-31:14
Pete Burke, Reporter (s) 4-26-32:13
Pete Kelly's Blues 8-03-55:6
Pete 'n' Tillie 12-13-72:15
Pete Seeger ... A Song and a Stone 2-02-72:16
Pete Smith's Scrapbook (s) 5-20-42:8
Peter 2-05-35:31
Peter Ibbetson 10-21-21:35
Peter Ibbetson 11-13-35:16
Peter im Schnee 8-04-37:25
Peter Pan 12-31-24:26
Peter Pan 1-14-53:6
Peter Rabbit and the Tales of Beatrix Potter (See: Tales of Beatrix Potter, The)
Peter the First 12-22-37:24
Peter the Great 6-28-23:22
Peter Vinogradov 5-08-35:45
Peter Voss, der Held des Tages 4-13-60:20
Peterson 8-28-74:20
Peterson and Bendel 9-26-33:20
Pete's Dragon 11-09-77:16

Planet of the Vampires 12-01-65:
20
Planete Sauvage, La 5-16-73:6
Plank, The 5-10-67:20
Planque, La 10-10-62:6
Planter's Wife, The 11-07-08:12
Planter's Wife, The 10-01-52:6
Plastered in Paris 9-26-28:14
Plasterers, The (s) 3-19-30:20
Plastic Age, The 7-21-26:14
Plastic Dome of Norma Jean, The
11-02-66:6
Platanov 1-19-77:22
Platinum Blonde 11-03-31:27
Platinum Blondes (s) 10-27-31:
19
Platinum High School 5-11-60:6
Play Boy, The (s) 8-31-30:15
Play Dirty 1-15-69:34
Play Girl 3-22-32:13
Play Girl 12-18-40:16
Play It Again, Sam 4-19-72:18
Play It As It Lays 9-13-72:24
Play Misty for Me 9-15-71:6
Play Safe 4-20-27:25
Play Time 12-27-67:7
Playboy of Paris, The 11-15-30:
30 (Also see: Petit Cafe, Le)
Players, The 8-06-75:17
Players 6-13-79:15
Playful Fun (s) 4-22-31:18
Playful Pan (s) 5-27-31:56
Playful Tenant 2-01-08:11
Playgirl 4-21-54:6
Playgirls and the Vampire, The
5-06-64:17
Playing Around 4-02-30:30
Playing Double 3-08-23:30
Playing It Wild 5-30-23:32
Playing Square 8-12-21:34
Playing the Game 4-19-18:44
Playing with Fire 4-28-16:28
Playing with Fire (s) 9-01-31:21
Playing with Souls 5-06-25:47
Playmates 11-12-41:9
Playmates (See: Femmes, Les)
Plaything of Broadway 3-18-21:
34
Playthings of Desire 5-13-25:39
Playthings of Passion 5-30-19:75
Playtime (See: Recreation, La)
Playtime (See: Play Time)
Playtime in Hawaii (s) 2-04-42:8
Plaza Suite 5-12-71:19
Plazmas (s) 6-02-26:15
Plea for Passion, A (See: Bigamist)
Pleasant Young Gentleman, A 11-
20-63:6

Pleasantville 8-25-76:22
Please Believe Me 3-11-50:12
Please Don't Eat the Daisies 3-
23-60:6
Please Excuse Me (s) 7-14-26:19
Please Get Married 11-07-19:97
Please (s) 11-14-33:17
Please Go 'Way and Let Me Sleep
(s) 8-04-31:18
Please Help Emily 11-30-17:45
Please Murder Me 2-08-56:6
Please, Not Now! (See: Bride Sur
le Cou, La)
Please Teacher 3-03-37:14
Please Turn Over 1-20-60:7
Pleasing Grandpa (s) 7-14-34:15
Pleasure 3-15-32:29
Pleasure at Her Majesty's, The
11-24-76:19
Pleasure Before Business 5-04-
27:22
Pleasure Buyers 2-17-26:41
Pleasure Crazed 7-17-29:53
Pleasure Cruise 4-04-33:15
Pleasure Game, The 3-04-70:18
Pleasure Garden, The 11-03-26:
20
Pleasure Girls, The 6-02-25:6
Pleasure Mad 1-10-24:26
Pleasure of His Company, The
5-10-61:6
Pleasure Palace 5-23-73:19
Pleasure Seekers, The 12-30-64:6
Pleasures of the Rich 4-14-26:38
Pledgemasters, The 9-01-71:26
Plein de Super, Le 4-07-75:26
Plein Soleil 3-23-60:6
Pleins Feux Sur l'Assassin 4-19-
61:6
Pleins Feux Sur Stanislas 10-13-
65:6
Pleneno Yato 5-30-62:6
Plern 5-30-79:26
Ples U Kisi 8-09-61:6
Pleure Pas la Bouche Pleine 11-
28-73:18
Pleut Sur Santiago, Il 12-10-75:
26
Pleut Toujours Ou C'Est Mouille,
Il 6-12-74:24
Ploetzliche Einsamkeit Des Konrad
Steiner, Die 7-07-76:16
Plokhoy Krhoshyi Chelovek 6-26-
74:22
Plomienne Serca 10-13-37:17
Plot Thickens, The 12-16-36:15
Plot to Kill Roosevelt, The 11-
03-48:14

347 •

Pork Chop Hill 5-06-59:6
Porn Flakes 3-23-77:24
Porno Pop 6-23-71:20
Pornografi--En Musical 8-18-71:22
Pornography Copenhagen 1970 4-29-70:176
Pornography in Denmark 4-15-70:17
Porr I Skandalskolan 8-14-74:16
Porridge 7-25-79:20
Port Afrique 5-23-56:6
Port de Desir, Le 6-29-55:6
Port of Call (See: Hamnstad)
Port of Desire (See: Fille de Hambourg, La)
Port of 40 Thieves 9-06-44:10
Port of Hate 8-16-39:16
Port of Hell 1-19-55:6
Port of Lost Dreams, The 4-03-35:17
Port of Missing Girls 8-01-28:18
Port of Missing Girls 4-06-38:14
Port of Missing Men 5-15-14:22
Port of Missing Point 10-29-30:27
Port of New York 11-23-49:25
Port of Seven Seas 6-29-38:12
Port of Shadows (See: Quai des Brumes, Le)
Port of Shame (See: Amants du Tage, Les)
Port Said 5-12-48:20
Port Sinister 2-18-53:6
Porte des Lilas 10-23-57:6
Porte du Large, La 11-25-36:15
Portentosa Vida Del Padre, La 9-13-78:21
Portes de Feu, Les 5-03-72:22
Portes de la Nuit, Les 12-18-46:14
Portia on Trial 11-10-37:19
Portland Expose 8-14-57:6
Portnoy's Complaint 6-21-72:24
Port Das Caixas 5-15-63:21
Portrait d'un Assassin, Le 1-18-50:6
Portrait d'un Assassin, Le 1-19-50:6
Portrait de Marianne, Le 10-14-70:30
Portrait de Son Pere, Le 2-24-54:6
Portrait from Life 12-22-48:6
Portrait in Black 6-08-60:6
Portrait of a Mobster 3-29-61:6
Portrait of a 60% Perfect Man 5-28-80:45

Portrait of a Woman 5-01-46:8
Portrait of Chieko 3-20-68:6
Portrait of Clare 8-02-50:16
Portrait of Fidel Castro 7-09-75:24
Portrait of Innocence 6-16-48:8
Portrait of Jason 10-04-67:12
Portrait of Jennie 12-29-48:6
Portrait of Lenin (See: Lenin v Polshe)
Portrait of the Artist As a Young Man, A 4-25-79:18
Portrait Robot 11-21-62:6
Portraits of Women (See: Naisenkuvia)
Portret S Dojdem 7-12-78:18
Ports of Call 3-25-25:39 and 5-06-25:47
Ports of Call (s) 8-25-31:24 and 9-01-31:21
Porzellan (s) 10-20-31:21
Poseban Tretman 5-14-80:19 and 5-21-80:21
Poseidon Adventure, The 12-13-72:15
Position and Backswing (s) 5-16-33:17
Poslednata Dounma 5-22-74:26
Posledni Ruze Od Casanovy 7-20-66:7
Posledno Liato 7-24-74:22
Poslizg 8-16-72:14
Posljednji Podvig Diverzanta Oblaka 8-09-78:22
Posowi Mnja W Dal Swjet Luju 7-05-78:17
Posse 5-28-75:18
Posse from Hell 3-15-61:6
Possedees, Les 5-16-56:6
Possessed 12-01-31:15
Possessed 6-04-47:16
Possession 2-10-22:34
Possession of Joel Delaney, The 5-17-72:20
Post Office Investigator 9-28-49:6
Postal Inspector 9-09-36:17
Postav Dam, Zasad Strca 3-05-80:26
Postava K Podpirani 5-06-64:16
Postgraduate, The 9-09-70:16
Postman Always Rings Twice, The 3-20-46:8
Postman Didn't Ring, The 6-03-42:9
Postman Goes to War, The (See: Facteur S'En Va-T-En Guerre, Le)

Postmark for Danger 1-25-56:6
Postmaster, The 3-17-26:30
Postmaster's Daughter, The 8-21-46:18
Posto, Il 9-06-61:6
Postschi 7-12-72:28
Pot-Bouille 12-04-57:22
Pot Carriers, The 5-30-62:23
Pot Luck 4-22-36:29
Pot O'Gold 4-09-41:16
Potash and Perlmutter 9-13-23:28
Potato Fritz 5-26-76:19
Potemkin (See: Cruiser Potemkin and Potemkin, The)
Potemkin, The 12-08-26:17 (Also see: Cruiser Potemkin)
Potere, Il 9-22-71:14
Poto and Cabengo 12-12-79:23
Potop 9-25-74:16
Potota, La 7-12-61:7
Pots, Pans and Poetry 3-04-11:18
Potters, The 1-19-27:18
Poudre d'Escampette, La 9-22-71:18
Poule, La 6-06-33:15
Pounce 1-12-72:14
Pound 8-19-70:16
Poupee, La 1-28-21:41
Poupee, La 5-09-62:7
Pour Clemence 8-31-77:30
Pour la Suite de Monde 5-15-63:6
Pour le Meilleur et Pour le Pire 10-01-75:26
Pour Reposer Ma Flute (s) 2-25-31:12
Pour un Sou d'Amour 3-15-32:21
Pourquoi Israel? 6-20-73:20
Pourquoi l'Amerique 11-05-69:15
Pourquoi Pas? 12-14-77:12
Pourquoi Viens-Tu Si Tard? 8-19-59:16
Pourvu Qu'On Ait l'Ivresse 10-16-74:18
Poussiere Sur la Ville 7-10-68:6
Poveri Ma Belli 2-27-57:6
Poverty in the Valley of Plenty 10-06-48:11
Poverty of Riches, A 11-25-21:43
Povestj Plamennykh Let 5-17-61:7
Povra Tak Otpisanih 8-17-77:22
Povratak 8-15-79:28
Powder Burns 4-07-71:24
Powder My Back 8-08-28:12
Powder River 5-13-53:18
Powder River Rustlers 2-08-50:11
Powder Town 5-13-42:8
Powdersmoke Range 3-11-36:15
Power 10-25-18:36
Power 7-18-28:31
Power 11-28-28:20

Power 10-09-34:18
Power, The 1-24-68:6
Power Among Men 3-11-59:6
Power and the Glory, The 8-23-18:41
Power and the Glory, The 8-22-33:22
Power and the Land 10-02-40:25
Power and the Prize, The 9-12-56:6
Power Behind the Nation, The (s) 9-17-47:16
Power Divide, The 9-27-23:30
Power Drive 4-09-41:16
Power of a Lie 1-05-23:41
Power of Darkness 10-31-28:31
Power of Evil, The 9-29-16:25
Power of Evil, The 8-14-29:31
Power of Labor, The 9-26-08:12
Power of Silence, The 12-05-28:27
Power of the Press, The 12-05-28:19
Power of the Press, The 2-24-43:14
Power of the Weak, The 6-16-26:18
Power of the Whistler, The 3-28-45:19
Power of Wong Fai-Hung Shakes the City of Five Goats, The 2-21-68:6
Power Play 8-30-78:28
Power Within, The 2-10-22:35
Powers Girl, The 12-23-42:8
Powers That Prey 3-15-18:44
Pozdravi Mariju, Sedmina 8-20-69:28
Pozegnania 7-29-59:6
Pozo, El (See: Well, The)
Pozor 3-14-33:14
Practen I Vejlby 9-20-72:18
Practically Yours 12-20-44:8
Praeriens Skrappe Drenge 9-30-70:24
Prairie, The 8-25-48:8
Prairie Badmen 7-24-46:26
Prairie Chickens 7-14-43:18
Prairie Express 12-03-47:11
Prairie Justice 11-30-38:12
Prairie King, The 5-25-27:21
Prairie Law 6-26-40:18
Prairie Moon 10-19-38:27
Prairie Pioneers 2-26-41:18
Prairie Roundup 1-24-51:6
Prairie Rustlers 1-23-46:12
Prairie Schooners 11-13-40:16
Prairie Stranger 9-03-41:17
Prairie Thunder 12-01-37:29

Prairie Wife, The 5-13-25:39
Praise Agent, The 8-08-19:48
Praise Marx and Pass the Ammu-
    nition 9-23-70:13
Pranke, Die 12-01-31:35
Prapanch 8-15-62:6
Prasad 12-31-75:15
Prata Palomares 5-10-72:20
Praterbuben 2-26-47:11
Pratidwandi 9-08-71:26
Prato, Il 9-05-79:23
Pratyusha 2-27-80:27
Prawo I Piese 7-29-64:8
Praznovanje Pomadi 8-16-78:18
Pre Istine 8-14-68:28
Prea Mic Prentru Un Rasboiu Atat
    de Mare 10-14-70:30
Prebroiavante Na Divite Zaitsi 8-
    21-74:22
Precipice, The 11-19-58:26
Prediction, The (s) 8-15-28:17
Predstava Hamlet U Mrdusi Donjoj
    8-22-73:19
Prefetto Di Fero, Il 11-16-77:21
Prehistoric Women 1-03-51:67
Prehistoric Women 1-25-67:6
Preis Fuer Ueberleben, Der 2-
    13-80:38
Prejudice 2-23-49:11
Prelude a la Gloire 7-12-50:16
Prelude to Fame 5-10-50:16
Prelude to Madness 11-02-49:22
Prelude to Victory (s) 1-06-43:
    50 (Also see: March of Time
    Newsreels)
Prelude to War 5-12-43:8 (Also
    see: "Why We Fight" Films)
Preludio a Espana 5-10-72:48
Preludio d'Amore 2-11-48:14
Premature Burial 3-14-62:6
Premia 12-03-75:28
Premier Rendez-Vous (See Her
    First Affair)
Premier Voyage 7-02-80:18
Premiere 2-24-37:19
Premiere Fois, La 12-01-76:38
Premieres Armes, Les 9-05-50:20
Premonition, The 11-26-75:20
Prenez Garde a la Peinture 5-16-
    33:25
Prep and Pep 12-26-28:24
Prepared to Die 12-27-23:27
Preparez Vos Mouchers 1-11-78:
    27
Presagio 10-09-74:19
Prescott Kid, The 10-21-36:17
Prescription for Romance 12-22-
    37:17

Presenting Lily Mars 4-28-43:8
President, The 1-23-29:43
President, Le 3-15-61:6
President Haudecoeur, La 5-08-
    40:22
President Vanishes, The 12-11-
    34:19
Presidentessa 12-10-52:18
President's Analyst, The 12-20-
    67:14
President's Lady, The 3-11-53:6
President's Mystery, The 10-21-
    36:15
President's Special, The 2-19-
    10:15
Pressed for Time 12-14-66:19
Pressure 12-01-76:38
Pressure of Guilt 2-05-64:16
Pressure Point 9-12-62:6
Prestige 2-09-32:19
Presuda 8-17-77:22
Prete Sposato, Il 1-20-71:13
Pretender, The 10-18-18:39
Pretender, The 8-20-47:16
Pretenders, The 8-25-16:23
Pretres Interdits 1-02-74:15
Pretty Baby 7-26-50:10
Pretty Baby 4-05-78:23
Pretty Boy Floyd 1-20-60:7
Pretty Clothes 1-18-28:19
Pretty Girl of Nice 9-18-09:13
Pretty Ladies 7-15-25:32
Pretty Maids All in a Row 3-03-
    71:22
Pretty Mrs. Smith 4-23-15:18
Pretty or Plain, They All Get
    Married 9-18-40:16
Pretty Poison 9-18-68:6
Pretty Polly 11-01-67:7
Pretty Sister of Jose, The 6-04-
    15:18
Preview Murder Mystery, The 3-
    25-36:15
Prey, The 10-01-20:35
Pri Nikogo 1-14-76:21
Price for Folly, A 6-04-15:18
    and 12-31-15:25
Price He Paid, The 11-21-14:27
Price Mark, The 10-26-17:29
Price of a Good Time, The 11-23-
    17:43
Price of a Party, The 11-26-24:
    52
Price of Applause, A 8-09-18:32
Price of Fame The 2-19-10:15
Price of Fame, The 11-03-16:25
Price of Happiness, The 2-25-16:
    23

Prisons de Femmes 11-09-38:17
Priu Cenusa Imperial 7-28-76:20
Privat-Sekretaerin Heiratet 12-09-36:13
Private Affairs 7-15-25:38
Private Affairs 6-12-40:16
Private Affairs of Bel Ami, The 2-26-47:10
Private Afternoons of Pamela Mann, The 2-26-75:20
Private Angelo 7-13-49:16
Private Beat 10-18-18:38
Private Benjamin 10-08-80:20
Private Buckaroo 6-03-42:8
Private Collection 6-28-72:18
Private Detective 12-06-39:14
Private Detective 62 7-11-33:15
Private Engagement, A (s) 10-08-30:22
Private Enterprise, A 11-19-75:18
Private Eyes, The 1-26-77:30
Private Eyes, The 11-26-80:15
Private Files of J. Edgar Hoover, The 1-11-78:27
Private Hell 36 9-01-54:6
Private Izzy Murphy 11-10-26:14
Private Jones 3-28-33:15
Private Lessons (s) 4-10-34:13
Private Life of a Cat, The (s) 10-06-48:11
Private Life of an Actor, The 9-01-48:20
Private Life of Don Juan, The 12-18-34:12
Private Life of Helen of Troy, The (See: Helen of Troy)
Private Life of Henry VIII, The (See: Henry VIII)
Private Life of Louis XIV, The 1-15-36:19
Private Life of Sherlock Holmes, The 10-28-70:17
Private Lives 12-22-31:15
Private Lives of Adam and Eve, The 1-18-61:6
Private Lives of Elizabeth and Essex, The 10-04-39:12
Private Navy of Sgt. O'Farrell, The 5-08-58:6
Private Number 6-17-36:23
Private Nurse 7-30-41:18
Private Parts 9-27-72:6
Private Pooley 12-19-62:7
Private Potter 1-02-63:6
Private Property 4-13-60:20
Private Right, The 12-21-66:6
Private Road 9-01-71:22

Private Scandal, A 6-17-21:34
Private Scandal, A 3-08-32:25
Private Scandal, A 6-19-34:27
Private Smith of the USA (s) 10-21-42:34
Private Snuffy Smith 2-25-42:8
Private War of Major Benson, The 6-01-55:6
Private Wives 6-20-33:11
Private Worlds 4-03-35:17
Private's Affair, A 7-22-59:6
Private's Progress, A 3-14-56:23
Privatesekretaerin, Die 2-04-31:43 and 6-23-31:19
Privilege 5-10-67:6
Prize, The 4-30-52:18
Prize, The 12-04-63:6
Prize Fighter, The 12-05-79:22
Prize of Arms, A 12-19-62:7
Prize of Gold, A 5-18-55:8
Prize Puppies (s) 7-23-30:19
Prizefighter and the Lady, The 11-14-33:17
Prkosna Delta 8-13-80:27
Pro Mou Lasku, Den 3-09-77:56
Proba de Microfon 7-30-80:23
Probation 4-12-32:15
Probation Wife, The 3-14-19:47
Problem Girls 3-11-53:18
Proces de Jeanne d'Arc 5-30-62:6
Procesado 1,040 8-12-59:19
Procesi K Panence 5-09-62:17
Proceso de Burgos, El 10-03-79:18
Processo di Verona, Il 4-17-63:7
Procesul Alb 7-20-66:7
Prodigal, The 6-30-31:20
Prodigal, The 3-30-55:8
Prodigal Daughter (s) 6-23-31:18
Prodigal Daughters 4-19-23:35
Prodigal Judge 2-10-22:34
Prodigal Liar, The 2-28-19:57
Prodigal Parson, A 8-08-08:11
Prodigal Son, The 11-13-09:13
Prodigal Son, The 2-22-23:42
Prodigal Wife, The 6-21-18:29
Prodigal Wife, The 1-03-19:38
Prodossia 5-26-65:7
Produced Trailers (s) 2-12-35:19 (Reprinted on: 2-27-35:27)
Producers, The 12-06-67:6
Professeur, Le 11-29-72:26
Profession: Aventuriers 6-13-73:16
Professional Soldier 2-05-36:12
Professional Sweethearts 7-18-33:36

Psychout for Murder 1-27-71:17
P'tit Vient Vite, Le 11-01-72:
30
Ptizi I Hrutki 10-29-69:28
Public Affair, A 3-28-62:6
Public Be Damned, The 6-29-
17:30
Public Cowboy No. 1 9-22-37:18
Public Deb. #1 8-28-40:20
Public Defender, The 10-05-17:
42
Public Defender 8-04-31:21
Public Enemies 1-28-42:8
Public Enemy, The 4-29-31:12
Public Enemy No. 1 1-16-57:18
Public Enemy's Wife, The 7-15-
36:31
Public Eye, The 7-12-72:17
Public Hero No. 1 6-12-35:12
Public Menace 9-25-35:12
Public Nuisance No. 1 3-11-36:
27
Public Opinion 10-30-35:14
Public Stenographer 1-30-34:12
Public Wedding 9-15-37:15
Publicity Madness 10-19-27:29
Puccini 5-20-53:16
Puddin'head Wilson 7-02-41:12
Pueblerina 8-10-49:8
Pueblito 7-11-62:27
Puente, La 8-10-77:16
Puerto Rico: U.S. Caribbean
Island 4-30-47:10
Puf der Goetter 7-24-57:7
Puff Your Blues Away (s) 11-24-
31:17 and 7-12-32:16
Puffs and Bustles (s) 5-30-33:15
Pufnstuf 6-03-70:17
Pugachev 7-13-38:17
Pugni In Tasca, I 8-25-65:6
Pugs and Kisses (s) 12-05-33:16
Puits Aux Trois Verites, Le 9-
27-61:7
Pukotina Raja 8-12-59:19
Pulgarcito (See: Tom Thumb)
Pull-Over Rouge, Le 12-12-79:23
Pulp 8-30-72:18
Pulsation, Une 2-25-70:20
Pulse of Life, The 3-23-17:25
Pumping Iron 1-19-77:22
Pumpkin Eater, The 5-20-64:20
Punatukka 7-08-70:15
Punch and Judy Man, The 4-17-
63:6
Punch Drunk (s) 8-21-34:17
Punishment, The (See: Punition,
La)
Punishment Park 6-30-71:22

Punition, La 5-08-63:26
Punition, La 7-18-73:14
Punk in London 3-28-79:22
Punk Rock Movie, The 6-21-78:
18
Punktchen Und Anton 1-20-54:18
Pupa, La 1-22-64:19
Puppe Kaputt 10-12-77:16
Puppet Crown, The 8-06-15:17
Puppet on a Chain 8-11-71:16
Puppets 9-22-16:36
Puppets 6-23-26:14
Puppets of Fate 4-22-21:40
Puppy Love 3-28-19:92
Pups Is Pups (s) 10-08-30:22
Purchase Price, The 7-19-32:25
Pure Feud (s) 4-24-34:14
Pure Grit 1-10-24:26
Pure Hell of St. Trinian's, The
12-28-60:6
Pure S 5-26-76:26
Purely Circumstantial (s) 12-25-
29:20
Purimspieler, Der 12-08-37:17
Puritain, Le 3-23-38:17
Purity 7-07-16:25
Purple Cipher, The 10-29-20:42
Purple Dawn 5-17-23:26
Purple Heart Diary 11-07-51:18
Purple Gang, The 1-13-60:7
Purple Heart, The 2-23-44:10
Purple Highway 7-26-23:27
Purple Hills, The 10-25-61:6
Purple Lady, The 6-16-16:22
Purple Lily, The 4-12-18:43
Purple Mask, The 6-01-55:6
Purple Night, The 10-01-15:19
Purple Noon (See: Plein Soleil)
Purple Plain 9-22-54:6
Purple V, The 3-24-43:20
Purple Vigilantes 2-02-38:17
Purpur und Waschblau 10-13-31:
15 and 7-12-32:17
Pursued 11-27-34:63
Pursued 2-19-47:8
Pursuing Shadow, The 8-06-15:17
Pursuing Vengeance, The 6-02-
16:16
Pursuit 10-09-35:14
Pursuit in the Steppe 6-25-80:21
Pursuit of Happiness, The 10-30-
34:16
Pursuit of Happiness, The 2-24-
71:26
Pursuit of the Phantom 1-09-15:
24
Pursuit to Algiers 10-31-45:17
Push Cart Race, A 11-14-08:13

Pusher, The   1-20-60:6
Pushover   7-28-54:6
Puss and Kram   9-27-67:6
Puss 'n' Boots (s)   6-17-42:20
Pussy Talk   11-19-75:26
Pussycat Cafe (s)   3-18-42:25
Pussycat, Pussycat, I Love You
      3-25-70:18
Pustolov Pred Vra-tima   8-30-61:
      16
Puszta Princess   2-25-39:13
Pusztai Szel   12-15-37:17
Put 'Em Up   5-02-28:15
Put on the Spot   9-16-36:17
Put U Raj   8-18-71:15
Put Up Your Hands   2-28-19:56
Putain Repectueuse, La   9-17-52:6
Puterea Si Adevarul   9-13-72:24
Putney Swope   7-09-69:6
Putovanje Na Mjesto   8-18-71:22
Puttin' On the Ritz   2-19-30:21
Putting It On (s)   10-10-28:15
Putting It Over   7-04-19:43
Putting It Over   8-25-22:34
Putting One Over   7-04-19:43
Puzzle of a Downfall Child   11-04-
      70:24
Puzzlegrafs (s)   8-07-33:14
Pyat'Vecherov   2-28-79:24
Pygmalion   9-07-38:13
Pygmies   10-17-73:14
Pygmy Island   11-22-50:18
Pyramide Des Sonnengottes, Die
      11-24-65:6
Pyramide Humaine, La   1-18-61:
      20
Pyretos Stin Asphalto   11-08-67:6
Pyro   4-29-64:6
Pyro (See: Fuego)
Pyx, The   10-03-73:14

Ragazza e il Generale, La 6-28-67:6
Ragazza in Pigiama Giallo, La 2-08-78:18
Ragazza in Vetrina, La 5-03-61:7
Ragazza Piuttosto Complicata, Una 1-22-69:6
Ragazze di San Frediano 4-15-55:9
Ragazzi del Massacro, I (See: Woman On Fire, A)
Ragazzo di Borgata 6-16-76:18
Rage 11-30-66:6
Rage 11-08-72:18
Rage at Dawn 3-09-55:6
Rage au Corps, La 3-31-54:6
Rage au Poign, La 2-26-75:20
Rage in Heaven 3-05-41:16
Rage of Paris, The 10-07-21:44
Rage of Paris, The 6-15-38:14
Rage to Live, A 9-15-65:6
Ragen 5-27-36:15
Ragged Earl, The 10-10-14:25
Ragged Edge, The 6-07-23:24
Ragged Heiress 4-07-22:42
Ragged Princess, The 10-20-16:25
Raggedy Ann and Andy 3-16-77:22
Raging Bull 11-12-80:26
Raging Moon, The 2-03-71:24
Raging Tide, The 10-17-51:6
Ragman's Daughter, The 5-24-72:26
Rags 8-06-15:17
Rags, Old Iron 3-12-10:39
Rags to Riches 9-29-22:41
Rags to Riches 9-13-41:18
Ragtime 12-28-27:20
Ragtime Cowboy Joe 10-02-40:12
Rah! Rah! Rhythm (s) 11-18-36:12
Rah! Rah! Thunder (s) 11-25-36:14
Rai Sanch Ha 7-11-79:19
Raices de Piedra 8-07-63:6
Raices de Sangre 6-20-79:19
Raid, The 6-02-54:6
Raid on Rommel 2-24-71:18
Raider Emden, The 5-02-28:15
Raiders, The 3-03-16:22
Raiders, The 7-08-21:27
Raiders, The 10-08-52:12
Raiders of Leyte Gulf 8-28-63:6
Raiders of Red Gap 5-03-44:23
Raiders of the Border 2-16-44:10
Raiders of the Seven Seas 5-29-53:6
Raiders of Tomahawk Creek 11-08-50:18

Railroad Follies (s) 8-20-30:14
Railroad Man, The (See: Ferroviere, Il)
Railroad Wretch (s) 2-14-33:12
Railroaded 6-14-23:23
Railroaded 10-08-47:8
Railroadin' (s) 10-09-29:23
Rails into Laramie 3-24-54:6
Railway Children, The 12-30-70:16
Railway on the Ice Sea 1-22-10:15
Rain 10-18-32:14
Rain for a Dusty Summer 9-15-71:6
Rain or Shine 7-23-30:19
Rain People, The 6-25-69:18
Rainbow, The 1-12-17:26
Rainbow 12-16-21:36
Rainbow, The 11-01-44:10
Rainbow Boys, The 4-11-73:20
Rainbow Bridge 3-29-72:30
Rainbow Island 9-06-44:10
Rainbow Jacket 6-09-54:6
Rainbow Man 4-02-29:13
Rainbow on the River 12-23-36:18
Rainbow over Broadway 12-26-33:11
Rainbow over Texas 5-08-46:8
Rainbow over the Range 11-06-40:16
Rainbow Princess, The 10-27-16:27
Rainbow Ranch 10-24-33:22
Rainbow Rangers 8-20-24:23
Rainbow Rhythm (s) 5-13-42:16
Rainbow 'Round My Shoulder 8-06-52:6
Rainbow Trail, The 10-18-18:39
Rainbow Trail, The 6-03-25:34
Rainbow Trail, The 2-02-32:15
Rainbow Valley 5-15-35:35
Rainbow's End 7-17-35:27
Rainey African Hunt 6-26-14:19
Rainha Diaba, A 10-01-75:28
Raining in the Mountain 7-18-79:14
Rainmaker, The 5-19-26:16
Rainmaker, The 12-12-56:6
Rainmakers, The 11-06-35:21
Rains Came, The 9-13-39:12
Rains of Ranchipur, The 12-14-55:6
Raintree County 10-09-57:6
Raisa and Rimi (s) 8-29-28:15
Raisces 6-01-55:22
Raise the Titanic 8-06-80:22
Raisin in the Sun, A 3-29-61:6

Raising a Riot 3-16-55:24
Raising the Roof (s) 7-03-29:17
Raising the Wind 9-27-61:7
Raison d'Etat, La 5-24-78:31
Raison du Plus Fou, La 4-04-73:
    26
Rak 4-26-72:6
Rak Kam Lok 5-24-78:40
Rak Otaroot 7-06-77:17
Rak Ri Sayar 6-20-79:18
Rakas 9-12-62:6
Rake's Progress, The 12-05-45:
    20
Rakoczi Indulo 10-28-36:15
Rallarblod 8-22-79:52
Rallare 2-18-48:9
Rally Round the Flag 12-18-09:15
Rally 'Round the Flag, Boys 12-
    24-58:6
Ralph Benefits by Others' Curiosity
    9-04-09:13
Ramble in Erin 11-21-51:18
Ramble Through Ceylon, A 12-03-
    10:14
Rambles in Paris 3-07-13:14
Ramblin' Kid, The 9-13-23:30
Rambling Ranger 8-03-27:19
Rambling Reporter (s) 8-25-31:24
Rambling Round Radio Row (s) 7-
    26-32:17; 1-17-33:14; 5-09-
    33:14
Ramon Ramos Orchestra (s) 5-06-
    36:19
Ramona 2-25-16:23
Ramona 5-16-28:13
Ramona 10-14-36:15
Rampage 8-14-63:6
Rampant Age, The 1-15-30:37
Ramparts We Watch, The 7-24-
    40:14
Ramrod 2-26-47:10
Ramshackle House 1-07-25:56
Ramuntcho 3-23-38:17
Ran & Ran 6-11-80:22
Ran Salu (See: Yellow Robes, The)
Ranch House Blues (s) 5-14-30:19
Ranch King's Daughter, The 1-
    29-10:13
Ranch Riders 12-14-27:26
Rancho Deluxe 3-26-75:18
Rancho Grande 12-07-38:13
Rancho Grande 3-27-40:17
Rancho Notorious 2-06-52:6
Randolph Family, The 3-14-45:16
Random Harvest 11-25-42:16
Range Beyond the Blue 3-12-47:
    12
Range Busters, The 11-20-40:18

Range Courage 7-20-27:19
Range Defenders 7-14-37:21
Range Feud, The 11-24-31:21
Range Justice 11-23-49:25
Range Land 3-01-50:16
Range Law 12-08-31:15
Range Law 8-16-44:26
Range War 8-30-39:14
Ranger, The 5-31-18:31
Ranger and the Lady, The 7-24-
    40:16
Ranger Courage 7-28-37:31
Ranger of Cherokee Strip, The 11-
    09-49:16
Ranger of the Big Pines 7-29-25:
    34
Ranger of the North 12-28-27:22
Ranger's Code 9-26-33:20
Rangers of Fortune 9-11-40:14
Ranger's Roundup 9-21-38:13
Rangers Step In 11-03-37:15
Rangers Take Over, The 3-31-43:8
Rangle River 1-20-37:14
Rango 2-25-31:12
Rani Radovi 7-16-69:6
Rank Cartoons 10-06-48:11
Rank Outsider, A 12-17-20:42
Rannstensungar 10-08-75:22
Ransom, The 1-14-16:19
Ransom 8-15-28:17
Ransom! 1-11-56:6
Ransom 4-24-74:18 and 3-26-75:
    20
Ransom's Folly 9-24-15:20
Ransomed; or, A Prisoner of War
    10-08-10:12
Ranson's Folly 6-02-26:14 and 6-
    09-26:17
Raoni 3-08-78:35
Raotsel des Silbernen Halbmonds,
    Das 8-23-72:6
Rapace, Le 4-24-68:26
Rape of Love (See: Mourir a Tue-
    Tete)
Raphael, ou le Debauche 4-14-
    71:16
Rapids, The 7-04-23:23
Rappel Immediat 7-12-39:13
Rapportpigen 2-27-74:16
Rapture 3-09-49:20
Rapture 8-25-65:6
Rare Breed, The 2-02-66:6
Ras le Bol 9-05-73:6
Rascal 6-11-69:6
Rascals 5-25-38:13
Rascel-Fifi 3-19-58:6
Rascoala 5-18-66:24
Rasho-Mon 9-19-51:24

Rashomon (See: Rasho-Mon)
Raspoutine 10-06-54:22
Rasputin 9-14-17:35
Rasputin 1-23-29:34
Rasputin 3-08-32:23
Rasputin 10-18-39:14
Rasputin and the Empress 12-27-32:14
Rasputin--The Mad Monk 4-27-66:6
Rasskaz Moei Materi 9-17-58:7
Rasskaz O Neisvestnon Celoveke 9-17-80:23
Rat, The 8-21-14:19
Rat, The 9-23-25:40
Rat, The 11-24-37:16
Rat 8-10-60:6
Rat d'Amerique, Le 5-29-63:6
Rat Fink 1-12-66:6
Rat Pfink and Boo Boo 9-14-66:6
Rat Race, The 5-04-60:6
Ratai 2-19-64:6
Ratas, Las 4-03-63:7
Ratataplan 9-05-79:30
Rationing 1-26-44:12
Raton Pass 2-28-51:13
Rats 10-29-10:14
Rats, The (See: Ratas, Las)
Rats of Tobruk, The 2-07-45:23
Ratten, Die 7-13-55:6
Rattle of a Simple Man 9-16-64:19
Raub der Mona Lisa 9-15-31:28 and 4-05-32:22
Raub der Sabinerinnen 2-10-37:15
Raubfischer In Hellas 11-25-59:6
Raulito, La 9-03-75:20
Rauschgift 12-20-32:55
Ravagers, The 12-08-65:6
Ravagers 5-30-79:17
Raven, The 11-12-15:22
Raven, The 7-10-35:19
Raven, The (s) 4-15-42:18
Raven, The 2-25-48:8
Raven, The 2-06-63:6
Raven's End (See: Kvarteret Korpen)
Ravishing Idiot, A (See: Ravissante Idiote, Une)
Ravissante 2-01-61:22
Ravissante Idiote, Une 4-01-64:23
Raw Deal 5-19-48:13
Raw Deal 2-09-77:26
Raw Edge 7-25-56:18
Raw Timber 11-09-38:17
Raw Wind in Eden 7-23-58:6
Rawhide 4-06-38:14
Rawhide 3-07-51:6

Rawhide Kid, The 1-18-28:19
Rawhide Rangers 8-20-41:9
Rawhide Years, The 6-06-56:6
Raymie 5-04-60:6
Raymond Hitchcock (s) 6-12-29:16
Raza, El Espiritu de Franco 11-23-77:19
Razlom 12-03-30:15
Razored in Kentucky (s) 10-29-30:17
Razor's Edge, The 11-20-46:22
Razumov 3-17-37:15
Razza Selvaggia 10-15-80:146
Razzia 6-16-48:20
Razzia in St. Pauli 6-07-32:25
Razzia Sur la Chnouf 6-08-55:6
Re Burlone, Il 4-08-36:17
Re: Lucky Luciano 11-14-73:16
Reach for Glory 8-08-62:6 and 11-14-62:7
Reach for the Sky 7-18-56:6
Reaching for the Moon 11-23-17:45
Reaching for the Moon 1-07-31:22
Reaching for the Sun 4-09-41:16
Ready for Love 12-04-34:12
Ready for the People 10-21-64:28
Ready in a Minute 4-30-10:16
Ready Money 11-14-14:25
Ready, Willing and Able 3-17-37:14
Real Adventure, The 6-30-22:33
Real Glory, The 9-13-39:12
Real Life 3-07-79:20
Real McCoy, The (s) 3-12-30:21
Realengo 18 7-04-62:63
Realization (s) 6-06-28:12
Really Big Family, The 3-08-67:6
Reap the Wind Wild 3-25-42:8
Reapers, The 3-31-16:25
Rear Window 7-14-54:6
Reason to Live, a Reason to Die, A 2-27-74:16
Reason Why, The 5-03-18:39
Reb Spikes' Band (s) 7-11-28:13
Rebecca 3-27-40:17
Rebecca of Sunnybrook Farm 9-07-17:34
Rebecca of Sunnybrook Farm 8-02-32:15
Rebecca of Sunnybrook Farm 3-09-38:14
Rebel, The 8-01-33:14
Rebel, The 3-15-61:7
Rebel City 5-13-53:18
Rebel in Town 6-27-56:6

Rebel Intruders, The   10-29-80: 18
Rebel Set, The   7-15-59:6
Rebel Without a Cause   10-26-55:6
Rebelde, El   3-14-45:16
Rebelion de los Colgados, La   9-08-54:22
Rebelle, Le   9-01-31:34
Rebelle, Le   12-03-80:26
Rebellion   5-04-38:15
Rebellious Daughters, The   4-11-19:55
Rebellious Daughters   9-21-38:13
Rebels Against the Light   11-18-64:6
Rebound   9-01-31:21
Rebozo De Soledad, El   10-01-52: 22
Recaptured Love   8-13-30:15
Recess   7-02-69:26
Recif de Corail   5-03-39:20
Reckless   4-24-35:12
Reckless Age, The   6-11-24:29
Reckless Age, The   8-30-44:10
Reckless Chances   1-20-22:35
Reckless Courage   4-29-25:36
Reckless Hour, The   8-04-31:21
Reckless Lady, The   1-27-26:42
Reckless Living   12-08-31:15
Reckless Living   6-08-38:17
Reckless Moment, The   10-19-49:8
Reckless Ranger   7-14-37:21
Reckless Roads   10-09-35:15
Reckless Romance   1-07-25:56
Reckless Sex, The   4-01-25:38
Reckless Speed   12-10-24:45
Reckless Youth   4-07-22:41
Reckless Youth   1-09-29:34
Reckoning, The   1-23-15:25
Reckoning, The   4-12-32:15
Reckoning, The   8-20-69:16
Reckoning Day, The   10-18-18:38
Recoil, The   4-27-17:27
Recoil   7-02-24:26
Recompense   4-22-25:34
Recommendation for Mercy   8-20-75:19
Reconstitiurea   3-17-71:28
Reconstruction of Palestine   9-04-29:31
Recontre a Paris   7-11-56:10
Record Boys (s)   1-30-29:14
Record Breakers (s)   9-16-42:20
Record of a Living Being (See: Ikimono No Koroku)
Recordando   9-27-61:6
Recours en Grace   6-15-60:18

Recreation, La   3-08-61:7
Recruit, The (s)   2-04-31:16
Recruits in Ingolstadt   10-13-71: 16
Recuperanti, I   2-18-70:17
Recurso del Metodo, El   5-31-78: 21
Red, La   5-13-53:22
Red   5-20-70:28
Red and the Black, The (See: Rouge et le Noir, Le)
Red and the White, The (See: Csillagosok, Katonak)
Red Angel   11-08-50:18
Red Apple   8-13-75:16
Red Badge of Courage, The   8-15-51:6
Red Ball Express   4-30-52:6
Red Balloon, The (See: Ballon Rouge, Le)
Red Barry (Serial)   10-26-38:15
Red Beard (See: Akahige)
Red Beret, The   8-19-53:6
Red Bizom a Felesegem   5-12-37: 13
Red Blood of Courage   6-12-35:41
Red Blossoms in the Tian Mountains   1-10-79:54
Red Canyon   2-02-49:12
Red Circle, The   11-26-15:23
Red Clay   4-20-27:25
Red Club, The   5-22-14:23
Red Courage   9-30-21:36
Red Cross Seal, The   12-24-10:16
Red Dance, The   6-27-28:14
Red Dancer, The   11-14-28:22
Red Danube, The   9-21-49:8
Red Desert, The   12-28-49:6
Red Desert, The (See: Deserto Rosso, Il)
Red Detachment of Women   9-15-71:6
Red Dice   4-14-26:38
Red Dragon, The   1-02-46:16
Red Dragon (See: Geheimnis der Drei Dschunken, Das)
Red-Dragon   6-14-67:7
Red Dust   11-08-32:16
Red Ensign   2-20-34:25
Red Fork Range   3-11-31:39
Red Garters   2-03-54:6
Red Hair   3-28-28:31
Red-Haired Alibi   10-25-32:54
Red Haired Cupid, The   6-07-18: 34
Red Head   11-20-34:17
Red Headed Baby (s)   12-29-31: 166

Red Headed Woman 7-05-32:14
Red Heads (s) 5-07-30:20
Red Heels 2-03-26:43
Red, Hot and Blue 7-06-49:9
Red Hot Dollars 1-02-20:75
Red Hot Leather 10-20-26:67
Red Hot Rhythm 9-10-30:29
Red Hot Romance 1-27-22:39
Red Hot Speed 2-04-29:18
Red Hot Tires 3-06-35:20
Red House, The 2-05-47:12
Red Kimona, The 2-03-26:37
Red Lane, The 7-16-20:32
Red Lantern, The 5-09-19:53
Red Lanterns (See: Kokking
   Fanaria)
Red Letter Days 11-29-67:6
Red Light 7-20-49:6
Red Lights 9-13-23:28
Red Lily, The 10-01-24:22
Red Line, The 8-19-59:6
Red Line 7000 11-10-65:6
Red Lips 10-17-28:24
Red Lips (See: Labbia Rosse)
Red Majesty 5-08-29:24
Red Man's Love, A 12-04-09:13
Red Mark 10-31-28:31
Red Meadows 1-25-50:18
Red Men Tell No Tales (s) 12-
   08-31:14
Red Menace, The 5-25-49:8
Red Mill, The 2-16-27:19
Red Mountain 11-14-51:6
Red Nichols' Pennies (s) 12-25-
   29:20
Red Olympiad, The (See: Sparta-
   kiada)
Red Pants, The (See: Culottes
   Rouges, Les)
Red Peacock 4-07-22:41
Red Pearls 3-05-30:35
Red Planet Mars 5-14-52:20
Red Pony, The 2-09-49:13
Red Raiders, The 10-12-27:24
Red Red Heart, The 3-29-18:46
Red Republic, The (s) 10-16-34:
   12
Red Riding Hood Rides Again (s)
   2-04-42:22
Red River 7-14-48:12
Red River Range 1-11-39:13
Red River Shore 12-30-53:6
Red River Valley 11-11-36:15
Red River Valley 12-31-41:8
Red Rope, The 7-21-37:19
Red Salute 10-02-35:16
Red Shadow, The (s) 1-02-33:19
Red Shoes, The 8-04-48:11

Red Signals 5-11-27:20
Red Skies of Montana 1-23-52:6
Red Sky at Morning 5-05-71:16
Red Snow 6-25-52:6
Red Square 8-25-71:16
Red Stallion, The 7-23-47:10
Red Stallion in the Rockies 3-16-
   49:11
Red Sun (See: Soleil Rouge)
Red Sundown 2-01-56:6
Red Sword, The 4-24-29:26
Red Tanks 6-10-42:8
Red Tent, The 7-28-71:14
Red Tomahawk 1-11-67:28
Red Town 2-25-21:42
Red Village, The 5-08-35:45
Red Virgin, The 9-24-15:21
Red Wagon 12-26-33:26 and 6-
   24-36:45
Red Warning 12-27-23:27
Red, White and Black, The 12-
   23-70:6
Red, White and Blue 3-03-71:22
Red, White and Blue Blood 1-04-
   18:44
Red Widow, The 4-28-16:28
Red Wine 3-20-29:28
Red Wing's Gratitude 10-16-09:
   12
Red Woman, The 2-02-17:24
Redeemed Criminal, The 1-07-
   11:13
Redeeming Sin, The 1-21-25:34
Redeeming Sin, The 2-20-29:14
Redemption 10-03-14:21
Redemption 5-04-17:28
Redemption 5-07-30:38
Redemption of David Carson, The
   4-17-14:22
Redes (See: Wave, The)
Redhead, The 4-24-14:20
Redhead 5-23-19:57
Redhead 7-02-41:18
Redhead and the Cowboy, The 12-
   13-50:8
Redhead from Manhattan, The 6-
   16-43:16
Redhead from Wyoming, The 12-
   24-52:14
Redheads on Parade 9-04-35:31
Redheads Preferred 12-29-26:17
Redman and the Child, The 8-01-
   08:13
Redskin 1-30-29:34
Reducing 1-21-31:17
Redwood Forest Trail 9-20-50:6
Reed Case, The 7-20-17:31
Reedham's Orphanage Festival 1910
   10-01-10:18

367 •

1-01-15:30
Return of the Vampire, The 2-02-44:18
Return of the Vikings 9-13-44:10
Return of the Whistler 3-03-48:8
Return of Wild Bill, The 7-10-40:12
Return of Wildfire, The 8-18-48:18
Return to Campus 10-29-75:17
Return to Life 8-10-38:27
Return to Macon County 7-16-75:21
Return to Paradise 7-22-53:6
Return to Peyton Place 5-03-61:6
Return to the Edge of the World 11-26-80:15
Return to Treasure Island 6-23-54:6
Return to Warbow 1-15-58:7
Return to Witch Mountain 3-15-78:20
Return to Yesterday 2-14-40:20
Reunion 12-02-36:18
Reunion, The (See: Rimpatriata, La)
Reunion in France 12-02-42:8
Reunion in Reno 10-03-51:6
Reunion in Vienna 5-02-33:12
Reunited at the Gallows 12-18-09:15
Reve, Le 8-04-31:21
Reveille with Beverly 4-28-43:8
Revelation 4-07-16:24
Revelation 3-01-18:41
Revelation 6-25-24:26
Revelers, The (s) 10-24-28:24; 1-30-29:14; 1-29-30:21; 4-15-31:20
Revenant, Le 12-04-46:13
Revenge 12-12-28:14
Revenge 9-08-71:16
Revenge 2-07-79:20
Revenge at Monte Carlo 5-02-33:13
Revenge Is Sweet (s) 6-09-31:18
Revenge of Frankenstein 6-18-58:6
Revenge of the Cheerleaders 7-14-76:20
Revenge of the Gladiators 9-01-65:6
Revenge of the Pink Panther, The 7-19-78:20
Revenge of the Zombies 9-01-43:20
Revengers, The 6-07-72:18
Revenue Agent 12-06-50:20

Revival Day (s) 1-01-30:15
Revolver, The (See: Blood in the Streets)
Revolt, The 2-06-15:23
Revolt, The 9-22-16:49
Revolt at Ft. Laramie 3-27-57:6
Revolt in the Bighouse 11-05-58:6
Revolt in the Desert 4-12-32:15
Revolt of Mamie Stover, The 5-02-56:6
Revolt of the Zombies 6-10-36:18
Revolte, Le 11-20-38:12
Revoltes de Lomanach, Les 5-26-54:18
Revolucion Matrimonial, La 4-09-75:20
Revolucion Mexicana, La 7-17-57:6
Revolution 5-15-68:30
Revolution d'Octobre 12-15-67:6
Revolution I Vand Kanten 4-07-71:24
Revolution Is in Your Head 3-18-70:27
Revolutionary, The 6-24-70:17
Revolutionary Family, A 8-02-61:7
Revolutionary Wedding 11-14-28:17
Revolutionists 12-30-36:11
Revolutionnaire, La 7-10-68:6
Revolutionshochzeit 11-14-28:17
Revolver aux Cheveux Rouges, Le 2-13-74:18
Revolveres Nao Cospem Flores 2-07-73:26
Revykoebing Kalder 12-12-73:20
Reward, The 7-02-15:16
Reward, The 9-22-65:6
Reward of Patience, The 9-22-16:37
Reward of the Faithless, The 2-02-17:22
Rey Del Joropo, El (See: King of the Joropo)
Rhapsodia Portuguesa 5-13-59:10
Rhapsody 2-17-54:6
Rhapsody in Blue 6-27-45:16
Rhapsody in Rivets (s) 2-04-42:22
Rhapsody of Steel (s) 1-20-60:6
Rheingold 2-22-78:34
Rheinlandmaedel, Das 9-22-31:26
Rheinsberg 12-27-67:20
Rhinefalls at Schaffhausen, The 4-09-10:15
Rhineland Memories (s) 3-08-32:14

Right Out of History--The Making
of Judy Chicago's Dinner
Party 9-03-80:25
Right That Failed 3-24-22:41
Right Timing, The (s) 12-02-42:8
Right to Happiness 9-05-19:61
Right to Lie, The 11-14-19:59
Right to Live, The 2-20-35:15
Right to Love, The 8-27-20:28
Right to Love, The 1-07-31:22
Right to Romance, The 12-19-
33:19
Right to the Heart 1-21-42:8
Right Way, The 11-04-21:41
Rights of Man, The 10-29-15:22
Rigolbouche 11-11-36:15
Rigoletto 11-16-49:16
Rikugun Nakano Gakko 6-22-66:6
Riley the Cop 12-05-28:19
Rim of the Canyon 9-07-49:11
Rimacs Rumba Orch. (s) 6-26-
35:23
Rimfire 3-30-49:13
Rimpatriata, La 7-03-63:18
Rimrock Jones 1-25-18:44
Rimsky-Korsakov 3-17-54:22
Rincon de las Virgenes, El 7-17-
74:18
Ring, The 10-19-27:28
Ring, The 8-20-52:6
Ring and the Man, The 6-12-14:
21
Ring Around the Clock 5-13-53:
20
Ring Around the Moon 2-19-36:
32
Ring of Bright Water 4-16-69:30
Ring of Fear 7-07-54:6
Ring of Fire 4-26-61:6
Ring of Spies 4-01-64:6
Ringards, Les 10-11-78:48
Ringer, The 9-12-28:27
Ringer, The 6-07-32:21
Rings Around the World 9-28-66:6
Rings on Her Fingers 3-11-42:8
Ringside 7-20-49:6
Ringside Maisie 7-30-41:18
Rink, The (See: At the Rink)
Rinty of the Desert 6-06-28:25
Rio 10-04-39:12
Rio Bravo 2-18-59:6
Rio Conchos 10-07-64:6
Rio Escondido (See: Hidden River)
Rio Grande 5-07-20:34
Rio Grande 1-11-39:13
Rio Grande 11-08-50:6
Rio Grande Patrol 11-08-50:18
Rio Grande Ranger 2-03-37:29

Rio Grande Romance 5-12-37:13
Rio Lobo 12-02-70:16
Rio Negro 8-03-77:22
Rio Rita 10-09-29:23
Rio Rita 3-18-42:8
Rio Zone Norte 8-27-58:6
Riot 12-11-68:6
Riot in Cell Block 11 2-10-54:6
Riot in Juvenile Prison 4-15-59:6
Riot on Sunset Strip 3-08-67:6
Riot Squad 1-07-42:45
Rip Tide 4-03-34:17
Rip Van Winkle 11-28-14:24
Rip Van Winkle 9-23-21:42
Ripe for Killing 2-09-55:11
Rip-Off 10-13-71:16
Rip-Tide 9-13-23:28
Riptide (See: Si Jolie Petite Plage,
Une)
Risa de la Ciudad, La 11-21-62:6
Risaia, La 7-25-56:6
Rise and Fall of Legs Diamond,
The 1-27-60:6
Rise and Fall of the World As
Seen from a Sexual Position,
The 6-28-72:26
Rise and Rise of Michael Rimmer,
The 11-25-70:13
Rise and Shine 11-19-41:9
Rise of Jennie Cushing, The 11-
16-17:51
Rise of Louis XIV, The (See:
Prise de Pouvoir Par Louis
XIV, La)
Rise of Susan, The 12-08-16:29
Rising Damp 3-12-80:22
Rising of the Moon, The 6-12-57:
18
Rising Sun 4-09-80:18
Riskiton Varjossa 5-15-46:8
Risky Business 12-10-20:35
Risky Business 9-08-26:17
Risky Business 3-29-39:14
Risky Road, The 4-12-18:42
Riso Amaro 11-16-49:29
Risque de Vivre, Le 5-28-80:44
Risques du Metier, Les 1-24-
68:6
Rita 2-22-50:18
Rita 8-27-58:6
Ritorna 5-21-69:18
Ritorno 10-03-73:15
Ritorno di Casanova, Il 10-04-78:
22
Ritorno di Ringo, Il 2-02-66:17
Ritratto di Borghesia in Nero
(See: Nest of Vipers)
Ritter der Nacht 11-14-28:17

Roadblock 7-25-51:18
Roadhouse Murder, The 5-03-32: 14
Roadhouse Nights 2-26-30:24
Roadhouse Queen (s) 5-16-33:17
Roads of Destiny 4-01-21:41
Roadside Impresario, A 6-22-17: 23
Roaming Cowboy 12-01-37:29
Roaming Lady 5-06-36:19
Roar, Navy, Roar (s) 1-06-43:50
Roar of the Crowd, The 5-20-53:6
Roar of the Press, The 6-25-41: 18
Roarin' Guns 7-08-36:28
Roarin' Lead 5-05-37:27 and 8-18-37:39
Roaring Lions and Wedding Bells 11-16-17:50
Roaring Fires 8-03-27:18
Roaring Rails 10-15-24:27
Roaring Ranch 5-21-30:27
Roaring Road, The 4-18-19:53
Roaring Six Guns 10-13-37:17
Roaring Timber 7-14-37:21
Roaring '20's, The 10-25-39:11
Rob Roy 10-27-22:42
Rob Roy 11-04-53:6
Rob the Bank (See: Faites Sauter la Banque)
Robbed the Chief of Police 9-11-09:13
Robber Baron, The 3-19-10:17
Robber Duke, The 11-13-09:13
Robber Symphony 1-27-37:12
Robbers and Giants of Bird Life (s) 8-25-31:24
Robbers of the Range 4-30-41:18
Robbers' Roost 3-21-33:27
Robbers' Roost 5-11-55:9
Robbery 10-04-67:6
Robbery Under Arms 10-23-57:6
Robby 8-21-68:26
Robe, The 9-23-53:6
Robert Chisholm (s) 10-09-29:23
Robert e Robert 6-28-78:23
Robert the Devil 9-17-10:12
Roberta 3-31-35:15
Roberte 8-23-78:30 and 4-18-79: 23
Robes of Sin 6-23-26:18
Robin and Marian 3-10-76:22
Robin and the Seven Hoods 6-24-64:7
Robin Hood 8-22-13:14
Robin Hood 10-20-22:40 and 11-03-22:42
Robin Hood 4-27-38:22

Robin Hood 3-12-52:16
Robin Hood 11-07-73:19
Robin Hood of El Dorado 3-18-36:17
Robin Hood of Texas 9-10-47:17
Robin Hood of the Pecos 1-15-41: 16
Robin Hood of the Range 8-18-43:26
Robinson Columbus 4-09-75:20
Robinson Crusoe 8-22-13:14
Robinson Crusoe, Jr. 9-03-24:25
Robinson Crusoe of Clipper Island (serial) 8-22-37:19
Robinson Crusoe on Mars 6-03-64:6
Robinson-Turbin Fight 7-18-51:22
Robot, The (s) 3-01-32:20
Robot Monster 6-17-53:16
Rocco and His Brothers (See: Rocco e Suoi Fratelli)
Rocco e Suoi Fratelli 9-14-60:6
Rock All Night 5-01-57:7
Rock Around the Clock 3-21-56:6
Rock Around the Clock (The Tommy Steale Story) 8-28-57:6
Rock 'n' Roll 1-10-79:54
Rock 'n' Roll High School 4-25-79:19
Rock 'n' Roll Wolf 6-14-78:20
Rock, Pretty Baby 11-21-56:6
Rock-Ribbed Maine (s) 2-23-27:19
Rock, Rock, Rock! 12-12-56:6
Rockabilly Baby 10-23-57:18
Rockabye 12-06-32:15
Rock-A-Bye Baby 6-04-58:6
Rockers 10-18-78:72
Rocket Man 5-05-54:6
Rocketeers (s) 5-17-32:14
Rockets Galore 9-24-58:6
Rocketship X-M 5-03-50:6
Rockin' the Blues 10-03-56:26
Rocking Horse Winner, The 12-21-49:8
Rockwell's Automatic Rocker (s) 12-26-33:10
Rocky 11-10-76:20
Rocky Horror Picture Show, The 9-24-75:22
Rocky Island Trail 5-03-50:6
Rocky Marciano-Ezzard Charles Fight (s) 9-22-54:6
Rocky Mountain 10-04-50:6
Rocky Mountain Big Game (s) 5-13-42:16
Rocky Mountain Mystery 4-03-35: 17
Rocky Mountain Rangers 7-03-40: 18

Rocky Rhodes 1-01-35:146
Rocky Road, The 1-08-10:13
Rocky Road to Dublin, The 5-15-68:7
Rocky II 6-13-79:14
Rod Stewart and Faces and Keith Richard 8-27-75:16
Roda Dagen 5-31-32:25
Rodeo 3-05-52:6
Rodeo Day (s) 11-13-35:16
Rodeo King and the Senorita 7-25-51:18
Rodeo Rhythm 12-17-41:8
Rodney Steps In 7-14-31:22
Roebe Kappe, Den 1-25-67:21
Roede Rubin, Den 3-11-70:24
Roetsel des Silbernen Halbmonds, Das 8-23-72:6
Roger Corman: Hollywood's "Wild Angel" 6-28-78:28
Roger la Honte 4-17-46:16
Roger Touhy, Gangster 5-24-44:10
Roger Wolf Kahn and Orch. (s) 6-20-28:14 and 10-31-28:24
Rogopay 9-25-63:6
Rogue Cop 9-01-54:6
Rogue in Love, A 10-27-22:42
Rogue of the Range 4-28-37:24
Rogue of the Rio Grande 12-17-30:63
Rogue River 2-21-51:16
Rogue Song, The 2-05-30:19 (Also see: Chant du Bandit, Le)
Rogues and Romance 1-28-21:40
Rogues Gallery 2-21-45:17
Rogue's March 12-31-52:6
Rogues of Sherwood Forest 6-21-50:8
Rogue's Regiment 10-06-48:11
Rogues' Tavern, The 7-15-36:55
Roi, Le 1-11-50:16
Roi de Coeur, Le 12-28-66:18
Roi des Champs Elysees, Le 1-22-35:15
Roi des Palaces, Le 10-18-32:19
Roi des Resquilleurs 12-17-30:63 and 6-14-32:17
Roi du Cirage 12-01-31:26
Roi et l'Oiseau, Le 4-23-80:24
Roi Sans Divertissement, Un 10-02-63:28
Rolande, or Chronicle of a Passion 3-15-72:6
Rolando Rivas, Taxista 10-30-74:44
Roll Along, Cowboy 6-01-38:12

Roll On Texas Moon 9-18-46:16
Roll, Thunder, Roll! 5-11-49:6
Roll Wagons Roll 12-20-39:47
Rolled Stockings 7-20-27:16
Roller Boogie 12-12-79:22
Rollerball 6-25-75:23
Rollercoaster 4-27-77:20
Rollickers (s) 1-16-29:14
Rollin' Home to Texas 2-26-41:18
Rollin' Plains 8-31-38:40
Rollin' Westward 8-23-39:20
Rolling Caravans 8-17-38:23
Rolling Home 6-09-26:17
Rolling Home 4-02-75:30
Rolling House (s) 10-08-30:22
Rolling Stones 8-25-16:25
Rolling Thunder 10-05-77:28
Roma 3-29-72:30
Roma a Mano Armata 4-14-76:27
Roma, Citta Aperta (See: Rome, Open City)
Roma, Ore 11 5-28-52:22
Roma Rivuole Cesare 10-02-74:22
Roman, The 2-19-10:15
Roman d'un Tricheur, Le 10-14-36:54
Roman Holiday 7-01-53:6
Roman Punch (s) 4-23-30:24
Roman Scandals 12-26-33:11
Roman Spring of Mrs. Stone, The 12-06-61:6
Romana, La 9-22-54:6
Romance 8-27-30:21
Romance (s) 7-26-32:17
Romance a l'Inconnue 3-18-31:34
Romance and Arabella 2-07-19:59
Romance and Riches 5-19-37:23
Romance and Rings 1-17-19:53
Romance De Luxe (s) 1-22-30:17
Romance de Medio Siglo 10-25-44:12
Romance in Flanders 9-22-37:19
Romance in Manhattan 1-22-35:14
Romance in the Andes 10-30-09:11
Romance in the Dark 2-16-38:15
Romance in the Rain 9-11-34:11
Romance Land 3-15-23:31
Romance of a Gypsy Camp 8-29-08:13
Romance of a Horse Thief 7-21-71:16
Romance of a Million 12-29-26:17

Romance of a Necklace, The 10-22-10:14
Romance of a Poor Girl 10-23-09:13
Romance of a Rogue 8-29-28:28
Romance of Aniceto & Francesca 11-02-66:19
Romance of Billy Goat Hill 9-29-16:24
Romance of Happy Valley, A 1-31-19:52
Romance of Hefty Burke, The 1-07-11:13
Romance of Hine Moa 10-02-29:22
Romance of History 10-27-22:42
Romance of Promoters, The 12-02-20:32
Romance of Rosy Ridge, The 7-02-47:13
Romance of Tarzan, The 10-18-18:38
Romance of the Air, A 11-15-18:45
Romance of the Limberlost 7-20-38:12
Romance of the Redwoods, A 5-18-17:24
Romance of the Redwoods, A 4-19-39:22
Romance of the Rio Grande 11-13-29:12
Romance of the Rio Grande 1-01-41:14
Romance of the Rockies 2-16-38:25
Romance of the Underworld, A 4-05-18:42
Romance of the Underworld 1-09-29:34
Romance of the West (s) 9-25-35:12 and 1-15-36:19
Romance of the West 2-13-46:10
Romance on the High Seas 6-09-48:12
Romance on the Range 7-29-42:8
Romance on the Run 5-11-38:16
Romance Por Kridlovku 7-26-67:24
Romance Ranch 7-16-24:44
Romance Rides the Range 12-23-36:62
Romance Road 10-21-25:38
Romance Sentimentale (s) 10-27-31:19
Romanoff and Juliet 5-10-61:7
Romans O Vljublennych 7-31-74:19
Romantic Adventuress, The

2-11-21:41
Romantic Age, The 12-21-27:25
Romantic Age, The 12-14-49:22
Romantic Englishwoman, The 5-28-75:19
Romantic Italy 9-11-09:12
Romantic Journey, The 12-01-16:28
Romantic Melodies (s) 7-18-33:36
Romantic Rogue, The 11-02-27:24
Romantik Paa Sengekanten 10-17-73:14
Romany Rye, The 7-31-14:16 and 4-23-15:18
Romanze 12-30-36:27
Romanzo Popolare 12-11-74:18
Rome Adventure 3-21-62:6
Rome Express 12-06-32:15 and 2-28-33:15
Rome, Open City 12-24-45:12 and 2-27-46:8
Romeo and Juliet 10-27-16:28
Romeo and Juliet 10-27-16:28
Romeo and Juliet (s) 11-05-30:23
Romeo and Juliet 8-26-36:20
Romeo and Juliet 9-08-54:6
Romeo and Juliet 5-18-55:9
Romeo and Juliet 10-05-66:6
Romeo and Juliet 3-13-68:6
Romeo and Juliet 9-04-68:6
Romeo, Julie a Tina 9-14-60:20
Romona's Father 1-14-11:18
Ronde, La 7-12-50:6
Ronde, La 10-28-64:7
Ronde des Heures 2-09-32:19
(Also see: Rondes des Heures)
Rondes des Heures 3-11-31:15
(Also see: Ronde des Heures)
Rondo 5-10-67:20
Ronny 1-12-32:28 and 4-19-32:15
Roof Garden, The (See: Terraza, La)
Roof of the World, The 7-23-30:31
Roof Tops of Manhattan (s) 3-04-36:27
Roof Tree 1-27-22:40
Roogie's Bump 9-22-54:6
Rooie Sien 5-14-75:35
Rookery Nook 2-26-30:42
Rookie, The (s) 1-03-33:19
Rookie, The 11-25-59:6
Rookie Cop, The 5-10-39:23
Rookie Fireman 9-06-50:8
Rookies 4-27-27:16

Rookies in Burma 12-08-43:8
Rookies on Parade 4-30-41:16
Rookie's Return, The 1-28-21:41
Room and Board 9-09-21:45
Room at the Top 1-28-59:6
Room for One More 1-16-52:6
Room 909 (s) 2-12-30:18
Room Service 9-14-38:15
Roommates 2-17-71:18
Rooney 4-09-58:6
Rooney and Bent (s) 5-23-28:21
Rooney Family (s) 10-23-29:17
Roosevelt in Africa 4-23-10:16
Roosevelt Reviewing the Troops
    11-05-10:14
Roosevelt Story, The 7-02-47:13
Rooster Cogburn 10-15-75:26
Root of All Evil 2-19-47:9
Rootin' Tootin' Rhythm 8-04-37:
    25
Roots of Heaven 10-22-58:6
Roots of Stone (See: Raices de
    Piedra)
Rope 9-01-48:14
Rope of Flesh 8-18-65:18
Rope of Sand 6-29-49:20
Roped 1-31-19:54
Ropin' Fool 11-11-21:37
Rosa Blanca, La 9-06-72:20
Rosa de America 6-19-46:22
Rosa de Francia 2-26-36:37
Rosa di Bagdad, La 9-28-49:15
Rosa Per Tutti, Una (See: Rose
    for Everyone, A)
Rosa Raisa (s) 6-20-28:14
Rosa Rossa, La 5-23-73:36
Rosa und Lin 12-06-72:20
Rosal Bendito, El 2-10-37:15
Rosalie 12-22-37:16
Rosary, The 3-31-22:40
Rosary, The 7-14-31:55
Rosas Del Milagro, Las 4-27-
    60:6
Rosaura a Las Diez 5-21-58:18
Rose, The 10-10-79:20
Rose Bernd 5-22-57:20 and 7-24-
    57:26
Rose Bowl 12-09-36:13
Rose Bowl Story, The 8-27-52:6
Rose de la Mer, La 3-19-47:12
Rose di Danzica, Le 10-03-79:18
Rose for Everyone, A 7-12-67:6
Rose-Marie 2-15-28:26
Rose Marie 2-05-36:12
Rose Marie 3-03-54:6
Rose o' Salem Town 10-01-10:18
Rose of Cimarron 3-12-52:16
Rose of Kildare, The 11-23-27:
    25

Rose of Nome, The 9-03-20:44
Rose of Paris, The 10-15-24:32
Rose of the Bower 8-31-27:24
Rose of the Golden West 9-28-27:
    25
Rose of the Rancho, The 11-21-
    14:27
Rose of the Rancho, The 1-15-
    36:18
Rose of the Rio Grande 7-13-38:
    15
Rose of the Sea 6-16-22:42
Rose of the South 11-24-16:30
Rose of the Tenderloin, A 11-27-
    09:13
Rose of the Tenements 4-13-27:
    22
Rose of the West 7-25-19:45
Rose of the World 1-11-18:42
Rose of the World 11-11-25:39
Rose of the Yukon 1-26-49:11
Rose of Tralee 10-26-38:15
Rose of Washington Square 5-10-
    39:14
Rose Tattoo, The 11-02-55:6
Rose von Istanbul, Die 7-08-53:
    18
Roseanna McCoy 8-17-49:8
Rosebud 3-26-75:18
Roseland (s) 9-17-30:21
Roseland 10-05-77:36
Rosemarie 9-17-58:7
Rosemary 12-10-15:21
Rosemary Climbs the Heights 11-
    01-18:38
Rosemary's Baby 5-29-68:6
Rosen fuer den Staatsanwalt 5-18-
    60:24
Rosenkavalier, Der 7-25-62:6
Rosenmontag 4-01-31:17
Roses and Ruses 5-11-27:24
Roses Are Red 11-05-47:8
Roses of Picardy 5-02-28:15 and
    12-11-29:39
Rosie! 11-01-67:6
Rosie O'Grady 2-09-17:28
Rosie O'Grady 9-22-36:16
Rosie the Riveter 4-05-44:14
Rosier de Mme. Husson, Le 3-
    01-32:21 (Also see: He)
Rosiere de Pessac, La 5-14-69:
    34
Rosita 9-06-23:22
Ross-Armstrong Fight (s) 6-08-38:
    26
Ross-Canzoneri Fight (s) 9-19-33:
    13
Ross-McLarnin Fight (s) 6-05-34:
    12 and 6-05-35:15

Ross-Petrolle Fight (s) 1-30-34: 12
Rossetto, Il 4-27-60:6
Rossini 2-04-48:21
Rosszemberek 2-28-79:26
Roswolsky's Sweetheart 10-14-21:44
Rotagg 11-27-46:28
Rote, Die 7-11-62:27
Rote Strumpf, Der 12-31-80:20
Rothapfel Unt 5-16-19:52
Rothschild 10-19-38:27
Rotten to the Core 7-21-65:7
Roue, La 1-19-23:47 (Also see: Wheel, The)
Rouge and Riches 2-13-20:45
Rouge Est Mis, Le 7-24-57:26
Rouge et le Noir, Le 12-01-54:6
Rouged Lips 8-30-23:27
Rough and Ready 4-19-18:41
Rough and the Smooth 10-14-59:6
Rough Cut 6-18-80:22
Rough Diamond 11-25-21:43
Rough House Rosie 5-25-27:20
Rough Lover, The 3-01-18:42
Rough Neck, The 1-25-19:45
Rough Necking (s) 6-12-34:19
Rough Night in Jericho 8-09-67:6
Rough on Rents (s) 12-02-42:22
Rough Riders, The 3-30-27:14
Rough Riders of Durango 2-07-51:18
Rough Riders' Roundup 4-12-39: 25
Rough Ridin' Rhythm 1-26-38:15
Rough Riding Red 11-14-28:30
Rough Romance 6-18-30:53
Rough Sailing (s) 9-22-31:22
Rough Seas (s) 6-02-31:14
Rough Shod 6-30-22:33
Rough Shoot 2-25-53:6
Rough, Tough and Ready 3-28-45:19
Rough, Tough West, The 6-25-52:6
Rough Waters 6-30-30:38
Rough Weather Courtship, A 9-10-10:14
Roughly Speaking 1-31-45:10
Roughneck, The 12-03-24:30
Roughshod 5-11-49:6
Roulette 2-28-24:22
Roumania (s) 5-06-31:22
Round the World in Song (s) 1-03-33:19
Round Trip 7-12-67:22
Rounder, The 8-06-30:21
Round-Up, The 9-10-20:35

Roundup, The 3-19-41:16
Roundup Time in Texas 7-07-37:25
Round-Up Time in Texas 8-04-37:19
Rousalochka 7-28-76:20
Roustabout 11-11-64:6
Route de Corinthe, La 10-25-67: 20
Route de Salina, La 11-18-70:14
Route Napoleon, La 11-25-53:24
Route Sans Issue 3-24-48:22
Routers du Sud, Les 5-03-78:27
Roveh Huliot 2-21-79:28
Rover Turns Santa Claus 8-28-09:13
Rover's Big Chance (s) 8-12-42: 20
Rovin' Tumbleweeds 1-10-40:16
Rowdy, The 9-23-21:42
Rowdyman, The 6-07-72:18
Roxie Hart 2-04-42:8
Roy Evans and Al Belasco (s) 11-20-29:12
Roy Likit 9-26-79:34
Roy Sedley (s) 5-15-29:20
Royal Affair, A (See: Loi, La)
Royal African Rifles, The 9-30-53:6
Royal American, A 8-10-27:26
Royal Ark 11-15-23:23
Royal Ballet 1-20-60:7
Royal Bed, The 2-04-31:16
Royal Box, The 5-22-14:23
Royal Box, The 1-01-30:24
Royal Cavalcade 4-17-35:15
Royal Divorce, A 5-12-38:19
Royal Family, A 8-20-15:20
Royal Family, The 12-24-30:20
Royal Flash 10-01-75:24
Royal Four Flusher (s) 7-02-30: 25
Royal Hunt of the Sun 10-01-69: 17
Royal Imposter, A 1-01-15:30
Royal Journey 1-23-52:22
Royal Mountain Patrol 12-31-41:8
Royal Pair, The (s) 9-25-29:17
Royal Rider, The 12-04-29:31
Royal Romance, A 4-23-30:39
Royal Scandal, The 9-25-29:17
Royal Scandal, A 3-21-45:10
Royal Symphony (s) 3-10-54:6
Royal Waltz, The 4-15-36:23
Royal Wedding 2-07-51:6
Royalut 7-25-79:16
Rozina the Loved Child 3-02-49: 20

Rozmarne Leto 6-19-68:6
Rubacuori 4-22-31:19 and 3-15-
32:14
Rubber 4-01-36:17
Rubber Gun, The 8-31-77:19
Rubber Heels 6-29-27:18
Rubber Racketeers 7-01-42:8
Rubber Tires 3-09-27:16
Rube and the Baron, The 3-14-
13:14
Rubens 7-13-49:16
Rubeville Night Club (s) 11-06-
29:19
Rubia's Jungle 3-17-71:26
Rubicon 9-22-31:26
Ruby 5-18-77:21
Ruby Gentry 12-24-52:6
Ruby Keeler (s) 6-06-28:12
Ruchome Piaski 4-09-69:8
Rude Boy 2-27-80:21
Rude Journee Pour la Reine 12-
12-73:20
Rudy Vallee and Orchestra (s)
3-27-29:12; 6-19-29:24;
7-12-32:16
Rue de l'Estrapade 5-20-52:16
Rue des Prairies 12-16-59:6
Rue du Pied-de-Grue 12-19-79:36
Rue Haute 4-28-76:30
Rue Sans Joie, La 6-01-38:13
Rue Sans Nom, La 1-23-34:21
Rufus 5-14-75:35
Rufus for President (s) 9-05-33:
19
Rug Maker's Daughter, The 7-09-
15:17
Rugged O'Riordans, The 12-14-49:
22
Rugged Water 6-22-25:32
Ruggles of Red Gap 3-15-18:43
Ruggles of Red Gap 9-13-23:28
Ruggles of Red Gap 3-19-35:15
Ruisseau, Le 11-30-38:13
Ruiter in die Nag, Die (See: Rider
in the Night, The)
Rule 'Em and Leave 'Em (s) 6-14-
32:16
Rule G. 2-06-15:23
Ruler of the Road 4-12-18:45
Rulers of the Sea 9-20-39:15
Rules of the Game (See: Regle du
Jeu, La)
Ruling Class, The 4-19-72:18
Ruling Passion, The 2-04-16:28
Ruling Passion, The 1-27-22:39
Ruling Passions 10-04-18:46
Ruling Voice, The 11-10-31:15
Rumble on the Rocks 11-28-56:6

Rumbo Al Cairo 11-06-35:21
Rumeur Publique 8-11-54:6
Rummy, The 9-29-16:24
Run, Angel, Run 4-23-69:6
Run Around, The (s) 2-14-33:12
Run for Cover 3-23-55:6
Run for the Hills 7-08-53:16
Run for the Money 1-28-70:23
Run for the Roses 11-15-78:79
Run for the Sun 7-25-56:6
Run for Your Life (See: Moglie
Americana, Una)
Run for Your Money, A 12-07-
49:20
Run Like a Thief 1-17-68:24
Run of the Arrow 5-29-57:6
Run Silent, Run Deep 3-26-58:6
Run the Wild River 6-16-71:22
Run Wild, Run Free 4-02-69:6
Run with the Devil (See: Via
Margutta)
Runaround, The 8-11-31:22
Runaround, The 6-05-46:13
Runaway, The 4-28-26:48
Runaway 11-18-64:6
Runaway Boys (s) 9-08-31:15
Runaway Bride 5-21-30:25
Runaway Bus, The 3-03-54:6
Runaway Daughters 1-16-57:6
Runaway Freight, The 11-14-13:
14
Runaway Girls 11-07-28:16
Runaway Wife, The 8-27-15:20
Runner Stumbles, The 4-11-79:21
Running 6-06-79:24
Running Away from a Fortune 1-
07-11:13
Running Empty 8-07-63:20
Running Fence 1-25-78:24
Running Fight, The 7-09-15:18
Running Man, The 8-07-63:6
Running Target 11-28-56:6
Running Water 10-27-22:42
Running Wild 6-15-27:20
Running Wild 11-02-55:6
Runoilija Ja Muusa 9-05-79:27
Rupert of Hentzau 7-12-23:29
Rupture, La 9-30-70:20
Rush Hour, The 2-08-28:24
Rush Hour Rhapsody (s) 10-21-36:
15
Rush to Judgment 6-07-67:6
Russ Morgan Orchestra (s) 7-29-
36:14
Russia 1-09-29:45
Russia 3-15-72:6
Russia Marches On 2-23-38:15
Russia on Parade 9-11-46:10

Safety in Numbers 9-07-38:12
Safety Last 4-05-23:36
Safety Match 4-13-55:9
Safo 11-17-43:20
Sag Mir, Wer du Bist 6-06-33:
15
Saga, En 1-12-38:15
Saga of Anatahan, The (See:
Anatahan and Devil's Pitch-
fork, The)
Saga of Death Valley 3-06-40:18
Saga of Hemp Brown 8-13-58:6
Sagar Sangame 7-15-59:6
Sagarana, O Duelo 7-03-74:24
Sage and the Cherub and the
Widow, The 10-15-10:12
Sage Brush Girls, The 11-28-14:
24
Sage Hen, The 2-04-21:43
Sagebrush Family Trails West,
The 4-17-40:16
Sagebrush Hamlet, A 8-01-19:53
Sagebrush Politics 5-21-30:27
Sagebrush Troubador 9-09-36:17
Saginaw Trail 8-26-53:6
Sahara 7-04-19:43
Sahara 9-29-43:8
Sahib, Bibi Aur Ghulam 7-03-63:
18
Sai Cosa Faceva Stalin Alle Donne?
9-17-69:23
Sai Thip 7-18-79:14
Said O'Reilly to McNab 7-14-37:21
(Also see: Says O'Reilly to
McNab)
Saiehaïeh Botan de Bad 5-16-78:19
Saignee, La 12-01-72:22
Saigon 2-04-48:13
Sail a Crooked Ship 12-20-61:7
Sailing Along 2-09-38:15
Sailor Be Good 2-28-33:39
Sailor Beware 12-05-51:6
Sailor Beware! 9-12-56:18
Sailor-Made Man, A 11-25-21:42
Sailor Takes a Wife, The 1-02-
46:8
Sailor Who Fell from Grace with
the Sea, The 4-14-76:23
Sailorizziemurphy 11-23-27:25
Sailor's Dog, The 8-15-08:11
Sailor's Holiday 10-23-29:17
Sailor's Holiday 3-15-44:32
Sailor's Lady, The 7.03-40:18
Sailor's Luck 3-21-33:27
Sailors On Leave 10-08-41:9
Sailor's Return, The 6-21-78:19
Sailor's Sweetheart 10-12-27:25
Sailors' Wives 2-29-28:27

St. Benny the Dip 6-27-51:9
St. Denis, Dans le Temps 10-21-
70:22
Saint, Devil and Woman 10-20-
16:27
St. Elmo 8-28-14:17
St. Elmo 11-29-23:26
Saint in London, The 7-12-39:13
Saint in New York, The 5-25-38:
12
Saint in Palm Springs, The 1-08-
41:24
St. Ives 7-21-76:22
Saint Jack 5-02-79:26
Saint Joan 5-08-57:6
St. Louis Blues (s) 9-04-29:13
St. Louis Blues 2-08-39:17
St. Louis Blues 4-09-58:6
St. Louis Kid, The 11-06-34:17
St. Matthew Passion, The 11-30-
49:6
Saint Meets the Tiger, The 8-04-
43:16
Saint-On Jamais 7-24-57:6
St. Pauli Report 3-22-72:20
Saint Prend L'Affut, Le 11-23-
66:6
Saint Strikes Back, The 3-01-39:
15
Saint Takes Over, The 4-24-40:
16
Saint Therese of Lisieux (See:
Little Flower of Jesus)
Saint Tropez Blues 3-08-61:6
St. Valentine's Day Massacre,
The 7-05-67:6
Sainte Famille, La 4-25-73:18
Sainted Devil, A 11-26-24:24
"Sainted" Sisters, The 3-10-48:
10
Saintes Nitouches, Les 8-28-63:
18
Saintly Sinner, The 2-16-17:25
Saintly Sinner 1-24-62:6
Saints and Sinners 6-16-16:26
Saints and Sinners 7-06-49:9
Saints and Their Sorrows 12-25-
14:42
Saint's Adventure, The 7-13-17:
26
Saint's Double Trouble, The 2-
14-40:20
Saint's Girl Friday, The 3-17-54:
22
Saint's Vacation, The 6-18-41:16
Sajenko--the Soviet 1-16-29:22
Sakada 4-07-76:28
Sakka Mat, El 10-26-77:20

Sal of Singapore 1-30-29:34
Sala de Guardia 5-28-52:24
Salach Shabati 6-24-64:20
Saladin 7-24-63:6
Salaire de la Peur, Le 4-29-53: 18
Salak Jitr 6-13-79:34
Salamander, The 12-17-15:18
Salamandre, La 7-07-71:18
Salammbo 4-16-15:19
Salamoniko 12-27-72:20
Salauds Vont en Enfer, Les 3-28-56:22
Sale Historie, Une 11-16-77:24
Sale Reveur 4-05-78:23
Sales Temps Pour les Mouches 3-22-67:6
Salesgirls' Idol, The 6-05-09:13
Saleslady, The 3-31-16:28
Saleslady 1-26-38:14
Salesman, The 9-11-29:18
Salesman 2-26-69:6
Salingit Mesra 4-25-79:19
Sally 3-18-25:40
Sally 12-25-29:20
Sally and Saint Anne 6-25-52:6
Sally Bishop 12-27-23:27
Sally Bishop 11-08-32:17
Sally Fieldgood & Co. 2-26-75: 22
Sally Fields (s) 9-05-28:14
Sally in Our Alley 7-21-31:34
Sally, Irene and Mary 12-09-25: 42
Sally, Irene and Mary 3-02-38: 15
Sally of Our Alley 7-28-16:24
Sally of Our Alley 11-02-27:21
Sally of the Sawdust 8-05-25:30
Sally of the Scandals 7-04-28:23
Sally of the Subway 2-23-32:19
Sally's Hounds 10-02-68:25
Sally's Irish Rose 11-26-58:6
Sally's Shoulders 12-26-28:27
Salo O la Centiventi Giornate Di Sodoma 12-03-75:22
Salo (The 120 Days of Sodom) (See: Salo O la Centiventi Giornate Di Sodoma)
Salo Mortale 9-01-31:34
Salome 2-28-13:15
Salome 10-11-18:45
Salome 1-05-23:42
Salome 3-18-53:6
Salome 9-13-72:34
Salome of the Tenements 2-25-25:31
Salome, Where She Danced 4-11-45:14
Salomy Jane 10-31-14:27
Salomy Jane 8-09-23:26
Salon Kitty 1-19-77:22
Saloon Bar 7-10-40:14
Salsa 4-07-76:23
Salt and Pepper 7-31-68:22
Salt Lake Raiders 5-17-50:16
Salt of the Earth 3-17-54:6
Salt Water Taffy (s) 9-12-33:17
Salto 9-08-65:68
Salto a la Gloria 8-12-59:6
Salto Mortale (See: Trapeze)
Salto Nel Vuoto 3-26-80:20
Salty O'Rourke 2-21-45:8
Saludos 12-09-42:8
Saludos Amigos (See: Saludos)
Salut en De Kost 10-30-74:44
Salut I Forca Al Canut 2-27-80: 26
Salut, Jerusalem 7-12-72:26
Salut l'Artiste 12-26-73:17
Salut, Voleurs 7-04-73:30
Salute 8-21-29:18 and 10-09-29: 38
Salute for 3 6-16-43:16
Salute John Citizen 9-02-42:34
Salute to Courage 1-21-42:18
Salute to the Marines 7-28-43:8
Salvage 6-17-21:34
Salvage (s) 9-30-42:20
Salvation Hunters, The 2-04-25: 33
Salvation Jane 5-11-27:21
Salvation Joan 4-07-16:21
Salvation Nell 8-20-16:19
Salvation Nell 7-01-21:29
Salvation Nell 7-07-31:25
Salvatore Giuliano 12-27-61:6
Salvo d'Acquisto 7-28-76:24
Salzburg Connection, The 8-02-72:18
Sam 8-12-59:6
Sam and His Musket (s) 11-13-35: 16
Sam Coslow (s) 3-27-29:12
Sam Langford and Jim Flynn Fight 4-23-10:16
Sam Whiskey 2-05-69:6
Samar 4-11-62:6
Samarang 7-04-33:16
Samaritan's Courtship, The 2-12-10:16
Samba Da Criacao Do Munco 2-21-79:20
Sambizanga 4-25-73:18
Same Jakki 5-22-57:20
Same Time, Next Year 11-22-78:22

Santa Fe Passage 5-11-55:9
Santa Fe Scouts 6-30-43:20
Santa Fe Stampede 12-07-38:13
Santa Fe Trail, The 10-22-30:35
Santa Fe Trail 12-18-40:16
Santa's Christmas Circus 11-02-66:22
Santa's Toy Shop (s) 12-25-29:20
Santa's Workshop (s) 12-27-32:14
Santee 10-03-73:14
Santfe Lauf, Der 6-28-67:6
Santi Veena 12-29-76:26
Santiago 6-20-56:6
Santo de la Espada, El 4-22-70:17
Santo Oficio, El 5-29-74:24
Sao 5 9-22-76:19
Sao Jom Tu 4-16-75:22
Sao Jomken 8-31-77:18
Sao Rang Sung 10-18-75:20
Sao Thang Tam 7-27-77:22
Sap, The 3-05-30:35
Sap from Syracuse 7-30-30:16
Saphead, The 2-18-21:40
Sapho 3-16-17:35
Sapho 12-30-70:16
Sapphire 4-29-59:6
Sappho 5-09-08:11
Sappho 10-14-21:44 (Also see:
Mad Love)
Sappho, Darling 3-12-69:6
Sapporo Winter Olympics 9-13-72:24
Saprofita, Il 10-30-74:44
Saps at Sea 5-01-40:20
Sara Akash 10-14-70:32
Sara Lar Sig Folkvett 2-23-38:15
Saraband Dance, The 3-19-10:18
Saraband for Dead Lovers 9-15-48:20
Saracen Blade 5-19-54:6
Sarah and Son 3-19-30:34 (Also
see: Hjartats Rost, Toute Sa
Vie, and Wiegenlied)
Saraha Eiga No Tomo Yo 11-07-79:40
Sarang Bang Sonnim Omoni 9-05-62:6
Sarati le Terrible 9-29-37:15
Saratoga 7-14-37:20
Saratoga Trunk 11-21-45:10
Sardines a la Carte (s) 10-16-29:17
Sarga Csiko 2-03-37:29
Sarge Goes to College 5-07-47:18
Sarie Marais 7-28-31:24
Sarong Girl 6-23-43:40
Sarten Por el Mango, La 3-21-73:18

Sartre Par Lui-Meme 12-15-76:22
Sarumba 3-22-50:20
Sarvasakshi 2-20-80:19
Sasaki Kojiro 5-10-67:21
Sasayaki No Joe (See: Whispering
Joe)
Saskatchewan 2-24-54:6
Sasom I en Spegel 1-03-62:6
Sasquatch 1-18-78:19
Sassy Cats (s) 2-23-14:33
Satan and Woman 3-21-28:26
Satan Bug, The 3-10-65:6
Satan in Sables 10-14-25:40
Satan Junior 3-07-19:66
Satan Met a Lady 7-29-36:14
Satan Never Sleeps 2-21-62:6
Satan Town 8-25-26:22
Satan's Brew (See: Satansbraten)
Satan's Cradle 11-09-49:6
Satan's Private Door 3-23-17:25
Satan's Sadists 1-14-70:20
Satan's Sister 6-17-25:38
Satansbraten 11-24-76:19
Satanis, the Devil's Mass 3-11-70:22
Satellite in the Sky 7-11-56:10
Satin Girl 12-06-23:26
Satin Woman, The 7-20-27:18
Satogashi Ga Kawareru Toki 7-12-67:22
Satori 1-02-74:15
Satri Ti Lok Leum 3-26-75:22
Satsujinkyo Jidai 3-29-67:26
Saturday Afternoon (s) 9-22-26:17
Saturday Island 3-26-52:6
Saturday Morning 5-05-71:16
Saturday Night 1-27-22:39
Saturday Night and Sunday Morning
11-09-60:6
Saturday Night at the Baths 4-16-75:22
Saturday Night Fever 12-14-77:12
Saturday Night in Apple Valley 11-17-65:6
Saturday Night Kid, The 11-20-29:30
Saturday Night Out 3-18-64:6
Saturday's Children 5-01-29:26
Saturday's Children 4-10-40:14
Saturday's Hero 8-22-51:10
Saturday's Heroes 9-29-37:14
Saturday's Millions 10-17-33:19
Saturn 3 2-20-80:19
Satyricon 9-17-69:13
Sauce for the Goose 8-30-18:40
Saucy Sue 6-12-09:13

385 •

Sauerbruch 11-10-54:6
Saul and David (See: Saul e David)
Saul e David 6-23-65:7
Saut de l'Ange, Le 10-20-71:22
Sauvage, Le 12-10-75:26
Sauve Que Peur la Vie 5-28-80: 15
Sauveur, Le 8-25-71:16
Savage, The 10-26-17:34
Savage, The 8-04-26:13
Savage, The 1-14-53:6
Savage Brigade 12-15-48:6
Savage Drums 7-11-51:6
Savage Eye, The 9-16-59:6
Savage Frontier 5-27-53:6
Savage Girl 5-02-33:13
Savage Gold 8-01-33:14
Savage Guns, The 12-19-62:7
Savage Horde 7-05-50:10
Savage Innocents, The 6-29-60:9
Savage Is Loose, The 10-16-74: 14
Savage Messiah 9-13-72:24
Savage Mutiny 1-21-53:18
Savage Pampas (See: Pampa Salvaje)
Savage Passions 6-08-27:15
Savage Sam 5-22-63:6
Savage Seven, The 5-15-68:28
Savage Shadows 6-11-69:40
Savage Splendor 7-27-49:12
Savage Wild, The 1-28-70:23
Savage Woman, The 8-16-18:38
Savages 5-17-72:30
Save the Children 9-19-73:16
Save the Tiger 2-07-73:18
Saved by Her Prayers 1-21-11:12
Saved by Wireless 11-05-15:22
Saved from the Quicksand 9-25-09:12
Saved from the Tide 2-26-10:15
Saved in the Air 6-25-15:20
Saving the Family Name 9-01-16: 21
Saviour, The 8-13-80:26
Savithri 2-13-80:16
Sawdust 7-26-23:28
Sawdust Paradise 8-29-28:15
Sawdust Ring, The 7-20-17:30
Sawdust Trail, The 7-20-24:24
Sax Appeal (s) 7-07-31:25
Saxofone 11-22-78:26
Saxon Charm, The 9-08-48:10
Say Hello to Yesterday 1-03-71: 24
Say It Again 6-09-26:16
Say It in French 11-30-38:12
Say It Isn't So (s) 7-18-33:36

Say It with Diamonds 6-08-27:19
Say It with Songs 8-14-29:18
Say One for Me 6-10-59:6
Say, Young Fellow 6-21-18:27
Sayama No Kuroi Ame 1-06-74:18
Sayarim 11-01-67:7
Sayat Nova 6-21-78:22
Sayonara 11-13-57:6
Says O'Reilly to McNab 2-02-38:17 (Also see: Said O'Reilly to McNab)
Sbandati 9-28-55:8
Sbatti Il Mostro In Primo Pagina 11-15-72:32
Scalawag 10-24-73:17
Scales of Justice 10-09-09:20
Scales of Justice 7-31-14:16
Scalphunters, The 3-06-68:6
Scamp, The 10-16-57:20
Scandal 7-16-15:17
Scandal 11-02-17:48
Scandal 4-24-29:22
Scandal 10-30-29:37
Scandal 8-20-80:20
Scandal at Scourie 4-29-53:6
Scandal for Sale 4-12-32:14
Scandal in Bad Ischl 2-12-58:18
Scandal in Paris, A 6-12-29:31 and 8-14-29:31
Scandal in Paris, A 7-10-46:8
Scandal, Inc. 8-08-56:6
Scandal Proof 7-08-25:39
Scandal Sheet 2-11-31:29
Scandal Sheet 1-10-40:16
Scandal Sheet 1-09-52:6
Scandal Street 7-28-26:16
Scandal Street 2-09-38:14
Scandale, Le 3-15-67:26
Scandale du Grand Hotel 4-25-33:18
Scandalous Adventures of Buraikan, The (See: Buraikan)
Scandalous John 6-23-71:46
Scandals 3-20-34:16 (Trailer reviewed on: 3-27-34:12)
Scandals of Clochermerle 3-22-50:6
Scano Boa 8-02-61:6
Scapegoat, The 7-22-59:6
Scapolo, Lo 7-18-56:6
Scar, The 4-04-19:68
Scarab King 7-22-21:36
Scaramouche 9-20-23:23 and 10-04-23:22
Scaramouche 5-14-52:6
Scarecrow 4-11-73:20
Scarecrow in a Garden of Cucumbers 2-23-72:6
Scared Stiff (s) 2-04-31:16

Schlagerparade 5-05-54:21
Schleppzug M. 17 5-09-33:17
Schlock 3-28-73:18
Schloss, Das 9-11-68:6
Schloss Gripsholm 3-18-64:6
Schloss Hubertus 2-27-35:26
Schloss in Flandern, Das 9-23-36:17
Schloss Vogeloed 5-13-36:15
Schluchtenflitzer 5-23-79:26
Schlussakkord 9-16-36:17
Schmeling-Uzcudun Fight (s) 7-03-
    29:17
Schneeglockchen Bluehn in September
    7-07-76:16
Schneeschuhsport in Sommer (s)
    8-25-31:24
Schneewittchen und die Sieben Gauk-
    ler 2-27-63:7
Schneider von Ulm, Der 5-30-79:26
Schoen Ist die Manoeverzeit 8-30-32:
    23
Schoene Abenteuer, Das 12-13-32:15
Schoene Abenteuer, Das 10-21-59:6
Schonzeit fueur Fuechse 5-04-66:6
School Boy's Revenge 4-10-09:13
School Days 12-09-21:36
School Days (s) 6-02-31:15
School Daze (s) 8-27-30:21
School for Brides 2-20-52:18
School for Danger 2-19-47:9
School for Girls 2-20-35:31
School for Husbands 8-25-37:23 and
    2-01-39:13
School for Love (See: Future Vedettes)
School for Romance (s) 4-10-34:13
School for Scandal 9-17-30:30
School for Scoundrels 10-26-60:17
School for Secrets 11-20-46:38
School for Sex 12-06-67:6
School for Suicide (See: Selvmor-
    derskolen)
School for Wives 4-01-25:38
Schoolgirl Diary 9-24-47:11
Schoolmaster of Mariposa, The 9-
    24-10:12
Schornstein Nr. 4 9-14-66:26
Schpountz, Le 5-18-38:12
Schrecken der Garnison, Der 6-07-
    32:25
Schrei der Schwarzen Woelfe, Der
    10-18-72:24
Schuberts Fruhlingstraum 6-28-32:15
Schuesse im 3/4 Takt 5-12-65:6
Schuetzenfest in Schilda 11-17-31:26
Schuldig 5-02-28:14
Schulde fuer Eheglueck 8-11-54:6
Schulmaedchen--Report 11-11-70:24
Schulmaedchen--Report III 3-22-72:36

Schuss im Morgengrauen 9-06-32:
    30
Schut, Der 11-04-64:18
Schwartz-Weiss-Rote Himmelbett,
    Das 1-16-63:20
Schwarz und Weiss Wie Tage und
    Maechte 9-20-78:34
Schwarze Hussar, Der 1-03-33:27
Schwarze Rosen 1-15-36:18
Schwarze Walfisch 3-20-34:31
Schwarzer Kies 6-07-61:6
Schwebende Jungfrau, Die 10-06-31:
    31
Schweik's New Adventures 9-22-43:
    12
Schweizermacher, Die 11-29-78:26
Schwestern, oder die Balance des
    Gluecks 10-10-79:20
Scipio L'Africano 9-08-37:19
Sciuscia 5-22-46:10 (Also see: Shoe
    Shine)
Scobie Malone 10-08-74:16
Scoffer, The 3-25-21:43
Scogliera Del Peccata, La (See: Cliff
    of Sin, The)
Sconosciuto di San Marino, Lo 2-18-
    48:9
Scopono Scientifico, Lo 10-18-72:24
Scorcher, The 5-04-27:22
Scorchy 10-06-76:21
Score 11-14-73:16
Scored Flesh 11-10-48:18
Scorpio 4-11-73:20
Scorpio Rising 5-25-66:6
Scorpio 70 5-27-70:20
Scotch Highball (s) 6-23-31:18
Scotch Love (s) 8-27-30:21
Scotch on the Rocks 6-16-54:6
Scotland Yard 10-22-30:23
Scotland Yard 4-09-41:16
Scotland Yard Commands 3-31-37:19
Scotland Yard Investigator 10-10-
    45:8
Scotland Yard Mystery 3-18-36:29
Scott Joplin 2-09-77:22
Scott of the Antarctic 12-08-48:11
Scoumoune, La 12-27-72:20
Scoundrel, The 5-08-35:16
Scram (s) 1-31-33:12
Scrambled Wives 5-27-21:35
Scrap for Victory (s) 8-26-42:18
Scrap Iron 6-03-21:40
Scrap of Paper, A 3-28-13:14
Scrap the Japs (s) 12-02-42:8
Scrapper, The 2-10-22:35
Scrappin' Kid 7-14-26:18
Scratch As Scratch Can (s) 11-03-31:
    17

389 •

Secret of Convict Lake 6-27-51:9
Secret of Deep Harbor 10-04-61:6
Secret of Dr. Kildare 11-22-39:14
Secret of Eve, The 3-02-17:28
Secret of Madame Blanche 2-07-33:
   12
Secret of Mayerling, The 5-16-51:18
Secret of Monte Carlo, The 8-09-
   61:6
Secret of My Success, The 9-29-
   65:6
Secret of Outer Space Island, The
   12-12-62:6
Secret of St. Ives, The 6-01-49:11
Secret of Santa Vittoria, The 10-
   01-69:17
Secret of Stamboul 10-21-36:23
Secret of the Blue Room 9-19-33:13
Secret of the Cellar 11-12-10:16
Secret of the Chateau 2-05-35:31
Secret of the Hills 11-04-21:41
Secret of the Incas 5-19-54:6
Secret of the Old Cabinet, The 4-09-
   15:20
Secret of the Purple Reef 11-02-60:6
Secret of the Storm Country 11-09-
   17:55
Secret of the Swamp, The 7-21-16:19
Secret of the Wastelands 9-24-41:8
Secret of Treasure Island (serial)
   5-11-38:16
Secret of Treasure Mountain 5-30-
   56:18
Secret Orchard, The 8-13-15:17
Secret Partner, The 3-15-61:7
Secret Patrol 6-24-36:45
Secret People 2-12-52:6
Secret Place, The 3-20-57:6
Secret Policeman's Ball, The 12-
   05-79:24
Secret Rites 10-20-71:20
Secret Rivals, The 7-07-76:16
Secret Scrolls (Part I) 5-22-68:28
Secret Scrolls (Part II) 5-29-68:20
Secret Service 6-27-19:45
Secret Service 12-15-31:14
Secret Service, The 5-20-53:16
Secret Service Investigator 6-02-48:
   12
Secret Service of the Air 3-08-39:18
Secret Seven, The 3-05-15:21
Secret Seven, The 8-14-40:14
Secret Seven, The 4-27-66:6
Secret Sinners 12-26-33:26
Secret Six, The 5-06-31:22
Secret Spring, The 8-04-26:16
Secret Strings 10-18-18:39
Secret Studio 6-15-27:21

Secret Valley 1-27-37:13
Secret Violence (See: Violenza
   Segreta)
Secret War of Harry Frigg, The
   2-28-68:6
Secret Ways, The 3-22-61:15
Secret Witness 12-22-31:15
Secret World 7-09-69:6
Secretary Preferred (s) 3-29-32:
   24
Secretas Intenciones, Las 9-30-
   70:24
Secreto Eterno 2-02-44:18
Secrets 3-26-24:26
Secrets 3-21-33:16
Secrets 11-01-78:40
Secrets d'Alcove 6-16-54:6
Secrets of a Ballerina 1-05-49:58
Secrets of a Co-ed 1-27-43:8
Secrets of a Model 4-17-40:16
Secrets of a Nurse 11-16-38:15
Secrets of a Secretary 9-01-31:
   31
Secrets of a Soul 1-18-28:23
Secrets of an Actress 10-12-38:
   15
Secrets of Life 9-13-23:34
Secrets of Life 10-17-56:6
Secrets of Monte Carlo 6-20-51:
   22
Secrets of Nature 8-28-29:31 and
   11-06-29:31
Secrets of Nature (s) 11-05-30:23
Secrets of Nature 9-13-50:6
Secrets of Night 3-25-25:38
Secrets of Paris 1-12-23:34
Secrets of Scotland Yard 6-14-
   44:10
Secrets of the French Police 12-
   13-32:14
Secrets of the Lone Wolf 11-26-
   41:9
Secrets of the Nazi Criminals 9-
   26-62:6
Secrets of the Orient 1-05-32:23
Secrets of the Underground 2-10-
   43:18
Secrets of Women (See: Kvinnors
   Vantan)
Secrets of Wu Sin 2-28-33:39
Section Speciale 5-14-75:27
Secuestador, El 9-17-58:18
Secuestro Sensacional 8-12-42:22
Security Risk 8-18-54:6
Sed de Amor 9-16-59:16
Seda, Sangre y Sol 5-20-42:8
Sedmi Kontinent 8-02-67:6
Sedmikrasky 8-03-66:7

391 •

Senor Americano 1-01-30:28
Senor Daredevil 8-18-26:60
Senor Fotografo, El 12-30-53:18
Senor Presidente, El 9-16-70:23
Senora de Perez Se Divorcia, La
    8-29-45:16
Senorita, The 11-06-09:13
Senorita 5-11-27:14
Senorita de Trevelez, Le 6-17-
    36:62
Senorita from the West 10-17-
    45:8
Sensation 12-30-36:11
Sensation Hunters 1-09-34:17
Sensation Hunters 11-28-45:10
Sensation in the Wintergarten 10-
    02-29:31
Sensation Seekers 3-16-27:17
Sensations 10-15-75:26
Sensations of 1945 6-21-44:12
Sense of Loss, A 10-11-72:18
Senso 10-13-54:6
Senso To Ningen 7-24-74:22
Sensual Man, The (See: Paolo Il
    Caldo)
Sensualita 10-29-52:24
Sensually Liberated Female, The
    11-25-70:22
Sentados Al Borde de la Manana
    Con Los Pies Colgando 2-07-
    79:26
Sentence, La 8-26-59:6
Sentimental Attempt, A (See: Ten-
    tativo Sentimentale, Un)
Sentimental Bloke 5-31-32:15
Sentimental Journey 2-06-46:12
Sentimental Lady, The 11-12-15:
    22
Sentimental Tommy 4-01-21:41
Sentimentalnyi Roman 1-12-77:44
Sentinel, The 2-16-77:24
Sentinelle di Bronzo 9-22-37:19
Sentinelle Endormie, La 2-23-66:6
Senza Bandiera 12-05-51:22
Senza Famiglia Nullatenenti Cercano
    Affetto 7-12-72:28
Separate Peace, A 9-13-72:20
Separate Tables 12-03-58:6
Separation 10-11-67:22
Sepia Cinderella 7-30-47:27
Sepolta Viva, La 6-01-49:20 (Also
    see: Buried Alive)
Sepoy's Wife, The 9-17-10:12
Seppuku 5-22-63:19
7 Fois.... (Par Jour) 6-09-71:22
Sept Hommes et Une Garce 4-05
    67:6
Sept Hommes, Une Femme

    9-30-36:29
Sept Jours Ailleurs 4-02-69:28
Sept Morts Sur Ordonnance 12-
    10-75:26
Sept Peches Capitals 6-04-52:6
    (Also see: Seven Deadly Sins)
Sept Peches Capitals 4-11-62:28
September Affair 9-06-50:8
September Storm 9-14-60:18
Septemberweizen 8-06-80:36
Septieme Ciel, Le 3-26-58:14
Septieme Commandment, Le 4-
    03-57:24
Septieme Compagnie Au Clair de
    Lune, La 12-28-77:24
Septieme Jure, Le 5-02-62:6
Sequestro Di Persona 4-10-68:22
Sequoia 2-27-35:12
Serafino 1-01-69:20
Serail 5-26-76:36
Seraphin 3-01-50:16
Serenade 9-09-21:44
Serenade 12-21-27:22
Serenade 4-03-40:16
Serenade 3-14-56:6
Serenade einer Grossen Liebe 5-
    27-59:6
Serenata a la Luz de la Luna 9-
    12-79:22
Serge 9-14-60:21
Sergeant, The 10-01-10:18
Sergeant, The 10-30-68:6
Sergeant Deadhead 8-11-65:6
Sergeant Madden 3-22-39:20
Sergeant Mike 2-07-45:23
Sgt. Murphy 12-22-37:17
Sgt. Pepper's Lonely Hearts Club
    Band 7-19-78:20
Sergeant Was a Lady, The 9-13-
    61:6
Sergeant York 7-02-41:12
Sergeant X, Le 4-19-32:25
Sergeant X 3-16-60:6
Sergeants Three 1-24-62:6
Serial 3-26-80:20
Serie Noire 4-20-55:6
Serie Noire 5-02-79:27
Serieux Comme le Plaisir 2-12-
    75:28
Serious Charge 4-15-59:6
Serment, Le 3-20-34:31
Serments 11-10-31:23
Serpent, The 1-28-16:23
Serpent, Le 4-04-73:26
Serpent of the Nile 4-15-53:22
Serpent's Egg, The 11-02-77:17
Serpente a Sonagli 8-19-36:17
Serpents of the Pirate Moon, The
    1-02-74:6

393 •

Seven Were Saved 2-19-47:9
Seven Women 12-08-65:22
Seven Women from Hell 10-18-61:6
Seven Wonders of the World 4-11-56:6
Seven Year Itch, The 6-08-55:6
Seventeen 2-21-40:12
1789 6-26-74:18
1776 11-08-72:18
1776, or Hessian Renegades 9-11-09:13
17th Parallel: Vietnam in War (See: 17e Parallele le Vietnam en Guerre)
Seventh Bandit, The 7-21-26:15
Seventh Cavalry 10-24-56:6
Seventh Continent, The (See: Sedmi Kontinent)
Seventh Cross, The 7-19-44:13
Seventh Dawn, The 6-24-64:6
Seventh Day, The 3-17-22:41
Seventh Heaven 5-11-27:14
Seventh Heaven 3-31-37:17
Seventh Juror, The (See: Septieme Jure, Le)
Seventh Noon, The 10-29-15:23
Seventh Seal, The (See: Sjunde Inseglet, Det)
Seventh Sheriff 12-20-23:26
Seventh Sin, The 5-15-57:22
Seventh Veil, The 10-31-45:17
Seventh Victim, The 8-18-43:26
Seventh Voyage of Sinbad, The 11-26-58:6
75 Years of a Cinema Museum 12-06-72:20
77 Park Lane 7-14-31:22
77 Rue Chalgrin 12-01-31:26
70,000 Witnesses 9-06-32:21
Severed Head, A 2-03-71:24
Sevres Porcelain 8-28-09:13
Sex 4-02-20:94
Sex and Astrology 1-20-71:13
Sex and the Single Gay 6-17-70:22
Sex and the Single Girl 12-23-64:6
Sex Demon 7-23-75:20
Sex En Gros 6-23-71:46
Sex Freaks 3-13-74:28
Sex-Jack 7-14-71:20
Sex Life of the Polyp, The (s) 8-01-28:12
Sex Lure, The 11-10-16:25
Sex O'Clock U.S.A. 8-04-76:20
Sex of Angels, The (See: Sesso Degli Angeli, Il)
Sex Perverse 9-30-70:22

Sex Power 7-08-70:15
Sex Shop, Le 10-18-72:24
Sex Thief, The 3-13-74:18
Sexe Fort, Le (s) 9-03-30:19
Sextanerin, Die 9-14-38:23
Sextet (See: Sekstet)
Sextette 3-08-78:31
Sextool 3-12-75:20
Sexual Customs in Scandinavia 3-01-72:20
Sexual Encounter Group 12-02-70:16
Sexual Freedom in Denmark 3-18-70:18
Sexual Liberty Now! 6-28-72:26
Sexual Practices in Sweden 11-18-70:40
Sey Seyeti 8-20-80:21
Sfida, La 9-17-58:18
Sh! The Octopus 12-08-37:16
Sha-Nu 5-28-75:18
Shabe Quzi 5-06-64:16
Shack Out On 101 11-30-55:6
Shackelton 8-08-28:23
Shackled 6-28-18:31
Shackles of Gold 5-12-22:33
Shades of Gray 2-04-48:13
Shades of Silk 12-12-79:23
Shadow, The 7-01-36:25
Shadow, The 12-22-37:24
Shadow Alley 12-03-47:11
Shadow Between, The 9-29-31:22
Shadow in the Sky 12-19-51:18
Shadow Man 12-09-53:6
Shadow of a Doubt 2-27-35:26
Shadow of a Doubt 1-13-42:8
Shadow of a Woman 8-14-46:10
Shadow of Doubt, The 4-07-16:24
Shadow of Evil (See: Banco a Bangkok)
Shadow of Fear 6-06-56:6
Shadow of Her Past, The 7-21-16:19
Shadow of Rosalie Byrnes, The 5-28-20:43
Shadow of Terror 11-21-45:18
Shadow of the Cat 5-03-61:26
Shadow of the Desert 3-26-24:44
Shadow of the Dragon (s) 6-02-31:14
Shadow of the Eagle 9-06-50:8
Shadow of the Hawk 7-14-76:20
Shadow of the Law 6-11-30:19
Shadow of the Past, A 11-19-10:13
Shadow of the Past 6-19-14:21
Shadow of the Sage 12-30-42:23
Shadow of the Thin Man 10-22-41:8

Shadow on the Wall 12-08-26:20
Shadow on the Wall 3-15-50:12
Shadow on the Window, The 2-27-57:6
Shadow over Angkor 7-30-69:6
Shadow Returns, The 8-28-46:14
Shadow Strikes, The 7-14-37:21
Shadow Valley 12-03-47:11
Shadowed into the Underworld 9-03-15:21
Shadows 6-25-15:20
Shadows 2-14-19:52
Shadows 11-03-22:42
Shadows 8-31-60:6 and 2-15-61:6
Shadows and Sunshine 11-03-16:29
Shadows Grow Longer, The (See: Schatten Werden Laenger, Die)
Shadows in the Night 8-02-44:20
Shadows of Conscience 3-17-22:42
Shadows of Fear 11-07-28:24
Shadows of Night 9-26-28:15
Shadows of Sing Sing 2-27-34:17
Shadows of Suspicion 5-09-19:52
Shadows of Suspicion 10-18-44:10
Shadows of the Law 4-21-26:35
Shadows of the Orient 10-13-37:16
Shadows of the Past 1-14-11:18
Shadows of the Past 8-27-15:19
Shadows of the Sea 1-06-22:42
Shadows of the West 9-28-49:6
Shadows of Tombstone 10-07-53:6
Shadows on the Stairs 4-16-41:16
Shadows over Chinatown 9-18-46:22
Shadows over Shanghai 12-07-38:12
Shady Lady 3-27-29:24
Shady Lady 9-05-45:15
Shaft 6-16-71:15
Shaft in Africa 6-20-73:20
Shaft's Big Score 6-21-72:18
Shaggy 4-14-48:8
Shaggy D.A., The 12-15-76:19
Shaggy Dog, The 2-25-59:6
Shah of Iran, The 1-16-80:31
Shake Hands with Murder 6-14-44:10
Shake Hands with the Devil 5-13-59:6
Shakedown, The 4-10-29:23
Shakedown 8-19-36:16
Shakedown 1-27-60:7
Shakedown 8-23-50:20
Shakespeare-Wallah 7-14-65:6
Shakespeare Was Right (s)

10-01-30:19
Shakiest Gun in the West, The 3-27-68:6
Shakuntala 1-07-48:56
Shalako 9-25-68:6
Shall We Dance? 5-12-37:12
Shall We Forgive Her? 10-05-17:40
Sham 5-20-21:41
Sham Battle Shenanigans (s) 4-08-42:20
Shame 11-16-17:52
Shame 8-05-21:25
Shame (See: Skammen)
Shame, Shame, Everybody Knows Her Name 8-19-70:24
Shameful Behavior? 10-20-26:67
Shameless Old Lady (See: Vieille Dame Indigne, La)
Shampoo 2-12-75:28
Shampoo the Magician (s) 12-13-32:14
Shamrock and the Rose 7-06-27:23
Shamrock Handicap, The 7-07-26:17
Shamrock Hill 4-20-49:11
Shams of Society 12-02-21:41
Shamus 1-31-73:18
Shane 4-15-53:6
Shanghai (s) 5-10-32:18
Shanghai 7-24-35:21
Shanghai Bound 11-09-27:21
Shanghai Chest 9-08-48:18
Shanghai Cobra, The 8-08-45:22
Shanghai Drama, The 1-17-45:14
Shanghai Express 2-23-32:13
Shanghai Gesture 12-24-41:8
Shanghai Lady 11-13-29:32
Shanghai Madness 9-26-33:20
Shanghai Rose 5-22-29:24
Shanghai Story 9-29-54:16
Shanghaied 10-22-15:23
Shanghaied 9-14-27:22
Shanghaied Baby, The 1-30-15:24
Shanghaied Love 11-10-31:23
Shanks 10-09-74:19
Shannons of Broadway 12-25-29:30
Shantata! Court Chaloo Ashey 9-20-72:18
Shantytown 4-21-43:8
Shaolin Abbot 11-21-79:25
Shaolin Avengers 7-21-76:22
Shaolin Rescuers 7-25-79:24
Shape of Things to Come, The 12-19-79:19
Sharen Sviat (Ipzit & Gola Savest) 8-30-72:26

Shark Master, The 9-09-21:45
Shark Monroe 7-12-18:36
Shark River 11-11-53:6
Shark Woman, The 6-04-41:15
Shark's Treasure 5-07-75:48
Sharkey-Loughran Fight (s) 10-02-29:19
Sharkey-Schmeling 6-28-32:14
Sharkfighters, The 10-31-56:6
Sharon Sviat (Ipzit & Gola Savest) 8-30-72:26
Sharp Shooters 1-25-28:12
Sharp Tools (s) 10-10-28:15
Sharps and Flats (s) 7-11-28:13
Sharpshooters 9-21-38:13
Shatranj Ke Khilari 12-01-77:14
Shattered 7-13-27:20 (Also see: Fragments)
Shattered Idols 6-16-22:41
Shattered Lives 7-08-25:40
Shattered Reputations 8-30-23:26
Shavlool 11-04-70:16
Shaw and Lee (s) 10-03-28:17
Shazdeh Ehte Jab 12-18-74:12
She 4-27-17:25
She 7-14-26:18
She 7-31-35:19
She 4-21-65:6
She and He 12-31-69:6
She Asked for It 9-01-37:22
She Couldn't Help It 2-25-21:42
She Couldn't Say No 2-19-30:33
She Couldn't Say No 1-22-41:16
She Couldn't Say No 1-13-54:6
She-Creature, The 9-05-56:6
She Defends Her Country 6-09-43:8
She Demons 3-19-58:16
She Devil 4-10-57:6
She-Devil Island 9-16-36:31
She Devils, The 12-06-18:39
She Didn't Say No! 10-08-58:6
She Done Him Wrong 2-14-33:12
She Gets Her Man 9-11-35:17
She Gets Her Man 1-10-45:10
She-Gods of Shark Reef 12-10-58:6
She Goes to War 6-12-29:29
She Had to Choose 9-25-34:14
She Had to Eat 7-14-37:21
She Has What It Takes 6-02-43:8
She Is Grown Up Now 8-06-75:18
She Knew All the Answers 5-21-41:15
She Loved a Fireman 11-17-37:16
She Loves and Lies 1-09-20:52
She Loves Me Not 9-11-34:11
She Made Her Bed 5-01-34:15

She Married a Cop 7-05-39:16
She Married an Artist 1-05-38:16
She Married Her Boss 10-02-35:16
She Shall Have Music 12-18-35:12
She Steps Out 3-19-30:34
She Wanted a Bow Wow 4-30-10:16
She Wanted a Millionaire 2-23-32:13
She Was a Lady 8-28-34:15
She Went for a Tramp (s) 4-01-31:16
She Went to the Races 10-17-45:8
She Who Gets Slapped (s) 7-16-30:15
She Wolf, The 7-11-19:60
She-Wolf, The 6-02-31:15
She-Wolf of London 4-10-46:16
She Wolves 8-19-25:37
She Wore a Yellow Ribbon 7-27-49:12
She Wrote the Book 5-15-46:8
Sheba Baby 4-23-75:18
Shed No Tears 7-14-48:12
Sheepman 4-23-58:6
Sheer Luck 6-02-31:31
Shehar Aur Sapna 8-12-64:22
Sheherazade 5-29-63:6
Sheik, The 11-11-21:37
Sheik Steps Out, The 7-28-37:27
Sheik's Wife, The 3-10-22:41
Sheila Levine Is Dead and Living in New York 2-05-75:20
Shell 43 7-28-16:25
Shell Game, The 3-08-18:43
She'll Have To Go 5-09-62:17
Sheltered Daughters 5-20-21:41
Shenandoah 4-14-65:6
Shenanigans 12-21-77:18
Shep Comes Home 1-12-49:8
Shepard King 12-13-23:23
Shepherd of Seven Hills 8-15-33:14
Shepherd of the Hills, The 2-22-38:20
Shepherd of the Hills, The 6-18-41:16
Shepherd of the Ozarks 4-08-42:8
Shepper-Newfounder 12-31-30:19
Sheriff, The 11-29-18:41
Sheriff of Fractured Jaw, The 11-05-58:6
Sheriff of Sage Valley, The 12-09-42:16
Sheriff of Tombstone, The 5-21-41:18
Sheriff of Wichita 3-02-49:8
Sheriff's Son, The 4-04-19:68
"Sherlock" Brown 8-11-22:33

397 ●

Sherlock Holmes 5-19-16:18
Sherlock Holmes 1-27-22:40 and
5-12-22:33
Sherlock Holmes 11-15-32:19
Sherlock Holmes and the Secret
Weapon 12-30-42:23
Sherlock Holmes and the Spider
Woman 1-12-44:24
Sherlock Holmes and the Voice of
Terror 9-09-42:14
Sherlock Holmes Faces Death 9-
08-43:16
Sherlock Holmes' Fatal Hour 7-
14-31:22
Sherlock Holmes in Washington
3-31-43:8
Sherlock, Jr. 5-28-24:27
Sherman Said It (s) 12-19-33:19
Sherry 6-11-20:35
She's a He (s) 5-14-30:19
She's a Sheik 11-23-27:22
She's a Sweetheart 1-10-45:10
She's Back on Broadway 1-28-53:6
She's Dangerous 3-24-37:17
She's for Me 12-08-43:8
She's Got Everything 12-29-37:17
She's in the Army 6-24-42:8
She's My Baby 6-08-27:17
She's My Cousin (s) 6-23-26:19
She's My Weakness 6-25-30:109
She's No Lady 8-18-37:27
She's Working Her Way Through
College 6-11-52:6
Sheshet Hayamin 4-10-68:22
Shield for Murder 9-01-54:6
Shield of Honor 12-14-27:23
Shifting Sands 8-30-18:38
Shigaon Shel Moledeth 5-21-80:24
Shijin No Ai (See: Chijin No Ai)
Shillingsbury Blowers, The 3-26-
80:24
Shin Heike Monogatari 8-09-61:16
Shinbone Alley 3-31-71:6
Shindig, The (s) 1-07-31:23
Shine On, Harvest Moon 3-15-39:
16
Shine On Harvest Moon 3-15-44:
21
Shinel 9-02-59:6
Shining, The 5-28-80:14
Shining Hour, The 11-16-38:15
Shining Victory 5-28-41:16
Shinju Ten No Amijima 9-10-69:
46
Shinjuku Dorobo Nikki 6-11-69:
42
Shinken Shobu 6-28-72:26
Ship a Hooey (s) 7-26-32:17

Ship Ahoy 4-22-42:8
Ship Cafe 11-27-35:14
Ship Comes In, A 9-05-28:28
Ship Dae Eui Ban Hang 11-09-
60:6
Ship from Shanghai, The 4-30-
30:38
Ship Is Born, A (s) 12-02-42:8
Ship of Condemned Women, The
(See: Nave Delle Donne
Maledette, La)
Ship of Doom, The 11-30-17:46
Ship of Fools 5-05-65:6
Ship of Lost Men 10-16-29:33
Ship of Wanted Men 11-21-33:20
Ship That Died of Shame, The 5-
11-55:9
Ship to India, A (See: Frustration
and Skepp Till Indialand)
Shipbuilders, The 1-19-44:30
Shipmates (s) 3-26-30:25
Shipmates 5-27-31:56
Shipmates Forever 10-23-35:12
Ship's Husband, The 11-12-10:16
Ships of Hate 7-28-31:24
Ships of the Night 3-27-29:24
Ships with Wings 1-07-42:45
Shipwrecked 7-07-26:17
Shipwrecked Among Cannibals 7-
09-20:28
Shipyard Sally 8-16-39:14
Shir Hashirim 10-23-35:13
Shiralee, The 7-24-57:27
Shirasagui 5-20-59:6
Shiraz 10-10-28:26 and 3-20-29:
13
Shirley Kaye 12-14-17:44
Shirley of the Circus 1-05-23:43
Shirley Thompson Versus the
Aliens 6-28-72:18
Shiroi Kyoto 11-02-66:6
Shiroi Sammyaku 5-22-57:20
Shivers (s) 1-22-35:15
Shiwjot Takoj Paren 7-05-78:16
Shmonah Be'ikvot Ekhad 12-16-
64:6
Sho O Suteyo, Machi E Deyo 10-
27-71:24
Shock, The 5-30-34:17
Shock 11-20-34:17
Shock 1-16-46:18
Shock Corridor 7-10-63:6
Shock Punch, The 5-13-25:37
Shock Treatment 2-26-64:6
Shock Troops (See: Homme de
Trop, Un)
Shock Troops for Defense (s) 8-
26-42:18

Shock Waves 10-08-80:22

Shocking Miss Pilgrim, The 1-01-47:14

Shocking Night, A 1-21-21:41

Shockproof 1-26-49:11

Shoe Shine 8-13-47:22 (Also see: Sciuscia)

Shoe String Follies (s) 4-10-35:17

Shoes 6-16-16:24

Shoes of the Fisherman, The 11-20-68:6

Shoes That Danced, The 3-01-18:42

Shogun Assassin 11-19-80:18

Shokei No Shima 7-27-66:6

Sholay 2-09-77:24

Shonen 6-26-69:24

Shoosh 5-11-27:24

Shoot 6-02-76:17

Shoot First 6-17-53:6

Shoot It: Black, Shoot It: Blue 12-04-74:22

Shoot Loud, Louder ... I Don't Understand 1-11-67:28

Shoot Out 5-26-71:20

Shoot the Piano Player (See: Tirez Sur le Pianiste)

Shoot the Works 7-10-34:13

Shoot to Kill 4-09-47:16

Shoot Yourself Some Golf (s) 4-22-42:18

Shootin' for Love 7-04-23:23

Shootin' Irons 4-25-28:29

Shootin' Mad 10-25-18:36

Shootin' Romance 2-10-26:41

Shooting High 3-06-40:16

Shooting in the Hunted Woods 1-15-10:13

Shooting Mermaids (s) 10-01-41:9

Shooting of Dan McGrew, The 5-14-15:19

Shooting of Dan McGrew, The 6-11-24:28

Shooting Stars 2-29-28:23 (2 reviews) and 6-13-28:12

Shooting Straight 7-30-30:17

Shootist, The 7-28-76:18

Shoot-Out at Medicine Bend 4-10-57:6

Shop Angel 5-03-32:15

Shop Around the Corner, The 1-10-40:14

Shop at Sly Corner, The 1-29-47:8

Shop Girl, The 6-23-16:21

Shop Girls of Paris 6-25-47:8

Shop on Main Street, The (See: Obchod Na Korze)

Shopworn 4-05-32:14

Shopworn Angel 1-09-29:11

Shopworn Angel 7-13-38:15

Shore Acres 10-24-14:22

Shore Acres 5-21-20:34

Shore Leave 9-16-25:40

Shore of Waiting 7-24-63:8

Shors 12-13-39:52

Short Cut to Hell 9-25-57:6

Short Eyes 10-05-77:36

Short Grass 12-06-50:20

Short Is the Summer 8-20-69:16

Short Shots (s) 9-22-36:17

Short-Sighted Mary 9-04-09:13

Shot Gun Wedding, The (s) 11-10-31:14

Shot in the Dark, A 5-22-35:16

Shot in the Dark, A 5-21-41:15

Shot in the Dark, A 6-24-64:6

Shot in the Talker Studio, The 8-13-30:15

Shotgun 3-30-55:8

Shotgun Pass 3-15-32:29

Should a Baby Die? 3-03-16:22

Should a Doctor Tell? 10-08-30:23 and 8-25-31:20

Should a Girl Marry? 9-18-29:55

Should a Girl Marry? 7-19-39:19

Should a Husband Forgive? 10-31-19:57

Should a Mother Tell? 7-16-15:18

Should a Wife Forgive? 11-05-15:23

Should a Wife Work? 2-03-22:42

Should a Woman Divorce? 1-01-15:30

Should a Woman Tell? 5-01-14:21

Should a Woman Tell? 1-23-20:61

Should Crooners Marry? (s) 3-07-33:14

Should Husbands Work? 7-26-39:15

Should Ladies Behave? 12-19-35:19

Should She Obey? 9-07-17:34

Shoulder Arms 10-25-18:36

Shout, The 5-24-78:34

Shout at the Devil 4-14-76:23

Show, The 3-16-27:17

Show Boat 4-24-29:13

Show Boat 5-20-36:12

Show Boat 6-06-51:6

Show Business (s) 11-08-32:16

Show Business 4-19-44:12

Show Business At War (s) 5-12-43:8

Siege of Pinchgut, The 7-08-59:6
Siege of Sidney Street, The 10-19-60:6
Siege of Syracuse, The 1-24-62:6
Siege of the Saxons 8-21-63:17
Siegel Gottes, Das 2-23-49:11
Sieger, Der 4-12-32:29
Siegerin, Die 3-06-29:15
Sierra 4-26-50:8
Sierra Baron 7-02-58:6
Sierra Maestra 9-17-69:22
Sierra Maldita 9-08-54:22
Sierra Passage 12-13-50:8
Sierra Stranger 5-01-57:6
Sierra Sue 11-12-41:9
Siete Locos, Los 7-11-73:18
Siete Pecados, Los 8-26-59:6
Sigfried 4-09-15:20
Sightseeing in New York (s) 12-01-31:15
Sign Invisible, The 3-01-18:41
Sign of Four 5-17-23:27
Sign of Four 8-30-32:21
Sign of Jack O'Lantern 2-10-22:34
Sign of the Cactus 3-04-25:39
Sign of the Cross, The 12-25-14:42
Sign of the Cross 12-06-32:14
  (Reissue notes: 8-16-44:16)
Sign of the Gladiator 10-28-59:6
Sign of the Pagan 11-10-54:6
Sign of the Poppy, The 12-01-16:27
Sign of the Ram, The 2-04-48:13
Sign of the Rose 3-10-22:42
Sign of the Virgin (See: Souhvezdi Panny)
Sign of the Wolf 9-03-41:8
Sign on the Door 7-22-21:36
Signal Tower, The 6-04-24:26 and 7-23-24:26
Signali Nad Gradom 8-09-61:6
Signe Arsen Lupin 2-03-60:6
Signe du Lion, Le 7-13-60:6
Signet Ring, The 10-29-10:14
Signor Max, Il 12-15-37:23
Signora di Montecarlo, La 1-04-39:14
Signora di Tutta 1-08-35:18
Signore e Signori 3-09-66:17
Signore e Signori, Buonanotte 1-19-77:22
Signori in Carrozza 12-05-51:22
Signpost to Murder 12-23-64:6
Signs of the Zodiac 7-24-63:8
Signum Laudis 7-30-80:28
Sikator 9-13-67:6

Silas Marner 2-25-16:23
Silas Marner 5-26-22:34
Silence 5-26-26:17
Silence 8-18-31:30
Silence (See: Milczenie)
Silence, The 10-02-63:6
Silence 5-01-74:18
Silence de la Mer, Le 5-18-49:20
Silence Est d'Or, Le (See: Man About Town)
Silence Has No Wings 11-09-66:6
Silence of Dean Maitland, The 8-27-15:20
Silence ... On Tourne 5-05-76:14
Silencers, The 2-09-66:6
Silencieux, Le 3-14-73:21
Silent Accuser, The 11-26-24:52
Silent Avenger, The 8-17-27:25
Silent Barriers 3-31-37:19
Silent Battle, The 7-21-16:19
Silent Call 11-18-21:42
Silent Call, The 6-21-61:6
Silent Command 9-06-23:23
Silent Conflict 4-07-48:10
Silent Cry, The 11-30-77:20
Silent Dust 2-09-49:20
Silent Enemy, The 5-21-30:19
Silent Enemy, The 3-12-58:7
Silent Hero, The 8-10-27:26
Silent Lady, The 11-23-17:43
Silent Lover, The 11-17-26:16
Silent Man, The 11-30-17:45
Silent Master, The 6-02-17:26
Silent Movie 6-23-76:16
Silent Mystery, The 11-29-18:40
Silent Partner, The 5-11-17:34a
Silent Partner, The 8-23-23:23
Silent Partner, The (s) 8-04-31:18
Silent Partner, The 6-07-44:19
Silent Partner, The 4-04-79:24
Silent Playground, The 4-22-64:102
Silent Plea, The 3-12-15:23
Silent Power 11-17-26:17
Silent Rider, The 12-10-18:36
Silent Running 3-08-72:24
Silent Sanderson 6-10-25:37
Silent Scream 1-30-80:28
Silent Sentinel 7-24-29:35
Silent Service, The (s) 9-19-45:12
Silent Strength 2-07-19:61
Silent Trail, The 3-20-29:31
Silent Village, The 7-14-43:22
Silent Voice, The 8-27-15:19

Silent Vow 5-12-22:33
Silent Watcher, The 10-22-24:23
Silent Witness, The 2-09-32:15
Silent Witness, The 9-27-78:20
Silent Woman, The 9-13-18:44
Silk Express, The 6-27-33:15
Silk Hat Harry 7-18-19:43
Silk Hat Kid 8-14-35:15
Silk Hose and High Pressure 11-05-15:23
Silk Legs 12-28-27:16
Silk-Lined Burglar, The 4-04-19:66
Silk Stockings 2-11-21:41
Silk Stockings 5-22-57:6
Silken Affair, The 10-17-56:6
Silken Shackles 5-26-26:19
Silks and Saddles 12-05-28:24
Silks and Satins 6-16-16:23
Sillon y la Gran Duquesa, El 9-29-43:8
Silly Billies 4-08-36:17
Silly Symphony (s) 11-20-29:12
Silna Voda 6-16-76:26
Silom Otac 8-19-70:24
Silouettes 11-08-67:24
Siluri Umani 4-27-55:6
Silver Bandit, The 3-29-50:11
Silver Bears, The 11-23-77:19
Silver Bullet, The 8-05-42:27
Silver Canyon 6-13-51:6
Silver Car, The 7-22-21:36
Silver Chalice, The 12-22-54:6
Silver City 10-03-51:6
Silver City Bonanza 3-21-51:7
Silver City Raiders 11-24-43:18
Silver Comes Through 5-25-27:21
     and 6-29-27:26
Silver Cord 5-09-33:14
Silver Darlings, The 9-10-47:17
Silver Dollar, The 12-27-32:14
Silver Dream Racer 4-02-80:24
Silver Fleet, The 3-24-43:20
Silver Horde, The 5-14-20:34
Silver Horde 10-29-30:27
Silver King, The 1-10-19:44
Silver King, The 9-04-29:31
Silver Lake 5-12-54:6
Silver Lining, The 1-28-21:39
Silver Lining, The 11-16-27:21
Silver Lining, The 5-31-32:25
Silver Queen 1-13-43:8
Silver Raiders 12-27-50:6
Silver River 5-05-48:8
Silver Skates 1-20-43:9
Silver Slave, The 1-18-28:13
Silver Springs (s) 8-30-32:14
Silver Spurs 4-01-36:17

Silver Spurs 7-21-43:22
Silver Stallion 6-18-41:16
Silver Star 3-02-55:9
Silver Streak, The 1-22-35:14
Silver Streak 12-01-76:18
Silver Threads Among the Gold 6-11-15:18
Silver Trail, The 1-05-38:16
Silver Trails 3-16-49:11
Silver Treasure 7-28-26:16
Silver Valley 11-02-27:21
Silver Whip, The 2-04-53:6
Silver Wings 5-26-22:33
Silvery Moon (s) 12-27-32:14
Simba 1-25-28:12
Simba 2-02-55:6
Simbaddha 7-12-72:30
Simchon Family, The (See: Mishpahat Simchon)
Simitrio 10-18-61:22
Simon 2-27-80:20
Simon, King of the Witches 4-07-71:18
Simon of the Desert (See: San Simeon Del Desierto)
Simon the Jester 10-01-15:19
Simon the Jester 11-25-25:39
Simone 4-23-10:16
Simone Barbes ou la Vertu 5-07-80:576
Simple Case of Money, A 2-06-52:20
Simple Charity 11-19-10:13
Simple Event, A 12-26-73:17
Simple Histoire, Une 9-30-70:24
Simple Mistake, A 10-01-10:18
Simple Rustic Tale, A 1-21-11:12
Simple Sis 6-08-27:17
Simple Souls 5-28-20:43
Simple Tailor 2-27-34:17
Simplemente Maria 10-07-70:22
Simply Killings (s) 1-21-31:17
Sin 8-08-13:8
Sin 10-08-15:21
Sin Cargo 12-08-26:20
Sin Flood 11-03-22:42
Sin Novedad En El Alcazar 1-22-41:16
Sin of Anna Lans 5-24-50:6
Sin of Harold Diddlebock, The 2-19-47:8
Sin of Madelon Claudet, The 11-03-31:17
Sin of Martha Queed, The 11-25-21:42
Sin of Nora Moran 12-19-33:19
Sin Ship 5-27-31:66

Sinner Take All 2-10-37:15
Sinners 4-30-20:43
Sinner's Holiday 10-15-30:25
Sinners in Heaven 9-10-24:27
Sinners in Love 11-21-28:30
Sinners in Paradise 5-04-38:15
Sinners in Silk 9-10-24:28
Sinners in the Sun 5-17-32:15
Sinners of Paris (See: Rafles Sin
   la Ville)
Sinners Parade 11-14-28:26
Sino-Japanese Curse (s) 3-01-32:
   20
Sins of Her Parent 11-10-16:24
Sins of Jezebel, The 11-18-53:6
Sins of Man 6-24-36:29
Sins of Men, The 5-19-16:20
Sins of Rachel Cade, The 9-14-
   60:18
Sins of Rome 6-30-54:23
Sins of Rosanne 10-15-20:41
Sins of Society, The 1-14-16:19
Sins of the Children 7-30-30:16
Sins of the Fathers, The 11-27-
   09:13
Sins of the Fathers 1-30-29:26
Sins of the Fathers 4-28-48:22
Sins of the Mothers 1-01-15:29
Sin's Payday 5-10-32:19
Sioux Blood 5-22-29:24
Sioux City Sue 11-27-46:28
Sir Arne's Treasure 12-02-25:43
Sir Arthur Conan Doyle (s) 5-29-
   29:14
Sir Henry at Rawlinson End 7-16-
   80:26
Siren, The 12-12-14:28
Siren, The 6-29-17:31
Siren, The 2-22-28:24
Siren Call 9-15-22:43
Siren of Atlantis 12-15-48:6
Siren of Bagdad 5-20-53:6
Siren of Corsica, A 4-02-15:21
Siren of Seville 11-19-24:30
Siren's Necklace 9-25-09:12
Sirene du Mississipi (sic), La
   7-02-69:24
Sirens of Syncopation (s) 9-04-
   35:31
Sirens of the Sea 8-31-17:30
Siripala and Ranmenika 1-26-77:
   50
Sirius 7-14-76:20
Sir-Loin 12-06-23:23
Sirocco 6-06-51:6
Sirocco d'Hiver 6-18-69:6
Siroco 12-01-31:35
Siroma Sam Al'sam Besan

8-12-70:14
Sis Hopkins 3-07-19:67
Sis Hopkins 4-09-41:18
Sissi 5-15-57:7
Sissignore 1-15-69:36
Sissle and Blake (s) 1-09-29:10
Sistemo L'America e Torno 2-
   27-74:18
Sister Against Sister 3-09-17:23
Sister Angelica 10-16-09:12
Sister Kenny 7-17-46:8
Sister Lieutenant, The 5-09-45:
   16
Sister of Mercy 3-20-29:28
Sister of Six, A 10-13-16:29
Sister to Assist 'Er, A 9-01-22:
   42
Sister to Assist 'Er, A 10-12-
   27:16
Sister to Assist 'Er, A 3-26-30:
   42
Sister to Salome, A 7-23-20:34
Sisters 4-07-22:41
Sisters, The 10-05-38:14
Sisters 3-21-73:26
Sisters of Eve 11-28-28:20
Sisters of the Golden Circle 6-
   28-18:31
Sister's Peat (s) 3-26-30:25
Sister's Sacrifice, A 1-22-10:15
Sisters Under the Skin 6-12-34:
   19
Sit Tight 2-25-31:22
Sitting Bull 9-15-54:6
Sitting Ducks 11-21-79:24
Sitting on the Moon 9-30-36:29
Sitting Pretty (s) 12-24-30:21
Sitting Pretty 12-05-33:16
Sitting Pretty 2-25-48:8
Sitting Target 2-23-72:6
Situation Hopeless--But Not Serious
   10-06-65:6
Six Bears and a Clown 7-14-76:
   20
Six Best Cellars 3-12-20:53
Six Black Horses 3-14-62:6
Six Bridges to Cross 1-19-55:6
Six Brown Bros. (s) 10-17-28:16
Six Card Stud 9-03-75:18
Six Cylinder Love 12-13-23:22
Six Cylinder Love 5-20-31:17
Six-Day Bike Rider 11-06-34:17
6-Day Grind, The (s) 1-15-36:19
Six Days 9-20-23:23
Six Fifty, The 9-27-23:24
Six-Gun Gold 8-27-41:20
Six-Gun Law 2-25-48:8
Six Gun Man 1-23-46:12

Six-Gun Rhythm 6-21-39:26
Six Hits and a Miss (s) 12-02-
    42:22
Six Hours to Live 10-25-32:15
Six in Paris (See: Paris Vu
    Par ...)
Six Lessons from Mme. La Zonga
    2-26-41:16
Six of a Kind 3-13-34:16
Six P. M. 2-06-46:12
Six Pack Annie 12-17-75:23
6. 5 Special 4-09-58:20
Six-Shooter Andy 3-15-18:44
Six Shootin' Sheriff 8-17-38:23
633 Squadron 6-03-64:6
Six Thousand Enemies 5-31-39:14
16 Fathoms Deep 1-23-34:21
16 Fathoms Deep 6-09-48:12
16 Sweeties (s) 3-12-30:21
16th Wife, The 5-11-17:34c
Sixth and Main 8-31-77:18
6th Commandment, The 6-25-24:
    26
Sixty Cents An Hour 5-17-23:22
60 Glorious Years 10-26-38:15
Sixty Years a Queen 4-24-14:21
65, 66 Och Yag 9-08-37:19
69 7-08-70:24
67 Days 8-06-75:17
Sjatte Budet 2-18-48:9
Sjoman Till Hast, En 11-05-41:
    24
Sjov I Gaden 8-27-69:34
Sjuget Dlja Nebolsciovo Rasskaza
    9-17-69:23
Skaerseldan 12-04-74:22
Skal Vi Danse Foerst 12-26-79:20
Skal Vi Lege Skjul? 4-08-70:24
Skammen 10-16-68:26
Skandal Um Eva 4-22-31:19
Skanderbeg 7-07-54:22
Skanor-Falsterbo 5-24-39:14
Skarabea 3-05-69:6
Skarb (See: Treasure, The)
Skas Pro To, Kar Zar Petr Arapa
    Shenil 12-08-76:19
Skateboard 3-22-78:24
Skatetown, U. S. A. 10-24-79:17
Skazany 4-14-76:23 and 12-08-76:
    19
Skeleton, The 2-05-10:35
Skeleton Dance, The (s) 7-17-29:
    42
Skeleton on Horseback 2-07-40:16
Skepp Till Indialand 10-22-47:13
    (Also see: Frustration)
Skeppar Jansson 10-31-45:17
Skezag 12-16-70:17

Ski Battalion 3-23-38:17
Ski Bum, The 1-20-71:13
Ski Champs 12-19-51:18
Ski-Faszination 12-07-66:22
Ski Fever 4-23-69:6
Ski on the Wild Side 8-02-67:22
Ski Party 6-16-65:16
Ski Patrol 5-22-40:14
Ski Troop Attack 5-04-60:6
Skid Proof 8-09-23:27
Skidoo! 12-18-68:26
Skier Training, A 10-15-10:12
Skin Deep 10-02-29:22
Skin Deep 10-04-78:19
Skin Game, The 3-18-31:38 and
    6-30-31:20
Skin Game 9-29-71:18
Skinner Steps Out 12-11-29:39
Skinner's Baby 8-03-17:23
Skinner's Big Idea 3-21-28:26
Skinner's Dress Suit 2-02-17:25
Skinner's Dress Suit 5-05-26:20
Skinny and Fatty 4-28-65:6
Skip Tracer, The 8-04-77:20
Skipalong Rosenbloom 5-23-51:6
Skipper & Co. 11-06-74:22
Skipper Surprised His Wife, The
    5-17-50:6
Skipper's Daughters, The 3-27-
    09:13
Skipper's Yarn, The 2-05-10:35
Skipping About the Universe (s)
    7-25-33:14
Skippy 4-15-31:33
Skirt Sky (s) 12-18-29:22
Skirts 8-25-16:25
Skirts 8-01-28:22
Skirts Ahoy! 4-16-52:6
Skrift I Snee 7-06-66:18
Skull, The 8-04-65:7
Skull and Crown 3-02-38:15
Skull Murder Mystery, The (s)
    3-08-32:14
Skullduggery 3-18-70:26
Sky Above--the Mud Below, The
    6-20-62:18 (Also see: Ciel
    et la Boue, Le)
Sky Boy (s) 12-25-29:20
Sky Bride 4-26-32:25
Sky Commando 8-26-53:6
Sky Devils 3-08-32:14
Sky Dragon 5-04-49:11
Sky Full of Moon 11-05-52:6
Sky Giant 7-20-38:12
Sky Hawk 12-18-29:22
Sky High 1-27-22:40
Sky High (s) 3-25-31:16
Sky High 4-16-52:16

Sky High 1-30-74:16
Sky Is Clearing, The 9-05-79:22
Sky Is Red, The 2-06-52:20
Sky Liner 8-03-49:16
Sky Murder 9-25-40:15
Sky Parade 4-22-36:14
Sky Patrol 11-29-39:18
Sky Pilot, The 4-22-21:40
Sky Pirate 2-11-70:16
Sky Princess, The (s) 3-11-42:
    20
Sky Raiders, The 6-02-31:31
Sky Ranger 11-14-28:26
Sky Rider, The 7-24-29:39
Sky Riders 4-14-76:21
Sky Scraping (s) 11-05-30:23
Sky Skidder 2-20-29:17
Sky Skippers (s) 2-26-30:24
Sky Spider, The 10-06-31:29
Sky Symphony (s) 5-23-33:15
Sky Trooper (s) 12-02-42:8
Sky West and Crooked 2-02-66:
    17
Skyhigh Saunders 12-14-27:26
Skyjacked 5-10-72:20
Skylark 9-10-41:8
Skylight Room, The 12-21-17:47
Skyline 10-06-31:29
Skyrocket, The 1-27-26:38
Sky's the Limit, The 11-17-37:
    17
Sky's the Limit, The 9-08-43:16
Skyscraper 4-11-28:12
Skyscraper Souls 8-09-32:17
Skytten 3-01-78:31
Skyway 10-24-33:22
Slacker, The 8-03-17:25
Sladkain Jentchina 2-09-77:36
Slaegten 1-10-79:54
Slalom 10-13-65:18
Slams, The 9-19-73:16
Slander 4-14-16:24
Slander 12-19-56:7
Slander House 10-05-38:59
Slander the Woman 5-30-23:24
Slantseto i Syankata 6-27-62:6
Slap, The (See: Gifle, La)
Slap Shot 3-02-77:22
Slapp Fangarne Loss Det Ar Var
    12-31-75:15
Slattery's Hurricane 8-03-49:16
Slaughter 8-23-72:6
Slaughter on Tenth Avenue 9-18-
    57:6
Slaughter Trail 10-17-51:6
Slaughterhouse-Five 3-22-72:20
Slaughter's Big Rip-Off 7-11-73:
    18

Slave, The 6-08-17:21
Slave, The 5-08-63:6
Slave Girl 7-16-47:14
Slave Hunt 6-22-07:13
Slave Market, The 1-05-17:27
Slave of Desire 12-13-23:22
Slave of Fashion, A 7-22-25:31
Slave of Love 3-20-14:24
Slave Ship 6-23-37:12
Slave Trade in the World Today
    (See: Schiave Esistano
    Ancora, La)
Slave's Vengeance 2-01-08:11
Slavera 5-25-77:24
Slaves 5-07-69:6
Slaves of Babylon 9-23-54:24
Slaves of Beauty 6-08-27:15
Slaves of Pride 1-16-20:61
Slaver, The 12-14-27:26
Slavey Student, The 9-03-15:21
Sledovateliat y Gozato 6-16-76:
    26
Sleep, My Love 1-14-48:10
Sleep Walker, The 4-14-22:41
Sleeper 12-19-73:12
Sleepers East 6-19-34:44
Sleepers West 3-19-41:16
Sleeping Beauty 1-21-59:6
Sleeping Beauty 5-04-66:6
Sleeping Car 6-27-33:15
Sleeping Car Murder, The (See:
    Compartment Tueurs)
Sleeping Car to Trieste 10-27-
    48:9
Sleeping City, The 9-06-50:8
Sleeping Dogs 10-19-77:26
Sleeping Dragon 5-14-75:31
Sleeping Fires 4-20-17:22
Sleeping Lion, The 6-27-19:45
Sleeping Memory, A 10-19-17:31
Sleeping Partners 4-02-30:30 and
    12-17-30:13
Sleeping Tiger 7-07-54:22
Sleeping Tonic 6-19-09:11
Sleepless Nights 11-15-32:23 and
    7-25-33:34
Sleepy Family 1-29-58:6
Sleepy Head (s) 2-11-31:14
Slender Thread, The 12-15-65:15
Sleuth 12-13-72:15
Sleuth and the Wig, The 10-16-
    09:12
Slick As Ever (s) 6-04-30:24
Slick Cylinders (s) 2-06-29:18
Slide, Babe, Slide (s) 5-24-32:29
Slide, Kelly, Slide 3-30-27:14
Slide, Nelly, Slide (s) 4-01-36:17
Slight Case of Larceny, A 5-06-
    53:6

Slight Case of Murder, A 2-09-38: 14

Slightly Dangerous 3-03-43:14

Slightly French 2-09-49:13

Slightly Honorable 1-10-40:14

Slightly Married 1-03-33:27

Slightly Scandalous 7-31-46:16

Slightly Scarlet 3-05-30:33

Slightly Scarlet 2-15-56:20

Slightly Tempted 10-30-40:14

Slightly Terrific 4-19-44:12

Slightly Used 10-19-27:29

Slike Iz Zivota Udarnika 9-16-72: 16

Slim 6-30-37:20

Slim Carter 10-09-57:6

Slim Princess, The 5-21-15:18

Slim Princess, The 7-02-20:27

Slim Shoulders 9-08-22:41

Slingshot Kid, The 12-28-27:22

Slip of the Watch, A (s) 4-26-32:13

Slipper and the Rose, The 6-15-76:27

Slipper Episode 6-01-38:13

Slippy McGee 6-14-23:23

Slippy McGee 1-28-48:11

Slipstream 4-17-74:20

Slipup 5-07-75:48

Slither 3-14-73:20

Slnchev Udar 8-09-78:22

Slogan 6-11-69:6

Slottet 9-09-64:22

Slovo Dlia Zaschity 1-19-77:38

Slow Beau (s) 5-14-30:19

Slow Dancing in the Big City 11-08-78:18

Slow Poison (s) 9-22-31:22

Slucajni Zivot 8-20-69:16

Slumber Party '57 2-09-77:26

Slums of Paris 2-29-08:12

Slums of Tokyo 7-09-30:31

Slunce v Siti 5-15-63:21

Sluzhebni Roman 7-19-78:20

Smak Wody 10-15-80:66

Small Back Room, The 1-26-49: 22

Small Change (See: Argent de Poche, L')

Small Circle of Friends, A 3-05-80:23

Small One, The (s) 12-13-78:26

Small Talk (s) 6-19-29:24

Small Town Boy 10-13-37:16

Small Town Deb 10-22-41:8

Small Town Girl 4-15-36:16

Small Town Girl 2-25-53:6

Small Town Idol 4-15-21:40

Small Town in Texas, A 6-09-76:23

Small Voice, The 11-24-48:14

Small World of Sammy Lee, The 4-17-63:7

Smallest Show on Earth, The 4-17-57:6

Smania Andosso, La (See: Eye of the Needle, The)

Smart Alecks 9-09-42:14

Smart Blonde 1-13-37:13

Smart Girl 8-21-35:31

Smart Girls Don't Talk 9-15-48: 20

Smart Guy 12-29-43:8

Smart Money 6-23-31:18

Smart Politics 2-04-48:20

Smart Set, The 3-07-28:28

Smart Sex, The 4-01-21:42

Smart Woman 10-13-31:14

Smart Woman 3-10-48:22

Smart Work (s) 7-12-32:16

Smartest Girl in Town, The 11-25-36:14

Smarty 6-26-34:16

Smash and Grab 10-06-37:13

Smash Your Baggage (s) 11-15-32:19

Smashing Bird I Used to Know, The 9-03-69:19

Smashing of the Reich, The 10-03-62:6

Smashing the Money Ring 11-22-39:16

Smashing the Rackets 8-10-38:12

Smashing the Spy Ring 1-18-39: 12

Smashing Through 6-14-18:30

Smashing Through 9-26-28:27

Smashing Time 12-27-67:7

Smashing Vice Trust 2-20-14:23

Smash-Up--The Story of a Woman 2-05-47:12

Smattes, Les 6-28-72:18

Smekmanad 7-12-72:17

Smertens Boern 10-26-77:38

Smesny Pan 12-24-69:14

Smic, Smac, Smoc 9-01-71:16

Smile 5-07-75:22

Smile, Brother Smile 8-31-27:22

Smile, Emil! 12-17-69:24

Smile Orange 3-31-76:14

Smiles 2-28-19:56

Smiles Are Trumps 3-17-22:42

Smiles of a Summer Night (See: Sommarnattens Leende)

Smiles of the City (See: Risa de la Ciudad, La)

see: So ein Maedel Vergisst
      Man Nicht)
So ein Maedel Vergisst Man Nicht
      10-02-35:17 (Also see: So
      ein Maedel)
So Ends Our Night 1-29-41:18
So Evil My Love 3-10-48:10
So Goes My Love 3-27-46:12
So Lange Leben in Mirist 7-27-
      66:7
So Little Time 4-30-52:18 and
      8-26-53:6
So Long at the Fair 6-14-50:34
So Long, Blue Boy 11-28-73:16
So Long Letty 2-12-30:19
So Near but Not Quite 1-21-11:12
So Proudly We Hail! 6-23-43:24
So Red the Rose 12-04-35:15
So-So 10-20-16:26
So This Is Arizona 4-14-22:41
So This Is College 11-13-29:12
So This Is Harris (s) 2-28-33:14
So This Is Hollywood (s) 10-11-23:
      27
So This Is London 5-28-30:21
So This Is London 3-29-39:14
So This Is Love 5-02-28:15
So This Is Love 7-22-53:6
So This Is Marriage 12-24-24:32
So This Is Marriage (s) 2-12-30:
      18
So This Is New York 5-12-48:8
So This Is Paris 8-18-26:58
So This Is Paris 4-25-33:15
So This Is Paris 11-17-54:6
So This Is Washington 8-18-43:26
So to Wed (s) 7-22-36:17
So Weit Das Auge Reicht 8-20-80:
      21
So You Think You Need Glasses
      (s) 2-03-43:14
So You Won't T-T-Talk (s) 1-08-
      35:18
So You Won't Talk 6-12-35:41
So You Won't Talk 10-23-40:14
So Young, So Bad 5-31-50:6
Soak the Rich 2-12-36:18
Soap Girl, The 6-14-18:30
Soaring Stars (s) 5-20-42:8
Soaring Wings (s) 2-09-27:17 and
      8-10-27:20
Sob Sister 10-06-31:29
Sobalvany 8-27-58:6
Sobrevivientes, Los 5-30-79:24
Sobstevennole Minienie 11-16-77:
      24
Social Ambition 5-10-18:43
Social Briars 5-31-18:31

Social Buccaneer, The 10-06-16:
      27
Social Celebrity, A 4-21-26:34
Social Code, The 1-17-24:27
Social Highwayman, The 4-14-16:
      26
Social Highwayman, The 6-16-26:
      16
Social Hypocrites 4-12-18:42
Social Leper, The 3-09-17:23
Social Lion, The 6-18-30:37
Social Pirate, The 5-09-19:52
Social Pirates, The 12-15-16:37
Social Quicksands 6-21-18:27
Social Register 10-09-34:18
Social Secretary, The 9-15-16:26
Society Architect 1-12-27:14
Society Detective 5-15-14:23
Society Doctor 2-05-35:31
Society Fever 11-27-35:30
Society for Sale 4-26-18:42
Society Girl 6-14-32:17
Society Goes Spaghetti (s) 9-17-
      30:21
Society Lawyer 4-05-39:15
Society Scandal, A 3-12-24:26
Society Sensation, A 10-04-18:49
      and 4-02-24:22
Society Smugglers 4-05-39:19
Society Snobs 3-18-21:34
Socrate, Le 4-24-68:26
Socrates 12-15-71:14
Sod Sisters 8-20-69:28
Soder Om Landsvagen 3-17-37:15
Soderkakar 12-23-36:62
Sodom and Gomorrah 2-28-24:37
Sodom and Gomorrah 12-05-62:6
Sodom and Gomorrah 2-25-76:39
Sodrasban 7-15-64:6
Soemaend Paa Sengekanten 10-
      20-76:39
Soennen Fra Vingaarden 2-26-75:
      22
Soeurs Bronte, Les 5-16-79:35
Sofi 11-01-67:20
Sofia 8-18-48:11
Soft Cushions 9-14-27:24
Soft Hands 7-15-64:22
Soft Living 2-29-28:23
Soft Shoes 3-25-25:38
Soft Skin, The (See: Peau Douce,
      La)
Sogni Muoino All'Alba, I 1-17-62:
      20
Sogni Nel Cassetto, I 10-09-57:6
Sogno Di Butterfly, Il 11-15-39:
      20 and 2-26-41:18
Soif des Hommes, La 5-24-50:20

Song 11-14-28:26
Song and Dance Man 2-03-26:37
Song and Dance Man 3-18-36:29
Song and the Silence, The 2-05-69:6
Song Drama, A (s) 9-17-30:21
Song for Miss Julie, A 2-21-45:8
Song Hits of Roy Turk (s) 1-16-34:15
Song Is Born, A 8-25-48:8
Song Is Ended, The 10-29-30:27
    (Also see: Lied Ist Aus, Das)
Song o' My Heart 3-19-30:20
Song of Arizona 3-13-46:10
Song of Bernadette, The 12-22-43:12
Song of Ceylon 8-18-37:39
Song of China 11-11-36:14
Song of Fame (s) 6-12-34:19
Song of Freedom 9-09-36:17
Song of Happiness 12-11-34:19
Song of Hate, The 9-17-15:25
Song of Idaho 3-31-48:22
Song of India 2-16-49:13
Song of Life 8-04-22:35
Song of Love, The 2-28-24:22
Song of Love 11-20-29:30
Song of Love 7-23-47:10
Song of My Heart 11-05-47:8
Song of My Heart 1-10-51:13
Song of Nevada 6-14-44:10
Song of Norway 11-04-70:16
Song of Old Wyoming 9-05-45:15
    and 4-10-46:16
Song of Paris 2-27-52:6
Song of Russia 12-29-43:8
Song of Scheherazade 1-29-47:8
Song of Sixpence, A 6-08-17:25
Song of Songs, The 2-22-18:44
Song of Songs 7-25-33:14
Song of Surrender 9-14-49:8
Song of Texas 6-02-43:16
Song of the Builder, The (s) 7-24-28:14
Song of the Cabellero 7-09-30:31
Song of the Canary 3-28-79:22
Song of the City 5-05-37:16
Song of the Cradle, The 11-06-09:13
Song of the Buckaroo 1-18-39:12
Song of the Eagle 5-02-33:13
Song of the Flame 5-14-30:19
Song of the Islands 2-04-42:8
Song of the Land 11-25-53:6
Song of the Nation (s) 9-02-36:18
Song of the Open Road 5-03-44:23
Song of the Road 5-08-40:12

Song of the Roses (s) 4-03-29:11
Song of the Saddle 3-25-36:63
Song of the Sarong 4-25-45:14
Song of the Siren, The 1-07-16:24
Song of the Soul, The 12-25-14:42
Song of the Soul, The 3-01-18:41
Song of the Soul 6-03-21:40
Song of the South 11-06-46:18
Song of the Thin Man 7-23-47:10
Song of the Trail 12-23-36:62
Song of the Wage Slave, The 9-24-15:21
Song of the West 3-05-30:21
Song of the Wildwood Flute, The 12-03-10:14
Song of the Woods 9-13-61:28
Song Plugger, The (s) 7-23-30:19
Song Remains the Same, The 10-20-76:38
Song Revue (s) 6-26-29:12
Song Shopping (s) 5-09-33:14
Song That Reached His Heart, The 10-15-10:12
Song to Remember, A 1-24-45:10
Song Without End 6-22-60:6
Song Writers' Revue (s) 1-08-30:89
Song You Gave Me 8-15-33:14
Songs of Central Europe (s) 12-01-26:34
Songs of Ireland (s) 9-29-26:19
Songs of Italy (s) 8-25-26:23
Songs of Mother (s) 5-14-30:19
Songs of Our Colleges (s) 1-22-35:15
Songs of Scotland (s) 8-25-26:23
Songs of Southern States (s) 9-22-26:17 and 10-05-27:25
Songs of the British Isles (s) 11-30-27:23
Songs of the Motherland (s) 11-10-31:14
Songs of the Soul 10-15-20:41
Songs of the South Seas (s) 1-24-33:12
Songs of the Steppes (s) 9-29-31:14
Songs That Live (s) 12-11-34:19
Sonne von St. Moritz, Die 9-01-54:22
Sonntagskinder 5-21-80:20
Sonny 6-02-22:34
Sonny and Jed 2-27-74:18

413 •

Sourdough 3-02-77:24
Souriciere, La 4-16-50:22
Sourire dans la Tempete, Un 5-02-51:12
Sourire Vertical, Le 7-04-73:18
Sous-Doues, Les 7-02-80:20
Sous la Lune du Maroc 1-24-33: 21 (Also see: Cinq Gentlemen Maudits)
Sous le Casque de Cuir 5-10-32: 19
Sous le Ciel de Paris 5-16-51:18
Sous le Ciel de Provence 5-01-57:7
Sous le Signe de Monte-Cristo 1-15-69:36
Sous le Signe du Taureau 4-16-60:6
Sous les Trois de Paris 5-14-30: 39 and 12-24-30:21
Sous les Yeux d'Occident 5-06-36:31
South American Journey (s) 7-19-32:24
South American Sports (s) 12-02-42:22
South of Algiers 3-25-53:6
South of Arizona 10-05-38:21
South of Caliente 10-31-51:6
South of Death Valley 7-12-50:6
South of Dixie 5-24-44:10
South of Pago Pago 7-17-40:16
South of Panama 6-18-41:16
South of Rio 8-10-49:8
South of St. Louis 2-16-49:13
South of Santa Fe 4-29-42:8
South of Suez 12-25-40:16
South of Suva 6-23-22:34
South of Tahiti 10-22-41:8
South of the Border 12-13-39:11
South of the Equator 1-07-25:54
South of the Northern Lights 2-08-23:42
South of the Rio Grande 5-10-32: 19
South of the Rio Grande 12-12-45:12
South Pacific 3-26-58:6
South Pacific Trail 11-12-52:6
South Riding 1-19-38:19 and 7-27-38:17
South Sea Adventure 4-05-32:23
South Sea Bubble, A 8-22-28:16
South Sea Love 1-17-24:26
South Sea Love 2-08-28:16
South Sea Pearl (s) 5-07-30:20
South Sea Rose 12-11-29:35
South Sea Woman 6-03-53:6

South Seas 5-28-30:35
South Seas Adventure 7-16-58:6
South Seas Sinner 1-04-50:63
South to Karanga 8-14-40:14
Southern India (s) 2-02-32:15
Southern Justice 5-25-17:23
Southern Love 2-21-24:19
Southern Revellers (s) 8-29-28:15
Southern Roses 10-21-36:17
Southern Tunis 10-08-10:12
Southern Yankee, A 8-11-48:8
Southerner, The 5-02-45:27
Southerners, The 5-29-14:21
Southside 1-1000 10-11-50:8
Southward Ho 6-07-39:12
Southwest Passage 4-14-54:6
Souvenir d'Italie 6-12-57:18
Souvenir of Gibraltar 5-07-75:52
Souvenirs d'En France 8-20-75: 14
Souvenirs Perdus 1-10-51:13
Souversivo, I (See: Subversives, The)
Soviet Border, The 3-01-39:45
Soviet Frontiers on the Danube 7-02-41:18
Soviet Power 9-10-41:18
Soviet Russia Today 9-27-39:14
Soviets on Parade 3-07-33:14
Sovsem Propashtshly 5-22-74:18
Sowers, The 3-31-16:25
Sowers and Reapers 5-18-17:25
Sowing the Wind 6-24-21:36
Sowing the Wind 3-20-29:22
Soy Mexico 9-18-67:22
Soy Puro Mexicano 6-09-43:8
Soy Un Delincuente 9-07-77:24
Soylent Green 4-18-73:22
Space Children 6-18-58:6
Space Coast 5-23-79:27
Space Cruiser Yamato 12-21-77: 30
Space Master X-7 7-23-58:6
Space Movie, The 3-05-80:23
Spaceflight IC-1 10-06-65:24
Spaceways 7-08-53:16
Spain in Flames 2-03-37:15
Spain's Maddest Fiesta (s) 10-15-30:25
Spalovac Mrtvol 7-16-69:28
Spangles 1-19-27:18
Spanische Fliege, Die 1-12-32:24
Spanish Affair 2-05-58:6
Spanish America (s) 3-06-34:14
Spanish Cape Mystery 11-20-35: 39
Spanish Dancer 10-11-23:26
Spanish Earth, The 7-21-37:5

Spanish Fiesta (s) 4-02-30:18
Spanish Gardener, The 1-02-57:6
Spanish Jade, The 3-05-15:21
Spanish Loyalty 11-26-10:18
Spanish Main, The 10-03-45:20
Spanish Onions (s) 5-07-30:20
Spanish Romance, A 10-17-08:11
Spanish Twist (s) 1-17-33:14
Spare the Rod 5-31-61:6
Spare Time in the Army (s) 2-18-42:8
Sparkle 4-07-76:26
Sparrows 9-22-26:14
Sparrows Can't Sing 4-03-63:7
Spartacus 10-12-60:6
Spartakiada 7-10-29:24
Spartan Girl, The 3-27-14:20
Spastel 9-10-80:30
Spawn of the Desert 5-10-23:22
Spawn of the North 8-24-38:12
Spaziergang Durch Wien (s) 5-16-33:17
Speak Easily 8-23-32:15
Speakeasy 3-13-29:28
Speaking of Animals and Their Families (s) 1-06-43:50
Speaking of Operations (s) 2-21-33:14
Spears of Death (s) 7-07-31:25
Special Agent 9-25-35:12
Special Agent 4-27-49:11
Special Agent K-7 9-08-37:19
Special Day, A (See: Giornata Speciale, Una)
Special Delivery 4-27-27:16
Special Delivery (See: Entrega Immediata)
Special Delivery (See: Vom Himmel Gefallen)
Special Delivery 7-07-76:16
Special Edition: Close Encounters of the Third Kind, The 8-06-80:22 (Also see: Close Encounters of the Third Kind)
Special Inspector 4-19-39:22
Special Investigator 4-29-36:15
Special Messengers (s) 9-18-34:11
Special Section (See: Section Speciale)
Special Servicer 5-10-67:21
Specijaino Vaspitanje 5-25-77:28
Speckled Band, The 3-25-31:71 and 11-10-31:23
Specter of the Rose 5-22-46:10
Spectre of Edgar Allan Poe, The 5-08-74:41
Spectre Vert, Le 5-21-30:19

Spectre at the Hour of Midnight 4-02-15:21
Speed 4-22-25:35
Speed 5-20-36:12
Speed Classic 12-26-28:42
Speed Cop 2-09-27:17
Speed Crazed 5-25-27:21
Speed Crazy 5-20-59:6
Speed Demon, The 8-12-35:33
Speed Devils 7-10-35:19
Speed Fever 9-20-78:26
Speed Girl, The 11-18-21:44
Speed Limit, The 5-19-26:16
Speed Limit, The (s) 6-09-31:18
Speed Limited 12-25-40:18
Speed Mad 12-09-25:43 and 5-05-26:21
Speed Madness 12-02-25:41
Speed Madness 10-11-32:20
Speed Maniac, The 9-26-19:60
Speed Reporter 4-06-38:14
Speed Spook, The 10-22-24:23
Speed to Burn 6-08-38:26
Speed to Spare 6-09-37:25
Speed to Spare 2-18-48:8
Speed Wings 4-03-34:27
Speeding Thru 10-27-26:68
Speeding Venus, The 10-06-26:54
Speedway 9-25-29:17
Speedy 4-11-28:12
Speedy Smith 12-14-27:26
Spell of the Yukon, The 5-12-16:20
Spellbinder, The (s) 1-09-29:10
Spellbinder 7-26-39:15
Spellbound 1-29-41:18
Spellbound 10-31-45:17
Spencer's Mountain 2-27-63:6
Spender, The 10-15-15:21
Spenders, The 1-28-21:41
Spendthrift, The 6-11-15:19
Spendthrift 7-29-36:14
Sperduti Nel Buio 5-18-49:20
Spermula 6-23-76:16
Spessart Inn, The (See: Wirthaus im Spessart, Das)
Spetters 4-02-80:22
Sphinx, The 2-18-16:22
Sphinx, The 7-11-33:29
Spiee of Life, The (s) 10-23-34:18
Spice of Life 1-13-54:6
Spider, The 2-11-16:24
Spider, The 9-08-31:15
Spider, The 2-07-40:16
Spider, The 10-10-45:8
Spider, The 11-05-58:6

Spookeasy (s) 4-23-30:24
Spooks (s) 6-24-36:29
Spork'schen Jaeger, Die 3-03-37:15
Sport of Kings, The 3-11-31:15
Sport of Kings, The 7-30-47:8
Sport Parade, The (s) 12-20-32:16
Sport, Sport, Sport 7-05-78:17
Sport Thrills (s) 1-03-33:19; 2-07-33:12; 2-28-33:14
Sporting Age, The 5-02-28:15
Sporting Blood 8-18-31:17
Sporting Blood 7-10-40:12
Sporting Brothers (s) 6-11-30:18
Sporting Chance, A 6-20-19:52 and 7-18-19:43
Sporting Chance, A 6-24-25:82
Sporting Chance, A 12-01-31:26
Sporting Double, A 7-21-22:53
Sporting Duchess, The 6-25-15:20
Sporting Duchess, The 3-05-20:62
Sporting Goods 2-15-28:26
Sporting Instinct 10-13-22:43
Sporting Life 9-20-18:45
Sporting Love 12-09-36:13
Sporting Lover, The 6-23-26:18
Sporting Venus 5-13-25:37
Sporting Youth 2-14-24:26
Sports and Travel in Central Africa 6-05-14:19
Sports in Java 9-18-09:13
Sports in the Rockies (s) 4-01-42:8
Sports Slants (s)
    6-16-31:21   7-05-32:14
    10-27-31:19   7-12-32:14
    12-01-31:15   7-19-32:24
    12-29-31:166   8-09-32:17
    3-28-32:24   8-30-32:14
Sportsman's World 3-05-69:28
Sposob Bycia 7-20-66:7
Spotkanie Na Atlantyky 9-24-80:22
Spotlight, The 11-30-27:18
Spotlight Sadie 4-25-19:90
Spotlight Scandals 7-21-43:20
Spots on My Leopard, The 7-30-74:16
Spreading Dawn, The 10-26-17:34
Spreading Evil, The 11-22-18:46
Spreading Sunshine (s) 3-29-32:24
Spreading Sunshine (s) 4-05-32:14

Spree 6-28-67:6
Spreewald Folk (s) 10-20-31:21
Spring 3-17-48:18
Spring Affair 12-21-60:6
Spring and Port Wine 2-25-70:15
Spring Fever 10-19-27:29
Spring Flood 7-19-67:6
Spring Has Came 9-11-09:13
Spring Kwangchow 2-05-75:20
Spring in Park Lane 3-31-48:15
Spring Madness 11-16-38:15
Spring Meeting 2-19-41:16
Spring Parade 10-02-40:12
Spring Reunion 3-13-57:6
Spring Shower 11-22-32:27
Spring Song 10-23-46:10
Spring Tonic 6-12-35:12
Spring Training (s) 9-15-31:14
Springer von Pontresina, Der 6-12-34:63
Springfield Rifle 10-01-52:6
Springtime 12-25-14:42
Springtime (s) 2-12-30:18
Springtime for Henry 10-23-34:25
Springtime for the Girls (See: Printemps de Jeunes Filles)
Springtime in the Rockies 11-24-37:16
Springtime in the Rockies 9-23-42:8
Springtime in the Sierra 7-23-47:10
Sprung von der Bruecke, Der 5-21-80:16
Sprung in den Abgrund 4-18-33:41
Spuds 5-04-27:24
Spukschloss im Spessart, Das 1-11-61:6
Spur eines Maedchens 9-06-67:20
Spurs 9-03-30:41
Spurs of Sybil, The 3-08-18:43
Spy, The 3-16-07:9
Spy, The 3-27-14:20
Spy, The 8-17-17:29
Spy, The 6-20-28:19 (Also see: Spies and Spione)
Spy Chasers 10-03-56:26
Spy Hunt 6-17-50:8
Spy in Black, The 3-29-39:14
Spy in the Sky 7-30-58:6
Spy in Your Eye 2-02-66:17
Spy of Mme. Pompadour 9-11-29:33
Spy of Napoleon 9-23-36:17
Spy of Odessa, The 7-03-29:30

Stairs of Sand   6-26-29:25
Stajnia Na Salwatorze   5-29-68:22
Stakeout!   8-21-63:6
Stalag 17   5-06-53:6
Stalker   9-19-79:19
Stalking Moon, The   12-18-68:26
Stallion Canyon   6-01-49:11
Stallion Road   3-19-47:12
Stamboul Quest   7-17-34:15
Stambul (s)   10-27-31:19
Stampede, The   9-11-09:13
Stampede   5-07-30:39
Stampede   9-09-36:17
Stampede   4-27-49:20
Stances a Sophie, Les   12-23-70:
   22
Stand and Deliver   4-04-28:28
Stand at Apache River, The   8-
   12-53:6
Stand By for Action   12-09-42:8
Stand Up and Be Counted   5-24-
   72:24
Stand Up and Cheer   4-24-34:14
Stand Up and Fight   1-11-39:12
Stand Up Virgin Soldiers   4-20-
   77:24
Standard Bearer   11-28-08:10
Standarte, Die   5-25-77:28
Stand-In   10-06-37:12
Standing Room Only   1-05-44:16
Standschuetze Bruggler   12-02-36:
   38 and 3-17-37:15
Stanley and Ginger (s)   9-18-29:
   15
Stanley and Livingstone   8-02-39:18
Stanotte Alle Undici   1-12-38:27
Stanza Del Vescovo, La   5-18-77:
   20
Star (s)   3-19-30:20 (Also see:
   Voice of Hollywood series)
Star, The   12-24-52:6
Star!   7-24-68:6
Star Dust   2-10-22:34
Star Dust   4-03-40:14
Star Dust Trail   4-29-25:36
Star for a Night   8-26-36:20
Star Globe Trotter   12-05-08:13
Star in the Dust   4-18-56:6
Star Is Born, A   4-28-37:15
Star Is Born, A   9-29-54:6
Star Is Born, A   12-22-76:20
Star Maker, The   8-23-39:14
Star Night at Cocoanut Grove
   (s)   3-27-35:15
Star of India   5-02-56:6
Star of Midnight   4-17-35:14
Star of Texas   1-14-53:6
Star of the Circus   3-23-38:16

Star over Night, A   11-28-19:56
Star Packer   10-23-34:25
Star Portraits (s)   6-03-42:24
Star Reporter   4-12-39:13
Star Rover, The   1-21-21:42
Star Spangled Girl   11-17-71:14
Star Spangled Rhythm   12-30-42:
   16
Star Trek--The Motion Picture
   12-12-79:22
Star Wars   5-25-77:20
Star Witness   8-04-31:21
Starci Na Chmelu   7-29-64:30
Starcrash   3-28-79:36
Stardust   9-04-74:20
Stardust Memories   10-01-80:20
Stardust on the Sage   5-27-42:8
Starhops   3-22-78:26
Stark Love   3-02-27:16
Stark Mad   7-03-29:32
Starke Ferdinand, Der   5-26-76:
   19
Starlift   11-07-51:6
Starlight over Texas   9-21-38:13
Starlit Days at Lido (s)   1-22-36:
   15
Staromodnaia Komedia   8-22-79:
   20
Stars and Stripes Forever   11-19-
   52:6
Stars and the Water Carriers,
   The   3-13-74:18
Stars Are Singing, The   1-28-53:6
Stars in My Crown   3-01-50:6
Stars in Your Eyes   12-26-56:6
Stars Look Down, The   1-03-40:
   40
Stars of the Russian Ballet   9-29-
   54:16
Stars of the Ukraine   7-15-53:18
Stars of Tomorrow (s)   7-01-36:
   12
Stars of Yesterday (s)   2-25-31:12
Stars on Parade   6-07-44:19
Stars over Arizona   1-12-38:15
Stars over Broadway   11-20-35:16
Stars over Texas   12-25-46:24
Stars, Their Courses Change   3-
   05-15:21
Starship Invasions   10-19-77:25
Start Cheering   2-09-38:15
Start the Revolution Without Me
   2-04-70:18
Starting of Around the World Auto-
   mobile Race, The   2-22-08:
   11
Starting Over   10-03-79:14
Starvation   1-16-20:61

22:34 and 12-22-22:35
Streets of New York, The 4-19-39:22
Streets of San Francisco, The 4-27-49:11
Streets of Shanghai 2-22-28:24
Streets of Sinners 9-04-57:6
Streets of Sorrow 7-06-27:22
Streghe, Le (See: Witches, The)
Strength of Donald McKenzie, The 8-11-16:26
Strength of the Weak, The 3-03-16:23
Stress Es Tres, Tres 9-18-68:6
Strich Durch die Rechnung 11-22-32:36
Strictly Business 1-19-32:29
Strictly Confidential 10-10-19:61
Strictly Confidential 11-11-59:6
Strictly Dishonorable 11-17-31:14
Strictly Dishonorable 7-04-51:8
Strictly Dynamite 7-10-34:13
Strictly in the Grove 1-11-42:8
Strictly Modern 5-07-30:21
Strictly Personal 3-21-33:27
Strictly Unconventional 7-16-30:29
Strife Eternal, The 12-10-15:21
Strike at the Steel Works, The 6-25-15:20
Strike It Rich 12-01-48:11
Strike Me Pink 1-22-36:14
Strike Up the Band 9-18-40:14
Strikers, The 1-16-15:27
Strikes and Spares (s) 5-29-35:14
String Beans 12-20-18:37
String of Strings (s) 8-10-27:20
Strip, The 8-08-51:6
Striporama 10-28-53:6
Stripper, The 4-24-63:15
Striving for Fortune 1-05-27:19
Stroemer 11-17-16:18
Strogoff 11-18-70:14
Strohfeuer 9-13-72:24
Stroke of Midnight, The 6-09-22:57
Stromboli 2-15-50:13
Strong Boy 4-03-29:20
Strong Man, The 9-08-26:16
Strong Revenge, A 3-07-13:14
Strong Way, The 1-04-18:44
Stronger Love, The 8-18-16:26
Stronger Than Death 1-23-20:61
Stronger Than Desire 6-28-39:14
Stronger Than the Sun 3-12-80:23
Stronger Vow, The 5-02-19:59

Stronger Will, The 4-11-28:13
Strongest Karate, The 5-12-76:34
Strongest Man in the World, The 2-05-75:20
Strongheart 4-17-14:21
Stronghold 2-06-52:6
Stroszeck 7-20-77:18
Struggle, The 4-07-16:23
Struggle, The 5-06-21:41
Struggle, The 12-15-31:21
Struggle Everlasting, The 12-21-17:45
Struggle for Life 6-26-35:26
Struktura Krysztalu 10-29-69:30
Stuckey's Last Stand 5-07-80:574
Stud 6-19-68:6
Stud, The 3-29-78:22
Stud Farm, The 6-25-69:18
Student Nurses, The 9-23-70:22
Student of Prague, The 11-24-26:19
Student Prince, The 9-28-27:24
Student Prince, The 5-26-54:6
Student Romance 10-21-36:23
Student Sein 5-06-31:23
Student Song, A 9-17-30:30
Student Tour 10-16-34:12
Studenten auf Schafott 9-06-72:18
Studentenlied aus Heidelburg (See: Student Song, A)
Student's Romance, A 8-07-35:62
Studio Girl, The 2-01-18:47
Studio Murder Mystery, The 6-12-29:29
Studs Lonigan 7-27-60:6
Study and Understudy (s) 3-25-36:15
Study in Scarlet, A 6-06-33:14
Study in Socks, A (s) 5-27-42:8
Stuerme der Leidenschaft 2-16-32:33
Stuerme Ueber dem Mont Blanc 2-15-31:22
Stuetzen der Gesellschaft 11-18-36:29
Stukas 8-25-43:10
Stumme, Der 8-25-76:68
Stumme von Portici, Der 1-19-32:25
Stunde Null 4-27-77:22
Stung (s) 12-01-31:15
Stunt Man, The 6-11-80:20
Stung Pilot 7-26-39:15
Stunts 6-08-77:23
Stupende Le Mie Amiche 10-08-80:22

Suicide Mission 11-07-56:6
Suicide of a Hollywood Extra (s)
  6-20-28:19
Suit Case Mystery, The 4-02-
  10:17
Suite California, Stops and Passes
  4-11-79:21
Suitor, The (s) 3-12-30:21
Suitor, The (See: Soupirant, Le)
Suitor's Competition 10-02-09:13
Suivez Cet Homme 5-20-53:16
Sujata 5-25-60:7
Sullivan's Empire 6-07-67:6
Sullivan's Travels 12-10-41:8
Sullivans, The 2-09-44:12
Sult 5-18-66:7
Sultans, Les 6-01-66:6
Sultan's Daughter, The 1-12-44:
  24
Sultan's Jester, The (s) 7-23-
  30:19
Sum Ga Egooli Manse! 7-11-73:18
Summer (s) 2-26-30:24
Summer and Smoke 9-06-61:6
Summer Bachelors 12-22-26:15
Summer Boarding 8-17-17:30
Summer Camp 6-06-79:24
Summer Flirtation, A 10-15-10:
  12
Summer Frenzy (See: Frenesea
  d'Estate)
Summer Girl, The 8-18-16:26
Summer Holiday 3-17-48:8
Summer Holiday 1-23-63:6
Summer Idyl, A 9-10-10:12
Summer Interlude (See: Sommarlek)
Summer Lightning 7-25-33:34
Summer Love 2-05-58:6
Summer Magic 6-26-63:6
Summer of '42 4-21-71:17
Summer of Secrets 12-29-76:14
Summer of the 17th Doll 3-30-60:6
Summer Paradise (See: Paradistorg)
Summer Place, A 10-07-59:6
Summer Rain, A 3-26-80:21
Summer Run 8-21-74:20
Summer Soldiers 10-04-72:18
Summer Stock 8-09-50:8
Summer Storm 5-24-44:10
Summer to Remember, A (See:
  Serge)
Summer Tragedy, A 9-24-10:12
Summer Wishes, Winter Dreams
  10-24-73:17
Summer's Children 5-16-79:35
Summerfield 9-07-24
Summerskin (See: Piel de Verano)
Summertime 6-08-55:6

Summertime Killer, The 7-12-
  72:26
Summertree 6-16-71:15
Summit 9-11-68:106
Sun Also Rises, The 8-28-57:6
Sun Comes Up, The 1-05-49:58
Sun Never Sets, The 6-07-39:12
Sun over Sweden 4-13-38:23
Sun Sets at Dawn, The 11-08-50:
  18
Sun Shines, The 3-15-39:18
Sun Shines Bright, The 5-06-53:
  16
Sun Tai Sil Ten Yin (See: Between
  Tears and Smiles)
Sun Valley Serenade 7-23-41:8
Sun Worshippers, The 11-01-23:
  30
Suna No Kaori 2-04-70:16
Suna No Onna 5-06-64:17
Sunbeam, The 11-17-16:23
Sunbonnet Sue 10-10-45:8
Sunburn 8-08-79:22
Sunce Tudeg Neba 8-21-68:6
Sunday, Bloody Sunday 7-07-71:14
Sunday Dinner for a Soldier 12-
  06-44:14
Sunday Funnies (s) 10-13-76:22
Sunday in New York 12-18-63:6
Sunday in the Country 4-09-75:
  20
Sunday Lovers 12-17-80:17
Sunday Punch 4-15-42:8
Sunday Too Far Away 5-28-75:19
Sundays and Cybele (See: Dimanches
  de Ville d'Avary)
Sunderin, Die (See: Sinner, The)
Sundown 12-03-24:27
Sundown 10-15-41:8
Sundown Jim 3-11-42:8
Sundown Kid, The 1-13-43:8
Sundown on the Prairie 3-15-39:
  18
Sundown Rider, The 11-18-36:29
Sundown Riders 10-11-44:12
Sundown Saunders 8-18-37:39
Sundown Slim 10-15-20:42
Sundown Trail, The 11-10-31:23
Sundown Valley 7-26-44:10
Sundowners 1-11-50:6
Sundowners, The 11-02-60:6
Sunflower, The 3-25-70:18
Sung Choonhyang 8-30-61:16
Sunken Submarine, The 10-01-10:
  18
Sunlight (s) 12-07-27:23
Sunny 12-31-30:19
Sunny 5-21-41:15

427 •

Sunny California (s) 7-18-28:15
Sunny Side of the Street 8-29-51: 20
Sunny Side Up 10-09-29:31
Sunny Skies 5-21-30:27
Sunny South (s) 5-06-31:22
Sunny Youth 8-21-35:31
Sunnyside 6-20-19:53
Sunnyside 6-06-79:20
Sunrise 9-28-27:21
Sunrise at Campobello 9-21-60:6
Sunrise Trail 4-01-31:60
Sunseed 5-23-73:28
Sunset 9-24-10:12
Sunset Boulevard 4-19-50:8
Sunset Derby, The 6-15-27:24
Sunset Hunter, The (s) 10-15-30: 25
Sunset Hunter, The (s) 10-15-30: 25
Sunset in El Dorado 9-26-45:14
Sunset in the West 9-27-50:8
Sunset in Vienna 7-07-37:25
Sunset in Wyoming 8-13-41:12
Sunset Legion 5-23-28:29
Sunset Murder Case, The 9-03-41:17
Sunset of Power 2-19-36:32
Sunset on the Desert 6-17-42:20
Sunset Pass 2-20-29:17
Sunset Pass 7-17-46:8
Sunset Range 5-15-35:35
Sunset Serenade 9-09-42:14
Sunset Sprague 12-17-20:41
Sunset Trail, The 9-28-17:38
Sunset Trail, The 11-12-24:25
Sunset Trail, The 5-17-32:15
Sunset Trail, The 10-26-38:13
Sunshine 1-16-29:25
Sunshine Ahead 2-12-36:18
Sunshine Alley 11-09-17:55
Sunshine and Gold 4-13-17:27
Sunshine Boys (s) 3-06-29:12
Sunshine Boys, The 10-29-75:16
Sunshine Dad 4-21-16:31
Sunshine Molly 3-12-15:23
Sunshine Nan 4-19-18:44
Sunshine of Paradise Alley 1-12-27:19
Sunshine Sammy (s) 4-03-29:11
Sunshine Sue 11-26-10:18
Sunshine Susie 12-29-31:167
Sunshine Trail, The 8-30-23:27
Sunstruck 1-24-73:18
Sunugin Ang Samar 9-25-74:16
Sun-Up 8-19-25:37
Suor Letizia 9-19-56:22

Suora Giovane, La 9-16-64:17
Sup Sap Bup Dap 10-15-75:26
Supe For Tva 4-23-47:18
Super, El 3-28-79:22
Super Cops, The 3-20-74:19
Super Flight, The 12-31-69:6
Super Sex 12-08-22:34
Super Sleuth 7-14-37:20
Super Snooper, The (s) 3-20-34: 16
Super-Snooper (s) 3-24-37:16
Super Speed 4-08-25:40
Super Stupid (s) 11-20-34:15
Super Super Aventura, La 6-18-75:16
Super Van 4-12-77:20
Super Vixens 3-12-75:20
Superbeast 10-04-72:18
Superdad 10-04-72:18
Superfly 8-02-72:18
Superfly T. N. T. 6-20-73:20
Supergirl 3-31-71:6
Supermacho, El 3-30-60:6
Superman 12-13-78:24
Superman II 12-03-80:22
Superman and the Mole Men 12-12-51:6
Supermarket 8-28-74:18
Supernatural 4-25-33:18
Supersonic Man 8-29-79:20
Superspeed 12-04-35:15
Superstars in Film Concert 8-18-71:15
Supply and Demand 6-02-22:34
Support Your Local Gunfighter 5-12-71:19
Support Your Local Sheriff 2-26-69:6
Suppose They Gave a War and Nobody Came? 5-27-70:20
Supreme Kid, The 8-04-76:22
Supreme Passion, The 3-15-23: 32
Supreme Sacrifice, The 3-17-16: 31
Supreme Temptation, The 3-24-16:24
Supreme Tests 12-20-23:26
Sur le Pave de Berlin 5-16-33: 21 (Also see: Berlin Alexanderplatz)
Sur un Arbre Perche 5-05-71:22
Surcouf, le Tigre des Sept Mers (See: Sea Pirate, The)
Sure Cure, A (s) 9-24-30:23
Sure Fire Flint 1-05-23:41
Surf, The 12-21-49:18
Surf Girl, The 8-11-16:26

433 ●

Tarzan the Ape Man 3-29-32:25
Tarzan the Ape Man 10-21-59:6
Tarzan the Fearless 8-15-33:14
Tarzan the Magnificent 6-15-60:6
Tarzan Triumphs 1-20-43:9
Tarzanova Smrt (See: Death of Tarzan, The)
Tarzan's Deadly Silence 7-15-70:20
Tarzan's Desert Mystery 12-08-43:8
Tarzan's Fight for Life 7-02-58:6
Tarzan's Greatest Adventure 6-17-59:6
Tarzan's Hidden Jungle 2-16-55:16
Tarzan's Magic Fountain 1-19-49:10
Tarzan's New York Adventure 4-15-42:8
Tarzan's Peril 5-21-51:6
Tarzan's Revenge 1-12-38:14
Tarzan's Savage Fury 3-19-52:6
Tarzan's Secret Treasure 11-19-41:9
Tarzan's Three Challenges 7-03-63:6
Tarzoon, La Honte de la Jungle 9-24-75:24
Tarzoon, Shame of the Jungle (See: Tarzoon, La Honte de la Jungle)
Task Force 7-20-49:6
Taste for Woman, A (See: Aimez-Vous les Femmes?)
Taste of Fear 4-12-61:6
Taste of Hell, A 12-12-73:20
Taste of Honey, A 9-20-61:6
Tate of Life, A 2-28-19:58
Taste of the Black Earth, The 7-08-70:14
Taste the Blood of Dracula 5-20-70:26
Tatlo, Dalawa, Isa 2-12-75:10
Tatoue, Arm Le 10-02-68:28
Tattered Dress, The 2-27-57:6.
Tattooed Arm, The 1-15-10:13
Tattooed Stranger, The 12-01-50:20
Tattooed Tears 12-13-78:24
Taugenichts 3-29-78:22
Taulois Maid, The (See: Padri e Figli)
Taut Bamispar 12-19-79:36
Tauwetter 12-07-77:20
Tavaszi Zapor (See: Spring Shower)
Tawny Pipit, The 5-31-44:20
Taxi 5-09-19:49

Taxi 1-12-32:15
Taxi 1-14-53:6
Taxi Dancer 3-09-27:16
Taxi di Notte 10-04-50:22
Taxi Driver 10-08-75:18
Taxi Driver 2-04-76:17
Taxi for Tobruk (See: Taxi Pour Tobrouk, Un)
Taxi Mauve, Un 5-25-77:21
Taxi, Master 4-21-43:8
Taxi Mystery, The 4-28-26:49
Taxi Pour Tobrouk, Un 6-07-61:20
Taxi Talks (s) 6-11-30:18
Taxi Tangle, A (s) 3-08-32:14
Taxi, Taxi! 2-16-27:19
Taxi 13 12-19-28:23
Taxi to Heaven 6-07-44:21
Taxi Troubles (s) 11-17-31:14
Taxichauffeur Baenz 7-24-57:27
Taxidi Toy Melitos 11-28-79:16
Taza, Son of Cochise 1-20-54:6
Tchaikovsky 7-15-70:14
Tchien Gnu You Houn 5-18-60:7
Te Csak Pipalj, Ladanyi 3-23-38:17
Te Necesito Tanito, A Mor 3-24-76:21
Te Quiero Para Mi 4-25-45:14
Tea and Sympathy 9-26-56:6
Tea for Three 11-02-27:20
Tea for Two 8-16-50:11
Tea with a Kick 10-11-23:26
Teacher from Vigerano, The (See: Maestro di Vigerano, Il)
Teacher's Pet 3-19-58:6
Teahouse of the August Moon 10-17-56:6
Tear Gas Squad 5-15-40:16
Tears of Happiness 2-27-50:16
Teaser, The 6-17-25:35
Teaserama 1-19-55:6
Technocracy (s) 1-10-33:15
Techo de Cristal, El 5-12-71:19
Teci, Teci, Kuza Moj 12-15-76:18
Teckman Mystery 8-24-55:6
Ted Brown Band (s) 9-11-29:18
Teddy Bears, The 3-09-07:8 and 12-31-30:18
Teddy Powell Orch. (s) 9-09-42:14
Tee for Two (s) 8-30-32:14
Tee Up (s) 9-03-41:17
Teen Age 6-21-44:12
Teen Kanya 8-15-62:6
Teenage Caveman 9-17-58:7
Teenage Cowgirls 2-21-73:24

Ten Commandments, The 10-10-56:6

10 Commandos 3-04-59:6

Ten Days That Shook the World 11-07-28:24

Ten Days to Die (See: Es Geschah Am 20 Juli)

Ten Days to Tulara 10-29-58:6

Ten Days Wonder (See: Decade Prodigieuse, La)

$10 Raise, The 5-13-21:43

$10 Raise, The 5-08-35:45

$10 or 10 Days (s) 3-08-32:14

Ten from Your Show of Shows 3-08-73:18

Ten Gentlemen from West Point 6-03-42:8

Ten Laps to Go 6-15-38:15

Ten Little Indians 12-29-65:6

Ten Little Indians 2-26-75:22

10. Mai, Der 12-11-57:14

Ten Minute Alibi 2-12-35:39

Ten Nights in a Bar-room 6-19-09:11

Ten Nights in a Bar-room 5-12-22:33

Ten Nights in a Bar-room 3-04-31:22

Ten North Frederick 4-20-58:6

Ten of Diamonds 8-31-17:30

10% Nadeja 1-26-77:50

10 Pin Parade (s) 3-25-42:18

10 Rillington Place 2-10-71:17

Ten Seconds to Hell 7-15-59:12

Ten Tall Men 10-24-51:6

10:30 P.M. Summer 10-19-66:20

10:32 in the Morning 2-23-66:6

Ten Thousand Bedrooms 2-20-57:6

Ten Wanted Men 2-09-55:10

Ten Who Dared 9-28-60:6

Ten Years 5-27-25:42

Tenant, The (See: Locotaire, Le)

Tenda Dos Milagres 7-13-77:18

Tender Comrade 12-29-43:8

Tender Hearts 1-26-55:7

Tender Hour, The 6-08-27:15

Tender Is the Night 1-17-62:6

Tender Scoundrel (See: Tendre Voyou)

Tender Trap, The 10-26-55:6

Tender Warrior, The 4-14-71:22

Tender Years, The 12-03-47:11

Tenderfoot 5-24-32:29

Tenderfoot Goes West 6-23-37:33

Tenderloin 3-21-28:18 (2 reviews)

Tenderly 1-15-69:36

Tendre Ennemie, La 4-06-38:14

Tendre et Violente Elisabeth 6-15-60:18

Tendre Poulet 12-21-77:21

Tendre Voyou 10-12-66:24

Tendres Cousines 12-03-80:26

Tendresse, La 6-18-30:53

Tendresse Ordinaire 4-25-73:18

Tenement Tangle, A (s) 6-11-30:18

Tengames la Guerra en la Paz 8-24-77:20

Tengo Fe En Ti 7-17-40:18

Tengoku To-Jigoku 9-04-63:20

Teni Zabytykh Predkov 9-08-65:68

Tennessee Champ 2-17-54:6

Tennessee Johnson 12-16-42:16

Tennessee's Pardner 2-11-16:24

Tennessee's Partner 9-28-55:8

Tennis Technique (s) 8-18-31:17

Tennis Topnotchers (s) 5-13-31:36

Tense Moments from Opera 7-14-22:40

Tense Moments from Plays 7-21-22:33

Tension 11-23-49:8

Tension at Table Rock 10-03-56:26

Tentacion Desnuda, La (See: Woman and Temptation)

Tentacles 6-15-77:20

Tentacles of the North 1-26-27:20

Tentation de Barbizon, La 4-17-46:16

Tentativo Sentimentale, Un 9-04-63:6

Tenth Avenue 10-10-28:22

Tenth Avenue Angel 1-21-48:20

Tenth Avenue Kid 8-31-38:18

Tenth Case, The 12-07-17:50

Tenth Man, The 9-02-36:21

Tenth Victim, The 12-22-65:6

Tenth Woman, The 10-22-24:26

Tenting Tonight on the Old Camp Ground 3-03-43:18

Tents of Allah, The 4-05-23:37

Teorema 9-18-68:6

Tercera Palabra, La 12-05-56:6

Tercera Puerta, La 9-29-76:34

Teresa 2-28-51:13

Teresa 12-16-70:26

Teresa la Ladra 10-24-73:22

Term of Trial 8-29-62:6

Terminal Man, The 5-29-74:24

Tero Nodim Parey 8-10-66:6

Terra Em Transe 5-10-67:20

Terra Madre 11-10-31:23

Terra Magazine (s) 11-17-31:14

Terra Trema, La 4-26-50:23

Terrace, The (See: Terraza, La)
Terrain Vague 11-23-60:6
Terraza, La 7-03-63:18
Terrazza, La 3-05-80:22
Terre Qui Meurt, La 6-24-36:45
Terreur des Dames, La 12-19-56:6
Terrible Beauty, A 5-18-60:6
Terrible Quarrel, or, I Did It, Mama 3-20-09:11
Territorie des Autres, Le 5-13-70:15
Terror, The 2-09-17:25
Terror, The 5-21-20:34
Terror, The 8-22-28:14
Terror, The 8-06-41:8
Terror 3-16-77:24
Terror 12-19-79:34
Terror at Midnight 4-18-56:7
Terror by Night 1-30-46:12
Terror From the Year 5,000 11-05-58:7
Terror House 6-09-43:8
Terror in a Texas Town 8-20-58:6
Terror in the Jungle 11-20-68:36
Terror Isle 4-30-20:43
Terror Mountain 10-17-28:27
Terror of Bar X, The 6-01-27:21
Terror on the Midway (s) 8-19-42:21
Terror Street 12-02-53:6
Terror Trail 2-14-33:12
Terror Train 10-01-80:22
Terrorist, The (See: Terrorista, Il)
Terrorista, Il 9-04-63:6
Terrorista, The (See: Ransom)
Terrornauts, The 10-18-67:6
Terrors of the Amazon (s) 5-16-33:17
Terrors on Horseback 4-17-46:32
Terry Whitmore, For Example 11-05-69:26
Tesha 9-12-28:12
Tesoro de la Isla Maciel, El 8-13-41:18
Tess 11-07-79:18
Tess of the d'Urbervilles 7-30-24:24
Tess of the Storm Country 4-03-14:21
Tess of the Storm Country 11-17-22:41
Tess of the Storm Country 11-22-32:17
Tess of the Storm Country 2-01-61:6

Tessie 9-23-25:39
Test of Honor, The 4-11-19:57
Test of Manhood, The 10-31-14:27
Test Pilot 4-20-38:15
Test Pilot Pirx 8-15-79:25
Testament 8-20-75:72
Testament d'Orphee, Le 3-02-60:6
Testament du Docteur Cordelier, Le 9-16-59:16
Testament of Dr. Mabuse, The 4-25-33:15 and 5-09-33:15
Testigos, Los 7-07-71:20
Testing Block, The 12-10-20:35
Testing Their Love 1-22-10:15
Tete Contre les Murs, La 12-24-58:6
Tete de Normande St. -Onge, La 5-19-76:23
Tetes Brulees, Les 12-20-67:15
Tetetoria 3-02-77:26
Tetto, Il 2-06-57:6
Teufeisinef, Die 9-22-76:19
Teufel Hat Gut Lachen, Der 12-28-60:6
Teufel in Seide 4-11-56:7
Teufel Spielte Balalaika, Der 7-19-61:6
Teufels General, Das 7-06-55:6
Tevya 12-27-39:45
Tex 12-10-20:36
Tex McLeod (s) 11-28-28:15
Tex Rides with the Boy Scouts 11-03-37:15
Tex Takes a Holiday 12-13-32:15
Texan, The 5-21-30:27
Texan Meets Calamity Jane, The 10-18-50:6
Texans, The 8-03-38:15
Texans Never Cry 3-07-51:18
Texas 10-08-41:9
Texas Across the River 9-14-66:6
Texas Bad Man 9-27-32:29
Texas Bad Man 2-24-54:6
Texas, Brooklyn and Heaven 7-14-48:12
Texas Buddies 11-15-32:23
Texas Carnival 9-12-51:6
Texas Chainsaw Massacre, The 11-06-74:20
Texas City 3-26-52:16
Texas Dynamo 6-14-50:22
Texas Gunfighter 5-31-32:62
Texas in 1999 (s) 4-29-31:12
Texas Kid, The 1-19-44:30
Texas Lady 11-30-55:6
Texas Lawmen 2-20-52:18

Texas Marshal 6-18-41:18
Texas Masquerade 1-26-44:12
Texas Pioneers 6-14-32:17
Texas Ranger, The 5-06-31:23
Texas Rangers, The 9-30-36:17
Texas Rangers, The 6-06-51:18
Texas Rangers Ride Again, The
11-06-40:16
Texas Stagecoach 3-27-40:17
Texas Stampede 6-07-39:12
Texas Steer, A 8-06-15:18
Texas Steer, A 1-11-28:20
Texas Terror 4-03-35:30
Texas Terrors 11-20-40:18
Texas to Bataan 10-14-42:8
Texas Tommy 8-14-29:31
Texas Tornado 3-06-34:27
Texas Trail, The 7-08-25:38
Texas Trail, The 12-22-37:24
Texas Wildcats, The 10-25-39:23
Thais 3-19-15:21
Thais 1-04-18:42
Thames, The (s) (See: Rank Cartoons)
Thampu 1-31-79:24
Thanassi Pare To Opio Sou 11-15-72:36
Thank God It's Friday 5-17-78:54
Thank You 10-07-25:44
Thank You Doctor (s) 8-20-30:14
Thank You, Jeeves 9-23-36:16
Thank You, Mr. Moto 1-12-38:15
Thank Your Lucky Stars 8-18-43:10
Thanks a Million 11-20-35:16
Thanks Again (s) 9-22-31:22
Thanks for Everything 12-07-38:12
Thanks for Listening 10-27-37:18
Thanks for the Buggy Ride 1-25-28:12
Thanks for the Memory 11-09-38:16
Thanksgiving Day (s) 10-31-28:24
Thanos and Despina (See: Patres du Disordre, Les)
Thar She Blows (s) 4-22-31:18
Thark 8-09-32:22
That Brennan Girl 11-20-46:38
That Certain Age 10-05-38:14
That Certain Feeling 6-06-56:6
That Certain Party 11-14-28:17
(Reprinted on: 8-07-29:69)
That Certain Something 6-18-41:18
That Certain Thing 5-02-28:26
That Certain Woman 8-04-37:19
That Chink at Golden Gulch 10-15-10:12

That Cold Day in the Park 5-28-69:36
That Dangerous Age 4-20-49:11
That Darn Cat 9-22-65:6
That Dirty Dog Morris 6-11-24:31
That Forsyte Woman 10-26-49:18
That French Lady 10-08-24:30
That Funny Feeling 6-23-65:26
That Gang of Mine 1-01-41:16
That Goes Double (s) 6-27-33:14
That Golden Fleecing 8-21-40:18
That Hagen Girl 10-22-47:12
That Hamilton Woman 3-26-41:16
That I May Live 5-12-37:13
That Kind of Woman 8-12-59:18
That Lady 3-30-55:9
That Lady in Ermine 7-14-48:12
That Lucky Tough 8-20-75:18
That Man Bolt 12-26-73:12
That Man from Tangiers 4-15-53:22
That Man George (See: Homme de Marrakech, L')
That Man in Istambul (See: Homme d'Istanbul, L')
That Man's Here Again 4-21-37:15
That Midnight Kiss 8-24-49:18
That Model from Paris 10-27-26:68
That Murder in Berlin 3-20-29:13
That Nazty Nuisance 6-02-43:8
That Night 7-24-57:7
That Night in Rio 3-12-41:14
That Night with You 9-19-45:12
That Obscure Object of Desire (See: Cet Obscure Objet du Desir)
That Old Gang of Mine (s) 7-07-31:25
That Other Woman 10-21-42:8
That Riviera Touch 4-06-66:24
That Royale Girl 1-13-26:40
That Scarlet Dove 6-13-28:13
That Sinking Feeling 9-19-79:19
That Something 4-08-21:40
That Splendid November 6-23-71:20
That Summer 7-04-79:25
That Surprising Fiddler (s) 3-27-29:12
That Tender Touch 11-26-69:26
That Touch of Mink 5-09-62:6
That Uncertain Feeling 3-19-41:16
That Way with Women 2-19-47:9
That Wild West 12-10-24:55
That Woman (See: Berlin Ist eine Suende Wert)

Therese and Isabelle 5-15-68:6
Therese Desqueyroux 9-12-62:6
Therese Raquin 6-13-28:13
Therese Raquin 10-07-53:6
These Are the Damned 7-14-65:6
These Charming People 8-11-31:22
These Dangerous Years 7-24-57:7
These Dry Days (s) 10-16-29:17
These Glamour Girls 9-06-39:14
These Thirty Years 5-29-34:13
These Thousand Hills 1-21-59:6
These Three 3-25-36:15
These Wilder Years 7-25-56:6
They All Came Out 7-05-39:14
They All Kissed the Bride 6-03-42:8
They Also Serve (See: British War Focus)
They Are Coming to Get Me (s) 7-11-28:13
They Are Not Angels 6-02-48:14
They Are Their Own Gifts 3-14-79:24
They Asked for It 7-05-39:16
They Call Her One Eye 6-26-74:22
They Call It Sin 10-25-32:15
They Call Me Mister Tibbs 7-08-70:14
They Call Me Trinity 11-03-71:16
They Came by Night 3-13-40:16
They Came from Beyond Space 10-11-67:22
They Came from Within 3-24-76:21
They Came to a City 9-13-44:10
They Came to Blow Up America 4-21-43:8
They Came to Cordura 9-23-59:6
They Came to Rob Las Vegas (See: Las Vegas 500 Milliones)
They Dare Not Love 4-30-41:16
They Died with Their Boots On 11-19-41:9
They Drive by Night 7-10-40:12
They Flew Alone 5-13-42:8
They Gave Him a Gun 5-19-37:22
They Go Boom (s) 2-26-30:24
They Got Me Covered 12-30-42:16
They Had to See Paris 10-16-29:17
They Just Had to Get Married 2-14-33:12
They Knew Mr. Knight 8-29-45:16
They Knew What They Wanted 10-09-40:16

They Knew Their Groceries (s) 12-04-29:15
They Like 'em Rough 8-04-22:32
They Made Her a Spy (s) 4-05-39:15
They Made Me a Criminal 1-25-39:11
They Made Me a Fugitive 7-02-47:13
They Made Me a Killer 1-30-46:12
They Met in a Taxi 9-16-36:16
They Met in Argentina 5-14-41:16
They Met in Bombay 6-25-41:16
They Met in Moscow 6-14-44:10
They Met in the Dark 5-23-45:19
They Met on Skis 12-25-40:18
They Might Be Giants 3-03-71:17
They Never Come Back 6-07-32:20
They Only Kill Their Masters 11-15-72:24
They Raid by Night 9-02-42:34
They Rode West 10-20-54:6
They Shall Have Music 7-12-39:12
They Shall Not Pass (s) 1-29-30:21
They Shall Overcome 1-01-75:16
They Shall Pay 8-26-21:35
They Shoot Horses, Don't They? 11-26-69:14
They Wanted Peace 1-17-40:24
They Wanted to Marry 2-24-37:17
They Went That-a-Way and That-a-Way 12-06-78:32
They Were Expendable 11-21-45:10
They Were Not Divided 4-05-50:22
They Were Sisters 5-30-45:16
They Were So Young 1-26-55:6
They Were Ten 11-09-60:19
They Were Ten 4-26-61:21
They Who Dare 2-24-54:6
They Who Step on the Tiger's Tail (See: Men Who Tread on the Tiger's Tail and Toro No O)
They Won't Believe Me 7-23-47:10
They Won't Forget 6-30-37:20
They're a Weird Mob 9-14-66:26
They're Off 9-07-17:32
They're Off 8-08-19:48
They're Off (s) 2-26-36:15
Thi Asimanton Aformin 11-06-74:22

Thicker Than Water (s) 10-09-35:15
Thief, The 12-25-14:42
Thief, The 9-24-52:6
Thief in Paradise 1-28-25:34
Thief in the Bedroom 7-13-60:6
Thief in the Dark 6-13-28:27
Thief of Bagdad, The 3-26-24:26
Thief of Bagdad, The 10-16-40:16
Thief of Bagdad, The 7-05-61:6
Thief of Damascus 3-26-52:6
Thief of Paris, The (See: Voleur, Le)
Thief of Venice, The 11-12-52:6
Thief Who Came to Dinner, The 2-28-73:20
Thieves 11-14-13:14
Thieves 11-07-19:100 and 12-19-19:45
Thieves 2-16-77:24
Thieves Fall Out 6-04-41:15
Thieves Gold 3-22-18:50
Thieves' Highway 9-07-49:11
Thieves Like Us 2-20-74:14
Thin Ice 7-04-19:43
Thin Ice 8-25-37:17
Thin Line, The 12-03-80:24
Thin Man, The 7-03-34:26
Thin Man Goes Home, The 11-22-44:10
Thin Red Line, The 4-22-64:6
Thing, The 4-04-51:6
Thing That Couldn't Die, The 5-07-58:6
Thing We Love, The 3-15-18:43
Thing with Two Heads, The 7-19-72:14
Things to Come 3-04-36:26 and 4-22-36:14
Think Fast, Mr. Moto 8-18-37:27
Thinker, The 8-18-22:41
Third After the Sun, The 7-25-73:6
Third Alarm 1-12-23:34
Third Alarm 12-24-30:20
Third Day, The 7-14-65:6
Third Degree, The 5-23-19:59
Third Degree 1-05-27:17 and 2-16-27:19
Third Finger, Left Hand 10-16-40:16
Third Generation, The (See: Dritte Generation, Die)
Third Kiss, The 9-19-19:54
Third Lover, The (See: Oeil du Malin, L')

Third Man, The 9-07-49:11
Third Man on the Mountain 9-16-59:6
Third of a Man 9-05-62:16
Third Secret, The 4-22-64:6
Third Time Lucky 1-19-49:10
Third Voice, The 1-27-60:6
Third Walker, The 9-20-78:24
Third Woman, The 3-19-20:53
Third World, Prisoner in the Street 8-13-80:26
Thirst (See: Torst)
Thirst 12-26-79:20
13, The 5-26-37:15 and 6-23-37:33
Thirteen Fighting Men 3-23-60:6
13 Frightened Girls 6-19-63:7
13 Ghosts 6-29-60:9
Thirteen Hours by Air 5-06-36:18
13 Jours en France 7-10-68:6
13 Kislany Moscolyog Az Egre 11-09-38:17
13 Lead Soldiers 5-05-48:8
13 Men and a Girl 8-18-31:30
13 Rue Madeline 12-18-46:14
13 Washington Square 2-01-28:22
13 West Street 5-09-62:7
13 Women 10-18-32:15
13th Chair, The 10-03-19:57
Thirteenth Chair, The 1-22-30:30
13th Chair, The (s) 11-12-30:21
13th Chair, The 6-02-37:15
13th Commandment, The 2-13-20:44
13th Girl, The 12-31-15:25
13th Guest, The 9-06-32:21
13th Hour, The 11-30-27:18
13th Juror, The 11-23-27:24
13th Labor of Hercules, The 6-08-17:21
13th Letter, The 1-24-51:6
13th Man, The 8-04-37:25
30th Piece of Silver, The 5-14-20:34
Thirty a Week 10-18-18:39
30-Day Princess, The 5-15-34:14
Thirty Days 12-01-22:34 and 12-15-22:40
30 Foot Bride of Candy Rock, The 8-12-59:18
30 Is a Dangerous Age, Cynthia 3-06-68:6
30 Seconds over Tokyo 11-15-44:8
Thirty Thousand 4-02-20:95
30 Years of Fun 2-13-63:6
39 East 9-17-20:35
39 Steps, The 6-19-35:21 and 9-

Three Friends, The 10-22-10: 14

Three Girls About Town 10-22-41:8

3 Girls from Rome (See: Ragazza di Piazza di Spagna, La)

Three Girls Lost 5-06-31:23

Three Godfathers, The 6-16-16: 23

Three Godfathers 3-11-36:15

Three Godfathers 12-01-48:11

Three Gold Coins 7-09-20:26

Three Green Eyes 4-25-19:80

Three Guys Named Mike 2-14-51:13

Three Hats for Lisa 5-26-65:14

Three Hearts for Julia 1-06-43: 50

Three Henchmen of Lampio (See: Tres Cabras de Lampiao)

Three Hours 11-22-44:10

Three Hours to Kill 9-08-54:6

365 Nights in Hollywood 11-13-34:15

322 10-29-69:30

300 Spartans, The 8-22-62:6

300 Year Weekend, The 3-03-71: 22

Three Husbands 11-08-50:6

Three in Exile 11-04-25:40

Three in One 8-01-56:6

3 in the Attic 12-25-68:6

Three into 2 Won't Go 6-25-69: 18

Three Is a Family 11-22-44:10

Three Jumps Ahead 5-30-23:37

Three Kids and a Queen 11-13-35:16

Three Legionnaires 7-14-37:21

Three Little Girls in Blue 9-04-46:10

Three Little Sisters 8-02-44:20

3 Little Swigs (s) 10-31-33:17

Three Little Words 7-12-50:6

Three Live Ghosts 1-06-22:43

Three Live Ghosts 10-02-29:19

Three Lives 10-20-71:22

Three Lives of Thomasina 12-18-63:17

Three Loves 6-02-31:26

Three Loves Has Nancy 9-07-38: 12

Three Married Men 9-30-36:17

Three Maxims 7-15-36:31

Three Men and a Girl 4-04-19:67

Three Men from Texas 1-15-41: 14

Three Men in a Boat 6-06-33:15

Three Men in a Boat 1-02-57:6

Three Men in White 5-03-44:23

Three Men on a Horse 12-02-36:18

Three Mesquiteers, The 4-07-37:14

Three Miles Up 9-28-27:25

Three Mounted Men 11-01-18:38

Three Moves to Freedom 9-21-60:6

Three Musketeers, The 1-16-14: 17

Three Musketeers, The 3-06-14: 21

Three Musketeers, The 9-02-21: 61

Three Musketeers, The 9-16-21: 35 (Also see: D'Artagnan)

Three Musketeers, The 11-06-35:20

Three Musketeers, The 2-08-39: 17

Three Musketeers, The 10-20-48:11

Three Musketeers, The 12-26-73:12

Three Must-Get-Theirs, The 9-01-22:41

Three Naked Flappers 1-16-29: 22

3 Notti d'Amore 12-30-64:20

3 November 1918 4-07-65:30

Three Nuts in Search of a Bolt 6-17-64:6

3 O'Clock in the Morning 2-28-24:22

Three of a Kind 7-01-36:23

Three of Many 12-08-16:28

Three of Them, The 9-17-10:12

Three of Us, The 12-25-14:42

Three on a Couch 6-08-66:6

Three on a Honeymoon 5-08-34: 21

Three on a Limb (s) 1-15-36:19

Three on a Match 11-01-32:12

Three on a Ticket 4-09-47:16

Three on a Week End 6-15-38:15

Three on the Trail 5-06-36:18

Three Pals 9-22-16:34

Three Passions 5-08-29:20

3 + 2 10-16-63:16

Three Queens and a Jack 2-26-10:15

Three Reasons for Haste 9-18-09: 13

Three Ring Circus 10-27-54:6

Three-Ring Marriage 10-03-28:23

Three Rogues 4-08-31:18

Today I Hang   3-11-42:20
Today Is for the Championship
    7-23-80:22
Today We Live   4-18-33:21
Todd Killings, The   8-18-71:15
Todd of the Times   1-25-19:46
Toddles (s)   11-02-27:25
Todesmagazin oder Wie Werde
    Ich ein Blumentopf   12-05-
    79:24
Todesschuesse am Broadway   6-
    11-69:6
Todo Modo   3-26-80:24
Todo un Caballero   8-13-47:22
Todo un Hombre   11-17-43:20
Together   10-11-18:46
Together   6-06-56:6
Together   1-12-72:26
Together? (See: Amo Non Amo)
Together Again   11-08-44:23
Together Brothers   8-14-74:16
Together for Days   12-06-72:16
Together We Live   10-23-35:13
Toho-Hero of Southern Bandung
    7-24-63:6
Tohottu Nuoruns   5-05-48:20
Toi Ashita   4-23-80:19
Toi Ippon No Michi   2-22-78:
    19
Toi Le Venom   11-19-58:26
Toilers, The   10-31-28:24
Toilers of the Sea   11-22-23:27
Tokaji Rapszodia   2-16-38:25
Toklat   12-29-71:6
Tokoloshe   10-27-71:18
Tokyo After Dark   2-04-59:6
Tokyo File 212   4-25-51:14
Tokyo Joe   10-12-49:6
Tokyo Olympiad   5-26-65:15
Tokyo Rose   12-05-45:16
Tokyo Senso Sengo Hiwa   7-21-
    71:24
Tokyo Siren, A   6-18-20:34
Tol'able David   1-06-22:42
Tol'able David   11-19-30:21
Told at Twilight   3-09-17:22
Told in the Hills   9-12-19:52
Toll Gate   4-16-20:43
Toll of Mammon   6-26-14:19
Toll of the Desert   1-15-36:19
Toll of the Sea   12-01-22:35
Tolldreisten Frauen des Honore
    de Balzac, Die (See: Bra-
    zen Women of Balzac,
    The)
Toller Einfall, Ein   5-31-32:25
Toller Hecht auf Krummer Tour
    2-21-62:6

Tolpatsch, Der (See: Lummox)
Tom   10-03-73:14
Tom and His Pals   1-19-27:18
Tom Brown of Culver   8-02-32:15
Tom Brown's Schooldays   6-26-
    40:16
Tom Brown's Schooldays   5-02-51:
    12
Tom, Dick and Harry   7-16-41:8
Tom Horn   4-02-80:22
Tom Jones   7-31-63:12
Tom Sawyer   12-07-17:50
Tom Sawyer   12-24-30:20
Tom Sawyer   2-16-38:15
Tom Sawyer   3-14-73:20
Tom Sawyer, Detective   2-15-39:
    13
Tom Thumb   12-03-58:6
Tom Thumb   10-25-67:20
Tom Thumb Church (s)   5-13-42:
    16
Tom Thumbs Down (s)   6-02-31:
    14
Tom Tom Trail, The (s)   1-19-
    32:25
Tomahawk   1-10-51:13
Tomahawk Trail, The   1-02-57:16
Tomalio (s)   12-19-33:19
Tomas--et Barn, du Ikke Kan naa
    12-03-80:24
Tomasa   10-01-69:30
Tombe du Ciel   9-04-46:10
Tombolo   12-28-49:6
Tomboy   5-15-40:16
Tombstone   6-17-42:8
Tombstone Canyon   4-11-33:20
Tommy   2-03-37:29
Tommy   3-12-75:18
Tommy the Toreador   1-13-60:6
Tomorrow   9-16-70:15
Tomorrow   2-02-72:16
Tomorrow and Tomorrow   2-02-
    32:15
Tomorrow at Seven   7-04-33:16
Tomorrow Is Another Day   8-15-
    51:6
Tomorrow Is Forever   1-16-46:18
Tomorrow Is My Turn (See: Pas-
    sage du Rhin, Le)
Tomorrow Is Too Late (See:
    Domani e Troppo Tardi)
Tomorrow Never Comes   3-01-78:
    27
Tomorrow the World   12-20-44:8
Tomorrow We Live   3-17-43:23
Tomorrow's a Wonderful Day   4-
    13-49:20
Tomorrow's Champions (s)   8-07-
    35:21

Tomorrow's Love 1-07-25:38
Tomorrow's Yesterday 4-15-64: 22
Tomoyuki Yamashita 7-08-53:18
Tong Man, The 12-19-19:44
Tongue of Scandal, The 4-09-10: 15
Tongue Twisters (s) 5-09-33:14
Tongues of Flame 12-20-18:37
Tongues of Flame 12-17-24:37
Tongues of Men, The 1-28-16:22
Tongues of Scandal 6-29-27:26
Tonguetied (s) 12-03-30:15
Toni 6-20-28:19
Toni 3-19-35:27
Tonight a Town Dies 8-02-61:7
Tonight and Every Night 1-31-42: 10
Tonight at Twelve 9-25-29:17
Tonight Is Ours 1-24-33:12
Tonight or Never 12-22-31:15
Tonight We Raid Calais 3-31-43:8
Tonight We Sing 1-28-53:6
Tonight's the Night (s) 6-02-26: 15
Tonio Kroeger 9-16-64:6
Tonite Let's All Make Love in London 10-04-67:12
Tonka 12-17-58:6
Tonka Sibenice 3-19-30:34
Tonnerre de Dieu, Le 10-06-65:6
Tonny on the Wrong Road 7-04-62:6
Tons of Money 1-14-31:34
Tonto Basin Outlaws 11-26-41:9
Tony America 10-11-18:44
Tony Draws a Horse 5-23-51:18
Tony Rome 11-08-67:6
Tony's Scrap Book (s) 4-05-32:14
Too Busy to Work 12-06-32:14
Too Busy to Work 11-01-39:14
Too Careless to Kiss (s) 10-04-32:15
Too Dangerous to Live 4-19-39: 22
Too Fat to Fight 12-06-18:38
Too Hard to Handle (s) 2-11-31: 14
Too Hot to Handle 9-21-38:12
Too Hot to Handle 9-28-60:26
Too Late Blues 11-08-61:6
Too Late for Tears 4-13-49:11
Too Late the Hero 5-06-70:15
Too Many Blondes 5-21-41:15
Too Many Crooks 7-04-19:41
Too Many Crooks 8-18-31:17
Too Many Crooks 2-18-59:6
Too Many Girls 10-09-40:16

Too Many Husbands 3-06-40:16
Too Many Kisses 3-04-25:36
Too Many Millions 12-13-18:41
Too Many on the Job 10-16-09: 12
Too Many Parents 4-22-36:29
Too Many Winners 6-04-47:18
Too Many Wives 4-28-37:15
Too Much Business 5-05-22:33
Too Much Champagne 3-14-08:13
Too Much Harmony 9-26-33:20
Too Much Money 3-24-26:39
Too Much, Too Soon 4-16-58:6
Too Much Water 10-01-10:18
Too Much Wife 1-27-22:40
Too Much Youth 5-13-25:38
Too Soon to Love 2-17-60:6
Too Tough to Kill 12-25-35:15
Too Young to Kiss 10-31-51:6
Too Young to Know 11-21-45:10
Too Young to Love 3-16-60:6
Too Young to Marry 5-06-31:23
Too Young, Too Immoral 8-15-62:6
Toolbox Murders, The 11-08-78: 28
Toot Sweet (s) 12-11-29:35
Toot, Whistle, Plunk and Boom (s) 9-30-53:6
Top Banana 1-27-54:6
Top Gun 11-30-55:6
Top Hat 9-04-35:14
Top Man 9-15-43:10
Top o' the Morning 7-20-49:6
Top of New York 6-23-22:34
Top of the Heap 5-31-72:6
Top of the Town 3-31-37:17
Top of the World 2-18-25:41
Top of the World 5-04-55:6
Top Secret 12-10-52:6
Top Secret Affair 1-16-57:6
Top Sergeant 9-23-42:8
Top Sergeant Mulligan 5-02-28: 26
Top Sergeant Mulligan 11-19-41: 20
Top Speed 9-03-30:41
Topaz 11-12-69:21
Topaze 2-14-33:21
Topaze 2-20-35:31 and 6-17-36: 23
Topical Spanish 11-21-73:12
Topics of the Day (s) 4-10-29:16
Topkapi 9-09-64:6
Tople Godine 11-02-66:22
Toplo 2-18-79:26
Topnotchers (s) 10-23-35:13
Topo, El 5-19-71:17

Touhazvana Anada (See: Adrift)
Touki-Bouki 5-23-73:34
Tour, Prends Barde!, La 5-07-58:22
Tourbillon de Paris (See: Whirlwind of Paris)
Touring the Canary Islands 4-23-10:16
Tourist Trap, The 3-21-79:28
Tournament, The 3-20-29:22
Tous a Poll Et Qu'on en Finisse 4-07-76:32
Tous les Chemins Menent a Rome 11-30-49:20
Tous Peuvent Me Tuer 2-12-58:18
Tous Vedettes 2-06-80:24
Tout, The (s) 1-09-29:10
Tout Depend Des Filles 6-25-80:20
Tout le Monde, Il Est Beau; Tout le Monde, Il Est Gentil 5-24-72:24
Tout l'Or du Monde 11-15-61:6
Tout Peut Arriver 10-15-69:26
Tout Va Bien 5-17-72:28
Toute la Ville Accuse 12-05-56:6
Toute Sa Vie 11-26-30:19 and 6-23-31:20 (Also see: Hjartats Rost, Richiamo Del Cuore, Sarah and Son, and Wiegenlied)
Toute une Vie 5-29-74:16
Toutes Folles de Lui 6-14-67:6
Toutons Flinguers, Les 12-25-63:16 and 4-15-64:22
Tovarich 12-08-37:16
Tovaritch 5-22-35:16
Toward the Unknown 9-26-56:6
Tower of Lies, The 9-30-25:42
Tower of London 11-22-39:14
Tower of Nelse 2-02-55:6
Tower of Terror 4-24-14:22
Tower of Terror 7-01-42:8
Towering Inferno, The 12-18-74:13
Towing 5-24-78:31
Town Bloody Hall 3-19-80:28
Town Called Hell, A 10-20-71:20
Town Like Alice, A 3-14-56:22
Town on Trial 2-06-57:6
Town Scandal, The 4-26-23:27
Town Tamer 8-04-65:7
Town That Dreaded Sundown, The 1-26-77:30
Town That Forgot God, The 11-03-22:42
Town Went Wild, The 4-11-45:20

Town Without Pity 10-11-61:6
Toxi 9-17-52:6
Toy Tiger 4-18-56:7
Toy Wife, The 6-08-56:7
Toymaker, the Doll, and the Devil, The 12-03-10:14
Toymaker's Secret, The 1-22-10:15
Toys (s) 4-09-30:22
Toys Are Not for Children 6-21-72:18
Toys in a Field of Blue (s) 10-18-61:22
Toys in the Attic 6-26-63:6
Tozi Istinski Musch 9-24-75:24
Tracassin, Le 1-31-62:6
Track of the Cat 11-10-54:6
Track of Thunder 2-14-68:16
Trackdown 3-31-76:15
Tracked 11-14-28:30
Tracked by the Police 6-15-27:25
Tracked in the Snow Country 7-22-25:32
Tracked to Earth 3-31-22:40
Tracks 5-19-76:27
Tracy's G-Men (serial) 8-16-39:16
Trade Winds 12-21-38:14
Trader Ginsberg (s) 12-17-30:13
Trader Horn 2-11-31:14
Trader Horn 6-13-73:16
Trader Hornee 6-17-70:24
Tradition 7-08-21:27
Tradition de Minuit, La 5-24-39:14
Traellenes Oproer 10-17-79:10
Traeumende Mund, Der 10-18-32:19
Trafic 5-05-71:22
Traffic (See: Trafic)
Traffic Cop, The 4-07-16:23
Traffic in Crime 10-09-46:14
Traffic in Hearts 6-25-24:26
Traffic in Souls 11-28-13:12
Traffic Regulations (s) 2-20-29:14
Traffic Tangles (s) 2-11-31:14
Traffic Troubles (s) 5-06-31:22
Tragedies of Crystal Globe 7-09-15:18
Tragedy at Midnight, A 3-04-42:8
Tragedy in the Career of General Villa, The 5-15-14:22
Tragedy of Everest (s) 3-01-32:20
Tragedy of Love 7-25-79:24
Tragedy of the H. M. S. Hampshire, The (s) 4-28-26:60
Tragedy of the Mill, The 1-15-10:13

455 •

Trigger, Jr. 7-05-50:10
Trigger Pals 1-11-39:13
Trigger Smith 4-05-39:19
Trigger Tricks 6-25-30:115
Trigger Trio 12-15-37:17
Trilby 9-10-15:21
Trilby 7-26-23:28
Trilogie des Wiederschens 5-23-79:25
Trimmed in Scarlet 4-19-23:36
Trinity Is Still My Name (See: Continuavano a Chiamarlo Trinita)
Trio 8-09-50:9
Trio 5-03-67:24
Trio Infernal, Le 5-15-74:28
Triomphe de Michel Strogoff, Le 1-17-62:7
Trionfo Dell'Amore, Il 4-06-38:15
Triorama 2-18-53:6
Trip Along the Rhine, A 3-26-10:15
Trip Through Germany, A (s) 6-12-35:12
Trip Through Scotland, A 11-12-10:16
Trip Through the Old Family Album, A (s) 4-05-32:14
Trip Through the Rocky and Selkirk Mountains in Canada, A 11-19-10:13
Trip Thru China, A 5-18-17:23
Trip to America, A 10-29-52:24 (Also see: Voyage en Amerique, Le)
Trip to Biarritz, The (See: Voyage a Biarritz, Le)
Trip to Mars, A 2-26-10:15
Trip to Mars, A 7-18-19:44
Trip to Paradise, A 10-07-21:42
Trip to Paramountown, A 7-07-22:60
Trip to Paris, A (s) 12-01-31:15
Trip to Paris, A 6-15-38:14
Trip to the Argentine, A 12-03-15:21
Trip to the Isle of Jersey 9-24-10:12
Trip to Tibet, A (s) 4-22-31:18
Trip to Yosemite, A 10-09-09:22
Trip with Anita, A (See: Travels with Anita)
Tripes au Soleil, Les 3-18-59:6
Triple Cross 12-21-66:6
Triple Echo, The 5-23-73:36
Triple Irons 10-17-73:14
Triple Mort du Troisieme Per-

sonnage, La 10-03-79:18 and 7-30-80:30
Triple Threat 9-29-48:18
Triple Trouble (s) 5-13-36:15
Triple Trouble 9-13-50:6
Tripoli 10-11-50:8
Triporteur, Le 3-12-58:7
Tripping Thru the Tropics (s) 9-11-34:11
Tristan et Iseult 7-18-73:14
Tristana 4-08-70:16
Triumph 9-07-17:33
Triumph 4-23-24:20
Triumph of Love 4-23-47:8
Triumph of Right 4-03-14:20
Triumph of Sherlock Holmes, The 5-29-35:14
Triumph of the Scarlet Pimpernel 12-05-28:24
Triumph of the Weak, The 5-10-18:43
Triumph of Venus, The 3-01-18:41
Trixie Friganza (s) 1-30-29:14
Trocadero 4-26-44:19
Trocadero Bleu Citron 9-27-78:22
Troe Sutok Posle Bessmertiya (See: Three Days After Immortality)
Trofej 8-15-79:28
Trog 9-30-70:15
Troika 12-10-69:20
Trois Chambres a Manhattan 9-15-65:95
Trois Enfants Dans le Desordre 6-15-66:6
Trois Femmes 5-14-52:20
Trois Font le Paire, Les 7-10-57:6
Trois Garcons, Une Fille 1-26-49:22
Trois Hommes a Abattre 11-12-80:26
Trois Hommes Sur un Cheval 1-14-70:38
Trois Jours a Vivre 5-07-58:23
Trois Masques, Les 11-20-29:30
Trois Milliards Sans Ascenseur 11-01-72:30
Trois Mousquetaires, Les 5-09-33:15
Trois Mousquetaires, Les 11-25-53:24
Trois Mousquetaires, Les 11-01-61:16
Trois Mousquetaires, Les (See: Three Musketeers, The)

Trois Valses 1-25-39:15
Trois Women 8-12-64:6
Troiseme Cri, Le 8-28-74:43
Trojan Brothers 1-02-46:16
Trojan Women, The 6-02-71:22
Troll 5-23-73:18
Trollenberg Terror, The 10-15-58:6
Tromba, the Tiger Man 11-19-52:16
Trompe l'Oeil 3-19-75:32
Troop B, 16th Cavalry in Maneuvers 1-22-10:14
Troop Train (s) 2-03-43:14
Trooper Hook 6-26-57:6
Trooper O'Neil 7-28-22:35
Troopers Three 2-19-30:33
Troopship 4-27-38:23
Trop C'est Trop 6-18-75:16
Trop Jolies Pour Etre Honnetes 12-20-72:18
Trop Petit Mon Ami 10-21-70:22
Troper Nachts 5-27-31:57 (Also see: Dangerous Paradise)
Tropic Fury 9-13-39:12
Tropic Holiday 7-06-38:15
Tropic Lure (s) 9-01-31:21
Tropic of Cancer 2-18-70:17
Tropic Zone 12-17-52:6
Tropical Ecstasy 10-07-70:22
Tropical Heat Wave 10-01-52:22
Tropical Nights 2-20-29:17
Tropici 10-02-68:26
Trotta 12-08-71:20 and 5-24-72:26
Trotte Teodor 1-26-32:27
Trottie True 8-17-49:22
Trotting Kings (s) 10-07-42:25
Trou, Le 4-13-60:6
Trou Dans le Mur, Un 6-18-30:37 (Also see: Nar Rosorna Sla Ut)
Trou Normand, Le 2-18-53:18
Troubador, The 3-26-10:15
Troubib, Le 12-12-79:38
Trouble 5-26-22:33
Trouble (s) 10-27-31:19
Trouble Ahead 10-21-36:23
Trouble Along the Way 3-18-53:6
Trouble at Midnight 11-10-37:19
Trouble Buster, The 10-12-17:40
Trouble-Fesses, Le 10-13-76:22
Trouble-Fete 5-20-64:6
Trouble for Two (s) 2-26-30:24
Trouble for Two 6-03-36:15
Trouble in Morocco 3-17-37:14
Trouble in Paradise 11-15-32:19
Trouble in Store 12-30-53:6

Trouble in Sundown 7-05-39:16
Trouble in Texas 7-07-37:25
Trouble in the Glen 6-30-54:6
Trouble Makers 12-22-48:6
Trouble Man 11-08-72:28
Trouble Preferred 1-19-49:10
Trouble Shots (s) 9-08-31:15
Trouble Spot (s) 8-19-42:21
Trouble with Angels, The 3-30-66:6
Trouble with Girls, The 5-14-69:30
Trouble with Harry, The 10-12-55:6
Trouble with Wives, The 8-05-25:32
Trouble with Women, The 7-16-47:14
Troublemaker, The 7-01-64:22
Troubles of a Bride 5-06-25:47
Troublesome Wives 9-12-28:27
Trouper, The 7-21-22:35
Trouping with Ellen 12-03-24:30
Trousseau, The (s) 6-29-27:27
Trovatore, Il 8-24-49:22
Truands, Les 6-13-56:6
Truant Husband, The 1-28-21:40
Truant Officer Donald (s) 9-03-41:17
Truchas, Las 3-15-78:21
Truck Busters 1-20-43:9
Truck It 2-21-73:24
Truck Stop Women 11-13-74:19
Truck Turner 6-20-74:18
True and the False, The 1-19-55:6
True As a Turtle 4-03-57:6
True As Steel 6-18-24:23
True Blue 6-07-18:33
True Confession 11-24-37:16
True Friends 12-22-54:6
True Gang Murders 12-06-61:18
True Grit 5-21-69:6
True Heart Susie 6-06-19:49
True Heaven 2-13-29:24
True Life Story of Lynn Stuart, The 2-19-58:7
True Love 10-23-68:6
True Nobility 3-24-16:29
True Story of Eskimo Nell, The 4-09-75:30
True Story of Jesse James, The 2-20-57:6
True to His Oath 1-22-10:14
True to Life 8-11-43:10
True to the Army 3-18-42:25
True to the Navy 5-28-30:35
Trueno Entre Las Hojas, El 9-04-57:26

Two Gun Man 6-16-31:34
Two-Gun of Tumblewood 7-27-27:21
Two-Gun Sheriff 4-23-41:16
Two Gun Troubador 7-12-39:13
Two Guns and a Badge 9-15-54:6
Two Guys from Milwaukee 7-31-46:16
Two Guys from Texas 8-04-48:11
Two-Headed Spy, The 11-26-58:6
Two Heads on a Pillow 10-09-34:18
Two Heartbeats 12-20-72:18
Two Hearts in Harmony 11-20-35:39
Two Hearts in 3/4 Time 4-02-30:35 (Also see: Zwei Herzen im 3-4 Takt)
200 Motels 11-03-71:24
Two in a Crowd 10-07-36:15
Two in a Crowd 10-07-72:24
Two in a Taxi 9-17-41:22
Two in Revolt 4-29-36:15
Two in the Dark 2-05-36:33
Two in the Steppes 11-04-64:18
Two Kinds of Women 2-03-22:42
Two Kinds of Women 1-19-32:25
Two Kouney Lemels (sic) 8-24-66:6
Two Ladies and a Beggar 5-08-09:13
Two-Lane Blacktop 6-23-71:46
Two Latins from Manhattan 10-01-41:9
Two Left Feet 5-19-65:30
Two Little Bears, The 12-20-61:6
Two Little Chinese Maids (s) 1-30-29:14
Two Little Imps 7-13-17:28
Two Little Vagabonds 2-04-25:39
Two Little Waifs 11-12-10:16
Two Lost Worlds 1-31-51:6
Two Lovers 3-28-28:30
Two Lovers and a Coquette 8-28-09:13
Two Loves 5-03-61:7
Two-Man Submarine 3-29-43:21
Two Men and a Woman 2-23-17:23
Two Men of Karamoja 5-08-74:37
Two-Minute Warning 11-03-76:26
Two Minutes to Go 10-28-21:34
Two Minutes to Go (s) 11-12-30:21
Two Minutes to Play 10-13-37:17
Two Mr. Whites, The 10-30-09:11
Two Moons 1-28-21:39
Two Mrs. Carrolls, The 4-02-47:16
Two Mules for Sister Sara

4-15-70:17
Two Natures Within Him, The 5-28-15:17
Two O'Clock Courage 4-18-45:12
Two of a Kind (s) 6-11-30:18
Two of a Kind 6-13-51:6
Two of Us, The 2-16-38:17
Two of Us, The (See: Vieil Homme et l'Enfant, Le)
Two on a Vacation 12-10-47:12
Two or Three Things I Know About Her (See: Deux ou Trois Que Je Sais d'Elle)
Two Orphans, The 9-10-15:21
Two Orphans, The 10-25-50:6
Two Outlaws 10-31-28:31
Two Paths, The 1-14-11:18
Two People 3-14-73:20
Two Plus Fours (s) 8-30-30:14
Two Raffles 12-12-10:17
Two Rode Together 6-21-61:6
Two Seconds 5-24-32:37
Two Senoritas from Chicago 6-23-43:24
Two Sides to a Story 12-04-09:12
Two Sinners 9-18-35:32
Two Sisters, The 9-17-10:12
Two Sisters 7-03-29:32
Two Sisters 12-14-38:15
Two Sisters from Boston 3-06-46:12
Two Smart People 6-05-46:13
Two Soldiers 8-02-44:20
Two Solitudes 8-23-78:30
Two Soul Woman, The 5-03-18:40
Two Tanks in Trinidad 3-25-42:8
2,000 Women 9-13-44:10
2001: A Space Odyssey 4-03-68:6 and 1-15-69:6
2076 Olympiad 6-22-77:17
2000 Years Later 2-26-69:30
Two Tickets to Broadway 10-10-51:6
Two Tickets to London 6-16-43:16
Two Tickets to Paris 9-26-62:6
2 x 2 3-27-46:12
Two Waifs and a Stray 9-24-10:12
Two-Way Stretch 2-03-60:6
Two Weeks 2-06-20:53
Two Weeks in Another Town 8-08-62:6
Two Weeks in September (See: A Coeur Joie)
Two Weeks Off 6-26-29:25
Two Weeds to Live 2-03-43:14

● U ●

U-Boat Prisoner 8-16-44:16
U-Boat 29 10-11-39:13
UFA Kabaret (s) 9-15-31:14; 11-
   10-31:14; 1-05-32:19; 2-22-
   32:15
U Gori Raste Zelen Bor 9-01-71:
   22
U Ozera 8-05-70:16
U. P. Trail, The 11-12-20:35
U Raskoraku 7-17-68:24
U. S. Smith 7-25-28:26
U. S. S. Teakettle 2-28-51:13
U. S. S. R. Newsreel 7-08-36:15
U. S. S. R. Today 4-22-53:6
U. S. C. vs. Tulane 1-26-32:23
U Toszezon 9-06-67:6
U-Turn 7-04-73:30
Ubagaruma 9-11-57:6
Ubangi 6-02-31:26
Ubistvo Na Svirep i Podmukao
   Nacin i Iz Nishkih Pobudaj
   8-26-70:22
Ubranie Prawie Nowe 10-07-64:6
Uccellacci e Uccellini 5-26-66:7
Uccidere In Silenzio (See: To Kill
   in Silence)
Uchujin Tokyo Ni Arawaru 12-25-
   57:6
Uden en Traevl 9-18-68:28
Udhetim Ne Pranvere 1-10-79:56
Udienza, L' 7-12-72:30
Udoli Vcel 7-24-68:20
Uebergang, Der 7-25-79:38
Ugetsu Monogatari 9-09-53:6
Ugly American, The 4-03-63:7
Ugly Dachshund, The 12-22-65:17
Ugly Ones, The 9-11-68:110
Uj Gilgames 7-15-64:6
Ukamau 8-03-66:7
Ukradena Vzducholod 10-01-69:30
Ukraine in Flames 4-19-44:12
Ukroschenie Ognia 8-16-72:14
Ukryty w Sloncu 10-15-80:14
Uli der Paechter 2-01-56:18
Ulica 1-31-33:29
Ulli und Marei 10-12-49:20
Uloga Moje Porodice U Svetskoj
   Revolluciji 8-18-71:15

Ultim Noapte a Copilarie 11-26-
   69:26
Ultima Cena, La 5-03-78:26
Ultima Notte d'Amore, L' 10-23-
   57:18
Ultimatum 11-30-38:12
Ultima Cinque Minuti, Gli 11-16-
   55:6
Ultima Tre Giorni, Gli 8-31-77:
   30
Ultimo Cuple, El 6-19-57:7
Ultimo Encuentro 5-17-67:18
Ultimo Incontro 1-09-52:20
Ultimo Paradiso, L' 7-24-57:6
Ultimo Refugio 9-17-41:22
Ultimo Uomo di Sara, L' 3-06-
   74:26
Ulysses 12-08-54:6
Ulysses 3-15-67:6
Ulzana's Raid 10-18-72:18
Um eine Nasenlaenge 9-15-31:24
Um Freiheit und Liebe 2-23-38:
   14
Um Sonho de Vampiros 10-14-70:
   32
Uma Abelha Na Chuva 8-02-72:
   24
Umberto D. 6-04-52:6
Umbrella, The 8-01-33:57
Umbrellas of Cherbourg, The
   (See: Parapluies de Cher-
   bourg, Les)
Um's Kap Horn (s) 12-01-31:15
Umsetzer, Der 5-11-77:9
Umut 8-02-78:20
Un de la Montagne 12-18-34:13
Un, Deux, Trois, Quatre! 8-31-
   60:6
Un Dia De Diciembre 10-31-62:6
Un et l'Ature, L' (See: Other One,
   The)
Una di Quelle 12-30-53:18
Una Vez en la Vida 8-27-41:20
Una Vida Por Otra 7-10-34:13
Unaccustomed As We Are (s) 5-
   08-29:20
Unanstaendige Profit, Der 4-27-
   77:22
Unappreciated Genius 4-10-09:13
Unashamed 7-19-32:25
Unashamed 8-10-38:12
Unattainable, The 8-25-16:23
Unbekannte, Die 12-16-36:21
Unbeliever, The 2-15-18:52 and
   5-03-18:40
Unblazed Trail 9-20-23:37
Unborn, The 6-23-16:20
Unbroken Promise, The 8-01-19:53

Veertig Jaren 9-21-38:25
Vegul 3-21-75:76
Veil of Happiness 5-02-28:15
Veiled Adventure, The 5-16-19:
52
Veiled Marriage 3-26-20:51
Veiled Woman, The 9-08-22:42
Veiled Woman, The 6-26-29:22
Veille d'Armes 1-08-36:13
Veils of Bagdad, The 9-30-53:6
Veinte Anos y Una Noche 8-06-41:8
Veliki i Mali 9-17-58:18
Vellos Sao Os Trapos 10-15-80:74
Velvet Paw, The 9-01-16:24
Velvet Touch, The 7-21-48:10
Velvet Vampire, The 8-18-71:22
Ven, Mi Corazon Te Llama 10-28-
42:8
Vendemaire 5-15-68:7
Vendetta 10-09-09:20
Vendetta, The 10-03-14:21
Vendetta 12-23-21:35
Vendetta 11-22-50:8
Venerable Ones, The (See: Vener-
ables Todos, Los)
Venerables Todos, Los 5-22-63:19
Venere di Cherone, La 3-19-58:16
Venere Imperiale 1-30-63:6
Venetian Affair, The 1-11-67:6
Venetian Bird 10-29-52:24
Venetian Holiday (s) 5-03-32:14
Venetian Night, A 9-26-14:22
Venezia, Ultima Serata di Carnevale
9-17-80:27
Venga a Prendere Il Caffe Pa Noi
10-28-70:30
Venganza, La 5-21-58:16
Vengeance 5-10-18:41
Vengeance (s) 2-05-30:19
Vengeance 3-05-30:33
Vengeance Alley 2-07-51:6
Vengeance Is Mine 2-04-16:28
Vengeance Is Mine 3-26-80:24
Vengeance of Durand, The 11-14-
19:60
Vengeance of Fu Manchu, The 1-
17-68:6
Vengeance of She, The 4-10-68:6
Vengeance of the Deep 4-19-23:36
Vengeance of the Deep 2-28-40:16
Vengeance of the Wilds, The 6-18-
15:18
Vengeance Trail, The 11-04-21:42
Venice and Die (See: Voir Venise
et Crever)
Venice of the North (s) 9-08-26:
20
Venita Gould (s) 6-20-28:14

Venner 7-06-60:6
Vent de l'Est, Le 5-20-70:28
Vent des Aures, Le 5-10-67:20
Vent Se Leve 3-04-59:6
Venta de Vargas 10-07-59:6
Vento Del Sud 9-14-60:20
Venus 6-26-29:29 and 10-16-29:17
Venus de l'Or, La 6-01-38:13
Venus in Furs 5-06-70:24
Venus in Peltz (See: Venus in Furs)
Venus in the East 1-31-19:54
Venus Makes Trouble 5-19-37:23
Venus Model, The 6-14-18:29
Venus of the South Seas 6-11-24:
31
Venus of Venice 5-04-27:20
Venusberg 5-15-63:20
Vera 10-03-73:15
Vera Cruz 12-22-54:6
Vera Holgk et Ses Filles 6-06-33:
15
Vera Romeyke Is Nicht Tragbar 7-
14-76:25
Vera, the Medium 1-05-17:27
Verbena de la Paloma, La 1-15-
36:19
Verboten! 3-25-59:22
Verbrande Brug 10-08-75:20
Vercingetorix, Gaul's Hero 4-10-
09:13
Verdad Sobre El Caso Savolta, La
5-28-80:14
Verdammt Gutes Leben, Ein 3-29-
78:28
Verdammt Zur Suende 12-02-64:6
Verden er Fuld at Boern 2-13-80:
16
Verdes Praderas, Las 7-04-79:25
Verdi (s) 3-04-31:14
Verdict, The 6-10-25:49
Verdict, The 11-06-46:18
Verdict 9-18-74:22
Verdugo, El 9-11-63:6
Vereda Da Salvacao 7-14-65:6
Vergine Per Il Principe, Una 3-
16-66:6
Verginita 4-22-53:6
Veri Az Ordog A Feleseget 11-16-
77:21
Verite, La 11-23-60:20
Verite Sur Bebe Donge, La 3-12-
52:16
Verkaufte Braut 5-01-34:15
Verklungene Traueme 12-10-30:26
Verklungenes Wien 12-05-51:22
Verliebte Firma, Die 3-22-32:61
Verliebte Lente 3-09-55:6
Verlobte, Die 7-23-80:20

Verloren Maandag 11-21-73:6
Verlorene, Der 9-05-51:6
Verlorene, Die 10-01-75:28
Verlorene Ehre der Katharina Blum,
  Die 10-01-75:28
Verlorene Engel, Der 10-01-80:
  26
Verlorene Paradies, Das 11-24-31:
  17
Verlorene Schuh 1-10-24:27 (Also
  see: Cinderella)
Verlorene Sohn 1-22-35:15
Verlorene Tal, Das 7-01-36:25
Verlorenes Leben 4-14-76:26
Vermilion Door 10-20-65:26
Vermillion Pencil 3-17-22:42
Vernon's Aunt (s) 5-28-30:21
Vernost Materi 12-27-67:7
Verona Trial (See: Processo di
  Verona, Il)
Veronicas Svededug 11-30-77:20
Veronique Ou l'Ete de Mes 13 Ans
  4-09-75:30
Verraeter 10-07-36:31 and 1-27-
  37:13
Verrohung, Die 3-26-75:22
Vers l'Extase 8-31-60:7
Versailles 9-11-09:13
Versprich Mir Nichts 10-13-37:
  16
Versteck, Das 3-12-80:23
Versuchen Sie Meine Schwester 6-
  23-31:19
Versuchung im Sommerwind 6-13-
  73:22
Verte Moisson, La 2-03-60:6
Vertreibung aus dem Paradies,
  Die 4-20-77:73
Vertige Pour un Tueur 9-30-70:22
Vertigine Bianca 4-18-56:7
Vertigo 7-03-46:10
Vertigo 5-14-58:6
Vertimmen (See: Hour of the Wolf)
Veruntreute Himmel, Der 12-17-
  58:6
Verwehte Spuren 11-02-38:23
Verweigerung, Der 9-20-72:14
Verworking Van Herman Durer
  (See: Demise of Herman
  Durer, The)
Very Big Withdrawal, A 5-23-79:
  24
Very Confidential 11-30-27:18
Very Edge, The 5-08-63:6
Very Good Young Man, A 8-08-
  19:48
Very Handy Man, A 12-14-66:6
Very Honorable Guy, A 5-22-34:29

Very Idea, The 8-06-20:26
Very Idea, The 8-28-29:31
Very Important Person 4-26-61:6
Very Impossible, The (s) 9-01-
  31:21
Very Natural Thing, A 5-29-74:
  14
Very Private Affair, A (See: Vie
  Privee, La)
Very Special Favor, A 7-07-65:6
Very Thought of You, The 10-18-
  44:10
Very Young Lady, A 4-30-41:16
Vespro Siciliano 1-28-50:6
Vessel of Wrath 3-16-38:15 (Also
  see: Beachcomber, The)
Vest with a Tail, The (s) 7-25-
  33:14
Vetar Je Stao Pred Zory 8-12-
  59:19
Vetchni Vremena 8-27-75:24
Veuve Couderc, La 10-27-71:24
Veuve en Or, Une 11-05-69:26
Vi Hemslavinor 6-07-44:21
Vi Som Gar Koksvagen 1-24-33:
  19
Via Express (s) 8-04-31:18
Via Margutta 11-09-68:19
Via Pony Express 5-09-33:15
Via Wireless 9-24-15:21
Viaccia, La 5-10-61:7
Viagem Ao Fim Do Mundo 10-30-
  68:6
Viager, Le 1-26-72:16
Viaggio, Il 9-25-74:18
Viaje, El 11-11-42:24
Viaje Al Centro de la Tierra 9-
  28-77:22
Viaje Fantastico en Globo 7-14-76:
  20
Vic Dyson Pays 7-22-25:32
Vica a Vadevezos 6-27-33:25
Vicar of Bray, The 5-26-37:15
Vicar of Wakefield, The 3-02-17:
  25
Vice and Virtue 5-14-15:20
Vice and Virtue 3-13-63:6
Vice et la Vertu, Le (See: Vice
  and Virtue)
Vice of Fools, The 12-03-20:32
Vice Racket 5-19-37:23
Vice Raid 12-16-59:6
Vice Squad, The 6-09-31:18
Vice Squad 7-08-53:6
Vichingo Venuto Dal Sud, Il 9-22-
  71:18
Vicious Circle, The 5-26-48:18
Vicious Years, The 2-22-50:6

Virginian, The 12-25-29:26
Virginian, The 1-30-46:12
Virginie 11-14-62:6
Virgins of Bali, The 12-13-32:15
Virgin's Sacrifice, A 6-16-22:43
Viridiana 5-24-61:6
Virilita 2-18-76:38
Virtue 11-01-32:13
Virtue's Revolt 5-27-25:41
Virtuous Husband 5-13-31:36
Virtuous Liars 4-02-24:22
Virtuous Men 4-11-19:55
Virtuous Model, The 9-19-19:54
Virtuous Sin, The 10-29-30:27
Virtuous Sinners 5-16-19:52
Virtuous Vamp, A 11-21-19:55
Virtuous Wives 1-03-19:37
Virus 5-28-80:43
Visages de France, Les 2-03-37:
   15
Viscount, The (See: Vicomte Regle
   Ses Comptes, Le)
Visionari, I 10-23-68:22
Visions of a Nag 11-27-09:13
Visions of Eight 5-30-73:12
Visions of Naples (s) 11-10-31:14
Visions of Spain (s) 11-07-28:15
Visit, The 5-13-64:6
Visit to a Chef's Son 3-20-74:18
Visit to a Small Planet 2-03-60:6
Visit to Biskra, A 9-11-09:13
Visit to the Nursery, A 4-25-08:
   13
Visit to Uncle, A 10-30-09:11
Visita, La 2-12-64:6
Visitatore, Il (See: Visitor, The)
Visiteurs du Soir, Les (See: Devil's
   Envoys, The)
Visitor, The 11-21-73:12
Visitor, The 3-26-80:27
Visitors, The 2-02-72:16
Viskingar Och Rop (See: Cries and
   Whispers)
Visnja Na Tasmajdanu 8-20-69:28
Vita, a Volte e Molto Dura, Vero
   Provvidenza? 11-15-72:32
Vita di Donizetti, La (See: Life of
   Donizetti, The)
Vita Difficile, Una 2-28-62:6
Vita Sporten, Den 10-15-69:15
Vital Question, The 3-31-16:28
Vitelloni, I 10-14-53:24 and 11-
   14-56:6
Viuda Montiel 3-05-80:26
Viva Cisco Kid 3-20-40:16
Viva Italia 7-12-78:18
Viva Jalisco Que Es Mi Tierra
   4-26-61:21

Viva Knievel 6-08-77:26
Viva La Clase Media 5-07-80:575
Viva la Muerte 3-17-71:26
Viva la Vida! 10-22-69:31
Viva Las Vegas 5-20-64:20
Viva Lo Imposible 9-17-58:7
Viva Maria! 12-08-65:6
Viva Max! 12-17-69:24
Viva Villa! 4-17-34:18
Viva Zapata! 2-06-52:6
Vivacious Lady 5-04-38:15
Vivan Los Novios 5-06-70:15
Vive Henri IV, Vive l'Amour 4-
   26-61:21
Vive la France 9-27-18:42
Vive la France 10-09-74:18
Vive la Liberte 6-26-46:11
Vive la Mort 10-22-69:32
Vive la Nation 2-14-40:20
Vivere 1-20-37:15
Vivette 7-12-18:39
Vivir Del Cuento 3-09-60:6
Vivre Ensemble 5-16-73:18
Vivre la Nuit 6-12-68:26
Vivre Pour Vivre (See: Live for
   Life)
Vivre Sa Vie, La 8-29-62:6
Vixen, The 12-08-16:29
Vixen 10-30-68:6
Vixens, The 1-29-69:6
Viza Privati, Pubbliche Virtu 5-
   26-76:20
Viza Zla 8-12-59:19
Vlad Tepes 5-30-79:16
Vladimir and Rosa 4-28-71:6
Vladimir et Rosa (See: Vladimir
   and Rosa)
Vlak Bez Voznog Reda 5-13-59:7
Vlak U Snijegu 8-18-76:24
Vlci Jama 9-17-58:18
Vlublennye 10-14-70:30
Voce Del Sangue, La 4-25-33:18
Voce Del Silenzi, La 4-22-53:6
Voce Nel Tuo Cuore, Una (See:
   Voice in Your Heart, A)
Voci Bianche, Le 10-21-64:6
Vodka Boatmen (s) 10-09-35:15
Voglia Matta, La 5-30-62:23
Vogliamo i Colonnelli 3-21-73:18
Voglio Vivere Con Letizia 2-16-
   38:25
Vogues of 1938 8-04-37:18
Voice from the Fireplace, A 2-
   12-10:16
Voice from the Minaret 2-08-23:
   41
Voice in the Fog, The 10-01-15:
   19

Voyage a Biarritz, Le 5-08-63:
28
Voyage au Bout du Monde, Le
12-08-76:18
Voyage d'Amelie, Le 1-29-75:16
Voyage de Noces, Le 5-05-76:22
Voyage du Pere, Le 10-12-66:6
Voyage en Amerique, Le 12-05-
51:22 (Also see: Trip to
America, A)
Voyage en Ballon, Le 9-07-60:6
Voyage en Douce, Le 2-06-80:22
Voyage en Grande Tartari e 3-
13-74:18
Voyage of Emperor Chien Lung,
The 10-25-78:20
Voyage of Silence (See: O Salto)
Voyage of the Damned 12-01-76:
18
Voyage Surprise 2-18-48:9
Voyage to Italy (See: Journey to
Italy)
Voyage to the Bottom of the Sea
6-28-61:6
Voyage to the End of the Universe
(See: Ikarie XBI)
Voyageur Trails (s) 5-08-34:14
Voyageuse Inattendue, La 2-08-
50:22
Voyol, Le 12-02-70:16
Vpervye Zamuzhem 7-30-80:23
Vrai Coupable, Le 8-01-51:18
Vrai Nature de Bernadette, La
5-17-72:30
Vrata Ostaju Otvorena 8-12-59:19
Vrazda Ingzenyra Certa 10-14-70:
28
Vrazda Po Cesku 6-28-67:22
Vrci Jana 8-27-58:6
Vreme Bez Rata 12-09-70:22
Vrhovi Zelengore 8-18-76:24
Vsichko e Lyubov 6-11-80:29
Vsichni Dobri Rodaci 5-28-69:34
Vski Roti 9-08-71:27
Vstuplenjie 9-04-63:20
Vu du Pont (See: View from the
Bridge, A)
Vuk Sa Prokletija 8-21-68:24
Vulture, The 1-25-67:6
Vynalez Zkazy 6-25-58:6 (Also
see: Fabulous World of Jules
Verne, The)
Vysoka Zed 8-05-64:7
Vyssi Princip 8-03-60:7 and 5-17-
61:6

Walk with Love and Death, A 9-10-69:48

Walkabout 5-19-71:17

Walking (s) 4-01-70:26

Walking Back 6-13-28:13

Walking Back Home (s) 6-26-34: 16

Walking Dead, The 3-04-36:26

Walking Down Broadway 2-02-38: 15

Walking Hills, The 3-02-49:8

Walking My Baby Back Home 11-11-53:6

Walking on Air 9-06-36:17

Walking Stick, The 3-18-70:26

Walking Tall 2-28-73:20

Walking the Baby (s) 7-11-33:15

Walking Up the Town 4-01-25:38

Walkower 5-19-65:31

Wall Between, The 4-07-16:22

Wall Flower 7-07-22:60

Wall of Noise 8-14-63:6

Wall Street 11-27-29:31

Wall Street Cowboy 9-06-39:14

Wall Street Mystery, The 5-28-20:43

Wall St. Mystery (s) 11-10-31:14

Wall Street Tragedy, A 8-18-16: 25

Wallflower 5-19-48:13

Wallflowers 4-04-28:29

Wallingford 12-09-21:36

Wallingford 10-13-31:14

Walls Came Tumbling Down, The 5-22-46:10

Walls of Fire 1-20-71:13

Walls of Gold 10-24-33:17

Walls of Hell, The (See: Intramuros)

Walls of Jericho, The 12-12-14:28

Walls of Jericho, The 7-04-48:6

Walls of Malapaga, The 3-29-50: 11

Walpi (s) 1-03-33:19 and 5-16-33: 17

Walter Donaldson (s) 9-26-33:15

Walter Huston and Co. (s) 5-01-29:17

Waltz Dream, The 7-28-26:16

Waltz of the Toreadors 5-18-62:6

Waltz Time 6-27-33:15 and 10-03-33:15

Waltz Time 7-04-45:8

Waltzes from Vienna 3-06-34:14 (Also see: Strauss' Great Waltz)

Waltzing Around (s) 5-15-29:20

Walzer fuer Dich, Ein 10-07-36: 31

Walzer un den Stefansturm, Ein 2-10-37:15

Walzer vom Strauss 2-16-32:33

Walzerkrug 11-20-34:17

Walzerparadies 3-07-33:54

Walzertraum, Ein 1-27-26:42

Wan Pipel 10-13-76:23

Wanda 9-02-70:32

Wanda Nevada 5-30-79:16

Wanda's Affair 11-12-20:36

Wanderer, The (s) 10-08-30:22

Wanderer of the Wasteland, The 5-21-24:26

Wanderer of the Wasteland, The 10-16-35:23

Wanderer of the Wasteland, The 9-26-45:14

Wanderers, The 1-07-16:23

Wanderers, The 7-11-79:19

Wanderers of the West 9-24-41: 18

Wandering Daughters 7-04-23:23

Wandering Fires 12-16-25:44

Wandering Footsteps 10-28-25:37 and 6-16-26:16

Wandering Girls 2-23-27:17

Wandering Husband, The 6-11-24: 29

Wandering Jew, The 4-22-21:41

Wandering Jew, The 6-21-23:25***

Wandering Jew, The 12-05-33:17 and 1-15-35:13

Wandering Jew, The 10-24-33:22

Wandering Thru China (s) 6-02-31:14

Wanderlust (s) 2-05-30:19

Waning Sex, The 9-01-26:15

Wanted 3-03-37:14

Wanted, a Child 10-09-09:20

Wanted--a Home 9-22-16:49

Wanted--a Husband 12-19-19:45

Wanted: A Master (s) 1-27-37:12

Wanted at Headquarters 10-22-20: 41

Wanted by Scotland Yard 7-12-39: 13

Wanted by the Law 5-07-24:25

Wanted by the Police 9-28-28:21

Wanted for Murder 12-13-18:40

Wanted for Murder 4-03-46:12

Wanted: Jane Turner 12-02-36:38

Wanted Men 7-15-36:55

Wanters, The 3-12-24:26

War Against Mrs. Hadley, The 8-05-42:8

War and Peace 8-22-56:6 (Credits reprinted in issue of 5-01-68: 25)

We All Loved Each Other So Much
(See: C'Eravama Tanti Amati)
We Americans 4-04-28:28
We Are from Kronstadt 5-06-36:
19
We Are Not Alone 11-15-39:18
We Are the Guinea Pigs 5-07-80:
575
We Are the Marines 12-09-42:8
We Can't Have Everything 7-12-
18:35
We Did It Ourselves (s) 3-07-56:6
We Dive at Dawn 6-02-43:8
We Do It Because (s) 2-04-42:8
We Go Fast 9-10-41:8
We Have Our Moments 5-05-37:16
We Joined the Navy 12-05-62:6
We Live Again 11-06-34:16
We Live Again 9-15-48:20
We Lived Through Buchenwald 2-
19-47:9
We Moderns 12-09-25:42
We Refuse to Die (s) 10-07-42:25
We Should Worry 7-05-18:31
We, the Animals, Squeak (s) 9-
03-41:17
We Two (See: Hum Dono)
We, We, Marie (s) 1-07-31:23
We Went to College 7-29-36:14
We Were Dancing 1-21-42:8
We Were Strangers 4-27-49:11
We Who Are About to Die 1-06-
37:40
We Who Are Young 7-17-40:16
We Will Come Back 10-20-43:12
We Will Remember (See: Senjo Ni
Nagareru Uta)
Weak and the Wicked, The 2-17-
54:6
Weak but Willing (s) 9-24-30:23
Weaker Sex, The 12-29-16:20
Weaker Sex, The 5-11-27:21
Weaker Sex, The 10-06-48:11
Weaker Vessel, The 7-25-19:43
Weakness of Man, The 7-07-16:
24
Wealth 7-01-21:27
Weapon, The 6-12-57:6
Weary River 1-30-29:14
Weaver of Dreams, A 2-22-18:45
Weaver of Miracles, The 7-04-
62:6
Weavers, The 10-09-29:82
Weavers of Life 12-03-20:32
Web, The 5-28-47:15
Web of Chance 1-31-20:56
Web of Danger 6-18-47:8
Web of Deceit 1-23-20:60

Web of Desire, The 2-23-17:23
Web of Evidence 9-09-59:6
Web of Fate 8-28-09:13
Web of Fate 2-01-28:22
Web of Fear (See: Constance aux
Enfers)
Web of Intrigue, A 11-08-18:41
Web of Life, The 4-06-17:24
Web of Passion (See: A Double
Tour)
Webb Singing Pictures 1-19-17:26
Webb's Electrical Pictures 5-08-
14:21
Weber and Fields (s) 9-12-28:12
Webster Boy, The 6-27-62:6
Websterian Students (s) 5-07-30:
20
Wechma 3-29-72:32
Wedding, A 9-06-78:22
Wedding Bells 8-19-21:35
Wedding Bells 6-29-27:18
Wedding Bills (s) 11-17-31:14
Wedding Certificate 7-14-65:7
Wedding Day, The 7-31-57:6
Wedding in Blood (See: Noces
Rouges, Les)
Wedding in Monaco, The (s) 5-16-
56:18
Wedding in White 10-18-72:24
Wedding March, The 10-17-28:16
Wedding March, The 2-06-29:19
Wedding Night, The 3-20-35:17
Wedding of Jack and Jill, The (s)
5-07-30:20
Wedding of Palt, The 3-03-37:14
Wedding of the Fairy Princess
8-01-56:6
Wedding of Zein, The 7-05-78:76
Wedding Party, The 4-09-69:28
Wedding Present 11-25-36:15
Wedding Rehearsal 10-28-32:26
Wedding Rings 5-14-30:39
Wedding Song, The 1-13-26:42
Weddings and Babies 9-17-58:7
Wedlock 7-19-18:38
Wednesday at the Ritz (s) 1-22-
30:17
Wednesday Children, The 6-20-
73:20
Wednesday's Child 12-18-34:13
Wedtime Story (s) 7-01-36:12
Wee Lady Liberty 8-31-17:30
Wee MacGregor's Sweetheart 8-
11-22:34
Wee Willie Winkie 6-30-37:20
Weed 5-17-72:28
Week's Leave, A 1-09-46:82
Weekend (See: Weekend, Le)

487 •

What's the Matter with Helen?
6-09-71:17
What's Up, Doc?   3-08-72:20
What's Up, Tiger Lily?   10-05-
66:6
What's Wrong with Women   12-08-
22:34
What's Your Harry?   8-20-20:35
What's Your Husband Doing?   11-
14-19:59
What's Your Racket   3-06-34:27
Wheel, The   3-11-25:43 (Also see:
Roue, La)
Wheel of Ashes   9-11-68:6
Wheel of Chance   7-04-28:16
Wheel of Karma, The   11-09-55:6
Wheel of Life, The   6-26-29:25
Wheel of the Law, The   10-06-16:
27
Wheeler Dealers, The   9-25-63:6
Wheels of Destiny   1-25-28:13
Wheels of Destiny   4-03-34:27
Wheels of Justice   10-16-09:12
Wheels of Justice, The   3-05-15:
21
When a Dog Loves   5-18-27:24
When a Feller Needs a Friend   4-
11-19:57
When a Feller Needs a Friend   5-
17-32:14
When a Girl Loves   3-14-19:44
When a Girl Loves   5-21-24:24
When a Man Loves   2-09-27:14
When a Man Rides Alone   12-26-
33:26
When a Man Sees Red   1-22-35:15
When a Man's a Man   2-07-24:22
When a Man's a Man   2-27-35:26
When a Stranger Calls   9-05-79:20
When a Woman Ascends the Stairs
(See: Onna Ga Kaidan O
Agaru Toki)
When a Woman Calls   6-04-75:19
When a Woman Loves   7-31-14:16
When a Woman Loves   9-13-61:28
When a Woman Sins   10-04-18:51
When a Woman Strikes   11-07-19:
97
When All Is Said (See: A Tout
Prendre)
When Broadway Was a Trail   10-24-
14:22
When Casey Joined the Lodge   6-
27-08:10
When Comedy Was King   3-02-60:6
When Danger Calls   1-18-28:28
When Danger Smiles   11-17-22:42
When Dawn Came   4-30-20:43

When Destiny Wills   9-16-21:35
When Devil Drives   7-07-22:60
When Dinosaurs Ruled the Earth
10-14-70:28
When Do We Eat?   10-25-18:35
When Dreams Come True   5-08-
29:24
When Duty Calls   1-09-29:34
When Eight Bells Toll   3-17-71:26
When Eve Came Back   9-29-16:27
When Fate Decides   5-30-19:75
When Fate Leads Trump   7-09-
15:17
When Fish Fight (s)   8-12-36:19
When G Men Step In   3-16-38:17
When Geisha Girls Get Gay (s)   8-
25-31:24
When Hell Broke Loose   11-05-58:6
When His Ship Came In   10-31-14:
28
When Husband's Deceive   8-25-22:
34
When Husbands Flirt   1-20-26:44
and 7-21-26:19
When I Grow Up   4-11-51:6
When in Rome (s)   6-14-32:16
When in Rome (s)   11-01-32:12
When in Rome   3-05-52:6
When Johnny Comes Marching Home
12-23-42:8
When Knighthood Was in Flower   9-
22-22:41
When Knights Were Bold   3-04-36:
27
When Ladies Meet   6-27-33:14
When Ladies Meet   8-27-41:8
When Lilacs Bloom   7-17-29:53
When London Burned   5-14-15:20
When Love Calls   10-13-48:11
When Love Comes   1-05-23:43
When Love Is King   2-11-16:22
When Love Is Young   4-21-37:14
When Love Was Blind   3-30-17:32
When Lovers Part   1-07-11:13
When Men Are Tempted   1-04-18:
44
When Moscow Laughs   9-18-29:32
When My Baby Smiles at Me   11-
10-48:15
When My Lady Smiles   8-27-15:
20
When Odds Are Even   4-30-24:36
When Peace Breaks Out (See:
Cuando Estallo la Paz)
When Romance Rides   4-14-22:39
When Rome Ruled   8-21-14:19
When Seconds Count   6-01-27:24
When Strangers Marry   5-30-33:15

Where the Red Fern Grows 5-29-74:24
Where the Sidewalk Ends 6-28-50:6
Where the Spies Are 12-08-65:22
Where the Sun Plays (s) 4-02-30:18
Where the Trail Begins 7-13-27:23
Where the Trail Divides 10-17-14:15
Where the Truth Lies (See: Malefices)
Where the West Begins 2-14-19:51
Where the West Begins 3-23-38:17
Where There's Life 10-08-47:8
Where Trails Divide 10-20-37:27
Where Was I? 8-10-25:37
Where Was Your Majesty Between 3 & 5? 3-24-65:6
Where Were You When the Lights Went Out? 6-12-68:6
Where Worlds Fail 8-11-48:8 (Also see: Donde Mueren las Palabras)
Where's Charley? 7-02-52:6
Where's Elmer? (s) 4-03-34:17
Where's George 8-21-35:21
Where's Jack? 4-09-69:28
Where's Mary? 10-10-19:61
Where's Poppa? 11-11-70:15
Wherever She Goes 2-04-53:6
Which Shall It Be? 4-09-24:18
Which Way Is Up? 11-02-77:17
Which Way to the Front? 7-29-70:15
Which Woman? 6-14-18:29
Whiffs 10-01-75:24
While I Love 10-22-47:13
While Justice Waits 1-12-23:34
While London Sleeps 12-22-26:18
While New York Sleeps 12-21-38:14
While Paris Sleeps 1-19-23:46
While Paris Sleeps 6-14-32:17
While Satan Sleeps 6-30-22:32
While the Captain Waits (s) 11-05-30:23
While the City Sleeps 10-24-28:24
While the City Sleeps 5-02-56:6
While the Patient Slept 3-06-35:20
While the Sun Shines 2-19-47:9
Whims for Society 2-08-18:43
Whip, The 3-30-17:31
Whip, The 9-19-28:28
Whip Hand, The 10-24-51:6
Whip Woman, The 2-15-28:27
Whiplash 12-22-48:6

Whipped 2-15-50:13
Whippet Racing (s) 8-04-31:18
Whipsaw 1-29-36:16
Whirl of Life, The 10-22-15:23
Whirl of Life, The 3-27-29:24 and 7-03-29:30
Whirl of Paris, The 6-20-28:19
Whirlpool, The 6-28-18:28
Whirlpool 5-08-34:21
Whirlpool 11-23-49:8
Whirlpool 3-25-59:6
Whirlpool 9-02-70:32
Whirls and Girls (s) 5-15-29:20
Whirlwind 4-04-51:6
Whirlwind 7-31-68:6
Whirlwind Horseman 6-06-38:15
Whirlwind of Paris 2-13-46:10
Whirlwind of Youth, The 6-08-27:15
Whirlwind Raiders 5-12-48:20
Whiskey Galore 6-22-49:20
Whispering Whoopee (s) 4-02-30:18
Whisper Market 9-03-20:45
Whispered Name 2-14-24:27
Whisperers, The 7-12-67:6
Whispering 3-01-39:15
Whispering Chorus, The 3-29-18:46
Whispering City 5-07-47:18 and 11-12-47:8
Whispering Death 4-21-76:23
Whispering Ghosts 4-22-42:18
Whispering Joe 5-08-68:36
Whispering Sage 4-06-27:24
Whispering Smith 6-16-16:24
Whispering Smith 5-12-26:16
Whispering Smith 2-19-36:12
Whispering Smith 12-08-48:11
Whispering Smith Vs. Scotland Yard 3-12-52:16
Whispers 7-02-20:29
Whist 9-17-10:12
Whistle, The 4-01-21:41
Whistle at Eaton Falls 8-01-51:6
Whistle Down the Wind 8-02-61:7
Whistler, The 5-03-44:23
Whistlin' Dan 6-28-32:15
Whistling Bullets 10-06-37:13
Whistling Hills 12-26-51:6
Whistling in Brooklyn 9-29-43:8
Whistling in Dixie 10-28-42:8
Whistling in the Dark 1-31-33:12
Whistling in the Dark 8-06-41:8
White and Unmarried 6-03-21:40
White Angel, The 7-01-36:12
White Banners 5-25-38:12
White Barbarian, A 2-22-23:42

White Bear, The 5-09-62:17
White Black Sheep, The 12-22-26:15
White Bondage 7-21-37:13
White Buffalo, The 9-21-77:18
White Caravan 5-20-64:20
White Cargo 2-26-30:24
White Cargo 9-16-42:8
White Christmas 9-01-54:6
White Circle 9-03-20:42
White Cliffs of Dover, The 3-15-44:32
White Cockatoo 1-15-35:63
White Corridors 6-27-51:9
White Cradle Inn 4-02-47:16
White Dawn, The 7-17-74:16
White Death 12-09-36:13
White Desert, The 7-08-25:36
White Devil, The 2-26-30:7 and 9-01-31:34
White Eagle 9-27-32:21
White Face 12-05-33:17
White Fang 7-22-36:17
White Feather 2-09-55:10
White Fire 2-10-54:6
White Flannels 3-23-27:18
White Flower, The 3-08-23:30
White Fury 3-26-69:30
White Goddess, The 3-19-15:21
White Gold 3-02-27:16
White-Haired Girl, The 9-06-72:26
White Hands 2-03-22:42
White Heat 6-19-34:27
White Heat 8-31-49:8
White Heather, The 5-09-19:53
White Hell 11-17-22:41
White Hell of Pitz Palu, The 12-11-29:42
White Hell of Pitz-Palu, The 1-02-52:68
White Hope 11-03-22:43
White Hope, The (s) 4-15-36:16
White Hunter 12-02-36:38
White Hunter 12-25-63:16
White in Bad Light 1-15-75:26
White Legion 12-23-36:62
White Lie, The 5-22-14:22
White Lie, The 9-27-18:44
White Lies 6-25-20:32
White Lies (s) 8-20-30:14
White Lies 1-01-35:18
White Lightning 3-04-53:18
White Lightning 6-06-73:18
White Line, The 12-10-52:18
White Line Fever 7-16-75:21
White Mane 12-23-53:16
White Man's Chance, A 8-15-19:70

White Man's Law, The 4-26-18:42
White Moll, The 7-23-20:33
White Monkey, The 6-10-25:37
White Moor, The 7-21-65:6
White Moth 6-18-24:23
White Nights (See: Notti Bianchi, Le)
White Oak 11-14-21:43
White Orchid 12-01-54:6
White Outlaw 9-16-25:41
White Panther 1-31-24:24
White Pants Willie 7-27-27:20
White Parade, The 11-13-34:15
White Pongo 12-05-45:16
White Rat 6-12-72:26
White Raven, The 1-19-17:26
White, Red, Yellow, Pink 11-30-66:6
White Rock 2-02-77:22
White Rose, The 5-14-23:23
White Rose of Hong Kong 12-29-65:6
White Savage 4-14-43:10
White Shadows in the South Seas 8-08-28:12
White Sheik, The 2-08-28:16 and 12-11-29:42
White Sheik, The (See: Sceicco Bianco, Lo)
White Shoulders 6-09-31:19
White Sin, The 5-07-24:25
White Sister, The 7-30-15:20
White Sister, The 9-13-23:30
White Sister, The 3-21-33:16
White Sister 3-14-73:21
White Slave Traffic 12-12-13:12
White Stallion, The 10-08-47:8
White Terror, The 7-23-15:18
White Tie and Tails 11-13-46:16
White Tiger, The 11-22-23:27
White Tower, The 6-14-50:8
White Unicorn, The 11-12-47:24
White Voices (See: Voci Bianche, Le)
White Warrior, The 2-01-61:6
White Way, The 10-03-56:6
White Wilderness, The 6-25-58:6
White Witch Doctor 6-17-53:6
White Woman 11-21-33:20
White Youth 12-17-20:41
White Zombie 8-02-32:15
Whitewashed Walls 4-25-19:80
Whither Germany? 4-25-33:18
Whity 7-14-71:24
Who Am I? 7-22-21:36
Who Are the DeBolts? (And Where Did They Get 19 Kids?) 10-12-77:16

Who Cares? 1-17-19:52
Who Done It? 11-04-42:8
Who Done It? 3-28-56:6
Who Fears the Devil? 11-01-72: 20
Who Goes There 1-23-17:44
Who Goes There! 6-25-52:20
Who Has Seen the Wind 11-16-77: 21
Who Hit Me? (s) 8-25-26:23
Who Is Boss 9-10-10:12
Who Is Harry Kellerman and Why Is He Saying All Those Terrible Things About Me? 6-16-71:15
Who Is Hope Schuyler? 3-11-42:8
Who Is Killing the Great Chefs of Europe? 9-20-78:24
Who Is "Number One"? 10-26-17: 33
Who Is to Blame 5-24-18:34
Who Is Your Servant? 2-27-20:47
Who Killed Aunt Maggie 11-06-40: 16
Who Killed "Doc" Robbin 5-05-48:20
Who Killed Gail Preston? 3-09-38:14
Who Killed John Savage 12-01-37: 29
Who Killed Mary Whats'ername? 11-10-71:16
Who Killed Max? 3-04-11:18
Who Killed Santa Claus? 4-28-48: 22
Who Killed Teddy Bear? 10-06-65:6
Who Killed Walton? 4-19-18:43
Who Knows 11-29-18:41
Who Loved Him Best 2-15-18:52
Who? Me! (s) 8-02-32:15
Who Owns the Rug? 10-08-10:12
Who Says I Can't Ride a Rainbow? 12-01-71:22
Who Shall Take My Life? 9-13-18: 45
Who Slew Auntie Roo? 12-22-71: 66
Who Was That Lady? 1-13-60:6
Who Will Marry Me? 1-25-19:45
Whole Town's Talking, The 3-06-35:20**
Whole Truth, The 8-06-58:7
Who'll Stop the Rain? 5-24-78:34
Wholesaling Along (s) 9-30-36:17
Wholly Moses 6-18-80:24
Whom the Gods Destroy 12-08-16:29

Whom the Gods Destroy 7-17-34:15
Whoopee 10-08-30:22
Whoops, I'm an Indian (s) 3-03-37:14
Who's Afraid of Virginia Woolf? 6-22-66:6
Who's Been Sleeping in My Bed? 12-04-63:6
Who's Cheating? 7-09-24:25
Who's Crazy 8-04-65:28
Who's Got the Action? 12-12-62:6
Who's Got the Black Box? (See: Route de Corinthe, La)
Who's Got the Body? (s) 5-21-30: 19
Who's Looney Now? (s) 12-02-36: 18
Who's Minding the Mint? 9-27-67: 6
Who's Minding the Store? 11-20-63:6
Who's That Knocking at My Door? 9-11-68:110
Who's the Boss (s) 10-01-30:19
Who's Who (s) 11-27-29:21
Who's Who in the Zoo (s) 3-25-42:18
Who's Zoo in Africa (s) 1-31-33: 12
Whose Baby Are You? (s) 10-28-36:15
Why Announce Your Marriage? 2-03-22:42
Why Be Good? 5-08-29:20
Why Blame Me? 2-08-18:40
Why Bring That Up? 10-09-29:31
Why Change Your Wife? 4-30-20: 43
Why Cry at Parting? 2-12-30:19
Why Does Herr Run Amok? (See: Warum Laeuft Herr R. Amok?)
Why Get Married? 8-06-24:25
Why Girls Go Back Home 5-19-26:16
Why Girls Leave 8-08-45:22
Why Girls Leave Home 10-02-09: 13
Why Korea? (s) 1-24-51:6
Why Leave Home? 9-18-29:25
Why Men Forget 1-27-22:39
Why Men Leave Home 10-13-22: 43
Why Men Leave Home 5-14-24:27
Why Not? (See: Pourquoi Pas?)
Why Rock the Boat? 10-09-74:19
Why Russians Are Revolting 6-03-70:20

493 •

Wild Westerners, The 6-17-62:6
Wild Wheels 7-23-69:26
Wild, Wild Planet 4-12-67:6
Wild, Wild Susan 8-05-25:31
Wild, Wild Winter 1-12-66:6
Wild, Wild World 8-18-65:6
Wild Winship's Widow 5-25-17:23
Wild Women 3-01-18:42
Wild Women of Borneo 4-26-32: 25
Wild Youth 3-22-18:52
Wildcat 9-02-42:18
Wildcat Bus 8-21-40:10
Wildcat Jordan 10-27-22:40
Wildcat of Paris, The 12-20-18:36
Wildcat of Tucson 2-26-41:18
Wildcatter, The 6-16-37:13
Wildente, Die 9-08-76:20
Wilder Reiter Gmbll 2-01-67:34
Wilderer, Der 3-17-26:30
Wilderness Trail, The 7-11-19:60
Wilderness Woman, The 5-12-26: 13
Wildfire 6-10-25:47
Wildfire 6-27-45:16
Wildwechsel 6-02-76:30
Wilful Youth 3-21-28:22
Wilhelm Tell 1-11-61:6
Wilkins Murder Case, The (s) 1-07-31:23
Will Any Gentlemen 9-02-53:6
Will Mahoney (s) 5-30-28:14 and 8-01-28:12
Will o' the Wisp, The 7-20-17:30
Will of a People, The (Spain Fights On) 2-15-39:21
Will Osborne (s) 2-05-35:14
Will Penny 2-28-68:6
Will Rogers in Dublin (s) 3-09-27:17
Will Rogers in Holland (s) 5-11-27:24
Will Success Spoil Rock Hunter? 7-31-57:6
Willard 6-16-71:22
Willard-Moran Fight 3-31-16:24
Willi-Busch Report, Der 11-28-79: 16
Willi und die Kameraden 5-23-79: 26
Willi Wird das Kind Schronchauein 8-16-72:28
William Comes to Town 1-12-49:8
William Jennings Bryan and John W. Kern 9-26-08:12
William O'Neal (s) 4-03-29:11
William T. Tilden (s) 8-25-31:14
William Tell 6-12-14:21

William Tell 5-20-25:47
Willie & Phil 8-13-80:23
Willie Dynamite 12-26-73:14
Willie's Wobbley Way 6-16-16:23
Willow Tree 1-23-20:61
Willy 1-01-64:6
Willy McBean and His Magic Machine 8-25-65:6
Willy Wonka and the Chocolate Factory 5-26-71:13
Willyboy Gets His 12-18-09:15
Wilson 8-02-44:10
Willst Du Ewig Jungfrau Bleiben? 5-07-69:258
Win That Girl 10-03-28:17
Winchester '73 6-07-50:8
Winchester Woman, The 10-24-19:60
Wind Across the Everglades 8-20-58:6
Wind and the Lion, The 5-21-75: 19
Wind Cannot Read, The 6-18-58:6
Wind from the East (See: Vent de l'Est, Le)
Windbag the Sailor 12-30-36:11
Windfall in Athens 10-03-56:26
Windflowers 2-21-68:6
Winding Stair, The 1-20-26:44
Windjammer 7-21-31:34
Windjammer 10-20-37:12
Windjammer 4-09-58:6
Windom's Way 1-01-58:6
Window, The 5-11-49:6
Window Cleaners, The (s) 5-07-30:20 and 11-05-30:23
Window Opposite, The 9-27-18:43
Windows 1-23-80:26
Winds of Change 8-19-25:36
Winds of the Pampas 12-21-27:24
Windsor Castle (s) 6-05-34:12
Windsplitter, The 6-23-71:46
Windwalker 12-10-80:34
Windy (s) 3-27-35:15
Wine Girl, The 3-22-18:47
Wine 9-17-24:28
Wine of Youth 8-13-24:21
Wine, Women and Horses 9-29-37: 15
Wine, Women and Song 3-27-34: 12
Wing and a Prayer 7-19-44:13
Wing Tou 3-11-21:32
Winged Horse, The (s) 7-12-32:16
Winged Horseman 5-29-29:58
Winged Idol, The 11-19-15:23
Winged Mystery, The 11-16-17:52
Winged Victory 11-22-44:10

Wings 8-17-27:21 and 12-17-80: 16

Wings for the Eagle 6-03-42:9

Wings in the Dark 2-05-35:14

Wings of a Moth, The 1-10-13:14

Wings of a Serf (See: Czar Ivan, the Terrible)

Wings of Adventure 8-13-30:31

Wings of Danger 3-26-52:16

Wings of Eagles, The 7-30-57:6

Wings of the Fleet (s) 4-11-28:13

Wings of Freedom (s) 6-17-42:20

Wings of the Hawk 9-02-53:6

Wings of the Morning 3-17-37:14

Wings of the Navy 1-18-39:12

Wings of the Turf 1-31-24:24

Wings of Time (s) 9-15-31:14

Wings of Victory 11-19-41:20

Wings over Africa 8-02-39:25

Wings over Ethiopia 10-16-35:22

Wings over Honolulu 6-02-37:15

Wings over Mt. Everest (s) 10-23-35:13

Wings over the Pacific 6-30-43: 20

Winnifred Wagner und die Geschichte des Hauses Wahnfried 1914-1975 6-23-75:17

Wink of an Eye 6-11-58:6

Winksome Widow, The 9-11-14: 22

Winner, The 10-10-14:25

Winner, The 12-03-47:11

Winner, The (See: Coeur Gros Comme Ca!, Un)

Winner Take All 12-31-24:26

Winner Take All 6-21-32:15

Winner Take All 4-05-39:15

Winners of the Wilderness 3-23-27:19

Winnetou, Part I 12-25-63:6

Winnetou, Part II 11-04-64:18

Winnetou, Part III 1-19-66:6

Winnetou und Sein Freund Old Firehand 4-05-67:6

Winnie Lightner (s) 8-15-28:17 and 9-12-28:12

Winning 5-07-69:6

Winning a Dinner 9-25-09:20

Winning a Wife 9-08-22:42

Winning Boat 10-02-09:13

Winning Coat 4-17-09:13

Winning Girl, The 3-28-19:93

Winning Grandma 8-09-18:33

Winning His Way (s) 7-02-24:26

Winning Oar, The 9-07-27:24

Winning of Barbara Worth, The 10-20-26:60

Winning of Sally Temple, The 2-23-17:24

Winning of the West, The 1-21-53:18

Winning Stroke, The 10-31-19:57

Winning Team, The 5-28-52:6

Winning the Futurity 5-21-15:18

Winning Ticket, The 2-12-35:39

Winning Wallop 10-20-26:66

Winslow Boy, The 9-29-48:18

Winslow of the Navy (serial) 1-07-42:45

Winsor McKay Animated Cartoons (s) 7-27-27:22

Winstanley 8-06-75:16

Winter A-Go-Go 11-03-65:6

Winter at the Zoo (s) 2-12-36:16

Winter Carnival 7-19-39:12

Winter in Eskimo Land (s) 9-03-41:17

Winter Kept Us Warm 12-15-65:6

Winter Kills 5-16-79:38

Winter Light 2-20-63:6 (Also see: Nattvardsgaesterna)

Winter Meeting 4-07-48:10

Winter Soldier 5-10-72:34

Winter Sports at Are 3-07-13:14

Winter Wind (See: Sirocco d'Hiver)

Winter Wonderland 5-28-47:15

Winterhawk 1-28-76:14

Wintermaerchen 10-27-71:24

Winternachtstraum 3-13-35:27

Winter's Tale, The 6-12-68:26

Winterreisen Im Olympiastradion 2-13-80:38

Winterset 12-09-36:12

Winterspelt 5-29-78:26

Wintertime 9-15-43:10

Wir Hau'n die Pauker in die Pfanne 9-30-70:20

Wir Kellerkinder 11-23-60:6

Wir Wunderkinder 8-26-59:6

Wir-Zwei 6-10-70:26

Wiretapper 1-11-56:22

Wirtin von der Lahn, Die 8-28-68:24

Wirthaus im Spessart, Das 3-01-61:15

Wise Blood 6-06-79:22

Wise Fool, A 6-03-21:40

Wise Girl 12-29-37:17

Wise Guy, The 7-28-26:16

Wise Husbands 8-12-21:34

Wise Kid, A 3-10-22:42

Wise Quackers (s) 2-02-32:15

Wise Wife, The 11-02-27:20

Wiser Sez, The 3-15-32:14

Wishing Ring, The 10-31-14:27

Wishing-Ring Man, The   2-28-19: 56

Wishing Stone, The (s)   1-15-36: 19

Wistful Widow of Wagon Gap, The   10-01-47:14

Witch, The   3-03-16:23

Witch Without a Broom, A   4-12-67:6

Witch Woman, The   3-29-18:44

Witchcraft   10-20-16:25

Witchcraft   8-30-23:30

Witchcraft   9-16-64:19

Witches, The   3-31-22:40

Witches, The   11-30-66:6

Witches, The   3-19-69:6

Witching Hour, The   11-24-16:30

Witching Hour, The   3-04-21:40

Witching Hour, The   5-01-34:15

Witchmaker, The   5-21-69:19

Witch's Cavern, The   11-06-09:13

Witch's Mirror, The (See: Espejo de la Bruja, El)

With a Song in My Heart   2-20-52:6

With Babies and Banners: Story of the Women's Emergency Brigade   4-11-79:24

With Byrd at the South Pole   6-25-30:109

With Car and Camera Around the World   12-25-29:32

With Her Card   8-21-09:17

With Hoops of Steel   5-10-18:40

With Lee in Virginia   3-21-14:13

With Love and Kisses   1-20-37:15

With Max Linder (See: Compagnie de Max Linder, En)

With Neatness and Dispatch   4-19-18:43

With Pleasure (s)   3-11-31:14

With Six You Get Eggroll   8-07-68:6

With Taft in Panama   3-06-09:13

With the Allies at Salonica   4-21-16:28

With These Hands   6-21-50:8

With This Ring   9-23-25:40 and 6-23-26:18

With Williamson Beneath the Sea (s)   1-31-33:12

Within Man's Power (s)   6-09-54: 20

Within Prison Walls   9-26-28:58

Within the Cup   3-22-18:49

Within the Gates   6-18-15:17

Within the Law   5-04-17:25

Within the Law   5-03-23:23

Within the Law   4-12-39:13

Within These Walls   6-06-45:12

Without a Home   4-19-39:23

Without a Soul   11-10-16:25

Without a Stitch (See: Uden en Traevl)

Without Apparent Motive (See: Sans Mobile Apparent)

Without Benefit of Clergy   6-24-21: 34

Without Dowry   4-17-46:32

Without Each Other   5-23-62:6

Without Fear   5-12-22:32

Without Honor   12-21-17:44

Without Honor   11-09-49:6

Without Honors   4-05-32:23

Without Hope   1-09-15:24

Without Limit   3-25-21:43

Without Love   3-21-45:10

Without Mercy   9-30-25:43

Without Orders   11-11-36:14

Without Pity   12-14-49:22

Without Prejudice   10-13-48:11

Without Reservations   5-08-46:8

Without Warning   4-02-52:6

Without Warning   9-24-80:18

Witness, The (s)   3-11-42:20

Witness Chair, The   4-22-36:14

Witness for the Defense   9-19-19: 54

Witness for the Prosecution   12-04-57:6

Witness to Murder   4-21-54:6

Witness Vanishes, The   10-25-39: 11

Witnesses, The   11-15-67:6 (Also see: Temps du Ghetto, Le)

Wits vs. Wits   6-11-20:35

Wives   2-27-14:23

Wives and Lovers   7-31-63:6

Wives and Other Wives   12-06-18: 37

Wives Beware   5-30-33:54

Wives, Etc. (s)   8-01-28:12

Wives Never Know   11-04-36:19

Wiz, The   10-04-78:18

Wizard, The   11-30-27:19

Wizard of Baghdad, The   12-14-60:6

Wizard of Oz, The (See: Dorothy and the Scarecrow of Oz)

Wizard of Oz, The   4-22-25:35

Wizard of Oz, The   8-16-39:14

Wizard of Waukesha, The   3-12-80:27

Wizards Apprentice, The (s)   6-04-30:24

Wizardland (s)   12-31-30:19

Wizards   2-02-77:24

Women of the World (See: Donna Nel Mondo, La)
Women of Twilight 1-28-53:6
Women They Talk About 10-17-28:24
Women Want Diamonds 4-27-27:17
Women Who Dare 5-09-28:17
Women Who Give 6-04-24:26
Women Who Wait 8-19-21:35
Women Without Names 2-21-40:12
Women Won't Tell 1-17-33:25
Women's Clothes 3-17-22:41
Women's Prison 1-26-55:6
Women's Wares 11-23-27:25
Won by a Holdup 1-29-10:13
Won in the Clouds 5-02-28:36
Won in the Desert 7-17-09:14
Won to Lose (s) 9-10-30:17
Won Ton Ton, the Dog Who Saved Hollywood 5-05-76:18
Wonder Bar 3-06-34:14
Wonder Boy 12-26-51:6
Wonder Man, The 6-04-20:28
Wonder Man, The 4-25-45:14
Wonder of It All, The 1-02-74:15
Wonder of Women 7-24-29:29
Wonderful Adventure, The 10-08-15:22
Wonderful Chance 7-21-22:35
Wonderful Country, The 9-30-59:6
Wonderful Day, The 7-04-28:23
Wonderful Lies of Nina Petrova, The 7-03-29:30; 7-31-29:23; 6-04-30:36
Wonderful Life, A 4-28-22:42
Wonderful Life 7-08-64:16
Wonderful Night, A 6-13-19:50
Wonderful Plates 12-03-10:14
Wonderful Thing 11-11-21:37
Wonderful Things 6-18-58:16
Wonderful Times 5-02-51:12
Wonderful World of the Brothers Grimm, The 7-18-62:6
Wonderful Year 6-02-22:33
Wonders of Aladdin, The 11-01-61:16
Wonders of Nature 8-28-09:13
Wonders of the Sea 3-22-23:29
Wonders of the Wilds 4-01-25:37
Wonderwall 1-15-69:6
Wood Chopping in Canada 3-28-08:13
Wooden Horse, The 8-02-50:16
Wooden Shoes 8-24-17:26
Woodstock 4-01-70:14
Wooing of Princess Pat, The 2-22-18:45
Wool Nymph, The 1-07-16:23

Word Is Out 3-08-78:31
Words and Music 10-02-29:34
Words and Music (s) 11-10-31:14
Words and Music 12-08-48:10
Words and Music By 5-23-19:57
Work 6-25-15:20
Work Is a Four-Letter Word 6-12-68:6
World Against Him, The 12-15-16:35
Working Man, The 4-25-33:15
World Accuses, The 3-27-35:31
World Aflame, The 8-01-19:53
World and His Wife, The 7-23-20:33
World and Its Woman, The 9-12-19:52
World and the Flesh 5-10-32:18
World and Woman 9-23-21:42
World at Her Feet, The 7-20-27:19
World at Prayer, The (s) 12-22-31:15
World at War, The 9-02-42:18
World by Night 8-16-61:6
World by Night No. 2 7-11-62:6 (Also see: Mondo di Notte, Il)
World by Night No. 3 (See: Mondo di Notte No. 3, Il)
World Changes, The 10-31-33:17
World Dances 11-10-54:6
World Flier, The (s) 12-08-31:14
World for Ransom 2-03-54:6
World Gone Mad 4-18-33:21
World in Flames 10-16-40:31
World in His Arms, The 6-18-52:6
World in My Corner 2-01-56:6
World in My Pocket, The 3-08-61:7
World in Revolt 6-12-34:19
World Is Full of Married Men, The 6-06-79:20
World Is Just a "B" Movie, The 3-17-71:26
World Madonna 7-21-22:35
World Moves On 7-03-34:26
World of Abbott and Costello, The 4-07-65:6
World of Apu, The (See: Apur Sanshar)
World of Folly, A 7-02-20:29
World of Henry Orient, The 3-18-64:6
World of Plenty 7-14-43:18
World of Suzie Wong, The 11-16-60:6
World Premiere 8-27-41:8
World Struggle for Oil 4-23-24:20
World Ten Times Over, The 11-13-63:6

• X •

Yellow Mountain, The 11-24-54:6
Yellow Pass, The 8-29-28:28 and
12-19-28:23
Yellow Passport, The 2-04-16:28
Yellow Robes, The 10-18-67:18
Yellow Rose of Texas, The 5-17-
44:20
Yellow Sands 7-20-38:13
Yellow Sky 11-24-48:6
Yellow Slippers, The (See: Historia
Zoltej Cizemki)
Yellow Stain 5-19-22:41
Yellow Streak, A 12-17-15:18
Yellow Submarine 7-24-68:6
Yellow Teddybears, The 8-14-
63:6
Yellow Ticket, The 5-24-18:35
Yellow Ticket, The 11-03-31:27
Yellow Tomahawk, The 5-19-54:6
Yellow Typhoon, The 5-14-20:34
Yellowneck 3-09-55:6
Yellowstone 9-23-36:16
Yellowstone Kelly 8-12-59:18
Yellowstone On Parade (s) 2-21-
33:14
Yelp Wanted (s) 1-05-32:19
Yes, Madam 11-23-38:14
Yes, Mr. Brown 2-07-33:13
Yes, My Darling Daughter 2-08-
39:17
Yes or No? 7-09-20:26
Yes Sir, Mr. Bones 8-01-51:6
Yes Sir, That's My Baby 8-10-
49:8
Yesterday 4-16-80:28
Yesterday and Today 3-03-54:6
Yesterday in Fact 11-04-64:6
Yesterday, Today and Tomorrow
4-01-64:23
Yesterday's Enemy 9-23-59:6
Yesterday's Hero 11-28-79:16
Yesterday's Heroes 10-09-40:16
Yesterday's Wife 11-29-23:26
Yeti 1-18-78:19
Yeux, Cernes, Les 9-30-64:6
Yeux de l'Amour, Les 2-03-60:20
Yeux Fermes, Les 4-26-72:6
Yeux Ne Veulent Pas en Tout
Temps Se Fermer ou Peut-
Etre Qu'un Jour Rome Se
Permettra de Choisir a Son
Tour 9-16-70:23
Yeux Noirs, Les 7-17-35:42
Yeux Sans Visage, Les 8-26-59:6
Yheden Miehen Sota 7-24-74:22
Yiddisher Boy, A 4-24-09:11
Yiddle with His Fiddle 1-06-37:
41

Yidishe Tochter 5-23-33:19
Yield to the Night 6-27-56:6
Yim Sawasdi 11-29-78:26
Yiskor 6-06-33:15
Yksityisalue 5-15-63:21 and 10-
14-64:22
Yo Baile Con Don Porfirio (See:
I Danced with Don Porfirio)
Yo Conoci Esa Mujer 1-28-42:8
Yo la Primero 2-12-75:36
Yo Mate a Facundo 8-20-75:73
Yo No Soy la Mata Hari 11-01-50:
18
Yo, Pecador 2-03-60:20
Yo Quiero Morir Contigo 8-20-
41:21
Yo Quiero Ser Bataclana 5-28-41:
16
Yod Manoot Computer 5-11-77:79
Yodelin' Kid from Pine Ridge 10-
13-37:17
Yoga-en Vej Til Lykee 4-30-75:
23
Yoho 2-24-65:6
Yojimbo 8-30-61:6
Yojohan Fusuma No Shitabari 1-
02-74:15
Yokel Boy 3-25-42:8
Yokel Dog Makes Good (s) 10-23-
34:18
Yokihi 6-15-55:20
Yoko Ono Film No. 4 8-30-67:6
Yolanda 2-21-24:18
Yolanda 1-20-43:9
Yolanda and the Thief 10-17-45:8
Yolanta 12-30-64:6
Yollymoon 7-10-63:6
Yomegareo Kinro 1-23-80:26
Yompaban Cha 2-01-78:24
Yoo Hoo (s) 9-20-32:14
Yoo Hoo Hollywood (s) 4-29-36:15
Yorck 11-29-32:18 (Also see:
York)
York 1-12-32:28 (Also see: Yorck)
Yoru No Onnatachi 9-11-57:6
Yoru No Tsuzani 6-25-58:6
Yosemite Trail 11-17-22:41
Yoshiwara 9-08-37:19
Yotsuya Kwaidan 8-10-66:6 (Also
see: Illusion of Blood)
Yotz' Im Kavua 5-30-79:24
You and Me 6-08-38:17
You Are Guilty 10-25-23:22
You Are in Danger 11-08-23:28
You Are the Woman That Every-
body Loves 4-24-29:22
You Are What You Eat 9-04-68:6
You Belong to Me 9-18-34:11

505 ●

You Belong to Me 10-29-41:9
You Better Watch Out 12-03-80:26
You Call It Madness (s) 11-08-32: 16
You Came Along 7-04-45:8
You Can't Beat Love 7-07-37:13
You Can't Beat the Irish 5-07-52:6
You Can't Beat the Law 4-04-28: 29 and 5-09-28:41
You Can't Believe Everything 7-12-18:33
You Can't Buy Everything 2-06-34:14
You Can't Buy Luck 5-19-37:23
You Can't Cheat an Honest Man 2-22-39:12
You Can't Escape Forever 9-23-42:8
You Can't Fool an Irishman 12-13-50:25
You Can't Fool Your Wife 4-26-23:25
You Can't Fool Your Wife 5-29-40:14
You Can't Get Away with It (s) 12-02-36:18
You Can't Get Away with Murder 1-25-39:15
You Can't Have Everything 7-28-37:27
You Can't Ration Love 3-01-44:20
You Can't Run Away from It 10-03-56:6
You Can't See 'Round Corners 2-26-69:30
You Can't Take It with You 9-07-38:12
You Can't Win 'Em All 7-22-70:20
You for Me 7-23-52:6
You Gotta Stay Happy 11-03-48:11
You Know What Sailors Are 2-17-54:6
You Light Up My Life 8-10-77:16
You Live and Learn 9-08-37:19
You Made Me Love You 8-15-33: 14; 6-05-34:29; 7-24-34:14
You May Be Next 3-04-36:27
You Must Be Joking 8-11-65:6
You Never Can Tell 10-08-20:41
You Never Can Tell 8-29-51:6
You Never Know Women 7-28-26:16
You Never Know Your Luck 11-14-19:58
You Never Saw Such a Girl 3-14-19:47
You Only Live Once 2-03-37:14
You Only Live Twice 6-14-67:6

You Only Love Once (See: Tu Seras Terriblement Gentile)
You Said a Mouthful 11-22-32:17
You Said It Sailor (s) 11-19-30: 21
You Were Meant for Me 1-21-48:8
You Were Never Lovelier 10-07-42:8
You Will Remember 1-01-41:16
You'd Be Surprised 9-29-26:14
You'd Be Surprised 5-14-30:43
You'll Find Out 11-20-40:16
You'll Like My Mother 10-11-72: 18
You'll Never Get Rich 9-24-41:8
Young America 7-07-22:60
Young America 5-10-32:18
Young America 1-07-42:44
Young Americans 9-06-67:20
Young and Beautiful 9-25-34:14
Young and Dangerous 10-16-57:6
Young and Innocent 12-08-37:17
Young and the Brave, The 5-15-63:6
Young and the Guilty, The 3-26-58:14
Young and Wild 3-26-58:14
Young and Willing 2-10-43:8
Young Animals, The 9-25-68:30
Young Aphrodites 7-03-63:18
Young As You Feel 8-11-31:19
Young As You Feel 3-06-40:16
Young at Heart 12-15-54:6
Young Bess 4-29-53:6
Young Bill Hickok 10-02-40:12
Young Billy Young 9-10-69:48
Young Blood 1-24-33:48
Young Bride 4-19-32:15
Young Buffalo Bill 5-01-40:20
Young Captives 2-11-59:6
Young Caruso, The (See: Enrico Caruso, Leggenda di una Voce)
Young Cassidy 3-03-65:7
Young Chopin 12-31-52:6
Young Cycle Girls, The 1-24-79: 22
Young Daniel Boone 3-01-50:16
Young Desire 7-30-30:17
Young Diana 9-01-22:41
Young Dillinger 6-16-65:16
Young Dr. Kildare 10-19-38:12
Young Doctors, The 8-23-61:6
Young Don't Cry, The 7-24-57:7
Young Donovan's Kid 5-27-31:56
Young Dynamite 12-15-37:17
Young Eagles 3-26-30:39
Young Forest 12-04-35:15

Young Frankenstein 12-18-74:13
Young Fugitives 7-20-38:12
Young Fury 2-03-65:6
Young Girls of Rochefort, The
 (See: Demoiselles de Roche-
 fort, Les)
Young Guard, The 12-28-49:6
Young Guns, The 8-22-56:18
Young Guns of Texas 11-07-62:6
Young Have No Time, The (See:
 Ung Leg)
Young Hollywood (s) 12-21-27:24
Young Ideas 7-23-24:27
Young Ideas 8-04-43:8
Young in Heart, The 11-02-38:15
Young Jesse James 8-10-60:6
Young Lady Chatterley 5-18-77:17
Young Lady's Fool, The 9-13-61:
 28
Young Land, The 4-22-59:6
Young Lions, The 3-19-58:6
Young Lochinvar 11-01-23:27
Young Love 3-11-36:15
Young Lovers 9-01-54:6
Young Lovers, The 10-14-64:6
Young Man of Manhattan 4-23-30:
 36
Young Man with a Horn 2-08-50:
 11
Young Man with Ideas 2-27-52:6
Young Master, The 2-27-80:20
Young Men's Fancy 8-16-39:16
Young Mr. Lincoln 6-07-39:12
Young Mr. Pitt, The 7-01-42:8
Young Mrs. Winthrop 3-26-20:54
Young Nowheres 10-09-29:38
Young One, The 5-18-60:7 and
 2-01-61:6
Young Ones, The 12-20-61:7
Young Onions (s) 9-06-32:15
Young People 7-17-40:16
Young People, The 7-21-71:16
Young Philadelphians, The 4-29-
 59:6
Young Pushkin 12-22-37:17
Young Racers, The 6-12-63:6
Young Rajah, The 11-10-22:42
Young Romance 2-06-15:23
Young Runaways, The 9-11-68:6
Young Sanchez 4-15-64:22
Young Savages, The 4-26-61:6
Young Sinner, The 6-09-65:6
Young Sinners 5-13-31:36
Young Soldier, The 7-21-65:6
Young Stranger, The 3-20-57:6
Young, the Evil and the Savage,
 The 8-21-68:6
Young Tom Edison 2-14-40:18

Young Torless (See: Junge Toerless,
 Der)
Young Want to Live, The 7-14-
 65:7
Young Warriors, The 4-12-67:6
Young Whirlwind, The 10-17-28:
 16
Young Widow 2-20-46:8
Young Winston 7-26-72:14
Young Wive's Tale 6-23-54:6
Young Woman of Bai-Sao, The
 7-24-63:8
Young Woodley 7-16-30:29 and
 10-01-30:19
Young World, A (See: Monde
 Nouveau, Un)
Youngblood 5-10-78:26
Youngblood Hawke 11-04-64:6
Younger Brothers, The 6-20-08:
 13
Younger Brothers, The 5-04-49:
 11
Younger Generation, The 3-20-
 29:12
Younger Years (s) 7-14-31:17
Youngest Profession, The 3-03-
 43:14
Your Best Friend 4-07-22:41
Your Cheatin' Heart 11-04-64:6
Your Friend and Mine 5-17-23:23
Your Girl and Mine 12-19-14:25
Your Money or Your Wife 4-06-
 60:6
Your Smiling Face 9-19-79:22
Your Three Minutes Are Up 8-
 29-73:14
Your Uncle Dudley 12-18-35:12
Your Wife and Mine 1-18-28:23
Your Witness 2-01-50:14
You're a Big Boy Now 12-14-66:
 19
You're a Lucky Fellow, Mr. Smith
 10-27-43:10
You're a Sweetheart 12-15-37:17
You're Fired 6-20-19:53
You're in the Army Now (s) 12-
 17-30:13
You're in the Army Now 4-21-37:
 14
You're in the Army Now 12-03-
 41:8
You're Killing Me (s) 8-23-32:15
You're My Everything 7-06-49:6
You're Never Too Young 6-15-
 55:6
You're Not So Tough 7-17-40:18
You're Only Young Once 1-12-38:
 14

507 ●

You're Out of Luck 3-12-41:16
You're Telling Me (s) 6-14-32:16
You're Telling Me 4-10-34:13
You're the One 2-05-41:12
Yours for the Asking 8-26-36:20
Yours, Mine and Ours 4-24-68:6
Yours to Command 8-03-27:19
Yours Truly Blake 1-12-55:6
Youth 10-15-15:21
Youth 7-20-17:30
Youth Aflame 9-05-45:15
Youth and Adventure 3-11-25:42
Youth Astray 5-30-28:30
Youth for Sale 9-03-24:25 and 10-15-25:32
Youth Must Have Love 11-03-27:42
Youth of Athens 11-02-49:22
Youth of Maxim 2-12-35:39
Youth on Parade 1-20-43:9
Youth on Parole 10-13-37:17
Youth on Trial 2-21-45:17
Youth Runs Wild 6-28-44:16
Youth Takes a Fling 9-28-38:14
Youth to Youth 7-21-22:33
Youth to Youth 10-27-22:40
Youth Will Be Served 11-20-40:16
Youthful Cheaters 7-26-23:29
Youthful Folly 4-02-20:94
Youthful Samaritan 8-01-08:13
Youthquake 5-25-77:24
Youth's Desire 10-15-20:41
Youth's Endearing Charm 9-01-16:24
Youth's Gamble 7-15-25:53
You've Got to Walk It Like You Talk It or You'll Lose That Beat 9-01-71:26
Yovita 6-28-67:22
Yowake No Kuni 10-18-67:6
Yukinojo Henge 8-02-78:18
Yukon Flight 1-10-40:16
Yukon Trail (s) 11-10-31:14
Yul 871 7-27-66:7
Yuppi Du 3-26-75:20
Yves Montand Chante 8-03-60:7
Yvette 4-27-38:23
Yvette Rugel (s) 10-23-29:17
Yvonne from Paris 7-18-19:42
Yvonne la Nuit 12-28-49:16

Zinker, Der 8-18-31:34
Zirkus Leben 1-03-33:27
Zirkus Prinzessin, Die (See: Last Princess, The)
Zivi Bili Pa Vidjeli 8-15-79:28
Zivot Je Masovna Pojava 9-30-70:24
Zizanie, La 4-05-78:23
Zizkowska Romance 6-04-58:6
Zlata Reneta 7-27-66:6
Zlate Kapradi 9-04-63:20
Zloto 7-31-63:12
Zmierc Prezydenta 2-22-78:19
Zmory 5-30-79:24
Znaki Na Drodze 8-15-71:16
Zo Monogatari 6-11-80:24
Zodiac Couples, The 7-15-70:20
Zoe 7-28-54:6
Zoe, a Woman's Last Card 4-24-14:22
Zoff 2-09-72:18
Zofia 6-08-77:23
Zoku Miyamoto Musashi (See: Samurai Part II)
Zoldar 11-30-66:6
Zombie 7-30-80:22
Zombies of Mora Tan 3-20-57:7
Zombies on Broadway 5-02-45:27
Zona Roja 6-23-76:17
Zongar 1-25-18:45
Zongora a Levegoben 3-02-77:26
Zonja Nga Qyteti 1-24-79:35
Zoo in Budapest 5-02-33:12
Zoological Gardens in Antwerp 9-10-10:12
Zoomar Newsreel (s) 10-08-47:18
Zorba the Greek 12-16-64:6
Zorns Lemma 9-16-70:15
Zorro 2-26-75:18
Zorro Contre Maciste (See: Samson and the Slave Queen)
Zorro Rides Again (serial) 11-10-37:22
Zosya 10-04-67:6
Zouzou 1-29-35:14
Zoya 4-18-45:12
Zozos, Les 1-17-73:20
Zrcadieni 8-02-78:18
Ztracena Tvar 8-04-65:7
Ztracenci 5-22-57:20
Zu Neuen Ufern 10-27-37:19
Zucchero, Miele e Peperoncino 12-03-80:22
Zucndschunuere 5-11-77:95
Zuffucht 11-14-28:17
Zukunft Ist Palling, Der 8-02-61:6
Zulu 1-29-64:6
Zulu Dawn 5-23-79:23

Zum Goldenen Anker 2-16-32:33
Zum Goldenen Ochsen 11-19-58:26
Zum Teufel mit der Penne 1-15-69:36
Zur Sache, Schaetzchen 10-09-68:26
Zuyder Zee (s) 4-01-31:16
Zvezda Putuje Na Jug (See: Hvezda ...)
Zvezdi V Kossite, Salzi V Ochiete 5-31-78:23
Zvoniat, Orkroyte Dver (See: Girl and the Bugler, The)
Zwaarmoedig Verhalen 5-14-75:35
20 Juli, Der 7-13-55:7
Zwanzig Maedchen und die Pauker 3-17-71:28
Zwei Herzen im 3-4 Takt 10-15-30:29 (Also see: Two Hearts in 3/4 Time)
Zwei Herzen in ein Schlag 3-15-32:21 and 9-13-32:19
Zwei in eimem auto 3-29-32:25
Zwei Kravaten 1-19-32:29
Zwei Menschen 12-29-31:167
Zwei Tage fuers Leben 2-02-77:34
Zwei und Furtzich (s) 12-26-28:11
Zwei und Vierzigste Strasse 6-23-31:18
42 Himmel, Der 12-19-62:7
Zwei Welten (See: Two Worlds)
Zweierlei Moral 1-28-31:40
Zweimal Hochzeit (See: Twice Wedding)
Zweimal Zwei im Himmelbett 2-16-38:25
Zweite Erwachen der Christa Klages, Das 6-21-78:19
Zweite Leben, Das 1-19-55:6
Zweree aus dem Ocean (s) 1-19-32:25
Zwischen Nacht und Morgen 9-01-31:31
Zwischen Nacht und Tag 7-30-75:22
Zwischengleis 10-11-78:48
Zwischenlandung in Paris 6-15-55:20
12 Maedchen und 1 Mann 10-07-59:6
Zycie Raz Jeszcze 8-04-65:6
Zycie Rodzinne 6-02-71:15
Zygmunt Koloscowski 11-19-47:8
Zywot Mateusza 5-22-68:27